FOUNDERS
OF
MODERN
NATIONS

A
BIOGRAPHICAL
DICTIONARY

FOUNDERS OF MODERN NATIONS

A
BIOGRAPHICAL
DICTIONARY

NEIL A. HAMILTON

ABC-CLIO

Santa Barbara, California
Denver, Colorado
Oxford, England

Library of Congress Cataloging-in-Publication Data

Hamilton, Neil A., 1959–
Founders of modern nations: a biographical dictionary / Neil A. Hamilton
p. cm. Includes bibliographical references and index.
1. Heads of state—Biography—Dictionaries. 2. Statesmen—Biography—Dictionaries.
3. History, Modern—Biography—Dictionaries. I. Title.
D226.7.H36 1995 920—dc20 95-43982

ISBN 0-87436-750-6 (alk. paper)

02 01 00 99 98 97 96 95   10 9 8 7 6 5 4 3 2 1

ABC-CLIO, Inc.
130 Cremona Drive, P.O. Box 1911
Santa Barbara, California 93116-1911

This book is printed on acid-free paper ∞ .
Manufactured in the United States of America

✦

This book is dedicated to my mother,
whose understanding and inspiration
have made the difference.

✦

Contents

Acknowledgments

This book could not have been written without the help of several dedicated professionals on the library staff at Spring Hill College in Mobile, Alabama. They went the extra mile in securing a great number of materials through inter-library loan and in directing me to numerous resources. In particular, David Bunnell and Bret Heim led me through the catacombs and uncovered material that, at times, seemed hopelessly unavailable. Dr. Alice Bahr, the Library Director, gave her full support to this project despite other demands on her, and that of her staff. Additionally, Brinin Behrend took time from his studies at the college to help in acquiring research materials. Special thanks goes to Dr. Milton Klein at the University of Tennessee-Knoxville for his valuable advice. Finally, I want to thank my editors at ABC-CLIO: Todd Hallman, for his attention to the final copy, and Henry Rasof, for giving birth to this book's concept and providing innumerable suggestions and valuable encouragement.

Neil A. Hamilton
Fairhope, Alabama

Preface

Any effort to compile a dictionary as far-ranging as *Founders of Modern Nations* involves establishing criteria. A modern nation is herein considered to be a political entity that exists today and that conforms to the characteristics of nation-states emergent in Europe as the Middle Ages came to an end, when, among others, Portugal, Spain, England, and France arose (ranging in time from the twelfth century onward). These entities displayed the critical modern developments whereby the citizens unite under one independent central government, share common cultural and economic interests, and usually establish an identity that revolves around the nation, thus recognizing themselves, for example, as Germans, Japanese, Brazilians, or Americans.

There is, then, no attempt in this dictionary to include the names of mythical or legendary founders who predate the modern era. Although ancient civilizations have had a substantial influence on today's nations, and many legends are insightful, this is a book about those leaders who helped bring into existence *modern* nations. Any reference to ancient heroes is peripheral and generally found in the descriptive nation entry. (Similarly, principalities are excluded as pre-modern.)

As another rule, defunct nations and their founders are omitted. This, of course, leaves out some prominent leaders, such as those involved in forming the Soviet Union, but the focus is on the current landscape. Hence, to be included, a national figure must have created the nation with the territorial boundaries as they still exist, or roughly so.

Additionally, the category *modern founders* includes leaders who changed their governments in revolutionary ways, provided such changes, even after some alteration, continue as a prominent feature. Cuba, for example, produced leaders for its initial founding in the late nineteenth century and for its radical shift to a Marxist-socialist system some fifty years later.

Finally, it should be recognized that, for many nations, it is impossible to include all the founders (let alone everyone involved in developing the political system over succeeding years). As one example, exhaustive coverage of the United States would, in itself, require a dictionary of formidable size. In seeking to present a worldwide survey, then, this work is restricted to the dominant figures as recognized by a wide number of authorities. Many secondary figures, however, are included within either the biographical or nation entries, and although the biographies constitute a "great men and women" approach, the narratives refer to impersonal social forces that affected human actions.

In sum, this dictionary is intended to serve as a starting point in learning about the founders of modern nations—providing a wealth of information within biographies that, it is hoped, will be intriguing enough to encourage further investigation. Perhaps, too, the reader will gain a sense of the great human diversity and the tremendous scale of nation building in the modern era, from the territorially smallest to the largest nations.

About the Dictionary's Organization

Founders of Modern Nations is divided into two parts: biographical entries and nation entries. The reader who already has a founder in mind can go directly to the alphabetically arranged biography section. Each listing contains a cross-reference to other relevant biographical entries. The biographies conclude with a notation of available books concerning the founder, either biographical works or general histories that provide context for the founder's actions.

As another option, the reader can turn to the nation entries—also arranged alphabetically—and find there a brief narrative outlining each country's history (including, where appropriate, mention of important secondary figures) and the listing for any biographies that appear in the dictionary. As an example, the South Africa entry directs the reader to see Louis Botha, Jan Smuts, Frederik Willem De Klerk, and Nelson Mandela. A chronology puts the founding of the world's nations in historical perspective, and continent maps show the locations of each country.

Entry Locator

MADAGASCAR
Ratsiraka, Didier
Tsiranana, Philibert
MALAWI
Banda, Hastings Kamuzu
MALAYSIA
Onn, Dato
Rahman, Tengku Abdul
MALDIVES
Nasir, Ibrahim
MALI
Keita, Modibo
MALTA
Mintoff, Dom
MARSHALL ISLANDS
Kabua, Amata
MAURITANIA
Daddah, Moktar Ould
MAURITIUS
Ramgoolam, Seewoosagur
MEXICO
Cárdenas, Lázaro
Iturbide, Augustín de
Juárez, Benito
Madero, Francisco
Morelos, José Maria
Zapata, Emiliano
**MICRONESIA
(FEDERATED STATES OF)**
Olter, Bailey
MOLDOVA
Snegur, Mircea
MONGOLIA
Choibalsang, Horloyn
Sukhebator, Damdiny
MOROCCO
al-Fasi, Allal
Mohammed V
MOZAMBIQUE
Machel, Samora
Mondlane, Eduardo
MYANMAR (BURMA)
Aung San
U Nu

NAMIBIA
Nujoma, Sam
NAURU
Deroburt, Hammer
NEPAL
Prithvinarayan Shah
THE NETHERLANDS
William I
NEW ZEALAND
Massey, William
NICARAGUA
Chamorro, Violeta

Del Valle, José Cecilio
Morazán, Francisco
Ortega, Daniel
NIGER
Diori, Hamani
NIGERIA
Awolowo, Obafemi
Azikiwe, Nnamdi
Balewa, Abubakar Tafawa
NORWAY
Michelsen, Christian

OMAN
Qābūs ibn Sa'īd

PAKISTAN
Jinnah, Mohammed Ali
PALAU
Nakamura, Kuniwo
Remeliik, Haruo
PANAMA
Amador Guerrero, Manuel
Torrijos Herrera, Omar
PAPUA NEW GUINEA
Somare, Michael
PARAGUAY
Francia, José Gaspar Rodríguez de
PERU
Bolívar, Simón
San Martín, José de
PHILIPPINES
Aguinaldo, Emilio
Bonifacio, Andres
Rizal, José
Roxas, Manuel
POLAND
Pilsudski, Józef
Walesa, Lech
PORTUGAL
Afonso I
Spinola, Antonio de

QATAR
Khalifah ibn Hamad Al Thani

ROMANIA
Brătianu, Ion
Iliescu, Ion
RUSSIA
Catherine II
Gorbachev, Mikhail
Ivan III
Peter I
Yeltsin, Boris
RWANDA
Kayibanda, Grégoire

ST. KITTS AND NEVIS
Simmonds, Kennedy
ST. LUCIA
Compton, John
**ST. VINCENT AND
THE GRENADINES**
Cato, Robert Milton
SAN MARINO
Onofri, Antonio
SÃO TOMÉ AND PRÍNCIPE
Pinto da Costa, Manuel
SAUDI ARABIA
Ibn Saud, Abd al-Aziz
SENEGAL
Guèye, Lamine
Senghor, Léopold Sédar
SEYCHELLES
René, France Albert
SIERRA LEONE
Margai, Sir Albert
Margai, Sir Milton
SINGAPORE
Lee Kuan Yew
SLOVAKIA
Meciar, Vladimir
Havel, Václav
SLOVENIA
Kucan, Milan
SOLOMON ISLANDS
Kenilorea, Peter
SOMALIA
Sayiid 'Abdille Hassan,
  Mohammed
Sayiid Barre, Mohammed
SOUTH AFRICA
Botha, Louis
De Klerk, Frederik Willem
Mandela, Nelson
Smuts, Jan
SPAIN
Ferdinand V
Isabella I
Juan Carlos
SRI LANKA
Bandaranaike, Solomon West
Ridgeway Dias
SUDAN
al-Azhari, Ismail
SURINAME
Arron, Henck
SWAZILAND
Sobhuza II
SWEDEN
Gustav II
SWITZERLAND
Furrer, Jonas

FOUNDERS OF MODERN NATIONS

A
BIOGRAPHICAL
DICTIONARY

Abdallah, Ahmed
(1919?–1989)
Comoros

Ahmed Abdallah inherited an extremely difficult situation: pressure to move toward independence amid political turmoil and poverty so extensive Comoros was referred to as a "Fourth World" nation.

Ahmed Abdallah was born around 1919 into a wealthy Islamic family in the Comoros Islands, where he became a prominent plantation owner and businessman. While he was a young man, France ruled Comoros, and Abdallah served as the area's representative to the French National Assembly from 1959 to 1972. Like many in the Comoros elite, he had a conservative ideology and a strong pro-French bias, yet in the 1960s, events pushed him toward supporting independence. Comorian expatriates living in Tanzania formed the Movement for the National Liberation of the Comores (MOLINACO). Their efforts struck a responsive chord, for many Comorians believed France neglected them and was responsible for the area's depressed economy.

Abdallah initially resisted independence through a conservative party he organized, the Democratic Union of the Comores (UDC). But he feared that an independence movement without proper direction from the elite, of which he was a part, would bring chaos and weaken the power of Comoros' traditional leaders. Hence, in 1972, after he became president of both the UDC and the Comores Governing Council, he agreed that the paucity of French financial support and the discontent among young Comorians required nationhood, which he called "a regrettable necessity." The UDC joined several other parties in a moderate coalition that cooperated with MOLINACO.

Abdallah then entered into negotiations with France, and in 1974 Comorians voted in a referendum in which they approved independence. The one exception was Mayotte. The outcome there, a largely Christian island as opposed to the rest of the Comoros that were largely Islamic, caused the French to delay further moves toward independence and to call for a second referendum. Angered, Abdallah reacted by declaring the Comoros Islands independent, and on 6 July 1975 the Comorian Parliament ratified his action.

Abdallah faced an immediate crisis when France suspended all financial assistance and closed all the French-run hospitals, schools, and water services. Amid this turmoil a reformer, Ali Soilih, the justice minister, enflamed anti-French opinion and staged a coup that in August 1975 toppled Abdallah, who fled into exile.

"Comorians, [unity] is not only the reunion among the political parties."

Soilih's attempt to radically change the political system, his emphasis on state power and extensive building programs, and his call for restraints on the Islamic religious leaders produced resistance, and several conflicts erupted that led to bloodshed. By the late 1970s, Soilih's popular support dwindled considerably and mercenaries, financed by Abdallah and led by a Frenchman, killed Soilih in his bed and overthrew the government.

With Soilih gone, Abdallah returned in May 1978 as president, a post he shared with Mohammed Ahmed. He restored Islam to its favored place, reasserted the protection of private property, and oversaw the writing of a new constitution, which created a federal Islamic republic (while Mayotte remained under French control). An election confirmed him as sole president, and he proceeded to develop a five-year plan for economic development and place restrictions on competing political parties. The instability continued, however, and in 1989, during yet another coup, Abdallah was killed.

Reference: Bunge, Frederica, M., ed., *Indian Ocean: Five Island Countries*, 1983.

Abdallah al-Salim al-Sabah
(1895–1965)
Kuwait

In the developments that led to Kuwaiti independence, no man played a more skillful role than Abdallah al-Salim al-Sabah. In his nation-state building and rise to power, he used his considerable administrative talents to overcome conflicts with family members and challenges from a new economy.

Abdallah al-Salim al-Sabah was born in 1895 to an illustrious family that included his grandfather Mubarak the Great, who ruled Kuwait in the early twentieth century, and his father Sheik Salim Mubarak, who ruled from 1917 to 1921. As a young man, Abdallah obtained his education through tutors, but he learned much more than any books contained: He learned the political skills of his elders. When his father ruled Kuwait, Abdallah helped him in tribal relations and in contacts with Britain—important since the British had gained a protectorate over Kuwait in 1899. This foreign presence diluted indigenous Kuwaiti authority but also offered protection from other avaricious powers, the latter a benefit appreciated by Kuwait's rulers.

When Abdallah's father died in 1921, the young son expected to become emir. This, however, did not happen as the Sabah family decided on another son, Ahmad, to rule. All during Ahmad's reign, which lasted until 1950, Abdallah assumed leadership positions and attempted to wrest power from the emir. When the British Petroleum Company struck oil in 1938 and new revenues began flowing into Kuwait, the Sabah family entered into deeper disputes. Abdallah allied himself with several leading merchants disaffected with Ahmad's rule. This erupted into an open rebellion, with demonstrations and additional demands for reform. But Ahmad turned back the dissidents and Abdallah retreated, although only temporarily.

Abdallah then developed another tact by which to gain power: He founded and developed the finance department, which supervised all oil revenues, and in overseeing their distribution he created political alliances. Abdallah headed this department from 1937 to 1950. He also had many wives, and this traditional custom allowed him to build family, tribal, and economic alliances over the years.

In 1950, Ahmad suffered a heart attack and died. Abdallah finally became emir and decided to undertake moderate reforms. In 1951, he negotiated a new agreement with British Petroleum and Gulf Oil to gain a greater percentage of the revenues for Kuwait. He reduced governmental corruption and obtained for Kuwaitis a share of the work done by British contractors on numerous projects. He also devoted vast sums to internal improvements, such as roads and schools, and provided all Kuwaitis with free health, education, and welfare benefits. This increased his popular support and kept Kuwaitis from turning to radical alternatives that might have ended Sabah family rule—the Nasserist movement, for example, envisioned a greater Pan-Arabism linked to Egypt.

Kuwait exhibited a subdued nationalist sentiment, and its nationhood came in 1961 when the British, seeking to reduce their presence in the Persian Gulf, took the initiative and gave the land its independence. Abdallah immediately faced a serious threat when Iraq threatened to invade Kuwait. The emir acted quickly: He got British and Arab League forces to intervene and prevent the Iraqi action.

In the area of political reform, Abdallah began a national legislature. The elections to this body resulted in several political opponents gaining seats and criticizing Abdallah. The emir allowed this open disagreement to continue, a move quite unlike his successors, who usually repressed dissent and even suspended the legislature.

On 24 November 1965, Abdallah died from a heart attack as another session of the national legislature began. His brother Sabah succeeded him. Abdallah left a legacy of firm but flexible rule and astute administrative decisions. He had guided Kuwait from a relatively poor state to a rich one bathed in post–World War II oil wealth. He did so without extravagance and with much foresight.

References: Abu-Hakima, Ahmad Mustafa, *The Modern History of Kuwait*, 1983; Crystal, Jill, *Kuwait*, 1992; Rush, Alan, *Al-Sabah: History and Genealogy of Kuwait's Ruling Family, 1752–1987*, 1987.

Adams, John
(1735–1826)
United States

When a committee presented the Declaration of Independence to the Continental Congress, John Adams provided guidance so crucial that THOMAS JEFFERSON later called him "the pillar of its support on the floor." Yet despite the radicalism implied in the document, this temperamental and stubborn New Englander desired a controlled, orderly revolution.

John Adams hailed from a family that had lived in Massachusetts Bay, a British colony, since the 1630s. He was born on 19 October 1735 in Braintree, a town near Boston. His father, John Adams Sr., was married to Susanna Boylston and, like the Adamses before him, worked the family farm. For over 20 years he also handled most of the town's affairs.

Young John obtained his advanced education at Harvard College. He graduated in 1755 and became the schoolmaster at Worcester, where he taught 50 boys in a one-room log house and for his work received a meager salary and lodging. Over the years, he kept a diary, one remarkable for its revelation of his puritanical mind as self-questioning filled his days.

Adams disliked the isolation of frontier Worcester and, ambitious, wanted to be more than a teacher. In 1756, he decided to study law and did so under a Worcester lawyer, James Putnam. After completing his studies in the fall of 1758, he returned to Braintree and from there traveled to Boston, where he gained admittance to the bar. Adams soon began his law practice in Braintree and quickly gained a reputation for intelligence and persuasiveness.

On 25 October 1764 he married Abigail Smith, who through the years exerted considerable influence on his politics and criticized the inferior legal position women held in society. Adams liked her intelligence and independent spirit, and these qualities contributed to a warm, strong relationship.

As Adams developed his legal practice in the 1760s, Massachusetts headed toward a revolutionary break with Britain. Protests occurred when Parliament tried to levy taxes on the colonists, and by 1765 Adams's cousin, SAMUEL ADAMS, joined the Sons of Liberty in promoting a radical course. For his part, John Adams displayed a greater distrust of the masses and preferred a more rational approach. Nevertheless, he opposed the Stamp Act, which required the colonists to pay a tax on printed material, and authored the Braintree Resolutions, which asserted the unconstitutionality of taxation without representation. In 1768, he moved to Boston, and his involvement in the Patriot cause deepened. That year, he defended John Hancock against British charges of smuggling. He won after basing his argument on the illegality of the Townshend Acts, under which Hancock had been charged, asserting they denied his defendant a trial by jury.

After the Boston Massacre in 1770, Adams defended Captain Thomas Preston, the British officer charged with murder. He did so, he claimed, not because he supported Britain, but because he supported liberty and order, and without the latter, the former could not survive. Preston, he determined, should not become the victim of an impassioned mob. Again, Adams emerged victorious when a jury acquitted the captain.

That same year, Adams won election to the General Court, or legislature, but served only until 1771, when he returned to Braintree. The move, he believed, would help his health and allow him to concentrate on law. Two events, however, drew him back into the revolutionary storm. First, in 1772, the Crown announced it would pay Superior Court judges directly. Adams considered this an attempt to reduce colonial influence over the judges by tying them directly to the Crown. Second, in 1773 Bostonians disguised as Indians boarded a British merchant ship and dumped its cargo of tea into the harbor. Adams rejoiced at the action and condemned the ensuing Coercive Acts, passed by Parliament to punish and isolate Massachusetts by suspending town meetings and closing the Boston port.

On 17 June 1774, Adams was chosen to serve as a Massachusetts delegate to the First Continental Congress in Philadelphia. Although he worried about independence bringing turmoil, he supported a break with England, and his position, along with a similar radical position taken by Samuel Adams, earned the colony a reputation for extremism. John Adams served on several committees but was disappointed to see Congress controlled by moderates. Upon his return home, he wrote articles in which he proclaimed the colonial legislatures supreme in America.

After the Revolution's first shots rang out at Lexington, Adams journeyed to the town and expressed his view that nothing could stem the move toward independence. He attended the Second Continental Congress and unsuccessfully tried to block the sending of another compromise petition to the king. On 14 June 1775, he rose in Congress and nominated GEORGE WASHINGTON to command the emerging army. In January 1776, THOMAS PAINE issued his pamphlet *Common Sense,* which captivated the colonists. Although Adams supported independence, he criticized Paine's work as too simplistic and inflammatory. The following month, he returned to Philadelphia and helped Congress prepare a resolution recommending that the colonies organize new governments. He considered this the final break with Britain, but the formal separation awaited the Declaration of Independence, written largely by Thomas Jefferson, although Adams served on the committee that reviewed it. At this point, he successfully led the effort to get the Declaration adopted by Congress, presenting a masterful speech that rebutted the moderates.

Adams served in Congress again the following year and worked tirelessly on its committees. Early in 1778, he departed for France as a commissioner assigned to handle relations with that nation, and lived in the same house occupied by BENJAMIN FRANKLIN. Adams considered the disputes among

> ## "I am a mortal and irreconcilable enemy to monarchy."

the commissioners injurious to American interests and recommended that one person be appointed to deal with the French government. Congress agreed and chose Franklin to handle the relations. Adams returned to Massachusetts in August 1779 and within days served as Braintree's delegate to a convention called to write a state constitution. The document largely reflected his ideas.

Adams did not stay at home long; Congress named him a minister to negotiate a commercial treaty and a general settlement with Britain. In November 1779, he sailed overseas, reaching Paris in February 1780.

Discord with Franklin soon occurred as the line separating the ministers' responsibilities blurred. In December, Congress made Adams minister to the United Provinces of the Netherlands, and in August 1781 he was instructed as minister plenipotentiary to negotiate a treaty of alliance with the Dutch. He also sought financial assistance for the United States, but made little progress until after British General Cornwallis surrendered in October 1781 to Washington at Yorktown. In October of the following year, Adams obtained the treaty and secured a loan.

After Britain agreed to open peace negotiations, Adams traveled to London where, in October 1782, he joined Franklin and John Jay in arranging the treaty that ended the war (an agreement which, at Adams's insistence, was completed without French acquiescence). Adams made important contributions to the document, including provisions dealing with land boundaries, fisheries, and the collection of debts owed British creditors. In 1785, Congress appointed him envoy to Britain but, unable to reach agreement on numerous disputes stemming from the previous treaty, he resigned in February 1788 and returned to Massachusetts.

As the Constitution took effect, the electoral college chose Washington as the nation's president and Adams as its vice-president. The latter referred to his position as totally "insignificant," but as president of the Senate he cast the deciding vote on several bills that shaped the new government. In 1791, he wrote *Discourses on Davila,* resoundingly attacked by Jefferson and many others in the newspapers as promoting monarchy and aristocracy. The following year, he was reelected vice-president, again serving under Washington.

In the early 1790s, America's politics polarized between two sides. The Federalist Party, led by ALEXANDER HAMILTON, promoted a strong national government and measures that favored a commercial elite. The Jeffersonian Republicans, or Republican Party (no relation to the modern Republican Party), opposed such an approach as creating a powerful, closed aristocracy. Jefferson and JAMES MADISON organized this party in reaction to the Federalists. But another issue worsened the political disagreement: The two sides took opposite stands on the French Revolution, with the Federalists condemning the uprising as a dangerous threat to orderly government and the Republicans supporting it as an extension of the American Revolution in its attack on monarchy and hereditary privilege.

Adams disliked the French Revolution, but this did not mean the Federalists were fully united. Although the New Englander preferred the Federalist orientation, he was not a party man and often took an independent path. This angered Hamilton, who opposed Adams's quest for the presidency in 1796. Adams won the office nonetheless, and the two men never reconciled their differences. In fact, Hamilton sought to secretly control Adams's administration by having three men in the president's cabinet—Timothy Pickering, James McHenry, and Oliver Wolcott—provide him with inside information and take action to redirect and disrupt Adams's efforts. For reasons unclear, even after the president realized the disloyalty of his three cabinet officers, he made no move to dismiss them until near the end of his term.

Adams had to deal with the continuing war between Britain and France, one which disrupted trade. After France increased its raids on American ships, he sent three commissioners to Paris. They tried to begin talks with the government there, but French officials first demanded they pay a bribe (a common practice in European diplomatic circles), and the Americans refused. After the Republicans in Congress accused Adams of not negotiating seriously with France, the president released the heretofore confidential correspondence revealing the bribe demand. Thus occurred the infamous XYZ Affair (the X, Y, and Z referring to the three American commissioners).

Directed by Hamilton, the Federalists in Congress put the United States on a war footing, establishing a large provisional army and, in 1798, passing the Alien and Sedition Acts that placed political restrictions on immigrants and made it illegal to "defame" Congress. To organize the army, Congress made Washington its leader, and when Hamilton maneuvered the former president to make him second-in-command, Adams fumed. On numerous occasions, rather than confronting Hamilton and his cabinet henchmen, Adams fled to his home at Quincy, complaining of ill health, but perhaps suffering from anxiety.

The Federalists also levied new taxes to pay for the army. When the impending French invasion never materialized, popular discontent with these taxes and the Sedition Act spread. Although not desirous of an immediate war with France, Hamilton wanted to maintain the pressure against a nation he despised. Adams, however, realized the growing unpopularity of this position and the damage it could do him and the Federalist Party. He also believed that war could destroy the United States. Hence, in 1800, he stunned Congress and sent another peace mission to France—a move that raised Hamilton's excitement and discontent to new heights.

In that year's presidential election, Hamilton split the Federalist Party by refusing to back Adams. Instead, he promoted his own Federalist candidate. The resulting disorder produced a tie in the electoral vote between Thomas Jefferson and Aaron Burr. Hamilton reluctantly supported Jefferson, and the Virginian became president.

A disgruntled Adams left office in March 1801, but not until after concluding a peace agreement with France. He retired to his home in Quincy, where he maintained extensive correspondence with notable Americans, including his son, John Quincy Adams, whose prestigious diplomatic and political career led to his election as president shortly before the elder Adams died. In his later years, Adams repaired his relations with Jefferson, who had considered the New Englander's presidential policies too Federalist, and the two men carried on an extensive correspondence. Adams died at Quincy on 4 July 1826, a few hours after Jefferson passed away at Monticello.

References: Howe, John R., and Edward H. Tebbenhoff, *John Adams*, 2 volumes, 1987; Peterson, Merrill, *Adams and Jefferson: A Revolutionary Dialogue*, 1976; Shaw, Peter, *The Character of John Adams*, 1976; Smith, Page, *John Adams*, 2 volumes, 1962.

Adams, Samuel
(1722—1803)
United States

Were it not for the American Revolution, Samuel Adams may have been a total failure. He certainly proved inept at business; he loaned money recklessly, squandered the inheritance received from his father, ruined the family distillery, and much preferred life in the pubs and at back-room political discussions than anything dealing with finances and everyday toil. Yet his personality fit the revolutionary era—his ability to excite united dissidents and stir them into making the monumental break with England.

Samuel Adams was born on 27 September 1722 in Boston, the son of Samuel Adams Sr. and Mary Fifield Adams. The elder Adams, referred to popularly as "Deacon" Adams, had established a comfortable living as a merchant and brewer; in fact, when he sent Samuel to Harvard, the youngster was ranked high in his class in an era when such ranking had nothing to do with academic performance and everything to do with social standing.

Samuel likely obtained some of his political rebelliousness from his father. Deacon Adams invested and lost money in the controversial Land Bank of the 1740s. On a financial level, the bank was founded to provide farmers and middling merchants with an inflated currency they could use to more easily pay their debts. On a political level, it represented a strong challenge to the power of the leading merchants, or aristocrats, and the officials who governed Massachusetts Bay as a colony within the British Empire. The Land Bank eventually failed, but the controversy resulted in political victories for its supporters, and likely infused Samuel with populist rhetoric and ideas.

Indeed, at that time he was enrolled at Harvard and in 1743 debated the affirmative side of the question "Whether it be lawful to resist the Supreme Magistrate, if the Commonwealth can not be otherwise preserved." The same year, Adams obtained his master's degree. Meanwhile, Deacon Adams arranged for the young man's employment in a countinghouse, where he could be trained as a merchant. He failed immediately at this venture, spending most of his time debating political issues rather than tending to business. His father then provided him money to invest, but Adams loaned much of it to a friend and lost it. Deacon Adams subsequently brought Samuel into the family brewery, but here again the young man exhibited little interest.

Samuel Adams's first political foray occurred in 1748, when he and several friends founded the *Independent Advertiser* to criticize the royal governor and condemn a wealthy elite for monopolizing power. In the peculiar conservatism that ran through Adams (and later the entire Revolution), he firmly supported traditional Puritanism and bemoaned its decline as permitting licentiousness. Adams progressed little in politics prior to the mid-1760s, however, holding only minor offices in Boston. In the meantime, he carried a heavy debt, and his family had to rely on gifts of food and clothes from neighbors and the shrewd household management of his wives, Elizabeth Checkley, who died in 1757 (they were married in 1749), and Elizabeth Wells, whom he wed in 1764.

When Parliament passed the Stamp Act in 1765, a measure which imposed a tax on printed material, Adams gained a wider audience for his views. He particularly attacked Thomas Hutchinson, the lieutenant governor, for acquiescing in the new law. In 1765, Adams won election to the colonial House of Representatives and was so effective at rallying support that in 1766 radicals gained a majority in the House. Before long, Adams emerged as the unquestioned radical leader and wielded enormous influence in shaping the Massachusetts response to British actions. The failed businessman knew the popular mind well, and the revolutionary campaign effectively drew on widespread discontent not only with Britain but also with the colonial elite.

In arguing against the Stamp Act, Adams asserted there could be no taxation without representation. He enjoyed meeting with the common people who congregated in the Caucus Club and he became its moderator, using it to advance his position. With the Stamp Act protest, he led a new organization, the Boston Sons of Liberty, that used mob action—including attacks on property owned by the man appointed to collect the tax—and organized the boycotts of British goods that caused Parliament to repeal the legislation.

Adams believed a conspiracy existed to deprive the colonies of their liberties. He accused Hutchinson of plotting with the king and royal advisors to advance the conspiracy. This emotional argument and the use of mobs caused problems for Adams when the violence threatened to get out of hand and become a general attack on Boston's wealthy. After a mob wrecked Hutchinson's house, Adams used his influence to calm the disorder; but the desire to use mobs, and the fear by the better sort that the masses would get carried away, remained a constant in the Revolution.

In 1768, Adams led an effective protest against the Townshend Acts that levied a series of taxes on imported items. After Parliament repealed this legislation, the situation in Massachusetts cooled, and Adams, like other revolutionaries, worried that the time to make further gains had passed. It is not clear when Adams concluded that the colonies should secede from the Empire, but in 1769 he publicly proclaimed: "Independent we are, and independent we will be."

By this time, Britain had taken a momentous step that strengthened the radical assertion about threats to liberty: It had dispatched troops to Boston. Adams's cousin, JOHN ADAMS, later asserted that this move convinced Samuel of the necessity to break with the mother country. Whatever the case, the troops helped excite the situation when, in 1770, they became involved in the infamous Boston Massacre. Historians believe Adams con-

tributed to the massacre through his incendiary propaganda in the weeks leading to the event, including letters purportedly written by the British, but actually forged by him, revealing a plan to have troops attack the colonists. After the massacre, he made fiery speeches in Boston's Faneuil Hall and praised the readiness of the Massachusetts militia.

Still, months passed without a final explosion, and the radicals worried they would lose momentum. For his part, Adams continued to work hard at building tensions. Under his guidance, the Boston town meeting appointed a committee of correspondence that issued a list of grievances and a declaration of rights, the latter drafted by him. The move infuriated many moderate dissidents, including John Hancock, who considered the list premature.

"This country shall be independent, and we will be satisfied with nothing short of it."

Adams, however, believed the committee essential in uniting Boston with the countryside and establishing intercolonial communication. His plan accomplished both of these goals (and occurred simultaneously with a similar plan advanced by Virginia, which took the lead in establishing committees outside New England). In 1773, Adams had the Massachusetts House release letters written by Hutchinson (now governor), which the radical had obtained from BENJAMIN FRANKLIN (who had instructed the letters remain confidential). The correspondence revealed little new, but Adams exaggerated its importance, insisting the letters proved Hutchinson's role in a conspiracy against liberty.

Then the British again inadvertently aided the radical cause by imposing the Tea Act, whose stipulations were seen by many colonists as a ploy by Parliament to get them to consume tea that already bore a disliked tax. On 5 November 1773, Adams wrote a resolution, adopted by the Boston town meeting, declaring all those involved in landing or selling the tea as enemies. On 16 December, he led a group disguised as Indians, boarded the merchant ship *Dartmouth,* and dumped its cargo of tea into Boston harbor. In retaliation, Parliament passed the Coercive Acts which, among other stipulations, closed the port of Boston.

Adams then pushed for an intercolonial congress, and in June 1774 the Massachusetts House agreed to participate in one. The legislature chose Adams as a delegate, and he traveled to Philadelphia—in clothes furnished by others because his finances were in such bad shape—and attended the First Continental Congress. There he supported the radical delegates and helped to defeat several compromise moves, partly by inflaming public opinion in Philadelphia and encouraging street demonstrations.

He attended the Second Continental Congress in May 1775 and raised a storm of controversy when he accused some members of being on the British payroll. When Congress hesitated in breaking with Britain, Adams threatened to take New England on its own course. In time, sentiment in Congress changed—partly influenced by the still intensifying reaction to the pamphlet *Common Sense*, written by THOMAS PAINE—and Adams voted for and signed the Declaration of Independence, authored mainly by THOMAS JEFFERSON.

Adams served in Congress until 1781, during which time he sat on numerous committees and helped to write the Articles of Confederation. He supported the appointment of GEORGE WASHINGTON to lead the military but also backed mediocre generals and interfered with the War Department. His "glory days" ended after his tenure in Congress; he remained politically active, but his influence waned, in part because he displayed little talent for statesmanship. He served as a delegate to the Massachusetts Constitutional Convention—where his conservatism showed in his failure to support the lowering of property qualifications for voting—and in the state senate. He opposed Shays' Rebellion, which erupted in 1785 when farmers in western Massachusetts protested high taxes and their precarious economic plight. When the French Revolution erupted overseas, he sympathized with it, and when the Confederation government faltered, he reluctantly sided with ALEXANDER HAMILTON and JAMES MADISON and supported the new Constitution.

Adams won election as lieutenant governor in 1789 and in 1793 became governor upon the death of John Hancock. The following year, he won election to the governorship in his own right. When in 1797 it became clear he would not win reelection, he retired from office. Adams died in Boston on 2 October 1803, remembered for his status prior to 1781 as the most powerful revolutionary in America.

References: Gerson, Noel B., *Grand Incendiary: A Biography of Samuel Adams*, 1973; Harlow, Ralph V., *Samuel Adams: Promoter of the American Revolution*, 1972; Maier, Pauline, *The Old Revolutionaries: Political Lives in the Age of Samuel Adams*, 1982; Miller, John C., *Sam Adams: Pioneer in Propaganda*, 1936.

Afewerke, Issayas
(b. 1946)
Eritrea

Late in April 1993, Eritreans flocked to the polls, excited and jubilant, anticipating a resounding affirmation of their more than 30-year fight for liberation from Ethiopia. Indeed, as results showed in May, they overwhelmingly endorsed independence and thus supported their nationalist leader, Issayas Afewerke.

Issayas Afewerke was born in 1946 in Asmera, where his father worked in the government bureaucracy. Issayas attended high school and University College in Addis Ababa but, attracted by Eritrea's fight for independence, he stayed only one year before joining the Eritrean Liberation Front (ELF), a group dedicated to achieving nationhood through the use of military force. In 1967, Afewerke traveled to China for military and revolutionary training, and upon his return he joined a combat unit. In 1970, however, the ELF fractured, and Afewerke sided with the breakaway organization, the Eritrean Popular Liberation Front (EPLF), which, like the ELF, fought for Eritrean independence, but was more ideological and developed a socialist program.

By 1972, Afewerke saw Eritrea's battle take another turn when a civil war began. ELF and EPLF units fought one another, largely suspending their attacks against Ethiopia. The situation changed again in 1974 when a military coup toppled Ethiopian Emperor HAILE SE-LASSIE and, encouraged by the surrender of Ethiopian army units at Asmera, Afewerke and his fellow rebels saw a new chance for victory. In 1977, the ELF and the EPLF reached an agreement creating a united front (although it proved tenuous, with some fighting between them occurring in 1979). The ELF and the EPLF also faced contention from other organizations, most notably the Eritrean Liberation Front-Popular Liberation Forces, but by 1978 the ELF and the EPLF had become the largest rebel groups.

Afewerke displayed a studious, calm manner and won numerous battlefield engagements that earned him widespread support within the EPLF. In 1977, he became deputy secretary-general, and ten years later he was elected secretary-general, making him overall leader of the EPLF.

Afewerke's leadership and the EPLF ideology, with its increasingly Marxist-Leninist line and condemnation of imperialism as evil, won an ever-

"Working together, fighting together, dying together creates a spiritual unity."

larger following. In 1991, Afewerke and his followers scored a military victory over Ethiopian forces and an agreement ensued scheduling a 1993 referendum to determine whether Eritreans wanted independence. Afewerke became chairman of a provisional government, and Eritrea became a nation on 24 May 1993.

To date, Afewerke has been an enormously popular leader. He has moderated his political views and gained a reputation as a pragmatist. His provisional government is at work on a constitution. Unlike many African nations, Eritrea has displayed a substantial amount of unity, promoted by a long struggle infused with strong nationalism. Yet Eritrea is a poor nation, heavily damaged by the armed fight that cost tens of thousands of lives and resulted in 750,000 Eritreans fleeing to neighboring lands. Eritrea's future may well rest on Afewerke's ability to overcome this substantial migration and repair his nation's economic fortunes. Toward this end, he is pursuing improved relations with Ethiopia.

References: Pateman, Roy, *Eritrea: Even the Stones Are Burning,* 1990; Sherman, Richard, *Eritrea: The Unfinished Revolution,* 1980.

Afonso I
(1109–1185)
Portugal

On his path toward founding Portugal, Afonso I had to contend with his mother, whose army he defeated, and with the Muslims, who dominated the Iberian Peninsula. His success resulted in Europe's first nation.

In 1109, Afonso was born Afonso Henriques (later oftentimes called Afonso the Conqueror) in a castle at Guimarẽs. In 1096, Alfonso VI, the emperor of Léon, a medieval kingdom, had granted a province called Portucalense, or Portugal, to Afonso's father, Henry of Burgundy. Since 711, Muslims had controlled most of the Iberian Peninsula on which Portugal was located, and the Christians were forced to the extreme north, into Portugal and nearby areas. Henry earned renown for successfully defending his province against a Muslim assault, which lasted from 1095 to 1112. By the 1120s, both Henry and Alfonso VI were dead and Afonso's mother, Teresa, ruled Portugal. Alfonso VII, the new king of Léon (and Afonso's cousin), tried to exert greater control over Portugal, but Teresa refused his demands. In 1127, however, she lost to Alfonso's invading army and had to submit to his political power.

At this time, nobles who were discontent with Teresa sided with Afonso, the heir to the province, who challenged his mother's rule. On 24 July 1128, he defeated Teresa's army at São Mamede and sent her to Galicia, where she died in exile.

A young man of only 20, resourceful and energetic, Afonso desired to break his connections to Léon and enlarge his territory. At first he met failure. After he invaded Galicia, then under Alfonso VII's control, and defeated several barons there, Alfonso VII retaliated. Because of pressure from the Muslims to the south, Afonso could not devote his full resources to this counterattack, and in 1137 he agreed to peace.

Afonso then warred with the Muslims. In 1139, he defeated a Muslim army at Ourique, after which his followers began calling him king. This chore completed, in 1140 he again attacked Galicia, prompting Alfonso VII to march his army into Portugal. At Arcos de Valdevez, Afonso defeated his enemy, and Alfonso VII recognized Afonso as Portugal's king.

Afonso then resumed his war against the Muslims and reconquered more territory than any

of the other Christian kings on the Iberian Peninsula. He built a castle at Leiria and moved farther south, capturing Lisbon in 1147, after a 17-week siege. In the battle, he received help from English, German, and Flemish crusaders. Between 1150 and 1169, he engaged in almost continuous warfare, capturing yet more territories from the Muslims. In the latter year, Afonso again attacked Galicia in an attempt to gain that area but suffered defeat and an injury when he broke his leg. Because his leg did not mend properly, he was unable to fight again. Portugal's military leadership then passed to his son, Sancho. In 1179, the pope recognized Afonso as king and assigned to him all lands on the peninsula that other kings could not prove were theirs.

Afonso died at Coimbra on 6 December 1185, ending a 57-year reign. Over the next 70 years Portugal expanded farther south, past Lisbon to Faro, thus filling an area equivalent to its present boundaries. In the late fifteenth century, King John II, called "The Perfect Prince," established royal absolutism by fully asserting his authority over the nobles. Over the ensuing years, Portugal underwent numerous additional political changes, achieving its present parliamentary system only after a revolution in the 1970s led by ANTONIO DE SPINOLA. The Portuguese, however, consider Afonso Henriques to be their nation's founder.

References: Livermore, H. V., *A New History of Portugal*, 1969; Nowell, Charles, *Portugal*, 1973.

Aguinaldo, Emilio
(1869–1964)
Philippines

Emilio Aguinaldo's career followed a curious course. He fought for Filipino independence, but quickly cooperated with American rule; he embraced the American system, but collaborated with Japanese invaders.

Born 23 March 1869, Emilio Aguinaldo grew up in Kawit, a town in Cavite Province. He obtained a college education at the University of Santo Tomás in Manila and then served as a city official

before becoming mayor of Cavite Viejo in 1896. Influenced by the great Filipino writer and reformer JOSÉ RIZAL, Aguinaldo became a nationalist and sought to end Spanish rule in the Philippines. During this long colonial period, Spain catholicized the Filipinos and exploited the land. The Filipinos had little say in the colonial government, and Spain provided few social programs.

In 1896, Aguinaldo became the local leader of

the Katipunan, a nationalist society founded by ANDRES BONIFACIO. After the Spanish executed Rizal in 1896, this organization took up arms, and Aguinaldo served as the most effective rebel military leader, scoring important victories. At this time, Aguinaldo had a falling out with Bonifacio, prompted by both Aguinaldo's declaration that he would lead any new national government and by Bonifacio's own military blunders. When Bonifacio refused to recognize Aguinaldo's position, Aguinaldo had him captured and executed for treason.

Aguinaldo's own military fortunes declined later in 1897, although in June he declared an independent republic at Biakna-Bato. In December 1897, the Spanish government arranged a truce with Aguinaldo and the other rebel leaders, whereby Spain agreed to enact substantial reforms and Aguinaldo agreed to go into exile in Hong Kong and receive financial support.

After Aguinaldo left, Spain proved reluctant to enact the reforms and, in any event, war erupted with the United States in April 1898. Aguinaldo arranged with American officials to return from exile to help fight the Spaniards in the Philippines. He fully expected that the United States would support nationhood for his homeland. On 12 June 1898, Aguinaldo proclaimed the Philippines independent, but in the Treaty of Paris signed between the United States and Spain in December, the Philippines became an American colony.

On 23 January 1899, Aguinaldo and a provisional assembly approved the Malolos Constitution for the Philippines. This document had been drafted by Apolinario Mabini, another leader in the Philippine Revolution. Mabini came from a peasant family but, like Aguinaldo, had attended the University of Santo Tomás. In 1896, he had emerged as Aguinaldo's most important advisor, urging him to cooperate with the United States in order to end Spain's rule. The Malolos Constitution even resembled America's.

When the United States rejected Aguinaldo's position, the nationalists again resorted to arms, this time against their American overlords, and Mabini joined Aguinaldo in the fighting. The war proved extremely bloody and hard-fought on both sides, with numerous atrocities committed by the Americans. In 1899, American reinforcements sent the rebels retreating to the north, away from Manila, but Aguinaldo used guerrilla warfare and the fighting lasted three more years. The combat declined sharply after the Americans captured Aguinaldo in northern Luzan on 23 March 1901, using a ruse that involved help from Filipino collaborators. The rebels surrendered completely in 1902.

After his capture, Aguinaldo took an oath of allegiance to the United States and was granted a pension. This decision veered sharply from that of Mabini. He, too, was captured by the Americans but refused any allegiance to the United States and was consequently exiled to Guam.

In 1935, Aguinaldo ran for president of the new commonwealth government, established to prepare the Philippines for independence, but lost handily. When the Japanese invaded the Philippines in 1941, Aguinaldo made several anti-American speeches. He even appealed to the American and Filipino forces on Bataan to surrender. After the war, the United States accused Aguinaldo of collaboration with the enemy, a charge he denied. He was arrested and imprisoned but within several months was freed in a general amnesty. In 1950, he was appointed to a board advising the president of the recently independent Philippines. He died in Manila on 6 February 1964.

References: Aguinaldo, Emilio, *A Second Look at America,* 1957; Wolff, Leon, *Little Brown Brother: How the United States Purchased and Pacified the Philippine Islands at the Century's Turn,* 1961.

Ahidjo, Ahmadou
(1924–1989)
Cameroon

As much as many Africans advocated breaking through artificial territorial boundaries imposed by European powers, they seldom accomplished it. Such was not the case, however, for Ahmadou Ahidjo, who presided over an independent Cameroon uniting French and British territories.

Ahmadou Ahidjo was born to a Fulani chief in August 1924 in Garoua, a northern regional capital, at a time when French rule of Cameroon followed a succession of European influences. France was attempting to create cultural and economic ties that would discourage any movement toward independence, and chiefs such as Ahidjo's father had little authority. They became government servants tied to the French administration, which developed Cameroon's economy but through forced labor and European financial domination severely limited any benefits for most Cameroonians.

During World War II, Ahmadou Ahidjo, who had received a secondary education in Garoua, became a radio operator in Cameroon's postal service, a job he held until 1953. As nationalism grew after the war, he became politically involved. He joined the Young Muslims at the same time reforms under the French Fourth Republic in 1946 provided for Cameroon's representation in the French Assembly and creation of a local legislature.

This, in turn, encouraged political parties, each advocating self-rule. The Union of the Populations of Cameroon (UPC), founded by Ruben Um Nyobeé and dominated by educated urbanites, took an outspoken nationalist position and had close ties to left-wing trade unions. In 1956, under Felix Moumié, the UPC followed a Marxist and violent strategy, and the French banned it. André-Marie Mbida organized the more moderate Democratic Cameroonians in 1956, and Ahidjo joined this group.

Meanwhile, Ahidjo won election to the territorial legislature from the Benoué region in 1947 and won reelection in 1952 and 1956. For three years, from 1953 to 1956, he also served as a Cameroonian representative to the Assembly of the French Union, where his colleagues chose him to be legislative vice-president.

In 1956, Ahidjo became president of the territorial legislature. This was the same year France instituted additional reforms under the *loi-cadre*, a reform act that established universal suffrage and an executive chosen by the territorial legislature. The UPC tried disrupting the elections to an expanded legislature but failed. The Democratic Cameroonians won, and Ahidjo became minister of the interior. The party, however, soon disintegrated, and in 1958 Ahidjo formed the Cameroonian Union (UC), a coalition of northern and southern groups that allowed him to organize a new government as premier. He advocated full independence and reunification with the British Cameroons—which bordered Nigeria—but only through nonviolent, cooperative tactics.

The UPC continued as Ahidjo's major opposition but split into two factions, one based in Cairo that called for new elections and another under Um Nyobeé that conducted violent attacks within Cameroon. Ahidjo met the UPC violence with French troops and promises of amnesty, both of which hindered the UPC. Nevertheless, armed revolt intensified again in 1959 when, suffering from poverty and land shortages, the Bamiléké people joined the UPC efforts. This uprising lasted three years and killed 10,000–20,000 Cameroonians.

Shortly before nationhood and amid Cameroon's internal strife, Ahidjo disbanded the legislature and ruled through decree. Independence came on 1 January 1960, followed by a referendum in February that provided for a new constitution. In a close election, the UC won 61 of 100 legislative seats, and Ahidjo was subsequently chosen to serve as president.

Ahidjo quickly confronted an unusual aspect of Cameroon's development: the existence of the separate British Cameroons. Residents of this area disagreed over the issue of annexation by

> *"We must realize the indispensable connections between tradition and progress . . ."*

Cameroon; many feared difficulties in linking a largely British territory with one largely French. In a 1961 United Nations plebiscite, the northern British Cameroon voted to merge with Nigeria while the southern British Cameroon voted to become a part of Cameroon. Hence, Ahidjo presided over an unusual unification of territories emerging from separate colonial rule.

As president, Ahidjo followed moderate economic policies (avoiding the state socialism found in several nearby countries), and encouraged substantial foreign investments. He established a largely stable government based on building coalitions and exerting authoritarian rule. Ahidjo consolidated power in the presidency through, for example, formation of a unitary state in 1972, and he greatly restricted freedom of speech and the press. He won reelection to the presidency five times but resigned on 6 November 1982, claiming physical exhaustion, and Paul Biya replaced him as president.

Ahidjo expected to continue ruling as UC party chairman, but to his surprise, Biya ousted him from that post in 1983 after uncovering, he claimed, a coup plot. Ahidjo lived his remaining years in exile, first in France, then in Senegal, where he died on 30 November 1989.

References: Le Vine, Victor T., *The Cameroons: From Mandate to Independence*, 1977; Rubin, Neville, *Cameroun: An African Federation*, 1971.

Akayev, Askar
(b. 1944)
Kyrgyzstan

As the Soviet Union collapsed and the forces of Kyrgyz nationalism strengthened, Askar Akayev left his profession as a scientist, where he had earned renown, and led his country's legislature in declaring independence.

In 1944, Askar Akayev was born in what was then the Kyrgyz Soviet Republic. He graduated from the Leningrad Institute of Precision Mechanics and Optics in the early 1960s, with a specialty in quantum optics, and then became a teacher in Kyrgyzia at the Frunze Polytechnic Institute. He excelled as a scientist and was named a department chair. In 1981, he joined the Communist Party and served briefly as head of the Central Committee's Department of Scientific and Educational Institutions. In 1989, he won election as president of the Kyrgyz Academy of Sciences. By this time, enormous changes were underway in the Soviet Union as the nation's leader, MIKHAIL GORBACHEV, initiated reforms to modernize the economy and make society more open. As a liberal, Akayev supported these changes.

> *"There are moments when I think Central Asia might become the biggest conflict zone on Earth over the next decade."*

But the leader of Kyrgyzia, Absamat Masaliev, preferred hard-line communism to Gorbachev's approach, and opposed loosening the republic's political system. When demonstrators for "Kyrgyzstan," an organization devoted to democracy, demanded change, he prohibited its members from meeting. Masaliev erred, however, in thinking he had more support in the republic's Supreme Soviet, or legislature, than he actually did, and in October 1990 he lost his bid for the newly created presidency when Akayev outpolled him and scored a stunning victory.

Akayev committed his administration to economic privatization and political democracy. He allowed Kyrgyzstan to meet and even appointed one of its members as his interior minister. Kyrgyzstan held a congress in February 1991, and the republic moved quickly toward a free-market economy and independence. The changes occurred so rapidly and peacefully that they were called the "Silk Revolution," akin to Czechoslovakia's "Velvet Revolution."

When in August 1991 conservative Communists in Russia attempted to overthrow the Gorbachev government, Akayev resoundingly condemned them. After the coup failed, he directed the Kyrgyz Supreme Soviet to declare independence, which it did on 31 August. Then he scheduled national elections and on 12 October won election to the presidency by a resounding 95 percent of the vote. The suddenness of the elections did not allow an opposition to organize, and he ran unopposed; however, he reaffirmed his commitment to developing a pluralistic political system.

Akayev received credit for reducing ethnic strife and allowing Muslims to worship freely—a policy that many believe defused the complaints of Islamic fundamentalists and prevented a religious-oriented revolution. Akayev lost some of his power in 1993 when Parliament created a strong prime ministry, and he faced numerous uncertainties concerning economic privatization, although early in 1994 voters approved market reforms. His administration remains committed to democracy in Central Asia.

Reference: Fierman, William, ed., *Soviet Central Asia: The Failed Transformation*, 1991.

Ali, Salim Rubay
(1934–1978)
Yemen

When in the 1960s revolutionaries battled Britain to gain South Yemen's independence, Salim Rubay Ali emerged as a supporter of radicalism. He favored a society modeled after the Chinese Revolution, and his country became the only Arab Marxist nation.

Little is known of Salim Ruby Ali's early life. He was born in Zinjibar, a town near Aden, in 1934 and by the late 1950s had been a farmer, teacher, and justice of the peace. He also joined the Arab Nationalist Movement and its South Arabian subdivision, called the National Liberation Front. This group believed that independence could come only through a violent revolutionary struggle as exemplified by MAO TSE-TUNG in China. It wanted an end to British rule and the elimination from power of all local rulers who supported Britain.

In 1963, after Britain formed the Protectorate of South Arabia to include South Yemen, the revolutionary armed struggle began, and Rubay Ali became one of its leaders. He embraced Maoist populism and relied heavily on popular uprisings. When, on 30 November 1967, South Yemen gained its independence, Rubay Ali obtained a secondary position in the new government. He represented the most extreme leftist elements, and in 1968 his opponents purged him from the government.

Rubay Ali, however, soon bounced back: As the government tottered, it called upon him and other leftists for support. In 1969, ABD AL-FATTAH IS-MAIL gained the position of secretary-general of the National Liberation Party (NL) , the most powerful position in South Yemen, and Rubay Ali was named the country's president. One year later, South Yemen became the People's Democratic Republic of Yemen (PDRY).

Rubay Ali had numerous differences with Ismail, and their cooperation was often strained. Both men supported economic nationalization and collectivization. Rubay Ali, however, encouraged the masses to engage in popular uprisings against landlords, and rather than a centralized, professionalized bureaucracy, he wanted extensive mass input in decision making. He also wanted the PDRY to be closer to China than to the Soviet Union.

Yet after 1972, Rubay Ali moderated his positions. The PDRY suffered enormous economic difficulties and threats from North Yemen and Saudi Arabia. Rubay Ali thus supported closer ties to the Soviet Union for purposes of economic and military assistance. To gain new trading outlets and oil money, he advanced better relations with Saudi

Arabia, Egypt, West Germany, and the United States. In 1977, he even visited Saudi Arabia on a diplomatic mission. Thus he displayed his willingness to be pragmatic in foreign affairs.

These efforts, however, backfired. Saudi aid never became significant and relations with the West bore few tangible results. Ismail promoted still closer ties with the Soviet Union and a hard line against Israel and its Western supporters. On top of this, several of Rubay Ali's domestic reforms collapsed as the PDRY economy worsened. Then on 24 June 1978, a bomb exploded in the office of North Yemen's president, Ahmad al-Ghashmi, killing him instantly. Accusations flew that Rubay Ali had planned the bombing to gain backing

within the NL, whose members envisioned a PDRY takeover of North Yemen. Whatever the case, on 26 June violent conflict broke out between Ismail's followers and those of Rubay Ali. Rubay Ali's forces lost, and he was captured, tried, and executed. In 1990, the PDRY and the Yemen Arab Republic (North Yemen) merged to form the Yemeni Republic. North Yemen had earlier gained its independence under the leadership of YAHYA and ALI ABDULLAH SALEH.

References: Bidwell, Robin, *The Two Yemens*, 1983; Kostiner, Joseph, *The Struggle for South Yemen*, 1984; Stookey, Robert W., *South Yemen: A Marxist Republic in Arabia*, 1982.

Aliyev, Heydar
(b. 1923)
Azerbaijan

For many years, Heydar Aliyev embraced the Soviet Union and the Communist Party; then he changed, demanding an independent Azerbaijan and a more open political system.

Just months before Heydar Aliyev was born, the Soviet Union, newly emergent after the Bolshevik Revolution, took over Azerbaijan and declared it to be part of the Transcaucasian Soviet Federated Socialist Republic. As a young man, Aliyev fully accepted this development and even changed the spelling of his first name from Geidar to Heydar, thus Russifying it. He joined the Communist Party and entered the KGB, or Soviet secret police. Over the years, he rose in its ranks and became a general.

In 1969, Aliyev was named first secretary of the Azerbaijani Communist Party, and his influence grew enormously when Leonid Brezhnev, the Soviet premier, accepted him into his inner political circle. Then in 1983, the Soviet leadership named him to the Central Politburo, an extremely powerful posi-

> *"I will devote the time God has left me to protect the independence of Azerbaijan . . ."*

tion since that body governed the Communist Party. He served as deputy prime minister under MIKHAIL GORBACHEV. In 1986, however, Gorbachev removed Aliyev, calling him corrupt and opposed to the openness and reforms necessary to improve Soviet society.

At that point, Aliyev disappeared from the political scene, but developments soon returned him to prominence, for the Soviet Union was crumbling. In 1990, Aliyev displayed a nationalist fervor he had not possessed earlier and led a demonstration in Moscow to protest Gorbachev's use of troops to quell disturbances in Azerbaijan.

By this time, the Azerbaijani Popular Front had emerged to obtain national self-determination. In 1991, the legislature, dominated by communists, gave in to this pressure and declared Azerbaijan independent. The new president, Ayaz Niyyaz Mutalibov, presided over a referendum that supported this decision. He, however, imposed stringent political restrictions, including press censorship and suspension of forthcoming elections. A revolt then erupted, led by the Popular Front, and Mutalibov was forced from office. Abulfaz Elchibey was elected president in June 1992, but he suffered from his failure to improve the economy and from Azerbaijan's battlefield defeats in a war with Armenia.

Meanwhile, Aliyev settled in Nakhichevan, an Azerbaijani republic, where he became chairman of the legislature. In that capacity he pursued numerous reforms, including use of the Latin alphabet to replace the Cyrillic script that had been imposed by Russia and the abolition of Soviet holidays.

When Elchibey found himself unable to govern effectively, he asked Aliyev to assume leadership of Azerbaijan, and in June 1993 the former KGB agent journeyed to Baku, where at age 70 he became chairman of Parliament. He did not force Elchibey from office, but clearly held the power. He promised to support a democratically elected president and committed himself to free-market reforms. Aliyev's authority was soon reduced, however, when, amid reverses in the war with Armenia, Surat Huseynov led a militia that ousted Elchibey from office. Huseynov became prime minister with widened power.

In October 1993, Aliyev won election to the presidency after obtaining 98.8 percent of the vote. At about the same time, he agreed to make Azerbaijan part of the Commonwealth of Independent States, a loose confederation of former Soviet republics. Although Azerbaijan still possessed substantial oil reserves, Aliyev faced enormous economic problems, including inflation exceeding 800 percent yearly and massive environmental pollution in the form of contaminated air and water, the latter most evident in the Caspian Sea where raw sewage and petroleum waste had been dumped for years.

Analysts questioned Aliyev's commitment to a competitive political system—some believed the former secret policeman had not changed that much. Whatever the case, Aliyev remains dedicated to Azerbaijani nationalism.

Reference: Alstadt, Audrey L., *The Azerbaijani Turks: Power and Identity under Russian Rule*, 1992.

Amador Guerrero, Manuel
(1835–1909)
Panama

In an unusual situation, Manuel Amador Guerrero gained Panama's independence from Colombia at the expense of domination by the United States.

Manuel Amador Guerrero, who was born on 30 June 1835 in Cartagena, Colombia, became leader of Panama because the United States wanted a canal built in his country. This became evident beginning in 1903. That year, while Panama was still a part of Colombia, the American government negotiated the Hay-Herrán Treaty that allowed it to construct a canal through the Panamanian isthmus. The Colombian legislature, however, refused to ratify the treaty, and at this point the United States encouraged the organization of a junta in Panama that could declare the area independent. Amador, who hailed from a prominent Panamanian family, emerged as the junta's leader, supported by José Augustin Arango, considered the strategist behind the Panamanian revolution.

In November 1903, Amador and the junta organized an uprising against Colombia. They were backed by the U.S. military, which prevented Colombian forces from entering Panama City. The Panamanian government then granted the United States extensive rights to build a canal, control it, and even intervene in Panamanian affairs as desired. Thus, to a large degree, Panama was created by the United States.

In 1904, Amador became president and represented the wealthy oligarchy that dominated politics. Under intense pressure from nationalist-minded Panamanians, he resisted American efforts to impose customs, tariffs, and postal services in the Canal Zone. This caused considerable friction with the United States and forced a compromise. The disaffection within Panama continued and Amador survived a coup attempt by liberal elements only because the American government supported him. Perhaps the most notable achievement under his administration was the health effort led by the United States to eradicate malaria and yellow fever. Amador died on 2 May 1909 in Panama. An oligrachy then ruled the nation, and substantial political change did not occur until the 1970s and 1980s under OMAR TORRIJOS HERRERA.

Reference: Niemier, Jean Gilbreath, *The Panama Story*, 1968.

Amanullah Khan
(1892–1960)
Afghanistan

Amanullah Khan led his country through dynamic changes. He obtained its independence and initiated important policies in foreign affairs and domestic politics.

Amanullah Khan was the third son of Afghanistan's ruler, Habibullah Khan. He was born on 1 June 1892 and seized power after political opponents assassinated his father on 20 February 1919. Under Habibullah Khan, Amanullah had maneuvered into a strong political position, supervising both the treasury and the army. He used this connection to circumvent his two older brothers and become emir, or prince. By the end of 1919 he had gained the support of most of the tribal leaders, extended his control into the cities, and imprisoned those family members who refused to swear loyalty to him.

Amanullah began his rule at a momentous time. As the Russian Revolution erupted, Britain and Russia assumed a position they had been accustomed to years earlier: competition over which nation would control Afghanistan. Back in the nineteenth century, Britain had established domination over the country, but Amanullah realized that conditions had changed, that the British had been exhausted by the recent world war, and that Russia might give him assistance. He launched a dramatic assault: At his coronation he declared Afghanistan fully independent and then attacked the British troops. Although the fight stalemated and Amanullah did not get all he wanted in both the ensuing armistice and a negotiated settlement in 1921, he did get some recognition from Britain of Afghanistan's right to make its own foreign policy, a course he began to pursue anyway.

In the 1920s, Amanullah established diplomatic relations with the Soviet Union and several other nations, and to show his country's real independence he elevated his title from emir to king. He got assistance from the Soviet Union, but it vacillated, being determined largely by what Russia considered the magnitude of the British threat.

On the domestic front, Amanullah modernized the military by establishing an air force in 1921 and sending troops to France, Italy, and Turkey for training. He advanced women's rights, abolished slavery and forced labor, introduced secular education, and began schools for the nomads. The Afghan constitution of 1923 guaranteed civil rights and established a national legislature.

With this, trouble soon erupted. Amanullah's reforms antagonized important elements in Afghan society. The tribes disliked his centralization of power; many traditional Muslims disliked his efforts to emancipate women; and the army disliked his reducing military pay. In 1928, tribesmen revolted in Jalalbad, and as the rebels advanced on Kabul, the capital, several army units deserted to their side. In January 1929, Amanullah abdicated in favor of his oldest brother who, after ruling for only three days, gave way to a Tajik tribal leader.

Amanullah tried to regain power later in 1929, when he led an army toward Kabul. He failed, however, and in May fled to India before going into exile in Italy. He died on 25 April 1960 in Zurich, Switzerland. A later king, Muhammed Nadir Shah, who ruled from 1929 to 1933, abolished most of Amanullah's reforms. In 1978, Afghani unity unravelled after a communist coup. The new Democratic Republic of Afghanistan, backed by the Soviet Union, alienated many with its Marxist policies, and rebel guerrillas fought to overthrow it. Soviet forces backed the communist regime, but withdrew in 1989. Even though rebel leaders gained power in February 1992, armed clashes continued among competing groups, and in 1995 a fundamentalist Islamic faction obtained power in several provinces. Despite this turmoil, Amanullah is still remembered for gaining Afghanistan's modern independence and developing a more progressive state.

References: Dupree, Lewis, *Afghanistan*, 1973; Gregorian, Vartan, *The Emergence of Modern Afghanistan, 1880–1946*, 1969.

Antall, József Jr.
(b. 1932)
Hungary

The type of revolution that swept through Hungary in the late 1980s was that preferred by József Antall Jr.: a peaceful one. As an academician he long embraced Western values; as a political leader he committed himself to developing them on a national scale.

József Antall Jr. was born on 8 April 1932 to József Antall Sr. and Irén Szucs Antall. As a boy, József witnessed the devastation of World War II and his father's struggles against the authorities. The Hungarian government sided with Hitler in the conflict, but the senior Antall risked his life helping Poles and Jews escape Nazi executions. After the war, both Poland and Israel honored him. József's father also opposed communism and won election to the national legislature on the ticket of the Smallholders, a conservative party that advocated land reform. József followed his father and joined the party's youth organization.

By 1948, however, the Communists gained control in Hungary, and with the backing of troops from the Soviet Union they suppressed their political opposition and established a one-party state. Young József, meanwhile, enrolled at Eïtvös University in Budapest. He graduated in 1954 and remained there to study for a doctorate. At the same time, he worked at various academic jobs, including the National Archives and the Institute for the Science of Education and also taught at the Eïtvös secondary school.

Antall soon got into trouble with the government. In 1956, Hungarians rose up in an attempt to overthrow the Communists. At first, it appeared they would succeed, but the Soviets sent in troops to topple the reformist Imre Nagy government and crush the rebellion. Antall participated in the anti-Communist demonstrations and was imprisoned briefly. The Communists labeled him a subversive and prohibited him from publishing any of his works, a ban that lasted until 1963.

Given this persecution, Antall decided to focus his career on medical history. Because it was a field lacking in political ideology, he believed his decision would spare him further harassment from the authorities. He worked several years at the Library of Budapest, continued his secondary teaching, and finally earned his doctorate in 1967. The following year, he became a senior research fellow and deputy director at the Semmelweis Museum, Library, and Archives for the History of Medicine. In 1972, he became its director. In that position, Antall earned a reputation for allowing diverse ideas, but the government did not persecute him because it had become more liberal.

". . . the most important root of our political thinking was American liberal democracy."

Economically, Hungary deteriorated under the state-controlled industrial system. This situation, coupled with news in the late 1980s of changes under way in the Soviet Union toward a reform economy and more open political discussion, encouraged Hungarians to form opposition groups. In October 1987, Hungarian intellectuals, including Antall, organized the Democratic Forum that emphasized nationalism and a free-market, Western-oriented economy. While violence rocked several Eastern European nations that were trying to cope with the collapse of the Soviet Empire, Hungary remained calm, and in March 1990 the national legislature decreed elections to establish a new government. The Democratic Forum chose Antall as its president, and he embraced a gradual approach toward economic reform and a neutral foreign policy.

Antall's main political opposition was the Alliance of Free Democrats (Alliance) that supported rapid economic change through the privatization of businesses and stressed Hungary's commonality with Europe rather than its distinctive nationalism.

In the 1990 elections, Antall deflected criticism that his party included anti-Semites and that it embraced a far-right agenda. He did so successfully, and in April his Democratic Forum soundly defeated the Alliance and entered a coalition with two other center-right parties.

Antall became prime minister and in May reached an agreement with the Alliance whereby their candidate, ÁRPÁD GÖNCZ, would serve as president (secondary in power to the prime minister). Antall faced enormous problems. He had to oversee the transition to a market economy and the question of what to do about property owners whose land had been confiscated by the Communists. On the latter issue, the National Assembly passed legislation proposed by Antall to compensate the owners, but on a gradual basis so as not to strain government finances. He also ended price supports for alcohol, tobacco, and gas—measures considered difficult but necessary in changing the economy.

Hungary, though, continued to struggle with capital shortages, antiquated industries, and high unemployment. In 1994, new elections ended Antall's government as the former Communists, running as reform socialists, obtained a 15-seat majority in the legislature.

References: Burant, Stephen, ed., *Hungary: A Country Study*, 1990; Hoensch, Jorg, *A History of Modern Hungary, 1867–1986*, 1988.

Apithy, Sourou-Migan

(b. 1913)

Benin

A man of modest origins, Sourou-Migan Apithy was a leading figure in Benin's politics for over 25 years. His actions reflected his homeland's unstable and difficult transition to independence and his own opportunism.

Sourou-Migan Apithy was born on 8 April 1913 at Porto Novo into a modest Goun clan family. At the time, France ruled this area as a colony called Dahomey. Young Apithy obtained an education at local mission schools, where he adopted a strong Catholic faith, and then journeyed to France. He attended colleges in Bordeaux and Paris and earned a degree in political science. After becoming a business accountant, he resided in France from 1933 until 1945.

When France adopted a new constitution in 1946, Dahomey became an Overseas Territory within the French Union, meaning it had its own assembly and could elect representatives to both the French Union Assembly and the French National Assembly. With this development, and after being pushed into prominence by local Catholic priests, Apithy entered politics and won election to Parliament. In 1946, he became a committee vice-president in the Rassemblement Démocratique Africain (RDA), which was a political organization for all of French West Africa. But two years later he withdrew from the RDA and organized a political group concerned exclusively with Dahomey. He became president of the Indépendants d'Outre-Mer (IOM) while still serving in the French National Assembly. Then in 1951 he organized Dahomey's first formal political party, the Parti Républicain Dahoméen (PRD). He soon linked this organization with several different West African interterritorial groups, constantly shifting his political alliances in search of opportunities.

Meanwhile, Apithy held several different offices. He remained in the French National Assembly until 1958, became councillor to the French West Africa Grand Council (1947–1957), and served as a member of the French delegation to the United Nations (1953), mayor of Porto Novo (1956), and deputy in both Dahomey's Conseil Général and the Assemblée Territoriale (1946–1960).

Elections occurred in 1957 to choose members of a colonial legislature whose powers had been expanded by a new French law, the *loi-cadre*. When the PRD won 35 of the 60 seats, Apithy became prime minister in a coalition arrangement with HUBERT MAGA. He joined with Maga in forming a new party, the Parti Progressiste Dahoméen (PPD).

When in 1958 France offered Dahomey and its other colonies the choice of becoming fully independent or remaining loosely joined to France in a French Community, Apithy supported the latter and successfully campaigned for it. He next worked against Dahomey joining its neighbors in a confederation, but his stand split the PPD and led him to resuscitate the old PRD.

Apithy's prime ministry tottered in 1958 when evidence of corruption surfaced. The following year, Maga became prime minister. Apithy served as minister of state but then left to form a new political party, the Parti des Nationalisttes du Dahomey (PND). To quell a challenge by another rival, Justin Ahomadégbé, Maga appointed Apithy minister of finance, and after new elections in 1960 made him vice-president. The two men joined in forming a new coalition party, the Parti Dahoméen de l'Unité (PDU).

In 1960, Dahomey became a completely independent nation under a strong presidency with Maga at the helm. Apithy's power waned, and although he continued as vice-president, he spent most of his time overseas as ambassador to France, Britain, and Switzerland.

Amid economic strife and nationwide strikes, a military coup deposed Maga in 1963. Apithy then returned to Dahomey and became president with Ahomadégbé serving as vice-president. Dahomey's political turmoil continued, however, and in 1965 the military overthrew Apithy. He remained in exile until 1970 when he returned and entered a presidential election in which he finished third. After the military annulled the election and civil war threatened, he took an unexpected course and supported efforts to separate Porto Novo from Dahomey and link it with Nigeria.

In April 1970 the military, Apithy, Maga, and Ahomadégbé agreed to a ruling triumvirate in which the three men would rotate the chairmanship. But this ended with another coup in October 1972 which forced Apithy into retirement. Dahomey subsequently underwent additional change when the coup began the Beninois Revolution. A Marxist-Leninist regime nationalized industries and placed most social activities under its control. Dahomey's name was also changed to its present form, Benin. The nation abandoned Marxism-Leninism in 1989.

Reference: Decalo, Samuel, *Historical Dictionary of Benin*, 1987.

Arron, Henck
(b. 1936)
Suriname

When Henck Arron became minister-president of Suriname in 1973, he faced a nation gripped by tension as racial groups eyed one another with suspicion and fear. When he advocated independence, he unleashed a political storm.

Henck Arron was born on 25 April 1936 in Paramaribo. At the time, Suriname was a Dutch colony heavily reliant on sugar, coffee, and cocoa agriculture and bauxite mining. Arron grew up as a Creole in a racially mixed society. The Creoles were the Negroid descendants of the slaves who had worked Suriname's plantations and received their freedom with abolition in 1863. Many Creoles were light skinned and had adopted European culture, yet the classification "Creole" became complex due to mixing with other ethnic groups. Indeed, Suriname developed a diverse culture as descendants of Hindustani, Javanese, and Chinese laborers populated the country.

". . . we will have to set up a monument, . . . a Suriname that is built up in unity and unanimity."

As political parties developed after World War II, they formed along largely racial lines. As a young man, Arron joined the Creole organization, the Suriname National Party (NPS). Political competition increased when, in 1954, the Netherlands granted Suriname autonomy in its internal affairs. In 1958, a coalition government gained power when the NPS, led by Johan Pengel, joined with the United Hindu Party (VHP). The coalition collapsed, however, in 1967 when the NPS refused VHP demands for more seats in the legislature. The NPS still ruled through a coalition with the Action Front, which represented East Indians. But this alliance collapsed when strikes rocked the government in 1969.

That same year, reforms within the NPS allowed Arron and other younger members to challenge the Pengel leadership. In June, Arron won election as the party's provisional chairman, and in December he became permanent chairman. Arron committed the party to cultural diversity and demanded the Dutch grant Suriname its independence within five years.

In 1970, Arron emerged as undisputed leader of the NPS after Pengel died. His continued calls for independence antagonized the VHP, which feared that nationhood would bring Creole domination. As unemployment and strikes soared, and as elections approached in 1973, Arron acted to regain power for the NPS by forming a united front with the Progressive Suriname People's Party (PSV), organized among working-class Creoles, and the Indonesian Peasants' Party (KTPI). They formed the National Party Alliance (NPK). Arron's strategy worked, and the NPK gained a legislative majority, making Arron minister-president. His victory displayed increased support for independence.

As Arron began his term, he faced a polarized nation with Hindustanis convinced they would be shut out of policy making. Indeed, Arron compiled a cabinet that failed to include one Hindustani. Then on 15 February 1974, he announced the government would obtain independence no later than

1975. The Dutch accepted this favorably as they wanted to grant Suriname its nationhood before the decade ended.

In May 1975, riots spread through Paramaribo, the main city and capital, as Hindustanis protested and set buildings afire. Meanwhile, Arron continued toward independence, reaching an agreement with the Dutch whereby they provided Suriname substantial economic aid. He then presented the legislature with a proposed constitution and stunned the opposition by publicly embracing its leader and inviting him to participate in Suriname's forthcoming appearance at the United Nations. He also agreed to changes in the proposed constitution that met several objections raised by the opposition. This led to a unanimous approval of the constitution, and on 25 November, Suriname became independent.

Arron's tenure as Suriname's leader proved brief. Although his party won the elections held in 1977, his failure to improve the economy weakened his standing. A military coup three years later deposed him and abolished the legislature. The coup leaders arrested Arron in 1980 but released him a few months later.

References: Buddingh, Hans, *Surinam: Politics, Economics, and Society*, 1987; Dew, Edward, *The Difficult Flowering of Surinam: Ethnicity and Politics in a Plural Society*, 1978.

Artigas, José Gervasio
(1764–1850)
Uruguay

As a young man and a daring cowboy, José Gervasio Artigas rustled cattle and smuggled goods. Then he joined the revolution against Spanish rule and emerged as the "father of Uruguay."

On 19 June 1764, José Gervasio Artigas was born in Montevideo, a town overlooking the Río de la Plata. His family was among the original Spanish settlers and had acquired substantial land. José lived both in Montevideo and on the nearby frontier, where he learned his skill as a horseman. After attending a Franciscan school, he traded in hides and became a notorious rustler and smuggler on the wild and largely unsettled interior plains of the Banda Oriental, a land abutting the R'o Uruguay.

At the time, Spain controlled Uruguay (long an area of contention with neighboring Portuguese Brazil) as a part of La Plata. In 1797, Artigas joined the Spanish military and fought against bandits. Two years later, he was named a regimental adjutant. Then in 1808, turmoil gripped Uruguay, as it did all of Spanish America, when Napoleon overthrew Spain's king. This sparked rebellion against the Spanish authorities in the colonies, and in Uruguay the rebels attacked the governor in Montevideo.

Artigas rallied his cowboys behind the rebellion but found his efforts frustrated when a junta in Buenos Aires signed a truce with the Spanish government. Artigas rejected this arrangement and began guerrilla attacks. When the leaders in Buenos Aires went further and agreed to end their rebellion against Spain and recognize the Spanish monarchy, Artigas and many in the Banda Oriental objected. Artigas withdrew from the Banda Oriental, as ordered by the Buenos Aireans, but plotted to keep his army intact. Most Orientales, some 16,000, or 80 percent of the population, decided to join his retreat to Entre R'os province; thus occurred the amazing "Exodus of the Orientales," as ox wagons loaded with household goods joined the military.

Artigas opposed both Spanish rule and Buenos Airean control. When before long the government in Buenos Aires again changed course and decided to attack the Spanish authorities, Artigas joined the fight. He took part in the siege of Montevideo that resulted in Spain's surrender, and then participated in a constitutional convention at

Buenos Aires. Although agreeing to a union of the La Plata lands, he demanded complete autonomy for the Banda Oriental. When the Buenos Aireans rejected this, a civil war ensued. In 1815, Artigas captured Montevideo and extended his control into central La Plata but blundered when he tried to annex Brazilian territory: Portuguese troops attacked him and in January 1817 captured Montevideo. In 1820, he retreated to Entre R'os, and the following year Brazil took over Uruguay. Artigas never returned to the Banda Oriental.

Determined to fight back, Urguayan exiles organized in Buenos Aires in 1825, and under Juan

Lavalleja they crossed the R'o de la Plata and attacked the Brazilians. In 1828, Brazil agreed to recognize Uruguay as an independent republic and, along with Argentina, to protect its sovereignty. Meanwhile, Artigas lived in Paraguay, where he died on 23 September 1850. Although his independent government was short-lived, he provided the impetus for the successful Uruguayan independence movement.

Reference: Street, John, *Artigas and the Emancipation of Uruguay,* 1959.

Attatürk
(1881–1938)
Turkey

A modernizer, a nationalist, a true Turkish patriot, a man who balanced power with fairness—all of this describes Attatürk. He is today ranked among the world's great revolutionaries.

Attatürk was born Mustafa in 1881 to a family of modest means in Salonika, a port in the Ottoman Empire (now called Thessaloniki and located in Greece). His father, Ali Riza, served in the militia during the Russo-Turkish War of 1877–1878, and his mother, Zubeyde Hanim, came from a nearby farming community. Mustafa's father died in 1888, yet left a deep impression on the boy by insisting he go to a secular rather than a religious school. This meant that Mustafa acquired a Western education, and he eventually carried this influence into politics and his reshaping of Turkey.

While in Salonika, Mustafa entered a military secondary school. His mathematics teacher gave him the nickname "Kemal," meaning "the perfect one." In 1895, he enrolled at a military school in Monastir (now called Bitola) and in 1899 attended the War College at Constantinople, where he encountered considerable discontent with the reigning sultan.

> *"The basis of liberty, equality, and justice is the sovereignty of the nation."*

Indeed, throughout Mustafa's youth the Ottoman Empire was known as "the sick man of Europe," a weak entity. Many Turks opposed the sultan as backward; they wanted a modernized, Westernized society that could compete with Europe. Additionally, reformist Turks considered the elite Ottoman rulers too removed, as more an imposed power than one truly reflective of their own society. Some began declaring "I am a Turk," rather than "I am an Ottoman." In short, Turkish nationalism stirred.

Kemal became an active part of this, beginning at the War College, where he helped put together a newspaper criticizing the Ottoman regime. The government discovered his activity but allowed him to graduate, which he did as a second lieutenant in 1902, ranked among the top ten in his class. He then went to the General Staff College and graduated from there in 1905. He idolized Napoleon and was considered a bright young officer, a future great leader.

At this time, Kemal joined with several other officers to begin a secret society that later merged with other organizations to form the Committee of

Union and Progress (CUP), also called the Young Turks. They desired restoration of the 1876 constitution, which had provided for a parliamentary political system. After a revolt erupted in Macedonia in 1908 led by Enver, a Turkish officer, the government agreed to the Young Turks' demand. In elections that followed, the CUP swept the contested seats, but in 1909 conservatives who backed the sultan disallowed the results. Young Turk army units then forced the sultan to abdicate, and he was replaced by his brother.

A split occurred among the Young Turks when some stressed an authoritarian nationalist regime and others demanded liberal reform. For the time being, Kemal remained aloof from this— the 1908 rebellion had occurred without his participation, and he concentrated on his military career. In 1910, he toured Europe, where he observed the French army. From 1912 to 1913, he commanded troops in two Balkan wars that resulted in the Ottomans losing territory. In 1915, during World War I, he helped defend Gallipoli against a British attack—one of the few Turkish victories in the war. Kemal's triumph brought him fame and promotion to general. Under Enver's direction, though, the government assigned him to Syria where, it was thought, he could be contained.

Several other tours of duty ensued, during which time he became seriously ill with kidney problems linked to gonorrhea. Meanwhile, the surrender of the Ottoman government in October 1918 caused its Young Turk leaders, Enver and others, to flee to Germany. In 1919, Kemal returned to Constantinople and found it occupied by British, French, and Italian troops. This strengthened his nationalist commitment and his desire to one day oust the intruders.

Kemal accepted appointment as inspector-general in the Ninth Army on the Black Sea coast, where he was supposed to supervise a postwar disarmament. He arrived on 19 May 1919, and almost immediately made contact with resistance groups that had taken up arms against the sultan. He publicly declared his break with the government, which he claimed had come under foreign control, and promised he would liberate Turkey.

Under pressure from the European occupiers, the sultan dismissed Kemal and ordered his arrest. He, however, resigned his commission and then marched with a small band of followers to Ezurum, where he obtained important support from General Kazim Karabekir, who provided him with 18,000 troops. On 23 July 1919, a congress of delegates from the eastern provinces met at Ezurum and chose Kemal as their chairman. By August, they completed the National Pact, a declaration of demands that included a complete rejection of any restrictions on Turkey's political, judicial, and financial rights. In January 1920 the Ottoman legislature approved the National Pact, but the occupying forces arrested many leading nationalists. Despite this setback, the nationalists convened a Grand National Assembly that met in Ankara and declared Kemal its president.

When Greek forces invaded Turkey, the nationalist army defeated them. As the nationalists gained more power, France and Italy withdrew from Turkey in 1921, and the Soviet Union signed a treaty recognizing Kemal's government.

In July, the Greeks launched another offensive, and this provided Kemal with a great challenge. General Kazim desired to unseat Kemal as the nationalist leader and thus maneuvered to make him commander of the army, expecting that the Greeks would win and Kemal's reputation would be ruined. Kazim then watched in amazement as Kemal surprised the Greeks at the Battle of Sakarya and launched his own offensive in August 1922 that pushed back the invaders.

By now, the Ottoman government in Constantinople had become isolated, and at Kemal's urging, the Grand National Assembly abolished the sultanate and, with it, the Ottoman Empire. The sultan fled, and on 2 October 1923 Kemal's forces occupied Constantinople. On 29 October the Grand National Assembly under Kemal's leadership proclaimed the Turkish republic, with its capital at Ankara.

Kemal determined to make Turkey a modern nation, and to do this he formed the People's Party with a platform called the Six Arrows or Kemalism: republicanism, nationalism, populism, reformism, etatism (state-owned and operated industries), and secularism. These were written into a new constitution in 1924 that provided for the Grand National Assembly to be elected under universal suffrage and have substantial legislative authority.

As president, Kemal initiated enormous change. Various laws emancipated women by granting them suffrage and allowing them to hold seats in the Assembly. Polygamy was made illegal, and civil marriage and divorce with equal rights for both parties were established. Kemal stunned Islamic conservatives by secularizing the state, thus removing religion from any direct role in the government. Toward this end, Holy Law and the holy courts were eliminated, and the Swiss civil code was adopted. He issued a decree banning the wearing of religious garb by anyone not holding a recognized religious office. These actions placed the state behind reform rather than behind Islam.

Among other domestic changes, in 1927 Arabic script was replaced by the Latin alphabet. This, along with more schools, greatly expanded literacy. Kemal toured the nation with chalk and blackboard, displaying the new alphabet and encouraging people to use it. His desire for Westernization included an order that the fez no longer be worn; hats and Western suits were to be the order of the day, the symbols of a new Turkey.

Economic reform included tariff laws in 1929 to protect and encourage Turkish production. Kemal sponsored state-run industries such as factories for textiles, paper, iron, and steel. Although these suffered from ineptitude and shoddy products, output did increase, and the economy exceeded the recent Ottoman performance.

Kemal announced a foreign policy dedicated to "peace at home and peace abroad." He negotiated friendship treaties with 15 nations, including a reconciliation with Greece, and in 1936 scored a diplomatic triumph with the Montreux Convention that allowed Turkey to refortify the Bosporus Straits and control the area while providing for freedom of trade.

These reforms did not go unchallenged. Religious conservatives especially disliked Kemal, and numerous clans opposed the centralization of authority. In the mid-1920s, Kurds led by the Dervish (a Muslim order) rebelled. Kemal crushed the revolt and hanged its leader. He also got the Grand National Assembly to provide him with emergency powers, which he held for four years. Kemal banned the opposition Progressive Republican Party, and after uncovering an assassination plot against him in 1926, numerous political opponents were arrested and executed. These actions, however, represented the only extensive domestic upheaval and the only violent repression by Kemal. He continued to focus on producing a modernized, Westernized state and insisted the military stay out of civilian affairs.

In 1934, the Grand National Assembly gave Mustafa Kemal the name Attatürk, meaning "Father of the Turks." When he died on 10 November 1938 from cirrhosis of the liver, the country fell into great shock and mourning. In 1939, the Turks lay his body in a mausoleum at Rasat Tepe, near Ankara. Attatürk, the man of great reform, always insisted his country do more, and for this he remains a guiding light, with his portrait still displayed in homes and businesses across the land.

References: Kinross, Patrick, *Atatürk: The Rebirth of a Nation,* 1981; Lewis, Bernard, *The Emergence of Modern Turkey,* 1968; Volkan, Vamik, and Norman Itzkowitz, *The Immortal Attatürk,* 1984.

Aung San
(1915–1947)
Myanmar

A thin, almost frail-looking man, frequently unwashed, but dynamic in his actions, Aung San led the military struggle for Myanmar's independence.

Aung San was born on 13 February 1915 in Natmauk. His father had participated in the resistance against British rule. Between 1826 and 1885, Britain made this country, formerly called Burma, a part of India. Because British and Indian companies dominated commerce, Burma failed to develop an entrepreneurial middle class; the small middle class that did exist came from the elite families tied to the once powerful Burmese kings and had little contact with the masses, a situation that for years stifled the emergence of a nationalist leadership.

In the 1930s, Burmese nationalism awoke, just as the British separated the country from India and allowed more Burmese responsibility. The Thakin, or Master, emerged as an extremist group especially popular among students at Rangoon University. The Thakin attracted Aung San, who edited the student newspaper *Oway* (Cry of the Peacock) and was expelled for writing an article attacking the college administration. Shortly after this, Aung Sang, along with U NU, led a student strike protesting British rule. More than 700 students marched through downtown Rangoon.

In 1938, Aung San, who was on the editorial staff of the English-language newspaper *New Burma,* won election to the general-secretary's position of Thakin. As such, he headed a diverse group including communists and those seeking Japanese help to end British rule. When in 1940 the British tried to arrest Aung San, he disguised himself and left the country aboard a Chinese ship.

He then traveled to Japan where the government offered to provide him and his followers military training. Aung San agreed and later returned to Burma to gather recruits. Again he journeyed surreptitiously, this time wearing a kimono, wig, and false teeth. He persuaded several Thakins to return with him to Japan, and this group became immortalized in Burmese history as the Thirty Companions. They received their training on Taiwan, and Aung San was chosen generalissimo.

In 1942, amid World War II, the Thirty Companions arrived in Thailand, where they gathered several hundred Burmese into an army. They believed they could expel the British without the Japanese and then proclaim a truly independent Burma. Japan, however, had other plans and intended to have its military enter Burma and secure the region under Japanese governance. The invading Burmese and Japanese armies defeated the British, and although in 1943 Burmese independence was declared, Japan held the reins.

In the new Burmese government, the nationalist figure Ba Maw served as president, Aung San became defense minister, and others among the Thirty Companions held additional positions. Aung San and several of his colleagues suspected Japanese intentions from the start, and as Japan weakened during the war, they developed a plan to support the approaching Allied forces. The Burmese army subsequently assisted the British, and early in 1945 Japan retreated. In the meantime, Aung San organized the Anti-Fascist People's Freedom League (AFPFL) to assist in the war effort and counteract a strong communist movement led by Than Tun. The AFPFL became Burma's governing party from the late 1940s to the late 1950s.

Once back in Burma, the British wanted to delay any discussions concerning independence, but Aung San, now deputy chairman of Burma's governing Executive Council (thus in effect serving as prime minister), insisted that a plan be developed to achieve nationhood. To support his position, he directed a paralyzing strike by Burma's police. Britain reluctantly agreed to Aung San's demand and in 1946 discussions began in London. Aung San led the Burmese delegation. In January 1947, an agreement provided for Burma's independence within one year. The following month, Aung San successfully negotiated with various hill tribes and secured their loyalty to a new government.

Then on 19 July 1947, shortly after Aung San introduced a constitution, he and most of his cabinet were assassinated as they met in a conference room. Gunmen hired by U Saw, a prewar prime minister who despised Aung San, carried out the bloody deed. U Nu became prime minister and guided Burma through its independence on 4 January 1948. The country changed its name to Myanmar in 1989.

References: Trager, Frank N., *Burma, From Kingdom to Republic: A Historical and Political Analysis,* 1966; U Maung Maung, ed., *Aung San of Burma,* 1962.

Awolowo, Obafemi
(1909–1987)
Nigeria

In striving for independence, Nigerians had to confront their deep-rooted ethnic and sectional antagonisms. Like so many other leaders in this land's independence movement, Obafemi Awolowo struggled with the internal fighting that reflected the weakness of nationalism and jeopardized Nigeria's existence as a nation.

Born in Ikenne in western Nigeria on 6 March 1909, Obafemi Awolowo inherited from his father, a descendant of Oduduwa, founder of the Yoruba kingdom, several royal titles and a privileged status. Obafemi began his schooling in Ikenne at the Church Missionary Society and Wesleyan School, but his father's death burdened him with family chores that slowed his education. Nevertheless, in 1925 he entered the Imo Methodist School in Abeokuta as a full-time student, and the following year enrolled at Wesley College. In 1927, he received a teacher's degree.

After a brief teaching assignment, Awolowo worked as a stenographer from 1930 to 1934, wrote for the *Motor Transporter and Produce Trader*, earned a bachelor's degree in communications, and studied law at the University of London, beginning in 1944. While there, he came into contact with fellow Nigerians and founded a Yoruba-based organization, Egbe Omo Odudua. He also wrote a nationalist work in 1947: *Path to Nigerian Freedom.* That same year, he obtained his law degree and entered the bar at Inner Temple. In 1948, he returned to Nigeria and became solicitor and advocate of the Superior Court, where he served until 1951.

When Nigeria's British rulers granted a series of constitutional changes, Nigerians acquired substantial political power and developed competing political parties reflecting both nationalism and ethnicity. Three of these parties sought eventual independence: the National Council of Nigeria and the Cameroons (NCNC), headed by NNAMDI AZIKIWE; the Northern Peoples' Congress (NPC), headed by Ahmadu Bello with the support of several Muslim modernists, including ABUBAKAR TAFAWA BALEWA; and the Action Group (AG), formed and led by Awolowo.

Awolowo had long been a member of the National Youth Movement (NYM), an organization that attracted a number of prominent young Nigerians and advocated national unity and Commonwealth status for Nigeria. In 1950, Awolowo merged the political activities of the NYM into his new Action Group, which was actually a political wing of Egbe Omo Odudua. Branches of Egbe Omo Odudua appeared in the North and East, and Awolowo further publicized his movement by founding a newspaper, the *Tribune.*

In 1951, the AG defeated the NCNC in Western Region elections and Awolowo became minister of local government there. In 1954, he began serving as premier and finance minister of the Western Region, a post he held for five years. He tried building the AG into a truly national party by forming alliances with minor parties and became an outspoken opponent of continued British rule, charging Britain with having appointed inferior, incompetent officials.

In the important federal nationwide election of 1959 preparatory to independence (obtained on 1 October 1960), Awolowo fought hard against the NPC and NCNC and, unlike his opponents, advocated a West Africa Federation with Ghana and Sierra Leone. His AG did not win the election but continued its solid base of support in the Western Region (one of three adminstrative regions established by Britain to create a federal system). Awolowo had to settle for a position as leader of the opposition in a NPC-NCNC coalition government.

In 1962, a serious confrontation emerged when Awolowo split with his fellow AG leader, Samuel Akintola, prime minister of the Western Region. Awolowo had offered bold proposals that the more conservative Akintola rejected. Awolowo appealed to Nigeria's younger, more educated voters, who suffered from inflation and rising unemployment, by advocating more state ownership of industry and commerce (although he remained committed to the business and professional class) and a less pro-Western foreign policy. Awolowo expelled Akintola from the AG and forced his resignation as prime minister. Akintola's removal provoked bloody riots in May, and an ensuing federal investigation charged Awolowo with misuse of public funds and plotting to overthrow the government. A trial found Awolowo guilty, and he was sentenced to ten years in prison, capping Akintola's victory in this dispute.

> *"West and East Nigeria are as different as Ireland from Germany."*

The conflict shattered the AG and, coupled with widespread criticism of Awolowo's trial and sentencing, destabilized the federal government. This, in turn, contributed to a military coup that overthrew the government in 1966 and triggered a civil war. Many northerners saw the coup as an attempt by the Ibo people, concentrated in the East, to take over the government. Anti-Ibo riots in the North resulted in much bloodshed. Consequently, Biafra, an eastern region dominated by Ibos, began an unsuccessful attempt at secession that racked Nigeria in the late 1960s. Amid this turmoil, the military regime released Awolowo from prison in 1966.

In the following years Awolowo, after much indecision, backed the federal government against the Biafran secessionists, and after the return of civilian rule in 1978, formed the Unity Party, running for the presidency twice, in 1979 and 1983, and losing both times. Another military coup on 31 December 1983 resulted in Awolowo's party being banned. He died on 9 May 1987 in Ikene, leaving a legacy of nationalist aspirations in a turbulent, divided country whose crosscurrents of nationalism, sectionalism, and ethnicity produced great instability.

References: Ajayi, J. F. A., and Michael Crowder, eds., *History of West Africa*, vol. 2, 1988; Awolowo, Obafemi, *Path to Nigerian Freedom*, 1947; Nicolson, I. F., *The Administration of Nigeria, 1900–1960: Men, Methods, and Myths*, 1969.

al-Azhari, Ismail
(1900–1969)
Sudan

After he graduated from Gordon Memorial College, Ismail al-Azhari experienced the oppression that came from British rule in the Sudan: Despite his education, the Europeans scorned him and treated him as inferior. This situation encouraged his nationalism and his desire to see Sudan independent.

Ismail al-Azhari was born in 1900 in Omdurman. He was the son of a prominent Muslim and attended Gordon College in Khartoum and the American University in Beirut. He then became a mathematics instructor and served as an administrator in the Condominium government that had been established by Britain and Egypt as a coopera-tive arrangement to control the Sudan. In 1938, Azhari became secretary to the Graduates' General Congress, a Sudanese political organization. By 1942, he emerged as leader of a radical faction within the group that condemened the Condominium. He distrusted any British promises of eventual independence and advocated unification with Egypt to end Britain's rule. Azhari organized Sudan's first political party, the Ashiqqa ("Brothers").

In the late 1940s, the British agreed to a national Sudanese legislative council. This angered the Egyptians, and in 1951 they proclaimed unilateral rule over the Sudan—a move that antagonized many Sudanese and damaged Azhari's unification platform. But Egypt's action faltered when the Egyptian revolution of 1952 brought to power GAMEL ABDEL NASSER, who as a rebel against foreign domination in his own land sympathized with Sudanese nationalism.

Britain and Egypt then signed an agreement in 1953 promising withdrawal of their troops from Sudan and establishing elections for a national legislature. Azhari's party, now called the National Unionist Party (NUP), still advocated a merger with Egypt, and he received the backing of Egyptians. He won an overwhelming victory over the Umma Party, which opposed unification with Egypt but had a pro-British reputation that disturbed many Sudanese. Also disturbing was the inclusion in Umma of Mahdists, who favored rejuvenating the old Islamic religious state of the late 1800s, which many modernists considered an antiquated idea.

The NUP victory made Azhari prime minister in 1954. He then stunned the Egyptians by reneging on all plans for eventual union. Azhari realized that popular opinion had turned against such cooperation, and that his victory had been largely anti-British, not pro-Egyptian. He became preoccupied, too, with problems in the southern Sudan. That area was different from the north: It was black African rather than Arab, and its religion was not primarily Islamic. Already southerners chafed under the northern domination of Azhari's national government in Khartoum and the use of northern district

> **". . . [the nation] was able . . . to extract its liberty . . . without having to resort to heavy bloodshed . . ."**

commissioners in the south. In 1955, the army in the south's Equatoria Province rebelled. The restoration of order resulted in hundreds of deaths.

Under Azhari's leadership, the NUP not only rejected unity with Egypt but also on 1 January 1956 adopted a Sudanese declaration of independence providing for a representative legislature inclusive of north and south. Azhari seemed to have ended Sudan's long reliance on authoritarian government.

Indeed, parliamentary rule became the symbol of nationalism and independence.

But this system of government proved fragile. The Umma Party advocated a strong presidential-style government, the rejection of unification with Egypt robbed the NUP of its main platform, and many southern Sudanese remained discontent. These factors weakened Azhari, and in 1956 he lost a vote of confidence in Parliament. Abdullah Khalil replaced him, but soon a military regime led by General Ibrahim Abboud supplanted the parliamentary government. Azhari opposed both regimes, and when, in 1964, Abboud resigned and party politics reappeared, he campaigned to again become Sudan's leader. Although his effort failed, he did serve for three years (from 1965 to 1968) in a largely ceremonial role as president. When Azhari died on 26 October 1969, the Sudanese remembered him as a principal architect of their independence.

References: Henderson, K. D. D., *The Making of the Modern Sudan*, 1952; Holt, P. M., *A Modern History of the Sudan*, 1979.

Azikiwe, Nnamdi
(b. 1904)
Nigeria

Rife with ethnic differences and affected by a British policy that discouraged radical alternatives, Nigerians never rallied around a strong leader in their quest for independence. Yet they had their voices of nationalism, and prominent among them was Nnamdi Azikiwe, affectionately called "Zik."

Nnamdi Azikiwe came from the Ibo ethnic group. He was born 16 November 1904 at Zungeru in northern Nigeria and received a good education, a reflection of his father's middle-class values as a government bureaucrat. Azikiwe attended Church Missionary Society's Central School at Onitsha and Hope Waddell Training Institute at Calabar before graduating from the Methodist Boys' High School in Lagos. His father then provided him money to attend college in the United States, so he began his higher education at Howard University in 1926. For his last two undergraduate years he attended Lincoln University in Pennsylvania, where he earned his B.A. in 1930. He pursued a graduate degree and received an M.A. in anthropology from the University of Pennsylvania in 1932.

Before returning to Africa, he worked for a short time as a reporter for the Baltimore *Afro-American* and the Philadelphia *Tribune*. Like many African students who obtained advanced degrees in the United States, Azikiwe experienced black American intellectual influences, including the ideas of Marcus Garvey, who believed all blacks should return to Africa, and of W. E. B. DuBois, who advocated Pan-Africanism—an independent United States of Africa.

Shortly after his return to Nigeria in 1937, Azikiwe joined a new nationalist organization, the National Youth movement. In 1944, he helped organize one of the several parties based on ethnicity and nationalism: the National Council of Nigeria and the Cameroons (NCNC), an Ibo-backed organization. Two other major parties emerged: the Northern Peoples' Congress (NPC), which had Hausa and Fulani support and represented a northern interest as expressed by reform Muslims; and the Action Group (AG), which had Yoruba backing.

The NCNC did not represent Nigeria's first stirrings of nationalism. In the 1920s, Herbert Macaulay had led the Nigerian National Democratic Party, which dominated elections from 1922 to 1938 and advocated self-government for Lagos. But although Macaulay is today considered the father of Nigerian nationalism, his appeal did not extend much beyond Lagos. The NCNC, then, was Nigeria's first truly national political party, and Azikiwe promoted it in several newspapers he owned as a part of Zik Enterprises, Ltd., including the *West African Pilot*, which he had established. Although greatly influenced by Pan-Africanism, Azikiwe advocated national unity and commonwealth status for Nigeria. He served as the NCNC's secretary-general from 1944 to 1946 (with Macaulay as president) and then as president from 1946 to 1960.

Azikiwe took part in several negotiations with Britain for constitutional changes, along with the leaders of the NPC and the AG. A new constitution in 1946 provided more power for a Legislative Council with separate legislative bodies in each of the three regions. This established a federal system reflective of Nigeria's diversity and regional interests. Azikiwe won election to the Legislative Council in 1947. He became NCNC opposition leader in the Western Assembly in 1952 but resigned the next year and won election to the Eastern Assembly. In 1954, he became eastern regional premier.

Azikiwe pushed for more self-government at the 1953 London Conference, and this materialized in the constitutional changes of 1954 and 1957 that, because they conceded so much power to Africans, kept Nigerian nationalism moderate. Further talks were held in London from 1957 to 1958 to prepare Nigeria for independence. The discussions included Azikiwe, OBAFEMI AWOLOWO, leader of the AG, and ABUBAKAR TAFAWA BALEWA, who headed the delegation.

Around this time, a scandal involving Azikiwe almost ended his political career. In 1956, accusations arose that he had diverted government funds to the African Continental Bank in an effort to keep it afloat. Azikiwe and Zik Enterprises held 28,000 shares in this bank. A British investigation found overwhelming evidence of Azikiwe's guilt, but the Nigerian fought back by dissolving the regional legislature and calling for new elections so he could take his case to the people. In the ensuing campaign, he triumphed handily after accusing Britain of plotting to protect European economic monopolies by ruining an African bank.

The federal elections of 1959, important as preparatory to independence, resulted in an NPC victory, but one that required a coalition to form a government. The NPC joined with the NCNC, making Balewa prime minister and Azikiwe president of the senate, a largely ceremonial position. After Nigeria became an independent nation within the British Commonwealth on 1 October 1960, Azikiwe, upon Balewa's recommendation, was appointed by the Crown as governor-general. In 1963, the Nigerian Parliament elected Azikiwe president, another largely ceremonial post that he held until January 1966, when a military coup overthrew the government.

In subsequent years, Azikiwe remained politically active, backing Biafra in its fight for secession from Nigeria in 1968, before switching and supporting the federal government; continuing as an opposition leader in the national legislature; and in 1979, after Nigeria's Second Republic emerged, running unsuccessfully for president as head of the Nigerian People's Party.

He wrote 13 books on topics such as forced labor in Nigeria and the nationalist struggle. Like most Nigerian nationalist leaders, Azikiwe occasionally made radical statements, but he usually proved moderate, reflective of his economic interests and the lack of a revolutionary movement in Nigerian politics.

References: Ajayi, J. F. A., and Michael Crowder, eds., *History of West Africa*, vol. 2, 1988; Azikiwe, Nnamdi, *Our Struggle for Freedom*, 1955; Nicolson, I. F., *The Administration of Nigeria, 1900–1960: Men, Methods, and Myths,* 1969.

Balewa, Abubakar Tafawa
(1912–1966)
Nigeria

Some observers claim that Abubakar Tafawa Balewa, protective of northern Nigerian interests and leery of national independence, underwent an important change after visiting New Orleans in the United States. He became convinced that the relatively harmonious racial and ethnic mixing in that city held hope for cooperative governance in his homeland and that Nigeria could survive as an independent nation.

In 1912, Abubakar Tafawa Balewa was born in Bauchi, located in heavily Islamic northern Nigeria. At age four, he moved to Tafawa Balewa along the Gongola River and, as was custom, adopted the village name as part of his. Abubakar's father, a member of the Geri tribe, held office as a minor official for the Emir of Bauchi, a position that enabled Abubakar to obtain extensive schooling, a notable achievement in a poor land where traditional Islamic beliefs disparaged modern education. Abubakar attended Tafawa Balewa elementary school and then Bauchi Provincial School, from which he graduated in 1925.

He continued his studies at Katsina Training College and earned his teacher's certificate in 1928. He returned to his former school in Bauchi and taught geography, history, and English. In 1944, he became headmaster of the school and one year later became supervisor of all schools in Bauchi province. He attended the London University Institute of Education from 1945 to 1946 and earned an advanced teacher's certificate.

By this time, Nigerian politics had undergone substantial change. A new constitution in 1946, approved by Britain, provided more power for Nigerians, with a protectorate-wide legislature and separate legislative bodies in each of three regions: East, West, and North. This established a federal system. That year, Balewa won election to the Northern Region House of Assembly and in 1947 was chosen as one of five delegates to the Central Legislative Council. In 1952, he was elected to the Nigerian House of Representatives. He served as minister of works for two years, beginning in 1952, and participated in the constitutional discussions in London in 1953. There he successfully gained Nigerian control over his homeland's rail system, which he later converted into a government-owned railroad corporation.

In the 1950s, Balewa, a devout Muslim, served as vice-president of the Northern Peoples' Congress (NPC), a political party representing the interests of the Islamic North, and on whose ticket he had been elected to the House. He angered some of the more conservative emirs with his modernist proposals for economic development, but he remained attached to his region's traditional power structure. Balewa served three years as minister of transport (from 1954 to 1957), during which time he made his trip to New Orleans and other points in the United States and studied the Mississippi River and Ohio River transportation systems.

Further constitutional revisions from 1950 to

1957 turned yet more power over to Nigerians, and in 1957 the NPC's primacy in the House of Representatives earned Balewa appointment as prime minister. Meanwhile, Britain agreed to a timetable for Nigerian independence, setting 1960 as the date. Nigeria's first national election occurred in December 1959 as preparation for nationhood. The NPC won a plurality of the vote, and Balewa formed a coalition government with an opposing party, the National Council of Nigeria and the Cameroons (NCNC). On 1 October 1960, Nigeria became an independent nation within the British Commonwealth.

As prime minister, Balewa continued his moderate policies, favoring a mixed economy over outright socialism and maintaining close relations with the United States. He rejected Pan-Africanism and insisted Nigeria should not relinquish any of its newly won sovereignty. He also supported sanctions against South Africa for its racist regime. But, tellingly, his power was constrained by a federal system that gave substantial powers to the regional governments.

In 1962, a political dispute in the Western Region unsettled Balewa's government. The federal government charged OBAFEMI AWOLOWO, a popular figure, leader of an opposition party (the Action Group), and potential successor to Balewa, with plotting to overthrow the government. The conspiracy trial that led to Awolowo's imprisonment seriously damaged public confidence in Balewa's rule. Corruption and intimidation permeated Balewa's administration—distrust grew between the NPC and the NCNC, with Balewa and NCNC leader (and Nigerian president) NNAMDI AZIKIWE unable to cooperate, and the coalition fell apart.

Late in 1965, the NCNC lost an election filled with voting irregularities. Protests and riots erupted, and Balewa proved unable to stop the violence in which some 2,000 people died. In January 1966 an army coup occurred, and Balewa was kidnapped from his home and killed. A civil war ensued that involved fighting between ethnic groups and the unsuccessful attempt of Biafra, a state led by the Ibo people, to secede.

References: Ajayi, J. F. A., and Michael Crowder, eds., *History of West Africa*, vol. 2, 1988; Nicolson, I. F., *The Administration of Nigeria, 1900–1960: Men, Methods, and Myths*, 1969.

Banda, Hastings Kamuzu
(b. 1902)
Malawi

Hastings Kamuzu Banda achieved a status admired by black Africans: He became a medical doctor in a white man's world. When Malawians sought independence, they turned to him for leadership and helped make him a political messiah.

Born in 1902 of Cewa parents in Kasungu district, Hastings Kamuzu Banda entered Livingstonia Mission in 1915 to become a teacher, but a controversy broke out over an exam he took and the mission expelled him. Banda then traveled to Southern Rhodesia, where he worked as an orderly, a move that convinced him to become a doctor. From there, he journeyed to South Africa and worked as an interpreter at a mine while attending night school. With the help of missionaries, he traveled to the United States and attended Wilberforce Institute in Ohio, from which he graduated in 1928. During the Great Depression, he lived on Chicago's South Side and assisted a professor at the University of Chicago, who was studying Bantu languages. Banda earned a bachelor's degree from the University of Chicago in 1931.

> *"In Nyasaland we mean to be masters, and if this is treasonable, make the most of it."*

He continued his studies at Meharry Medical College in Tennessee, where he obtained an M.D. in 1937. This, however, did not qualify him to practice in British territories, so he journeyed to Scotland in 1938, where he obtained additional medical training. During World War II, he practiced medicine for the National Health Service in Liverpool and at the Mission for Colored Seamen in Tyneside. After the war, he began a successful practice at Harlesden, a London suburb, where he served mainly white patients. Banda's office soon became a gathering place for African expatriates and intellectuals.

Meanwhile, nationalism in Banda's homeland grew. The work of Scottish missionaries stimulated it by emphasizing individualism and the worth of African culture. Friction over land and money was also an important factor. After World War I, the population of Malawi (it was then called Nyasaland) increased, and Africans began moving onto land that Europeans owned but had left fallow. The Europeans, in turn, required many of these squatters to pay high rents—the *thangata* system—that continued a cycle of African impoverishment. Monetarily, wages for European civil servants and other workers far outstripped those of Africans in the same positions (a disparity ameliorated by British reforms in 1959).

But the real spark to nationalist activity was the British drive to federate Nyasaland with Northern and Southern Rhodesia. Although racial discrimination existed in Nyasaland, conditions in Southern Rhodesia were worse, with, for example, restrictive travel regulations requiring blacks to possess a "pass." Furthermore, to many Africans amalgamation with Southern Rhodesia signified establishment of a permanent white state with no hope of eventual independence. Africans protested, but in 1953 Britain went ahead and joined the three colonies into the Federation of Rhodesia and Nyasaland.

British action brought to life the Nyasaland African Congress (NAC), a largely quiescent political group that now began to advocate peaceful protest against the Federation. In this, Banda played a leading role. In 1953, he moved to Ghana, where he continued practicing medicine and helped direct NAC activities. But the NAC strategy of peaceful protest failed when violence broke out in 1954. The organization subsequently abandoned its effort.

In 1955, Britain allowed five African delegates to Nyasaland's Legislative Council, and the NAC won all of these positions. Several NAC leaders, including Kanyama Chiume and Masuako Chipembere, urged Banda to return home. They wanted a dynamic political leader who could appeal to the masses. Banda agreed, and as he toured Nyasaland in 1958 he received an enthusiastic welcome from his countrymen, who cheered whenever he excoriated the Federation. He became president-general of the NAC, with enormous powers to make internal policy. Militant radicals, particularly Chiume and Chipembere, supported him as their hope for independence.

Late in 1958, Banda attended the All-African Peoples' Congress in Ghana. There he renewed ties with KWAME NKRUMAH, whom he had known in London. Nkrumahist ideas influenced him, ideas about creating mass parties and developing Pan-Africanism. Banda returned to Nyasaland and promoted intertribal unity. Then in January 1959, he demanded an African majority in the Legislative Council. After Britain refused, several riots broke out in February, and the Federation government launched Operation Sunrise, banning the NAC and arresting Banda and over 300 other NAC members. Banda was sent to Southern Rhodesia and detained there.

After an outcry in the British Parliament by Liberals who opposed the ruling Conservative government's support of the Federation's action, an investigation began. The subsequent Devlin Report called Operation Sunrise excessive and thus discredited the colonial government. Britain subsequently released the detainees and freed Banda on 1 April 1960.

After he returned home, Banda helped develop a nationalist organization founded in 1959: the Malawi Congress Party (MCP), a successor to the NAC. As MCP leader, Banda attended the London Constitutional Conference in 1960. He wanted a constitution that would provide Nyasaland's

African population with full suffrage; Britain, however, agreed only to extend voting rights to 200,000 blacks, while permitting an African majority in the Legislative Council.

In 1961, the MCP won nearly all the African seats in Nyasaland's Legislative Council, and Banda became minister for natural resources, an important post in which he oversaw agricultural policies. Under yet another constitutional change, he became prime minister in 1963, still within the Federation government.

For all practical purposes, Banda and the MCP had run Nyasaland since 1961. On 31 December 1963, Britain ended the Federation and set Nyasaland's independence for 6 July 1964. On this date, Nyasaland became Malawi, and Banda became prime minister of an independent British Commonwealth nation.

In 1964, pressure built against Banda's tactics. He stressed economic cooperation with white-run Rhodesia and South Africa and operated several government ministries directly. Many believed he had abandoned Pan-Africanism and had become an autocrat. Chipembere and Chiume, two of Banda's most prominent ministers, led this criticism and called for reform. Such strife put the MCP in disarray and produced several violent clashes. Banda then cracked down; he dismissed Chipembere and Chiume, who were encouraged to leave Malawi. Chiume did, but Chipembere organized an ill-fated clash with Banda's military forces. After his defeat, he also left Malawi, thus ridding Banda of another of his most prominent opponents.

A constitutional change in 1966 declared Malawi a republic and voters elected Banda president. By now, he had established an autocratic one-party regime. He frequently jailed his political opponents, and there is evidence he may have ordered several of them to be executed. He continued his moderate policies toward Rhodesia and South Africa and focused on building Malawi's infrastructure and diversifying its agricultural production. In 1971, a constitutional amendment made him president for life.

Into the 1990s, Malawians treated Banda as a chief of chiefs. He followed the many traditional customs accorded tribal leaders, such as carrying a fly whisk in his hand and having women precede him as he walked, sweeping his path with brushwood. In his paternalistic manner, he issued strict orders against practices he considered immoral, such as long hair on men, and his face adorned coins and bank notes and the walls of nearly every shop and office. In addition to the presidency, he held several ministerial positions including those of agriculture, foreign affairs, justice, and public works. He also presided over a huge monopoly of tobacco farms, factories, oil producers, banks, and insurance companies. Through high fees he restricted education, and his policies largely ignored the health services. At the same time, he spent lavishly on himself and built 13 palaces, including one that had 150 rooms and cost $120 million.

Then his hold weakened. The United States, which supported him as a barrier against Soviet expansion during the cold war, cooled toward him as the communist threat decreased; student and labor protests against his autocracy erupted; several opposition newspapers began publishing; and, in 1993, Malawians voted in a referendum to allow a multiparty system. The following year, Banda lost the presidency in an election to Bakili Muluzi, who subsequently released all political prisoners. Banda, however, remained a father symbol of African independence.

References: Pike, John G., *Malawi: A Political and Economic History,* 1968; Rotberg, R. I., *The Rise of Nationalism in Central Africa,* 1966.

◆

Bandaranaike, Solomon West Ridgeway Dias
(1899–1959)
Sri Lanka

Although Solomon West Ridgeway Dias (S. W. R. D.) Bandaranaike did not preside over Sri Lanka's independence, he played a truly revolutionary role in its political development. Bandaranaike so altered Sri Lanka's government that he is considered the founder of his homeland's post-Western era.

S. W. R. D. Bandaranaike, who was born on 8 January 1899 in Colombo, obtained his advanced education at Oxford in England. This would indicate he had a deep attachment to British culture, but he actually broke with that culture as his political career progressed.

In 1925, Bandaranaike joined the bar and returned to Sri Lanka, where he practiced law and entered politics. In 1951, he won election to the State Council, a legislative assembly. Bandaranaike allied himself with the Ceylon National Congress (Congress) and pressed for reforms, but he took a different tack in 1937 when he organized Sinhala Maha Sabha, a group within the Congress that promoted Sinhalese culture (as opposed to the minority Tamils, who also lived on the island).

In 1944, Britain announced its intention to relinquish Sri Lanka, and negotiations began with D. S. Senanayake, who headed the State Council. In 1947, the Independence Act formalized Sri Lanka's nationhood and provided membership in the British Commonwealth. Senanayake became prime minister as leader of the United National Party (UNP), a grouping of disparate religious and ethnic groups.

Bandaranaike had worked with Senanayake in gaining Sri Lankan independence and won election in 1947 to the new House of Representatives as a prominent UNP candidate. Senanayake then appointed him minister of health and local government.

But in July 1951, Bandaranaike broke with Senanayake and the UNP and formed the Sri Lanka Freedom Party (SLFP). Bandaranaike wanted a leftist economic development and a "Sinhalese first" movement. When Senanayake died in an accident in 1952, so too did the symbol of Sri Lankan unity, and politics became more splintered. In elections that year, Bandaranaike and the SLFP lost to the UNP, but just four years later Bandaranaike led his party to an overwhelming victory (allied with other radical groups as the People's United Front). He then began what some call a social revolution. Over the years, Bandaranaike had been moving away from his Western background, and he publicly emphasized the Buddhist faith, dominant among the Sinhalese. He accused the UNP and the Catholic Church of working to destroy Buddhism.

He also called the Independence Act a fake because it tied Sri Lanka to the British Commonwealth. This link, he asserted, should be severed. Furthermore, he wanted greater state control of the economy and, in a highly emotional appeal, demanded that Sinhala be the only official language. This last position struck not only at English and the Westernized elite who embraced it, but also at the minority Tamils, who were Hindu. They considered Bandaranaike's stand a dangerous assault on their culture, intended to make them powerless.

As prime minister, Bandaranaike instituted his program. The Official Language Act deepened the rift with the Tamils, while his welfare programs and food and fuel subsidies drained the treasury. Bandaranaike nationalized many industries and redistributed land to peasants, an act that decreased the concentration of wealth and won him much popular support. In his move away from the West, he established diplomatic relations with many communist nations.

Eventually, Bandaranaike's emotional appeal to the Sinhalese proved his undoing. His policies unleashed Sinhalese-Tamil violence, and in 1959 he was forced to reach an agreement with a Tamil leader to provide considerable autonomy for the Tamils in the north. Although this agreement never took effect, it angered many Buddhists. On 25 September 1959, a Buddhist extremist who believed Bandaranaike had deserted the Sinhalese cause attacked the prime minister, and he died the following day. Yet Bandaranaike's social revolution had turned back many Western influences, and his widow, Sirimavo Rarwatte Dias Bandaranaike, continued his policies when she became the world's first woman prime minister in 1960.

References: de Silva, Chandra Richard, *Sri Lanka: A History*, 1987; Jeffries, Charles, *Ceylon: The Path to Independence*, 1963; Wilson, A. Jeyaratnam, *Politics in Sri Lanka, 1947–1979*, 1979.

Barrow, Errol
(1920–1987)
Barbados

Errol Barrow came from a privileged family, but still identified with the workers and promoted social reform, which he linked to Barbadian independence.

Errol Barrow was born on 21 January 1920 in St. Lucy. His father, Reginald Grant Barrow, an Anglican minister and head of a school, had married into wealth when he wed Ruth O'Neal, the daughter of a plantation owner. Errol received the best of educations: He attended Primary Danish School in the Virgin Islands and then enrolled at Wesley Boy's School in Barbados. From there he attended Combermere, a prep school, and in 1934 began his studies at Harrison College. Upon graduation in 1939, he taught school for a year.

In 1940, Barrow joined the Royal Air Force and went to Canada, where he received training as a navigator. While stationed in England during the Second World War, he flew 53 missions over Europe. Barrow continued in the air force until 1947, when he undertook a demanding academic program and studied at the London School of Economics while reading law at Lincoln's Inn. In 1949, he passed his bar exam and the following year obtained a degree in economics.

Barrow returned to Barbados in 1950, began practicing law, and quickly proved successful. He also entered politics, joining the Barbados Labour Party, dedicated to socialist reform, and in 1951 he won election to the House of Assembly from St. George Parish. However, Barrow soon ran into trouble with Grantley Adams, the party leader. He criticized Adams and his supporters for their excessive conservatism (including their close relationship with the British governor) and became leader of a dissident faction. Adams retaliated by accusing Barrow and the dissidents of communist leanings.

Barrow aligned himself with the Barbadian workers and launched an anticolonial program. In March 1954, he broke completely with Adams and formed the Democratic Labour Party (DLP). He called for lowering the disparity in wealth, widening worker participation in economic decisions, diversifying the economy, and expanding education to help the lower class. In the 1956 elections his party won only 4 out of 23 seats, and he lost his own district, eliminating him from the legislature. Two years later, after he supported the island's sugar workers in their demands for increased wages, and Adams led Barbados into joining several other Caribbean islands to form the West Indian Federation, Barrow was returned to the House, and the DLP scored impressive gains (although he lost his race for a seat in the new federation legislature).

In 1959, Barrow became chairman of the DLP and was appointed finance minister in the Barbadian cabinet. Then in 1961 his party won half the legislative seats, and he was named premier. The victory reflected his effort in building support among the workers, the middle class, and young people in the urban areas. In 1962, the West Indies Federation collapsed, and Barrow attempted to unite Barbados in a modified federation with the Leeward and Windward Islands. At the same time he asked Britain to grant the federated islands their independence.

The new federation, however, soon collapsed, a victim of economic differences and fears among the other states that Barbados would dominate. In 1965, Barrow pushed for Barbados to gain independence on its own. The following year, Britain agreed to Barrow's proposal, and on 30 November 1966 Barbados became an independent nation within the British Commonwealth. Barrow was named prime minister and successfully obtained membership for his nation in the Organization of American States and the UN.

Barrow had built an anticolonial and nationalist reform movement whose momentum he used in gaining internal changes. He always considered national independence to be linked to social independence. Most importantly, he reformed the educational system by providing free secondary schooling, so that social mobility increased. While he advocated more power for the workers, he attracted tourist dollars and developed a friendly investment atmosphere. Barbados emerged as the center for international finance in the eastern Caribbean.

Barrow lost the prime ministry in 1976 but was returned to office a decade later. When he died on 1 June 1987, the nation had lost its founder and one of the most notable reformers in the Caribbean.

Reference: Beckles, Hilary, *A History of Barbados: From Amerindian Settlement to Nation-State*, 1990.

Barton, Edmund
(1849–1920)
Australia

Initially, Edmund Barton focused on politics in his home colony of New South Wales, but the Australian expanded his vision and emerged as a great statesman and nationalist who unified his country.

When Edmund Barton was born in Sydney on 18 January 1849, Australia was a disparate grouping of colonies under British rule. As a young man, Barton obtained from his father, a moderately successful financier, enough backing to attend the University of Sydney. There he excelled in the classics and in 1870 graduated with a master of arts degree. In search of a career, he decided to study law and in 1872 was admitted to the bar. He remained in Sydney and practiced commercial law.

In 1877, Barton lost his first bid for a seat in the New South Wales legislative assembly, but he won two years later. In 1883, he was chosen Speaker of the House, a position he held until 1887, and one which brought him attention throughout the colony. He then served on the Legislative Council, or Upper House, and twice as attorney general, in 1889 and from 1891 to 1893. At this time, he began actively campaigning for national unity. A convention organized by Henry Parkes and Samuel Walker Griffith in 1891 failed to achieve unification, but an economic depression stimulated the desire for an efficient, coordinated government, and Barton, joined by Alfred Deakin of Victoria, put together a new national convention. In doing so, he overcame strenuous objections from legislators in New South Wales, his home colony, and addressed some 300 meetings to rally support.

In 1897, voters chose delegates to the national convention, and Barton won an enormous victory in New South Wales. His popularity caused the delegates to choose him leader of the convention and chairman of the committee assigned to draft a constitution. The completed document, however, ran into opposition from New South Wales and Western Australia, and amendments had to be made, including an agreement to locate the national capital in New South Wales. Barton then headed the campaign to get the constitution ratified by the voters. All the colonies except Western Australia voted yes, and even that region recanted and, in July 1900, approved the document. Meanwhile, Barton led a delegation to London to get British approval of the constitution. Parliament agreed, and on 1 January 1901 the Commonwealth of Australia Constitution took effect. Britain still handled Australia's foreign affairs, but a united nation had emerged.

Under the constitution, Barton was named prime minister, with important support from Deakin, who became attorney general. Barton persuaded Parliament to pass the first federal tariff and an act that effectively blocked Asian immigration. In 1903, he tired of the bickering in Parliament and agreed to resign the prime ministry and serve on the Australian High Court. He took office in September and held the position until his death on 7 January 1920.

References: Deakin, Alfred, *The Federal Story: The Inner History of the Federal Cause, 1880–1900*, 1943; Reynolds, John, *Edmund Barton*, 1948.

Batlle y Ordóñez, José
(1856–1929)
Uruguay

In a nation accustomed to leadership by strong-men, or *caudillos*, José Batlle y Ordóñez, as writer and president, insisted on democracy and constitutionalism with a strong commitment to morality. He quelled a civil war and led his countrymen in instituting bold social and economic reforms.

At the time José Batlle y Ordóñez was born, on 21 May 1856, Uruguay was suffering great turbulence: Ever since independence in 1828, the nation had experienced interference from neighboring Argentina and Brazil, and internal contention between liberals and conservatives, with the latter dispute based not on ideology, but on selfish grabs at power.

José grew up in a prominent political family. His father, Lorenzo Batlle y Grau, supported the liberals and in 1868 became Uruguay's president. José attended preparatory school in Montevideo and then in 1873, one year after his father was overthrown in a coup, studied at the National University. José never obtained a degree and in 1879 journeyed to Paris. He returned in 1881 and worked as a journalist for a newspaper in Montevideo, *La Nación.* Shortly after this, in July, he founded his own newspaper, *El Día,* the voice of the liberals, or Colorado Party.

Batlle's pen proved extremely influential as he expressed the need to regenerate Uruguay through moral force. He supported order, democracy, and assistance to the disadvantaged. In 1887, he was named political chief of the Department, or state, of Minas, but lost his bid for a seat in the Chamber of Deputies. In 1890, he won election as a Colorado Party deputy from Salto Department. Building his support among the middle class and European immigrants, he developed a liberal wing within the Colorado Party and molded it into a cohesive group. At this time, a civil war erupted between the liberals and the conservatives, tensions which would carry into the twentieth century. In 1898, Batlle won election to the Senate, and after an intense political fight the Senators chose him to be their president. On 1 March 1903, he became president of Uruguay.

Batlle immediately faced a rebellion when the conservatives, or Blancos, under Aparicio Saravia took up arms. On 1 September 1904, government forces defeated Saravia, who died in battle, and the conflict ended. Batlle subsequently worked to reunite the nation and develop moderate reforms. In 1905, he reduced income taxes for low-salaried public workers and over the next two years promoted the building of secondary schools and obtained a law liberalizing divorce procedures for women.

After his presidential term ended in 1907, Batlle went to Europe, where he studied the institutions and laws of the Swiss government. He returned to Uruguay in 1911, brimming with ideas to change the nation. Almost immediately upon his return, Uruguayans, attracted by his stand against corruption, elected him president.

Through the newspaper *El Día,* Batlle revealed his bold social and economic program that included guaranteeing freedom of speech and the press, expanding suffrage, creating compulsory free rural schools, and opening college education to women. Significantly, he advocated state ownership of some private companies to lessen the dependence on foreign capital and help the workers.

Legislation to develop his program passed the congress: In 1912, the State Insurance Bank was created, and it provided fire, life, and workers' compensation insurance; the government took over the electric utilities and lowered rates in Montevideo; and Batlle also got the government to build and operate a railroad system, one hampered by unexpectedly high fees. In 1915, he oversaw creation of the National Administration of the Port of Montevideo, which operated that city's important shipping facilities, and he established the eight-hour work day. Although conservatives opposed these programs as extreme, Batlle rejected the more radical demands among liberals to redistribute large landholdings.

Batlle left the presidency in 1915 but remained the foremost leader of the Colorado Party and an enormous influence. With great controversy, he encouraged the writing of a new constitution. Batlle believed that a powerful presidency threatened dictatorship and he wanted it contained. A constitutional convention agreed to limit presidential authority to bureaucratic matters, foreign policy, and defense, while giving to a committee, the National

Council of Administration, power over commerce, public works, industry, and finances. The proposal, which Batlle supported, split the Colorado Party and angered conservatives, yet in 1919 the change was adopted. He also obtained a constitutional separation of church and state.

Batlle served only one term on the National Council of Administration, in 1919, but continued as the guiding force in Uruguayan politics until his death on 20 October 1929. While his programs did not always produce the desired results, his emphasis on social justice and democracy shaped Uruguay after the civil war years into the modern nation it is today.

Reference: Vanger, Milton I., *José Batlle y Ordóñez of Uruguay: The Creator of His Times, 1902–1907,* 1963.

Belgrano, Manuel
(1770–1820)
Argentina

A Creole intellectual, Manuel Belgrano served in the revolutionary junta that gained Argentina its independence, and he became commander of the army.

Manuel Belgrano was born on 3 June 1770 in Buenos Aires. As a young man, he studied law in Spain and then returned home to serve as secretary to the Buenos Aires merchants' guild. In that capacity and heavily influenced by Enlightenment ideas, he railed against trade restrictions imposed on Argentina, then a Spanish colony and part of the Viceroyalty of the R'o de la Plata.

> *"Our liberty can have as many enemies as it likes . . . these experiences form our national character."*

Developments in Europe stimulated discontent in Spanish America: In 1808, Napoleon overthrew Spain's king and by 1810 had crushed the last resistance. That same year, Belgrano, along with MARIANO MORENO and BERNARDINO RIVADAVIA, deposed the viceroy and formed a revolutionary junta. Not everyone in La Plata agreed with this action, which created resistance to the junta in outlying provinces, including present-day Uruguay and Paraguay. Belgrano led the army into Paraguay and tried to gain that region's acquiescence, but he was unsuccessful. This, in turn, caused the junta to collapse, replaced by a triumvirate under the guidance of Rivadavia.

As commander of the army, Belgrano led a successful expedition against pro-Spanish, or royalist, forces in the northwest. He won a major victory at Tucumán on 24 September 1812. The following year, however, he suffered a reverse in Upper Peru (present-day Bolivia). At the same time, the revolution continued to change and JOSÉ DE SAN MARTÍN became its leader, replacing Belgrano as army commander. Belgrano and San Martín both pushed for a declaration of independence from Spain (which did not come until 1816). Later, Belgrano displayed his intense nationalism by designing the blue and white flag of Argentina.

Belgrano had hoped to establish a monarchy in Argentina, and in 1814 he journeyed with Rivadavia to Europe in search of a suitable ruler. This mission, however, ended in failure. Belgrano died on 20 June 1820 in Buenos Aires. Some analysts believe his studiousness made him unsuitable to be a general and that he should be remembered first and foremost as an intellectual leader in the revolution.

Reference: Levene, Ricardo, *A History of Argentina,* 1937.

Ben Bella, Ahmed
(b. 1918?)
Algeria

A secret militant organization, years in prison, radical socialism, and election as premier—all reflect Ahmed Ben Bella's tumultuous life as a revolutionary nationalist.

Amid the mountains of western Algeria, Ahmed Ben Bella was born around 1918. His father was a merchant and landowner. As a boy, Ahmed attended a government elementary school in Maghnia, his home town, and then a high school in Tlemcen. He played soccer with such skill that he considered becoming a professional. When he failed his diploma exam at age 15, he returned to Maghnia and worked on his father's farm. While still in his teens, the nationalist movement attracted him.

Wherever Ben Bella looked in his homeland he saw a European elite suppressing Muslims. Under French Algeria, many Muslims lost their land to the colonizers, Christians who settled the coastal area and, out of fear for retaliation by the Muslims, strongly supported French supremacy.

With World War II, Ben Bella and many Algerians experienced intensified nationalist pressures that had been mounting over decades and coalesced into three different groups: liberal assimilationists who wanted equal rights with Frenchmen; Islamic reformists, as represented by Sheik Abdelhamid Ben Badis, who stressed not immediate independence but religious and national consciousness; and radical anticolonial nationalists led by Messali Hadj, who demanded complete separation from France and, toward this end, organized the infamous North African Star, which advocated a socialist future. In 1937, Hadj had formed the Algerian Peoples' Party (PPA), a mass-based nationalist socialist party.

Ben Bella served in World War II as a sergeant-major with the French army, and at Monte Cassino he saved his commander and directed his battalion. At war's end, he received five decorations for bravery, but when he applied for a commission as a regular army officer the French turned him down: They did not believe Algerians should attain such status. This discrimination and the French crushing of a nationalist rebellion in eastern Algeria convinced Ben Bella that independence must come—and through the barrel of a gun.

First, he joined Hadj's PPA and, after it was outlawed, he joined its successor, the Movement for the Triumph of Democratic Liberties (MTLD) and won a seat on the Maghnia Municipal Council. But the MTLD strategy emphasized working within the political structure. This and Hadj's authoritarian manner rankled Ben Bella. Then, in 1947, he was forced to flee Maghnia after he shot and wounded a man who had laid claim to his farm through falsified documents. Ben Bella lived under an assumed name in Algiers and joined five other dissidents to form the Secret Organization (OS). Still linked with the MTLD, the OS sponsored armed insurrection, and Ben Bella soon became its leader.

In February 1950, Ben Bella led a raid on the post office at Oran that netted a considerable sum of money. The French soon discovered and destroyed the OS, and in May they arrested Ben Bella. In March 1952, he was sentenced to prison but fled in a daring escape, using a saw smuggled to him in some food. He secretly traveled to France, then to Egypt. In 1954, he and several other rebels formed the Revolutionary Committee for Unity and Action (CRUA), and he earned a reputation as a "historic chief" or founding father of the Algerian Revolution. (There were nine other such chiefs.) The CRUA leaders were all dedicated to violent action, and the emergence of this organization is considered by many as the start of the Algerian Revolution.

Presently, the CRUA became the Algerian Front of National Liberation (FLN) and developed a military wing, the Army of National Liberation (ALN). Ben Bella commanded the forces and procured arms and, in 1954, a coordinated attack was launched on police posts, utilities, and other sites. To build solidity, he ordered the execution of politicians who favored a negotiated settlement. His methods raised opposition within the movement, however, even producing a reprimand from FLN leaders in 1956.

The revolutionary fighting involved brutality on both the French and ALN sides and did not go well for the rebels. By 1957, Ben Bella's forces numbered nearly 40,000 and used guerrilla tactics. But France had erected a barbed-wire boundary between Algeria and Morocco and was effectively using reinforcements and forcibly relocating residents to prevent their helping the ALN.

"Every Algerian is a potential guerrilla if he could get a gun."

The French even captured Ben Bella. On 22 October 1956, French pilots diverted to Algiers a Moroccan commercial airplane carrying him and four other leaders. They took Ben Bella to Paris and placed him in prison without a trial. Despite this, he continued his contacts with his fellow revolutionaries and gained heroic stature among many Algerians.

Although suffering numerous setbacks, the FLN emerged victorious, partly because nationalist sentiment continued to grow in Algeria, partly because of international pressures on France, and partly because the war had disrupted many French families. Indeed, the French position became tenuous when, in 1958, the FLN announced formation of a provisional government (GPRA)—a government-in-exile based in Tunis—and it received recognition from many Arab and Third World nations. Finally, a cease-fire occurred in March 1962, and the French released Ben Bella.

As independence neared in July, Ben Bella had a falling out with the provisional premier, Benyousef Ben Khedda, and tried to get him removed. Ben Khedda favored a more cooperationist stance with France while Ben Bella took a militant socialist position. Soon Ben Bella usurped Ben Khedda. He returned to Algeria on 11 July 1962, and at a rally announced his desire for a one-party state. A few days later, he formed a seven-member commission to govern Algeria, and in early August Ben Khedda stepped down. Ben Bella further consolidated his power in the September elections when his candidates captured Parliament which, in turn, elected him president. In his climb, Ben Bella acquired crucial support from the ALN and Colonel Houari Boumédienne.

As president, Ben Bella initiated "autogestion"—a plan to establish the workers' management of the workplace and move Algeria toward a socialist system. Although economic chaos from the revolution remained a vexing problem, Ben Bella brought increased order to a politically unstable environment and provided substantial monies for education. He was a pronounced supporter of the Soviet Union in the cold war and received the Lenin Medal.

Ben Bella raised much opposition when he acted to increase his power. In April 1963, he assumed the general-secretary's position in the FLN. Later that year, he led a constitutional change that centralized his power, and he assumed the title of military commander in chief. His actions stirred factionalism in the FLN and antagonized Boumédienne, who feared Ben Bella would usurp his military authority. The army, which had been so important in Ben Bella's rise to power, turned against him and, in June 1965, removed him from office.

Boumédienne subsequently assumed the presidency and ordered Ben Bella detained. For the next 14 years while Boumédienne ruled and developed a more moderate socialist state, Ben Bella lived in isolation, kept under guard at various army camps. Not until Boumédienne's death in 1978 was Ben Bella transferred to house arrest, and not until 30 October 1980 was he released. Ben Bella spent ten years in exile in France and Switzerland and returned to Algeria in 1990.

References: Entelis, John P., *Algeria: The Revolution Institutionalized*, 1986; Merle, Robert, *Ben Bella*, 1965.

Ben-Gurion, David
(1886–1973)
Israel

A devout Zionist while still in his teens, David Ben-Gurion later delivered Israel's Declaration of Independence and has since been hailed as his nation's Founding Father.

David Ben-Gurion was born David Gruen on 16 October 1886 in Plonsk, Poland. His father, Victor Gruen, had emerged as a leader in the Lovers of Zion, a movement that advocated a return of Jews to their original homeland in Palestine. David received an education at an Orthodox Hebrew school and in his early teens began leading Zionist meetings. He believed that Jews should create a state by developing farms in Palestine. In 1903, he helped begin a branch in Poland of Workers for Zion. So dedicated had he become that in 1906 he emigrated to Palestine, where he worked on Jewish farms in Galilee and changed his name to the ancient Hebraic, Ben-Gurion. At that time, the Turks controlled Palestine, yet he organized the Palestine Labor Party, which had a socialist orientation, and in 1910 edited *Unity*, its official publication. Three years later, he studied Turkish law at Ottoman University.

World War I changed both the situation in Palestine and Ben-Gurion's life. The Turks were ousted, replaced by British rule. Britain obtained a mandate over Palestine in 1922 from the League of Nations and issued the Balfour Declaration that called for a Jewish homeland in the area. At first, few Jews emigrated there, but with the holocaust in Europe the flow of settlers increased in the mid-1930s. Soon the Yishuv, or Jewish community in Palestine, became formidable in terms of economic development and population, and the Arabs grew fearful of Jewish power. They attacked Jews violently, including assaults at the sacred Wailing Wall. In reaction to this dangerous animosity, Britain issued its White Paper, which established limits on Jewish immigration.

Ben-Gurion was intimately involved with these developments. Once the Balfour Declaration was issued, he organized the Jewish Legion of Volunteers to fight in World War I. He enlisted in 1918 (one year after marrying Paula Munwess, a medical student he had met in New York), earned promotion from private to corporal, and participated in the Middle East operations against the Turks, although the fighting had ceased and he did not see battlefield action. In the 1920s, he and Isaac Ben-Zvi expanded the Labor Party and founded Histradut, the General Federation of Jewish Labor, an organization they used to unite the Jewish immigrants into an identifiable polity. Ben-Gurion became the general-secretary of this group in 1921 but resigned in 1933 to join the Jewish Agency for Palestine, which he headed beginning in 1935. The Jewish Agency was the executive branch of the Zionist movement.

Meanwhile, in 1930, he had become leader of Mapai, a re-aligned Israeli Labor Party, and reacted strongly to the White Paper. He called upon Jews to rise up against Britain, and, indeed, the Zionists violated the immigration restrictions and waged a terrorist campaign against the British, including sabotage.

In 1942, Ben-Gurion convened a conference of Zionists at the Biltmore Hotel in New York. In what was called the Biltmore Program they, for the first time, declared their intention to establish an independent Jewish nation. Early in 1947, Britain referred the Palestine issue to the United Nations. The UN, with American agreement, decided to support a partitioning of Palestine into two states—one for the Jews, the other for the Arabs. Yet Arab rejection of this arrangement led to a civil war marked by terrorist activities on both sides. Late in 1947, the British began withdrawing from Palestine, and as they did so the Jewish settlers gained the military advantage over the Arabs.

On 14 May 1948, Ben-Gurion read in Tel Aviv the Israeli Declaration of Independence, and on

16 May the Jewish Council elected CHAIM WEIZ-MANN president of a provisional government. During that year, the military conflict widened as the Arab nations adjacent to Israel waged war against the new nation. Early in 1949, however, the Jews prevailed, and the Arab nations signed an armistice.

As Israel formed a Parliament, the Knesset, and held elections in 1949, Ben-Gurion organized a political coalition that won a majority. He subsequently became prime minister and in that position proved more strident and militant than Chaim Weizmann and several other leaders. He considered Israel to be a renewal of the Jewish homeland, destroyed 2,000 years earlier by the Roman diaspora. He focused on building a strong state economically, educationally, and militarily, with rapid and firm reprisals against any Arab attacks, or threatened attacks.

For health reasons, he resigned as prime minister in 1953, but he accepted appointment as minister of defense in 1955 and when his party, Mapai, won a parliamentary majority he again became prime minister. A new crisis soon confronted him. In 1956, Egypt announced its nationalization of the Suez Canal, a move that greatly angered Britain and France. Ben-Gurion flew to the latter nation, where he met secretly with British and French leaders and agreed to join with them in attacking Egypt. In the ensuing war, the Israeli army captured the Sinai Peninsula. Upon American insistence, the UN intervened and convinced Ben-Gurion to relinquish the Sinai in return for placing UN forces on patrol along the Egyptian-Israeli border.

> *"We shall fight the war as if there was no White Paper."*

In subsequent years, Ben-Gurion engaged in numerous unsuccessful efforts to arrange a general peace and security agreement with the Arab nations. In June 1963, a political controversy forced him from the prime ministry when, in the Lavon Affair, Israelis argued over his responsibility for ordering attacks in 1954 against British and American property in Egypt. The implication that Ben-Gurion had done something wrong tore Mapai apart. When he resigned, Levi Eshkol became prime minister. A prominent member of the Zionist movement, he was secretary to Mapai during World War II and from 1948 to 1963 headed the settlement department of the Jewish Agency. After his election to the Knesset, he served under Ben-Gurion as finance minister. Two years after resigning, Ben-Gurion formed a political party, the Rafi, to challenge Eshkol. Although his effort failed, he still served in the Knesset until 1970.

Ben-Gurion published many of his speeches and several works about the Jewish community. These included *Ourselves and Our Neighbors* (1920), *The Labor Movement and Revisionism* (1933), *The Working Class and the Nation* (1933), *The Struggle* (1949), and *Israel at War* (1950). He was a guiding light in the Zionist movement and a strong, determined leader. The other prominent nationalist leaders, Chaim Weizmann, MOSHE DAYAN, and GOLDA MEIR, all stood beholden to Ben-Gurion, who died on 1 December 1973.

References: Bar-Zohar, Michel, *Ben-Gurion: The Armed Prophet*, 1967; Kurzman, Dan, *Ben-Gurion: Prophet of Fire*, 1983.

◆

Berisha, Sali

(b. 1944)
Albania

A heart surgeon turned politician, Sali Berisha helped organize a political party that challenged the Communist system and its totalitarian hold on Albania. In so doing, he created a new nation struggling to shake off years of isolation.

Sali Berisha was born in the Gjakova Highlands on 15 October 1944, a time when Albania emerged from World War II and a Marxist state developed under Enver Hoxha. During Hoxha's rule, Albania followed an independent foreign policy and a staunch Stalinist ideology. Hoxha received assistance from fellow communist nations Yugoslavia, China, and the Soviet Union, and at various times denounced each for their revisionism or corruption of communism. He closed Albania's borders to most outside contact and imposed a strict totalitarianism that left his nation isolated and impoverished.

In 1967, Berisha graduated from the medical school at the University of Tirana. He was then appointed to Tirana Hospital as a teacher and physician in the cardiology department. In 1986, he was elected to the European Committee on Medical Scientific Research, headquartered at Copenhagen. The following year he obtained a doctorate from the University of Tirana.

Meanwhile, Hoxha died in 1985, and liberal tendencies in Eastern Europe along with the collapse of the Albanian economy shattered the system he left behind (despite modest reforms by the new leader Ramiz Alia).

In 1990, Berisha entered the tumultuous political fray when he published articles in the Albanian press criticizing the Communist system and calling for freedom of expression and political pluralism. On 8 December, he joined in the demonstrations by students and workers against the government and founded the Albanian Democratic Party (ADP) with Aleksander Meksi. It was the first party to oppose the Communists, presently reorganized as the Socialist Party of Albania (SPA). In the spring of 1991, the ADP won a third of the legislative seats in an election restricted by Communist-imposed rules, and later in the year Berisha agreed to have

his party join the SPA in a coalition government. But policy differences and continued economic deterioration convinced Berisha to withdraw the ADP from the arrangement. In new elections held in March 1992, Berisha and the ADP scored an overwhelming victory, and on 8 April the legislature elected him president. He, in turn, appointed Meksi as premier.

Berisha, one of several activists and intellectuals in Albania who rose to leadership positions while possessing little government experience, founded a new nation, sharply different from its Communist predecessor. He supported shock treatment for the Albanian economy: rapid and deep changes to construct a free market. Businesses were privatized, collective farms dismantled, the budget deficit reduced, and the volume of exports increased. Yet Albania suffered from outmoded industries and shortages of farming equipment. The SPA consequently criticized Berisha, arguing some industries should have remained under state control and reforms should have been introduced gradually. In July 1992 the SPA made gains in local elections.

"The President of one of the world's poorest countries should live like the rest of its citizens."

The following spring, Berisha dismissed several of his ministers and there occurred a marked shift in appointments to persons with more government expertise. These moves earned widespread approval among Albanians.

Berisha also had to face problems with Yugoslavia. When ethnic Albanians in Kosovo, a province in the Yugoslav republic of Serbia, declared their independence in 1991, Albania officially recognized them (the only nation to do so). Serbia reacted to the rebellion by repressing the Kosovo Albanians, and Berisha worried that the Serbs would attack Albania or ignite a general Balkan war. He thus moved closer to Turkey, and in December 1992 Albania joined the Organization of the Islamic Conference. He also tried to develop closer ties with Western Europe through the North Atlantic Treaty Organization (NATO), urging that NATO troops be stationed in Kosovo. In April 1993, Berisha's government extended diplomatic recognition to Macedonia, a former Yugoslav republic that had a large number of ethnic Albanians. He developed cordial relations with two other Yugoslav breakaway republics: Slovenia and Croatia. On the other hand, relations with Greece worsened as controversies emerged over the treatment received by ethnic Greeks in Albania and the emigration of thousands of Albanians who sought work in Greece.

Berisha claims that the restoration of order and public confidence is the most important task

awaiting him. He rejects opulent living and insists on humble surroundings befitting, he said, an impoverished land. Albania's problems could overwhelm many a leader. Whether Berisha will conquer or give in to them remains to be seen.

References: Biberaj, Elez, *Albania: A Socialist Maverick*, 1990; Kaplan, Robert D., *Balkan Ghosts: A Journey through History*, 1993; Zickel, Raymond, and Walter R. Iwaskiw, eds., *Albania: A Country Study*, 1994.

Bird, Vere Cornwall
(b. 1910)
Antigua and Barbuda

When Vere Cornwall Bird appeared at his nation's independence ceremony wearing a tuxedo and sandals, he told those who questioned his unusual appearance that he always dressed to be comfortable. Many observers, however, considered Bird's action indicative of an eccentric style that permeated his politics.

Vere Cornwall Bird was born on 7 December 1910 on Antigua and attended St. John's Boys' School. As a teenager he joined the Salvation Army, received his training in Trinidad, and worked for the charitable organization on Grenada.

In the 1930s, Bird returned to Antigua and became active in the trade union movement. From 1943 until 1967, he served as president of the Antigua Trades and Labour Union. During this time, Antigua, a British colony, experienced considerable political change, and Bird developed an impressive public career. In the 1940s, he served several times on the island's Legislative Council and was reelected to it after Britain instituted universal suffrage. In 1967, Antigua gained

associate status, meaning the island had full control of its internal affairs while Britain handled foreign policy and defense. This resulted in the island obtaining a premier and a House of Representatives to replace its Legislative Council. As leader of the Antigua Labour Party (ALP), Bird obtained the premiership.

Many Antiguans contemplated independence. Bird, however, rejected any rapid moves toward this goal. He believed Antigua's economy remained too underdeveloped. In 1971, Bird lost his office after the ALP finished second to the Progressive Labour Movement (PLM), led by George Walter. In the 1976 elections, Walter championed immediate independence while Bird continued his cautious stand. The ALP emerged victorious, and Bird regained the premiership while one of his sons, Lester Bird, became deputy premier.

In 1978, Bird declared Antigua and Barbuda ready for independence, and two years later the ALP won 13 of 17 legislative seats preparatory to nationhood. Many in Barbuda opposed linkage to Antigua, but Britain rejected Barbudian pleas for a separate status. On 1 November 1981, Antigua and Barbuda officially became independent with Bird as their first prime minister. He stressed economic development, including new hotels and improvements at the airport to boost tourism. He also pursued diversification to lessen the nation's reliance on imports.

Bird developed a powerful political organization, but in the 1980s scandal engulfed his administration. In 1989, he won reelection amid charges of voting irregularities, charges confirmed by an investigation. In April 1990, one of Bird's sons, Vere Bird Jr., who served in the government as public works minister, was implicated in a deal that provided weapons for a drug cartel in Colombia. The prime minister was forced to dismiss his son and in November accepted recommendations from a committee of inquiry that prohibited Vere

> *". . . after 350 years, if we're not ready to look after our own destiny . . . then we never will be."*

Bird Jr. from ever holding public office and committed the prime minister to a campaign against governmental corruption.

In 1992, demonstrations and strikes erupted against Bird after reports revealed that he had misappropriated government funds. The ALP held an emergency meeting to select a new leader, but Bird held onto his post. Controversy struck again when Bird acted to nullify anticorruption legislation. The prime minister announced his intention not to seek reelection, and in September 1993 the ALP selected Lester Bird as its new leader, while Vere Bird accepted a secondary position as party chairman. Critics saw the action as perpetuating a family political monopoly. Nevertheless, Lester Bird won election as prime minister on 8 March 1994.

Reference: Griffiths, John, *The Caribbean in the Twentieth Century*, 1984.

Bismarck, Otto von
(1815–1898)
Germany

Otto von Bismarck exemplified *realpolitik* as he cajoled, bribed, and lied his way to German unification. He built a powerful industrial, military state; yet he knew his goals and rejected a conquest of the European continent in favor of a strong empire within secure borders.

On 1 April 1815, Otto von Bismarck was born to Ferdinand von Bismarck and Wilhelmina Mencken at the Schönhausen family manor in Brandenburg state. His father was a Brandenburg squire, and his mother came from a wealthy family. In 1816, Otto's parents moved to Kniephof, a family estate in Prussian Pomerania. At age seven, he went to Plamann's Institute, a preparatory school. In 1832, he entered the University of Göttingen and in

1834 transferred to the University of Berlin. He did not excel and contemplated a military career, but his mother influenced him to join the civil service. Bored by his bureaucratic duties and shaken by his mother's death in 1839, followed by family financial problems, he became lord of the Schönhausen estate. In 1847, he began a long, happy, and close marriage to Johanna von Puttkamer.

Soon his political reputation grew. The same year as his marriage he was appointed to the legislature for Prussian domains and showed his conservatism when he chastised those liberals and democrats who had protested monarchical power. Bismarck proclaimed that the existing political structure, which included enormous influence for the elite Junkers (the landed aristocracy), represented the natural order. A statesman, he asserted, should protect this order—the crown must rule through a hereditary aristocracy or else liberalism would destroy Prussia.

He remained steadfast in this belief amid the populist revolutions that shook central Europe in 1848 and threatened to shatter the German Confederation. When the Diet, or Confederation legislature, began debating how to strengthen the union, which consisted of Prussia, Austria, and numerous smaller states and free cities, Bismarck, as a Prussian representative, favored a "Small German" program. Under it, Prussia would avoid federating with Austria and instead dominate the smaller states. He also worked hard to block any Austrian designs and supported neutrality in the Crimean War of 1854 to 1856, in which England and France joined Turkey in fighting Russia. He did this to win the support of Russia in any maneuvers against Austria.

In 1862, King William I appointed Bismarck prime minister of Prussia and minister of foreign affairs. In this capacity, he began his domination of Prussian politics. As the king had expected and desired, Bismarck rode roughshod over the Prussian legislature, illegally collecting taxes and spending revenues to enlarge the army. He suppressed opposition newspapers and had some opposition representatives arrested.

Bismarck pursued his main goal of ending the German Confederation and building a Prussian empire separate from Austria, and his success in this allowed him to assure the power of the king and nobility over the middle class. In 1864, he manipulated Austria into joining with Prussia in a war against Denmark, from which they obtained several duchies. He then turned on the Austrians, claiming they improperly administered one of the duchies, Holstein. He subsequently ordered Prussian troops into Holstein and provoked a war.

The conflict lasted only seven weeks, largely because Bismarck had signed a secret treaty with Italy (in violation of the German Confederation), and the Austrians thus found themselves fighting on two fronts. The Austrian defeat led to Prussia annexing several states, including Hanover, Hesse-Cassel, and Schleswig-Holstein. Yet Bismarck overruled those Prussians who wanted to severely punish Austria, for he realized he might need that nation's help or at least forbearance in the future.

The Peace of Prague, signed in 1866, replaced the German Confederation with a North German Confederation organized by Prussia and consisting of states north of the Main River. Several states south of the river were to form a separate South German Confederation, but Bismarck violated the treaty and signed secret agreements with those states that, in effect, placed them under Prussian control. Badsen, Bavaria, and Wurtemberg soon joined this arrangement, and by 1871 Bismarck had unified Germany under Prussian leadership.

The new Confederation adopted a constitution under Bismarck's direction that allowed a legislature, but it had few real powers, and its decisions could be vetoed by the Federal Council, which had delegates from all the member states. Prussian votes dominated, so that the king of Prussia really ruled Germany. In this arrangement, Bismarck became chancellor.

In the meantime he provoked yet another war. In a move Bismarck knew would anger France, he attempted to get a Prussian-backed prince elevated to the Spanish throne. This greatly worried the French, who believed Prussia was trying to surround them. When France opposed Bismarck's move, the Prussian leader unleashed a virulent anti-French campaign in the German newspapers, raising tensions further, and provoking France into declaring war in July 1870.

In this Franco-Prussian War, Bismarck's army defeated the French early in 1871, and the chancellor obtained Alsace and most of Lorraine, two mineral-rich provinces. The war solidified the attachment of the South German states to the North, and on 18 January 1871 the German Empire was declared with William I as emperor. Bismarck continued as chancellor and foreign minister, and was also made a prince.

After the French loss, Bismarck refrained from any additional territorial conquest. He had defeated his most powerful enemies and now worked to secure Germany against any other threats. He modernized German society by developing railroads and a central bank. In the 1870s, he struck against the Center party, which consisted mainly of Catholics, by initiating anti-Catholic legislation in his Kulturkampf campaign. (He repealed these laws in the 1880s to gain Catholic support against the Liberals and Social Democrats, who had by then become his main opponents.)

In 1879, Bismarck established a protective tariff to help German industry and agriculture. To contain labor unrest, particularly by the socialists, he promoted legislation to assist workers. In 1882, the government enacted compulsory insurance against illness, and in 1884 a similar bill was passed to cover accidents. A social security system soon followed, with insurance for old age. Also in the 1880s, Bismarck formed an alliance with Austria to guard against any French attack, an action he always thought possible.

In 1888, William II ascended to the German throne. The new emperor, headstrong and limited in talent, nevertheless wanted to exert his authority and soon collided with Bismarck. They had numerous policy differences, and in March 1890 William obtained Bismarck's resignation.

Bismarck retired to his estate at Friedrichsruh, where he wrote his memoirs and criticized government policy. He died on 30 July 1898, leaving behind an empire whose autocracy reflected his own disdain for democratic institutions. Although the German Empire fell in World War I, and there followed several changes in governmental structure and territorial configuration, including foreign occupation after World War II, Bismarck had laid the foundation for a German nation rebuilt and revitalized in the 1990s under HELMUT KOHL.

"The object of war is to conquer peace . . ."

References: Crankshaw, Edward, *Bismarck,* 1983; Kent, George O., *Bismarck and His Times,* 1978; Robertson, C. Grant, *Bismarck,* 1969.

Boganda, Barthelemy
(1910–1959)
Central African Republic

For years, French colonialists had plundered Oubangui-Chari, the current Central African Republic. When the Oubanguians elected Barthelemy Boganda in 1946 as their representative to the French Assembly, they expected change, and Boganda looked forward to a receptive audience in Paris. Yet many French officials considered him an agitator, and their opposition smashed Boganda's idealistic hopes, producing a political awakening for him and his homeland.

On 4 April 1910, Barthelemy Boganda was born in Boubangui, a poor village in a poor land. He experienced substantial hardship, including the murder of his mother by guards who supervised the rubber harvest for a French business. Such cruel treatment was not unknown to others in this isolated land—ever since the French had turned the countryside over to huge concessionary companies that used forced labor and virtually controlled the political system.

Despite his mother's death as a result of the exploitive arrangement, Boganda did not develop an early or intense dislike toward France. Catholic missionaries adopted him in 1922 and encouraged the intelligent young man to become a priest. He received ordination in 1938 and served at various missions. His work earned him prominence as an Oubangui leader, and in 1946 the Bishop of Bangui suggested he run for a seat in the French National Assembly.

After his election, Boganda brought with him to Paris numerous reform proposals. They included eliminating all forced labor (which the Assembly made illegal although several companies continued the practice for years afterward), ending racial segregation, and reducing the heavy taxes that had hurt Oubangui-Chari's already impoverished population. When the Assembly offered strong resistance to most of his efforts, Boganda decided that the masses in his homeland needed political education and activation.

In 1950, a personal development also influenced him when he married Michelle Jourdain, a Frenchwoman. This brought racial slurs against him from French political opponents and further stimulated his fight against white supremacy. But his marriage also reinforced his long-held sympathy for French culture and institutions.

"Zo kew zo—a man is a man."

Boganda aimed at weakening the grip held by the concessionary companies. In 1948, he organized the Socoulolé, a cooperative of small property holders. French advisors helped him, and the organization received some government funding, but the Socoulolé soon collapsed. Its officials embarrassed Boganda by misusing funds, the staff had little knowledge of production or management practices, and many larger companies refused to cooperate, fearing the Socoulolé would weaken their power.

Boganda organized politically when, in 1949, he and several of his followers met in Bangui and formed the Movement for the Social Evolution of Black Africa, or MESAN. He condemned exploitive practices that had stripped the land and impoverished society, and he equated the continuing forced labor with slavery. Yet Boganda did not push for independence. MESAN focused more on cultivating black identity than on nationalism.

When in 1951 a French district official arrested Boganda and his wife during a dispute between Portuguese traders and the Socoulolé, the Oubanguian became more than a leader—he became a hero, to many a messiah. Even French officials recognized his enormous influence. In April 1954, a riot broke out in Berberati against a white employer accused of murdering two of his workers. The French governor asked Boganda's help in restoring peace. Boganda agreed, traveled to the area, and in a display of his popular support calmed the protestors, probably averting a massacre of whites and a severe French retaliation.

On 18 November 1956, Boganda became mayor of Bangui when, much to the chagrin of French officials, he defeated the white candidate who had received European support. The next year Boganda became head of the Grand Council for the French Equatorial Africa. At this time, the French Assembly passed the *loi-cadre* or Enabling Act, reform legislation that transferred more power to the territories and established assemblies and an executive branch or Council of Government in each one. In March 1957, MESAN won all the seats in the Oubangui-Chari legislature, and as party leader Boganda headed the Council of Government. He quickly encountered more problems as he lacked sufficient numbers of trained Oubanguians to serve in offices, the local French officialdom opposed the Council, and his reputation suffered when he engaged his government in an unsuccessful effort to expand coffee production.

Then a development caught Boganda by surprise. In 1958, France announced a new policy toward the territories whereby they could become part of a French Community. France would control foreign policy, currency, and common economic concerns, but each territory would have its own constitution and government. A territory could reject Community membership and opt for complete independence, but it would lose all French military and economic assistance. France insisted that each territory within French Equatorial Africa vote separately from all others on the issue of Community status.

The situation put Boganda in a difficult spot. He preferred Community status to the uncertainties of complete independence, but not with Oubangui-Chari as a separate entity; a divided central Africa, he believed, would make economic progress more difficult and greatly hamper his landlocked homeland, which lacked ports and other transportation facilities. Boganda advocated forming within the Community a united republic comprising Oubangui-Chari, Gabon, the Congo, and Chad that would in turn be federated with Rwanda, Burundi, Angola, and Cameroon in a United States of Latin Africa. But he could not get the various territories to agree, and France rejected the plan. He then reluctantly supported formation of the Central African Republic, consisting only of Oubangui-Chari. On 1 December 1958, the constitution of the Central African Republic took effect, and the country assumed its position within the French Community.

Boganda began initiating numerous reforms. He moved to establish local district councils with substantial authority and to convert the territorial legislature into one operating within a republican framework. He called for elections in April 1959 and organized MESAN for the campaign. Then on 29 March 1959, after a political stopover at Berberati, Boganda boarded an airplane. The following day searchers discovered its wreckage strewn near the Lobaye Valley. Boganda and all aboard had been killed. The plane apparently had suffered an explosion of a suspicious—and still undetermined—origin.

The Central African Republic had lost a charismatic leader whose appeal had surmounted regional and tribal differences. Under Boganda's successor, DAVID DACKO, the Republic gained full independence on 13 August 1960.

References: Kalck, Pierre, *Central African Republic: A Failure in De-Colonisation*, 1971; O'Toole, Thomas, *The Central African Republic: The Continent's Hidden Heart*, 1986.

Bolívar, Simón
(1783–1830)
Colombia, Ecuador, Peru, Venezuela

In 1805, Simón Bolívar, later called "The Liberator," visited Rome, where he climbed the heights of Monte Sacro, fell to his knees, and pleaded with God to witness his declaration: He would free his homeland from Spain.

Simón Bolívar was born on 24 July 1783 in Caracas to a wealthy family of Spanish descent. Spain ruled his country, Venezuela, as it had since the beginning of the sixteenth century. By the time Simón reached age nine he had lost both his parents, and his maternal uncle, Carlos Palacios, supervised his upbringing. From a tutor he learned Enlightenment ideas and was especially attracted to the philosophy of Rousseau. In 1799, he was sent to Europe, where he completed his education. He lived in Spain for three years and married Maria Teresa de Toro, the daughter of a Spanish nobleman. Tragedy soon struck, however, for soon after Bolívar returned to Venezuela in 1802, his wife died of yellow fever.

Bolívar again journeyed to Europe in 1804 and visited Italy and France, where Napoleon's grandeur infused him. He traveled to the United States in 1807 and then sailed to Venezuela.

The following year, the Spanish Empire trembled when Napoleon conquered the Iberian Peninsula and appointed his brother ruler of Spain. In Spanish America, confusion resulted: Although the colonies unanimously refused to recognize the new ruler, some colonists opted to remain loyal to the deposed king, while others decided to fight for independence. Bolívar sided with the latter, and in 1810 joined a revolutionary group that expelled the Spanish governor from Venezuela. The ruling junta then sent Bolívar to England in search of assistance. Although the English refused Bolívar's requests, the revolutionary convinced FRANCISCO DE MIRANDA, a prominent Venezuelan nationalist, to return home and help in the rebellion.

In 1811, Venezuela declared its independence, and early the following year Miranda became head of the revolutionary government (and the rebel Congress eventually granted him dictatorial powers). Bolívar won an important battle at Valencia, an engagement that earned him the loyalty and admiration of his men. But a split developed in the revolutionary leadership: Miranda gained Bolívar's enmity when he signed an armistice with Spain—a move engendered in part by Bolívar's having lost a harbor fortress to the enemy. Bolívar then delivered Miranda to the Spanish. In gratitude, Spain decided not to jail Bolívar and instead rewarded him with passage to Curacao, a Dutch Caribbean island.

After journeying to New Grenada (Colombia),

Bolívar planned another attack and in August 1813 led an army triumphantly into Caracas, proclaimed the country a republic, and was made its leader with the title of "Liberator." He had not, however, secured his position, and in 1814 the Spanish, supported by Venezuelan *llaneros,* or cowboys, defeated the Liberator, who fled to Jamaica. Bolívar then wrote one of the important works in Latin American history, "The Letter from Jamaica," in which he expressed his grand scheme to establish republics throughout Spanish America with representative bodies and presidents chosen for life. Anxious to continue the fight, he obtained weapons and money from Haiti and in March 1816 sailed for Venezuela. Spanish forces, however, again turned him away.

"I desire to see America fashioned into the greatest nation in the world . . ."

Despite this setback, several factors converged to work in Bolívar's favor. For one, the *llaneros,* led by JOSÉ ANTONIO PÁEZ, a daring cavalryman who became one of the founders of Venezuela, shifted their loyalty to the revolutionaries. Second, Bolívar changed his strategy to focus on the resource-rich Orinoco River basin, rather than Caracas with its heavy fortifications. Third, several thousand adventurers arrived from England to help the Liberator.

In 1817, Bolívar led his army into the Orinoco region and established a temporary capital, Angostura. He then surprised the Spanish by attacking New Grenada: In 1819, he and his men trekked through steamy tropical jungles and across the frigid 11,000-foot Andes and, on 7 August, met the enemy at Boyacá and scored a stunning victory.

Even though Spain still held substantial territory, Bolívar audaciously formed Gran Colombia, encompassing Colombia, Venezuela, and Ecuador. By now, the Liberator held the initiative, and turmoil within Spain disrupted the Spanish war effort. In June 1821, Bolívar, leading an army of 6,500 men, won a crucial battle at Carabobo, and the following year ANTONIO JOSÉ DE SUCRE, Bolívar's foremost general, defeated the Spanish at Pichincha, in Ecuador. On 16 June, Bolívar marched his army into Quito. Thus Gran Colombia had been liberated, and Bolívar ruled under a new constitution that made him president.

Spain still maintained control of Peru, though, and at this point Bolívar met with JOSÉ DE SAN MARTÍN, the great Argentinean revolutionary who had liberated his homeland and Chile. San Martín had already entered Lima and declared Peruvian independence, but the Spanish retained a grip on the interior. On 26 July 1822, Bolívar and San Martín conferred at Guayaquil, in Ecuador. Details of their discussion have been lost, but San Martín left Ecuador, apparently resigned to Bolívar's dominance, and went into exile.

In August 1824, Bolívar and Sucre defeated the Spanish at Junin in Peru, and four months later Sucre defeated them at Ayacucho. The country was now free, and Bolívar was president of Gran Colombia and Peru. In 1825, Sucre eliminated the last Spanish opposition in Upper Peru, which upon independence became Bolivia, named after Bolívar. The Liberator drafted the constitution for that republic, complete with a weak legislature and a lifetime president, a position filled by Sucre (after Bolívar ruled on an interim basis for five months).

Bolívar, meanwhile, battled severe illness and a spreading discontent with his rule. In 1826, he crafted a league of Hispanic-American states that held a congress in Panama. Colombia, Peru, Mexico, and the Central American Federation sent delegates, and they agreed to a treaty of alliance. Plans for a joint military and a regular congress proved unsuccessful.

Civil war soon erupted in Gran Colombia when Venezuelan and Colombian forces clashed. Bolívar quickly left Peru and arranged a new constitution that granted Venezuela greater autonomy. Elections to a national convention in 1828 produced more opposition to Bolívar, who then assumed dictatorial powers over Gran Colombia. That autumn, dissidents tried to kill Bolívar but failed. As the Liberator battled tuberculosis, Venezuela seceded from Gran Colombia in September 1830, followed by Ecuador.

On 3 May 1830, Bolívar left Bogotá, headed for exile in Europe, but he made it only to Santa Marta on the Caribbean coast, where he died on 17 December. Grandiose in his schemes, headstrong and difficult, Bolívar nevertheless conquered enormous obstacles in gaining South American independence.

References: Angell, Hildegarde, *Simón Bolívar: South American Liberator,* 1930; Del Rio, Daniel, *Simón Bolívar,* 1965; Johnson, John J., *Simón Bolívar and Spanish American Independence, 1783–1830,* 1968; Masur, Gerhard, *Simón Bolívar,* 1969; Trend, J. B., *Bolívar and the Independence of Spanish America,* 1946.

Bolkiah, Haji Hassanal
(b. 1946)
Brunei

Haji Hassanal Bolkiah proved a reluctant nationalist, wary of any changes that might threaten his power and the enormous wealth that came from his country's oil reserves.

As the son of the youngest brother of Brunei's reigning sultan, Haji Hassanal Bolkiah was born a prince on 15 July 1946. While growing up, he lived amid sumptuous surroundings, in the Palace of the Abode of Peace, whose spacious grounds abutted the Brunei River. When in 1950 the sultan died, the boy's father, Penigran Omar Ali Saifuddein, ascended to the throne and because of his many building projects gained a reputation as the "architect of modern Brunei."

Despite this modernization, Prince Hassanal was raised in a traditional Muslim environment and at age 13 was sent to the Jalan Gurney School in Kuala Lumpur. He entered the Victoria Institution, in the same city, two years later.

By this time, nationalist pressures were growing in Brunei and threatening the conservative sultanate. Indeed, the country suffered an identity crisis in seeking to determine its relations with Britain, which controlled it as a protectorate, and with its neighbors. The Brunei People's Party (PRB) under Sheikh A. M. Azahari criticized the arrangement with Britain and advocated self-government.

Then, in 1961 the issue of whether to federate with Malay (later Malaysia) took a central position: The sultan favored it and the PRB opposed it (preferring, instead, a merger with Borneo). Political tensions soon led to a rebellion. The sultan requested assistance, and by late 1962 some 2,000 British troops crushed the uprising. The crisis convinced the sultan to abandon his federation plan and, importantly, it convinced Prince Hassanal of the need to make political reforms.

In 1963, the prince entered the Sultan Omar Ali Saifuddein College in Brunei. From there, he enrolled in the Royal Military Academy at Sandhurst in England, a training school for elites associated with the British Empire. His stay was interrupted when his father abdicated the throne in 1967.

The prince, installed on 5 October as Sultan Bolkiah, worked to weaken opposing political parties. Perhaps his greatest challenges were the need to mend relations with Malaysia and determine Brunei's future status as a British protectorate. By 1966, Britain indicated strongly its desire to grant Brunei more autonomy. Sultan Bolkiah continued as a restraining force, nervous that independence might imperil the small country's security in the face of threats from Malaysia and left-wing elements.

Finally, in 1978 Sultan Bolkiah reached an agreement with Britain whereby Brunei was to gain full independence five years later. This arrangement was made possible after Malaysia began moderating its relations, thus lessening its threat to Brunei. On 1 January 1984, Brunei obtained its nationhood, with the sultan declaring the country a democratic Muslim monarchy. He served as both ruler and prime minister, and he appointed the cabinet, thereby retaining his enormous power.

Sultan Bolkiah's accomplishments included beginning a campaign against drug abuse, establishing the University of Brunei Darussalam, increasing the number of schools, opening a new hospital, reinforcing Islamic law, and planning economic diversification, particularly the enhancement of farming. Most significantly, he expanded the Seria oil field that made the sultanate enormously wealthy. Citizens received free health care and schooling, and interest-free loans to buy homes and cars. Sultan Bolkiah may face a crisis, however, when oil reserves are exhausted, probably near the year 2010.

Reference: Chalfont, Arthur Gwynne Jones, Baron, *By God's Will: A Portrait of the Sultan of Brunei*, 1989.

Bonifacio, Andres
(1863–1897)
Philippines

Andres Bonifacio took the Philippine Revolution further than his nationalist predecessors. Eschewing mere reform, which itself was bold against an intransigent Spanish colonialism, he advocated full independence.

Born 30 November 1863 of poor parents in Manila, and lacking much formal education, Andres Bonifacio became a warehouse worker and later an agent selling rattan and various items for a trading company. As an avid reader, he constantly tried to improve himself and was particularly attracted to works on the French Revolution.

In the late nineteenth century, a nationalist rebellion emerged in the Philippines, stimulated by the writings of JOSÉ RIZAL, who pushed the Spanish colonial rulers for civil liberties and other changes. Bonifacio joined Liga Filipina, an organization begun by Rizal to promote a reformist agenda. Spain reacted to this nationalist protest by arresting Rizal in 1892 and executing him in 1896. Rizal's arrest encouraged Bonifacio's radicalization, and in 1892 he founded the Katipunan, an organization whose secret ceremonies he modeled after the Masons. The Katipunan did not advocate Rizal's limited reforms; instead, it sought full independence for the Philippines and changes in an oppressive class structure. Indeed, Bonifacio wanted to promote the principles of the French Revolution. By 1896, the Katipunan had some 10,000 members, mainly from the working and lower classes.

With Rizal's death, Bonifacio launched an armed insurrection against Spanish rule, beginning with an attack on Luzon. Spain reacted harshly to Bonifacio's uprising and by 1897 forced the contingent of rebel troops under his command into the hills, while other troops under EMILIO AGUINALDO fought more effectively. Later that year, a truce halted the fighting. Meanwhile, a serious dispute had split the rebels when, earlier in 1897, Aguinaldo declared himself the leader of a new government whose political structure would be determined later. Bonifacio considered Aguinaldo's action a usurpation of power and refused to recognize the declaration. When he tried to establish his own government, Aguinaldo had him arrested and, on 10 May 1897, executed for treason.

Despite his failure as a military leader and what many analysts consider his excessive adventurism, Bonifacio is considered one of the three great leaders of the Philippine Revolution, along with Rizal and Aguinaldo. He formed the radical organization essential to the uprising, and although this revolution failed in its goal of immediate independence, it set in motion continuing nationalist forces that, after World War II, brought nationhood under MANUEL ROXAS.

References: Agoncillo, Teodoro, *The Revolt of the Masses: The Story of Bonifacio and the Katipunan*, 1956; Agoncillo, Teodoro, *The Writings and Trial of Andres Bonifacio*, 1963; Karnow, Stanley, *In Our Image: America's Empire in the Philippines*, 1989.

Bonifácio, Jose Andrada e Silva
(1763–1838)
Brazil

An ardent nationalist, Jose Bonifácio instilled in his homeland's emperor a commitment to Brazilian interests and promoted among his people a national identity.

Jose Bonifácio (also known by his full name, Jose Bonifácio Andrada e Silva) was born on 13 June 1763 in São Paulo. As a young man, he obtained a law degree at Coimbra and then journeyed to Europe where he studied natural science in Prussia, Denmark, Sweden, and several other countries. When, during the Napoleonic Wars, France invaded Portugal, he fought on the Portuguese side.

The French conquest of Portugal in 1807 produced a monumental change in Brazil, at the time a Portuguese colony. Portugal's royal family, including the regent ruler, settled there to live in exile, and in 1815 Brazil was declared a partner in the United Kingdom of Portugal, Brazil, and Algarve. This development stimulated Brazilian nationalism as the colonists felt equal to the Europeans. In 1816, after the defeat of France, Portugal's regent ruler returned to Iberia and reigned as King João VI. He left his son, Prince Dom Pedro, behind to govern Brazil. In 1821, the Portuguese Parliament attempted to return Brazil to its colonial status and ordered Dom Pedro back to Portugal. He, however, refused and in 1822 organized a new cabinet that included Bonifácio, who had returned home in 1819 with an outstanding reputation as a lawyer, intellectual, and soldier.

Brazil remained under Portuguese control, if only nominally, but Bonifácio's nationalism influenced Dom Pedro and produced further change. As minister of the kingdom, Bonifácio convinced the prince to consider himself first and foremost a Brazilian. He also moved quickly to centralize authority by placing the provinces under the control of Rio de Janeiro. After Dom Pedro made it known he would nullify any unfavorable legislation emitting from the Portuguese Parliament, Bonifácio sent a letter to several foreign governments urging them to establish direct relations with Brazil. Clearly, independence approached, and it reached fruition after Portugal declared a reduction in Dom Pedro's powers, and Bonifácio urged the prince to pronounce Brazil a separate nation. Dom Pedro agreed, and on 1 December 1822 he was crowned Emperor of Brazil as PEDRO I.

Bonifácio ran into trouble when he condemned slavery and criticized the emperor for being too closely tied to Portuguese interests. Although wanting to maintain the monarchy, Bonifácio supported additional power for the largely ineffectual legislature—not a popular position with Dom Pedro—and this led in 1823 to his imprisonment and then deportation to France.

In 1831, Dom Pedro abdicated in favor of his son, who ruled as PEDRO II. He returned to Portugal but left his four children behind and appointed Bonifácio as their tutor. Bonifácio died on 6 April 1838. Most Brazilians looked fondly on him as protector of their interests, and he was later considered the primary founder of their nation. Later that century, in 1889, the Brazilian monarchy collapsed and MANUEL DEODORO DA FONSECA established a republic.

References: Correa da Costa, Sergio, *Every Inch a King: A Biography of Dom Pedro I*, 1964; Macaulay, Neill, *Dom Pedro*, 1986.

Botha, Louis
(1862–1919)
South Africa

A nationalist committed to South African unity, Louis Botha forged white solidarity by oppressing the black majority.

Louis Botha was born on the frontier, near Greytown in Natal, on 27 September 1862. His father was a farmer who had migrated inland to obtain land and escape the infusion of British immigrants into the Cape area. At this time, South Africa was not a single entity; rather, Europeans had developed four separate colonies: Cape Colony, Natal, Transvaal, and the Orange Free State. Britain controlled the first two; Voortrekkers, or Afrikaner pioneers, persons of largely Dutch descent, created the latter two. Many Voortrekkers, however, such as the elder Botha, settled in Natal. The settlers in the Cape Colony allowed considerable political influence for the majority black population, but the Voortrekkers in Transvaal and the Orange Free State created a strict color line.

Shortly after Botha was born, his family moved to the Orange Free State. Botha obtained little formal schooling on the frontier. In 1884, he became involved in a civil war when he joined a military unit of Boers (another name for the Dutch settlers) that fought for a faction among the Zulus. As a result of backing the winning side, the Boers received several million acres of land from the Zulus. Botha then helped organize the area politically and it became part of Transvaal. In 1897, he won election to the legislature, where he favored a conciliatory policy toward English settlers.

Tensions continued to build, however, between the English and the Afrikaners, and in 1899 the Boer War erupted. Botha served as aide-de-camp to General Lucas Meyer and commanded the army at Ladysmith after Meyer fell ill. In two battles he decimated the British forces, although eventually they reinforced Ladysmith. Early in 1900, Botha became deputy to the commander of all the Boer forces, and several weeks later obtained the full command. Britain's army, however, gained the upper hand, and in 1902 the Boers agreed to negotiate. Botha was a signatory to the Peace of Vereeniging, which brought Transvaal and the Orange Free State under British control.

After the war, Botha joined with JAN SMUTS to form a political party, Het Volk (The People). He sought to unite the four South African colonies into a single nation. In 1907, he became prime minister of Transvaal after Britain allowed the colony internal self-government. He and Smuts headed a convention the following year to pursue union, and in 1909 Britain agreed to the creation of an independent republic. The Union of South Africa subsequently emerged in 1910.

A national convention chose Botha as South Africa's first prime minister. Perhaps his most serious challenge involved race policy. The whites in South Africa were a minority and questions arose as to how they would relate to the nonwhite majority of blacks, mixed-race ("Coloureds"), and Indians. Botha also had to decide Afrikaner-English relations.

He supported segregationist policies to maintain white supremacy and cooperationist policies to ease animosities among the whites. He built the South African Party in 1911 to advance this approach. Conservative Afrikaners who disliked cooperation with the English were angered, however, and James Hertzog organized the Orangia Union to oppose him. (Other opposition came from the largely English Unionist Party.)

When, with the advent of World War I, Botha decided to side with Britain and attack German South West Africa, some Afrikaners started an uprising. Botha crushed it and in 1915 proceeded to defeat the Germans. Upon the request of Britain, he accepted a seat in that nation's War Cabinet and in 1919 participated in the peace conference at Versailles, where he inveighed against any harsh treatment of the Germans. On 27 August, he died in Pretoria.

In subsequent years, racial segregation and tensions increased after the Afrikaners solidified the system of white supremacy in the 1940s and 1950s. This produced a strident campaign by blacks for democratic reforms. NELSON MANDELA emerged as the African leader who, in the 1990s, pressured FREDERIK WILLEM DE KLERK to make revolutionary changes in the South African government, changes that led in 1994 to Mandela's election as president.

References: Engelenburg, Frans V., *General Botha*, 1929; Spender, Harold, *General Botha: The Career and the Man*, 1916.

Bourguiba, Habib Ben Ali
(b. 1903)
Tunisia

By the 1950s, the French had concluded they could not do without Habib Ben Ali Bourguiba's help. For two decades he had led Tunisia's nationalist movement; now he could bring internal auotonomy through peaceful means.

Habib Ben Ali Bourguiba was born the son of an army officer in Monastir, a fishing village, in 1903. He was educated in Tunis, where he graduated from a French high school. He then pursued a law degree at the University of Paris, and upon his return to Tunis in 1928 was admitted to the bar.

In Bourguiba's youthful years, Tunisia experienced turmoil and change. The French had landed troops in 1881 and forced upon the monarch, or bey, a treaty that established a protectorate. Then in 1919, Abd al-Aziz Thaalbi wrote *La Tunisie Martyre,* a book that claimed Western influences had destroyed Tunisia's golden age. He organized Dustur, or the Constitution Party, which called for a Tunisian legislature with substantial power. Bourguiba joined Dustur but soon considered it too moderate. In 1932, he and others published a newspaper, *L'Action Tunisienne,* and defended traditional Tunisian customs while advancing modern nationalism and developing a populist appeal. In March 1934, he met with other disaffected Dusturs in Ksar Hellal and organized the Neo-Dustur (New Constitutional) Party. France, however, outlawed the organization and arrested Bourguiba.

Despite this, Bourguiba's crusade was aided by a worsening economy. French settlers had appropriated large landholdings and the worldwide depression in the 1930s struck Tunisia, particularly damaging its wheat, olive oil, and wine exports.

In 1936, a leftist government in France released Bourguiba but did not agree to any Neo-Dustur proposals. Abd al-Aziz Thaalbi tried to regain control of the nationalist movement, but Bourguiba's appeal proved too strong. In 1938, a riot caused the French to again imprison Bour-

guiba. He was not released until World War II, when the German occupiers in France let him go.

He returned to Tunis in 1943 and advocated home rule. In 1944, he, the Dusturs, and the communists together issued the "Manifesto for the Tunisian Front" that called for self-rule and a national assembly, but stopped short of demanding independence. When France rejected this appeal, Bourguiba decided on a renewed effort in 1945; two paths were open to him: He could lead a violent internal revolt or encourage external pressure on France. Bourguiba opted for the latter. At the same time, he distanced himself from the extreme left and led his trade union followers out of the communist-dominated workers' confederation.

Bourguiba traveled to the United States in 1951 and made a speech supporting Tunisian independence. The French, however, still rejected autonomy, and in January 1952, they once more arrested Bourguiba. In 1954, France allowed reforms in Tunisia, yet the Neo-Dustur opposed them as insufficient. Riots then erupted in the cities, and as the situation worsened France released Bourguiba in 1955 and agreed to new negotiations.

In April, an agreement was reached that provided additional power for Tunisians, and Bourguiba considered this an important step toward independence. The French, indeed, soon went further, largely because of a worsening situation in Algeria that drained their resources. France thus agreed in 1956 to Tunisian independence, officially obtained on 20 March 1956. The Neo-Dustur won a majority in legislative elections that year, and Bourguiba became prime minister. In 1957, he had the legislature end the monarchy and declare Tunisia a republic with himself as president.

Bourguiba stressed modernity and progress, and in this he and the Neo-Dustur conflicted, for many Tunisians emphasized traditional Islam. Nevertheless, nationalism had an enormous influence and often brought the disparate sides together. Bourguiba created a unified judicial system, modernized schools, and placed many mosques under government control. He also diversified the economy to produce less reliance on agriculture and implemented socialist planning. When, however, the government approached insolvency in the 1970s, Bourguiba shifted direction to emphasize private investment that made Tunisia heavily reliant on foreigners. Bourguiba entered the 1980s with his nation suffering high inflation and unemployment. Still, he retained a high degree of power through the Neo-Dustur. Throughout his presidency, he pursued his programs by often circumventing the legislature and issuing decrees.

In 1987, Bourguiba appointed General Zine el-Abidine Ben Ali as prime minister. Late in the year, a team of doctors declared Bourguiba, now an old man, as medically unfit to hold office. He stepped down and Ben Ali became president in what some referred to as a bloodless coup.

Reference: Perkins, Kenneth J., *Tunisia: Crossroads of the Islamic and European Worlds*, 1986.

Brătianu, Ion
(1821–1891)
Romania

With King Carol I, Ion Brătianu united Moldavia and Walachia to create Romania as a unified nation.

Ion Brătianu was born on 2 June 1821 in Pitesti, a town located in Walachia. At the time, Walachia was experiencing considerable turmoil, and in the year of Brătianu's birth, a nationalist uprising by Romanians occurred against the ruling Greek princes. By 1848, Brătianu had joined many of his countrymen in their desire for a united, independent Romania. That year, revolutions erupted in Europe and Romanian peasants rebelled in Transylvania. Brătianu demanded that Moldavia and Walachia be joined, and he supported a revolutionary platform calling for universal suffrage and freedom of speech, association, and assembly.

In 1856, shortly after the Crimean War, France backed Brătianu, after he lobbied Emperor Napoleon III, and in 1859, Moldavia and Walachia united under Prince Alexandru Cuza. The prince initiated numerous reforms, including the end of serfdom and forced labor, but he antagonized wealthier Romanians, and when he secularized monastic property he antagonized the Greek Orthodox Church. Brătianu founded the Liberal Party to oppose the prince and, in 1866, Brătianu helped direct a coup that overthrew the prince.

He subsequently nominated Prince Karl of Germany's Hohenzollern-Sigmaringen family to become the new prince (Karl would rule until 1914). Brătianu was appointed minister of finance in the government and immediately went to work formulating a new constitution. When completed, it established a bicameral legislature and included guarantees of basic liberties, such as freedom of speech, religion, and assembly.

Brătianu was discredited in the prince's eyes when a faction of his Liberal Party acted amid the Franco-Prussian War of 1870 to depose him. The prince put down the revolt, but the Liberal Party became more outspoken against the ruler. Beginning in 1876, Brătianu served as premier and was instrumental in getting the European powers that met at the Congress of Vienna in 1880 to recognize Romania as independent.

In 1881, the Romanian Parliament declared the nation a kingdom and Karl as King Carol I. Although Romania now had a full-fledged monarchy, Brătianu held most of the power, and from 1881 to 1888, he dominated Romanian politics. Under his guidance, foreign trade increased and new port facilities were built. But there was also a continued maldistribution of land and persecution of Jews. After Russia annexed southern Bessarabia, Brătianu supported cooperation with Germany and Austria-Hungary to offset Russian power.

Brătianu retired from office in 1888 and died at Florica on 16 May 1891. Romania had been united and after World War I the nation doubled in size, acquiring Transylvania and other areas. Yet it lost land in 1938 to Russia, Hungary, and Bulgaria and after World War II fell to Russian domination until ION ILIESCU helped topple the Communist regime.

References: Kaplan, Robert D., *Balkan Ghosts: A Journey Through History*, 1993; Riker, T. W., *The Making of Roumania*, 1971.

Brown, George
(1818–1880)
Canada

As an influential newspaperman, George Brown initially derided French influence in Canada. Later, though, he underwent a transformation and promoted national unity.

George Brown was born in Edinburgh, Scotland, on 29 November 1818 and at age 19 emigrated to New York City, where he lived until 1843, when he moved to Canada. The following year, he began the *Globe*, a newspaper in Toronto. Brown used the *Globe* as a means to promote reform, particularly the separation of church and state. Just four years earlier, Britain had created the Province of Canada by uniting Canada East (today, Québec) with Canada West (today, Ontario) and Brown worried that the French, who predominated in the former area, would dominate the government. His criticism of the Roman Catholic Church and its influence won him many enemies in Canada East.

In 1857, Brown was elected to a seat in the Canadian Parliament as an independent from Kent County. In his drive to separate church and state, he led a successful campaign to end the policy of setting aside Crown land to support the clergy. He put together a Liberal Party organization that resulted in his becoming premier for a brief period in 1858.

At this time, he developed a broader vision and advocated a united Canada that would consist of the Province of Canada and the Maritime Provinces of New Brunswick, Nova Scotia, and Prince Edward Island. In 1861, he was defeated in his reelection bid but two years later returned to Parliament; by now his disgust with the Province of Canada system had intensified—the government seemed paralyzed, wracked by sectional disputes between Canada West and Canada East made worse by the arrangement that gave each side equal representation in Parliament despite Canada West's greater population. Constitutional reform appeared more urgent than ever.

In 1864, Brown joined JOHN ALEXANDER MACDONALD, the prime minister for the Province of Canada, and attended a meeting in Charlottetown on Prince Edward Island with several other leaders. The most prominent leaders included: GEORGE ÉTIENNE CARTIER from Canada East, SAMUEL TILLEY from New Brunswick, and CHARLES TUPPER from Nova Scotia. The delegates agreed to convene another meeting in Québec to discuss a national union. This conference, held in September, resulted in resolutions to form a confederation.

Brown, meanwhile, joined Macdonald's cabinet and then resigned from the government in 1865 to protest the terms of a trade and fisheries reciprocity treaty with the United States. After the Dominion of Canada officially came into existence on 1 July 1867, Brown ran for a seat in the new Parliament, but lost.

Brown envisioned Canada stretching to the Pacific Ocean and helped acquire the Northwest Territory from Britain. In 1873, he entered the Senate and under the Liberal prime minister, Alexander Mackenzie, journeyed in 1874 to Washington, D.C., where he negotiated a new reciprocity agreement with the United States that was rejected by the American Senate.

Shortly thereafter, Brown left the government and devoted his time to the *Globe.* On 9 May 1880, a disgruntled employee shot and killed him. Brown, a founder of the Liberal Party, was also one of the "fathers of confederation," and his conversion to a national vision did much to create a united Canada.

Reference: Creighton, Donald, *The Road to Confederation: The Emergence of Canada, 1863–1867,* 1965.

Burnham, Forbes
(1923–1985)
Guyana

Soon after Forbes Burnham presided over Guyana's independence, he changed his course from moderation to declaring a cooperative republic: a country socialistic and aligned with the communist world.

Forbes Burnham was born on 20 February 1923 in Kitty, Guyana. His father was a politically astute headmaster at that town's primary school, and as a result the younger Forbes was exposed at an early age to his homeland's leading political issues. At that time, Britain ruled what is now Guyana as the colony of British Guiana, and there existed distinct racial differences between the Indo-Guyanese and the Afro-Guyanese. Forbes belonged to the latter group and championed it in his political career.

After compiling an impressive academic record, young Forbes attended law school at the University of London, where he obtained his degree in 1947. When he returned home two years later, he entered politics and provided much-needed leadership to the Afro-Guyanese commu-

> *"The final control of economic development of any country must be the responsibility of the state."*

nity. Along with CHEDDI JAGAN, Burnham formed the People's Progressive Party (PPP) and became its chairman. He ran for a seat on the Georgetown council in 1950, but lost, and he helped develop the party's platform that criticized British practices and supported socialist development.

In 1955, Burnham split with Jagan and formed a separate wing within the PPP. He followed a more moderate course than his former ally and appealed directly to the Afro-Guyanese, particularly in advocating that Guyana join a proposed West Indies Federation. Burnham lost to Jagan in the 1957 elections and he subsequently merged his faction with the United Democratic Party to form the People's National Congress (PNC).

After Jagan became prime minister in 1961, Burnham directed the PNC in staging demonstrations and even riots to disrupt the government. This upheaval was supported by money and guidance from the United States Central Intelligence Agency. In 1964, the British reapportioned the colonial legislature, and this allowed the PNC to capture additional seats in that year's election. Although the PNC finished second to the PPP, Burnham formed a coalition with a third party and on 14 December 1964 became prime minister after the British, under U.S. pressure, ousted Jagan from office.

At first, Burnham moderated Jagan's policies and even ended relations with Communist Cuba. He endorsed Guyana's push for independence, and nationhood came on 26 May 1966 amid an expanding economy. Elections in 1968 resulted in a decisive PNC victory. At that point, Burnham shifted his policies and committed his administration to socialism.

In 1970, Burnham declared Guyana a "cooperative republic" and called for self-reliance. To achieve this, he began nationalizing industries, such as the bauxite mines and sugar plantations. He also reestablished relations with Cuba, condemned imperialism, and praised liberation movements in southern Africa. Domestically, he consolidated his power by declaring the government inseparable from the PNC.

Two dramatic developments, however, undermined Burnham. In 1978 religious fanatics under Jim Jones, an American, killed a United States congressman, Leo J. Ryan, at their settlement in western Guyana, and they then committed mass suicide in fear of retaliation. Investigations revealed a close relationship between Jones and the Guyanese government, and this damaged Burnham's reputation. Second, Burnham's administration was implicated in the death of a prominent opposition leader.

On top of this, the Guyanese economy declined as public services deteriorated and Burnham ran up a huge debt. In voting widely held to have been fraudulent, Burnham won election in 1980 to the newly created presidency, a position much stronger than prime minister. Five years later, as economic stagnation gripped the country, Burnham became ill, and on 6 August 1985 he died. His radical course was eventually abandoned by his successor, Desmond Hoyte.

Reference: Merrill, Tim, ed., *Guyana and Belize: Country Studies*, 1993.

Bustamante, William
(1884–1977)
Jamaica

A man with a varied career as a soldier, businessman, labor organizer, and political leader, William Bustamante sought to direct Jamaica's development along conservative lines.

William Alexander Bustamante was born William Alexander Clarke on 24 February 1884 in Blenheim. His father, an immigrant from Ireland, was a planter who struggled to make ends meet, and his mother was of Arawak Indian blood. At age 15, Colonel Arnulfo Bustamante, a Spanish officer visiting Jamaica, adopted William and took him to Spain, where the youngster obtained an education.

Young Bustamante then enlisted in the Spanish army and fought in Morocco. From there, he traveled to many different places and engaged in a wide variety of jobs. He went to Havana, Cuba, where he was the police inspector, and then to Panama, where he managed a tramway system. In 1923, he traveled to New York City and worked as a dietician in a Harlem hospital. He took his savings and invested carefully in the stock market, taking advantage of price declines during the 1929 collapse. In an era when people desperately needed cash, he began lending money, and by 1932 he had acquired some wealth.

He subsequently returned to Jamaica and entered the labor movement. Amid unrest in the late 1930s, he rallied the workers against unjust laws administered by the British, who governed Jamaica as a Crown Colony. His fiery speeches encouraged more protests and endeared him to many workers, who nicknamed him "Busta." He founded the Bustamante Industrial Trade Union (BITU) in 1938, and made it Jamaica's largest labor organization. In 1939, he led a massive strike, which ended when the British declared it illegal.

Some radicals, meanwhile, believed him to be self-aggrandizing, too dictatorial, and too moderate. Under Norman Manley, Bustamante's cousin, they organized the Trade Union Advisory Council linked to the Peoples' National Party (PNP), a socialist group. Whatever Jamaicans thought, the British did not like Bustamante's labor agitiation, and they detained him for 17 months, beginning in 1941, on charges of disrupting the government amid World War II. After his release in 1943, he formed the Jamaican Labor Party (JLP) to counteract the PNP.

In 1944, Britain reacted to the labor strife by granting Jamaica more internal self-government, and in elections that year Bustamante advanced a conservative agenda. While many workers supported him, so too did the sugar companies and the upper class. The JLP outpolled the PNP by a comfortable margin, winning 23 of 32 seats in the lower house. Bustamante won a seat and in 1947 was elected mayor of Kingston. Two years later, he won reelection to the House.

In 1953, a constitutional change created the post of chief minister, and Britain named Bustamante to the position. The PNP, however, defeated the JLP in 1955, and Norman Manley succeeded Bustamante as chief minister. Bustamante opposed the PNP effort to include Jamaica in a new West Indies Federation, fearing the smaller islands would join together and dominate it. After a referendum supported his position, he called for Jamaican independence within the British Commonwealth. In 1962, he again became chief minister, or prime minister as it was then called, after the JLP defeated the PNP in new elections.

> *"We are determined to rule ourselves. We must have independence . . . within the British Commonwealth."*

Bustamante oversaw the writing of a constitution, preparatory for nationhood, and on 6 August 1962 Jamaica became independent. He launched economic programs to alleviate the island's high unemployment, and he sided strongly with the United States, condemning FIDEL CASTRO and encouraging American investments. After 1964, Bustamante's health declined, and he handled few daily decisions.

Despite some economic gains, Jamaica continued suffering from high unemployment and soaring inflation. Investments decreased and factionalism within the JLP worsened. Nevertheless, the JLP defeated the PNP again in 1967, although Bustamante decided not to run. In 1972, the PNP regained primacy under MICHAEL MANLEY and initiated a radical departure from Bustamante and the JLP. Bustamante, meanwhile, retired from politics. He died on 6 August 1977 after having guided a conservative course in Jamaica's emergence as an independent nation.

References: Levi, Darrell E., *Michael Manley: The Making of a Leader,* 1989; Nettleford, Rex, *Caribbean Cultural Identity: The Case of Jamaica,* 1980.

✦

Cabral, Amilcar
(1924–1973)
Guinea-Bissau

After Amilcar Cabral became a nationalist, one event in particular converted him to militancy: the 1959 massacre of protestors by the Portuguese military. Cabral not only won independence for his homeland but also is renowned as a revolutionary theorist.

Amilcar Cabral came from Bafata, where he was born on 12 September 1924. He attended a secondary school at São Vicente and from there enrolled at the University of Lisbon where, in 1950, he graduated with honors and received a degree in agronomy.

By this time, Cabral's homeland had been ruled by Portugal for several decades. When Cabral returned to what was then called Portuguese Guinea in 1950, he entered the colonial agricultural service to which he applied his college training. He also became intellectually involved with African nationalists whom he had met during his studies in Lisbon. In his ideology he reflected the discontent of the *assimilados*—Africans who had received European education and adopted many European practices. He was also influenced by his Portuguese wife, who adopted a revolutionary outlook. Cabral's work with the agricultural service involved travel across the country that allowed him to learn much about the land and its people.

In 1954, Cabral organized the Movement for the National Independence of Portuguese Guinea (MING). It represented his early entry into nationalist politics and was a clandestine organization consisting mainly of commercial workers and civil servants. At this time, a fascist regime reigned in Portugal, and it opposed all efforts at independence by its overseas colonies.

Then, in the mid-1950s, Cabral joined with his intellectual friends from other Portuguese colonies in forming the Anti-Colonialist Movement (MAC). Stepping up his activities further, in September 1956 he met with his brother Lu's and with other nationalists in Bissau to form the African Party for the Independence of Guinea-Bissau and Cape Verde (PAIGC). Lu's Cabral became a significant nationalist leader in his own right—in the 1960s, he

> *"The people . . . are fighting to win material benefits, to live better and in peace . . ."*

became a member of the PAIGC War Council, and after Amilcar's death he became deputy secretary of the PAIGC and his nation's first president.

Although the PAIGC had only 50 members in 1958, Amilcar Cabral organized nationalist labor strikes. One of these greatly affected him and his movement. On 3 August 1959, Pijiguiti dock workers in Bissau demonstrated and made nationalist demands. Portuguese soldiers reacted by firing into the crowd, killing 50 and injuring over 100 strikers. The Portuguese government then convicted 21 people accused of subversion. Over the next few years, Cabral faced a determined effort by the Portuguese to make arrests and repress the PAIGC. Shocked by the dock worker massacre, Cabral turned to armed fighting in 1961, including sabotage within Guinea-Bissau, and proclaimed a revolutionary doctrine based on mobilizing the peasant masses. He always emphasized that the PAIGC must revolutionize people's lives by improving local economies, gaining higher prices for the peasants' produce, and advancing health care and education. Wherever the PAIGC went, it worked at these concerns and brought in trained doctors and technicians from the Soviet Union to help.

Cabral's PAIGC made substantial military gains within a short time. In April 1964, a 65-day offensive resulted in Portugal evacuating thousands of troops, and by the following year the PAIGC controlled half the countryside. From 1962 to 1973, Cabral served as secretary-general of the PAIGC and thus directed the liberation fight. He also wrote several acclaimed works on African culture and revolution. Cabral extended his concerns beyond Guinea-Bissau by uniting with other Africans in their struggles against Portuguese rule, most notably the movements in Angola and Mozambique.

On 1 July 1970, Cabral met with the pope in Rome, a move that greatly angered Portugal. The Portuguese retaliated by launching a raid against PAIGC headquarters and trying to kill Cabral and his colleagues. The raid failed after bloody fighting

and only led to a more violent response by Cabral, who oversaw a military offensive in 1971. At last, in 1972 Portugal granted more autonomy to both Guinea-Bissau and Cape Verde—but it was too little too late. Cabral had the initiative and a widening base of support, and new weapons from the Soviet Union even allowed him to attack Portuguese aircraft.

In August 1972, the PAIGC held elections in the liberated zones and established a Peoples' Assembly. Cabral then traveled to the United States where he announced that Guinea-Bissau would soon proclaim its independence. It appeared a moment of great triumph for Cabral, and most observers expected he would become the leader of his independent homeland. But that did not happen, for dissidents within the PAIGC joined with Portuguese intelligence officials to plot and carry out an assassination. On 23 January 1973, Cabral was shot and killed while visiting the city of Conkary. In May the PAIGC launched Operation Amilcar Cabral, a successful assault that seized a fortified base.

After Amilcar Cabral's death, the PAIGC continued under Lu's Cabral, and in September 1973 Guinea-Bissau proclaimed its independence. By October, over 60 nations had extended diplomatic recognition, and a year later Portugal officially recognized Guinea-Bissau's new status. Cabral's birthday, 12 September, is today a national holiday in Guinea-Bissau.

References: Cabral, Amilcar, *Our People Are Our Mountains: Amilcar Cabral on the Guinean Revolution*, 1971; Chabal, Patrick, *Amilcar Cabral: Revolutionary Leadership and Peoples' War*, 1983.

Cárdenas, Lázaro
(1895–1970)
Mexico

Lázaro Cárdenas grew up in a poor village and as an adult remembered the dirt-floor dwellings in which the villagers lived and the small corn plot his father worked. This experience shaped his political outlook and his radical reforms.

On 21 May 1895, Lázaro Cárdenas was born in Jiquilpan in western Michoacán. Like other peasants, his family struggled in poverty, and he received little education. In his youth, Lázaro witnessed a nation in turmoil. In fact, Mexico had experienced considerable instability ever since the early 1800s when the revolutionary efforts of JOSÉ MORELOS arose, followed by the independence movement led by AUGUSTÍN DE ITURBIDE. Although BENITO JUÁREZ initiated several reforms in the mid-1800s to stabilize Mexico, the nation suffered from economic problems, including a maldistribution of wealth, that fomented a revolution in 1910.

This uprising brought FRANCISCO MADERO to power, but he failed to establish his democratic goals. As the revolution continued, Victoriano Huerta established a dictatorship supported by conservatives who opposed reform. Venustiano Carranza took up arms against Huerta. Although Carranza had little humanitarian desire to promote reform, he portrayed himself as a liberal in order to attract followers and gain power. In 1913, Cárdenas joined a revolutionary army led by Guillermo Garc'a Aragón, but he joined Carranza after the latter split with Aragón.

In July 1914, Carranza captured Mexico City, and he soon initiated several radical reforms, including the 1917 constitution that allowed restrictions on private property in order to lessen the concentration of wealth. Some revolutionaries still fought Carranza, thus Cárdenas continued to serve the president in the army. In 1920, he was promoted to general and continued to fight against various uprisings well into the decade.

In 1928, Cárdenas won election as governor of his home state, Michoacán. The next year, he joined Plutarco Elías Calles, who had become president in

1924 and served until 1928, in forming a political organization, the National Revolutionary Party (PNR). Cárdenas thus became part of Calles's political clique, one that controlled the presidency irrespective of who actually held the office. In 1931, Cárdenas served briefly as interior minister under Ortiz Rubio, and in 1933 he became war and marine minister under Abelardo Rodríguez. President Rodríguez represented the decline of the country's revolutionary movement: Like Calles, he had accumulated much wealth, partly by investing in casinos, and cared little for reform.

As Rodr'guez's term neared its end, discontent with the PNR intensified. Critics accused it of having abandoned land redistribution, and unions demanded labor reform. Nevertheless, in 1934 the PNR acquiesced in Calles's choice for president: Cárdenas. Calles thought he had another pliant leader, but Cárdenas surprised him by pursuing an independent course of vigorous change so substantial it was called the Second Mexican Revolution. Although Cárdenas had no opposition in the 1934 presidential campaign, he traveled the nation anyhow, spending considerable time with peasants and factory workers and building popular support.

Throughout 1934 and into 1935, his first year in office, Cárdenas worked to consolidate his power and isolate Calles. He did so skillfully and accomplished his task by June 1935. The following year, he ordered the former president to leave the country, which he did. Cárdenas then launched his reforms. He did not stay in Mexico City; in fact, most of the time he traveled to different localities, where he set up his presidential office. This "mobile presidency" reinforced his popular standing and displayed his sincere attachment to the people, particularly the disadvantaged. Early on, he promoted unions to protect industrial workers and encouraged them to strike. Consequently, workers' wages increased, although inflation eradicated most of the advance.

Fulfilling the desire of the heroic 1910 revolutionary EMILIANO ZAPATA, he transferred land from *haciendas* (large estates) to peasant *ejidos* (village communal landholdings). In 1937, he nationalized the railroads and promoted union ownership of some industries.

That same year, he engaged in a showdown with the huge American and British companies that controlled Mexico's oil industry. A governmental board investigated the companies and found that wages to Mexican workers had decreased in the 1930s, while wages to workers in the United States had increased, and that the profit margin for the companies in Mexico was considerably greater than for those in the United States. Because of this, the board ordered a substantial hike in wages paid Mexican workers. The oil companies objected, but Cárdenas backed the board, and on 18 March 1938, after the companies still refused to meet the wage demands, he abruptly nationalized them.

> *"If employers weary of the social struggle, let them turn over their plants to the . . . workers."*

He did so not simply in reaction to the wage dispute, but out of a sense that the companies had exploited Mexican resources. The nationalization, a radical move, drew only mild protest from the American government, which was more concerned with maintaining good relations with Mexico as war erupted in Europe. Cárdenas's action won widespread approval in Mexico, and people referred to 18 March as the "Declaration of Economic Independence."

The oil industry suffered immensely, however, as production dropped, in part because foreign companies boycotted Mexican oil. Conditions improved after Cárdenas established public corporations to operate the industry.

In 1938, Cárdenas reorganized the PNR, making it more open to industrial workers and farmers. Although Mexican politics remained far from competitive, the organization, renamed the Party of the Mexican Revolution (PRM), increased popular influence. Unlike most previous Mexican presidents, Cárdenas did not seek to run the presidency from behind the scenes after his departure in 1940. He largely retired from politics, returning only to serve as defense minister from 1943 to 1945, during the crisis of World War II. In his later years, he remained widely respected and symbolized the Mexican left. He criticized American economic power in his nation and in 1959 supported FIDEL CASTRO's revolution in Cuba. Cárdenas died on 19 October 1970 in Mexico City. A bold and talented leader, his political coalition and reforms reshaped Mexico and continue to greatly influence the nation's development.

References: Newton, Clarke, *The Men Who Made Mexico*, 1973; Townsend, William Cameron, *Lázaro Cárdenas: Mexican Democrat*, 1979.

Carrera, Rafael
(1814–1865)
Guatemala

Uneducated and illiterate, Rafael Carrera nevertheless created an independent Guatemala under his control. A deeply religious man, Carrera protected the Catholic Church and won its enthusiastic support through his dictatorship.

Rafael Carrera was born on 24 October 1814 in Guatemala City, into a poor family of mixed white and Indian heritage. He never received a formal education and remained illiterate throughout his life. While a young man, his country was in disorder, and he determined to establish a religious government. In 1823, Guatemala had joined with four other states to form the United Provinces of Central America. When Liberals, an organized group of educated professionals, gained power in 1829, they ended state support for the Catholic Church and tried to reform property holding. This angered the priests and the wealthy, who, organized as Conservatives, encouraged poor Indians attached to Catholicism to rebel.

Carrera took up this appeal. A religious fanatic, he encouraged the Indians to follow him in overthrowing Mariano Gálvez, leader of the Liberals and the United Provinces. Carrera formed a guerrilla army and fought in the jungles. When in 1834 cholera caused many deaths in Guatemala, Carrera blamed it on Gálvez. He asserted that the deaths were not a result of disease but of poisoned medicine distributed by Gálvez to eliminate his enemies.

Carrera suffered a major military defeat in 1837 at Santa Rosa. Nevertheless, after Gálvez began arbitrarily consolidating his power, some discontent Liberals turned to Carrera for help. Using rusty muskets, defective pistols, clubs, and machetes, Carrera's militia invaded Guatemala City in 1839, and on 2 February they toppled Gálvez.

The Liberals remained in power, however, and tried placating Carrera by making him a general. But this arrangement did not last long. Disdainful of the Liberals, Carrera gathered his peasant army and on 13 April attacked Guatemala City a second time. He later boasted that he had begun his revolt with "13 men armed with old muskets, which they were obliged to fire with cigars."

> *"Long live religion and death to the foreigners!"*

After his victory in Guatemala City, he crushed insurgent groups in Los Altos state and in Quezaltenango, where he executed the city officials. Carrera acted to establish order, protect property, and make Guatemala a Catholic citadel. In 1839, he officially declared his nation independent and dissolved the national legislature, replacing it with a subservient council that elected him president in 1841. He ended the reform laws that had been passed by the Liberals—such as the legalization of civil marriages—reopened the monasteries, and invited the exiled Jesuits back.

In 1848, Carrera resigned the presidency and retired to Mexico after an attempted coup. The Liberals regained power, but only momentarily. Under General Mariano Paredes, the Conservatives overthrew the Liberals and invited Carrera back to Guatemala as commander in chief of the army. He returned on 7 August 1849 and two years later became president, elected to that position for life by the new Guatemalan legislature.

The church and the wealthy strongly supported Carrera, as did the impoverished Indians, who considered him godlike. He initiated few progressive reforms and ignored educational development. He did, however, build roads, improve agricultural practices, and reduce the national debt. In 1852, he declared the Catholic Church the official state church, and shortly after this the pope decorated him for his loyalty and faith.

Carrera focused mainly on protecting Guatemala from foreign invasion while undertaking his own intervention in surrounding nations: He turned back attacks by Nicaragua, Honduras, and El Salvador, tried repeatedly to place conservatives at the head of those countries, and stopped an attempted annexation by Mexico. In 1863, he invaded El Salvador with 6,000 men and was initially defeated but fought back and installed a conservative ruler there.

Carrera continued as president until his death in Guatemala City on 4 April 1865. Although often brutal, he had presided over independence and brought order. After his death, the

Liberals regained power, but Guatemala's history became generally a succession of dictatorships in which the differences between Liberals and Conservatives proved minor.

References: Calver, Peter A., *Guatemala*, 1985; Painter, James, *Guatemala*, 1989; Rosenthal, Mario, *Guatemala*, 1962.

Cartier, George Étienne
(1814–1873)
Canada

As a young Canadian of French descemt, George Étienne Cartier joined a rebel group that took up arms against the English-speaking inhabitants of Québec. After the attack failed, he fled into exile. Then he moderated his views, and on his eventual return he developed a distinguished political career as a champion of Canadian unity.

George Étienne Cartier was born on 6 September 1814 in St. Antoine, Lower Canada (today, Québec). He completed his higher education at Saint Sulpice College in Montréal and began practicing law in 1835. At the time, Lower Canada was one of several colonies that comprised British North America, and due to its French heritage it had a distinct cultural background. Cartier proudly defended this culture and in 1837 joined Joseph Papineau in an armed rebellion against the English. Only several hundred French joined in the uprising, however, and the British military quickly crushed it. Cartier fled to the United States, where he lived in Burlington, Vermont.

In 1838, after the British declared an amnesty, Cartier relocated to Montréal and resumed his legal career. He gained a reputation as an excellent corporate lawyer specializing in railroad companies and played an important role in developing the Grand Trunk Railway that eventually ran from Lake Huron to some 120 miles below Québec. In 1840, the British government united Lower Canada, renamed Canada East, and Upper Canada, renamed Canada West, into one entity, the Province of Canada. Eight years later, Cartier entered politics and won election to the Canadian legislature. In 1855, he became the provincial secretary for Canada East.

Cartier's career then took a crucial turn: He developed a close working relationship with JOHN ALEXANDER MACDONALD, the leading political figure in Canada West and head of the Conservative Party. The two formed a political alliance in 1856 based on their commitment to Canadian unity—with a full partnership between English and French—and economic growth. Together, these two men would craft the Canadian confederation.

Cartier served with Macdonald as co-prime minister of the Province of Canada. When, in 1864, the Maritime Provinces decided to hold a conference at Charlottetown on Prince Edward Island to pursue union among themselves, Macdonald requested that he and a delegation be allowed to attend and discuss the issue of a wider confederation. After the Maritime Provinces agreed, Macdonald and Cartier attended the meeting. The two men presented their argument cogently: that stability

and economic development necessitated the formation of a greater Canada. Also present at the meeting were other men who became leaders in the union movement, such as GEORGE BROWN, CHARLES TUPPER, and SAMUEL TILLEY. Cartier's presence was crucial because it showed the Maritimers that different views could coexist in a larger union—for like Macdonald, Cartier favored national unity, but unlike him, he stressed protecting local institutions. From this meeting came an agreement to gather at Québec. This conference occurred in September and resulted in resolutions to establish a confederation. Cartier had again proved influential as his clear arguments and forceful personality bolstered the union argument.

Yet many in Canada East had reservations about the proposed union, especially the French who feared domination by a national English majority. Cartier responded with his usual energy and persuasiveness. He pointed out that Britain existed as a nation encompassing diverse nationalities—English, Irish, Scots, and Welsh—and so, too, could Canada. In 1865, the Canada East legislature approved confederation.

Opposition still existed in the Maritime Provinces, but after another meeting, held in London in December 1866, and guided by Cartier and Macdonald, the British North America Act, modeled closely after the Québec Resolutions, was agreed upon and created the Dominion of Canada, which came into existence on 1 July 1867. Macdonald was chosen the first prime minister and Cartier served in the cabinet as minister of militia. Along with Macdonald, he promoted the effort to build the Canadian Pacific Railway through British Columbia to connect the East and Far West. In 1869, he secured the purchase of western lands from the Hudson's Bay Company to pursue the railroad project and expand Canadian control.

In 1873, Macdonald's prime ministry collapsed after it was revealed that a year earlier Cartier had obtained campaign monies for the Conservative Party from a businessman who received the contract for building the Canadian Pacific Railway. At this time, Cartier suffered declining health and traveled to England for medical advice. On 20 May 1873 he died in London. Remembered as one of the "fathers of confederation," it is quite possible that without his ability to lead French Canadians into a union with the English, a united Canada would never have emerged.

> *"We all desire that these provinces should be as great as possible."*

References: Boyd, John, *Sir George-Étienne Cartier: His Life and Times,* 1914; Wade, Mason, *The French Canadians, 1760–1945,* 1968.

Castro, Fidel
(b. 1926)
Cuba

As a college student, Fidel Castro immersed himself in revolutionary ideology and violent attacks against oppressive regimes——he participated in a failed attempt to assassinate one dictator and riots to overthrow another. As a national leader, he established a revolutionary government committed to Marxism.

Fidel Castro was born on 13 August 1926 in Cuba's easternmost Oriente Province, on a plantation situated along the northern coast. Although not wealthy, his father, Angel Castro y Argiz, lived a comfortable life raising sugar on some 23,000 acres. His mother, Lina Ruz González, was a cook with whom his father had an affair. Fidel attended boarding schools in Santiago and the leading Jesuit preparatory school in Havana. He was not only an outstanding student but also excelled in sports and particularly liked baseball.

He enrolled in 1945 at the University of Havana and five years later obtained a law degree. During those years he became heavily politicized, convinced of the need for social and political reform in Cuba and elsewhere in Latin America. He headed the University Students' Association and in 1947 took part in an expedition that sailed to the Dominican Republic to overthrow the dictatorship of Rafael Trujillo, but the effort failed. In 1948, he helped organize a student conference at Bogotá, Colombia, and participated there in a violent demonstration.

In 1950, Castro began a law practice in Havana, where he specialized in representing the disadvantaged. He joined a new party, the Ortodoxos, which advocated social reform. Competitive party politics, however, came to an end after Fulgencio Batista staged a coup and in October 1952 began a military dictatorship. Castro boldly submitted a petition to the Cuban high court that asserted Batista should step down because his government was illegitimate. Predictably, the court rejected the petition.

Castro then began his struggle to overthrow Batista and install a revolutionary regime. On 26 July 1953, he led 165 men on an attack against the Moncada army barracks at Santiago de Cuba, but was captured (along with his brother, Raúl) and sentenced to 15 years in prison. He later claimed that JOSÉ MARTÍ was the "intellectual author" of the Moncada attack. For months, Castro languished on the Isle of Pines, seemingly silenced. Yet when Batista increased his repression of dissidents, a backlash occurred that led to demands for the release of political prisoners. In July 1955, Batista freed Castro, who went into exile in Mexico. There the political rebel planned a new assault.

In Mexico City, Castro organized the 26th of July Movement and joined with one of the great tacticians of the Cuban Revolution, Che Guevara. On 2 December, Castro, Guevara, and 82 armed followers invaded Oriente Province. Batista's army crushed the attack and nearly captured Castro. He, however, hid in a cane field, covered himself with a layer of leaves, and talked incessantly in whispers to the few revolutionaries left nearby, formulating his escape and expressing his plans to reorganize the rebel army. While Batista announced Castro had been killed, the Cuban revolutionary retreated safely to the Sierra Maestra Mountains and proclaimed total war on the dictator.

Batista felt so confident after his defeat of Castro that he went ahead with a presidential election scheduled for 1958, and his candidate won in voting rife with fraud. Castro subsequently moved quickly and with his peasant supporters launched a new offensive while the United States, long a backer of the Cuban regime, recoiled at Batista's flagrant election abuses and repression. As American aid dwindled and Castro's men scored impressive victories that encouraged uprisings in the cities, Batista's support faded, and on 1 January 1959, the revolutionaries marched into Havana in triumph.

On 16 February 1959, Castro became prime minister. After he resigned in July in a dispute with the revolutionary president, crowds rallied behind him, and on 26 July he resumed the prime ministry. Coupled with the selection of a new president, this marked Castro's success in consolidating his power, and he moved to radically transform Cuban society. He ordered Batista supporters arrested and in some instances executed, established revolutionary bodies to replace the former power structure, and launched a massive land redistribution program to help the peasants. He also reached an aid agreement with the Soviet Union, with the Soviets consenting to purchase sugar. In July 1960, after the United States cancelled Cuba's quota for sugar, Castro nationalized American holdings, including the utility companies, oil refineries, and banks.

In 1961, Castro announced his commitment to Marxism, and the United States responded by ending diplomatic relations while secretly planning to invade Cuba and remove the revolutionary from power. This plan materialized in 1962 with the Bay of Pigs Invasion, a disastrous failure that embarrassed American President John F. Kennedy and strengthened Castro's position at home. It also moved Castro closer to the Russians for protection, and he soon allowed the Soviet Union to erect nuclear missiles in Cuba aimed at the United States. Kennedy reacted by demanding the missiles be removed, and American naval ships blockaded Cuba and turned away Soviet vessels. The crisis nearly brought the United States and the Soviet Union into a nuclear war, but the Soviets agreed to dismantle the missiles in return for Kennedy's promise to respect Cuban sovereignty. (The United States later broke this promise when the Central Intelligence Agency attempted to assassinate Castro.)

In the mid-1960s, tension between Cuba and the Soviet Union mounted as Castro remained angered about the Russians having bypassed him in reaching the agreement with Kennedy. The Cuban leader rejected the Russian model of economic development through technocrats, and he collectivized production and sponsored revolutionary movements in other Latin American countries as part of his belief that socialism could not exist in isolation. He established closer relations with Communist China and adopted several of its programs.

As various economic experiments failed, however, he again moved closer to the Soviet Union. After Che Guevera was killed in Bolivia in 1967, where he had gone to organize a leftist revolution, Castro ceased exporting rebellion to Latin America, although he continued to provide military aid, including advisors, to Nicaragua and El Salvador and tried to increase Cuban influence in Grenada.

After 1970, Castro relied more on the Soviet model for development, and in 1975 he sponsored a new constitution modeled after the Soviet one: It legitimized a one-party system, described Cuba as a socialist state, and committed the nation to developing communism. Castro also expanded his

"Condemn me. It does not matter. History will absolve me!"

foreign adventures, sending troops to help communist rebels in Angola and to back the Marxist government of Ethiopia in its war against Somalia.

In 1980, Castro allowed discontented Cubans to leave for the United States, and a massive exodus known as the Mariel Boatlift occurred. Among those who fled were hardened criminals and mental patients, deported by Castro as a way to eliminate their burden on Cuba and as a coy effort to retaliate against the United States for its recent attempts to reverse improved relations with him. Castro obtained recognition in the 1980s as the chairman of the Nonaligned Movement and spoke to the United Nations General Assembly, where he called for developed nations to assist the Third World. Domestically, he continued to improve Cuba's educational and health systems, both ranked among the best in Latin America. The Cuban economy, however, suffered from poor planning and problems with several sugar harvests.

Enormous setbacks occurred in the 1990s after the Soviet Union collapsed—a development that robbed Castro of a crucial trading partner and leading source of financial aid. Coupled with a continuing American trade embargo, the nation's economy tottered, and in 1994 Castro allowed thousands more Cubans to flee across the Florida Straits to the United States. Although Castro expanded trade with many European and Latin American nations, observers wondered if his economic problems would soon cause his downfall and reverse his revolution.

References: Dominguez, Jorge I., *Cuba: Order and Revolution*, 1978; Szulc, Tad, *Fidel: A Critical Portrait*, 1986.

◆

Castro Madriz, Jose Maria
(1818–1892)
Costa Rica

In his brief tenure as president, Jose Maria Castro Madriz built upon the success of the great Central American liberator FRANCISCO MORAZÁN and declared Costa Rica an independent nation.

Jose Maria Castro Madriz was born in 1818 and as a young man received his law degree in Nicaragua. He returned to Costa Rica committed to improving his country's schools and fostering a democratic system. He was one of the founders of the University of Santo Tomás and was its president for over a decade. He also began Costa Rica's first newspaper. During this time, in the 1840s, political turmoil gripped his nation. Some Costa Ricans sought to revive the Central American Federation, the short-lived alliance Costa Rica had been a member of in the 1820s. This effort, however, failed, and in 1847 the congress turned to Castro Madriz to serve as president.

He was the first chief executive to have this title, and his administration marked the emergence of Costa Rica as a nation distinct from its neighbors. In 1848, he officially declared Costa Rica an independent republic, with no intentions of reviving a federation. He then began several reforms to shape Costa Rica's national status. He abolished the army and replaced it with a national guard, a minimal force intended to preserve internal order, and guaranteed freedom of expression and association. His action against the military won him the enmity of many army officers, and his liberalism angered the conservative coffee planters. In 1849, they banded together and forced him to resign.

For many years after, the coffee barons dominated politics, and Costa Rica remained an ill-defined country with a weak national identity. This changed in 1857 when the Costa Rican army joined with other Central American troops and defeated William Walker, an adventurer from the United States who had established a dictatorship in Nicaragua aimed at controlling Central America. This National Campaign, as Costa Ricans called it, produced a battlefield hero in Juan Santamaria, a mulatto drummer boy, and pushed regional interests to a secondary position.

In 1859, Castro Madriz led a legislature that wrote a new constitution. Seven years later, after he served as head of the Supreme Court, his countrymen returned him to the presidency. During another brief term he again focused on reforms. He developed an elementary school system, opened the Bay of Limón to trade, and began the first telegraph network. But he once again ran afoul of the conservative military, and in November 1868 the army overthrew him. He died in 1892, honored by his country's highest award, the Benemérito de la Patria. By this time, Costa Rica had developed the democratic polity Castro Madriz desired, although it was nearly ended in 1948, and then saved by JOSE FIGUERES FERRER.

Reference: Nelson, Harold D., *Costa Rica: A Country Study*, 1983.

Catherine II
(1729–1796)
Russia

Catherine II, called "the Great" by her admirers, immersed herself in the Enlightenment, even corresponding with Voltaire and Diderot, among others. She determined to liberate Russia from the shackles of superstition and barbarity—yet liberation extended only to the privileged. To the masses, she extended poverty and oppression.

Catherine was not Russian by birth; she was born on 2 May 1729 in Anhalt-Zerbst, a principality in Germany. Her father, Christian August, served as a general in the Prussian army, and her mother was Princess Johanna Elizabeth of Holstein-Gottorp. Catherine received a limited formal education from a tutor, who taught her religion, history, and French.

At age 15, she traveled to Russia, where she met Grand Duke Peter, the future Tsar Peter III, who was then 16. A marriage had been arranged between the two, and after the meeting she consented to the union. She had little interest in Peter—who, in fact, exhibited instability bordering on madness—but keen interest in becoming Russia's ruler. In 1745, she married Peter. The couple quickly grew apart; she found him boring and obnoxious and disdained his intellect, which remained that of a child. He often played with wooden soldiers and attended church, only to mock the priest and emit rude sounds during the service.

In 1761, Peter became tsar, and Catherine maneuvered to depose him. Although Peter did not realize it, he helped her scheme when he announced his intention to marry his mistress and send Catherine to a convent. This alienated the *streltsy*, or royal guard, and Catherine plotted with it. In 1762, she went to the Winter Palace, announced the end of Peter's rule, and installed herself as empress. Peter did not oppose her but retired to his country estate, where one week later he was killed.

Catherine brought to the throne an attachment to the French Enlightenment, and, perhaps more than any ruler who preceded her, she influenced the spirit of the times. Her initial attempts to reform Russia displayed her own commitment to the liberal faith in order, reason, progress, and human perfectibility. She believed Russia needed to be Westernized and thus saw herself as continuing the efforts of Tsar PETER I (Peter the Great).

Catherine gained the attention of European intellectuals and political leaders when, in 1767, she called together a commission to compile a new code of laws and provided the delegates with a *Nakaz*, or set of instructions, so voluminous and liberal it surprised many. She had worked on the *Nakaz* for two years, writing much of it but borrowing heavily from Enlightenment authors. She asserted that all subjects should be equal before the law, that torture should be abolished and capital punishment used only in extreme circumstances, and that religious dissent should be tolerated. She did not advocate dismantling serfdom but did raise questions about its legitimacy.

Thus Catherine exhibited the Enlightenment principles and policies that marked her early reign. The commission, however, suffered from interminable disagreements, and after meeting for several years it accomplished nothing.

Despite this setback, Catherine successfully initiated several domestic reforms. In 1775, she reorganized the administrative structure, changing the division of Russia from 8 to 50 *gouvernements*, or provinces, and subdividing them into districts. This allowed greater local representation, although she appointed the top officials. In 1785 she issued the Charter of the Nobility that ended the obligations of noblemen toward the government. Furthermore, they were exempted from direct taxes and corporal punishment.

The empress made modest advances toward a freer market, ending the monopolies that Peter I had promoted in his plan to stimulate industry.

Catherine encouraged competition and invited foreigners to begin factories and, indeed, Russian commerce expanded. She also developed new towns and cities, which she believed should epitomize a modern nation. At one point, she visited the Crimea and marvelled at the structures being built, not knowing that in some instances the "buildings" were merely false fronts hastily put together under the direction of her chief advisor as a ploy to impress her.

Catherine's reforms also encompassed education: She began elementary schools in some districts, high schools appeared in the major cities, and she organized a college of medicine at the University of Moscow. In the field of health, she encouraged the use of inoculations and quarantines, effective against smallpox.

"What I want is not slavery, but obedience to the law."

Unlike Peter I, Catherine pursued reform systematically. Where Peter had been haphazard, she planned her moves to agree with Enlightenment ideas. Always concerned with what Western nations thought about her and Russia, she portrayed her country as modernizing and prosperous, an image many Europeans accepted.

Had they looked closer, however, they would have found many limitations, most notably the increasing oppression and misery of the peasants. In relying on support from the nobles and merchants, Catherine consolidated serfdom so pervasively that the peasants had no rights. Furthermore, she expanded the geographical area of serfdom, taking it into White Russia and the Ukraine, where previously it had not been entrenched.

As under previous tsars, the peasants, mired in poverty, bore an enormous tax burden and owed military service. In the 1770s, while Catherine was displaying her Enlightenment reforms, a massive peasant uprising erupted in the southeast, between the Volga and the Urals, led by a Cossack, Emelian Pugachev. He claimed to be Peter III and thus the true tsar. The uprising began in the autumn of 1773, and some 30,000 rebels captured towns and cities, burned the houses of noblemen, and tortured government officials. For two years, Pugachev ruled a wide area, but Catherine's army finally captured him and crushed the rebellion. Pugachev was taken to Moscow, displayed in chains, and then beheaded.

Ever since IVAN III, Russia had followed a strongly expansionist policy, and Catherine continued this approach. She handled foreign relations realistically and aggressively. Catherine annexed territory along the Baltic coast almost to the Prussian border. She then set her sights on Poland, not intending to partition it but to gain dominance in Warsaw and obtain territory she considered a legitimate part of her nation: White and Red Russia. Partitions, however, occurred. After Catherine stationed Russian troops in Poland to put down a movement for a liberal government, tensions with Turkey increased; in 1768, the Turks and Russians went to war. When Catherine emerged victorious, Prussia convinced her to acquire land mainly from Poland rather than from Turkey. Catherine did not prefer this plan, but with the Pugachev uprising she felt pressured to reach a quick settlement. Consequently, in 1772 Russia, Prussia, and Austria engaged in the first partition of Poland, whereby Catherine acquired the White Russian territories in the Dvina and Dnieper regions.

In 1793, she again sent Russian troops into Poland and in cooperation with Prussia arranged a second partition. This time, Catherine obtained most of Lithuania and the western Ukraine. A third partition occurred in 1795 after an uprising by the Poles. The arrangement gave Catherine the rest of Lithuania and the Ukraine, along with Courland, while Prussia and Austria also received substantial territory. Poland was thus eliminated as an independent nation; all told, the partitions resulted in Russia gaining 190,000 square miles.

Catherine's second expansionist success involved Turkey. She wanted to obtain Bessarabia and control the Black Sea, Constantinople, and the Dardenelles. She even hoped to establish a grand empire in the Balkans. While Catherine did not accomplish all of this, she did gain much. As noted above, the first war with Turkey, which began in 1768, ended in a great Russian triumph, and although she acquired land mainly from Poland, the 1774 Treaty of Kuchuk-Kainardji that ended the conflict also gave Russia land between the Bug and Dnieper Rivers. (But it returned to Turkey the Russian conquests in Bessarabia, Moldavia, and elsewhere.) In 1783, she obtained the Crimea from that principality's khan, a crucial acquisition that established Russian power on the Black Sea. There she soon established Odessa, which fulfilled the Russian desire for an important warm-water port.

Unsatisfied, Catherine was determined to end the Turkish presence in Europe. In 1787, Russia (allied with Austria) and Turkey again went to war.

A treaty five years later resulted in the Turks finally withdrawing their troops from between the Bug and Dnieper Rivers, which despite an earlier agreement they had refused to do, confirming Catherine's complete control of the Crimea.

The empress always kept a firm hold on her power. Conscientious and hard working—given to 12-hour days—she never delegated important matters to others. Although she had many lovers—her voracious sexual appetite caused scandalous talk—and on numerous occasions accepted their advice in the political realm, she maintained control. Grigory Potemkin, her chief minister from 1774 until 1791, with whom she had an affair for two years, was the one man among her advisors who exerted great power and was the architect of the Crimean acquisition. Still, she did not give him carte blanche authority; they worked together as a team.

Catherine's "enlightened absolutism" never encompassed republicanism—indeed, she opposed the French Revolution as too extreme. For the most part, her Enlightenment reforms did not extend beyond society's upper levels and tensions long present in Russia worsened. To the casual observer, Catherine appeared highly successful, gaining territory and forging both a truly national state and a European power. But the upper class dominated society, the peasants suffered enormously, and the government functioned chaotically. When Catherine died in St. Petersburg on 5 November 1796, she left behind a nation whose exterior appearance hid enormous internal problems. These eventually contributed to the 1917 Revolution that established the Communist Soviet Union, itself altered, under MIKHAIL GORBACHEV and BORIS YELTSIN, by the forces in Russian society that frequently transcended its rulers.

References: Alexander, John T., *Catherine the Great: Life and Legend,* 1989; Grey, Ian, *Catherine the Great: Autocrat and Empress of All Russia,* 1961.

Cato, Robert Milton
(b. 1915)
St. Vincent and the Grenadines

In the prevalent cold war atmosphere then gripping the Caribbean, Robert Milton Cato rejected extremism and committed his homeland to a moderate course.

Robert Milton Cato was born on 3 June 1915 on St. Vincent and from 1928 to 1933 attended the island's grammar school. At that time, St. Vincent was under British control, as it had been since 1763, and Cato followed the established colonial route to success. He began studying law in Kingstown, St. Vincent, until World War II intervened. During the conflict, he joined the First Canadian Army and as a sergeant saw active service in France, Belgium, and Holland. After the war, he resumed his law studies, entering London's Middle Temple in 1945. Three years later, he was admitted to the bar.

When Cato returned to St. Vincent, he began a law practice and immersed himself in the island's politics. In 1952, he became chairman of the Kingstown Town Board, and continued on it until 1959. He also served as chairman of the Labour Advisory Board and a member of the Public Service Commission and Central Housing and Planning Authority.

Cato helped organize the St. Vincent Labour Party in the 1950s, and as its leader pursued moderate socialist reform to fight the island's economic stagnation. When, in 1967, St. Vincent joined the West Indies Associated States as an internally self-governing entity, Cato was elected his homeland's chief minister. He became premier in 1969, after St. Vincent gained considerable home rule from Britain. In 1972, however, Cato lost his bid for re-election. Two years later, the voters returned him to the premiership, and in 1978 he led a delegation to London for a conference on Vincentian nationhood.

The following year, St. Vincent, joined with the Grenadines, gained complete independence. Cato became prime minister after his Labour Party captured 11 of 13 seats in Parliament.

Unlike some radical Caribbean leaders, Cato rejected close relations with Communist Cuba and declared nonalignment. He did, however, participate in the Regional Security System, an alliance crafted by the United States. In the 1980s, Cato's health declined, and his inability to effectively lead his party contributed to his defeat in 1984. James Mitchell, leader of the New Democratic Party, became prime minister and tried unsuccessfully to unify St. Vincent with the neighboring Windward Island states. Meanwhile, Cato retired from politics, remembered as the man who guided his country to independence.

Reference: Griffiths, John, *The Caribbean in the Twentieth Century,* 1984.

Cavour, Camillo Benso di
(1810–1861)
Italy

A brilliant diplomat and an ardent proponent of a unified Italy, Camillo Benso di Cavour rejected extremism and idealistic populism and instead pursued realistic politics to accomplish his goal.

Camillo Benso di Cavour was born on 10 August 1810 in Turin, then under French control. His father, a nobleman, held a prominent position in French society, while his mother came from Geneva and influenced him with that city's cosmopolitan heritage. In 1820, young Camillo enrolled in the Military Academy of Turin.

While in his youth, Camillo read about the liberals, who wanted to advance popular power, and showed republican sympathies that his family considered dangerous. In fact, at one point they tried to keep him from associating with a friend who seemed too liberal. Camillo even disputed with the royal court and won its enmity for many years.

In 1826, Cavour served as a lieutenant in the corps of engineers for Savoy and Piedmont. During an assignment in Genoa, he associated with radical republicans and developed more completely his dislike for absolutism and the entrenched aristocracy and clergy. He quit the corps in 1831 and held a minor mayoral appointment. Increasingly, his attention turned to Europe's disadvantaged, and in 1834 he wrote a book about poverty and the "poor laws." He also criticized extremists who sought progress through violence and reactionaries who opposed reform. As a moderate, he preferred gradual change to revolutionary cataclysm. He gained additional attention with his promotion of economic improvements, including railroad and steamship development, and his engagement in progressive agricultural techniques on his family estate.

In the late 1840s, Cavour founded *Il Risorgimento,* a newspaper whose name meant resurgence and reflected the burgeoning nationalism in Europe. When King Charles Albert of Sardinia-Piedmont showed an interest in reform, Cavour used *Il Risorgimento* to promote change. He influenced the king to adopt a liberal constitution that protected basic liberties, such as freedom of speech and the press, and established a Parliament.

Cavour sought to use the power of Sardinia-Piedmont in an effort to weaken Austria, which at that time dominated the disparate Italian states. He considered this a necessary step in uniting the states and creating one nation. In 1848, he won election to the new Parliament and during his campaign, when amid revolutionary fervor Milanese nationalists rebelled against foreign rule, he advocated that King Charles Albert declare war on Austria. The king did so, but the war effort failed, and in 1849 Cavour opposed those who wanted to renew the conflict. In 1852, he was named prime minister of Sardinia-Piedmont, serving under the nationalist king VICTOR EMMANUEL II. Over the years, he initiated numerous reforms to modernize his homeland, including improved banking, expanded credit, better schools, and the end to monasteries and the privileges enjoyed by the Catholic Church.

Cavour rejected the idealism of GIUSEPPE MAZZINI, an Italian nationalist from Genoa, and planned a realistic political approach to unify Italy under Sardinia-Piedmont with the help of France. In a secret agreement with the French ruler Napoleon III (the 1858 Pact of Plombieres), Sardinia-Piedmont joined France in provoking Austria into war, which erupted in 1859. Much to Cavour's chagrin, Napoleon withdrew from the conflict before the defeat of Austria could be accomplished. Nevertheless, Sardinia-Piedmont gained territory and power by wresting Lombardy from the Austrians, and in 1860 an additional agreement with France gained Tuscany, Parma, Modena, and portions of the Papal States. Sardinia-Piedmont was now the most powerful state in Italy and poised to dominate unification.

At this point, GIUSEPPE GARIBALDI launched an invasion of Sicily to end the monarchical rule there. He succeeded, and it appeared that he and Cavour might become rivals and disrupt the drive toward Italian unification. Cavour quickly regained the initiative, however, when he sent an army into the Papal States, captured them, and prevented Garibaldi from marching on Rome. This strategy resulted in cooperation between the two men and created a unified Italy.

Cavour died in Turin on 6 June 1861 as he was trying to establish Rome as the Italian capital. Through his persuasiveness and complex diplomatic strategies, he had created Italy as a modern nation.

References: Salvadori, M., *Cavour and the Unification of Italy*, 1961; Smith, Dennis Mack, *Victor Emanuel, Cavour, and the Risorgimento*, 1971; Whyte A. J., *The Early Life and Letters of Cavour, 1810–1848*, 1976; Whyte A. J., *The Political Life and Letters of Cavour, 1848–1861*, 1975.

Chamorro, Violeta
(b. 1929)
Nicaragua

Violeta Chamorro incorporated in her politics an ideology stemming from Catholic mysticism. As such, she saw her main political opponents as demons and envisioned a strongly Christian, and conservative, government.

Violeta Barrios de Chamorro was born on 18 October 1929 in Rivas. Her parents were wealthy and her father owned a huge cattle ranch. She was expected to follow the traditional course for an upper-class woman: some practical education, an advantageous marriage, and life as a devoted wife and mother. But unexpected developments altered this script.

She attended a high school in the United States

"I have enormous faith in God. He will . . . show me how to do what my conscience dictates."

in San Antonio, Texas, and then enrolled in the secretarial program at Blackstone College in Southside, Virginia. She left after only one year, however, when her father died. Then in 1950 she married Pedro Chamorro, who edited and published a leading newspaper, *La Prensa*. He was heavily involved in political issues, defiantly opposing the Somoza dictatorship that ruled Nicaragua. This stirred Violeta Chamorro's interest in politics. In 1957, the Somoza regime exiled the Chamorros to a remote town. They escaped to Costa Rica, where they lived until 1960, when they returned home.

Pedro Chamorro continued his opposition, and in 1978 he was assassinated under mysterious circumstances, likely by persons connected to the Somoza regime. Violeta Chamorro determined she would not let her husband's death be in vain; she took up the fight against the dictatorship and directly entered the political fray. By this time, the Sandinista National Liberation Front (FSLN), a revolutionary political and military organization, had arisen to fight the Somoza regime. Although dedicated to a leftist agenda, the FSLN won support from wealthy Nicaraguans angered by the assassination, and Violeta Chamorro contributed $50,000 and the support of *La Prensa* to the cause.

When in July 1979 the Somoza regime collapsed and the Sandinistas took power, they asked Violeta Chamorro to join the five-person civilian junta that would govern until elections, and she agreed. By 1980, however, she had fallen out with the Sandinistas; she saw them as too Marxist and feared they would follow the Communist Cuban model. She used *La Prensa* to attack the FSLN and its leader DANIEL ORTEGA.

She and other conservatives soon received help from the United States, where in 1981, Ronald Reagan became president and committed his administration to overthrowing the Sandinistas. Although Ortega kept the more radical FSLN Marxists at bay and followed a generally cautious socialist program, Reagan organized former Somoza National Guardsmen, now called Contras, to fight the Sandinistas, and the United States soon boycotted all trade with Nicaragua.

The Contras failed to amass a popular following, but economic restrictions and the need for the Sandinistas to build the military to counter the American threat greatly damaged the government. Inflation surpassed 36,000 percent annually and many Nicaraguans tired of the war and the economic hardship. Violeta Chamorro advanced her ideas and ingratiated herself with the United States by promoting a right-wing attack. She and many of her associates were members of The City of God, a fundamentalist Catholic cult that proclaimed its faith in mysticism and condemned the Sandinistas as demons. She often claimed she spoke with her dead husband.

Violeta Chamorro advocated Christian education in the schools, opposed legalizing abortions, and saw a woman's proper place as in the home. She worked secretly with the Central Intelligence Agency to undermine the Sandinistas, including accepting money for *La Prensa* channeled by the U.S. government through the National Endowment for Democracy. On several occasions the Sandinistas closed or censored her newspaper.

Violeta Chamorro's stand against the Sandinistas caused a split in her family as other Chamorros disagreed with her. Meanwhile, Ortega, who had been elected president in 1984, announced new elections for 1990. He guaranteed that they would be open and competitive. To oppose the FSLN, 14 parties, mainly conservative but also including disaffected communists, joined to form the National Opposition Union (UNO). The party chose Violeta Chamorro as its presidential candidate to run against Ortega.

She accused the Sandinistas of breaking their promises and promoting Marxism. Many neutral observers noted she seemed to know little about political details and in embarrassing moments even forgot the names of prominent leaders. Her vague and general campaign nevertheless benefited from her personal warmth and, more importantly, the continuing economic downturn and an infusion of American money. On 25 February 1990, Nicaraguans elected her president, and, as promised, Ortega accepted the decision.

The FSLN still held a large number of seats in the legislature, and in a conciliatory move Violeta Chamorro allowed Humberto Ortega, the Sandinista brother of Daniel, to continue as head of the army. While she promised to respect the agrarian land policies of the previous Sandinista administration, she moved quickly to privatize other areas of the economy, in part to gain economic assistance from the United States. By 1991, she began firing government employees connected to the Sandinistas and dismantling the agrarian reform. These moves and continued economic chaos, with inflation still high, led to rioting. She brought the military directly under her command, but found herself battling an often recalcitrant National Assembly.

Violeta Chamorro substantially redirected the revolution against the Somoza dictatorship to advance a conservative reaction. Some of the Sandinista programs continue, and the era of dictatorships has ended—but for how long, in a polarized political setting, remains a great question.

References: Collins, Joseph, *Nicaragua: What Difference Could a Revolution Make?*, 1986; Walker, Thomas, *Nicaragua: The First Five Years*, 1985; Walker, Thomas, *Nicaragua: The Land of Sandino*, 1991; Zwerling, Philip, and Connie Martin, *Nicaragua: A New Kind of Revolution*, 1985.

Chamoun, Camille
(1900–1987)
Lebanon

Lebanon has long been torn by religious differences. Camille Chamoun recognized these and worked to develop a pragmatic, balanced government for his homeland.

Lebanon's religious antagonisms mainly involved two sects: the Druze and the Maronites. As a Muslim sect, the Druze, largely concentrated in Lebanon's Shuf Mountains and west Beirut, had adopted some elements of Christianity. As Christians, the Maronites, largely concentrated in the northern mountains and east Beirut and constituting two-thirds of Lebanon's population, had pledged their loyalty to the Roman Catholic Church. Like most religious disputes, this one also had roots in economics as the Druze leaders were generally feudal chieftains who held power over their peasants, and the Maronite leaders were generally wealthy merchants.

Camille Chamoun, born in 1900 at Deir el-Kamir, was a Maronite, but he came from the Shuf district where many Druze lived, and thus understood the mixed nature of Lebanese society. He obtained his elementary education at a Catholic school in Deir el-Kamir and graduated from high school in Beirut, the product of a French education. During World War I, the Chamoun family was exiled for anti-Turkish activities on the part of Camille's father. After World War I, Lebanon became a French mandate and France thus became the object of Lebanese nationalists.

Under French rule, the Lebanese economy expanded considerably and Camille immersed himself in it. After graduating from the Faculty of Law at the University of Saint Joseph in Beirut and obtaining his law license in 1923, he became a successful lawyer, businessman, and property holder. He also wrote articles for a newspaper, *Le Reveil-* where he began expressing his political views.

Although the economy expanded, there was much about French rule for the Lebanese to dislike, including press censorship and a dominant role for French investors. Chamoun wanted this situation changed. In 1929, he won his first election campaign and became an elector, whose duty it was to help choose delegates to Lebanon's Chamber of Deputies. That year he also married Zelpha Tabet, whose family had important connections in British social circles. Chamoun subsequently learned English and developed contacts with British politicians.

Chamoun's nationalism intensified, and after he won election to the Chamber of Deputies in 1934, he sided with the Constitutional Bloc led by Sheikh Bechara al-Khouri, which sought an end to French domination. Chamoun won reelection in 1937 and was appointed minister of finance (although the Constitutional Bloc was a minority party).

During World War II, Chamoun emerged as a crucial architect of Lebanese independence. In 1941, French and British forces invaded Lebanon and ousted the Vichy-controlled government (which had collaborated with Nazi Germany). Britain supported Lebanese independence, a move France opposed. Chamoun lobbied the British to assure their continued support for nationhood and even won the label "agent of British intelligence."

Finally, in 1943 France agreed with Britain to allow Lebanon's independence. Elections that year made the Constitutional Bloc the majority party and Bechara al-Khouri was voted in as president. Chamoun emerged as a powerful figure in the administration. He was appointed minister of finance and then, because of his close ties to the British, he was made minister plenipotentiary to London. He displayed a political acumen that led to an important success: getting Britain to back the withdrawal of French troops at a time when France had second thoughts about totally relinquishing Lebanon. He also obtained his country's membership in the United Nations.

Chamoun, now enormously popular, expected to become president, but Khouri moved to amend the constitution to allow himself another term. Chamoun subsequently resigned and cooperated with the opposition Socialist National Front Party led by Kamal Jumblatt, a Druze. Khouri remained president, but by 1951 his opponents gained a bigger following and widespread discontent with him led to his resignation in 1952. With Jumblatt's support, Chamoun won election in Parliament as president.

Chamoun ran into a formidable problem: He had antagonized his Constitutional Bloc followers and many Maronites by having cooperated with Jumblatt, and when he tried to win back these people, he antagonized Jumblatt and many Druze suspicious of his Maronite background. Nevertheless, he initiated several reforms: a change in the election system that weakened the domination of public office by landholding aristocrats and urban elites; suffrage for women; and an independent judiciary. The economy expanded under Chamoun,

and he promoted a free exchange of ideas, including total freedom of the press.

Yet many Muslims disliked his refusal in 1958 to join Lebanon with the United Arab Republic, and demonstrations shook his presidency while aggravating underlying religious tensions. As armed rebellion spread, and Chamoun's power and even Lebanese unity were imperiled, he called in American troops, who prevented a coup. This action, however, brought charges that he was a tool of Western imperialism and too close to the pro-Israeli United States.

In 1958, Chamoun's term as president ended, but he remained politically active. He formed a new opposition organization in 1959, the National Liberal Party, and won election to Parliament in 1960, 1968, and 1972. He successfully maneuvered Suleiman Franjieh into the presidency in 1970 and gained several ministerial posts.

Then, in 1975, Lebanon's longstanding religious differences again blew up into a civil war, and Chamoun obtained Israeli support for the Maronite forces. The bloodshed continued, and when Amin Gemayel became president in 1982, he turned to Chamoun to help restore a national unity government. Chamoun served once again as minister of finance, but the civil war—which by the end of the decade took some 130,000 lives—overwhelmed him, as it did all of Lebanon's national leaders. Chamoun died of old age in 1987. Three years later, a government of national unity took power and a tenuous peace returned to most of Lebanon.

Chamoun had thus led Lebanon through the intricacies of international politics in the 1940s to gain nationhood and as president had tried to balance the various religious groups. His actions made him a symbol of national unity.

References: Gilmour, David, *Lebanon: The Fractured Country*, 1983; Gordon, David C., *The Republic of Lebanon: Nation in Jeopardy*; Mackey, Sandra, *Lebanon: The Death of a Nation*, 1989.

Charles, Eugenia

(b. 1919)
Dominica

Eugenia Charles raised strong emotions among Dominicans. This was evident by the way in which they referred to her: "Ma Eugenia," "Iron Lady of the Caribbean" and "Lady Dracula." As a black female nationalist leader in a world of white male diplomats, she seemed both a revolutionary and a conservative, defending Dominican independence while rejecting radicalism.

Eugenia Charles was born amid comfortable family surroundings on 15 May 1919 in Pointe Michel on Dominica, at that time an island colony within the British Empire. Her father had risen from a modest background to own substantial land and several businesses. In 1921, Eugenia's parents moved the family to Roseau, the main town. At age four, Eugenia began her schooling at the Convent of the Sisters of the Faithful Virgin. As a child, she was considered energetic and headstrong, quite forceful in her views, and unwilling to acquiesce easily to male authority. She obtained her secondary education at the Convent High School and received a certificate in 1935. She continued at the school for another year while trying to determine what path she would pursue.

Charles soon obtained work as a clerk in the Treasury Department, taught herself Latin, and then decided to obtain a law degree. To prepare for the matriculation exam, she attended the Convent High School on Grenada. From there, she went to the University of Toronto, which had a special program for West Indian students. In 1946, she obtained a bachelor's degree in law and then proceeded to the Inner Temple in London to complete her legal studies. In October 1947, she passed her bar finals, and in 1949 returned home and gained admittance to the Dominican bar.

By this time, Dominica's relations with Britain were undergoing change, and in the process the island's politics became more competitive. The British sponsored constitutional reforms that in 1951 provided full suffrage. This, and the growth of trade unions, stimulated formation of the Dominica Labour Party (DLP).

While Charles practiced law, she also became

> *"I believe in free enterprise, but I also believe a Caribbean government has to do things . . ."*

attracted to politics. Two developments in 1967 and 1968 stirred her activism: Dominica obtained control of its internal affairs, and the chief minister, Edward LeBlanc, had the legislature pass a bill restricting the right of Dominicans to criticize their government. Charles helped form the Freedom Fighters to oppose this legislation. She organized demonstrations and a petition drive and presented an unscheduled speech at a rally that attracted widespread notice.

In October 1968, Charles and her supporters reshaped the Freedom Fighters to form a new political organization, the Dominica Freedom Party (DFP). Yet her effort met substantial resistance from Dominicans who considered her and the DFP to be elitist. Labour seemed to be the party that cared for the workers. In 1970, the DLP defeated the DFP handily in elections to the House. Charles then became leader of the opposition.

As DFP president, Charles supported developing tourism and building low-cost housing. Ideologically, the DFP did not differ greatly from the Labour Party—the point of contention was frequently over Labour Party corruption and the "outs," that is the DFP, wanting power. If anything, Charles held economic views more conservative than the DLP and strongly defended private property ownership. In December 1970, the DFP won all the seats on the Roseau town council, an important victory.

In the mid-1970s, the black power movement erupted. Labour and the DFP both condemned the movement, and Charles criticized the radicals' assaults on whites. In 1974, after a fight among the Labour Party members, PATRICK JOHN became premier. He advocated independence for Dominica, a position Charles supported. The DLP again defeated Charles in 1975, winning 16 of 21 seats in the House. Charles still served as the opposition leader in Parliament, but the DFP had suffered a setback.

In August 1976, John formally announced his plan to obtain independence, and Charles supported the concept but called for a referendum. Although John rejected the demand, the House accepted Charles's proposal that independent Dominica be a true republic without any allegiance to the British monarchy. Dominica officially gained its nationhood in November 1978.

John served as premier of the new nation, but soon got into trouble when he involved himself in a deal with a foreign investor to turn over a large land area to private development. At the same time, he mismanaged government funds. In May 1979, a protest turned tragic when Dominican troops fired on an unarmed crowd. John backed the army in its action, and the discontent spread. After these developments, Charles and the DFP entered the 1980 elections with renewed vigor and won. She served not only as prime minister but also as minister of finance and foreign affairs.

Charles faced an unstable political environment and endured two attempted coups against her rule, both occurring in 1981. The rebellions resulted in the imprisonment of John for conspiring to overthrow the government. She also faced great economic challenges: devastation from two recent hurricanes and an empty treasury. She rejected socialism and welcomed investments and aid from the United States. Charles reacted to opposition from the Dominican military by disbanding it. She won worldwide attention when, in 1983, she stood beside the American president, Ronald Reagan,

and proclaimed her support for sending U.S. troops into Grenada to crush that island's radicals.

Charles won reelection by a large margin in 1985, and her conservative approach to foreign affairs continued. She praised the Monroe Doctrine and its use by the United States to prevent subversive movements in the Western Hemisphere, and in 1989 she supported the American invasion of Panama to oust that nation's ruler. Dominica was the only Caribbean nation to support the U.S. position. She developed close ties not only with the United States but also with Britain, Canada, Israel, and Taiwan. In the 1990 elections, she again led the DFP to victory, but this time her party maintained only a one-vote majority in the House and faced a challenge from a new organization, the Dominica United Workers' Party.

Charles has brought many advances to Dominica, including better roads and utilities, a sounder financial system, and improved schools and hospitals. Yet the economy has not diversified and tourism lags. In reaction to this, Charles continues to privatize state enterprises. Despite her problems, she remains a symbol of Dominican independence and stability.

Reference: Higbie, Janet, *Eugenia: The Caribbean's Iron Lady*, 1993.

Chiang Ch'ing
(1913?–1991)
China

Chiang Ch'ing stirred waves of youthful Red Guards with her fiery speeches promoting Maoism. Radical in her beliefs, she accepted no compromise with capitalism, no retreat from building China along the lines advocated by her husband, MAO TSE-TUNG.

The details surrounding Chiang Ch'ing's childhood are unsettled. She was born Luan Shumeng about 1913 in Chu-ch'eng, located in Shantung Province, and was raised by her grandfather in Tsinan. She attended primary and secondary schools affiliated with the Shantung Normal

School. During her childhood, China went through tumultuous change as the Nationalists, led primarily by SUN YAT-SEN, tried to build a united Chinese government, freed from years of foreign domination. After Sun's death in 1925, CHIANG KAI-SHEK deposed fellow Nationalist WANG CHING-WEI and headed the movement. In trying to consolidate his power in the late 1920s, he purged the Communists.

This turmoil affected nearly all aspects of Chinese life, including the seemingly apolitical theater, which had attracted Chiang Ch'ing. In 1929, she studied at the Shantung Experimental Drama

Academy in Tsinan and joined a theater troupe, but her activity in a Communist organization led to her arrest in 1933. After her release in 1934, she played minor roles in movies produced by the leftist Tien Tung Motion Picture Company. In 1935, she began working for the Lien Hua Motion Picture Company, where she played the female lead in *Wang Lao Wu* (1937) and costarred in *Lien Hua's Symphony* (1937).

In 1937, Japan attacked China and Chiang Ch'ing fled to Chungking where the Nationalists, who agreed to an alliance with the Communists to fight the Japanese, had headquartered the Chinese government. There she worked for the Nationalist-controlled Central Movie Studio. But she also entertained Mao Tse-tung's Communist troops in Yenen and soon broke with the Nationalists. She taught drama at an art academy where, about 1939, she met Mao, who gave a talk to the school. The two fell in love and in a controversial move, Mao divorced Ho Tzu-chen, his third wife, who had been a Communist Party loyalist and was now seriously ill, and married Chiang Ch'ing. The hierarchy of the Chinese Communist Party (CCP) especially objected to this, but Mao quieted the protestations when he agreed that his new wife would abstain from participating in politics.

Chiang Ch'ing remained quiescent politically until the mid-1960s. In 1964, she demanded that plays be cleansed of their bourgeois content, and eight plays in the Peking drama series were subsequently replaced. Then, in October 1965, she wrote a critique condemning a play written by an associate of several CCP leaders as anti-Mao. This helped ignite the Cultural Revolution during which students demonstrated, protesting capitalist revisionism and chanting the sayings of Chairman Mao. Purges began among teachers, writers, and reporters to make China ideologically pure. Many politicians in the CCP were forced to publicly admit their errors; many were imprisoned and tortured, and some were executed.

Chiang Ch'ing developed an enormous influence with the students, soldiers, and workers who had organized into cadres called the Red Guards. In 1966, she led several mass meetings in Peking where she praised Mao and LIN PIAO, who had undertaken to make the army reflect Maoist thought. This entire effort amounted to Mao and his supporters bypassing the CCP bureaucracy, which they believed too cumbersome, self-absorbed, and

"Last year was the time to kindle the flames of revolution."

compromising toward capitalist practices that resembled the influence of revisionists tied to the Soviet Union. Mao intended to rely on his direct contacts with the people and on the reformed army to strengthen his power, some of which he had lost in the 1950s, and to reshape China.

Chiang Ch'ing became cultural advisor to the army and her importance equaled that of Lin Piao and the premier, CHOU EN-LAI. In 1967, she demanded that Mao's enemies be "wiped out."

But the Cultural Revolution threatened to go too far. Mao worried that the Red Guards and other groups bordered on anarchy as they took their attacks against authority, and their questioning, to extremes. Furthermore, the establishment within the CCP retaliated, deepening the chaos. Political power began shifting to more moderate leaders, such as Chou En-lai. By the beginning of 1968, Chiang Ch'ing was advising calm to control the excesses.

As the Cultural Revolution subsided, so too did Chiang Ch'ing's influence, but she remained formidable and in 1969 was elevated to the powerful CCP Politburo. In the early 1970s, her ranking within the Chinese hierarchy dropped, and Chiang Ch'ing struggled with Chou En-lai for influence with Mao. By 1975, Chou had emerged firmly in control. Then in 1976 his death, and that of Mao, shattered Chinese politics. For the radicals the loss of Mao meant the loss of their champion and their shield. In October, less than a month after Mao's death, the moderates purged the radicals, which entailed removals from office and arrests. Four prominent radicals—labeled the Gang of Four—were designated the main culprits in damaging China. Most notable in this group was Chiang Ch'ing, who was expelled from the CCP in 1977.

At her public trial in 1981, Chiang Ch'ing denied the voluminous accusations against her, including having forged Mao's will and fomented disorder during the Cultural Revolution. Strident and adamant, she denounced the court and China's leaders for straying from Maoist ideology. The court handed down a suspended death sentence, changed in 1983 to life imprisonment. She died on 14 May 1991 in prison. According to the Chinese government she committed suicide.

Reference: Karnow, Stanley, *Mao and China: Inside China's Cultural Revolution*, 1972.

Chiang Kai-shek
(1887–1975)
China

In his pursuit of unifying his country, Chiang Kai-shek followed in the footsteps of SUN YAT-SEN, the father of modern China. Unlike Sun, however, Chiang could not control the selfishness in his Nationalist movement nor could he understand the need to help the peasants. His strident belief in his own invincibility ultimately destroyed him.

Chiang Kai-shek was born on 30 October 1887 in Ch'i-k'ou, a town located in Chekiang Province. His father, a moderately prosperous salt merchant, died in 1896.

In the time of Chiang's boyhood, China underwent enormous upheaval as the ruling Ch'ing dynasty had been disgraced and weakened by foreign encroachments on Chinese sovereignty. Many Chinese blamed this on Ch'ing traditionalism and backwardness and believed China had to become more modern to expel the foreigners and regain its power and dignity.

Chiang agreed with this. When he traveled to Japan in 1907 to train for a military career at the Shikan Gakko Military Academy, he came into contact with other Chinese students who advocated reform. Chiang even joined the revolutionary group founded by Sun Yat-sen, T'ung-meng hui (United Alliance), committed to overthrowing the Ch'ing dynasty and establishing a republic.

Chiang served in the Japanese army from 1909 to 1911. When on 10 October 1911 revolution erupted in Wuhan, Chiang returned home to fight under Ch'en Ch'i-mei against the Ch'ing. The revolutionaries overthrew the dynasty, and on 1 January 1912 Sun Yat-sen proclaimed the Republic of China. Sun, however, did not have the military power necessary to unite China. Yüan Shih-kai, a political boss based in the north, possessed the most military might, and so Sun agreed to his becoming president. Yüan quickly ignored the national legislature controlled by Sun's political party, the Kuomintang (KMT, or Nationalists). Instead, Yüan developed a dictatorship and moved militarily against the Na-tionalists. In 1913, this produced a "second revolution" in which Sun and Chiang fought against Yüan's forces, but by the end of the year Sun had lost and Chiang was forced to flee to Japan.

Chiang led a secretive existence from 1916 to 1917, during which time he apparently involved himself with the Shanghai underworld and associated with a group called the Green Gang. In 1918, he rejoined Sun Yat-sen's movement and developed a close relationship with the Nationalist hero.

By this time, Yüan had died and his government had disintegrated, ushering in a chaotic period in which various warlords exerted power in their territories. Sun led a Nationalist government, which existed only in name, so he still struggled to unite China under his banner. In the early 1920s, Sun reorganized the Nationalist Party along the lines of the Communist revolutionaries in Russia. In 1923, Sun sent Chiang to Moscow to study Soviet military methods and the close political arrangement between the army and the Communist Party.

Chiang returned to China late in 1923 and directed the Whampoa Military Academy, established near Canton with the help of Soviet advisors. CHOU EN-LAI headed its political department and LIN PIAO enrolled as a cadet. So important had the Communists in China become that Sun admitted them into the Nationalist Party.

In March 1925, Sun Yat-sen died and Chiang, for some time considered Sun's heir apparent, used the support of the Whampoa army in a political stuggle with his main rival in the Kuomintang, WANG CHING-WEI, to emerge as the new Nationalist leader. Nevertheless, he still had an important threat to his position: the Communists. In 1927, Chiang took the Nationalist army into northern China, where he gained control of the lower Yangzi Valley. He then moved on Shanghai and captured that city after a Communist-led uprising of workers paved the way for his entry. In a surprise move on

12 April 1927, Chiang attacked the labor unions and captured the Communists, killing several hundred of them. He had broken openly with the Communists and the leftist faction in the Nationalist movement, and now increasingly allied himself with the right.

Chiang did this for several reasons: He feared the Communists would grab power from him, particularly since many Nationalist troops sympathized with them; he was convinced that the Communists were more concerned with promoting the interests of the international Communist movement than those of China; and he needed the support of warlords who disdained the Communists. Chiang forced two leading competitors in the Nationalist Party to retire: Wang Ching-wei, sympathetic to the left wing, and MAO TSE-TUNG, Communist head of the propaganda department. After several additional military assaults, by October 1928 Chiang's forces had control of nearly all of China.

In 1930, Chiang married Mei-ling (he had earlier divorced his first wife), whose Westernized family convinced him to become a Christian. The marriage drew him closer to the conservatives in Chinese society.

Chiang claimed he supported economic reform, but he never initiated any major changes. His Nationalist government sided with the business interests and the landed gentry. In a country where most people were peasants and most of those were suffering great hardship, his policies won little popular support. At the same time, his rule became known for its widespread corruption. Chiang committed a serious blunder in his policy toward Japan. The Japanese captured Manchuria in 1931 and showed every intention of invading northern China and beyond. Rather than prepare his army primarily for this invasion, Chiang decided to concentrate on the Communists and eliminate them from the scene. But the Communists, led by Mao Tse-tung, eluded Chiang and won a substantial following by focusing their attention on the despised Japanese. The Nationalists and Communists eventually united against Japan, but only after General Chang Hsueh-liang captured Chiang and forced him to accept such an arrangement.

In 1934, Chiang began a New Life Movement, trying to get the Chinese to adopt Confucian values mixed with puritanical Protestantism. But this ideology paled in appeal next to the radicalism, particularly the land reform, offered by the Marxists.

When Japan finally did invade China in 1937, the Communists rallied the countryside and the Red Army grew enormously. Millions of Chinese who little understood Marxism found in Mao a hero who would protect China. Chiang worsened his situation by withholding his army from much of the fighting. He let the Communists and later the Allies bear the brunt, thinking he would save his men for the postwar struggle against Mao. In the meantime, his army grew indolent and overconfident. Chiang was mortified when, in 1944, the Japanese attacked Nationalist forces with devastating results: 700,000 men lost, along with 100,000 square miles of territory in seven months.

In 1946, the Nationalists and Communists engaged in fierce fighting, ignited when Chiang blocked Mao's troops who sought to move from central China to the north, where they could reinforce Communist units in Manchuria. For three years the combat continued, and for three years Chiang made serious military mistakes, the most damaging being his decision to move his army into Manchuria, thus overextending his supply lines. Furthermore, he blundered when he outlawed reform movements and consequently convinced many liberals to support the Communists.

Even Mao expressed surprise at how fast the Nationalists disintegrated. In 1949, Chiang fled to Taiwan, an island near China's southeast coast, where with U.S. backing he founded the Republic of China. While Mao and the Communists ruled mainland China and, with the help of Mao's wife, CHIANG CH'ING, developed a cultlike Maoist ideology, Chiang insisted that his Nationalists constituted the legitimate Chinese government—a claim only the United States took seriously—and for many years Taiwan held the Chinese seat in the United Nations.

Under Chiang, Taiwan developed a prosperous capitalist economy, helped greatly by massive infusions of American aid and military protection. Although Taiwan had a representative assembly, Chiang ruled the island as his personal domain.

Chiang claimed he would recapture the mainland, but it never came about, and he grew more isolated. In 1972, Communist China regained the Chinese seat in the UN, and throughout the 1970s the United States normalized its contacts with the mainland. Chiang did not live to see the United States sever its formal ties with Taiwan in 1979, when it established diplomatic relations with mainland China. He died on 5 April 1975 and was succeeded as Taiwan's leader by his son, Chiang Ching-kuo.

References: Crozier, Brian, *The Man Who Lost China: The Full Biography of Chiang Kai-shek,* 1976; Hedin, Sven Anders, *Chiang Kai-shek, Marshall of China,* 1975.

Choibalsang, Horloyn

(1895–1952)

Mongolia

Born on Mongolia's spacious, arid eastern plains, Horloyn Choibalsang ran away from his monastic schooling to pursue revolution. In time, his organizational brilliance linked his country with the Marxist-Leninist ferment under way in Russia.

In 1895, Horloyn Choibalsang was born into a poor family. His parents placed him in a Buddhist monastery when he was 13, but after three or four years he ran away to Urga, the Mongolian capital, where he entered a school for interpreters.

For many years, Russia and China had competed for influence in Mongolia, with the Chinese gaining the upper hand. When Choibalsang arrived in Urga, however, he found Chinese control rapidly deteriorating. The fall of China's Ch'ing dynasty to an internal revolution led Outer Mongolia to declare its independence in December 1911. But Russia moved quickly to make Outer Mongolia a tsarist protectorate. The situation changed again in 1913, when China and Russia agreed to an autonomous Mongolia under Chinese oversight.

Then the tsarist regime in Russia fell to the Bolsheviks, and Mongolia became ensnared among Chinese, White Russians (opposed to the Bolsheviks), and Japanese, all maneuvering to gain control. This turmoil further stimulated Mongolian nationalism, and in 1919 Choibalsang, who had completed his schooling in Siberia, where he heard much about the Russian Revolution, headed a secret revolutionary organization that competed with one headed by DAMDINY SUKHEBATOR. Choibalsang had already embraced Marxism and considered the Russian Revolution a vanguard of worldwide rebellion. He desired not only to end foreign control in Mongolia but also bring about a social transformation.

When Choibalsang first met Sukhebator he knew they would complement each other—he as the political organizer, Sukhebator as the military leader. The Communist International in Moscow urged the two men to unite, and in 1920 they formed the Mongolian People's Party, with Sukhebator as its overall head. The party's revolutionary

"For Mongolia, Russia is the most loyal friend . . . and we ought to work . . . to strengthen our friendship."

army drove several foreign armies from Mongolian soil, and on 14 September 1921 the People's Government of Mongolia proclaimed the nation's complete independence, with Dogsomyn Bodoo as premier and Choibalsang serving under Sukhebator as deputy commander in chief of the military. The revolutionaries defeated the last White Russian forces in January 1922. That same year, Choibalsang helped organize a secret police force for Mongolia.

In the early 1920s, the ruling Mongolian People's Party experienced an internal struggle between those who, like Choibalsang, wanted to continue close ties with Soviet Russia and those who wanted to distance Mongolia from the neighboring nation. Amid the struggle, Choibalsang was studying military tactics in Moscow. After Sukhebator died in 1923 under mysterious circumstances (he may have been poisoned), Choibalsang, his ally in the party fight, isolated the anti-Soviet faction. As a result, in 1924 he became commander in chief of the army, and four years later, with his faction backed by the Soviet Union, he became head of the nation's standing legislative body, the Little Hural.

As his power increased, Choibalsang attacked the nobility with a vengeance. As an extreme leftist he wanted to end the feudal property system and collectivize the farms. His crusade included attacking the Buddhist monks, who from their monasteries held considerable property and power. He also collectivized the herdsmen, which caused this fiercely independent group to rebel. The economy soon spiralled downward, beset by crop failures and a wasteful slaughter of animals. Food shortages spread and civil war threatened.

In 1932, Choibalsang announced a change that he called the New Turn Policy—a gradualist approach toward collectivization. Private enterprise was allowed to resume, and the herdsmen were generally left alone. The state regulated much internal trade and encouraged cooperatives, but Choibalsang developed only a few state farms.

Choibalsang built Mongolia's army with substantial Soviet assistance, and he developed the school system. In 1921, Mongolia had only 1 elementary school; by 1952 it had 426. The first university was founded in 1947. He also destroyed many monasteries and ordered that the abbots be arrested, tried, and executed for their opposition to the revolution.

Although on paper Choibalsang did not always hold the highest positions in the party (for example, in 1940 the Tenth Party Congress chose Yumjaagiyn Tsedenbal as general-secretary), by the end of the 1930s he was premier, minister of war, and the most powerful man in Mongolia. He engaged in fierce power struggles with his opponents, used terror tactics to survive, and developed a personality cult. This led some observers to call him "Mongolia's Stalin."

Choibalsang died on 26 January 1952. The transition to a new leader brought more purges and, in the mid-1950s, a repudiation of Choibalsang for his excesses.

References: Lattimore, Owen, *Nationalism and Revolution in Mongolia,* 1955; Lattimore, Owen, *Nomads and Commissars: Mongolia Revisited,* 1962; Rupen, Robert, *How Mongolia Is Really Ruled: A Political History of the Mongolian People's Republic, 1900–1978,* 1979.

Chornovil, Vyacheslav
(b. 1937)
Ukraine

As a political dissident who advocated Ukrainian nationalism, Vyacheslav Chornovil spent many years in prison, incarcerated by his Soviet oppressors.

Vyacheslav Chornovil was born in 1937 and as a young man became a journalist. He wrote stories detailing Russian discrimination against Ukrainian culture and the persecution of Ukrainian nationalists. In the mid-1960s, he authored *The Chornovil Papers,* and in 1967 the Soviets reacted to the book by imprisoning him. They released him in 1969, whereupon he continued writing and presenting his views. In 1972, the government jailed him again, this time for editing *The Ukrainian Herald.* Chornovil was not released until 1985.

In the late 1980s, after the Soviet Union undertook internal reform to promote greater openness, Ukrainian nationalism surged, and in 1989 when the poets Ivan Drach and Pavlo Movchan founded Rukh, or "The Movement," Chornovil joined them. At first moderate, Rukh soon condemned the Communist Party and sought democracy, a market economy, respect for human rights, and Ukrainian sovereignty, either within the Soviet Union or, preferably, as a separate nation. In an election to choose delegates to the Ukrainian Supreme Soviet—the republic's legislature—Rukh captured one-third of the seats, a victory that caused the Communist Party to change its position and support national sovereignty. That same year, Chornovil worked as a member of the Ukrainian Helsinki Union to advance human rights, and the Soviets labeled him an "extremist."

In 1990, a hard-line Communist who had become a reformer, LEONID KRAVCHUK, was elected chairman of the Supreme Soviet. When conservatives in Russia tried to overthrow the Soviet government, Kravchuk condemned the action—but he did so only after it was clear the coup had failed. This convinced Chornovil that Kravchuk was not sincerely committed to Ukrainian nationalism and reform—that he was an opportunist. In December 1991, Chornovil ran against Kravchuk for the Ukraine presidency. In a multicandidate race he lost, obtaining 23 percent of the vote compared to Kravchuk's 62 percent. At the same time, the Soviet Union collapsed and Ukraine officially declared its independence.

Chornovil continued his opposition and attacked Kravchuk for being weak toward reform; he decried what he called an "unfinished revolution" and believed that Kravchuk was appointing too many communist bureaucrats to the new government. Chornovil organized a strong faction within Rukh and in December 1992 won election as its leader by a wide margin. However, he faced opposition from moderates led by Ivan Drach, who supported Kravchuk as the only politician with the expertise and support to protect Ukrainian independence.

In 1994, Chornovil still commanded Rukh and appeared to be converting it into a powerful opposition party. As the Ukrainian economy experienced enormous difficulties with skyrocketing inflation, Chornovil remained committed to rapid democratization and a free market. Observers wonder, however, whether many Ukrainians still prefer the security of state-run industries, particularly in light of Leonid Kuchma's recent election to the presidency that seemed to signal a go-slow approach to reform.

Reference: Solchanyk, Roman, ed., *From Chernobyl to Sovereignty: A Collection of Interviews*, 1992.

Chou En-lai
(1898–1976)
China

A leader in building modern China, Chou En-lai was also an adept survivor who manuevered through the divisions within the Chinese Communist Party to wield substantial power as premier and foreign minister.

Chou En-lai was born in Huaian, Kiangsu Province, in 1898. His father was a moderately wealthy landowner. Since both of Chou's parents died while he was still a child, he was raised by an uncle in Shao-hsing, Chekiang Province. There he attended elementary school before graduating from a middle school in Tientsin and going to Japan in 1917 to continue his studies.

Japan had become a hotbed for Chinese students who wanted reform in their homeland. Since the nineteenth century, the Ch'ing dynasty had been declining, mired in traditional practices that made China a weak country, divided into spheres of influence by several foreign nations. Some of the student reformers wanted to get rid of the dynasty in order to move China into a modernized, Westernized future. Chou engaged in the reform discussions, which included Marxist ideas.

> *"Struggle by violent means merely touches people's flesh. Only struggle through reason can touch their souls."*

In 1919, the May Fourth Student Movement erupted in China, and Chou returned to Tientsin to join in the protest. This movement aimed at the corrupt and power-hungry regime in Peking that a few years earlier had overthrown the Ch'ing dynasty and grabbed power from the leader of the Kuomintang, or Nationalist, movement, SUN YAT-SEN. The students also condemned the Treaty of Versailles ending World War I, which they believed forced China to accept Japanese seizures in their country. Chou edited a radical student newspaper and then was arrested in 1920 for his participation in a demonstration.

After four months in prison, Chou went to France under a work-and-study program. There he met French and Chinese socialists and joined the Chinese Socialist Youth Corps, a communist organization. In 1922, he founded the organization's Berlin branch and was elected to the European branch of the Chinese Communist Party (CCP).

In 1924, Chou returned to China, a land beset with a choatic political situation as warlords and competing parties vied for control. Sun Yat-sen continued his efforts to unite China behind his Koumintang and in the 1920s looked increasingly to the Communist success in the Russian Revolution as a model for his own efforts. He accepted advice from Soviet Russia and admitted Communists into the Nationalist Party. Chou subsequently joined the Kuomintang.

In 1925, he married Tung Ying-chao, a student activist who emerged as a powerful member of the CCP. At this time he also was appointed deputy director of the political department at the revolutionary Whampoa Military Academy, where CHIANG KAI-SHEK served as director and LIN PIAO trained as a cadet. He also became special commissioner for the East River District of Kwangtung Province. Chou lost this position in 1926, when Chiang Kaishek, now Sun Yat-sen's successor as Nationalist leader, began moving against the Communists.

Chou then went to Shanghai in 1927 to lead a Communist uprising of the workers there, an upheaval which, ironically, made it easier for Chiang Kai-shek to capture the city. When Chiang started arresting and killing Communists in Shanghai, Chou fled to Wuhan, where the Fifth National Congress of the CCP elected him to the Politburo and made him head of the military committee.

Chou commanded a military unit and led a Communist uprising in Nan-ch'ang on 1 August 1927, but the Nationalist forces captured the city, and Chou fled again, this time to Shanghai. From there he went to Moscow, where he won reelection to his party positions. He returned to China in 1929 and in 1932 became political commissar of a communist army linked MAO TSE-TUNG. In 1934, he participated with Mao in the infamous Long March, during which the Communist forces, hemmed in and nearly defeated by Chiang Kai-shek, retreated to northern China.

Chou initially had policy differences with Mao, but when Mao emerged as the CCP leader in 1935 after the Long March, Chou moved into close cooperation with him and became his trusted ally thereafter. Chou proved to be a consummate negotiator for the CCP. By this time, Japan was threatening to invade northern China, and Chou arranged a cease-fire with powerful General Chang Hsueh-liang that led to Chang's kidnapping Chiang Kai-shek and convincing the Nationalist leader to join in a united front against Japan (thus rebuking another Nationalist, WANG CHING-WEI, who advocated a peaceful agreement with the Japanese). Chou proved instrumental in the negotiations with Chiang Kai-shek, and also in saving the Nationalist leader from execution by Chang. From 1937 until 1943, Chou served as the CCP's chief representative with the Nationalists, and he led the negotiations after World War II that attempted, unsuccessfully, to reach a political settlement with them.

After Chiang Kai-shek's government fell to the Communists in 1949, Chou became premier of the People's Republic of China. He worked closely with Mao, who held the political reins as chairman of the CCP. He developed the bureaucarcy and, at the same time, served as foreign minister (a post he maintained until 1958). In February 1950, Chou signed a 30-year treaty of alliance with the Soviet Union. Between 1956 and 1964, he traveled extensively in Asia and Africa, promoting the need for revolutions against capitalism.

During the 1960s and 1970s, he softened and eventually contained the extremism produced by the Great Leap Forward and the Cultural Revolution promoted by Mao and his wife, CHIANG CH'ING. In particular, he directed substantial economic growth that reversed the downturn from Mao's excessive collectivization, and he helped restore to power moderates who had been impugned. Until 1969, he was the third-ranking Chinese leader; he moved up to second when, in 1971, his major rival, Lin Piao, had a falling out with Mao and was killed in an airplane crash.

Although not officially foreign minister in the 1970s, Chou still exerted great influence in that area and oversaw the thawing of relations with the United States. In 1971, he negotiated skillfully with the American secretary of state and helped arrange the 1972 visit of President Richard Nixon.

On 8 January 1976 Chou died from cancer. Since 1949, he had been a prominent force in the CCP, a talented negotiator who kept the party together and helped restore China as a major power, once again independent of foreign domination.

References: Kai-yu Hsu, *Chou En-lai: China's Gray Eminence,* 1968; Li Tien-min, *Chou En-lai,* 1970; Roots, John M., *An Informal Biography of China's Legendary Chou En-lai,* 1978.

Chulalongkorn
(1853–1910)
Thailand

In 1897 and again in 1907, Chulalongkorn toured Europe and the monarchies there received him warmly. For Chulalongkorn the trip and the receptions signified what he wanted: Thailand's continuing Westernization and acceptance as a modern nation.

Chulalongkorn was born on 20 September 1853, the ninth son of King MONGKUT. From his father, Chulalongkorn inherited an important legacy: the molding of Thailand (then called Siam) into a modern nation based on Western principles. Mongkut had initiated this development and expected his successor to continue it. As such, he had his sons educated extensively in Western ways while maintaining an attachment to Buddhism. Like his father, Chulalongkorn was for a time a Buddhist monk.

When Mongkut died in October 1868, Chulalongkorn, then only 15, succeeded him. For five years, he ruled under a regent, during which time he learned court procedure and traveled to Malaya, Burma, and India, where he studied British administration. His journey continued his father's efforts at liberalizing and opening up the monarchy, since Thailand's kings did not traditionally leave their country.

Chulalongkorn's reforms began immediately upon his coronation in 1873 when he announced that Thais would no longer have to lay prostrate before their king. He quickly began other reforms, including changes in the judiciary and finances, that copied Western procedures. Conservatives, however, revolted against him late in 1874. Although Chulalongkorn suppressed the uprising, he was forced to move more cautiously in making additional changes.

In 1888, he began a gradual conversion of the government to a cabinet system with 12 ministries. His interior minister subsequently changed the provincial governments to replace a semifeudal system with a centralized administration.

Chulalongkorn promoted Western education. He established three European-style schools for the children of government officials, developed specialized schools to train civil servants, encouraged study in Europe, and began compulsory primary education for all Thais. One of his most important later reforms was to abolish slavery (although emancipation proceeded gradually over a 20-year period).

Chulalongkorn oversaw the development of Thailand's first railroad, completed between Bangkok and Ayutthaya in 1897, and the establishment of a postal service and telegraph system. He also instituted universal military conscription. In all, he wanted Thailand to be accepted as a modern nation. Part of his motivation came from a desire to maintain his homeland's independence against European encroachments in Southeast Asia. He did not, however, fully succeed in this: The French forced him to relinquish Thai claims in Laos and Cambodia, and in 1909 he had to cede four Malay states to Britain. Nevertheless, he balanced his relations with the Western nations and kept Thailand from European control.

Chulalongkorn died on 23 October 1910 after having ruled longer than any king in Thailand's history. Along with his father, Mongkut, Chulalongkorn is remembered as the founder of modern Thailand.

Reference: Chomchai, Prachoom, *Chulalongkorn the Great*, 1990.

Collins, Michael
(1890–1922)
Ireland

A wave of terrorism swept Ireland in 1920. The Irish Republican Army had adopted a new plan for attacking the country's British occupiers, one dubbed the Active Defensive Strategy, and under it Michael Collins sent his execution squad into action. In July, 11 officers in the British army were killed. Then in November, Bloody Sunday erupted when gunmen in trench coats murdered 14 British agents, and the army retaliated by firing into a crowd at a football game.

Michael Collins was born in County Cork, Ireland, on 16 October 1890. After attending the local primary schools, he obtained a job as a postal clerk in London in 1906, where he lived for the next ten years, and joined the Irish Republican Brotherhood, one of several secret societies dedicated to overthrowing British rule in Ireland. Collins returned to his home country in 1916 and participated in the infamous Easter Week uprising that earned him a brief imprisonment in North Wales.

During World War I, Collins emerged as the military leader of Sinn Fein (Ourselves Alone), a strident nationalist organization, while EAMON DE VALERA served as its political leader. Collins became noted for his administrative abilities, boundless energy, and ruthless tactics. He liked living on the precipice of danger, daring the British to capture him as he cycled along Dublin's streets, important papers hidden in his socks. In 1916, as director of intelligence for the Irish Republican Army (IRA), the military group dedicated to gaining independence, he began building a network that infiltrated the British government.

In 1919, Collins's special execution squad launched a spectacular assault on the British viceroy in Ireland as he disembarked from a train and entered a car. The attackers lobbed hand grenades at their intended victim, but he emerged uninjured. The Irish rebels considered themselves struggling freedom fighters for an independent Ireland; many Britons, however, considered them citizens of the United Kingdom who had become law breakers and terrorists.

After King George V called for a truce, Collins acceded to De Valera's request and joined the peace delegation. He believed it unlikely the British would recognize an independent Irish republic, and so he expected failure from the negotiations. As it turned out, Collins and the other delegates likely could have gained complete independence for all of Ireland, including Ulster, but Prime Minister Lloyd George successfully bluffed them. He threatened total war within days if the Irish delegates did not accept terms giving Ireland autonomy but keeping it within the British Empire and continuing Parliament's direct control over Ulster.

> *"They think when they get me everything will be over."*

Collins did not believe that the IRA and the Irish people in general could withstand an all-out war. He considered the proposed treaty a starting point toward total removal from the Empire.

Although the Dail, or Irish Parliament, accepted the treaty, De Valera and his Republicans did not. As the British evacuated Ireland, Collins attempted reconciling the differences between the Irish Free State government, as it was called, and De Valera, but failed. He then used force against the Republicans and a brief but bloody civil war ensued that proved tragic for Collins when, on 22 August 1922, he was killed in an ambush. While Collins left an important legacy, others were important in the Irish fight for freedom, including DANIEL O'CONNELL, CHARLES STEWART PARNELL, and PATRICK PEARSE.

References: Dangerfield, George, *The Damnable Question,* 1976; O'Connor, Frank, *The Big Fellow: Michael Collins and the Irish Revolution,* 1937.

Compton, John
(b. 1926)
St. Lucia

John Compton sought an independent St. Lucia that would reject radicalism and develop along a moderate path.

At the time of John Compton's birth in 1926 in neighboring St. Vincent and the Grenadines, St. Lucia was a British colony. Compton obtained his higher education at the London School of Economics and in 1951 began practicing law on St. Lucia. Three years later, he won election to the Legislative Council and joined the St. Lucia Labour Party (SLP), which governed the island into the 1960s.

In 1961, Compton resigned from the SLP to form a conservative organization, the National Labor Movement, which presently became the United Workers' Party (UWP). He became leader of the UWP in 1964, the same year that his party defeated the SLP, and was elevated to chief minister. In 1967, Britain implemented internal self-government in St. Lucia, while continuing to handle the island's foreign affairs and defense. The change in status resulted in a House of Assembly replacing the Legislative Council and the chief minister becoming premier.

Compton favored independence and applied to the British Parliament for it. Initially, the SLP opposed nationhood without first holding a referendum, but in 1978 it changed its position. On 24 October, the St. Lucia legislature approved the draft constitution arranged weeks earlier in London, and the island became independent on 22 January 1979. Compton served as prime minister pursuant to elections.

> *"We have no illusions about our impact on world affairs. . . . we are getting to manhood and we expect the benefits it provides."*

On 2 July 1979, however, he suffered a stunning defeat: The UWP unexpectedly lost the legislative elections to the SLP, which had called Compton's organization "antinational" for its over-reliance on foreigners to develop the island economy. Allan Louisy succeeded Compton as prime minister, and the UWP founder became leader of the opposition. At political rallies, extremists attacked Compton, hurling rocks and bags of excrement at him, and the disorder increased with attacks on private businesses. The SLP, meanwhile, pursued socialist policies and closer ties to leftist governments—moves that stirred considerable controversy. In 1982, Compton, promising economic growth based on agriculture, tourism, and light industry, returned to the prime ministry after the UWP captured 14 of the 17 legislative seats.

Compton won reelection in 1987, but only by a one-seat margin. An improved economy helped his party gain additional seats in the 1992 elections. Many critics, though, maintained that Compton had not lived up to his promise regarding economic diversification. Educated young people especially considered themselves either underemployed or totally shut out of the economy. Compton continues to face this discontent, along with demands he crack down on the local drug trade.

Reference: Griffiths, John, *The Caribbean in the Twentieth Century*, 1984.

Cristiani, Alfredo

(b. 1947)

El Salvador

When Alfredo Cristiani won election to the presidency, many outside observers worried he would endorse a right-wing reign of terror and fail to restore peace to a nation shattered by revolution. But Cristiani steered a middle course en route to establishing a new, more stable El Salvador.

Alfredo Cristiani was born on 22 November 1947 in San Salvador. He came from a wealthy family, which was involved in coffee, cotton, and pharmaceutical businesses. He attended the American School in San Salvador, obtained a degree from Georgetown University in Washington, D.C., and spent a good deal of his time in recreational activities, mainly sports and motorcycle racing. After college, he entered his family's business endeavors, but did not handle them with dedication.

During these years, turmoil engulfed El Salvador, produced by a growing gap between the wealthy elite and the impoverished masses, and by a small but increasingly restless middle class anxious to gain some political power. In 1980, the government came under the control of an alliance between the military and the Christian Democratic Party (PDC), which sought middle-class goals of economic growth and political stability. Several leftist guerrilla organizations opposed this arrangement by forming the Farabundo Marti National Liberation Front (FMLN).

As violence escalated in 1980, it directly affected Cristiani. He and several other businessmen were held hostage by the guerrillas for two weeks. In 1982, the PDC won the largest number of seats in Parliament, but four right-wing parties joined forces to have the legislature elect Roberto D'Aubisson Arrieta president. He represented the rightist National Republican Alliance (ARENA). Two years later, Cristiani joined this group and tried to moderate its extremist actions, particularly those of D'Aubisson, who was linked with the right-wing death squads.

"We won't roll back land reform."

ARENA lost the 1984 elections to the PDC as many voters were attracted by that party's candidate, José Napoleón Duarte Fuentes, who offered moderate reform and opened peace talks with the guerrillas. Cristiani continued his efforts at moderation, and D'Aubisson, convinced he would never win election, stepped aside as ARENA leader, allowing Cristiani to assume the position. Duarte's administration suffered from spiraling inflation, tax increases, and labor unrest, and this allowed Cristiani to lead ARENA to victory in the 1988 elections. He won a seat in the Assembly and prepared to run for president.

In 1989, Cristiani won the presidency and then tried to end the civil war by entering into negotiations with the FMLN. An agreement was reached in 1992 whereby the rebels promised to disband, and the government promised to distribute land to the peasants in rebel-held areas. El Salvador faced a trying recovery: The civil war had cost some 75,000 lives and untold economic destruction.

The question remained as to whether Cristiani had founded a new order. Critics accused him of siding with extreme right wingers and working to continue an elitist political system that operated to keep most Salvadorans impoverished. Their criticism seemed legitimate when in 1993 the National Assembly granted amnesty to all persons who had committed atrocities during the civil war. The following year, Calderón Sol replaced Cristiani as president but continued his predecessor's efforts at peace.

Reference: Haggerty, Richard A., ed., *El Salvador: A Country Study*, 1990.

Dacko, David
(b. 1930)
Central African Republic

By all accounts, as first president of the fully independent Central African Republic (CAR) David Dacko restricted his homeland's autonomy by allowing the former French rulers enormous influence in exchange for their support of his power. This working quid pro quo dominated the CAR's early years.

David Dacko was born 24 March 1930 in Bouchia. His father had worked as a night watchman for one of the foreign companies that dominated the area. Dacko attended a French school in the Middle Congo, returned home a teacher, and became head of a school in Bangui and a militant member of the teachers' trade union. He later joined MESAN, the political party formed by BARTHELEMY BOGANDA, a relative of his. After Boganda became president of the CAR, established in 1958 as a republic within the French Community, Dacko held office as minister of the interior and minister of economic affairs.

". . . the present disorder would never have taken root if our regime had been harsher from the beginning."

When on 29 March 1959 Boganda died in an airplane crash, the recently formed government entered a tumultuous period. Dacko and several other politicians pursued the presidency. French officials and Boganda's widow backed Dacko, and the CAR Assembly made him president. France supported him because he appeared more pliable than Abel Goumba, a nationalistic contender.

Dacko soon began amassing extralegal powers and dismantling Boganda's republican government. He removed the Assembly leader from office for trying to censure him.

Dacko continued Boganda's efforts at forming a confederation with the surrounding states, but cooperation proved futile, and on 13 August 1960, in a move Dacko did not expect for its rapidity, France granted the CAR full independence. Dacko then forced through the CAR Assembly measures that outlawed subversive writings and allowed a suspension of political parties. He appointed himself head of MESAN and appropriated Boganda's mantle.

Dacko deflected attention from the worsening economy and his own power grab by expelling the advisory French high commissioner—a move, he claimed, that proved his own independence from France. His action appealed to many within the CAR who held animosity toward France. But Dacko's move was more form than substance as he surrounded himself with French bureaucrats and entered an agreement with France permitting that nation's domination of foreign affairs and finances.

Dacko allowed wasteful spending by his advisors while the economic crisis in his homeland worsened. In the early 1960s, diamond production increased but only through the severe exploitation of peasant labor, while cotton, coffee, and other segments of the economy suffered. Dacko tried some economic reforms, but by December 1965 bankruptcy threatened. On 1 January 1966 a military coup ended his presidency.

References: Kalck, Pierre, *Central African Republic: A Failure in De-Colonisation*, 1971; O'Toole, Thomas, *The Central African Republic: The Continent's Hidden Heart*, 1986.

Daddah, Moktar Ould

(b. 1924)

Mauritania

In his public career, Moktar Ould Daddah mirrored the general support of French West African leaders for the institutions of France while he navigated through a Mauritanian society deeply divided by ethnic differences.

Moktar Ould Daddah, born on 25 December 1924 in the town of Boutilimit, came from a wealthy family, part of the indigenous elite favored by the French, who controlled the colony. He obtained a university education in Paris and became his homeland's first lawyer.

While Daddah was getting his education, France began reforming its colonial policies. In 1946, this included separating Mauritania from Senegal and allowing a territorial assembly and political parties. Horma Ould Babana headed the Mauritanian Entente, the territory's first political party, and linked it to the French Socialists. Many within the Moor ruling class, however, distrusted socialism, and with the cooperation of the French government they formed the Mauritanian Progressive Union and won control of the territorial legislature in 1952.

When Daddah returned from Paris in the mid-1950s, he joined this conservative party. Another French legislative reform in 1956, the *loi-cadre* or Enabling Act, expanded the power of the Mauritanian legislature and for the first time allowed an executive branch, called the Council of Government, chosen by the legislature. In 1957, the Mauritanians chose Daddah to head the Council and thus serve as prime minister. His pro-French credentials pleased the colonial power.

Daddah represented West Africa's modernizing elite. He advocated cultural independence; by this, he meant a stronger Islam, a bilingual system of Arabic and French, and a greater role for women in government.

In 1958, France gave her overseas territories the option of becoming semiautonomous members of a new French Community or becoming fully independent. Community status would mean economic assistance, whereas independence would preclude it. Daddah reacted by forming the Mauritanian Regroupment Party that supported Community membership and sought to unite the politically dominant Arabic Moors with the black Africans, who lived mainly south of the Senegal River.

The party also rejected Moroccan claims to Mauritania. Some Moors actually favored absorption of Mauritania by Morocco in hopes of unifying with fellow Arabs and diluting the black African influence. In all, Daddah positioned himself as the only person able to keep a divided Mauritania together.

In October 1958, the Islamic Republic of Mauritania emerged as a member of the French Community with Daddah as prime minister. But Daddah's political party soon splintered. As nationalistic sentiment swept through colonial Africa, some of his party members formed the Mauritanian National Renaissance Party (Nahda), whose platform advocated a complete break with France. Daddah outlawed this party in 1959, yet he and his followers gave in to the nationalist forces at work, and on 28 November 1960 Mauritania left the Community and became a completely independent nation with Daddah as president.

"Keep together the Mauritanian fatherland!"

While Daddah eliminated opposing political parties, he also developed an inclusive administration that tried to heal Mauritania's divisions. Thus, for example, he appointed black Africans to important cabinet positions. In 1961, he disbanded his old political party and formed yet another to promote national unity: the Mauritanian People's Party (PPM).

As president, Daddah followed three main courses of action. First, he enhanced his powers and developed a strong presidency by becoming secretary-general of PPM and ruthlessly crushing student and worker demonstrations over economic and ethnic issues. Second, he nationalized several important industries, including iron mining. Third, he pursued a contradictory policy toward Western Sahara (a territory bordering Morocco and Mauritania). When Spain withdrew from Western Sahara in the late 1960s, Morocco claimed the region. Daddah reacted by insisting on self-determination for Western Saharans. Then, to please his Moor supporters, he claimed all the area for Mauritania. Indeed, many Moors believed that annexing Western Sahara would benefit them by enhancing their power against the black Africans.

But Daddah also recognized the superior military strength of Morocco, and so he soon changed his position and claimed he would settle for only part of Western Sahara. Under the Madrid Agreement of 1975, Morocco obtained the northern two-thirds of Western Sahara, and Mauritania received the southern one-third. At this point, rebels in Western Sahara made war on both Morocco and

Mauritania, but they attacked Mauritania the hardest because of its weaker military position.

Daddah's Western Saharan policy became his downfall. The war greatly drained Mauritania financially while drought and famine ravaged the area. Daddah was forced to rely on huge loans from Arab nations to keep Mauritania afloat. Protests increased as most black Africans considered this an Arab war unjustly costing them their lives. These tensions produced a military coup that ended Daddah's regime on 10 July 1978.

Reference: Gerteiny, Alfred G., *Mauritania*, 1967.

Dayan, Moshe
(1915–1981)
Israel

As a child, Moshe Dayan experienced the double edge of Arab-Jewish relations. He developed a friendship with an Arab boy from a neighboring tribe, and he watched, at age five, as the Jewish settlement of Degania burned after an Arab attack.

Moshe Dayan was born 20 May 1915 on Palestine's first kibbutz and raised at Nahalal, a cooperative farm settlement. He had a trying childhood, experiencing much illness. This he overcame in a distinguished military career that began in 1937. He learned guerrilla warfare from a British officer and then joined squadrons that attacked Arab lands in Palestine. These squadrons were the beginning of a Jewish army. Dayan believed that a Jewish state would never be allowed by Arabs through peaceful evolution; consequently, he joined the Hagnah, a military group that had been declared illegal by Palestine's ruler, Britain. British authorities arrested Dayan in 1939, and he remained in prison until 1941, when he was released to participate in an allied assault on the Vichy French in Syria. During this operation, Dayan was struck by a bullet and lost his left eye.

When Israel's war for independence began in 1948, Dayan served as commander of Jerusalem

and successfully defended it against a siege. He participated in negotiations with Jordan's king that produced an armistice between Israel and Jordan.

With Israel officially a nation under DAVID BEN-GURION as prime minister and CHAIM WEIZMANN as president, Dayan served from 1950 to 1953 as commander of the Southern and Northern Command of the Israel Defense Forces (IDF) and, shortly thereafter, head of the General Branch of Operations in the General Staff, which made him second in rank within the IDF. On 6 December 1954, Ben-Gurion appointed Dayan chief of staff. From this position Dayan, a quiet and often diffident man, directed the 1956 invasion of the Sinai Peninsula that coordinated with a British and French attack on Egypt in retaliation for that nation having nationalized the Suez Canal. His success made him enormously popular in Israel.

Dayan obtained election to the Knesset (Parliament) in 1959, representing the Israeli Labor Party coalition, Mapai. Ben-Gurion appointed him minister of agriculture, a post he held until 1964, and through which he established long-range agricultural planning and developed water allocations. He resigned in a political dispute but again won election to the Knesset in 1965 as a member of Rafi, a new party headed by Ben-Gurion.

It appeared as if Dayan's military days had ended, but in 1967 Egypt prepared to invade Israel and broke the existing armistice by shelling Israeli soldiers. Prime Minister Levi Eshkol then appointed Dayan defense minster. Dayan and Yitzhak Rabin, the chief of staff, directed Israel's strategy in a war that lasted only six days (5–10 June) and brought a resounding defeat for Egypt and its Arab allies. Once again, Israelis embraced Dayan as a hero. But he generated controversy when he established an Open Bridges Policy that permitted people and goods to journey between Jordan and the West Bank and Gaza Strip without hindrance. This risked an Arab infiltration of militia and weapons and contrasted with the prevailing Israeli policy (particularly before 1963) of curtailing most Arab liberties within Israel proper.

A great blow occurred to Dayan's prestige when, in 1973, Egypt and Syria launched a surprise attack on Israel. Many Israelis criticized him for having delayed the mobilization of forces, but prime minister GOLDA MEIR continued Dayan in his position as defense minister. Indeed, Dayan had been nervous about Egyptian and Syrian troop movements and had ordered some measures, but he and other Israeli leaders were misled by intelligence reports that insisted the Arabs would not at-

tack. After Yitzhak Rabin became prime minister in 1974, Dayan was forced out of office. For the next three years he again served in the Knesset.

When Menachem Begin gained the prime ministry in 1977, he appointed Dayan foreign minister. Dayan later exerted an enormous influence in the Camp David Accords, the historic peace agreement signed in 1978 between Israel and Egypt: He desired autonomy for Arabs in the West Bank and Gaza Strip, and although Begin rejected this idea, it was agreed that Palestinian Arabs would participate in future negotiations with Egypt, Jordan, and Israel to determine the future status of the West Bank and Gaza.

Dayan resigned his post in 1979 after strenuously opposing Begin's plan (not culminated) to annex the West Bank that, although occupied by Israel, was legally a part of Jordan. In 1981, Dayan formed Telem, a new political party, advocating Israel's withdrawal from all lands occupied after the 1967 Six Day War. He died 16 October 1981 from cancer. His career had many highs and lows, but his military if not also his political leadership proved instrumental in the establishment of Israel and its defense against antagonistic Arab neighbors.

References: Dayan, Moshe, *Story of My Life*, 1976; Dayan, Yael, *My Father, His Daughter*, 1985.

De Gaulle, Charles
(1890–1970)
France

In 1958, when the Fourth Republic collapsed, Charles de Gaulle let it be known that he would agree to step forward and serve as France's leader. The French people accepted his offer, and one year later, the egotistical, strongly nationalistic World War II hero established the Fifth Republic.

Charles de Gaulle was born in Lille on 22 November 1890 and grew up in Paris, where his father worked as a teacher at a Jesuit school, the College of

the Immaculate Conception. Charles, who at age 13 developed a desire for a military career, attended secondary school in Paris and then entered Saint-Cyr, the French military school from which he graduated in 1911 with a commission as a second lieutenant. He then served under Colonel Henri Pétain in the Thirty-Third Infantry Regiment.

De Gaulle fought in World War I and earned a reputation for valor. He was wounded three times and, in 1916, was captured by the Germans at Verdun. After the war, he joined with other French volunteers to help the Poles fight the Russian Red Army.

After the Polish army defeated the Russians in 1921, de Gaulle returned to Paris and attended the War College, where he promoted controversial military tactics that called for more flexibility in the heat of battle, especially in the use of tanks, than his superiors thought best. They also considered him too conceited and unwilling to accept criticism, hence they assigned him a low grade. Pétain, now a general, supported de Gaulle, appointed him to his own staff, and had him give lectures at the War College. From 1929 to 1931, de Gaulle headed French military operations in Syria, Egypt, Iraq, and Iran. When he returned home, he gained appointment as secretary-general of the Higher Council of National Defense and was promoted to lieutenant colonel. He was assigned to preparing a study on the mobilization of France during a war crisis.

Many observers believe that de Gaulle exhibited great military insight in the 1930s when he warned about developments in Europe. In his book *The Army of the Future,* he criticized France's reliance on the Maginot Line for defense against Germany and called for the formation of mechanized armored columns. He asserted that "any defender who limited himself to static resistance by old-fashioned elements would be doomed to disaster." His advice went largely unheeded, and in June 1940 German forces easily entered France.

De Gaulle was promoted that year to brigadier general and in a tank operation momentarily turned back the Germans at Laon and Abbeville. He was named undersecretary of national defense and war and went to London for discussions with the British prime minister, Winston Churchill. He refused to accept the truce that the French government had worked out with the Germans and later in 1940 announced the formation of a French government-in-exile headquartered in London. He became president of Free France, and the British recognized him as commander of the Free French Army.

Back in Paris, the collaborationist Vichy government pronounced a death sentence against de Gaulle. On 7 August 1940, he signed an agreement with Churchill whereby the British promised to help France regain its independence. Within Free France, de Gaulle had competition from General Henri Honoré Giraud. The American president, Franklin D. Roosevelt, had close relations with Giraud and favored him to lead the French action in North Africa. In 1943, de Gaulle and Giraud met at Casablanca and shortly thereafter they agreed to cooperate in forming the French Committee of National Liberation, with the two men serving as cochairs. But in a series of maneuvers with Giraud and the Allies, de Gaulle soon gained command of the committee and in May 1944 emerged as the overall leader and president of the newly reorganized provisional government of the French Republic.

After the Normandy invasion, de Gaulle returned to Paris in August 1944. He continued as president of the provisional government and guided France through its writing of a new constitution. He desired a strong executive branch and a weak legislature, and when early in 1946 opposition to his views prevailed, he resigned the presidency. In October, the French people approved the constitution for the Fourth Republic.

De Gaulle, meanwhile, said it would not work and organized the Rally of the French People (RPF) to compete in elections and fight for change. In 1947, voters made the RPF the most popular party in France, but in 1953 it suffered a severe loss in municipal elections, and de Gaulle resigned the party presidency and retired from politics to begin writing his memoirs.

In 1958, a revolt in French-held Algeria along with inflation and financial instability within France shattered the Fourth Republic. The nation stood ready for yet another transformation, one of several since its formation in the fifteenth century under LOUIS XI. De Gaulle announced that if the people desired, he would end his retirement and lead France. Many army officers supported him, for they believed that as a fellow military man he would buttress the French presence in Algeria, at that time precarious.

De Gaulle

In May 1958, the French president asked de Gaulle to form a government. He did so after Parliament approved his ascension. De Gaulle then pushed for a new constitution to shift most power from the legislature to the executive and thereby create a strong presidency rather than a parliamentary government. In a plebiscite the French approved such a document, and the Fifth Republic was born with de Gaulle chosen president in an election on 21 December.

De Gaulle had enormous powers, but although enemies called him a dictator he always fought to maintain the Republic and resisted pressure to become an emperor. As a strong nationalist he sought to strengthen his country financially and militarily. The economy moved ahead with inflation under control. At the same time, de Gaulle proceeded with the development of nuclear weapons. To do this, he pushed aside objections from the United States and asserted that France needed the nuclear capability in order to be truly independent against American and Soviet power.

De Gaulle believed that French security and the safety of Europe required a balance between the United States and the Soviet Union, and in his view America had become too powerful. Hence, he withdrew French forces from the North Atlantic Treaty Organization, the American-dominated alliance to protect Western Europe from Soviet expansion. He also twice vetoed the entry of pro-American Britain into the Common Market.

To the surprise of many in the French military, he opposed a continued French presence in Algeria, an involvement that he felt was weakening his nation, and sought to extricate France from its existing colonial system. In 1958, he accomplished the latter by forming the French Community, an arrangement that gave the colonies internal autonomy. (With regard to Algeria, he agreed to that country's independence in 1962.)

De Gaulle frequently antagonized the United States, such as when he established diplomatic relations with Communist China. He considered France to be the leader of continental Europe and bristled at American efforts to "run the show."

"We must condemn capitalism, capitalist society. . . . We must found a new way: participation."

While many French criticized his heavy-handed manner, they supported his efforts to restore French prestige. He visited the United States on several occasions, including a meeting with President John Kennedy in 1961, during which he displayed his perceptive analysis in warning against an increased American involvement in Vietnam—an involvement, he claimed, that would turn into "an endless process."

In 1968, violent demonstrations by university students rocked de Gaulle's government. The protestors demanded not only changes in the college curriculum but also in French society. They rebelled against de Gaulle's authoritarianism and the inequities in wealth and employment. Clashes occurred with the police, and in March many industrial workers joined the students, paralyzing France with a general strike. The Fifth Republic tottered, but de Gaulle moved troops toward Paris, advocated reform, and called for new elections. He expressed his desire to see more participation by labor in economic decisions. His tactics worked; the student uprising quickly collapsed when a huge demonstration occurred supporting him and when French voters, fearful the disorder would lead to a communist takeover, provided de Gaulle with a sizable election victory.

Yet the rebellion underscored deep political and economic differences in French society and showed the limits to de Gaulle's administration. Discontent resurfaced, fueled by serious governmental financial problems; the criticism of de Gaulle increased, and in a pique when he lost a referendum on a reform proposal, the general resigned the presidency in 1969. He retired to Colombey-les-Deux-Eglises, where he resumed writing his memoirs. He died from a heart attack on 9 November 1970. The Fifth Republic, however, continued—the result of de Gaulle's leadership in a trying postwar Europe.

References: Crozier, Brian, *De Gaulle,* 1973; De Gaulle, Charles, *The Complete War Memoirs,* 1964; De Gaulle, Charles, *Memoirs of Hope,* 1971; Lacouture, Jean, *De Gaulle: The Rebel, 1890–1944,* 1990.

De Klerk, Frederik Willem
(b. 1936)
South Africa

Frederik Willem De Klerk grew up in a privileged family and early in his political career advocated conservative white views. Thus, his change in support of a new South Africa that dismantled racial inequality proved all the more startling.

Frederik Willem De Klerk was born on 18 March 1936 in Johannesburg, the son of Jan De Klerk and Corrie Coetzer De Klerk. His father, like the De Klerk men before him, was prominent in politics and eventually served in two cabinets and led the Senate. As an Afrikaner (a person of Dutch or German descent), he was a member of the National Party, which dominated politics.

F. W. De Klerk graduated from Monument High School in Krugersdorp and then attended Potchefstroom University. He displayed his political bent as a college student when he joined the Afrikaanese Studentebond, the youth organization of the National Party. In 1958, he obtained his law degree and shortly thereafter practiced law, primarily in Vereeniging, a mining town. In 1972, De Klerk was elected to Parliament.

De Klerk initially supported the system of racial segregation, or apartheid, that had advanced in the early twentieth century under JAN SMUTS and LOUIS BOTHA—the founders of the Union of South Africa—and that the National Party had codified in various laws beginning in 1948. Apartheid restricted South Africa's black majority (and other nonwhites) and protected white supremacy. De Klerk hewed closely to the party line and displayed no support for reform. In 1978, he was appointed minister of posts and telecommunications under Prime Minister John Vorster. He held numerous cabinet positions under Vorster's successor, P. W. Botha, including internal affairs from 1980 to 1982, and national education and planning from 1984 to 1989. During the latter period, he became leader of the House of Assembly.

Meanwhile, demonstrations, strikes, and violence escalated as the African National Congress (ANC), headed by NELSON MANDELA, pushed to end apartheid. Although Mandela had been imprisoned by the government in 1962, he remained a powerful leader and symbolized the oppression blacks suffered.

Amid the turmoil, the National Party splintered and the Conservative Party formed as a strident defender of apartheid after Prime Minister Botha initiated reforms to allow Asians and persons of mixed race (or "coloreds") to participate in the political system. In the controversy, De Klerk sided with Botha and was named party leader in the Transvaal region. Then early in 1989, Botha suffered a stroke and the National Party chose de Klerk as its leader. Botha did not relinquish all of his leadership duties, however, until the fall, after parliamentary elections returned the National Party to power by a slim margin.

As foreign nations boycotted South African trade and the economy deteriorated, De Klerk proclaimed his support for greater changes. He permitted peaceful protests, which had been previously prohibited, and met with black opponents of apartheid, including Archbishop Desmond Tutu, to discuss possible negotiations with Mandela and the ANC. On 2 February 1990, the government lifted its ban on the ANC—which had been in effect since 1960—and a few days later released Mandela. In August, De Klerk and Mandela signed the Pretoria Minute, moving South Africa toward a new constitution, and the government released political prisoners while the ANC suspended its violence. The following month, De Klerk surprised many whites by announcing his support of a one-man, one-vote rule, a position that would end apartheid.

In June 1991, Parliament dismantled the

apartheid laws that restricted property ownership, and shortly thereafter it ended several other restrictions. In February 1993, De Klerk appointed the first blacks ever to serve in a South African cabinet. He did this to attract African voters in the upcoming elections. In 1994, however, Mandela and the ANC swept De Klerk and the Nationalists from office. Although De Klerk dismantled apartheid only after intense pressure from African nationalists and foreign nations, his actions nevertheless paved the way for Mandela's ascension and the creation of a new South Africa.

Reference: Lodge, Tom, *Black Politics in South Africa since 1945*, 1983.

De Valera, Eamon
(1882–1975)
Ireland

Near the end of World War I, Eamon De Valera sat in Britain's Lincoln Jail imprisoned on charges of conspiring with Germans to disrupt the war effort. He and some accomplices had developed a plan for escaping, and now he acted. He stole a key from the prison sacristy, carefully traced an outline of it on paper, and enclosed the outline in a letter. His accomplices then made a duplicate key, concealed it inside a cake, and smuggled it into prison. A spectacular jail break followed, and De Valera became a full-fledged hero among Irish nationalists. This episode displayed the mix of determination, resourcefulness, and daring that made De Valera an important leader in Ireland's fight for independence.

In 1879, De Valera's mother, Kate Coll, emigrated to the United States where she worked as a domestic. Soon she met Vivion Juan De Valera, an exile from Spain and a friend of her employer. In 1881, they married, and on 14 October 1882 she gave birth to Edward, who later changed the form of his first name to the Irish, Eamon.

After his father died in the 1880s, Eamon was sent by his mother to live in Ireland with relatives. There, as a child in Bruree, he tended the cows and took the milk to market. Later he enrolled at University College in Blackrock, and after graduation, at age 21, became a teacher. After the National Uni-

"The sovereignty of Ireland . . . cannot possibly be given away by Irish Republicans."

versity of Ireland was founded in 1909, he taught there as professor of mathematics.

But his thoughts went well beyond math. As a Catholic and an Irishman, he became enamored with his homeland's language and, along with it, the drive to restore Irish culture to prominence. In 1908, he joined the Gaelic League and advocated teaching Irish in public schools. He also fell in love with one of his Irish language teachers, Sinead Flanagan, whom he married in 1910.

As World War I began, Britain announced limited home rule for all of Ireland, but Protestants in Ulster (Northern Ireland) objected, claiming this would place them under a Catholic majority. The Protestants even set up a provisional government, and this resistance greatly affected De Valera, convincing him that home rule would only come through violent protest. He joined the Irish Volunteers, a group dedicated to organizing militarily for independence, and in 1916, after Britain formally announced a delay in home rule, his revolutionary resolve stiffened.

De Valera entered Sinn Fein (Ourselves Alone), a militant political wing of Irish nationalism. This group imported arms and became intertwined with the Irish Volunteers. In 1916, De Valera helped lead the infamous Easter Week Rebellion that had as its goal capturing Dublin. During the uprising, The Irish Volunteers (who soon became the Irish Republican Army, or IRA) proclaimed a provisional government headquartered at the post office, but British troops rounded up the plotters, and De Valera experienced his first jail term. After his release, Sinn Fein's members chose him as their leader.

When the British arrested him a second time in 1918 and sent him to Lincoln Jail without trial, most Irish considered the effort a ludicrous attempt to stifle a formidable foe. After De Valera's escape, the rebels organized the Dail, or Irish Parliament, and chose him president of Ireland. While MICHAEL COLLINS handled military strategy and violent conflict continued in Ireland, De Valera traveled to the United States, where he rallied thousands of Americans in sympathy to the Irish cause and established an organization to raise money.

Then, in 1921, King George V called for an end to the bloodshed, and De Valera conferred with British Prime Minister Lloyd George. Formal negotiations soon began, and Britain agreed to Irish independence, although exclusive of Ulster. Most Irish nationalists supported the agreement, and the Dail ratified it in January 1922. De Valera, however, opposed the partitioning of Ireland and disliked other provisions of the treaty that limited Irish sovereignty. After he resigned the presidency, fighting broke out between the Free State government that supported the treaty and De Valera's group, the Republicans.

De Valera lost the battle and was arrested by the Irish government; nevertheless, he ran for a seat in the Dail and won. In 1924, he formed the Fianna Fail Party whose platform rejected any oath of allegiance to the king (required because of Ireland's membership in the British Commonwealth), demanded a reunited Ireland, and promoted the revival of Irish language and culture. De Valera's party obtained a majority in the Dail in 1932, and he became head of government.

Shortly thereafter, De Valera led a successful movement to write a new constitution. Throughout the remainder of his life he was a dominant figure in Irish politics; as head of the majority party in the Dail he also headed Ireland for most of the period until 1959, when he relinquished party leadership for the more ceremonial presidency. He held this position until his retirement in 1973. He died two years later, on 29 August 1975. De Valera represented the heroism behind the Irish independence effort, also evident in the actions of Collins, DANIEL O'CONNELL, CHARLES STEWART PARNELL, and PATRICK PEARSE.

Reference: Earl of Longford and Thomas P. O'Neill, *Eamon De Valera,* 1976.

Del Valle, José Cecilio
(1770–1834)
Costa Rica, El Salvador, Guatemala, Honduras, Nicaragua

Although José Cecilio del Valle, a Honduran, did not push specifically for his homeland's nationhood, he advocated independence for all of Central America and was one of its prime architects.

José Cecilio del Valle was born on 22 November 1770 in the Honduran town of Choluteca. When he was nine, his parents, part of a wealthy ranching family, took him to Guatemala, where he could obtain a good education. José graduated from the University of San Carlos de Guatemala and obtained a law degree there in 1793. But although he developed a thriving practice, he soon considered legal issues dull and throughout his adult life pursued intellectual development through extensive reading.

When, in 1820, Central Americans began organizing against Spanish rule, del Valle edited a newspaper, *El Amigo de la Patria,* that cautioned against immediate independence. But the following year he shifted his position, and when the Central American provinces declared their separation from Spain, he helped write the Act of Independence. As Spanish rule crumbled, del Valle opposed efforts by Mexico to annex Central America. He served in the regional congress that defended Central American rights, and when the Mexican government took over the provinces, it imprisoned him.

Mexican rule did not last long, though, and del Valle spent only six months in confinement. In 1824, he helped compile the first constitution for the United Provinces of Central America, and until 1826 served on a provisional triumverate and concentrated on economic development. After FRANCISCO MORAZÁN became the federation's president in 1829, del Valle served in the legislature. As a member of the movement, he had several differences with Morazán, who was a Liberal. Morazán supported a less elitist government and a separation of church and state. Del Valle wanted the opposite, and in 1830 ran against Morazán for the presidency. In a close election, he lost. He was defeated a second time later that year. In 1833, however, he defeated Morazán in yet another election. Del Valle, however, never served: In 1834, he died at his home near Guatemala City. Four years later, the federation collapsed, and Honduras declared its independence as a separate nation under FRANCISCO FERRERA.

Reference: Bumgartner, Louis E., *José Cecilio del Valle of Central America*, 1963.

DeRoburt, Hammer
(1923–1992)
Nauru

The size of Hammer DeRoburt's homeland, a small island in the Pacific, belied its great resource: enormous phosphate deposits. In the 1960s, DeRoburt worked to end the foreign exploitation of these deposits and acquire both independence and more wealth for Nauruans.

Hammer DeRoburt was born on 25 September 1923 on Nauru. He obtained his education at the Nauru Secondary School and then studied at the Geelong Technical College in Victoria, Australia. He returned home in 1940 and became a teacher. In 1942, however, the Japanese invaded Nauru and evicted the British, who had controlled the island. They also deported nearly all the Nauruans to Truk, in the Caroline Islands, to build airstrips, and DeRoburt was among this group. The Japanese treated the Nauruans brutally, and only 737 from the original group of 1,200 survived.

After World War II, the United Nations established a trusteeship over Nauru on behalf of Britain, New Zealand, and Australia, with the latter administering the island. DeRoburt and the other dislocated Nauruans were returned home. The British Phosphate Company (BPC) resumed the mining of Nauru's phosphate deposits, which it had begun earlier in the century. The phosphate, perhaps of the highest quality in the world, was used as fertilizer, mainly in Australia and New Zealand. The BPC obtained the phosphate at a very low cost, imported Chinese laborers, and provided no executive positions for Nauruans.

> *"Step by step, our message began getting through."*

In the 1950s, nationalism appeared as DeRoburt, who served on the local government council beginning in 1955, and other Nauruans, especially Timothy Detudamo, questioned foreign control of the phosphate mining. By 1961, DeRoburt was advocating that Nauruans be allowed to purchase the phosphate industry and also govern themselves. So strongly did he favor independence that his nationalism exceeded in importance the dispute over phosphate. In 1965, DeRoburt became chair of the local government council and Nauru's head chief. In 1966, Nauru—

with a population of about 7,000—was permitted internal self-rule, and on 31 January 1968 it gained its complete independence. DeRoburt became the nation's first president.

Under the terms of the 1968 Nauru constitution, the president was elected by Parliament. DeRoburt held onto the presidency until 1976 when opponents with the Nauru Party, led by Bernard Dowiyogo, defeated him. DeRoburt called the election procedure unconstitutional, and in 1978 first Dowiyogo and then his successor, Lagumont Harris, resigned. This forced new elections, and DeRoburt once again became president. He established an extensive power base by also heading the ministries of aviation, external and internal affairs, public service, and island development and industry.

DeRoburt oversaw substantial prosperity as the government acquired the phosphate mines from the BPC and revenues grew. Unlike most South Pacific islands, Nauru became wealthy; the government consequently provided free education and health care for all its citizens and subsidized imports that would otherwise be expensive.

(Nearly everything had to be transported in, including fresh water.) DeRoburt founded Nauru Airlines that serviced several South Pacific islands and built a $45 million office building, 52 stories tall and called Nauru House, in Melbourne, Australia. Yet amid the prosperity complications emerged: The phosphate deposits dwindled, and Nauruans suffered increased health problems from the consumption of rich, imported foods. DeRoburt started a program to get his people exercising more and tempering their diets.

In 1986, DeRoburt resigned the presidency after losing a vote of confidence in Parliament. He returned just two weeks later, but then lost the elections in December. When the government stalemated, however, he won new elections in January 1987 and resumed his presidency. In August 1989 DeRoburt again lost the presidency in a no-confidence vote. He died in July 1992.

Reference: Bunge, Frederica M., and Melinda W. Cooke, *Oceania: A Regional Study,* 1984.

Dessalines, Jean-Jacques
(1758?–1806)
Haiti

After winning Haitian independence, Jean-Jacques Dessalines made himself emperor. An ardent black revolutionary, he declared war on whites in his country and sought to exterminate them.

Jean-Jacques Dessalines was born around 1758 in West Africa and brought to the French colony of Haiti (then called Saint Dominque) as a slave. He worked as a field hand for a black master until 1791. That year, slaves rebelled in Haiti, stimulated by their own oppression and by the ideas of liberty and equality emanating from the French Revolution. Dessalines joined the uprising. The black slaves attacked whites and mulattos and fought to

> *"Behead heads, burn the cities."*

end French rule. Their actions reflected the complex Haitian society in which whites, blacks, and mulattos had enormous differences.

Dessalines proved to be a brilliant tactician and allied himself with the emerging black leader TOUSSAINT L'OUVERTURE. Their new government, linked nominally to France, freed those still enslaved. By 1801, Toussaint controlled nearly all of Haiti and neighboring Santo Domingo, but the French retaliated by launching an attack under General Charles Leclerc in January 1802, aimed at restoring their rule and reestablishing slavery. At first, Dessalines fought alongside Toussaint in battling the French and the Haitian whites, mulattos, and blacks who allied with the Europeans. But after Leclerc scored important victories and offered amnesty, Dessalines deserted Toussaint and accepted French rule. Toussaint surrendered later in 1802 and was imprisoned in France.

When in 1803 Napoleon made public his plan to reestablish slavery in Haiti, and the French escalated their attacks to slaughter and eliminate thousands of black and mulatto opponents, Dessalines and his supporters revolted. A yellow fever epidemic that decimated the French troops and the assistance of the British, who had renewed an intermittent war with France, proved crucial in the conflict. Dessalines pushed the French out of the country and on 1 January 1804 declared Haiti an independent nation.

The French remained in Santo Domingo, and in response to their presence and to the atrocities perpetrated earlier by Leclerc and other French officers, Dessalines ordered that the 3,000 or so whites still in Haiti be murdered, and nearly all were. In September, he declared himself emperor for life, thus continuing the dictatorial system begun under Toussaint. He issued a constitution in 1805 that established a military government, prohibited whites from owning property, and stipulated that all Haitians be referred to as "blacks" (an attempt to erase the distinction between blacks and mulattos). On many plantations, although slavery no longer existed, Dessalines continued Toussaint's policy of using forced labor.

Despite the racial equality between blacks and mulattos implied in the constitution, Dessalines restricted the mixed-race Haitians, and widespread discrimination existed between the mulattos, who owned much of the country's property, and the blacks, who, for the most part, had only recently arrived from Africa. The tensions proved so great that Dessalines faced a mulatto revolt led by Alexandre Sabés Pétion. On 17 October 1806, Pétion's men ambushed Dessalines at Jacmel, killed him, and mutilated his body, throwing the remains into a ditch.

References: Bellgarde-Smith, Patrick, *Haiti: The Breached Citadel*, 1990; Nicholls, David, *From Dessalines to Duvalier: Race, Colour, and National Independence in Haiti*, 1979.

Diori, Hamani
(1916–1989)
Niger

In the development of Nigerien nationalism, Hamani Diori helped establish a dual strategy: cooperation with FÉLIX HOUPHOUËT-BOIGNY, the nationalist leader in Côte d'Ivoire, and pursuit of moderate political policies.

Born on 6 June 1916 in Soudouré, Hamani Diori was influenced by his father's pro-French leanings. Sidibá Hamani had welcomed France's arrival in Niger, joined the French civil service, and saw to it that his son's education included studying at Senegal's famed École William Ponty.

In 1936, Diori returned from Senegal to Niger and for ten years taught at schools in Maradi and Niamey, except for one year in Paris at the École d'Outre Mer. At Niamey, he became headmaster of the École de Filingue. Already a renowned Nigerien educator, Diori entered politics in 1946.

By this time, Niger was permitted its own legislature and political party formation occurred. The Nigerien Progressive Party (PPN) did not emerge from the masses but instead received its impetus from wealthy Nigeriens who had adopted French culture. Issoufou Saidou, a young nobleman, led in organizing the PPN and became the party's first president. Boubou Hama also helped found the PPN and became a powerful politician. Diori joined Saidou and Hama in forming the PPN, which they linked to the African Democratic Rally (RDA), a regional party founded by Côte d'Ivoire's Félix Houphouët-Boigny for all

French West Africa (AOF). It sought equality with France.

When, as part of de Gaulle's reforms, France allowed African representatives in the French National Assembly, Diori, in 1946, won election. In 1951, however, a split within the PPN doomed his reelection bid. That year, France accused the RDA of communist leanings and Houphouët-Boigny declared a purge of radicals. This produced two factions within the PPN, one led by Djibo Bakary, who in 1950 formed a Marxist party, the Nigerien Democratic Union (UDN), and the other led by Diori, who supported Houphouët-Boigny's move.

The UDN gained most of its support from West Niger, where Bakary supported the area's peanut farmers. Bakary's UDN scored impressive election victories and, in alliance with another party, won a majority in Niger's 1957 legislative election. In 1958, the UDN formed yet another alliance and changed its name to SAWABA, meaning freedom.

After his election defeat, Diori returned to teaching and directing a school in Niamey (a position he held until 1958). In 1956, Diori regained his seat in Parliament, defeating Bakary by a narrow margin. The following year, he won election to the Niger Territorial Assembly, became municipal councilor of Niamey, and was elected deputy-speaker of the French National Assembly. Bakary then made a political blunder. He allowed Diori to again gain much support among the traditional tribal chiefs, who feared any radicalism that might undermine their authority, and in 1958, while heading the territorial government, he campaigned against making Niger a semiautonomous state within the French Community, opting instead for complete independence. De Gaulle had warned that rejecting this status would result in Niger losing all French military and economic assistance. Reminding voters of this possibility, Diori led the PPN to an overwhelming victory, gaining 54 seats in the legislature as opposed to SAWABA's 4.

Now in power as prime minister, Diori moved quickly against Bakary, banning SAWABA, arresting many of its leaders, and sending Bakary into exile. Bakary launched several attacks from Mali, trying to topple Diori, but he failed. After constitutional changes in 1960, Diori became Niger's president. That same year, France agreed to Niger's independence, officially obtained on 3 August. Diori then signed cooperative economic agreements with France.

As president, Diori earned a reputation as a mediator in inter-African disputes. He served as president of the African Entente from 1967 to 1974 and chair of the West African Community from 1973 to 1974. But in the early 1970s, many Nigeriens disagreed with his authoritarian manner and disliked Niger's worsening economy. They protested when, as a severe drought gripped Niger, Diori mishandled food relief and condoned, or at least tolerated, extensive government corruption. In 1974, a military coup toppled Diori, and he lived for a time under house arrest. In 1987, he moved to Rabat, Morocco, and in April 1989 died there.

References: Decalo, Stephen, *Historical Dictionary of Niger*, 1979; Fuglestad, Finn, *A History of Niger, 1850–1960*, 1983.

Duarte, Juan Pablo
(1813–1876)
Dominican Republic

An idealistic liberator, Juan Pablo Duarte formed a secret society and led the fight to end Haitian rule in Santo Domingo.

In 1813, Juan Pablo Duarte was born in the Dominican Republic, then called Santo Domingo. This land, which occupies the island of Hispaniola with Haiti, had been acquired by the French in 1795 and at Duarte's birth was emerging from a tumultuous era. A few years earlier, Haitian rebels under TOUSSAINT L'OUVERTURE and JEAN-JACQUES

DESSALINES invaded Santo Domingo, and from 1804 until 1809 the Haitians, French, Spanish, and British fought for its control.

The battles were extremely bloody, with the Haitians attacking white plantation owners and the Europeans exacting a severe retribution. The British sided with the Spanish, and together they pushed the Haitians westward and placed Santo Domingo under Spanish rule. In 1821, the Dominicans overthrew the Spaniards, but the following year Haiti again invaded and caused such destruction that the episode would, for decades, remain a source of enmity between the two lands.

In 1828, during the Haitian occupation, Duarte went to Paris for his education. His studies reinforced his disgust with the cruel treatment of his country by the Haitians, who wanted black supremacy at almost any cost, levied heavy taxes, and forced young men into the Haitian army. In reaction, he committed himself to gaining independence for his people. When he returned home in 1833, he organized a secret society, La Trinitaria, ("The Trinity," referring to "God, Fatherland, and Liberty") to win nationhood and establish democratic reforms. A natural disaster helped Duarte's effort: In 1842, an earthquake destroyed much of his homeland, and the unrelieved suffering under Haitian rule stirred others to support his crusade.

Duarte solicited and received financial help from Venezuela, and in 1843 he and his followers attacked the Haitian garrisons. This effort failed, however, and he fled into exile. In a second effort in 1844, his followers defeated the Haitians. Duarte returned to Santo Domingo in February, hailed as a hero, and proclaimed the Dominican Republic independent.

Duarte failed to move quickly to solidify his power, and when he hesitated, others seized control. Within weeks he was forced into exile, and two military generals, Buenaventura Baéz and Pedro Santana, marched into the capital and declared themselves *caudillos,* or dictators, beginning the "era of the two *caudillos.*" In the 1860s, Santana announced he would allow Spain to rule the Dominican Republic. This produced another rebellion under Gregorio Luperón in 1864, who met only weak resistance from Spain. There followed a series of short-lived governments.

Meanwhile, Duarte who was then living in Caracas, Venezuela, returned to his homeland during the 1864 upheaval and for one year represented the tenuous government on a diplomatic assignment. He then returned to Caracas, where he died in 1876.

Like its neighbor Haiti, the Dominican Republic has been governed mainly by dictators, the most infamous one being Rafael Trujillo, who ruled from 1930 to 1961. Despite this troubled past, Dominicans owe their nationhood to Duarte, the man called "the father of Dominican independence."

References: Rodman, Selden, *Quisqueya: A History of the Dominican Republic,* 1964; Wiarda, Howard J., and Michael J. Kryzanek, *The Dominican Republic: A Caribbean Crucible,* 1992.

Faisal I
(1885–1933)
Iraq

Many in Iraq's nationalist movement criticized King Faisal I as too pro-Western, a criticism related to his peculiar position of being an outsider brought into Iraq by British politicians. But although Faisal did indeed owe his accession to Britain, he exhibited nationalist goals tied to his Pan-Arabic views.

Faisal was born on 20 May 1885 in Mecca as the son of Husayn ibn 'Ali, who ruled the Hejaz (a region in present-day Saudi Arabia). As a boy, Faisal first lived for several years among the Bedouin, where he learned tribal customs and the qualities expected of a leader, and then obtained an education from tutors in Mecca. He thus absorbed both rural and urban culture.

In the early 1900s, the Ottoman Turks controlled the Hejaz, as they did the Middle East in general. Shortly before World War I, Faisal represented the Hejaz in the Ottoman Parliament. As Arab nationalism spread, he served as a liaison between his father and the nationalist movement. At one point, he arranged an agreement whereby Husayn ibn 'Ali would lead a revolt. While some within the nationalist movement enthusiastically supported an alliance with Britain to help oust the Turks, Faisal did so only reluctantly, seeing it as a necessary evil. When the revolt against the Turks began in 1916, Faisal served as an important military leader. In 1918, an Arab force occupied Damascus in Syria, and the nationalists declared Faisal king, expecting British support for their position in return for concessions. But France, also a power in the Middle East, had its own agenda and in 1920 occupied Syria and deposed Faisal, who went into exile, eventually living in London.

Britain's expansionist desires in 1914 led it to occupy Iraq. Initially, the British allowed little involvement in the government by Iraqis. But in 1920, a nationalist rebellion occurred, and the British decided to revamp the government. They brought in Faisal, and under pressure, the Iraqi Council of State declared him king within a representative political system. Faisal's coronation occurred on 27 August 1921.

The British expected a fully compliant ruler, but Faisal proved otherwise. The new king recruited Iraqi nationalists for government positions, partly because of his Pan-Arab sentiments and partly because as an outsider he needed to build his domestic support. When the British proposed a new treaty in 1922 that left them largely in control of Iraq's fiscal and foreign policies, urban nationalists protested, and Faisal encouraged demonstrations. The treaty took effect in 1924, but only after enormous opposition in the Constituent Assembly.

Nationalist pressures continued, however, and by 1929 the British refusal to allow more Iraqi autonomy resulted in a crisis so severe that Faisal's prime minister and the entire cabinet resigned. Then, in 1930, Britain signed a treaty with Faisal's government under which Iraq gained independence, but with numerous restrictions. For example, Britain still maintained enormous leverage in foreign affairs, obtained two air bases, and forced Faisal to employ British advisors. Although many Iraqi nationalists objected to this arrangement, Faisal supported it, and he gained important backing when in 1933 the opposition Ikhā Party agreed to the treaty in return for Faisal permitting its leaders to form a cabinet.

Instability characterized the remainder of Faisal's rule as nationalists continued agitating for a complete break with Britain, and minority groups, most notably the Assyrians, rebelled against the government. Numerous conflicts between the army and the Assyrians resulted in ruthless tactics on both sides and much bloodshed. Since most Iraqis embraced an anti-Assyrian position, Faisal's disdain for the conduct of his military commanders and the Ikhā cabinet in this episode cost him substantial support. In September 1933, Faisal, depressed and in poor health, traveled to Europe. On 7 September a heart attack struck him in Geneva, where he died. Faisal's son, Ghāzī, assumed the throne and proved even more reluctant to follow British policies.

While Faisal refused to take Iraq down the extreme nationalist path, he did much to weaken the British presence and balance internal animosities so as to allow Iraq's transition into a new era of autonomy. Radical change awaited the revolutions of 1958 and the 1960s, the first under ABDUL KARIM QASSEM and the second under SADDAM HUSSEIN.

References: Helms, C. M., *Iraq: Eastern Flank of the Arab World*, 1984; Marr, Phebe, *The Modern History of Iraq*, 1985.

al-Fasi, Allal
(1910?–1974)
Morocco

In Morocco's conservative and traditional society, Allal al-Fasi reflected the crosscurrents of devout Islam and modern nationalism. As a thinker and political activist, he endured a nine-year exile for his defiance of French rule.

Allal al-Fasi did not grow up impoverished; on the contrary, he came from a wealthy, prominent family. His father was a professor at Qarawiyin University, curator of the library there, a substantial property owner, and close associate to the sultan's advisors. He was also strongly Islamic and saw that his son received a traditional religious education.

Allal al-Fasi was a precocious learner, wrote political poetry at age 15, and was instructed by Mulay al-Arabi al-Alawi in Islamic piety as part of the Salafiya movement. Allal attended Qarawiyin University, where he received a divinity degree and the title of scholar. Even as a student, he displayed his activism. He helped form the Students' Union, a secret organization dedicated to Islamic purity and reforms in the curriculum. And in 1928, he gained public attention when he wrote a letter opposing plans proposed by France, the colonial power, to divert river waters in order to irrigate several French-owned farms. His opposition grew strident in 1930 when the French issued a decree, the *dahir*, that limited the use of Islamic laws among the Berbers, who lived in the mountainous areas of Morocco. Many Muslims considered this action an assault on Islam.

For his part in the protests against the Berber dahir, Allal al-Fasi was exiled to Taza for two months. Upon his return, he resumed teaching at Qarawiyin, where he had taught briefly in 1930, but his fervent style in support of Islam and criticism of French actions led, in 1933, to his removal. Fasi subsequently traveled to France, where he associated with nationalistic Arab students before obtaining permission from the colonial power to return home. He resumed his teaching, but his ideas again brought dismissal.

This propelled Allal al-Fasi to organize the National Action Bloc, or Kutla, Morocco's first nationalist political party. He did not demand independence, but he did demand substantial internal reforms, including widespread suffrage. In 1936, the French arrested him and other nationalist leaders, a move that produced riots that forced his release. Allal al-Fasi had now emerged as the most prominent nationalist and he won election as Kutla's president.

In 1937, a crisis struck when demonstrations again led to rioting. The French arrested Allal al-Fasi and exiled him to Gabon, where he lived for nine years. During his exile, the nationalist movement became radicalized and demanded independence. The Independence Party, or Istiqlal, issued a manifesto in 1944 demanding Moroccan nationhood. In 1946, al-Fasi gained his release and returned home. Under political pressure, he stayed only briefly, moving to Cairo, a city he used as a base for organizing his nationalist appeal. He visited the United Nations in 1952 and in 1953, when the French deposed MOHAMMED V, he declared his support for the sultan, supported armed resistance against the French, and openly endorsed guerrilla tactics.

Such violence and an increasing crisis in Algeria convinced France to negotiate with Moroccan leaders and agree to both a restoration of Mohammed V and independence, which came in March 1956. Allal al-Fasi returned to Morocco and sought unity with Mohammed V. The sultan's insistence on real rather than ceremonial power caused a rift, however, and Allal al-Fasi, who in 1961 had become minister of Islamic affairs, resigned his position late in 1962. He won election to Parliament in 1963 and served until Mohammed's successor, King Hassan II, dissolved the legislature two years later.

Allal al-Fasi then formed a new National Bloc Party and strongly opposed the king's attempts to form a constitution that allowed only limited parliamentary government. Despite this opposition, the constitution took effect in 1972. In another policy area, Allal al-Fasi maintained a strong vision of a Greater Morocco encompassing Mauritania and other areas, and became outspoken in supporting Morocco's claim to Spanish Sahara and Tindouf in Algeria.

Allal al-Fasi was a noted author and scholar in his own right, and in his essays advocated a return to Islamic values and an egalitarian religious socialism. He died of a heart attack on 13 May 1974 while visiting Romania.

References: Ashford, Douglas E., *Political Change in Morocco*, 1961; al-Fasi, Allal, *The Independence Movements in Arab North Africa*, 1954; Halstead, John P., *Rebirth of a Nation: The Origins and Rise of Moroccan Nationalism, 1912–1944* , 1968.

Ferdinand V
(1452–1516)
Spain

Along with Queen ISABELLA I, Ferdinand brought several kingdoms on the Iberian Peninsula together to form Spain.

Ferdinand was born on 10 March 1452 at Sos in Aragon, one of three Christian kingdoms that dominated the Iberian Peninsula. Over the years, the Aragon kings had acquired Sicily and lands along the Mediterranean. Another kingdom, Castile, larger and more populous than Aragon, had led in expelling Muslim invaders from areas of the peninsula. Along the Atlantic coast lay the peninsula's third Christian kingdom, Portugal, also important in the wars against the Muslims.

Ferdinand was heir to the crown of Aragon and cousin to Isabella, heiress to the throne of Castile. Isabella had strong ambitions to unify Spain and considered marriage to Ferdinand to be the best way to advance this agenda. After she proposed this strategy to him, he agreed, and they married on 19 October 1469, creating a formidable partnership that would alter world history.

When Isabella's brother, Henry IV, died in 1474, Ferdinand and Isabella became joint monarchs of Castile. Then in 1479 Ferdinand's father, John II of Aragon, died, and Ferdinand also ruled that kingdom. Although Ferdinand held important titles, he did not have absolute power in either Aragon or Castile, and the two rulers and their kingdoms had many differences. Linguistically, the people in these areas spoke different Spanish dialects. Strategically, Aragon had long been focused on the Mediterranean, and Castile on the Atlantic. Furthermore, Ferdinand differed from Isabella in his skepticism toward religion and his tendency toward tolerance in that area. These differences were underscored when Ferdinand agreed, in a document called the "Capitulations," to make no wars or alliances unless Isabella approved of them and to appoint only Castilians to high office in Castile.

The arrangement signified that Castile had the greatest wealth and the most prominent position in the political linkage.

Ferdinand had great abilities as a statesman and applied his penchants for deceit, crassness, and opportunism. He and Isabella realized that to strengthen the crown they needed new sources of revenue. They turned to the church, and in 1486 the pope granted them patronage rights over bishoprics to be established in the areas from which the Moors, or Muslims, had been driven out. The pope also issued bulls, or decrees, in 1493, 1501, and 1508, granting them control over ecclesiastical appointments and revenues in the Americas. This would prove to be a lucrative source for the crown. The church thus became an important tool in developing royal absolutism. In return, Ferdinand and Isabella strongly supported the pope's prerogative in spiritual matters, a loyalty that earned them the title The Catholic Sovereigns, granted by Pope Alexander VI.

Ferdinand guided the final conquest of the Moors, beginning an assault on Grenada in 1481. This stronghold fell in 1492, the same year the crown agreed to back Christopher Columbus on his westward journey across the Atlantic.

While Isabella consolidated royal power in Castile, Ferdinand continued the Aragonese involvement in the Mediterranean. In 1494, he helped put together a coalition of Italian states to defeat the invading army of France's Charles VIII. Ferdinand also arranged the defeat of Louis XII when, in 1500, that French king tried to capture Naples. In 1504, Louis was forced to recognize Ferdinand's control there after devious maneuvering by the Spanish monarch. Louis later complained that he had been deceived twice, and Ferdinand replied that the Frenchman had lied—that in truth he had been deceived ten times!

That same year Isabella died, a development

that threatened Ferdinand's authority in Castile. Isabella had willed Castile to their daughter Joanna, who had married Philip of Burgundy. Ferdinand thus temporarily lost control of Castile, and in 1505 he married a niece of Louis XII. Joanna, however, went insane, and after Philip died in 1506, Ferdinand again ruled Castile, this time as regent for his mad daughter. In 1512, he conquered the kingdom of Navarre and three years later annexed it to Castile.

Although the marriage of Ferdinand and Isabella and the subsequent unification of Aragon and Castile left each kingdom with its own laws and institutions and recognized Isabella's primacy in Castile, a new European power had been created. Like other early nations emerging from the Middle Ages, Spain was substantially a dynastic state; that is, a state created more from royal maneuvering and connections among dynasties than from nationalist sentiment. Furthermore, it still contained many medieval attributes and would undergo numerous changes before reaching the stage of a democratic constitutional monarchy under JUAN CARLOS. Nevertheless, Ferdinand and Isabella effectively put together a new nation—their rule marked the birth of Spain, and at his death on 23 January 1516 at Madrigalejo in Estremadura, Ferdinand was the most powerful monarch in Western Europe.

Reference: Miller, Townsend, *The Castles and the Crown: Spain, 1451–1555*, 1963.

Ferrera, Francisco
(1794–1851)
Honduras

Francisco Ferrera led the Conservative forces that opposed a united Central America and favored an independent Honduras.

Francisco Ferrera was born on 29 January 1794 in San Juan de Flores. He came from an impoverished family and was orphaned in 1801. A parish priest taught him to read and write and then sent him to Tegucigalpa, where he learned music. Upon his return home, he became a musician for the Catholic Church. Later, he worked as a tailor and studied some law, earning an appointment as advisor to the mayor. Shortly before 1820 he entered the military.

In 1823, Honduras joined its neighboring provinces to form the United Provinces of Central America. This entity quickly fell prey to internal fighting among the states and between two organized groups, Liberals and Conservatives. The former favored economic diversification, governmental institutions similar to those in the United States, and a separation of the government from the Catholic Church. The Conservatives wanted a more elitist political system and favored clerical power. In 1830, the great Honduran leader FRANCISCO MORAZÁN, a Liberal, became president of the federation. Although challenged by the Conservative JOSÉ CECILIO DEL VALLE, he initiated numerous reforms. At this time, Ferrera fought alongside Morazán and became a lieutenant colonel.

Membership in the United Provinces brought turmoil to Honduras as factions fought for power, and when the federation began unravelling, Hondurans opted for separate nationhood, which was declared on 26 October 1838. For reasons not entirely clear, but in part owing to his attachment to Catholicism and his dismissal as vice-chief of Honduras, Ferrera broke with Morazán and, as a Conservative, commanded the Honduran army in an 1839 attack against the Federation president, whose rule had become limited to El Salvador. Morazán defeated Ferrera twice in the summer, but in 1840 the Liberal was beaten by another force, and he went into exile.

In 1841, Ferrera became the first president of

the Republic of Honduras, a post he held with some interruption until 1847. After he left the presidency, he continued as the actual ruler, using his position as armed forces chief and minister of war to establish a dictatorship. Ferrera sought to undo Liberal programs and maintain a close relationship between the state and the Catholic Church. He died on 10 April 1851 in Chalatenango, El Salvador.

Reference: Rudolph, James D., ed., *Honduras: A Country Study*, 1984.

Figueres Ferrer, Jose
(b. 1906)
Costa Rica

Jose Figueres Ferrer stands alongside FRANCISCO MORAZÁN and JOSE MARIA CASTRO MADRIZ as a founder of Costa Rica. He presided over his nation's politics for nearly four decades and in the process promoted democratic and social reforms to build a more equitable society.

Jose Figueres Ferrer was born in 1906 to an immigrant family in San Ramón. As a youth, he traveled to the United States, where he attended some classes at the Massachusetts Institute of Technology. When he returned to Costa Rica he purchased a ranch in San José Province and turned it into a successful venture. He advanced not through family connections but through hard work and opportunistic decisions, and as such appealed to those Costa Ricans looking for new leaders. He gained much attention in 1942 when, in a radio speech, he criticized President Calderón Guardia's administration for taking Costa Rica into World War II without adequately securing the nation's defenses, and for failing to enact proposals for widespread social reform. His speech caused the government to exile him, and he went to Mexico where he broadened his political contacts.

In 1944, the Social Democratic Party (PSD) was formed, a left-of-center group that turned to Figueres for leadership. He returned from exile in May of that year and tried to build the party, but it did not grow, and in 1946 he joined the Democratic Party (PD), which was dedicated to reform. His attempt to become its leader failed when the PD members instead chose Fernando Castro Cervantes. Figueres left the PD and proceeded with plans he had formulated in Mexico to overthrow the government. He did this out of his conviction that the political leaders would never allow a real reformer to win at the polls.

Figueres signed a pact in 1947 with exile groups from other countries, and in return for their support he agreed to help them liberate their homelands, namely Honduras, Nicaragua, Venezuela, and the Dominican Republic. The 1948 election in Costa Rica bore out Figueres's fears: After losing in a disputed vote count, the existing government, backed by Calderón, refused to relinquish its power. Figueres led his National Liberation Army into action, and on 12 March the fighting began. In April, after his infamous "phantom march" along ox trails, he captured Puerto Limón. On 19 April the government agreed to surrender, thus ending the 1948 Civil War, often called the War of National Liberation.

On 8 May, Figueres became head of the Founding Junta of the Second Republic and asserted he would revolutionize Costa Rica. He imposed an excess wealth tax and imprisoned former government officials. In December, he joined several other nations in signing the Rio Treaty, which provided for collective security. After turning back a coup attempt in 1949, Figueres proceeded with a new constitution that established a unitary state with a clear separation of powers among the branches of government and an elected presidency. It also established a special council to oversee elections and prevent fraud. In November, Figueres relinquished the government to the candidate who had won the presidential election the previous year in opposition to Calderón.

In 1951, Figueres formed a new political group, the National Liberation Party (PLN), which he affiliated with the Socialist International. Two years later, he won the presidency in a landslide election and began his radical changes. He negotiated a contract with the powerful United Fruit Company to get more profits for Costa Rica, raised the minimum wage, and expanded education and public housing. Figueres's supporters christened him "Don Pepe," an affectionate nickname. His social programs, however, raised the national debt and activated his critics, who called him a communist.

Insurgents invaded Costa Rica in 1955 and nearly toppled Figueres, but he received help through the Rio Treaty from several nations, primarily the United States. In 1958, he completed his term as president but remained active in politics and in 1970 ran again for the presidency, which he won as a self-styled "democratic left" candidate. He established diplomatic relations with the Soviet Union and launched new social reforms, but he got into trouble when stories circulated he had engaged in illegal dealings with an unscrupulous American financier, Robert Vesco. The charges against Figueres were never proved, and he completed his four-year term as president.

Once again, he remained politically active, inadvertently helping a conservative to become president in 1977, after he had a falling out with the PLN candidate. Don Pepe remained a political force into the 1980s, but was best remembered for his establishment of free elections and radical reforms after the Civil War.

References: Ameringer, Charles D., *Don Pepe: A Political Biography of Jose Figueres of Costa Rica*, 1978; Bell, John Patrick, *Crisis in Costa Rica: The 1948 Revolution*, 1971; Creedman, Theodore S., *Historical Dictionary of Costa Rica*, 1991.

Flores, Juan José
(1800–1864)
Ecuador

Illiterate and capricious, Juan José Flores followed an erratic course through which he imposed autocratic rule and shaped Ecuadorian politics for 20 years.

Juan José Flores grew up in poverty. He was born in Venezuela, then a Spanish colony, at Puerto Cabello on 19 July 1800, the illegitimate son of a wealthy merchant. When his father departed for Europe, young Juan was left penniless. He worked in a Spanish military hospital and then, at the age of 14, joined the army. In his capacity as a sergeant he fought against SIMÓN BOLÍVAR and the revolutionaries who wanted to liberate Venezuela, and South America in general, from Spanish rule. But he was captured by the rebels in 1817 and decided to fight for their cause. He proved a valuable leader, contributing substantially to the crucial victory at Carabobo in 1821. Bolívar promoted him to lieutenant colonel and later to colonel and governor of a province. In 1825, after he became a brigadier general, he led the capture of Guayaquil, an important seaport in Ecuador.

Under Bolívar's plan, Ecuador, along with Venezuela and Colombia, was to be a part of Gran Colombia. In this arrangement, Flores was made *intendente* of Quito (placing him in charge of administering justice, collecting taxes, and organizing the militia), and along with ANTONIO JOSÉ DE SUCRE he turned back an invading Peruvian army on 27 February 1829 at the Battle of Tarqui. By this time, regional pressures were already tearing Gran Colombia asunder, and Flores added to them when, boosted by his strategic marriage to a member of the local aristocracy, he called together an assembly in Quito. On 13 May 1830, this group declared Ecuador independent, and shortly thereafter a constitutional convention met in Riobamba and named Flores president and military chief. In 1831, Flores tried, but failed, to annex Colombia's Cauca Valley.

As president, Flores had the backing of many aristocrats and the Venezuelan army in Ecuador and used these to enforce an autocratic rule. Nevertheless, he encountered difficulties from a depleted treasury, a dislike among many Ecuadorians toward the Venezuelan "outsiders," and uprisings in Quito and along the coast. He quashed the coastal rebellion when he captured its leader, Vicente Rocafuerte, and then gained his support by offering him the presidency. Rocafuerte accepted, agreeing that he would hold the office in a four-year rotation with Flores, who proceeded to defeat the revolutionaries in Quito early in 1835.

While Rocafuerte served as president, Flores continued as military chief. In 1839, Rocafuerte became governor of Guayas, an important province, and Flores resumed his presidency. Four years later, Flores decided to end his agreement with Rocafuerte by formulating a new constitution and getting himself reelected to an eight-year term. Rocafuerte opposed this, but Flores prevailed after he provided his opponent substantial money to leave the country. Flores's presidency proved short-lived, however, when a revolt backed by Rocafuerte exiled him to Europe in 1845.

Flores tried to regain power in 1852 when he led an invasion, but was easily defeated. For several years, chaos prevailed in Ecuador; then, in 1860, a decision by Ecuador's most prominent leader, Guillermo Franco, to cede land to Peru ignited a civil war. Amid this turmoil, a faction headed by Gabriel Garcia Moreno asked Flores to return and command an army. Flores agreed, and his forces ousted Franco and crushed the revolt. Flores was named president of a constitutional convention held in 1861, which recognized his colleague Moreno as the nation's ruler.

Flores's military adventures continued. When war erupted between Ecuador and Colombia, Flores entered the fray, but was defeated in 1863 at Guaspud. The following year, he returned to the battlefield to put down another internal uprising. He was, however, captured by the rebels and on 1 October 1864 died on board a ship taking him back to Guayaquil.

Reference: Blanksten, George I., *Ecuador: Constitutions and Caudillos,* 1964.

Fonseca, Manuel Deodoro da
(1827–1892)
Brazil

Manuel Deodoro da Fonseca served as Brazil's president for only a short time, but he is remembered as the leader who ended the nation's monarchy and began a self-proclaimed republic.

Manuel Deodoro da Fonseca was born in Alagôas on 5 August 1827, just five years after Brazil had gained its independence from Portugal under PEDRO I and his chief minister, JOSE BONIFÁCIO. Fonseca was the son of an army officer and followed in his father's footsteps by entering the military. He graduated from the Brazilian Military Academy in Rio de Janeiro and first gained prominence when he fought in the War of the Triple Alliance against Paraguay. This six-year battle, which lasted from 1864 to 1870, resulted in a Brazilian victory.

After the war, PEDRO II, the emperor who had solidified Brazil as a nation, encountered numerous problems. The treasury had been exhausted, and his drive to end slavery antagonized wealthy planters. Furthermore, many Brazilians believed the emperor had become too despotic. Most challenging to Pedro II, however, was the increasing power of the army. In 1887, Fonseca became president of the Military Club and thus the recognized spokesman for the military leadership.

In 1888, Pedro II appointed Afonso Celso his prime minister. Celso was a liberal who wanted to contain the military and even considered reducing the army. This prompted a crisis and fueled a republican drive to rid Brazil of the emperor. Fonseca supported the republicans after he was persuaded that reform could come only by ending the monarchy, and he heard rumors that the emperor might arrest him for his outspoken criticism.

On 15 November 1889, Fonseca and Floriano Peixoto led a military revolt that deposed Pedro II and declared Brazil a republic. He served as provisional president until February 1891, when the national legislature chose him president. Under his leadership, the government separated church and state, declared religious freedom, and abolished all titles of nobility. The president sought to combine the conservative emphasis on order with the liberal desire for progress.

Despite his support for the republican movement, Fonseca displayed a heavy-handed approach to governance, and at one point his entire cabinet resigned when he ignored its protest over awarding a public works contract to one of his friends. After his election in February, he tried to consolidate his power by abandoning the republican constitution, and on 3 November 1891 dissolved the Congress, which had opposed him on numerous issues.

In effect, Fonseca grabbed dictatorial powers. But the Congress and navy joined together to oppose him. When in late November he suffered a heart attack and naval ships threatened to bombard Rio, he relinquished the presidency. Fonseca tried to launch a revolt and return to the presidency in January 1892, but his successor, Peixoto, turned him back. The man who had toppled the emperor and helped found the republic (albeit a limited one) faded from public attention and died in Rio de Janeiro on 23 August 1892.

Reference: Simons, Charles Willis, *Marshal Deodoro and the Fall of Dom Pedro II*, 1966.

Francia, José Gaspar Rodríguez de
(1766–1840)
Paraguay

After José Gaspar Rodríguez de Francia led Paraguay to independence, he developed a cruel and relentless dictatorship, arresting and punishing people for merely criticizing his rule. Obsessed by fears of outside influences, he quarantined Paraguay, creating what some analysts called a "hermit nation," but he also revolutionized society to help the masses.

When José Gaspar Rodríguez de Francia was born in Asuncíon on 6 January 1766, Spain controlled the territory, which in the 1770s became part of an administrative unit, the Viceroyalty of the Río de la Plata. Asuncíon was a small town, only a shadow of its once thriving self, reduced in part by a recent expulsion of the Jesuits and by the growth of Buenos Aires.

As a young man, Francia obtained his education in theology and law. He attended the College of

Monserrat and the University of Córdoba. He taught theology at the Seminary of San Carlos in Asunción in 1790, but he soon gave this up to practice law.

Francia collected the works of Voltaire, Rousseau, and other French thinkers and possessed the largest library in Asunción. As a lawyer, he helped the poor, and his interest in social issues involved him in politics. By 1809, he was head of the Asunción town council.

As an ardent nationalist, Francia criticized Spain and attempts by Argentina to control his homeland. Under Spanish rule, many Paraguayans suffered from high taxes and strict trade regulations. After Napoleon invaded Spain, the colonial system crumbled rapidly. In July 1810, revolutionaries pushed for independence, and their army defeated a force invading from Buenos Aires. In June 1811, the Paraguayans officially declared their independence, and Francia emerged as the nation's prominent leader with control over the army.

At the forefront of a five-man revolutionary junta, Francia enlarged his power, and in 1814 a democratically elected Congress, consisting largely of the rural poor who made up most of Paraguay, agreed to make him dictator. Two years later, the legislature named him "dictator for life." Francia considered himself a utopian revolutionary and idolized the French Revolution. He aimed to weaken the elite and greatly strengthen the masses.

Although Francia tried at first to expand Paraguay's trade, he quickly adopted an isolationist policy and condemned most contacts with other countries. He restricted the river traffic with Buenos Aires and forbade Paraguayans from leaving the nation, while prohibiting foreigners from entering.

Francia stressed self-sufficiency, confiscated lands held by wealthy Spaniards, ended most aristocratic privileges, and broke relations with the pope by appointing his own clergy. His anti-clericalism included the expulsion of all religious orders and the confiscation of church property. He allowed no dissent and jailed, murdered, or exiled those who questioned his authority. Paraguayans suspected of disloyalty might find themselves tortured in the infamous Chamber of Truth. In 1821, he arrested some 300 elites and threw them in jail, not releasing them until they paid fines so high their wealth and power were broken.

Amid these developments, he encouraged agriculture through scientific farming, and production increased. Francia leased government land to the peasants at low rates and even gave them cattle. In all, he founded what has been called the world's first state-run socialist system and thus initiated an internal revolution that exceeded the changes occurring in the other former Spanish colonies. He developed shipbuilding and textiles, and his centrally planned economy achieved efficiency, although the trade restrictions retarded any development beyond a subsistence level. Francia wanted to create a new society, and toward this goal he forced the elite to marry Indian women—he believed the increase in mestizos (persons of mixed Indian and European blood) equalized Paraguayan society.

In foreign affairs, Francia shrewdly protected his nation's independence by developing close relations with Brazil to offset Argentina's power. Most importantly, his refusal to intervene in those two nations maintained peace.

Francia ran his administration with great financial responsibility, honesty, and frugality. When his dictatorship ended, a surplus existed in the treasury. Indeed, his absolutism ceased only with his death on 20 September 1840. Even then, Francia's influence continued as Paraguayans, accustomed to a strong ruler, developed political passivity and a pattern of dictatorial government.

"These unfortunate times of oppression and tyranny have ended at last."

References: Pendle, George, *Paraguay: A Riverside Nation,* 1967; Williams, John Hoyt, *The Rise and Fall of the Paraguayan Republic, 1800–1870,* 1979.

Franklin, Benjamin
(1706–1790)
United States

While in Paris, Benjamin Franklin wore his fur cap only rarely; but the image stayed indelibly in the minds of many, both in Europe and America: Here was a man of wisdom who bespoke the truth emanating from a wilderness country; here was the man of nature who heralded a republican nation, positioned to provide the world with fresh visions.

Josiah Franklin sailed from England to the British colony of Massachusetts Bay around 1682 , and after his first wife died married Abiah Folger. They lived in Boston, and on 17 January 1706, Benjamin Franklin was born to them. Josiah taught Benjamin to read and write at an early age (at seven he was composing poetry) and sent him to the Boston Grammar School and, after that, a private school.

In 1716, Benjamin began working in his father's shop as a tallow chandler and soap boiler. Two years later, he worked as an apprentice in the printing shop owned by his half-brother, James. Although young, Benjamin developed a talent for printing and committed himself to a rigorous program of self-improvement focused on extensive reading. He earned acclaim after an essay of his appeared in James's newspaper, under the pseudonym "Silence Dogood." Benjamin and James did not get along, however, and in 1723 the young man left Boston for Philadelphia.

Franklin had little money and found employment in a print shop. His talents and gregarious nature resulted in many friends and connections, and in 1729 he became owner of *The Pennsylvania Gazette.* The following year, he married Deborah Read. She was illiterate, and the couple had a difficult time relating intellectually. Although they cared for each other, Franklin did not maintain absolute fidelity; indeed, over the years he engaged in several extramarital affairs and fathered two illegitimate children.

Franklin developed his business interests and engaged in extensive self-promotion. His success represented the American ethic of climbing up from humble beginnings, and his writings reinforced it. *Poor Richard's Almanack,* which he published from 1732 until 1757, communicated numerous homilies and sayings that permeated American culture, and he was never at a loss to tell people how to live. His advice included: "Speak not but what may benefit others or yourself; avoid trifling conversation"; "Lose no time, be always employed in something useful; cut off all unnecessary action"; and "Eat not to fullness, drink not to elevation." Later critics considered him the pontificator of conformity and a man who measured success by social acceptance and material gain.

The Enlightenment influenced Franklin greatly, and he developed a keen interest in practical science. Although he defended pure research, he believed science should be useful to mankind. Most famous among his diverse inquiries were his experiments with electricity. The idea that lightning produced electricity did not originate with him, but he did propose a way to test this assertion by placing an iron rod on a tower. The experiment worked in 1752 when tried in France. That summer Franklin conducted a modified experiment in Pennsylvania using a key and a kite. His publications on electricity brought him recognition as a scientist, and Harvard, Yale, and William and Mary awarded him masters of arts degrees.

Franklin had the time to engage in these activities because he delegated the daily operations of his printing firm to someone else. Not really interested in business, he preferred intellectual and political endeavors. In the 1730s, he founded the first circulating library in the colonies, and over the next two decades he began or helped begin numerous projects to improve Philadelphia. These included the American Philosophical Society, a city hospital, the Academy for the Education of Youth, a city police force, and improved roads.

In 1754, Franklin served as the Pennsylvania delegate in the Albany Congress, an intercolonial gathering intended to unite the colonists against the French and Indians. There he advanced his infamous Albany Plan to establish a colonial union, but although the Congress adopted it, the individual colonies did not. In 1757, he was sent to England to resolve a controversy between the Pennsylvania Assembly and the proprietors of the colony, who appointed the governor. The Assembly disliked this control over the governor, for it resulted in proprietary lands being exempt from taxes. Franklin convinced Parliament in 1760 to tax the lands. During his stay, the Pennsylvanian enjoyed English society, establishing friendships with scientists and philosophers. He also wrote an influential article, which argued Britain should obtain Canada rather than the Caribbean island of Guadeloupe in the French and Indian War then under way.

Franklin returned to Philadelphia in 1762, but the Assembly again sent him to England to settle another dispute with the proprietors. Shortly after he arrived, the first in a long series of crises erupted between the colonies and Britain when, in 1765, Parliament passed the Stamp Act. Radicals such as SAMUEL ADAMS led a protest in Massachusetts against the tax, which was imposed on printed material used in the colonies; and even moderate men, such as JOHN ADAMS, criticized the measure.

Franklin did not like the Stamp Act but recommended the colonists abide by it and named a friend to serve as the stamp distributor in Philadelphia. As it turned out, he had underestimated the colonial opposition, perhaps a result of his long absence from home, and this undermined his reputation in America. He soon recovered, however, when he offered a strong defense of the colonial position in Parliament. His views were published throughout the colonies.

Shortly after Parliament repealed the Stamp Act in 1766, Georgia, New Jersey, and Massachusetts appointed him as their agent in London. When differences with the British government continued, he worked to reconcile the opposing sides. Gradually, he saw the futility of trying to compromise with Parliament and in 1770 expressed the opinion that the colonies should be autonomous,

linked to Britain only by a common allegiance to the king.

Franklin contributed to the tension in 1772 after a friend in Parliament showed him six letters written by Massachusetts governor Thomas Hutchinson in which the royal official advocated limiting that colony's English liberties. Franklin sent the letters to a friend in America who, against the Pennsylvanian's wishes, published them. The ensuing uproar played into the hands of the radicals.

"They that can give up essential liberty to obtain a little temporary safety deserve neither liberty nor safety."

Franklin returned to Pennsylvania in May 1775 (several months after his wife died) and was immediately chosen to serve as a delegate in the Second Continental Congress. In that capacity, he helped organize the post office and served on committees that advised GEORGE WASHINGTON (then head of the army) and drafted the Declaration of Independence, largely written by THOMAS JEFFERSON. In September 1776, he sailed for France as one of three commissioners appointed to negotiate a treaty with that nation.

The French received him enthusiastically. To them, he epitomized the Enlightenment and the possibility of a better future. John Adams later remarked, with some jealousy, that France hailed the Pennsylvanian as some kind of savior. Franklin's standing obviously helped him in his negotiations with the government. France wanted to weaken Britain's position in Europe, but moved warily, concerned that the colonies might settle for something less than independence, or that they might quickly collapse. After the British suffered a defeat at Saratoga in New York, France entered intense negotiations with the American commissioners, and early in 1778 the two sides signed a treaty of commerce and alliance.

In September 1778, the Continental Congress named Franklin minister plenipotentiary, and he worked to secure loans from France, money that was crucial in the Revolutionary War. As the British position in America deteriorated, particularly after Lord Cornwallis's defeat in 1781 at Yorktown, Franklin and two other commissioners, John Adams and John Jay, undertook negotiations with the enemy. Franklin had long been partial to France and had promised that the United States would not negotiate with Britain except in coordination with the French government. Adams and Jay, however, disagreed with this approach and, wanting to distance the United States from France, they persuaded Franklin to proceed with independent negotiations. The peace agreement was signed on 3 September 1783, but Franklin continued until 1785 as minister to France.

Shortly after Franklin returned to the United States, Pennsylvania chose him as a delegate to the Constitutional Convention, which began meeting in May 1787. Over 80 years old at the time, he was eclipsed at the convention and in the subsequent ratification effort by such men as JAMES MADISON and ALEXANDER HAMILTON. Nevertheless, his prestige carried substantial weight, and he served on the committee that resolved the dispute over how to determine the congressional representation from each state.

After the Constitutional Convention, he retired to his home in Philadelphia, where he lived with his daughter and dabbled in inventions. He died on 17 April 1790, his diverse, rewarding life a testament to his ambition, intellect, and the challenging times that complemented his talents.

References: Crane, Verner W., *Benjamin Franklin and a Rising People,* 1962; Franklin, Benjamin, *Autobiography of Benjamin Franklin* (ed. L. W. Labaree et al.), 1964; Hawke, David F., *Franklin,* 1976; Ketcham, R. L., *Benjamin Franklin,* 1965; Lopez, Claude-Anne, and E. W. Herbert, *The Private Franklin,* 1975; Wright, E., *Benjamin Franklin: His Life as He Wrote It,* 1990; Wright, E., *Franklin of Philadelphia,* 1986;.

Frederick VII
(1808–1863)
Denmark

In 1848, revolution swept Europe, tied to national and liberal goals. Although Denmark did not experience a massive upheaval, a sentiment for change affected its society, and Frederick VII presided over substantial political reform as "the giver of the constitution."

Frederick was the son of Denmark's future king Christian VIII and Charlotte of Mecklenberg-Schwerin. He was born on 6 October 1808 at Amalienborg Castle in Denmark and educated by tutors. His schooling, however, did not go beyond the basics, and he had a reputation for coarseness and eccentricity. In 1839, he received appointment as governor of Fyn, a large island near the mainland's southeast coast. Frederick had a tumultuous private life, entering two unhappy marriages that ended in divorce.

On 20 January 1848, Frederick succeeded his

father as king. His ascension occurred in a historic year as revolution affected most of Europe. These uprisings contained a dual appeal: to nationalism, which stimulated a romantic love for country, and to liberalism, which advocated democratic reform through new constitutions. Under Frederick's father, Christian VIII, many Danes had anticipated a shift away from royal absolutism, but the king had proved conservative and unwilling to go beyond some administrative reforms.

In 1848, popular demonstrations erupted in Denmark, and agitators and reformers led by Jens Andersen Hansen and Anton Frederik Tscherning placed pressure on Frederick. Tscherning formed the Society of the Friends of the Peasants, which evolved into the Liberal Party. Frederick subsequently organized the March Cabinet that included Liberal Party leaders

Orla Lehman and Ditlev Gothrad Monrad. Demands for a free constitution led Frederick to call a constituent assembly. From this group came a constitution that abolished the 190-year-old absolute monarchy by providing for a bicameral legislature elected through a popular vote. The constitution created an independent judiciary and guaranteed freedom of the press, religion, and association. Frederick signed the document on 5 June 1849, a move that made him enormously popular. Although he had not initiated the reform movement, he had, unlike his father, agreed with it and even supported it. Denmark thus experienced a relatively peaceful transition into a democratic era.

Frederick also involved himself in important foreign policy decisions. He incorporated the territory of Schleswig into the new Danish state, a move that ignited a rebellion by Germans there, who obtained Prussian help. Frederick's action conformed with the liberal movement, which found in this issue an expression of its nationalist sentiment. The conflict resulted, however, in Schleswig maintaining its autonomy and eventually, in 1864, being absorbed by Prussia.

Frederick died on 15 November 1863 at Glucksburg Castle. In his later years he had become engaged in numerous conflicts with the Liberal Party, particularly over who should be his successor. The king had married Louise Christine Rasmussen, a ballerina, in 1850, but remained childless. Despite the political disputes, to many Danes Frederick remained if not the initiator, then at least the symbol of reform and a new Denmark.

References: Kjersgaard, Erik, *A History of Denmark*, 1974; Oakley, Stewart, *A Short History of Denmark*, 1972.

◆

Furrer, Jonas
(1805–1861)
Switzerland

For centuries Switzerland had existed as a confederation of cantons, but in 1847 civil war threatened to tear apart all unity. Jonas Furrer, however, brought to the political scene moderate ideas that produced a widely respected federal constitution.

Jonas Furrer was born on 3 March 1805 at Winterthur. After graduating from law school in Germany, he gained an outstanding reputation in the legal profession, particularly noted for his adeptness at constructing rational arguments. In 1839, he emerged as the leader of the liberals in Zürich. Stirred into action by the 1830 Revolution in Paris, this group advocated more democracy

through a truly representative government and societal regeneration through educational reform. The Liberals also wanted a more unified state to promote economic development. Switzerland had not yet emerged as a modern nation; power resided primarily in the several small states, or cantons, and most people identified first and foremost with their canton. Furrer and the other Liberals wanted to change this, and from his position as a delegate in the Zürich cantonal assembly he pushed for constitutional reform. He became vice-president of the assembly in 1842 and president in 1846, the same year he served as president of the confederation Diet.

In Zürich, Furrer headed a commission that, like those in several other cantons, produced a liberal constitution protecting basic liberties and affirming the people as the source of sovereignty. He helped reform the primary schools and establish a university. But these developments produced tensions between the reformers and conservatives made worse by religious differences as the Liberals acted to suppress Catholic orders, with the more radical among them forming anti-Jesuit societies. The Catholic cantons, in turn, protested, and when the liberal cantons reached agreements for mutual protection, the former did the same, creating the Sonderbund.

"The authorities recognize neither friends nor opponents but only fellow-citizens and confederates."

Although a Liberal, Furrer disagreed with the radicals and the mounting polarization. After the radicals gained a majority in the federal Diet, they decided to move militarily against the Sonderbund. There followed in 1847 a brief civil war in which conservative Lucerne was captured and the radicals emerged victorious. Furrer then served on the Reform Commission (headed by Ulrich Ochsenbein) to write a new constitution, and as such sought to heal differences by moderating radical demands.

The new constitution established a legislature, called a Council of States, and an executive, called a Federal Council. The old confederation gave way to a federation of states that for the first time (excepting a short-lived Napoleonic republic) created an integrated Swiss nation. The constitution went into effect on 12 September 1848. Furrer won election that year as the republic's first president and was reelected in 1852, 1855, and 1858. Furrer died on 25 July 1861 at Baad Ragaz.

The Swiss wrote another constitution in 1874 that increased the power of the central government. Furrer's original effort, though, signified Switzerland's emergence as a unified modern nation.

References: Bonjour, Edgar, et al., *A Short History of Switzerland*, 1955; Kohn, Hans, *Nationalism and Liberty: The Swiss Example*, 1956.

Gairy, Eric
(b. 1922)
Grenada

Eric Gairy built a mass political party in Grenada, authoritarian and heavily dependent on his personal appeal. "Gairyism" became a catch word that referred to his fanaticism.

Eric Gairy was born into a poor family on 18 February 1922 near Grenville. He received little education and did not show an intellectual bent. In 1942, Gairy left Grenada for Trinidad, where he got a job helping to build an American military base. Then he journeyed to Aruba and worked at an oil refinery. He became a trade union organizer and ran into trouble with the Dutch authorities who governed the island. Consequently, he returned to Grenada in 1949 and the following year organized the Grenada People's Party (GPP).

In so doing, Gairy took advantage of recent changes in the political system. The British, who governed Grenada, allowed universal adult suffrage beginning in 1951, and this eventually enabled Gairy to convert his enormous personal appeal into victories at the ballot box. While he built his political party, he gained his first popular recognition as a labor leader and by late 1951 organized well over 20,000 Grenadians. He especially appealed to the rural workers and stressed the need for blacks to obtain acceptance from whites and mulattos as equals.

In his early efforts, he displayed neither a socialist outlook nor a strongly nationalistic one. While he had his political party behind him, he relied more on personal appeal than formal organization. In fact, this situation got him into trouble several times when he miscalculated his ability to get supporters to the polls based solely on his charisma.

Gairy's successful leadership in 1951 of a widespread strike that brought Grenada to a standstill elevated him from a trade union leader to a political leader and boosted his party organization. Later that year, the GPP captured six of the eight seats in the legislative council. He repeated this feat in the 1954 election, although the percentage of the popular vote on his side declined substantially. He fared worse in 1957, losing seats to competing parties. Meanwhile, he served not only on the legislative council but also as minister of trade and production. In 1960, after Britain allowed a new constitution, Gairy called for elections. He won these handily, but the British refused to name him chief minister.

Although Gairy did not promote a socialist agenda, many in Grenada interpreted his actions as radical. He talked about land for the landless, and his championing of black businessmen challenged the white and mulatto power structure. Meanwhile, Gairy's power faded as his organization languished and Grenadians were attracted to other issues he did not champion, such as forming the West Indies Federation (a union of several Caribbean islands) that took effect in 1961. When it collapsed a year later, Gairy's appeal was again eclipsed by talks concerning a merger of Grenada with Trinidad. After that union failed to materialize, Gairy grabbed the political reins, won the 1967 election, and became premier.

Gairy's supporters called him "Uncle Gairy," but his critics condemned him for violating financial regulations, using public monies to buy luxury

"I knew that some day I must become a famous leader, but I didn't know it would come so soon."

items, and harassing opponents. The British even removed him from office for mismanaging funds.

Gairy supported independence for Grenada, which was obtained in 1974, and at this point he became prime minister. Some observers claimed he had supported the break with Britain without providing sufficient measures to protect constitutional rights, and that in doing so he had shown a concern for advancing his own power rather than a sincere attachment to nationhood.

In the 1970s, Gairy's administration became more authoritarian and militaristic. He formed the "Mongoose Gang," a special security group that attacked and beat troublesome critics. Several political opponents mysteriously "disappeared." In 1978, he greatly restricted the right of trade unions to strike, and so constrained the House of Representatives that it became a powerless institution. The opposition against him began to mount: union leaders who disliked his restrictions, church leaders who criticized his indulgent behavior, young professionals who considered him an embarrassment, and radicals who desired a socialist society. In 1979, Gairy, who was out of the country, was overthrown in a leftist coup.

Instability continued in Grenada. In 1983, another coup led by dissident leftist revolutionaries deposed and executed the Marxist prime minister, Maurice Bishop. The United States, worried about a possible link between the rebels and Communist Cuba, invaded Grenada and established a moderate government. In the 1988 election, Gairy led his United Labour Party while claiming to be a mystic and follower of voodoo and an African religion, Shango. He was unsuccessful in his bid to become prime minister.

Reference: Lewis, Gordon K., *Grenada: The Jewel Despoiled*, 1987.

Gandhi, Indira
(1917–1984)
India

As with many other Indian nationalists, Indira Gandhi was strongly influenced by MOHANDAS GANDHI (not a relative). As a child she mimicked Gandhi's nonviolent tactics; as a woman she broke through traditional gender boundaries and helped lead her country through its formative years.

Indira Nehru Gandhi was born 19 November 1917 in Allahabad, the only child of Jawaharlal and Kashmir Nehru. Her family, a wealthy one, had important ties to India's nationalist movement. Her grandfather, Motilal Nehru, had helped organize the Indian National Congress, a political party that sought more autonomy for Indians from the colonial power, Britain. Her father, JAWAHARLAL NEHRU, joined Congress.

Indira spent several years of her childhood without her parents, whom the British imprisoned off and on for their political activities. When as a little girl she played with her dolls, it was unlike most other children: She arranged them in Mohandas Gandhian-style demonstrations. She also delivered political speeches to her family's servants.

Even as a child she became involved in the nationalist movement. At age 12 she formed a children's organization to write messages of protest against Britain, and over the years her father's letters from prison educated her as to the moral commitment necessary and the British oppression that prevailed.

In 1936, after schooling in Switzerland, Indira Gandhi entered Somerville College at Oxford University. In England she joined the British Labor Party, which had a more liberal policy toward India than the ruling Conservatives, and came into contact with V. K. Krishna Menon, a leading Indian nationalist. Before she could complete her college education, ill health forced her return to India. In 1938, she joined Congress and in 1942 supported the Quit India movement, which demanded Britain relinquish its rule. That year she also married Feroze Gandhi, a journalist and Congress Party activist. (They separated in the 1950s and he died in 1960.) Later that year, Britain imprisoned both her and her husband for subversive activities, and she spent 13 months in jail.

On 15 August 1947, India gained its independence. This provoked rioting between Hindus and Muslims, and Indira Gandhi stepped in to arrange meetings that quelled the violence in several communities.

After Jawaharlal Nehru became India's first prime minister, Indira Gandhi filled the position of first lady (her mother had died several years earlier and her father had not remarried). She did more than take care of social affairs. She traveled with her father on several diplomatic missions and then in 1955 joined the executive body of Congress. This gave her a prominent political role, and four years later she won election as Congress Party president. In this capacity, she maneuvered to end the Communist Party rule in the state of Kerala and to make Congress dominant there.

In 1960, poor health forced her to resign the presidency. Then early in 1964, after her father became sick, she took over most of the prime minister's duties. When Nehru died in May, the new prime minister, Bahadur Shastri, asked her to serve as foreign minister, but she rejected the request and, tired by her personal tragedy, instead accepted the lesser, and less demanding, position as minister of information and broadcasting. For the next two years she worked to reform the bureaucracy in her ministry.

When on 11 January 1966 Shastri died, Congress turned to Indira Gandhi and on 19 January elected her prime minister (as party leader in Parliament). She raised much controversy when, that year, she agreed to create a separate state within India for the Sikhs, who had protested their domination by Hindus. Many of the militant Hindus denounced her.

Another controversy erupted in 1969 when she supported a candidate for India's president different from the one endorsed by traditional leadership of the Congress. As a result, Congress expelled her from the party, but she formed her own party, Congress-N, and gained much public support when she nationalized all banks. In 1971, her Congress-N won a sweeping election after she promised additional economic and social reforms.

Indira Gandhi gained still more popular support when, in December 1971, India soundly defeated Pakistan in a war that produced independence for Bangladesh. She wielded considerable power within Congress-N, building the party's strength through a youthful leadership. Yet problems ensued in 1972 and 1973 when the economy sagged due to crop failures and higher oil prices, among other factors. To gain loans from the International Monetary Fund, she shifted to more conservative economic policies that angered many of her partisans.

When in 1975 the Supreme Court ruled that Indira Gandhi had violated electoral rules four years previous and thus could not hold her seat in Parliament, she proclaimed a state of emergency and suspended civil rights while censoring the press. To combat widespread governmental corruption, she and Parliament announced reform drives and imprisoned wrongdoers. In 1977, she

> *"I don't see the world as divided into right and left. I think most of us are in the center."*

released her opponents from jail and Parliament announced new elections. Her Congress-N party lost, and she had to relinquish the prime ministry.

Then in June 1979 the ruling coalition splintered, and elections the following year resulted in Indira Gandhi's return as prime minister under a new party banner, Congress-I. Although in 1982 she visited both the Soviet Union and the United States, she steered a course toward closer relations with the latter.

In 1983, violence swept Punjab State as Sikh nationalists demanded more autonomy. Then, in Assam State, Hindus rioted to prevent Bangladeshi refugees from voting in upcoming elections. While Indira Gandhi quelled these disturbances with much difficulty, the violence soon ended her rule. In March 1983, she hosted a conference of Third World nations, which met in New Delhi, and the meeting raised her international standing. Then in June 1984 she decided to strike against the Sikh nationalists. The army raided their headquarters at the Golden Temple, the holiest Sikh religious structure, in Amritsar. Her action angered Sikh extremists, and in October two Sikh members of her own security force assassinated her. Her son, Rajiv Gandhi, was sworn in as the new prime minister.

References: Butler, F., *Indira Gandhi*, 1986; Hiro, Dilip, *Inside India Today*, 1979; Masani, Zaheer, *Indira Gandhi*, 1976.

Gandhi, Mohandas Karamchand
(1869–1948)
India

The leader of modern Indian nationalism, Mohandas Gandhi infused the movement with Hindu spirituality. To Gandhi, moral values always superseded material ones, and the improvement of human souls was a necessary precursor to the improvement of a nation.

Mohandas Gandhi's life began on 2 October 1869 at Porbandar, a city in British-ruled western India. His father, Karamchand Gandhi, a man of modest means, worked as an administrator for the local chief minister. His mother, Putlibai, followed a devout religious life noted for fasting; at a later date,

Gandhi claimed his mother's religiosity was the biggest influence on his life. Mohandas learned as a boy to worship the Hindu god Vishnu and to abide by the Jainist teaching of nonviolence. His family's religious beliefs included respect for all living things and required strict vegetarianism.

As a youngster, Mohandas was not a good student. He did not show enthusiasm for either his studies or sports. Furthermore, his schooling suffered disruption when in 1882, at age 13, he was married by arrangement. Like many adolescents, Mohandas went through a rebellious period during which he adopted Western ways, ate meat, smoked, and told lies. Each time he did these things he suffered great guilt, and he soon returned to his Hindu teachings and renounced his irreligious behavior.

In 1887, Mohandas barely passed a matriculation exam and began studying at Samaldas College in Bhavnagar. His family felt he should study law, and although Mohandas had some desire to become a doctor he agreed, partly as a way to get away from Samaldas, which he did not like. Legal studies required that he journey to England, and this he did with dreams he would live amid a culture of great poets and philosophers. What he found, however, dismayed him: prejudice against his Indian background.

In 1888, Gandhi entered the Inner Temple, a law college in London. He felt awkward with Western food and practices and focused more on the social issues confronting him than on legal obscurities. His vegetarianism, often criticized, became a source of strength for him in maintaining his Hinduism. He even joined the London Vegetarian Society and wrote articles for its journal. He also began reading the Hindu *Bhagavadgita,* which had an increasing influence on him.

Gandhi returned to India and obtained admission to the bar in 1891. He had no enthusiasm for the law, however, and made a miserable appearance in the courtroom. As a result, he scratched out a living by preparing petitions for litigants. The next year, he agreed to journey to Natal in South Africa to work as a lawyer for a firm there.

Gandhi's South African experience proved momentous in his personal development and, by extension, in India's history. This British-ruled colony discriminated severely against its Indian residents, and as Gandhi traveled he found his movements restricted. Yet he resisted segregation, refusing in one instance to give up his seat on a stagecoach to a European, a decision that resulted in his being beaten by the white driver. These experiences made Gandhi determined to fight social injustice. Almost overnight he became a dynamic leader, and in 1894 he petitioned the British government to reject a bill that would deny Indians the right to vote. Although his effort failed, he organized the Natal Indian Congress and activated Indian resistance to injustices. His frequent petitions drew world attention to the discrimination in South Africa. He lived a life of great self-discipline, residing in a self-supporting settlement called Tolstoy Farm.

In 1906, the government proposed legislation, enacted the following year, requiring that Indians register and be fingerprinted with the authorities. Gandhi and most Indians considered this insulting, and he organized an opposition drive that focused on *satyagraha,* meaning Soul Force. This strategy stressed weaning the oppressor from his unjust practices through nonviolent protest that would make him see the error of his ways. In this instance, Gandhi did not win the repeal of required registration. In continued protests, Gandhi was arrested and while in jail he read Henry David Thoreau's "Civil Disobedience," which influenced him greatly.

In 1914, Gandhi won a compromise settlement for Indians in South Africa. It included the end to the tax on former indentured Indian workers, the recognition of Hindu and Muslim marriages as legal, and a prohibition against importing indentured Indian labor. Gandhi then returned to India in 1915, enlightened by the many lessons he had learned in South Africa.

During World War I, Gandhi refrained from any attacks on British rule in India. He even helped Britain recruit Indian soldiers, yet he disagreed with British actions injurious to his countrymen. By this time his Hindu philosophy had developed further, assisted by a spiritual advisor. Gandhi embraced *aparigraha,* requiring a rejection of material possessions that hindered spiritual development (an extension of his belief developed at Tolstoy Farm that life close to the earth was best); and he embraced *samabhava*, requiring he work his deeds without emotion, without any desire to defeat an enemy. In fact, Gandhi always preferred winning over an opponent to conquering him. Furthermore, he adopted a celibate life; sex, he believed, interfered with discovering God, and sexual restraint must be included with restraints in diet, speech, and emotions. He may have been acting from a more practical consideration, too, as his wife, having borne him four sons, developed physical problems that impaired sexual activity.

When Britain announced new legislation after the war that provided for imprisoning Indians suspected of sedition, Gandhi announced a *satyagraha*. His effort soon turned to alarm when, in 1919, protestors engaged in violence, and the British retaliated by slaughtering 400 Indians meeting at Amritsar in the Punjab. Gandhi called off the *satyagraha*, but he soon entered a more activist political phase. In 1920, he became leader of the Indian National Congress, a political party that had developed a cooperative effort by Hindus and Muslims to get concessions from Britain. Gandhi completely reorganized the group, making it less elitist and stronger. A mass organization evolved, wedded to his *satyagraha*. He called for widespread boycotts of British goods with a turn to self-reliance and material simplicity. Once again, though, when his efforts sparked violence, this time in 1922, he suspended them. The British arrested Gandhi for his activities, and he served two years in prison until his release in 1924 for poor health.

After his prison term, Gandhi focused on a *satyagraha* to help the untouchable caste. He won them the right to use a temple road in a southern state and declared that untouchables, as children of God like all human beings, must have the same rights as everyone else. Meanwhile, the Congress Party split apart as Muslims and Hindus went their own separate ways with one faction led by Chitta Ranjan Das, a Muslim, and another led by Motilal Nehru, a Hindu. The political situation heated again when, in 1928, Britain announced the formation of a commission to study reforms. The commission did not have a single Indian representative, and at that point Congress, under Gandhi's direction, demanded Indian independence. To

support this Gandhi promoted a *satyagraha* in 1930 that sought to eliminate the tax on salt—a tax that especially harmed India's poor. His efforts led to new discussions with Britain, but these produced only modest results, and, in any event, his protests earned him another term in jail.

In 1934, Gandhi resigned completely from Congress, as leader and member. He claimed that the party had abandoned his strategy by supporting nonviolence only as a means rather than a principle. He refocused his efforts to uplift India by encouraging his countrymen to live simply, reject manufactured goods, and develop their own handicrafts. He lived as he preached, residing at Sevagram, a small central Indian village, where he spun cotton and reduced his material possessions to the minimum.

In the mid-1930s, Britain accelerated reforms that Indianized the government. A limited franchise that had been granted Indians years earlier was expanded slightly and more Indians were brought into the bureaucracy. But to many Indians the changes seemed too slow and too meager, and they left them as second-class citizens in their own country.

"No cause that is intrinsically just can ever be described as forlorn."

Gandhi raised considerable controversy during World War II when, during Britain's fight against Germany, he demanded that the British withdraw and grant his country its complete independence—the Quit India movement. Critics accused him of hampering the war effort, but Gandhi was reacting to British delays in transferring power to Indians and British tactics intended to inflame the differences between Hindus and Muslims. The British reacted harshly; in 1942 they jailed Gandhi and the entire Congress leadership. Gandhi remained in prison until 1944.

The following year, the Labor Party came to power in Britain and changed the policy toward India. Henceforth, steps would be taken to grant the country its independence. Much to Gandhi's regret, however, the procedure adopted provided for two separate states, with Pakistan to be given its own autonomy as a predominantly Muslim state. Britain decided this while violence between Hindus and Muslims mounted within India. When Congress approved the plan, it deserted Gandhi.

With independence promised for no later than June 1948, Gandhi toured India in 1947 and again the following year, attempting to end the religious fighting. He began a fast to convince Hindus they should be nonviolent, even when provoked by Muslims, and declared he would not end his protest until the violence ceased. The rioting, centered in Delhi, came to an end, but his efforts won him the animosity of many Hindus and Muslim extremists. On 30 January 1948, as Gandhi walked to a platform from which he was to address a prayer meeting, a Hindu fanatic, Nathuram Godse, shot him. Gandhi said "Oh, God," and died instantly.

In his time, Gandhi had obtained the name "mahatma," meaning great soul. He was the leader of Indian nationalism, but his efforts clearly transcended the political realm. He envisioned a better society, founded on compassion and respect for all, a new moral order for his people and the world.

References: Erikson, Erik H., *Gandhi's Truth: On the Origins of Militant Nonviolence*, 1969; Fischer, Louis, *Gandhi: His Life and Message for the World*, 1954; Fischer, Louis, *The Life of Mahatma Gandhi*, 1983; Gandhi, Mohandas, *The Story of My Experiments with Truth*, 1983; Green, Martin B., *Tolstoy and Gandhi: Men of Peace*, 1983; Nanda, Bal R. *Mahatma Gandhi: A Biography*, 1968; Payne, Robert, *The Life and Death of Mahatma Gandhi*, 1969.

Garibaldi, Giuseppe
(1807–1882)
Italy

The military hero behind Italian unification, Giuseppe Garibaldi pursued an exciting adventure of intrigue and bravery. He roamed South America as a soldier and pirate and later gathered his Red Shirts and conquered Sicily.

Giuseppe Garibaldi was born on 4 July 1807 in Nice, France, the son of a ship's captain. As a youth, he sailed the Mediterranean and Black Seas and followed in his father's footsteps. In the early 1830s, he entered the navy of Sardinia-Piedmont and also joined Young Italy, a nationalist organization that was founded by GIUSEPPE MAZZINI to promote Italian unification. At the time, Italy did not exist as a nation but rather as several different entities, largely under Austrian control.

> *"The Rome that I beheld with the eyes of youthful imagination was the Rome of the future . . ."*

For Young Italy and Garibaldi, *risorgimento* became the leading idea—meaning resurgence, in this case a resurgence of Italy through unity and republicanism. In 1834, after Garibaldi participated in a failed Mazzini-inspired uprising against the monarchical Sardinia-Piedmont government, he took refuge in France. Then he sailed for South America in 1836, where he served as a soldier and a pirate for the province of Rio Grande in its unsuccessful battle to secede from Brazil. In an adulterous arrangement, he courted Anna Maria Ribeiro da Silva, who was already married; the two wed, and she became his companion in his military endeavors. In 1842, he headed the Uruguayan navy in that nation's war against Argentina, and the following year he commanded its legion, consisting of Italian volunteers. The legend of Garibaldi spread—a hero clad in his infamous long red shirt.

Garibaldi learned in 1848 of an uprising against Austria by Milanese nationalists supported by Sardinia-Piedmont. He returned to Italy and joined the rebels in what turned out to be a losing cause. In 1849, he fought for Mazzini's newly formed Roman Republic against French forces that sought to block the formation of a unified Italy. His brave stand against a numerically superior army won him admiration among Italians. In July, he retreated and tried to escape capture, a move that resulted in his wife's death.

Exiled in the early 1850s, Garibaldi lived in the United States for a short time, employed as a candle maker, then went to Peru, where he served in the military. In 1855, Garibaldi returned to Italy and met with CAMILLO BENSO DI CAVOUR, the prime minister of Sardinia-Piedmont, who had convinced that country's king to establish a republican government. Cavour actively promoted Italian unification and wanted Garibaldi on his side. The adventurer consequently became a general in the Piedmontese army. When war erupted in 1859, Garibaldi's reputation soared after he helped drive the Austrians from northern Italy. In the subsequent peace agreement, Sardinia-Piedmont acquired Lombardy, an important step in the unification effort.

Garibaldi's most brilliant military move soon followed. With Sardinia-Piedmont as his base, he invaded Sicily (part of the Kingdom of the Two Sicilies centered in Naples) in May 1860 with a band of 1,000 guerrillas called the Red Shirts. He quickly defeated the Neapolitan army and in September captured Naples itself, thus making him ruler of the Two Sicilies. Desirous of Italian unity, he turned the Two Sicilies over to Victor Emmanuel, the king of Piedmont-Sardinia, whom he now considered to be the ruler over united Italy.

Cavour, however, feared that Garibaldi would march on Rome, a city still held by France, and ignite a dangerous war that could challenge Emmanuel's leadership. Through political and military maneuvering, he prevented Garibaldi from doing this.

Garibaldi's fame spread throughout Europe and even to the United States, where Abraham Lincoln, embroiled in the Civil War, offered the Italian nationalist a command in the American army. Ever the staunch republican, Garibaldi refused because Lincoln did not completely renounce slavery.

Garibaldi's efforts in a new war with Austria from 1864 to 1866 resulted in the acquisition of Venice. In 1867, he led forces into the Papal States, but France intervened and defeated him. His final military campaign occurred in 1870 when he helped France fight Poland. His accomplishments in that effort resulted in his election to the French National Assembly.

The completion of a unified Italy occurred in 1870 through an agreement with the pope, an action that did not directly involve Garibaldi. The new Italy was not truly republican and more closely fit the description of a parliamentary monarchy. Nevertheless, Italy now encompassed Rome, and Garibaldi's military prowess had proved crucial in building the nation.

Throughout the remainder of his life, Garibaldi advocated change. He voiced republican sentiments while cautioning against excessive parliamentary power, promoted women's rights, and embraced socialism. His death on 2 June 1882 marked the passing of Italy's great military leader and famous hero of *risorgimento*.

References: Parris, John, *The Lion of Caprera*, 1962; Ridley, Jaspar, *Garibaldi*, 1974; Smith, D. Mack, *Garbaldi: A Great Life in Brief*, 1956.

Giap, Vo Nguyen
(b. 1912)
Vietnam

As a young boy, Vo Nguyen Giap had a fascination with military strategy and knew every detail of Napoleon's battles. As a revolutionary, he won his own military fame, beating the French at Dien Bien Phu and later defeating South Vietnam and the United States.

Vo Nguyen Giap was born 1 September 1912 at An Xa, a village in central Vietnam. His father, a peasant, worked at growing rice. The young Giap grew up under an oppressive French colonial regime. By the 1900s, nationalism stirred in Vietnam, and at age 14 Giap joined a secret nationalistic group, the Tan Viet Cach Menh Dang, at Hue, where he attended high school. Giap conversed frequently with a legendary nationalist, Phan Boi Chau, from whom he adopted many anticolonialist views.

The French arrested Giap in 1930 for his revolutionary activity but released him after a few months. He then enrolled at the Lycée Albert Sarraut in Hanoi and graduated from the University of Hanoi in 1937 with a law degree. He wrote articles for two nationalist newspapers and taught history at the Lycée Thanh Long, where he also effectively proselytized his revolutionary views. Here he showed, too, his detailed grasp of Napoleon's battles.

Around this time, Giap joined the Indochinese Communist Party, founded by HO CHI MINH. In 1939, he escaped French persecution of the party members by fleeing to China. The French, however, captured his wife and sister-in-law. They sentenced his wife to a life term for her political activities, and in 1942 she died in prison; they guillotined his sister-in-law.

Giap joined with Ho Chi Minh in China and became his military aide. Together they formed the Vietnam Doc Lap Dong Minh Hoa (League for the Independence of Vietnam), dedicated to liberating Vietnam from foreign control and developing a socialist state. This group became popularly known as the Viet Minh.

Giap built a Viet Minh liberation army in China and allied with Chu Van Tan, leader of the Tho, a tribal group in mountainous northern Vietnam. Chu Van Tan had already begun fighting against the French and had won an important battle. In 1944, Giap staged a bold raid on two French security posts, overrunning them and earning notoriety for his fledgling militia.

During World War II, the Viet Minh assisted the United States against the Japanese, with Giap's troops helping to find downed American pilots and joining in battles. Under Giap, the Viet Minh gained control of the countryside, and in August 1945 they entered Hanoi, capturing it from the Japanese. At that time, Ho declared Vietnam an independent nation—the Democratic Republic of Vietnam—and made Giap minister of the interior (with Chu Van Tan minister of defense).

France, however, refused to recognize this development and determined to maintain a grip on Vietnam. The French reached an agreement with Ho in 1946, granting Vietnam some autonomy but continuing French economic domination. The agreement unravelled when many Viet Minh balked and when the French began violating it. Conflicts between French and Viet Minh forces followed, and on 20 December 1946 Ho called for a war of national resistance. Giap, commander of the Viet Minh army, now also became minister of defense.

Giap built his army into an effective fighting force. He realized that any war against France would likely be lengthy, and he taught his men to prepare for it. He stressed guerrilla warfare to stretch out the enemy and attack its vulnerable points. He believed in ambush and diversion and a defensive effort to prepare for a later offensive stage with more conventional combat.

"The life or death of a hundred . . . tens of thousands . . . even our compatriots, means little."

In 1954, he scored a stunning victory when he defeated a French army of 12,000 men at Dien Bien Phu. In this effort, his troops had dragged massive howitzers up mountainous slopes—his military had little mechanization—and aimed them at the French gathered in the valley below. The defeat convinced the French to end their rule and led, in the same year, to the Geneva Accords that called for national elections to unify Vietnam in 1956. The United States, however, sabotaged the elections and they were never held. This caused Vietnamese in the south, where the United States had established a government at odds with the Viet Minh, to organize a group, called the Viet Cong, with its goal to liberate the region.

By 1965, the United States committed ground troops to South Vietnam, and Giap sent divisions of Viet Minh regulars to fight them. He took over direct planning of the war in 1967 and masterminded another stunning military move: As at Dien Bien Phu, he decoyed the enemy. This time, he made the Americans believe he was preparing to attack at Khe Sanh. But he diverted his troops, and beginning on 31 January 1968, during the Tet religious holiday, he assaulted American forces throughout South Vietnam, even gaining access to the United States Embassy in Saigon.

Although the United States beat back the attackers, Giap had shown that despite years of American air attacks and the presence of 500,000 ground troops, the Vietnamese revolutionaries had widespread support and could strike most anywhere. Giap believed that militarily the war had reached a stalemate, but he intended to fight decades longer, if necessary, and bleed the U.S. forces dry. In America, Tet fueled the antiwar movement and helped convince President Lyndon Johnson to begin negotiations with Ho for an eventual withdrawal of American forces.

Giap continued leading his troops to victory, forcing the Americans to leave Vietnam in 1973 and bringing the collapse of South Vietnam two years later. At last, Vietnam was unified and free from foreign rule. In 1976, Giap became minister of defense and deputy prime minister in the new government, positions he held until 1980. He also served on the powerful politburo of the Viet-

namese Communist Party until 1982, when a stagnant economy encouraged more youthful party members to retire several of the older leaders. Giap was subsequently hailed as one of the greatest military leaders in world history.

References: Kahin, George McTurna., *Intervention: How America Became Involved in Vietnam,* 1987; Karnow, Stanley, *Vietnam: A History,* 1983; O'Neill, Robert J., *General Giap,* 1969; Sheehan, Neil, *A Bright Shining Lie: John Paul Vann and America in Vietnam,* 1988; Vo Nguyen Giap, *Dien Bien Phu,* 1962; Vo Nguyen Giap, *People's War, People's Army,* 1961.

Gligorov, Kiro
(b. 1917)
Macedonia

As a Communist, Kiro Gligorov wanted to see socialist Yugoslavia continue, but as the nation fell apart, he supported Macedonian nationalism while rejecting demands for a greater Bulgaria.

Kiro Gligorov was born on 3 May 1917 in Stip. He attended the University of Belgrade where, after graduating, he taught economics. In those years his homeland was under Serbian control. During World War II, Gligorov fought against the Nazis and supported the creation of Yugoslavia, a nation welded together largely by Josip Broz Tito. Gligorov served in Tito's Communist government, first in 1946 as deputy secretary-general, then in 1947 as assistant minister of finance. Eight years later, he became deputy general of the Executive Council for General Economic Affairs. He continued to rise in government circles after that, applying his economic expertise. From 1962 until 1967, he served as federal secretary for finance and from 1967 to 1969, as vice-president of the Federal Executive Council. In the late 1970s, he became president of the Yugoslav Parliament, deputy prime minister, and finance minister.

> *"This is all we seek from the European Community—to . . . recognize the Republic of Macedonia."*

Upon Tito's death in 1980, conditions changed in Yugoslavia. Leadership was turned over to a collective presidency that lacked the power to contain the ethnic and religious tensions traditionally a part of the Balkan Peninsula. By 1990, Yugoslavia was disintegrating—much to Gligorov's regret. He did not display the intense nationalism expressed by neighboring Serbia and Bosnia. He considered that, as a poor country, Macedonia's best interest was to remain in a federation with cooperative economic ties.

Late in 1990, Gligorov ran for a seat in Parliament as a member of the League of Communists of Macedonia–Party for Democratic Transformation (LCM–PDT, later called the Social Democratic Alliance). He won the election and his party captured 31 seats, finishing second to the Internal Macedonian Revolutionary Organization–Democratic Party for Macedonian National Unity (IMRO–DPMNU), which won 37 seats. The IMRO–DPMNU favored a Greater Bulgaria, a position opposed by the minority Albanian and Muslim populations. In January

1991, the Assembly declared sovereignty, but not complete independence, and with support of the IMRO–DPMNU, Gligorov won election as Macedonia's president.

Even as Yugoslavia collapsed, Gligorov sought to keep Macedonia linked to some type of federation. But tensions worsened among Serbia, Croatia, and Slovenia, and in September, Macedonians voted in a referendum for nationhood. Parliament declared independence on 9 September, and on 17 November it approved a constitution.

Gligorov immediately confronted a formidable crisis: Neighboring Greece protested the use of the name "Macedonia" as duplicating the name attached to its northern province. Furthermore, the Greeks believed that Gligorov's nation chose "Macedonia" because it intended to annex Greek territory. Greece thus refused to recognize Macedonia, worked to block its entry into the United Nations, and began economic pressure, such as boycotts. Gligorov traveled extensively to gain recognition for his nation. In 1992, he won the support of Bulgaria, Turkey, and Russia. Recognition finally came in 1993 from the European Community and the United States.

Gligorov faced a worsening economic situation. Inflation hit 200 percent and unemployment soared. He pushed for expanded ties with other European nations and especially the former Yugoslav republics. War in the Balkans, however, threatens Macedonia's security, and observers wonder if Gligorov can maintain the loyalty of the minority Albanians, who prefer linkage with their homeland, and control the continuing tensions with Greece.

References: Cvicc, Christopher, *Remaking the Balkans,* 1991; Kaplan, Robert D., *Balkan Ghosts: A Journey through History,* 1993.

Göncz, Árpád
(b. 1922)
Hungary

A writer turned political activist, turned president—for many Hungarians Árpád Göncz represented the moral consciousness of their nation against communist domination; for many, he embodied Hungarian nationalism, the yearning in this proud land for a truly independent country.

In 1922, Árpád Göncz was born in Budapest and grew up while Hitler was rising to power in Germany. When Hungary officially allied with Hitler, Göncz deserted the Hungarian army and joined the anti-Nazi underground. He was wounded by the Germans in 1944.

After the war, he earned a law degree and joined the Independent Smallholders' Party, a group that advocated land reform, for whom he edited the party newspaper. The Smallholders won a majority in the first postwar elections, but in 1948 the Communists gained power, and the Soviet Union dominated Hungary. Göncz criticized the Communists and the end of free elections, and the government responded by denying him employment except in menial positions. He worked on farms and also as a welder and pipe fitter.

The repression Göncz suffered did not stifle his criticism; in fact, it strengthened it, and in 1956 he participated in a widespread revolt to liberalize the regime and topple Soviet domination—a rebellion that Göncz later called the high point of his life, one that gave his existence essential meaning. The Russians responded to the protestors by occupying Budapest and crushing the rebellion. The Hungarian government then arrested Göncz and charged him with treason. He was sentenced to a life term in prison as part of a purge that, all told, resulted in 25,000 imprisonments and 2,000 executions.

While in jail, Göncz learned English with the help of books brought to him by his wife. Around 1960, he began working from his prison cell translating English works into Hungarian for the interior department, including World War II memoirs and the speeches of John F. Kennedy. After this, he translated *The Forsyte Saga,* a novel by John Galsworthy. His wife smuggled the completed manuscript out of prison and had it published, earning Göncz his first money as a translator. He later claimed that prison was endurable because his nation's best minds were there.

In 1963, the government released Göncz during a general amnesty for political prisoners. He then translated more works, using the money earned to help his children attend college. Among others, he translated the works of E. L. Doctorow, William Faulkner, Ernest Hemingway, William Styron, John Updike, and Edith Wharton. Over time, Göncz also wrote six plays, several short stories, and a novel.

When in the late 1980s the Soviet Empire crumbled, Göncz joined other dissidents in calling for open elections in Hungary. That desire was met, and in May 1990 the nation's legislature convened, the first freely elected one in 40 years. The Democratic Forum, a center-right party, held the majority and JÓZSEF ANTALL JR. became prime minister. But the Forum agreed to support Göncz for the less powerful presidency in order to establish unity with the party Göncz had founded, the Free Democrats. Göncz obtained 339 of the 370 votes in the National Assembly to become president.

In 1990, Göncz traveled to the United States where he met President George Bush and received an honorary degree from the University of Indiana. Göncz, also head of Hungary's National Writers' Association, conferred with several American authors.

As Hungary's president, Göncz supported a neutral foreign policy and his nation's withdrawal from the Soviet-led Warsaw Pact. He proved to be an outspoken executive, often criticizing the Democratic Forum as too authoritarian. In one instance, he refused to sign orders issued by Antall to dismiss some of the heads of the state-run radio and television stations. Although Göncz supported privatization, he warned that its social costs had to be addressed, particularly the high unemployment among Hungary's young people. In May 1994, the legislative elections resulted in a majority for the Socialists, formerly the Communists, but Göncz continues in office and seeks to help steer a moderate reform program.

Reference: Hoensch, Jorg, *A History of Modern Hungary, 1867–1986,* 1988.

Gorbachev, Mikhail
(b. 1931)
Russia

In 1985, Mikhail Gorbachev, recently named leader of the Soviet Union, stunned Westerners when he visited Canada and engaged in a frank discussion with members of that nation's Parliament. Never before had a Communist ruler seemed so outgoing, intellectual, and committed to reform. The meeting displayed Gorbachev's desire to change the Soviet Union in ways he could control—but just five years later, impersonal forces overpowered him, the Soviet Union collapsed, and he stood politically obsolete.

Mikhail Gorbachev was born on 2 March 1931 in Privolnoye, a village in the northern Caucasus of the Soviet Union. For many years, the region in which he lived, Krasnogvardeisky, had exhibited an independent spirit; it did not willingly accept the 1917 Communist revolution, and it resisted Joseph Stalin's collectivization program. Perhaps something of this atmosphere influenced young Mikhail, for despite his loyalty to communism he desired substantial changes in the system.

Mikhail's parents were peasants, and as a boy he endured many hardships. Possessing little money, he had to combine schooling with farm work. At age ten, he witnessed German troops invade Krasnogvardeisky amid World War II. His father fought against the Germans, an action Mikhail referred to proudly in future years.

The war devastated Mikhail's homeland and necessitated even harder work to raise a crop. He excelled at the challenge, however, and in 1949 earned the Order of the Red Banner for his contribution to that year's harvest. At the same time, he did well in school, earning a silver medal for his work, and in 1950 he entered law school at the Soviet Union's prestigious Moscow State University.

Law was not a leading field in the Communist nation, but Mikhail apparently considered it a vehicle for his political goals. Fellow students considered him friendly, outgoing, and ambitious—looking to advance in the Communist hierarchy. The young man found his first professional outlet in the Komsomol, or Communist Youth League, in which he became active as an organizer, and in 1952 he joined the Communist Party.

Gorbachev graduated from law school in 1955 and then advanced rapidly and impressively. He served as first secretary of the Komsomol in Stavropol from 1956 to 1958, and in the latter year became the organization's first secretary for the entire Stavropol region. He then shifted his efforts to the Communist Party and in 1962 worked as an organizer for the collective farm administration, thus returning to his rural background. At the same time, he attended Stavropol Agricultural Institute, where he studied agronomy. In 1966, he became first secretary for Stavropol and the following year obtained his agronomy degree. Just three years later, he was the party's first secretary for the Stavropol region and in 1971 was named a member of the Central Committee of the Communist Party—a young man within a politically powerful body dominated by older leaders.

During his tenure in Stavropol, he gained a substantial following among workers on the collectives. He introduced reforms that allowed the farmers more power in making decisions and encouraged larger private plots, where they could grow food for the open market. His measures increased production, and this won the attention of party officials. Fyodor Kulakov, the agriculture sec-

retary, noticed Gorbachev's talent and promoted his career. So, too, did Yuri Andropov, who later became the Soviet Union's leader as Communist Party general-secretary, the most powerful position in the nation. Gorbachev's good standing with influential men was evident in the 1970s, when party officials sent him overseas on three occasions, including in 1976 as head of a delegation visiting Paris.

Gorbachev's career progressed again in 1978 when Fyodor Kulakov died. The party chose Gorbachev to fill Kulakov's position—once more unusual for a man so young. The following year, while still serving as agriculture secretary, he gained appointment to the Politburo, the party's inner circle, as a nonvoting member. In this position he applied his law background and, as requested by the Communist leadership, proposed new rules for the Supreme Court and the Prosecutor's Office. In 1978, he backed the decision to send Soviet troops into Afghanistan in support of the Communist regime fighting a rebellion.

As agriculture secretary, Gorbachev faced a major problem: Grain harvests had dropped precipitously. He applied innovations, such as decentralizing decision making and awarding workers monetarily for production increases. Although the harvests continued poorly, in 1980 Gorbachev advanced to full membership in the Politburo and championed a new agricultural plan that resulted in yet more freedom for the farmers to develop private plots. This approach, criticized by conservatives as too radical and injurious to the collectives, lasted less than a year.

Meanwhile, Leonid Brezhnev, the Communist Party's general-secretary, suffered deteriorating health. He died in 1982 and Yuri Andropov, Gorbachev's mentor, became the new secretary.

Gorbachev's power subsequently increased, and he ranked as one of only three men who held both a Politburo position and a position as a national party secretary. Gorbachev helped Andropov carry out a purge of corrupt officials—considered necessary as the economy worsened and the party stagnated—and the general-secretary revived Gorbachev's plan to increase agricultural production through incentives.

As Andropov's health worsened throughout 1983, Gorbachev assumed more duties, making important speeches and leading a delegation to Canada, where he confronted the members of Parliament. Many observers believed that Gorbachev would succeed Andropov, but when the leader died the party chose another from among its Old Guard, Konstantin Chernenko. Gorbachev supported Chernenko, while taking charge of ideology and economics. In 1984, he added to his duties when he became chairman of the Foreign Affairs Committee of the Supreme Soviet (the national legislature), a development that displayed his diverse expertise and confirmed his importance beyond agricultural matters.

Then suddenly, in March 1985, another shock hit the Soviet leadership—Chernenko died. Although Gorbachev had substantial power, it was not at all clear that he would become the new general-secretary. Several in the Old Guard opposed him, but in the end, the Politburo elevated him. Gorbachev set about changing the personnel and structure of the Soviet system, making appointments to the Politburo and bringing fresh blood into prominent positions, such as naming EDUARD SHEVARDNADZE as his foreign minister. Perhaps nothing so symbolized the need for reform than the catastrophic meltdown at the Chernobyl nuclear power plant in 1986—a disaster stemming from shoddy procedures and one whose initial cover-up resulted in additional casualties.

As Gorbachev faced enormous internal challenges, he pursued an easing of tensions with the United States. He met several times with the American president, Ronald Reagan, and negotiated arms control measures. In all, Soviet-American relations improved considerably.

Within the Soviet Union, pressures intensified from troublesome forces that had permeated the land for many years. Since the fifteenth century, when IVAN III founded the Russian state, expansion and consolidation had been tempered by fragmentation and dissonance. The masses felt alienated in an autocratic system, a feeling that intensified as their economic suffering and loss of autonomy increased in the sixteenth and seventeenth centuries under PETER I and CATHERINE II. At the same time, as the Russian state expanded in size, it encompassed an ethnically diverse population that often found itself at odds with Russian and, in general, Slavic

culture. In 1917, the Russian Revolution established the Communist Soviet Union, whose leaders believed their system would end the nation's economic problems and unify its people behind an idealistic crusade against capitalism. The economy, however, did not perform as desired and ethnic pressures continued.

Thus in many ways Gorbachev, like previous Russian leaders, fell victim to forces well beyond his control. Yet he also unleashed new ones—intended to save the Soviet Union but actually contributing to its demise. In short, he became the unwilling creator of a revolution. This materialized with his policies of *glasnost* and *perestroika*. The first meant openness, the latter meant reform.

With *glasnost*, Gorbachev allowed intellectual and political debate. Books previously banned in the Soviet Union were now allowed, including critical works by the prominent Russian dissident, Aleksandr Solzhenitsyn. Newspapers displayed editorials questioning government policies and people gathered at meetings where they freely debated issues.

> *"In short, comrades, what we are talking about is a new role for public opinion in this country."*

With *perestroika*, Gorbachev pursued extensive political and economic change. In 1989, he initiated competitive elections for a new Congress of Peoples' Deputies, which had the responsibility of electing the more powerful Supreme Soviet. Furthermore, whereas in the past the Supreme Soviet seldom met—the Politburo within the Communist Party approved all major decisions—it now was to convene regularly. The same year, Gorbachev added to his duties that of chairman of the Supreme Soviet, meaning he served as the legislature's speaker. More importantly, in 1990 the Supreme Soviet created the office of national president as a powerful position and made it elective—a crucial development in weakening the Politburo. (This office existed previously, but as a ceremonial one, usually held by the party's general-secretary.) Initially, Gorbachev was elected to the presidency by the Congress of Peoples' Deputies, but subsequent elections were to be by popular vote.

Gorbachev also promoted an increased role for leaders from the republics that made up the Soviet Union. They represented different ethnic groups, and Gorbachev intended to calm their secessionist desires.

In the economy, Gorbachev lessened the state's role and developed plans to introduce free-market practices. He moved cautiously, however, ever fearful that reforms, such as the end to price controls and guaranteed jobs, would lead to inflation and unemployment, and consequently social unrest.

Overall, *glasnost* encouraged criticism, and rather than calm separatist desires in the outlying republics, it intensified ethnic pride and nationalism. *Perestroika,* despite its modest nature, produced economic dislocation and angered both conservatives, who detected an assault against Communism, and liberals, who believed the economy needed quicker, more extensive change—a "shock treatment." Gorbachev seemed unable to advance beyond his Communist outlook, his belief that the system in which he advanced his career should not be totally dismantled. Furthermore, by 1990, his effort to subordinate the military to other interests produced rumblings of discontent from powerful generals.

Amid these developments, the Soviet domination of Eastern Europe collapsed. Forces similar to those in the U.S.S.R. had been at work there, and nations such as Poland, Hungary, and Czechoslovakia ended their Communist regimes and exerted their independence. As promoter of *glasnost,* and beset with internal difficulties, Gorbachev, for the most part, let these nations go their own way, even agreeing to the reunification of Germany. He took a firmer stand toward the Baltic republics, where many ethnic Russians lived, but these nations also gained their independence.

At home, Gorbachev faced an uprising in the Russian Republic, the largest of the Soviet republics, when its leader, BORIS YELTSIN, demanded more radical reform. Then on 19 August 1991, con-servative Communists tried to overthrow Gorbachev. They isolated him while he was away from Moscow and cut his communications. Yeltsin, however, rallied the Russian people, promoting a general strike and huge demonstrations. His supporters surrounded and fortified the Parliament building. On 21 August, the coup attempt collapsed and Gorbachev resumed his presidency. Within days, he resigned as general-secretary, and the government suspended all Communist Party activities. Meanwhile, several republics declared their independence, including Russia, Ukraine, and Kazakhstan, and others prepared to do the same.

Yeltsin, not Gorbachev, emerged the hero. His courageous stand and his call for democracy and a market economy won him an enormous following. At the same time, the coup attempt was the death blow to the Soviet Union, which formally collapsed in December 1991. Gorbachev and Yeltsin cooperated in forming the Commonwealth of Independent States, a loose confederation consisting of Russia and ten other former Soviet republics. With the Soviet Union defunct and Yeltsin as Russia's leader—confirmed by a huge election victory just weeks before—Gorbachev retired from the political scene.

Although a reluctant revolutionary, Gorbachev proved crucial in advancing massive change. *Glasnost* and *perestroika,* added to other forces, produced a new Russia, which faces a troubling future.

References: Butson, Thomas G., *Gorbachev: A Biography,* 1985; Smith, Hedrick, *The New Russians,* 1990; Talbott, Strobe, et al., *Mikhail S. Gorbachev: An Intimate Biography,* 1988.

Gorbunovs, Anatolijs
(b. 1942)
Latvia

Although as a young man Anatolijs Gorbunovs joined the Communist Party, he always prized his Latvian heritage, and in the late 1980s, he took a bold stand to break with the Soviet Union.

Anatolijs Gorbunovs was born in 1942 in Latvia's Ludza district. At that time, the Soviet Union controlled Latvia, having acquired it by force in 1940. As a boy, Gorbunovs joined the Komsomol, or Communist Youth League, and later the Communist Party. Gorbunovs worked as a construction engineer from 1959 to 1962, at which point he entered the army. Soon after leaving the military in 1965, he enrolled in the Riga Polytechnic Institute, where he obtained a degree in 1970. He then studied at the Moscow Social Sciences Academy. From 1978 until 1982, he served as first secretary of the Latvian Communist Party, and after that held several important positions within the organization. In 1985, he became secretary of the party's Central Committee, in charge of ideology. Gorbunovs did not side with the Communist conservative wing, but rather supported reform. This position made him enormously popular among Latvians, who considered Soviet rule oppressive. Indeed, the Russians had suppressed Latvian culture and given important leadership positions to Russified Latvians.

In 1988, the Popular Front of Latvia appeared, challenged the Communist Party, and the following year, scored an election victory so big that Gorbunovs became chairman of the Latvian Supreme Soviet, or Parliament. Gorbunovs steered Latvia toward independence, but decided he would avoid the extreme stand taken by the other Baltic states in their drive for nationhood. Unlike Estonia and Lithuania, he refused to suspend the Soviet constitution. Instead, when in May 1990 Parliament declared it would restore Latvia to its status as a nation, Gorbunovs announced that the Soviet constitution would remain in effect until the independence process was complete. He expected his move would forestall a full-scale Soviet invasion, but thousands of Soviet troops were sent into the country and an economic embargo was imposed.

In January 1991, a Russian paramilitary unit attacked Latvian government buildings in Riga. After four people died, Latvians barricaded the buildings to protect them, and the Russians backed away. Gorbunovs presided over a referendum in March through which Latvians overwhelmingly supported independence. When conservatives in Moscow tried in August to overthrow the Soviet government, Gorbunovs announced his opposition to the coup. After the rebels failed, his position in Latvia and with the Soviet leaders was strengthened. During this upheaval, Latvia officially declared its independence, and in September, the Soviets recognized it as a nation. Three months later, the Soviet Union dissolved.

Gorbunovs allowed political party development, and he privatized areas of the economy. In foreign relations, he developed closer ties to Scandinavia and sought membership in the European Community. Gorbunovs continued economic ties to Russia, particularly in acquiring oil. The large Russian minority within Latvia was a challenge to him, and he had to balance that ethnic group with the Latvians to maintain national unity. In 1993, Gorbunovs lost his reelection bid.

> *"Neither a new constitution for the republic nor economic laws will be adopted without consulting with everyone . . ."*

References: Brown, Archie, ed., *The Soviet Union: A Biographical Dictionary*, 1990: Loeber, Dietrich Andre, et al., *Regional Identity under Soviet Rule: The Case of the Baltic States*, 1990.

Gouled, Hassan
(b. 1916)
Djibouti

Buffeted by ethnic rivalries and external pressures, Hassan Gouled nevertheless held his people together to begin building a nation in an impoverished, barren land.

In 1916, Hassan Gouled was born in Djibouti Town. He grew up receiving little formal education. At the time, France ruled his homeland, which was then part of French Somaliland, and Gouled spent most of his adult life in politics, representing Djibouti in the French Senate from 1952 to 1958, and then in the French National Assembly until 1962. In the latter year, he returned to Djibouti and served as minister of education under Ali Aref.

"There will be no tribal constitution."

Shortly thereafter he broke with Aref and supported independence. Aref was an Afar, and Gouled came from the Issa ethnic group, which for years had been at odds with the Afars. (In the 1960s, France renamed this land the French Territory of Afar and Issa.) The Issas resented the French for erecting a fence around the town of Djibouti to keep them out. They also resented election laws that gave the Afars representation disproportionate to their numbers and protected their dominant power. Gouled founded the African People's League for Independence (LPAI) to challenge the largely pro-French Afars.

In 1975, France announced its intention to pull out of French Somaliland, and Ali Aref organized his Afar followers into a new party, the National Union for Independence (UNI), even though the Afars supported nationhood reluctantly and still desired close ties with the French. In 1976, tensions mounted when guerrillas highjacked a bus carrying 30 French schoolchildren. Aref blamed neighboring Somalia for the attack (the Somalis had designs on Djibouti) and accused Gouled and the LPAI of being in league with them. Gouled then sponsored mass demonstrations in support of independence.

Aref's position became untenable when several members of his cabinet resigned. They criticized Aref's obstructionism in the movement toward independence and asserted that an Afar-Issa coalition government was needed to reduce ethnic rivalry. In July 1976, while Aref clung to office, armed clashes occurred between Afars and Issas. Later that month, the Djibouti legislature removed Aref from office, while Gouled called for independence early in 1977, reform of the election system, and dismantling of the fence around Djibouti Town.

On 24 June 1977, the Djibouti Chamber of Deputies named Gouled their nation's first president, and three days later Djibouti officially became independent. Gouled named an Afar as prime minister (most power was held by the president) and appointed several Afars to his cabinet to build widespread support. He had, however, a stiff challenge from militant Afars who organized in Ethiopia and attacked across the border. He also confronted the Djibouti Popular Liberation Movement (MPL), a Marxist Afar group that was blamed for bombing a cafe and killing several people. Gouled outlawed the MPL, arrested its leaders, and ruled by decree. His Afar ministers then resigned, although early in 1978 several of them returned to the cabinet.

Gouled presided over a nation with few natural resources and with an economy heavily dependent on outside aid from France and Saudi Arabia. Unemployment hovered around 40 percent, and to ease this situation Gouled promoted Djibouti as a free port for neighboring nations. He acquired money to expand the shipping facilities, but unemployment in Djibouti Town reached 80 percent, and refugees from the Ethiopian-Somalian war produced additional burdens.

In the 1980s, Gouled continued to tackle the vexing economic problem, while maintaining an ethnically mixed cabinet and allowing representation from several political parties. He rejected Afar attempts to dilute his authority and create a powerful prime ministry, a move he believed would inhibit national identity and favor tribalism. In fact, he worked to "detribalize" his country and in 1980 dismantled the LPAI to form a party encompassing both Issas and Afars, called the Popular Assembly for Progress.

Gouled also traveled the Arab world, where he obtained additional aid for Djibouti, and brought his nation into the Arab League, a move that resulted in substantial financial and technical help. He also improved relations with Ethiopia, important because that nation used the Djibouti port as an outlet to the sea. In all, Gouled estab-lished stability in a nation few outside observers considered a candidate for survival. He won re-election in 1993 and continues in office.

Reference: Tholomier, Robert, *Djibouti: Pawn of the Horn of Africa*, 1981.

Guèye, Lamine
(1891–1968)
Senegal

A man of intellectual brilliance, Lamine Guèye helped modernize Senegal's politics after World War II and propelled his country toward in-dependence. Yet his status as a privileged member of the citizen class under French rule eventually caused him political problems.

Lamine Guèye was born in 1891 in Médine and, because of his family's background, was one of those select black Africans whom the French colo-nial power designated a "citizen"—a status that en-abled him to vote for candidates in representative bodies, including the city councils, and to hold po-litical office. (These rights were extended to other blacks in the mid-1940s.) Senegal was the only colony in which France allowed such participation, which dated back to the mid-nineteenth century when the French placated black mercantile interests by allowing them a political role in Senegal's cities (a policy not followed in the countryside).

In the early 1920s, Guèye studied law in Paris. He returned home determined to gain more political power for the Senegalese, particularly for younger men who were shut out of the existing power struc-ture. He obtained substantial political experience when, in 1925, he won election as mayor of Saint Louis, a position he held for two years. In 1928, he called for a new local political leadership that would support developing public housing and organizing labor unions. That year, he also made his first con-tacts with the French Socialist Party. Then in 1931, wanting to advance his legal career, Guèye accepted appointment by the French government as a judge at Réunion, an island located in the Indian Ocean.

After his return, Guèye formed Senegal's first modern political party in 1936, the Senegalese So-cialist Party. It became an important political force in association with the French Socialist Party (SFIO). In 1945, Guèye and his colleague LÉOPOLD SÉDAR SENGHOR won seats in the French National Assembly. Senghor owed his victory largely to Guèye's efforts. Shortly thereafter, Guèye's SFIO won a majority in Senegal's territorial legislature. As a delegate, Guèye pushed for extending to black Africans the same rights enjoyed by Frenchmen.

The SFIO splintered in 1948 when Senghor left to form the Senegalese Democratic Bloc (BDS). Sen-ghor had protested Guèye's close ties with the French Socialists as infringing on Senegalese au-thority. He also believed the SFIO leadership re-flected the power and interests still held by the old "citizen" elite as opposed to the majority of blacks, who, like him, were commoners.

Senghor effectively organized the BDS among rural farmers, and it soon emerged as the dominant party. In 1951, Guèye lost his seat in the French As-sembly to the BDS. From this time on, Senghor eclipsed him politically. In 1958, Guèye merged his SFIO with Senghor's party. The following year, France allowed Senegal and its other overseas terri-tories membership in a new French Community. Under this arrangement, Senegal composed its own constitution that established a new National As-sembly. Guèye won election to this Senegalese As-sembly in 1958 and served as its president until his death in Dakar on 10 June 1968.

Reference: Ajayi, J. F. A., and Michael Crowder, eds., *History of West Africa*, 2 volumes, 1974.

Gustav II

(1594–1632)
Sweden

Contemporaries called Gustav II "The Lion of the North." Devoutly religious, he led an army that sang hymns as it marched through Europe; and while fighting to make the Baltic a Swedish sea and protect Protestantism, he laid the foundations for modern Sweden.

Gustav (or Gustavus Adolphus, a name by which he is widely known) was born in Stockholm on 9 December 1594. A mere 17 years later, he succeeded his father, Charles IX, as king of Sweden. At the time, turmoil beset Sweden, both internally and externally. Within the country, Charles had ruled arbitrarily and harshly, and the nobles subsequently pressed for constitutional reforms. They forced Gustav to promise he would consult their representative body, the Estates, before undertaking any important action. This was stated in a charter that Gustav signed in 1612. By an organic law promulgated in 1617, the country's four main classes—nobles, clergy, burghers, and peasants—had their positions in society defined, with the nobles protecting an exclusive right to hold high office (a right stated formally in a later law).

Outside the country, Charles had embroiled Sweden in wars against Poland, Russia, and Denmark—wars still under way when Gustav became king. The war with Denmark had gone badly, and Gustav decided to end it quickly. He signed the Peace of Knäred in 1613, by which he relinquished claims to the Arctic coastline of Scandinavia, and for a large monetary payment, one that crippled Sweden financially, gained possession of Älvsborg, a fortress that guarded Sweden's access to the Atlantic.

He also suspended the war against Poland so he could turn his attention to the continuing conflict with Russia. From this war he learned much about military strategy. The results on the battlefield proved mixed, but when Russia experienced internal difficulties, Gustav altered his objectives from a defensive emphasis to the acquisition of territory. The Peace of Stolbova in 1617 gave him In-

"If I draw a pail of water from the Baltic, am I supposed to be desirous of drinking up the whole sea?"

gria and Kexholm and blocked Russia from the Baltic Sea, thus protecting Swedish interests there.

Coincident with his war acitivities, Gustav supported additional reforms within Sweden that established a modernized state. Working with his chancellor, Axel Oxenstierna, he organized the government into departments, each headed by an official responsible to the king. Indeed, Gustav stressed a businesslike administration with full-time civil servants. In 1614, he created a court of appeals that standardized the judiciary. He also improved education: Secondary schools, or gymnasiums, were founded in the cities, and Gustav supported the teaching of modern subjects such as law, history, politics, mathematics, and science. In the 1620s, he gave land to the University of Uppsala, which saved it financially. At Gustav's insistence, the university increased its endowed chairs and broadened its course offerings. Later, he established the University of Dorpat in Swedish Estonia, an important center of learning, especially in training graduates to serve in the civil administration.

He reformed the military, stressing Sweden's power as a maritime nation. By 1624, the Swedish fleet reached parity with the Danes. Gustav's navy had bigger ships, heavier guns, and more recruits than under Charles IX. Gustav introduced new weapons into the army and reformed the draft system so as to greatly reduce exemptions.

Gustav also vigorously developed the Swedish economy. New industries appeared, often tied to his military needs. Copper production expanded to the point that Sweden had nearly a monopoly on the product in Europe, and iron also became a leading export. Gustav even developed new cities to encourage commerce within his country. This was financed substantially by Dutch capital and displayed the shift under way in Europe from a precommercial medieval economy to a capitalist one. In all, Gustav got along well with the budding merchants and the nobles who recognized in the king a leader willing and equipped to support a more participatory state, one different from Charles's reign.

In 1621, shortly after he married Maria Eleonora of Brandenburg, Gustav had renewed his war with Poland. He wanted to effectually end the claims of a ruler there, Sigismund, to the Swedish throne. He also desired to protect Protestantism, since the claimant was Catholic. As a devout Lutheran, Gustav saw the various struggles in Europe not only in political terms but also religious ones. Protestants throughout the continent feared the Habsburgs in Germany, who were ardent Catholics, and many looked to Gustav to save their cause.

In Poland, Gustav captured Riga and gained Livonia. The Treaty of Altmark ended his efforts there in 1629, and he then focused on the Habsburgs, who had recently defeated Denmark and pushed toward the Baltic. For religious and strategic reasons, Gustav could not let this happen. The Estates in Sweden backed his decision to launch an offensive, and in 1630 the nation entered what later became known as the Thirty Years' War, actually a series of wars that had been under way for some time.

Gustav brought into battle a large army of 23,000 men, highly disciplined and using innovative tactics, including flexible formations and the first easily maneuverable light artillery. He gained some important allies—France, Brandenburg, and Saxony—and in September 1631 a Swedish-Saxon army defeated the Habsburg force led by General Tilly at Breitenfeld. By the end of 1631, Gustav con-trolled half of Germany and aimed to liberate the Protestant Habsburg states in the south. He also developed a plan to create a Protestant League headed by himself. The latter especially worried many Germans (and several European leaders) concerned that he would depose the Habsburg ruler, Ferdinand II (officially the Holy Roman Emperor), and develop a vast new empire. There is, however, no proof he desired this, and in any event the Protestant League did not materialize as an effective organization.

In 1632, Gustav captured Munich. When the enemy launched an attack against Saxony, Gustav responded, and the Battle of Lützen ensued on 6 November. The Swedish army won, but Sweden lost a heroic leader. In the heat of battle, while trying to ease the pressure on his left flank, Gustav led a cavalry charge and was attacked from behind. One enemy soldier shot him in the back, and after he fell from his horse another shot him through the head. Plunderers then stripped his body.

Gustav had protected the Protestants, defended Swedish interests in the Baltic, and developed innovative military techniques. He had created the most advanced administration in Europe and, in this, stood above his predecessors in establishing the modern Swedish nation.

References: Ahnlund, Nils, *Gustav Adolf the Great*, 1940; Roberts, Michael, *Gustavus Adolphus and the Rise of Sweden*, 1973.

Haile Selassie
(1892–1975)
Ethiopia

The modernization of Ethiopia had begun in the nineteenth century under Emperors Tewodros IV and MENELIK II. Haile Selassie continued this development but in the process unleashed a conflict that eventually ended his 44-year reign.

Haile Selassie was born Tafari Makonnen at Harar in 1892, the son of Ras Makonnen, who hailed from Shewan nobility and was Emperor Menelik's most trusted advisor. As a boy, Tafari journeyed several times to Europe, and he received a largely European-style education. In 1903, Tafari was introduced to the court at Addis Ababa. His father died in 1906, but by this time Tafari had already been appointed a district governor. Emperor

Menelik subsequently made Tafari governor of Salale. At age 17, he became governor of Sidamo. Then in 1911, he obtained the governorship of Harar, where he applied a modernist approach, sponsoring programs to foster economic development and land reform. To weaken old feudal relationships he began a salaried civil service.

In 1913, Menelik's grandson Eyasu became emperor, yet he raised serious concerns both within and outside Ethiopia when he appeared to support Islam. The Ethiopian Christian Church, which was a powerful force in politics, opposed any pro-Islamic leanings, and Britain and other European nations feared that Eyasu might lead an Islamic uprising in East Africa. Consequently, Tafari helped a group of Ethiopian noblemen depose Eyasu in 1916. They proclaimed Menelik's daughter Zauditu empress, and appointed Tafari regent and heir apparent.

Many conservative noblemen expressed wariness toward Tafari's reformist leanings, which they believed could weaken their power. They appointed a conservative minister of war, Habta Giorgis, who kept watch on Tafari. In effect, a ruling triumvirate emerged. Under Tafari's influence Ethiopia became one of the first member countries of the League of Nations. By 1928, Tafari had maneuvered himself into a commanding position over public affairs, and upon Empress Zauditu's death in 1930, Tafari became Emperor Haile Selassie I.

Haile Selassie emphasized modernization. He stressed an efficient army, a trained, centralized bureaucracy, expanded education, and an infusion of European capital. He made progress in each of these areas and in 1931 oversaw enactment of Ethiopia's first constitution. The emperor, however, had to constantly battle the centrifugal forces of Ethiopia's recalcitrant provincial governors.

Haile Selassie faced an external challenge in the 1930s when Italy, as it had during the reign of Menelik II, coveted his nation. Fascist dictator Benito Mussolini believed that conquering Ethiopia would deflect domestic attention from Italy's economic problems. When a border clash occurred between Ethiopian and Italian soldiers late in 1934, Selassie went to the League of Nations for help. But neither Britain nor France, two powerful League members, supported him. Subsequently, in 1935 Italy invaded Ethiopia with 120,000 troops, 350 airplanes, and 100,000 irregulars from surrounding Eritrea and Somalia. They defeated Ethiopia's forces and in seven months swept Haile Selassie from power. In 1936, he fled to exile in London.

Under Italian rule, Ethiopia ceased to exist as an independent nation. Italy poured money into Ethiopia's economic development, including building 2,000 miles of excellent roads. While some Ethiopians cooperated with the Italian occupiers, others formed guerrilla bands and waged war from the secluded hillsides.

Haile Selassie worked with Britain in forming a British-Ethiopian assault force that entered Ethiopia from the Sudan during World War II, attacked the Italian occupiers, and ejected them. Selassie returned as emperor in 1941, his prestige bolstered by his stand against fascism. He continued his modernization program in the 1950s, using professional civil servants trained in Western schools, establishing a new national court system, and promoting a revised constitution. But he did not sweep away the tradition of personal rule. In fact, the constitution of 1955 reaffirmed full sovereignty as vested in the emperor.

Haile Selassie played an important role in African affairs. In 1963, he helped form the Organization of African Unity, and Addis Ababa, the Ethiopian capital, housed its headquarters. He mediated the Algeria-Morocco crisis of 1963 and the southern Sudan crisis of 1972. He also promoted the complete absorption of Eritrea that occurred in 1962 (a move that generated much opposition among Eritreans).

By encouraging economic development and education, Haile Selassie inadvertently set into motion forces that challenged his rule and led to his overthrow. He had placated neither modernists, who believed he had failed to go far enough in promoting change, nor traditionalists, who believed he had undermined conservative practices. Despite his reforms, Haile Selassie relied on personal control. He failed to set long-range goals to deal with problems. Furthermore, he restricted dissent and limited political participation.

While on a state visit to Brazil in 1960, members of the Imperial Guard, backed by a rising tide of social discontent, staged a coup against him, but loyal army and air force senior officers crushed the coup. After this, Haile Selassie feared additional threats to his power, mainly from progressives. He announced new reforms, particularly a land program. This foundered, however, when he failed to adequately back it against the opposition from conservative noblemen.

Protests against Haile Selassie came from three areas. Students, some of them Marxists, complained that he obeyed too many traditionalists; labor grew discontented over low wages and a stagnating economy; and enlisted men and junior officers demanded higher pay and better working conditions. This latter group proved the most effective in its protests. In January 1974, a serious drought and accelerated inflation ignited mutinies within the army. Although Haile Selassie granted pay increases, reformist junior officers demanded additional land reform, a free press, and legalized political parties. The emperor tried to crush this activism, but by then the junior officers had gained substantial power.

In 1974, these dissidents formed the Coordinating Committee of the Armed Forces, Police, and Territorial Army (Derg). The group arrested 300 of Haile Selassie's supporters and forced the emperor to appoint new government ministers. After this success, the Derg charged Haile Selassie with having looted Ethiopia's wealth. On 17 September 1974, the Derg overthrew Haile Selassie and declared itself in power as the Provisional Military Administrative Council (PMAC). Haile Selassie spent the rest of his life as a prisoner in his own palace and died 27 August 1975 under suspicious circumstances.

PMAC subsequently dissolved the legislature, suspended the constitution, made all strikes and demonstrations illegal, and in 1975 declared an end to the monarchy. The government detained labor and education leaders who protested military rule. Lieutenant Colonel Mengistu Haile Mariam emerged as Ethiopia's ruler and began socialist reforms, most notably a land redistribution program that appreciably helped formerly landless peasants. He later adopted a Marxist line and then in 1991 was deposed.

Emperor Haile Selassie did much to establish Ethiopia as a modern nation. He advanced his predecessors' reforms and in so doing promoted a centralized government and weakened the old feudal structure. His efforts in professionalizing the bureaucracy and advancing education have particularly left a substantial impact on Ethiopia.

References: Greenfield, Richard, *Ethiopia: A New Political History*, 1965; Spencer, John H., *Ethiopia at Bay: A Personal Account of the Haile Selassie Years*, 1984.

Hamilton, Alexander
(1757–1804)
United States

Alexander Hamilton thirsted for glory; during the American Revolution he helped lead the assault at Yorktown that resulted in a British surrender. He eventually received the important place in history he always felt beckoned him, and with it the controversy attached to his grandiose style.

Alexander Hamilton's life began in controversy. He was born 11 January 1757 on Nevis, a British colony in the Leeward Islands, and was the offspring of an adulterous relationship between his father, James Hamilton, and his mother, Rachel Fawcett Lavien, who was married to John Lavien (although separated from him). James came from a prominent Scottish family but failed at his business endeavors and, near the time of Alexander's birth, declared bankruptcy. Furthermore, his relationship with Rachel soon unravelled, and in 1765 he abandoned his family, leaving them destitute.

When Rachel died in 1768, young Alexander found himself deserted, and this situation may have shaped his view that life required conquest. The boy's salvation came through the intervention of Nicholas Cruger, a merchant who employed the youngster as a bookkeeper. Alexander had obtained some education from his mother and a clergyman, and to Cruger he seemed unusually bright.

When Cruger departed the island temporarily, he appointed Alexander the manager of his firm, a position that gave the boy substantial authority over businessmen and lawyers many years his senior. Despite his managerial success, Alexander considered his job boring and longed to sail for America and advance his education. The opportunity came in October 1772 after Cruger and Hugh Knox, a Presbyterian clergyman, supported him with money and letters of recommendation.

Like his revolutionary colleague THOMAS PAINE, Hamilton arrived in America only a short time before war erupted against British rule. Already the colonies had been stirred by Parliament's attempts to tax them, the arrival of British troops in the cities, the outbreak of demonstrations and boycotts, and the fervent pleas of Patrick Henry and SAMUEL ADAMS. Hamilton, however, did not immediately embrace revolution; in fact, after gaining some education at a preparatory school in Elizabethtown, New Jersey, he enrolled at King's College (today Columbia University) in New York City, partly because of its Loyalist sympathies. Ironically, revolutionary fervor soon interrupted his college work.

Historians debate the point at which Hamilton adopted a revolutionary position, with some arguing it occurred in 1774, after he journeyed to Boston, studied the situation there, and met with the city's radical leaders. Whatever the case, that summer, at age 17, he began writing articles strongly critical of British actions and in December anonymously authored a prominent pamphlet so perceptive in its analysis that several observers thought it had been penned by an older, more experienced revolutionary.

In March 1776, Hamilton obtained a commission in the New York militia as an artillery commander. He trained his men effectively and fought

"Real liberty is neither found in despotism nor the extremes of democracy, but in moderate governments."

alongside General GEORGE WASHINGTON's troops on Long Island. He participated in their ensuing retreat and won the general's attention for his dedication and intelligence. In March 1777, Washington made Hamilton his aide-de-camp with the rank of lieutenant colonel. Once again, the young man proved insightful, handling an enormous workload and becoming Washington's main advisor. This experience gave him considerable knowledge about America's military and financial condition. In January 1778, he issued a brilliant report on the need to reorganize the army.

Despite his prestige and influence, Hamilton craved the glory of the battlefield and bemoaned his relegation to a desk job. Ambitious and, to a degree, vainglorious, he constantly pushed Washington to grant him a command. When the general proved reluctant, Hamilton provoked a dispute with him and in February 1781 quit as aide-de-camp. The previous year, he had married Elizabeth Schuyler, daughter of Philip Schuyler, one of the most prominent men in New York. The union ended Hamilton's meager financial situation and boosted his social standing. Now he retreated to his home and wrote extensively, including a proposal for a national bank. He expressed his preference for a representative government, but one with a strong executive.

Retirement to home and hearth, however, was not for Hamilton, and he still awaited military glory. Fortunately for the New Yorker, Washington relented and allowed him to lead an infantry regiment attached to the Marquis de Lafayette's force. Late in 1781, Hamilton commanded an attack upon a British redoubt at Yorktown, a successful maneuver whose prominence earned him greater recognition.

As the war neared its end, Hamilton served in the Continental Congress in November 1782, and expressed his disgust with the disorder and weakness of the national government. In 1783, he began practicing law in New York City but continued his interest in national politics. He remained a vocal critic of the Articles of Confederation, condemning them for their ineffectiveness and wary that turmoil and excessive popular power would prevail. When several states proposed a commercial convention at Annapolis in September 1786, Hamilton won appointment as a New York delegate and formulated the plan to hold another meeting in

Philadelphia dedicated to political matters. Hamilton had in mind jettisoning the Articles and writing a new constitution.

A populist uprising in Massachusetts, called Shays' Rebellion, added momentum to the Philadelphia meeting, and as a representative in the New York Assembly, Hamilton got his colleagues to support a constitutional convention. The legislature named him one of the state's three delegates to Philadelphia. At the Constitutional Convention, Hamilton, with such notables as JAMES MADISON and BENJAMIN FRANKLIN present, pushed for a powerful executive, one who could serve for life. As an ardent nationalist, he wanted all state laws subject to federal laws.

Yet he was not a leading figure at the convention; rather, his most important work occurred in New York, where he rallied support for the new constitution through adroit political maneuvering in the state ratification convention, and through his writing of several articles that, along with those of Madison and John Jay, became known as *The Federalist Papers.* Eighty-five in number, they appeared between October 1787 and May 1788.

Meanwhile, he again served in the Confederation Congress as it prepared to accede to the new national government. He supported Washington for the presidency and fully expected a top-level appointment in the administration. In September 1789, Washington chose him to serve as secretary of the treasury.

Hamilton immediately confronted the main problem facing the new government, namely its finances. He crafted his proposals based on three beliefs: first, that financial reform was imperative to the government's survival; second, that loyalty to the government rested far more on economic concerns than patriotic ones; and third, that the wealthy elite must be linked closely to the government.

His proposals entailed assuming the state debts, funding the national debt, establishing a national bank, and levying excise taxes. He believed these measures, each interrelated, would give the elite a stake in the government's survival, for if the government should collapse the bonds held by the elite would decline in value and the money that they invested in the national bank would disappear. Hamilton's proposals passed Congress in 1790 and 1791, but only after great controversy. In particular, Madison and Secretary of State THOMAS JEFFERSON accused him of creating an overbearing national government and an aristocracy.

In building support for his program, Hamilton created the Federalist Party. In opposition to it, Jefferson and Madison organized the Jeffersonian Republicans, or Republican Party (no relation to the modern Republican Party). Differences between these two groups intensified amid the French Revolution. Hamilton considered the Revolution evil, as threatening to undermine order everywhere. Jefferson saw it as good, as an extension of the American Revolution in its fight against entrenched aristocracy. When war erupted between Britain and France, Hamilton, biased toward the British side and opposed to America being pulled into the conflict, convinced Washington to issue a proclamation of neutrality.

Late in 1791, Hamilton presented to Congress his infamous Report on Manufactures. In it, he proposed government help to developing industries through protective tariffs and bounties. The report, cooly received in the agrarian South, further stirred the Republicans, who believed it would bias the national government against agriculture.

Hamilton's financial program caused a protest called the Whiskey Rebellion, when farmers in Pennsylvania refused to pay the tax on distilled liquor. The New Yorker used the uprising to exert national authority, and in 1794 he and Washington led an army into the backwoods. The rebellion collapsed, and Hamilton claimed he had proved the primacy of the federal government.

Meanwhile, the differences between Hamilton and Jefferson had reached a breaking point. The New Yorker constantly interfered in the State Department, and shortly before the Whiskey Rebellion, Jefferson quit the cabinet. Early in 1795, Hamilton resigned, partly because of exhaustion. He never again held public office, although for years he remained the most powerful man in the Federalist Party. He returned to his law practice and was soon making substantially more money than he had while serving in the federal government.

Controversy, however, dogged him and in 1797 opponents charged he had mishandled treasury business. Hamilton denied these accusations but admitted he had paid money to silence the husband of a woman with whom he once had an affair. This infamous scandal involving Maria Reynolds embarrassed Hamilton's wife and encouraged scurrilous remarks about the New Yorker, but his marriage remained intact.

Hamilton tried to secretly direct Washington's successor as president, JOHN ADAMS. He did so by having Secretary of State Timothy Pickering, Secretary of War James McHenry, and Secretary of the

Treasury Oliver Wolcott act as his spies, providing him information and working to undermine Adams's orders. When Adams discovered the situation and criticized Hamilton, the New Yorker broke completely with the president—a fellow Federalist—and set out on a path to destroy him.

In 1798, after it appeared France might attack the United States, Congress enlarged the army and appointed Washington to lead it. Hamilton maneuvered the Virginian into naming him second-in-command, a move that greatly angered Adams. The New Yorker developed grandiose plans to attack South America and establish an American empire there, but before he could act, tensions with France eased, particularly after Adams sent a peace delegation to Paris, a decision Hamilton vehemently opposed.

Hamilton worked hard in 1800 to deny Adams reelection as president. In so doing, he split the Federalist Party and sent the election into the House of Representatives. Congress had to choose the new president from among the two top vote-getters, both Republicans: Jefferson and the New York politician Aaron Burr. Hamilton disliked both men but despised Burr more and so used his power to swing the election to Jefferson.

Thereafter, Hamilton's influence at the national level waned, and in 1802 he began building a new home, The Grange, located in Manhattan, and focused his attention on family matters. Two years later, however, he entered the state political fray by opposing Burr's bid to become governor. He believed that his nemesis intended to join with malcontents in New England and take New York out of the union. Burr lost his bid, and the animosity between the two men grew deeper.

During the election, Burr discovered statements made by Hamilton accusing him of being a dangerous man who could not be trusted. Burr demanded a retraction, but Hamilton refused. There followed on 11 July 1804 a duel between the two men at Weehawken Heights in New Jersey. Burr's shot struck Hamilton, who fell mortally wounded. He was taken to the home of William Bayard in New York City, where he died the next day. Hamilton's quick intelligence and forceful determination had helped gain America's independence and forged a vibrant national government.

References: Cooke, Jacob, *Alexander Hamilton*, 1982; Flexner, James, *The Young Hamilton*, 1978; McDonald, Forrest, *Alexander Hamilton: A Biography*, 1979; O'Brien, Steve, *Alexander Hamilton*, 1989; Rossiter, Clinton, *Alexander Hamilton and the Constitution*, 1964; Stourzh, Gerald, *Alexander Hamilton and the Idea of Republican Government*, 1970.

Havel, Václav
(b. 1936)
Czech Republic

A playwright who became a revolutionary—that is the unusual path followed by Václav Havel. Although his outspoken criticism of communism brought him imprisonment and restrictions that forced him to take menial jobs, he never shirked his fight for freedom, which gained momentum and prominence after an incident involving a rock group.

Václav Havel was born to wealthy parents on 5 October 1936 in Prague. His father owned extensive real estate and operated a prominent restaurant. Yet this wealth worked against Václav when, in 1948, the Communists gained control of Czechoslovakia. They confiscated his family's properties (reducing his father to an office clerk and forcing Václav's mother to work as a tour guide) and tried to prevent Václav from continuing his education. Nevertheless, the young man overcame this opposition and completed secondary school. He then worked as a laboratory technician from 1951 to 1955, after which he attended a technical school and the Prague Academy of the Arts. He had his first essay published at age 19—a critical analysis of Josef Capek, a renowned Czech writer and artist.

In the early 1960s, events worked to enhance Havel's career when the Czech government decided to ease its restrictions on free expression. The Theatre on the Balustrade in Prague began producing Czech works, and Havel joined it as a stagehand and electrician. He later worked as a secretary and a manuscript reader. Then the theater staged one of his plays, entitled *Hitchhiking.* There followed another play in 1963, *The Garden Party,* which received such acclaim it was translated into many other languages, including English.

Havel's plays emphasized society as absurd, particularly that under totalitarianism. In *The Memorandum,* produced at the Balustrade in 1965, he criticized systems that destroy human personality and as such took aim at the Communist bureaucracy that existed to serve itself rather than the people.

> *"Where total control over society is sought, the first thing to be suppressed is its culture."*

In 1968, the Czech government granted Havel permission to travel to the United States. *The Memorandum* was staged in New York City, and Havel received the Obie Award for that year's best off-Broadway foreign play. But Havel's literary freedom soon ended. In August, the Soviet Union decided to crack down on Czech liberalism, and its troops invaded Prague. Havel addressed the world from an underground radio station and pleaded for help, but his calls went unanswered. The Communists then banned production of Havel's plays and revoked his passport. During the 1970s, he was repeatedly harassed, imprisoned, and forced to work in a brewery, where he stacked barrels.

He still wrote plays, including two partly autobiographical works, *A Private View and Interview,* which he produced illegally for private audiences. He and his friends also smuggled his manuscripts outside the country.

In 1977, the Czech government's persecution of a rock group, The Plastic People of the Universe, persuaded Havel and hundreds of Czech intellectuals and artists to sign a document called Charter 77. In it, they called for the Czech government to abide by the recent Helsinki Accords, under which the United States, the Soviet Union, and European nations—including Czechoslovakia—had agreed to recognize human rights. Havel claimed that the restrictions on speech and writing violated the Accords.

This action earned Havel widespread recognition within and outside Czechoslovakia as a proponent of a free nation based on liberty. In 1978, he formed the Committee for the Defense of the Unjustly Persecuted; the following year the government arrested all of its members. Havel was charged with subversion and sentenced to nearly five years of hard labor. After serving all but ten months of his sentence, he fell ill to pneumonia, and under international pressure the government released him.

In the late 1980s, the Soviet Union began to unravel, and the Communists in Czechoslovakia lost their outside support. This stimulated a peaceful revolt called the Velvet Revolution that began in 1989 when mass demonstrations erupted in Prague, and the Charter 77 group reorganized as the Civic Forum with Havel as its leader. Presently, Havel sat across from the government officials who had imprisoned him and negotiated a transfer of power to a transitional government consisting of Communists and dissidents. Marian Calfa, a Slovak, was appointed premier, and on 29 December 1989 the new Parliament chose Havel for the more powerful position of president.

Havel immediately began normalizing relations with the West, and in 1990 he oversaw Parliamentary elections in which 23 parties competed freely. The Civic Forum finished first, and Parliament subsequently reelected Havel as president. He pursued economic reforms to encourage a free market, restructured the bureaucracy, and supported policies to promote democracy within the crumbling Soviet Union.

Despite these efforts, Czechoslovakia itself soon fell apart. Slovaks complained that their republic within the federated nation was not receiving equal treatment. Havel tried to obtain constitutional changes to give parity to the Czech and Slovak states, but he failed. He then introduced legislation in Parliament for a referendum on continuing the national union, but the representatives refused to approve it. On 17 July 1992 Slovakia proclaimed its independence. Within the Czech Republic, Havel's popularity declined, and on 20 July 1992 he resigned rather than preside over the finalization of Slovakia's withdrawal. VLADIMIR MECIAR led the Slovak nation.

Reference: Leff, Crol, *National Conflict in Czechoslovakia: The Making and Remaking of the State, 1918–1987,* 1988.

Henry VII
(1457–1509)
Great Britain

As a child and young man, Henry VII lived a perilous existence, fleeing would-be captors who wanted to make sure he never became king. But Henry did become king, ending a destructive civil war and laying the foundation for a united England.

Henry was born 28 January 1457 at Pembroke Castle in Wales, three months after his father, Edmund Tudor, died fighting for the Lancastrians in the conflict known as the Wars of the Roses. Henry's mother, Margaret Beaufort, was a 13-year-old heiress. By inheritance, Henry was Earl of Richmond.

Henry unwittingly became embroiled in the Wars of the Roses, a conflict between two lordly houses, the House of Lancaster and the House of York, over who would rule England. The conflict had erupted in 1455 and reflected the increasing tendency of noblemen to use liveried, or paid, retainers gathered in armies to settle disputes by attacking castles and fighting on battlefields. This occurred in a setting where the king had become weak and unable to prevent disorder.

When Henry was still a child, his mother left him in the care of her brother, Jaspar Tudor, the Earl of Pembroke, who supported the Lancastrians. A few years later, the Yorkists captured Pembroke Castle; Jaspar fled but Henry was captured. From his exile in France, Jaspar Tudor looked for the appropriate moment to rescue Henry. When in 1469 a Lancastrian king, Henry VI, ousted the Yorkist king, Jaspar returned to Wales and took Henry to London.

More trouble ensued, however, when the Yorkists scored a major battlefield victory and Edward IV became king. Jaspar Tudor and Henry fled across the English Channel to Brittany. There Henry received an education from tutors, but he lived precariously, always fearful that the Brittany ruler, Duke Francis, would turn him over to Edward IV who, in turn, would kill him to prevent him from claiming the throne.

Indeed, at one point, the Duke's advisor, Pierre Landois, acceded to the demands of Edward's successor, Richard III, to deliver Henry to him. When Jasper Tudor heard of this he acted to save Henry,

> ## *"I am Henry by the grace of God, King of England."*

arranging for Henry's retinue to head for the French border while leaving Henry behind in Brittany. As Jaspar expected, Landois thought Henry to be with the retinue, and he and his men followed them. Meanwhile, Henry, dressed as a servant, rode furiously toward the French border, following a circuitous path to fool any pursuers. Landois discovered the deception and dispatched a troop of horsemen after Henry, but they did not catch up with him until just after he had crossed into France.

In 1485, Lancastrians anxious to unseat Richard III convinced Henry to invade England. Supported by these men, Henry sailed on 1 August, and as he marched eastward across the country he gained more supporters. Henry met Richard III in combat at Bosworth Field in what became the last great battle in the Wars of the Roses. Henry's army killed Richard and defeated his forces. This led to Henry's coronation at Westminster Abbey on 30 October 1485, beginning the Tudor line of monarchs.

Henry inherited a chaotic, impoverished country, devastated by the long wars. A shrewd and sagacious man, he determined to unite his subjects, first by healing the wounds from the conflict. He pledged himself to marry Elizabeth, the eldest daughter of King Edward IV, the Yorkist. The marriage took place at Westminster on 18 January 1486. He also gathered around him men who had served the Yorkist kings and called the Parliament into session to formally confirm the line of succession to reside in him and his heirs. Later in 1486, he undertook a "progress," or royal journey, to the north, a region where the Yorkists had been especially strong. There he used force, enticement, and the splendor of his office to secure loyalty. At one point in the progress he put down a minor rebellion.

So effective was Henry that by 1487 he had command of his kingdom. Of course, conditions helped him. Many middle-class merchants longed for order so they could develop England economically and garner wealth. Hence, they eagerly supported Henry as a savior from war, and the king, in turn, linked himself to their fortunes.

Nevertheless, Henry's rule did not go without challenge. Some Yorkists, led by Margaret of Burgundy, plotted to overthrow him. They promoted pretenders to the throne, such as Lambert Simnel, whom they proclaimed to be Edward VI. Margaret sent an army from Germany to march on London in support of Simnel, but most Englishmen refused to back it. On 16 June 1487, Henry decisively defeated the invaders at East Stoke. The king captured Simnel and made him a lowly spit turner in his kitchen.

The Yorkists supported yet another pretender in the 1490s, Perkin Warbeck. He tried three times to defeat Henry and on one occasion, in 1497, received support from the King of Scotland. Henry dealt Warbeck his final defeat that year at Cornwall, and the pretender was captured and hanged. This was the last major revolt against Henry.

Henry made sure that his nobles remained secondary to him. Like his predecessors, he had a council consisting of peers, bishops, knights, and lawyers. The royal council advised him on policy and helped him administer the realm, but he determined who among this group would meet with him daily as the inner council. In short, he took the initiative and made sure the council reacted to his wishes.

In addition to this, Henry kept Parliament in line. He realized that the more he relied on the legislature for monies, the less his authority, so he developed creative ways to raise funds. Through various forfeitures Henry greatly expanded his landholdings, an important source of revenue. Increased foreign trade, which he encouraged, resulted in a sizable income from customs duties. Furthermore, he imposed heavy fines on law violators, sold pardons, and vigorously collected debts. In all, he nearly tripled the Crown revenues, a feat that not only meant infrequent sessions of Parliament but also enabled him to relieve his subjects from high taxes and further win their loyalty, or at least prevent antitax uprisings.

To more swiftly enforce the law, Henry used the Star Chamber, a council created under an earlier king and named after the room in Westminister where it met—a room ornamented with stars. The Star Chamber could supersede the courts, holding hearings without juries or counsel for the defendants, deciding guilt or innocence without further review, and using torture to gain confessions. But Henry rarely used the Star Chamber to initiate a prosecution and relied mainly on the courts and the justices of the peace to maintain order. In 1495, Parliament granted the justices the power to try without jury those accused of rioting.

The wool and cloth trade expanded considerably during Henry's reign, and he negotiated treaties with Spain and France that opened new markets—accomplishments that endeared him with the merchants. He also encouraged shipbuilding and constructed warships of his own. In a daring overseas venture he supported John Cabot's efforts to open trade westward across the Atlantic with the Far East. Like Columbus, Cabot did not find his sought-after route, but in 1497 he did land at Newfoundland.

At the same time, Henry adroitly allied himself with Spain when he arranged for his son Arthur, born in 1486, to marry Princess Catherine of Aragon, daughter of King FERDINAND V and Queen ISABELLA I. In 1503, he improved relations with both France and Scotland when he married his daughter to the Scottish King James IV. The French, with whom Henry had warred briefly in 1492, were angered since Scotland had long been their ally.

Henry had extravagant and peculiar habits, some still tied to medieval customs. Through his Welsh grandfather he traced his lineage to ancient kings and considered himself to be the successor to the semimythical Arthur (hence the name for his eldest son). He adopted the red dragon of Wales as part of the royal coat of arms, even though he was only one-quarter Welsh. He spent enormous sums on his own upkeep, seeing that he and his court had the finest clothes, and built a huge palace, added on to other palaces, gambled heavily, and entertained lavishly.

Yet in many respects Henry was much the modern ruler. Despite some scattered outbreaks of disorder, he brought stability and unity to England. In all, he did not so much innovate as take existing institutions and practices and apply to them a vigorous, strong leadership, thus building the structure by which successor Tudor kings and queens developed a more modern nation. Henry died at Richmond on 21 April 1509. In the seventeenth century, England experienced a revolution that strengthened Parliament and led to the famous Bill of Rights under King WILLIAM III.

References: Chrimes, Stanley Bertram, *Henry VII*, 1972; Elton, G. R., England under the Tudors, 1974; Storey, R. L., *The Reign of Henry VII*, 1968.

Ho Chi Minh
(1890–1969)
Vietnam

For several years, Ho Chi Minh traveled clandestinely in Asia, dressed as a Buddhist monk, a beggar, and a businessman. Rumors spread in the 1940s that he had died. But the mysterious figure lived, organizing Communist groups and planning Vietnam's liberation from the French.

Ho Chi Minh came from a family of modest means in Kim Lien, a small village in central Vietnam. Born Nguyen That Thanh on 19 May 1890, he experienced firsthand the economic deprivation suffered under French rule. His father, a civil servant and menial farm worker, struggled financially, eventually abandoning his family. Ho attended grammar school in Cap Vinh and at age nine had already involved himself in the anticolonial movement, serving as a messenger for a nationalist organization. His outspoken criticism of French occupation brought his expulsion from Lycée Quoc Hoc, a secondary school in Hue.

In 1910, Ho began the frequent travels that along with his solitude—he never married and rarely talked to his kin—characterized his life. He worked briefly as an adjunct teacher at Lycée Dac Than in Phan Thiet, then moved on and for several months attended a trade school in Saigon (today, Ho Chi Minh City). To escape the French authorities, he boarded a steamer in 1911 or 1912 and worked as a cook. This adventure took him first to Indian and African ports and then to Boston and New York. (At one point he worked in Brooklyn as a laborer.) From 1915 to 1917, Ho lived in London, where he worked as a snow cleaner and an apprentice chef at the Carlton Hotel and joined a Chinese-led anticolonial organization, Lao Dong Hai Ngoa. During World War I, he moved to Paris, where he again held several jobs, working at various times as a gardener, waiter, and photo retoucher.

Ho remained in France until 1923 and during that time engaged in intellectual discussions with leading radicals, including Communists. He assumed the name Nguyen Ai Quoc (Nguyen the Patriot) and in 1919 joined the French Socialist Party. When, that same year, he tried unsuccessfully to attend the Versailles Peace Conference and demanded that all Indochinese have rights equal to the French, he earned praise from many Vietnamese.

In 1920, he helped found the French Communist Party in the hope that Russia would in some way assist with Vietnam's liberation. He later said patriotism stirred him to do this, more so than Communist ideology. Ho traveled throughout Europe, speaking to groups and writing pamphlets. One publication in particular was later distributed in Vietnam and made him a hero among nationalists there. He also edited *Le Paria*, a newspaper for Indo-Chinese exiles, and composed plays, including a comedy disparaging France.

The anti-imperialist pronouncements of Lenin in Russia drew Ho to Moscow late in 1923, and there he wrote a moving farewell to the Russian revolutionary, who died in January 1924. He met Stalin and Trotsky and attended the revolutionary University of Oriental Workers. That summer, he represented the French Communist Party at the Communist International, where he spoke strongly against colonialism and asserted that the oppressed peasantry could be a vanguard of revolution, and that underdeveloped countries could even be more revolutionary than industrialized ones.

In December 1924, Ho left for Canton, recruited members for a Vietnamese nationalist movement, and formed the Vietnam Thanh Nien Cach Menh Dong (Vietnamese Revolutionary Youth Association), more popularly known as Thanh Nien. He taught his followers to organize political cells and to avoid vague or intellectual theorizing in appealing to the peasants. In 1927, however, China expelled all Communists in Canton, and Ho returned to Moscow before traveling in 1928 to Brussels, Paris, and then Thailand.

The following year, Ho helped organize the Indochinese Communist Party (PCI) in Hong Kong, after members of Thanh Nien had taken the initiative to develop it. The PCI demanded Vietnamese independence and socialist reform. The French, fearing Ho's revolutionary appeal, sentenced him to death in absentia and tried to get him extradited from Hong Kong, but he escaped and returned to Moscow. There is much speculation as to his travels in the 1930s. He seems to have journeyed incognito to Singapore and other areas in Southeast Asia, where he helped organize revolutionary groups. At one point, he escaped imprisonment in Hong Kong by getting an employee in the prison infirmary to report him as dead. Using this cover, he returned to China.

In any event, World War II changed the situation in Indochina. When Japanese troops invaded, Ho aligned himself with the Allies. He went to South China and early in 1941 slipped into Vietnam—his first return to his country in 30 years—where he met nationalist colleagues VO NGUYEN GIAP and Pham Van Dong in a cave and told them it was time to fight the Japanese and then the French. They put together the Vietnam Doc Lap Dong Minh Hoa (League for the Independence of Vietnam), a grouping of socialist and nationalist exile forces popularly called the Viet Minh. At this time, he also changed his name to Ho Chi Minh (Bringer of Light) to hide his identity and shape his image.

Late in 1941, Chinese forces arrested Ho, and while he sat in jail he wrote his *Notebook from Prison,* a stirring call to revolution. Ho gained his release in 1943 when his colleagues convinced a Chinese warlord to set him free so that he could fight against any French return to Indochina. Ho subsequently went to Vietnam and cooperated with the United States against Japan. The Viet Minh guerrilla fighters battled the Japanese in the mountains near China and also near Hanoi. On 19 August 1945, after Japan had surrendered in World War II, the Viet Minh forces entered Hanoi, and on 2 September, Ho declared Vietnam independent.

Ho expected the United States to support Vietnam against any French reconquest. He admired many American institutions and modeled the Vietnamese Declaration of Independence after the American one. In elections held on 6 January 1946, the Vietnamese chose Ho as president, and the Viet Minh won 230 out of 300 seats in the national legislature. The new constitution resembled the U.S. Constitution, and Ho awaited both French acquiescence and international recognition.

Instead he got opposition. Ho initially reached an agreement with France in March 1946 whereby Vietnam would have a semiautonomous status within the French Union, provided the Viet Minh allowed multiparty elections. French troops in Vietnam would remain, although within enclaves, and France would still dominate the southern rice and rubber trade. Despite this agreement, the French, with American backing, used Japanese troops to suppress the Viet Minh, and they violated terms referring to revenue collections. French and Vietnamese forces clashed in November, and in December a French ship and French aircraft opened fire on Haiphong, a Viet Minh stronghold, slaughtering 6,000 Vietnamese civilians.

> *"Nothing is as dear to the heart of the Vietnamese as independence and liberation."*

On 20 December, Ho declared a national war of resistance to gain complete independence. France determined to reconquer Vietnam and soon got the full backing of the United States. Thus began what is called the First Indochina War, and in it the United States provided some 80 percent of the supplies and finances used by France. Gripped by cold-war hysteria, the American government considered Ho a dangerous Communist threat who had to be stopped.

Ho directed his government from remote back areas in North Vietnam and Giap commanded the Viet Minh military. Giap's guerrilla warfare strategy proved brilliant, and soon the Viet Minh controlled the countryside in the north and launched major assaults on the cities. On 7 May 1954, the Viet Minh defeated the French at the infamous battle of Dien Bien Phu, and France now decided to leave Vietnam.

Ho attended negotiations held in 1954 at Geneva, and although the Viet Minh held most of Vietnam, he did not push for full control. He agreed to participate in elections scheduled for 1956 to determine whether the Viet Minh or another party would rule Vietnam. The Geneva Accords, as the agreement was called, divided Vietnam into two temporary zones, North and South, until the elections, and placed Ho in charge of the North and a government friendly to France and the United States in power in the South. The Accords stipulated that no nation could provide military assistance to either zone.

The United States violated the Accords almost immediately, sending 8 tons of military weapons to the South under the guise of humanitarian supplies. By 1956, the United States was fully backing the dictatorship in South Vietnam with military supplies and money. In contradiction with the Geneva Accords, the United States claimed South Vietnam was an independent nation. Furthermore, America decided to block the 1956 elections—Ho would win and that could not be allowed.

Meanwhile, Ho, serving as president of the Viet Minh government while Pham Van Dong served as premier, needed economic assistance for North Vietnam, a poor area, and got it from the Soviet Union and Communist China. He also launched a repressive agricultural reform crusade in 1955 that stirred a peasant uprising and resulted in 50,000 deaths. Ho blamed the bloodshed on radicals within Lao Dong, the Workers' Party, and determined to stem any abuses, he took direct charge of the organization.

Ho had to balance the influence of the Soviet Union and Communist China. He did not want either one to dominate Vietnam, nor did he want to worsen the rivalry between them. He also had to deal with an insurgency in South Vietnam. There the Viet Cong had taken up arms to fight against the American-backed government. Like these southern rebels, Ho wanted the United States out of Vietnam, but he realized that the Viet Cong, a collection of Marxists and nationalists, some of whom had been in the Viet Minh, could challenge his primary role as Vietnam's liberator. In 1959, as American resistance to the Geneva Accords continued, Ho decided to send weapons and men south to help the Viet Cong, who had requested his assistance.

At the same time, Ho relinquished his party leadership—considered to be the focus of power in the North—and concentrated on his presidential role. Considerable dispute exists as to how much power he still wielded, with some analysts saying control was more in the hands of his colleagues, such as Vo Nguyen Giap and Pham Van Dong, and others saying he still exerted enormous influence behind the scenes. In any event, he had become a great symbol of Vietnamese unity and nationalism, admired by many in his country as "Uncle Ho."

As the fighting went badly for the South Vietnamese government, American President Lyndon Johnson announced in August 1964 that North Vietnam had attacked U.S. destroyers in the Gulf of Tonkin. While a minor attack had occurred, it was not to the extent portrayed by Johnson. Furthermore, Johnson failed to tell the American people that the U.S. ships had first committed aggression against North Vietnam by bombarding its coast. Johnson used the assault as a pretext to launch air attacks on North Vietnam and eventually commit American ground troops to a combat role in the South. The Second Indochina War was well under way.

By 1965, the United States had launched raids on the North by B-52 bombers that devastated the land, and by 1968 America had 500,000 troops in South Vietnam, attacking Ho's forces there in free-fire zones (in which entire villages were destroyed and all within them were killed) and using napalm, defoliants, and numerous other destructive devices. Ho continued sending men and arms, largely Soviet weapons, to the South along what became known as the Ho Chi Minh Trail, while rallying the North to withstand the American air strikes (which by the end of the war exceeded in tonnage all bombs used in all the world's previous wars combined).

As protests against the war mounted in the United States and as Ho stood firm, President Johnson announced in 1968 the beginning of negotiations to end the fighting. Ho died shortly after these began on 2 September 1969. Although Ho did not live to see the American defeat and evacuation that led to a unified, independent Vietnam under the Viet Minh, he left an enormous legacy as a nationalist and revolutionary, a hero of peasant-based revolutions and of Asian dignity against Western power.

References: Fenn, Charles, *Ho Chi Minh*, 1973; Halberstam, David, *Ho*, 1987; Kahin, George McTurna, *Intervention: How America Became Involved in Vietnam*, 1987; Karnow, Stanley, *Vietnam: A History*, 1983; Neumann-Hoditz, Reinhold, *Portrait of Ho Chi Minh: An Illustrated Biography*, 1972; Sheehan, Neil, *A Bright Shining Lie: John Paul Vann and America in Vietnam*, 1988.

Houphouët-Boigny, Félix
(1905–1993)
Côte d'Ivoire

When in the wake of World War II West Africans pressured France for reforms, the grievances in Côte d'Ivoire emanated most prominently from a peculiar oppression: wealthy planters discriminated against by French administrators who favored European economic interests. Félix Houphouët-Boigny came from this group of wealthy planters and led his country on a course often at odds with his fellow West African leaders.

Along with repressive measures, French rule brought Ivoirians increased education, including schooling in France. This fostered development of an intellectual elite of which Félix Houphouët-Boigny became a member. Houphouët-Boigny's background was a privileged one: His father was both a tribal chief and businessman who owned cocoa plantations. Félix, born on 18 October 1905 in Yamoussoukro, attended École Primaire Supérieure at Bingerville and then went to Senegal, where in 1925 he received a diploma from the School of Medicine at Dakar. For 15 years he worked as an intern and a medical assistant, but racial discrimination prevented him from becoming a doctor. Frustrated, he returned in 1940 to his family's plantations.

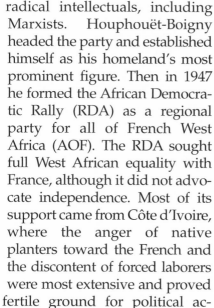

By this time another source of discontent influenced him: the conditions facing planters and workers. French laws discriminated against Ivoirian planters by allowing Europeans use of forced labor and access to protected markets. In some instances the French compelled Ivoirian planters to give up their lands to Europeans. At the same time, the system of forced labor impoverished native workers.

In 1940, Houphouët-Boigny entered politics and won a position as chief of his canton (a colonial administrative subdivision). In 1944, he and other planters put together one of the most important organizations in Ivoirian history, the African Agricultural Union, which became the genesis for native political power. The following year, reforms permitted an Ivoirian delegate in the French National Assembly. The territory's African voters chose Houphouët-Boigny. As a major reformer, he sponsored the law passed in 1945 forbidding forced labor.

After the French allowed party politics in 1946, Ivoirian leaders organized the Democratic Party of Côte d'Ivoire (PDCI), which grew out of the African Agricultural Union. It attracted many radical intellectuals, including Marxists. Houphouët-Boigny headed the party and established himself as his homeland's most prominent figure. Then in 1947 he formed the African Democratic Rally (RDA) as a regional party for all of French West Africa (AOF). The RDA sought full West African equality with France, although it did not advocate independence. Most of its support came from Côte d'Ivoire, where the anger of native planters toward the French and the discontent of forced laborers were most extensive and proved fertile ground for political activism. The French government considered both PDCI and RDA (which worked together cooperatively) as enemies to French rule.

When the territorial government rigged elections against PDCI and dismissed workers affiliated with the party, Houphouët-Boigny organized boycotts of European goods and held mass rallies. In 1949, violence erupted after government troops fired on African demonstrators. The French political and military retaliation and the alliance of PDCI with the French Communist Party, which was firmly opposed by the colonial power and had alienated moderate supporters of Ivoirian rights, endangered the existence of Houphouët-Boigny's party. Consequently, in 1951 Houphouët-Boigny ended relations with the French Communists and dropped his militant tactics. These moves strengthened both the PDCI and the RDA and encouraged French political concessions.

Houphouët-Boigny's reputation rose within

the French government. In 1956, he became minister designate in Prime Minister Guy Mollet's administration, a position with full cabinet rank. He later served brief terms as minister of state and minister of public health. He cosponsored the *loi-cadre*, or reform legislation, which brought more change, including universal suffrage and a semi-autonomous status for Côte d'Ivoire and other overseas territories.

In the process, he angered RDA leaders outside Côte d'Ivoire by rejecting arguments that the *loi-cadre* had weakened AOF and had served French interests by balkanizing West Africa. In 1957, Houphouët-Boigny served on the French delegation to the United Nations. Meanwhile, the RDA won an absolute majority of seats in AOF assemblies and Houphouët-Boigny obtained additional duties as president of the AOF Grand Council (although his continued stand against any federation of West African territories caused much opposition from neighboring leaders). At the same time, he served as mayor of Côte d'Ivoire's most populous city, Abidjan.

When in 1958 Charles de Gaulle's government moved to establish a French Community, Houphouët-Boigny and the Côte d'Ivoire elite supported it enthusiastically. Indeed, Houphouët-Boigny helped prepare the document establishing the Community. For West Africa, Community status meant an end to AOF with each member territory becoming a separate republic. France still controlled foreign affairs, currency, and economic concerns of mutual importance, but each republic established its own constitution and executive.

Houphouët-Boigny and most Ivoirian leaders believed complete independence at this stage would damage their country by ending important economic links with France. Indeed, Houphouët-Boigny argued strenuously against the position of KWAME NKRUMAH, leader of Ghana (a British colony), who advocated immediate independence for West Africa. The Ivoirian leader insisted this would only mean economic and political isolation for the region. He advocated interdependence between Africa and Europe and also opposed the call of West African leaders such as Senegal's LÉOPOLD SÉDAR SENGHOR for a strong federation among the region's republics. He feared his poorer neighbors might drain wealth from the relatively prosperous Côte d'Ivoire.

> *"Competition is healthy for sport, but in politics what must triumph is team spirit."*

In March 1959, Côte d'Ivoire adopted its first constitution as a self-governing republic in the French Community. The PDCI won all of the seats in the newly formed unicameral legislature, and Houphouët-Boigny resigned from the French cabinet to head his homeland's government as prime minister. Perhaps to protect his regional prestige, he grouped Côte d'Ivoire into a loose economic alliance with Niger, Dahomey (now Benin), and Upper Volta (now Burkina Faso), called the Council of the Entente.

Houphouët-Boigny saw his stand against independence erode when France permitted any member of the French Community to become fully autonomous in 1960, and both Senegal and Mali subsequently opted for nationhood. He reacted by withdrawing Côte d'Ivoire from the French Community, and the republic proclaimed full independence on 4 August 1960. In October of that year, Côte d'Ivoire adopted a new constitution that created a presidency, which Houphouët-Boigny won.

While Houphouët-Boigny claimed he supported democratic measures, he and other PDCI leaders equated stable government with unanimous allegiance to their party. Houphouët-Boigny preferred strong bureaucratic rule to the bickering and uncertainties of parliamentary governance. As president, he began acquiring enormous powers. By the late 1960s he had gained the right to choose all the members of Côte d'Ivoire's National Assembly. He also greatly limited the Assembly's prerogatives and organized a military whose more complete loyalty he gained in 1974 by appointing officers to important governmental positions.

Under Houphouët-Boigny's leadership, Côte d'Ivoire underwent substantial economic growth as he supported unrestrained free enterprise and followed a pragmatic foreign policy that included commercial ties with South Africa. Yet tensions within the country grew: Important economic positions remained within French hands, Abidjan prospered but the rural regions did not, the new wealth failed to reach the lower levels of the population, and the government encouraged the importation of large numbers of cheap laborers from surrounding countries. This latter development caused a particularly violent reaction from native Ivoirian workers, who despised the added competition for jobs.

In 1963, Houphouët-Boigny defeated an attempted military coup. He subsequently used more extensive patronage appointments and played on ethnic differences within the nation to maintain power. In 1969, he effectively crushed student protests critical of what were called neocolonialist relations with France. He also defeated a secessionist move by the Agni tribe in the eastern Sanwi region.

Houphouët-Boigny adroitly used the French bureaucratic organization inherited from the days of Côte d'Ivoire's territorial government as a means to maintain power into the 1990s, and a large number of French bureaucrats and entrepreneurs resided in the nation and maintained close relations with the president. Houphouët-Boigny won continuous reelection within a system that discouraged popular political competition. To many Ivoirians, he assumed godlike proportions, and when he died of old age on 7 December 1993, the country mourned the passing of a great leader with one of the most elaborate state funerals in recent world history.

References: Ajayi, J. F. A., and Michael Crowder, eds., *History of West Africa*, 2 volumes, 1974; Jackson, Robert H., and Carl Rosberg, *Personal Rule in Black Africa*, 1982.

Hussein ibn Talal
(b. 1935)
Jordan

In the Arab nationalist movement King Hussein I (Hussein ibn Talal) has held an ambiguous position. He has been identified with the cause of Arab independence, yet he has often relied on Western help to maintain his power.

Hussein ibn Talal was born 14 November 1935 in Amman to Talal ibn Abdullah, Crown Prince of Transjordan. His family had been intimately involved in Arab efforts to end foreign domination. Years earlier, Abdullah ibn Hussein, the young Hussein's grandfather, had helped lead the Arab revolt that erupted in 1916 against Turkish rule and emerged as emir of Transjordan after Britain agreed to recognize and support his government. In effect, under Abdullah a British protectorate existed with Britain overseeing most government functions. Although the emir identified himself with the greater Arab nationalist movement, nationalism within Transjordan was weak

and the emir too beholden to British interests to be considered by many Arabs as their leader.

As a young man in this environment, Hussein attended classes at an Islamic school in Amman and received tutorials in Arabic and religion. At the time he reached age 11, Transjordan gained its independence from Britain and Abdullah ibn Hussein became king. British authority, however, remained paramount. Then, as Hussein continued his education at Victoria College in Alexandria, the nation of Israel was created along Transjordan's western border, an event that would greatly affect the young man in his years as ruler.

In 1950, Abdullah conducted secret negotiations with Israel and gained Israeli approval to annex the West Bank. In reaction, on 20 July 1951 a Palestinian, angered by Abdullah's contacts with Israel, assassinated the king. Hussein's father, Crown Prince Talal ibn

Abdullah, subsequently became king of Jordan (which had shortly before this changed its name from Transjordan). His rule proved short-lived, as most people believed it would, for Talal suffered from a mental illness, schizophrenia. Meanwhile, Hussein was sent to Harrow, an elite school in England. Then on 11 August 1952, the Jordanian Parliament replaced Talal with Hussein, although a regency council ruled for another year until the young monarch could attain his majority and complete his education, which he did at Sandhurst, the premier military academy in Britain. In May 1953, Hussein officially assumed his duties as king.

Hussein's monarchy proved a moderate one, protective of Jordan's independence but, like his grandfather's rule, often sympathetic to Western influences. As a member of the Hashemite family he obtained important advice and leadership training from his Hashemite relatives.

Hussein established his nationalist credentials in 1956 when he ended the Jordanian treaty with Britain. He talked strongly about his dedication to Arab independence and reaffirmed his commitment to Islam. Yet in 1958, when Pan-Arab Nasserists threatened to overthrow him, he acquiesced in the use of British troops to maintain his power. Around 1960, he accepted an increasing amount of American assistance to develop his military and economy. Furthermore, he was often at odds with Palestinians in Jordan who complained about his dictatorial rule and who never identified with the Hashemite family.

In the 1967 Arab-Israeli War, Hussein committed his nation to the fight on the Arab side, and in the ensuing defeat lost all of Jordan's territory west of the Jordan River, including Jerusalem. In the early 1970s, he had to battle Palestinian guerrilla groups within Jordan, which he defeated. Through the 1970s and into the 1980s, Hussein's relations with his fellow Arab nations fluctuated based on the Arab-Israeli relationship and on his own needs for military and economic help. Jordan supported Iraq in the Iran-Iraq war that erupted in 1980, and in the Persian Gulf War of 1991 he gained the enmity of the United States and many Arab nations, particularly Saudi Arabia, by condemning the retaliatory attack against Iraq for its invasion of Kuwait. Hussein, however, did not ally with the Iraqis, and he did support the economic sanctions imposed against Iraq.

In all, Hussein continues the general approach of his grandfather, King Abdullah. His nationalism in guiding Jordan through its early years of nationhood and into the 1990s can only be described as cautious, but he recently showed a mark of boldness in his agreement to officially end his nation's state of belligerency toward Israel and pursue with that nation a far-ranging peace treaty.

References: Hussein ibn Talal, *Uneasy Lies the Head: The Autobiography of His Majesty King Hussein I of the Hashemite Kingdom of Jordan*, 1962; Snow, Peter, *Hussein: A Biography*, 1972; Wilson, Mary C., *King Abdullah, Britain, and the Making of Jordan*, 1987.

Hussein, Saddam
(b. 1937)
Iraq

As a young man, Saddam Hussein embraced extreme actions to advance Iraqi nationalism and his own power: He participated in riots to depose Iraq's king and an assassination attempt against an Iraqi dictator. Both efforts failed, but his steely, often harsh resolve to reshape Iraq's government carried into his later years and eventually prevailed.

Saddam Hussein was born on 28 April 1937 in Tikrit and was raised by his mother and maternal uncle. His family lacked land and wealth, and young Saddam, already impoverished, felt the consequences of foreign domination, such as the flood of cheap British goods that hurt the Tikrit textile industry and depressed the economy. At this time,

Iraq had its own monarchy under King FAISAL I, but Britain restricted his power, and the king himself exhibited a pro-Western mentality. Saddam's uncle gained notoriety in 1941 when he participated in a nationalist uprising against the king. Faisal crushed this rebellion, but as Saddam got older he admired his uncle's action and imbibed his family's hatred for foreign influence in Iraq and throughout the Arab world.

Saddam obtained his early schooling in Tikrit but in 1955 went to Baghdad, where he attended the al-Karkh secondary school. He had already become politicized, and in 1956 he engaged in the demonstrations and riots that were part of a coup against King Faisal II. This uprising failed, but the following year Hussein joined the Ba'ath Party, which promoted Pan-Arab nationalism and socialist reforms. In 1958, the AB-DUL KARIM QASSEM regime, which had overthrown the monarchy, placed Hussein in jail for six months because of his participation in Ba'ath Party demonstrations.

Shortly after his release, Hussein joined several other Ba'athists in plotting to kill Qassem, who was disliked for his alliance with Iraqi communists and opposition to Pan-Arabic nationalism that would link Iraq with Egypt. In 1959, Hussein and his coconspirators attacked Qassem, but the assassination attempt failed. In the fracas, Qassem's guards shot Hussein and a bullet lodged in his leg. He went into hiding and had a friend remove the bullet with a penknife, all the while enduring the pain and providing the necessary instructions.

Sentenced to death, Hussein fled Iraq, riding a donkey across the desert into Syria. From there he went to Cairo, where GAMAL ABDEL NASSER's revolutionary ideology reinforced his desire for an Arab world free of Western control.

While in Cairo, Hussein completed secondary school and in 1962 enrolled in the Cairo University Law School. He also served on the executive committee of the Ba'ath Party. Before he completed his first year of law school, Ba'athists overthrew Qassem, and the young Iraqi returned home to participate in the new government. Hussein held a minor position, however, and in any event the Ba'athists were themselves soon overthrown. Hussein then went underground, but Iraqi authorities found him and sent him to prison. He spent two years in jail, during which time he resumed his law studies. In 1966, he

"The Mother of Battles will be our battle of victory and martyrdom."

escaped from prison and began writing revolutionary pamphlets.

The Iraqi government continued in turmoil, a situation that played into Hussein's desires. On 17 July 1968, another coup led by Ba'ath Party militias that Hussein had organized resulted in the Ba'athists regaining power. Major General Ahmed Hassan al-Bakr became president, and Hussein became his secretary and deputy chairman of the Revolutionary Command Council. He worked assiduously and quickly to become the real power in Bakr's regime and to advance revolutionary change. He envisioned Iraq taking the mantle of Pan-Arab leadership from Egypt, and in accordance with Ba'athist ideology, he worked to develop a socialist state.

Hussein displayed a behavior pattern that characterized his political leadership. He had a penchant for conspiratorial activities, and his secrecy along with his distrust of outsiders permeated everything he did. He also brutally crushed any serious challenge to his power and developed a reputation as a man to be feared. The latter appears in a story about his obtaining his law degree. He showed up for his final examination in 1969 accompanied by bodyguards and wearing a pistol in his belt. The examiners got the message and understood the necessity of passing him.

Under the Bakr-Hussein leadership, Iraq followed a radical foreign policy by supporting the Marxist regime in South Yemen to agitate the conservative Saudi Arabian rulers, demanding two islands from Kuwait (and even occupying the northwest corner of that country until the Arab League secured a withdrawal), and developing close ties to the Soviet Union, not because of an ideological attachment to Marxism, but because it needed Soviet weapons and wanted to counteract Western influence in the Middle East. In 1972, Hussein traveled to Moscow and signed an Iraqi-Soviet friendship treaty.

By 1973, Hussein eclipsed Bakr in power, and that year Iraq took a radical economic turn in nationalizing its oil industry. This move reinforced the Western view that Iraq was an unreliable state, but it produced greater oil profits.

On 16 July 1979, Bakr resigned and Hussein took over as president. He held other positions too: chairman of the Revolutionary Command Council, prime minister, commander of the armed forces, and secretary-general of the Ba'ath Party. A highly personalized and centralized regime emerged with a strong cult of personality. Hussein's photograph appeared everywhere, and Iraqis saw him on television, kissing babies, acting fatherly toward children, and granting favors to petitioners.

Hussein used Iraq's oil revenues to make massive internal improvements. Agricultural modernization, water purification, rural electrification, highways, hospitals, schools—all these and more improved the average Iraqi's standard of living. But throughout, he maintained a dictatorial regime marred by extensive human rights abuses.

Amid these developments, Iraq's longstanding feud with Iran exploded into open warfare. AYATOLLAH RUHOLLA KHOMEINI, the Iranian leader, called on Shiite Muslims to rise up against the Sunni-dominated Ba'athists (which as a party had distanced itself from any religious agenda). Hussein expelled or imprisoned thousands of Shiites. He considered Iran a grave threat and desired a government there under Iraqi domination. Toward this end, in September 1980 he launched an attack on Iran, expecting a quick victory but finding that his enemy, although in the throes of an internal revolution, could withstand the invasion. The Iran-Iraqi war dragged on for years, ending in 1988 without victory for either side. During the war, Hussein used chemical weapons against the Iranians, and also against rebellious Kurds within Iraq's own borders.

In 1990, Hussein determined to resolve Iraq's longstanding dispute with oil-rich Kuwait. His troops subsequently invaded that country, and he announced its annexation. Both the United Nations and the United States reacted, denouncing Hussein's aggression and enacting an embargo against him. Early in 1991, American troops, with assistance from Arab League members, forced Hussein to retreat after an intense air assault on Iraq. Although the United States did not aim to capture Baghdad, it did hope to topple Hussein (portrayed by the Americans as the world's new Hitler). The Iraqi leader, however, withstood the assault. After the war, he rebuilt the areas destroyed, a difficult task given that a nearly total economic embargo continued against his nation, and ruthlessly crushed two rebellions: one by the Shiites in the south (encouraged to rebel by Iran) and another by the Kurds in the north (encouraged to rebel by the United States). Furthermore, he continually hampered United Nations teams sent to Iraq to investigate nuclear and chemical weapons development under the terms of the cease-fire.

Even though many of Hussein's modernization projects had been destroyed, his nation economically and politically isolated, his military embarrassed, and his program to make nuclear weapons halted, he remains in power, a testament to his autocratic strength and his ability to use brute force.

References: Hiro, Dilip, *Desert Shield to Desert Storm: The Second Gulf War*, 1992; Iskandar, Amir, *Saddam Hussein: The Fighter, the Thinker, and the Man*, 1980; Marr, Phebe, *The Modern History of Iraq*, 1985.

Ibn Saud, Abd al-Aziz
(1881–1953)
Saudi Arabia

Abd al-Aziz Ibn Saud inherited much from his ancestors, particularly a commitment to his family's legacy as rulers and a determination to spread Islam. He combined these in founding an independent Saudi Arabian kingdom.

In 1881, Abd al-Aziz Ibn Saud was born the son of Abd al-Rahman, the ruler of the second Saudi state. Well before al-Rahman's time, the Saud family had committed itself to spreading the Islamic Wahhabi creed, which advocated a purified Islam free of popular, particularly Western, corruptions. The Wahhabis believed that Muslim life should dominate the state and that laxity in worshipping God should not be tolerated. Ibn Saud's father led a Saudi state that fell to the competing Rashidi Dynasty of the Shammar tribe centered in Hail, northwest of Riyadh. The collapse sent Abd al-Rahman and his family into exile, arriving in Kuwait City in 1891.

Ibn Saud grew up there in a royal setting. He joined the entourage of Kuwait's ruler and learned riding, fighting, and regal customs. He married at age 15, and after his wife died, remarried at age 18; shortly thereafter, he had his first son. As was custom, Ibn Saud would over the years have many wives. In his youth, he imbibed the Wahhabism that his father followed and learned of the former Saudi state, its power and glory. He sought to spread his Islamic belief and renew his family's rule.

In 1902, Ibn Saud raided Riyadh and, amid shouts of "Al Saud!" and "God is Great!," he and his men captured the town from the Turks, who had controlled the area under the Ottoman Empire. Thus began the military and political effort to build the Saudi state, and within eight years Ibn Saud's rule extended into the region called Qasim. In this expansion, Ibn Saud did not allow his religious faith to obliterate his pragmatism. He well knew that Arabia was a sensitive area, where Turkish and British strategic concerns mixed with tribal objectives. Since the Turks supported the Rashidis and since the British, who supported the Hashemite sheikhs, sought additional ways to counteract Turkish power, Ibn Saud considered his future as best linked to Britain. In his military campaigns he always avoided attacks on tribes allied with Britain, and he actively sought British recognition.

After he captured Riyadh, Ibn Saud, entangled in a family rivalry, survived a poisoning attempt by two of his nephews, and formed alliances with surrounding tribal groups. He also sent his forces into battle and in 1913 captured al-Hasa, the Persian Gulf region, from the Turks. He gained Britain's attention because the Persian Gulf was considered a vital maritime connection to India.

Then World War I altered the Arabian picture. It eliminated the Ottoman Empire as a factor, and since during the war Ibn Saud backed Britain, he now received rewards. In a 1915 treaty, the British agreed to help Ibn Saud against any aggression by outside powers, and they recognized the Saudi state as an independent entity. For his part, Ibn Saud promised not to attack any of the British-supported principalities in the area.

This new relationship brought with it money from Britain and permitted Ibn Saud to attack Rashid, knowing Britain looked favorably upon the action; he thus expanded his territorial control. Then in 1920, he uncovered a plot on the part of the Hashemite family and the sheikh of Kuwait to kill him. He subsequently intensified his assaults, capturing towns near Kuwait City and conquering the Rashidi capital. In 1925, he expanded his control to include Asir. The next year, he laid siege to Mecca and Jidda and gained control over them. Thus the Saudi state had been revived.

Ibn Saud solidified his power within his new state by having his brothers marry many different women, creating alliances among leading families. He modernized his state by organizing government offices and developing telegraph communication and highways. He decreased the reliance on Kuwait City for trade by developing Jubail and Qatif.

In the early 1930s, he successfully crushed two rebellions led by competing tribes, one in Hejaz and the other in Asir. The latter involved war with Yemen, and Ibn Saud's army advanced into that area. Under British pressure, however, the Saudi forces withdrew. This led to Ibn Saud pursuing a policy of stabilizing relations with nearby states, and in the 1930s he signed treaties of friendship with Iraq and Jordan. Meanwhile, on 16 September 1932 Ibn Saud declared his realm the Saudi Arabia Kingdom and officially was crowned King Abd al-Aziz.

World War II brought yet another change to the Arabian Peninsula. As Britain emerged from the war weakened, Ibn Saud concluded he must move closer to the United States, and in the ensuing cold-war atmosphere America reciprocated. Meanwhile, a momentous economic event had occurred in 1933 when Ibn Saud signed a 66-year oil lease with Standard Oil, which in the late 1940s joined several American oil companies to organize the Arabian American Oil Company (ARAMCO). In 1950, ARAMCO completed an oil pipeline that traversed Saudi Arabia and Syria and reached the Mediterranean. The development of oil drilling and transportation by ARAMCO brought considerable wealth into the kingdom and enriched both the Saudi rulers and the population as a whole. But Western dollars and personnel brought another problem: a conflict between modern practices and the traditional Islam to which Ibn Saud had committed himself. Indeed, this problem intensified as the king engaged in extravagant living (linked to the custom that all the kingdom's income belonged to him) and introduced new technology to his homeland—everything from telephones to the latest military weapons.

Ibn Saud suffered a prolonged illness in 1953 and died on 9 November. His eldest son, Saud bin Abdul Aziz succeeded him but immediately ran into opposition from another of Ibn Saud's sons, Faisal bin Abd al-Aziz. King Saud abdicated the throne to Faisal in 1964, and the new king undertook reforms to end slavery, modernize the administration, and establish a local governmental system. Ibn Saud had established a kingdom whose vitality and oil wealth remains a crucial strategic concern to the United States and other Western nations, as well as those of the Middle East.

References: Almana, Mohammad, *Arabia Unified: A Portrait of Ibn Saud*, 1980; Bligh, Alexander, *From Prince to King*, 1984; Holden, David, and Richard Johns, *The House of Saud*, 1981.

Iliescu, Ion
(b. 1930)
Romania

A dedicated Communist, Ion Iliescu led a rebellion that overthrew the existing Communist regime, but he likely did so more out of a drive for personal power than a commitment to reformist principles. He used authoritarian tactics and continued the existence of a brutal secret police.

Ion Iliescu was born on 3 March 1930 in Oltenita, a town in southeastern Romania. While he was still a child, Romania, which had gained unity and independence in the nineteenth century under ION BRĂTIANU and had grown greatly in size after World War I, lost much land to Russia, Hungary, and Bulgaria in the first year of the Second World War. During the war, Romania initially supported Hitler, but after Russian troops invaded in 1944 and the Romanian dictatorship was overthrown, the nation sided with the Allies. In the same year, Iliescu joined the Union of Communist Youth, and the following year the Communists successfully gained power in a coup backed by the Soviet army. The Communist and Soviet postwar domination of Romania thus began. By 1948, the Communists eliminated most political opposition and supported by the Securitate, the secret police founded by them, they had firm control of the nation.

In 1952, Gheorghiu-Dej gained dictatorial

> *"Our entire economic and social policy must rely on . . . the truth."*

powers, and although Iliescu's father ran into trouble with the new government, Iliescu himself benefited greatly as he loyally served the Communist leadership and became an official member of the Communist Party in 1953. He obtained a degree in business administration from the Bucharest Polytechnic Institute and then continued his studies in the Soviet Union, where he earned an engineering degree at Moscow State University.

After Iliescu returned to Romania, he became secretary of the Union of Communist Youth in 1956 and in the early 1960s earned appointment as deputy chief of health and education of the Communist Party's Central Committee. In 1965, he headed the propaganda division and became eligible to sit on the Central Committee itself.

But his status soon dropped. In 1965, Nicolae Ceausescu gained the most powerful position in Romania as secretary-general of the Communist Party and developed the most oppressive dictatorship in Soviet-bloc Eastern Europe. He also gained a degree of independence from the Soviet Union, especially in economic matters, and against Russian wishes he industrialized his country. To build support, Ceausescu developed a personality cult—a move that alienated Iliescu. At first, in the early years of Ceausescu's reign, Iliescu continued to advance, and in 1968 he gained full membership on the powerful Central Committee. Despite his credentials with Ceausescu, Iliescu attracted a following among Romania's youthful intellectuals when he complained about Ceausescu's rigidity—his unwillingness to allow any ideological variance. In 1971, Ceausescu removed Iliescu from his posts, except for the Central Committee, and sent him to Timisoara, a town in western Romania, to serve as regional party secretary.

Ceausescu liked to protect his power through frequent reassignments of officials, and in 1974 he sent Iliescu to Iasi, near the Soviet border. These moves only angered Iliescu more and increased his discontent. In 1979, Ceausescu demoted Iliescu again, making him director of the National Council for Water Resources. The downward slide continued when, in 1984, Iliescu was appointed director of an obscure publishing house and removed from the Central Committee.

Iliescu joined the disaffected, a number growing in size as Ceausescu's arbitrary rule ruined careers and as Romania's economy, which had expanded greatly in the 1960s and 1970s, fell apart. The last straw for many came when Ceausescu imposed a stringent austerity program and rejected the liberalization then under way in the Soviet Union. In 1989, Romania exploded with protests, and Ceausescu retaliated by ordering his army to fire into the crowds. One such event in Timisoara late in 1989 ignited bloody fighting between government troops and the protestors. Shortly thereafter, the military deserted Ceausescu and his regime fell. Ceausescu escaped angry mobs by boarding a helicopter and fleeing Bucharest, but he was captured within hours and several days later was executed.

Shortly after Ceausescu fled, Iliescu arrived at the ransacked Central Committee building where he took over the government. He and his supporters formed the National Salvation Front and promised to begin a democracy. Although the Front included dissidents of diverse views, the former Communists, such as Iliescu, dominated it. One of Iliescu's first acts was to release a videotape displaying the bullet-riddled bodies of Ceausescu and his wife. The state television played it repeatedly to show Romanians that Ceausescu was dead and also to show the power of the Front. On 26 December the provisional government named Iliescu interim president, and he again promised open elections. He immediately ended Ceausescu's unpopular stringent economic measures, declared the Securitate dissolved, and promised he would end the collective farm system.

Yet Iliescu had many opponents who distrusted him and his Communist past. His main opposition came from the cities, and large demonstrations occurred against him early in 1990. He appeased the demonstrators by promising to ban the Communist Party, but within days he reneged on the promise. He did permit elections in May, noted for the diverse array of parties that participated. Yet he allowed these parties little room in which to present their views: The Front controlled the newspapers and encouraged thugs to assault opposition headquarters. Needless to say, Iliescu won the election overwhelmingly with 85 percent of the vote.

Several hundred demonstrators continued to protest in Bucharest after the election. Iliescu ordered the police to arrest them, but as they did more protestors arrived. Fearing that the military was too unreliable and might gain too much power if used too often, Iliescu bypassed the army and transported 10,000 miners into Bucharest to eliminate the protestors. The miners and others in Romania's rural areas strongly supported Iliescu, and he knew they would do his bidding. For two days the miners wielded clubs, attacked the protestors, and destroyed opposition headquarters. All told, the miners killed 21 people while injuring hundreds more.

Romania did not have a heritage of political competition and only gradually did a united opposition arise to contest Iliescu's power. The Civic Alliance formed, led by intellectuals and labor activists, and sponsored massive demonstrations. Iliescu, however, maintained his power, moving cautiously toward free-market reforms, depending on many former Communists for his support, and continuing to operate the Securitate he had ostensibly dissolved. Despite the controversies surrounding Iliescu, he won reelection in 1992 and remains notable as the leader in ending Soviet domination and forming a new Romania, more autonomous than at any other time since the end of World War II. The degree to which he has broken with the past remains to be seen.

Reference: Bachman, Ronald D., ed., *Romania: A Country Study*, 1991.

Isa Bin Sulman al-Khalifah
(b. 1933)
Bahrain

In the 1950s, a nationalist movement containing radical elements emerged in Bahrain to demand independence and challenge the traditional emirate government. As heir apparent to the emir and later as ruler in his own right, Sheikh Isa Bin Sulman al-Khalifah adopted a moderate stance, open to reform but protective of his family's rule.

Sheikh Isa was born on 4 June 1933 into the al-Khalifah family, which ruled Bahrain, then under control by Britain. He was educated by British tutors and traveled with his father on several occasions to India. In 1942, Sheikh Isa's father, Sheikh Sulman bin Hamad, became emir, and in 1956 he appointed his son to the presidency of the municipal council overseeing Manama, the largest city in Bahrain. Sheikh Isa successfully quelled disturbances occurring between Bahrain's two Islamic sects, the Sunni and the Shiites.

In the late 1950s, Sheikh Isa's responsibilities increased after his father suffered a series of heart attacks. Sheikh Isa became acting head of the al-Kahlifah family and in that position gained control over his homeland's oil revenues, which he distributed to family members and favorites in a way to build his support. On 16 December 1961, Sheikh Isa became emir, little more than a month after his father died.

In the late 1960s, Britain, too strapped financially to maintain a political and military presence, decided to withdraw from its position in the Persian Gulf. Sheikh Isa subsequently prepared for Bahrain to gain its independence. This goal had actually been sought earlier in the 1950s when nationalists led by 'Abd al-Aziz Shamlan and 'Abd al-Rahman al-Bakir demanded both Britain's ouster and reforms to make the emir less autocratic. Now antigovernment riots propelled Sheikh Isa to reconsider the structure of his government and Bahrain's relationship to its neighbors. In 1970, the emir created a cabinet, a modern device, but one that hardly lessened autocracy. In fact, he appointed his brother prime minister.

With regard to the nearby emirates, it appeared initially as if Bahrain might join Qatar and the British Trucial States (later the United Arab Emirates) in a federation, but fearing restrictions on his homeland's autonomy, Sheikh Isa decided to go it alone. On 14 August 1971, he declared Bahrain an independent nation.

Still feeling the pressure from opponents who wanted a more open government, Sheikh Isa proved himself a liberal reformer. He declared formation of a convention to draft a constitution and on 2 June 1973 approved the new document, which recognized the legitimacy of trade unions, declared women equal to men, and established an elective national legislature. On the other hand, when in 1975 the legislature severely criticized Sheikh Isa's policies, he suspended it and granted legislative powers to his cabinet. In 1993, he yielded again to reform pressure and allowed a 30-member consultative council.

Sheikh Isa supports technological modernization to help his people and directs much oil revenue to social programs. Autocratic, he is also benevolent and steers a largely pragmatic course in directing Bahrain's independence and development.

References: Lawson, Fred H., *Bahrain: The Modernization of Autocracy*, 1989; Nakhleh, Emile A., *Bahrain: Political Development in a Modernizing Society*, 1976.

Isabella I
(1451–1504)
Spain

Strong-willed and decisive, Isabella determined to unite her kingdom of Castile with Aragon to dominate the Iberian Peninsula. Out of her subsequent union with FERDINAND V came the nation of Spain.

Isabella was born 22 April 1451 in Madrigal, the daughter of John II of Castile and Isabella of Portugal. She was the half-sister of Henry IV, who became king of Castile in 1454. Isabella obtained an education at a convent, where priests and tutors were her teachers. As a pastime she developed a talent for crafts, such as weaving and embroidering, and also became an excellent horsewoman. In 1462, she was brought to the court, meaning that for several years she traveled with the monarchs across Castile.

Despite attempts by court officials to marry her to someone else, Isabella determined that she would wed Ferdinand, the heir to the throne of Aragon, which along with Castile and Portugal was one of the three major Christian kingdoms on the Iberian Peninsula. Since she was heiress to the Castilian throne, Isabella realized that her union with Ferdinand would produce a powerful kingdom.

Unfortunately for Isabella, Henry IV wanted her to marry the king of Portugal. When she defied his wishes and married Ferdinand in 1469, the king announced that his successor would not be Isabella, but rather his daughter Juana. When Henry died in 1474, Isabella claimed the throne, igniting a civil war between those who supported her and those who supported Juana, including the Portuguese king, Afonso V. Isabella's army defeated Afonso's forces at the Battle of Toro in 1476, thus ending the conflict and securing Isabella's rule.

When, in 1479, Ferdinand became king of Aragon, the union of the two kingdoms was completed. But Castile and Aragon did not stand as equal partners and much work lay ahead in order for Isabella and Ferdinand to consolidate their power. In fact, at the time of their marriage,

Ferdinand signed a document called "The Capitulations," in which he recognized Isabella's primacy in Castile by agreeing to make no wars or alliances without the queen's approval and to appoint only Castilians to office in Castile.

Isabella took the lead in solidifying crown rule in Castile, motivated by her fervent Catholicism, a religious faith that well exceeded her husband's. Isabella summoned the Cortes, a consultative body of the nobles and clergy, only sparingly. She revoked the pensions and many land grants given to the nobles and redirected tax monies into the royal treasury. She also reformed the currency to eliminate counterfeit coinage, improved the roads, and held trade fairs. These moves increased commerce and with it customs receipts, which enriched the royal coffers.

Her strong Catholicism mixed with her pursuit of power appeared most evident in religious policies. In 1478, she initiated the Inquisition against Muslims and Jews as primarily a royal rather than papal device to promote Spanish unity by enforcing the Catholic faith. It soon became persecution, and Jews in 1492 were offered two alternatives: accept baptism into the Catholic Church or leave Spain. Many went into exile and lost their property. Ten years later, the Muslims were given the same alternatives. The Inquisition prepared her and Spain for the attack on Grenada, the last Moorish, or Muslim, stronghold on the Iberian Peninsula. The assault began in 1481 and culminated successfully in 1492, resulting in additional territory being annexed by Castile.

Isabella sponsored Christopher Columbus's voyage westward across the Atlantic. When he sailed from Spain in 1492, he saw a boatload of exiled Jews leaving the country—a juxtaposition that, although he did not realize it, symbolized the monarchy's qualities of conquest and intolerance. Columbus's discoveries in America opened new revenues for the crown and new sources of power.

Isabella had five children, including Catherine of Aragon, who married Henry VIII of England, and Joanna, who married Philip of Burgundy. Joanna went insane and after Isabella's death ruled Spain only through Ferdinand, who served as her regent. Isabella died on 26 November 1504. She had crafted with Ferdinand a new nation, still a transitional state from the Middle Ages—one that exhibited many qualities of personal allegiance rather than nationalism. Except for a brief interruption of his authority in Castile, Ferdinand continued to rule Spain as king until his death in 1516. Over the years the nation experienced additional political changes, and in the twentieth century it became a democratic constitutional monarchy under JUAN CARLOS.

Reference: Miller, Townsend, *The Castles and the Crown: Spain, 1451–1555*, 1963.

Ismail, Abd al-Fattah
(1939–1986)
Yemen

In the struggle over the nature of independent South Yemen's development, Abd al-Fattah Ismail took an intractable stance. Against great opposition, he fought for a Soviet-style Marxist state.

Abd al-Fattah Ismail actually came from North Yemen. He was born in the al-Hujariyah district in 1939 but traveled south to Aden, where he attended Aden Technical College. In 1957, he obtained employment as a schoolteacher at the British Petroleum complex.

Ismail soon got involved with the struggle to throw off British rule. He joined the radical National Liberation Front (NLF), which advocated an armed fight for independence. Ismail alone among the NLF's early leaders took a pro-Soviet Marxist stand and pursued a violent strategy linked to a tightly organized vanguard organization. He also stood firmly against any merger of the NLF with more moderate opposition groups.

Ismail fought not only the British but also the competing People's Socialist Party (PSP). By late 1967, he defeated the PSP in several street battles in the city of Aden and captured an important district from Britain. When in November the British withdrew, the NLF assumed power, and in the initial government for South Yemen, Ismail was appointed minister of culture, guidance, and Yemeni unity. This government, however, was more moderate than Ismail, and his opponents ousted him from office in March 1968.

The next year, Ismail maneuvered to successfully overthrow the moderates, and he became the secretary-general of the NLF, his new country's most powerful political position. At the same time, SALIM RUBAY ALI became South Yemen's president. Numerous tensions arose between the two men; although they agreed on a socialist future for South Yemen, they disagreed regarding strategy, with Ismail embracing a Soviet-style Marxism and Rubay Ali adhering to a Chinese model. Ismail also preferred a more centralized, bureaucratic party than that desired by Rubay Ali.

In 1970, Ismail and the NLF, now called the National Front (NF), declared South Yemen to be the People's Democratic Republic of Yemen (PDRY). In 1978, Ismail consolidated his power, arresting Rubay Ali, having him executed, and purging his followers. He converted the NF into the Yemeni Socialist Party (YSP), which relied heavily on advice from Soviets and East Europeans. Ismail signed a 20-year friendship pact with the Soviet Union in 1979, obtained financial assistance from that nation, and developed a planned economy.

Yet Ismail aroused significant opposition. His absorption by Marxist theories distanced him from many Yemenis, who continued their traditional tribal lives linked to Islam. His economic programs proved disruptive and Soviet aid too meager. Furthermore, his close ties to the Soviets meant he could not obtain substantial help from oil-rich

Saudi Arabia. Finally, in April 1980, Ismail's opponents removed him from office while he was traveling outside the country.

For five years he lived in Moscow, but when another power struggle occurred in his homeland he returned, arriving in 1985 and serving on the YSP Central Committee Secretariat. For several months, Ismail and his supporters engaged in a political fight with an opposing faction. This climaxed on 13 January 1986, when assassins opened fire on Ismail's group at a meeting, fatally wounding Ismail.

Despite an often destructive obstinacy, Ismail had been the leader in advancing Marxist thought in his country, which became the only Arab Marxist nation. He founded the YSP and in so doing left a residue of party ideology and organization that remains an influence in the Yemeni Republic, the nation formed in 1990 from the merger of the PDRY and the Yemen Arab Republic (North Yemen), whose own independence had been shaped greatly by YAHYA and by ALI ABDULLAH SALEH.

References: Lackner, Helen, *P.D.R. Yemen: Outpost of Socialist Development in Arabia*, 1985; Page, Stephen, *The Soviet Union and the Yemens: Influence in Asymmetrical Relationships*, 1985; Stookey, Robert W., *South Yemen: A Marxist Republic in Arabia*, 1982.

Ito Hirobumi
(1841–1909)
Japan

Ito Hirobumi crafted Japan's modern constitution and guided his country away from its medieval practices.

When Ito Hirobumi was born on 2 September 1841 in Tokamura, a village in western Honshu, Japan was largely closed to foreigners under the Tokugawa shogunate. The country had a feudal land system and possessed a strong anti-Western bias.

As a young man, Ito adopted this attitude. He studied at a private academy, Shoin Yoshida, and criticized those who took a weak stand toward the West, a particularly trenchant issue when, in 1854, the American commodore, William C. Perry, arrived with a powerful naval fleet, forcing the Japanese to open their borders to trade and, as a result, to Western influence. Ito went to Tokyo (then called Edo) in 1859 and participated in

demonstrations against foreigners, including an attack on the British legation.

But in the 1860s he changed. The shogunate and its traditional practices seemed increasingly backward. Ito came to believe that Western technology needed to be developed. In 1863, he journeyed to London, where the modern inventions impressed him. He urged the leaders in Japan's feudal Choshu domain, his place of birth, to accept the foreign intrusion. Although he had only a minor role in it, he fully supported the overthrow of the shogunate (the government under shogun, or warrior, leadership) and the restoration, under MEIJI in 1867, of the powers of the emperor. Japan's modern political faction intended this move to shake the country from its medieval society and use the emperor as a vehicle for Westernized reform.

Ito's political connections with the new government led him to journey to the United States in 1870, where he studied tax and budget systems. Back home, he helped institute several reforms, including a banking system and such internal improvements as telegraphs and railroads. He earned so much renown that in 1878 he became minister of home affairs, a powerful position that moved him to the forefront of Japanese politics.

In the 1880s, he served three years as premier and used his various political positions to promote constitutional reform. In 1882, he visited Europe, where he studied political theory and its practical application. When he returned home, he established the Office for the Study of the Constitution. But before he proceeded further, he undertook numerous changes in the political system to strengthen the monarchy and prepare it for the shift to a more popular system. For example, he established a body of peers, elite leaders who passed on legislation (and would later be the upper house in the national legislature), and in 1888 an oligarchical privy council to advise the emperor. He desired a mix of liberal democratic arrangements and more conservative ones, with the greatest emphasis on the latter. The Japanese constitution that emerged under his guidance in 1889 gave almost all state legal powers to the emperor, but it also allowed the cabinet substantial control over policy and established a national legislature, or Diet, that included a popularly elected lower house with power over taxes.

Ito served again as premier from 1892 to 1896 and oversaw two important developments in foreign affairs. First, he got Britain and other Western nations to agree that their nationals residing within Japan would be subject to Japanese laws—a concession that placed his nation on equal legal footing with the outsiders. Second, he led Japan into war against China in 1894 and acquired Formosa (Taiwan) and reduced the Chinese influence in Korea.

In 1896, Ito left the government to form a political party, the Seiyukai. He envisioned it as a broad unifying party that would counteract the warring political parties in the Diet, ones he considered obstructionist in blocking cabinet nominations and opposing various proposals. Ito succeeded in gaining a majority of seats for his party in the lower house, and in 1900 he once again became premier, but he encountered unexpected problems when factions in the upper house opposed him. Frustrated by this, he resigned the party presidency and the premiership in 1903.

From 1905 to 1909, Ito served as Japan's resident general in Korea, meaning he managed that land's foreign affairs. He opposed calls within Japan to annex Korea. At the same time, he encouraged the Koreans to modernize and Westernize their society. He intervened directly in Korea's internal affairs, and when the Koreans formed a guerrilla group to oppose Japan, Ito ordered Japanese troops to attack them. In all, Ito neither pleased the annexationists in Japan, who carried out their plan in 1910, nor the nationalists in Korea, who disliked both Western influences and Japanese interference. On 26 October 1909, a Korean nationalist attacked and killed Ito at a train station in Harbin. He left Japan with a new constitution and a modernized society, but also an aggressive one later devastated by World War II and rebuilt under YOSHIDA SHIGERU.

References: Akita, George, *Foundations of Constitutional Government in Modern Japan, 1868–1900,* 1967; Hamada Kengi, *Prince Ito,* 1936.

Iturbide, Augustín de
(1783–1824)
Mexico

In 1820, the Spanish government ordered Augustín de Iturbide to lead his army into southern Mexico and crush an uprising. Iturbide led the troops but turned on the government and joined forces with the rebels in a drive that resulted in Mexican independence.

Augustín de Iturbide came from a privileged position. He was born on 27 September 1783 in Valladolid (today Morelia) to aristocratic parents. His father was Spanish and his mother Creole (a person of Spanish descent born in Mexico). Raised as a strict Catholic, he obtained his education at the seminary in Valladolid and then became manager of his father's haciendas (large estates).

At the time, Spain controlled Mexico and reserved the most important leadership positions for Spaniards and thus restricted the Creoles. This caused discontent among Creoles such as Iturbide. In 1808, when Napoleon overthrew the Spanish monarchy, the subsequent disruption in the colonial government caused a struggle between Spaniards and Creoles over who would control Mexico. Amid the turmoil, Father Miguel Hidalgo organized a rebellion to gain Mexican independence. Some Creoles backed Hidalgo, and he asked Iturbide to join him. Iturbide refused, perhaps dissuaded by what he saw as a radical movement when Hidalgo joined forces with JOSÉ MORELOS and gathered around him Mexico's impoverished. A staunch conservative, Iturbide wanted nothing to do with social reform. So he instead joined the Spanish Royalist forces and fought against Hidalgo. In 1814, he helped defeat Morelos in a battle that ended the first phase of the Mexican fight for independence.

Yet neither the capture of Morelos nor the collapse of Napoleon in Europe and the return of the Spanish monarchy quelled the disturbance in Mexico. Rebel armies continued to fight, albeit weakened, and more significantly for Iturbide, the Creoles united in their protest against Spanish domination. Iturbide sensed this before he accepted his military orders in 1820 to lead a Royalist army into southern Mexico and battle one of the rebels, Vicente Guerrero. After Iturbide journeyed south, his vanity and opportunism held sway, as did his fear that recent changes in the Spanish government would bring liberal reforms to Mexico, such as land redistribution.

Iturbide decided now was the time to create a nation under conservative direction. Hence, rather than fight Guerrero, he signed a pact with him, and the two joined forces against the Spaniards. (A hero of the Mexican independence movement in his own right, Guerrero eventually broke with Iturbide, and in 1829, several years after the latter's fall from power, briefly held the presidency as a reformer.) Iturbide needed money for his campaign and so raided a caravan carrying silver pesos.

> *"I have always been successful in war. . . . I have never lost an action."*

Thus emboldened, in February 1821 he issued his Three Guarantees: allegiance to Catholicism, loyalty to a monarchy (perhaps under the Spanish royal family but with greater Mexican autonomy), and equality for Creoles. He said nothing about Indians, mestizos, or others in Mexico's lower class. As the Creoles rallied behind Iturbide, the Spanish government agreed to a treaty that recognized Mexico's independence with a monarchical political system, and on 27 September 1821 Iturbide entered Mexico City triumphantly. In 1822, the Mexican Congress chose him to be ruler. In a grand ceremony on 21 July, he received the crown as Emperor Augustín I.

Iturbide's power was short-lived. He weakened his position by launching an invasion of Central America in 1821, which gained territory but overextended his resources. Importantly, Mexico had little money, and Iturbide was unable to pay his soldiers. In addition to this, a small liberal group in Congress protested against the monarchical government and pushed for a republican state. In October 1822 Iturbide dissolved Congress, but later in the year Antonio López de Santa Anna, supported by fellow generals and troops, called for a republican constitution. In March 1823, Congress removed Iturbide from office and exiled him to Italy.

Iturbide did not stay there long and in 1824

returned to Mexico, where he urged the people to rebel against the government. Few rallied to his cause, and he was captured, found guilty of treason, and on 19 July 1824 executed by firing squad. Iturbide had won Mexico's independence, but his narrow, egotistical goals doomed his government and sullied his reputation. Reform awaited the efforts of BENITO JUÁREZ in the mid-nineteenth cen-

tury and the Mexican Revolution of the twentieth century, led by FRANCISCO MADERO and EMILIANO ZAPATA, which stimulated the radical changes under LÁZARO CÁRDENAS.

References: Caruso, J. A., *The Liberators of Mexico*, 1954; Robertson, William Spence, *Iturbide of Mexico*, 1952.

Ivan III
(1440–1505)
Russia

In 1480, Ivan III faced his enemy, the army of the great Golden Horde, on the banks of the Ugra River. By this time, he had expanded Russian power and stood poised to end Tatar rule. Then, inexplicably, he retreated toward Moscow. The criticism of his act—as weak and vacillating—made him fearful to enter the city, but to his benefit the Tatar khan, lacking an ally, also retreated. Thus marked the emergence of a Russian state free from foreign control and, as historians have claimed, "the beginning of her national consciousness."

When Ivan III was born Ivan Vasilyevich in Moscow on 22 January 1440, Russia was still in its formative period, with the Moscow princes paying tribute to their Mongol, or Tatar, overlords. Despite this, expansion to the east, across the Volga River, and to the southeast, across the treeless steppe, had already begun and resulted in Slavic domination in those areas. As they invaded the frontier, farmers tackled the often inhospitable land by developing communal agriculture based on collective ownership of the fields.

In his youth, Ivan experienced a precarious situation. His father, Grand Prince Vasily II, faced a rebellion in Muscovy led by an uncle, Iuri. In 1446, the rebels captured Vasily and blinded him (thus his appellation, Vasily the Dark). Vasily's supporters then hid Ivan in a monastery. Some of those he trusted, however, betrayed him and turned him over to his father's enemies. The following year,

discontent within Moscow forced the rebels to release both Vasily and Ivan, and in a political arrangement Ivan, age six, was promised to the daughter of the grand prince of Tver, a shrewd move that boosted the boy's alliances. Ivan's youth remains shrouded in mystery, but a few facts are known. In 1452, he married the Princess of Tver, and six years later his first son was born. In 1458, he led an army against a Tatar horde and prevented it from crossing the Oka River. The victory won him considerable renown.

Meanwhile, Vasily continued to expand Moscow's power, and the city became the greatest in Russia. By the time of his death in 1462, he had gained control of the Upper Volga and Oka; and the principality of Novgorod, although independent, was forced to pay tribute to Moscow.

After Vasily died, Ivan ascended to the throne and expanded his father's policies. He ruled autocratically and at times brutally. At one point, after his brothers and nephews conspired against him, he put them to death. He kept the upper class, or *boyars*, in line by torturing some of them; rebellious Poles, and even princes, he ordered whipped or burned alive. Yet he did not like going into battle and usually avoided leading his men in such assaults.

In 1470, Novgorod challenged Ivan when the princes in that great northwestern city decided to pledge their allegiance to the Polish ruler and deny the ecclesiastical supremacy of Moscow. (This was not a unanimous decision as many in Novgorod preferred annexation by Ivan.) The rulers of Muscovy had for decades considered it their right to name Novgorod's leaders. Ivan reacted to this challenge by sending an army in 1471 to crush the rebellion. His men soundly defeated the Novgorodians. The Muscovites destroyed farms and burned towns, but in all, Ivan's settlement with Novgorod was lenient, eliminating its ability to conduct foreign relations but neither punishing its people with heavy fines or wholesale executions nor annexing large amounts of territory.

Shortly after Ivan departed, the Novgorodians again proved resistant. A second assault, concluded in 1478 with no military resistance from the Novgorodians, silenced them, and in the end Novgorod lost its independence to Moscow, which consequently gained an outlet to the Baltic Sea and dominated the lucrative trade in the northwest.

In 1480, Ivan broke with the Golden Horde of the Tatars, whose power had been deteriorating over the years. After arranging a series of alliances with neighboring khans, Ivan refused to exhibit homage to the Tartars—at one point taking a picture of Khan Akhmed presented to him by Tartar emissaries and throwing it to the ground. More significantly, he refused to pay his customary tribute. This led to the famous confrontation on the Ugra. As the opposing armies faced each other, the river froze over. Ivan believed the Tatars would attack, so he ordered a hasty retreat—whether this was from trepidation or a strategic ploy is not known with certainty. In any event, the sound of the Muscovites breaking camp confused the Tatars, and they also retreated. Thus such a non-battle ended the Tatar yoke.

Historians generally consider this event to mark the emergence of Russia as a nation. In the 1480s and into the early 1500s, Ivan chipped away at Lithuania, gaining the allegiance of several princes in that land and obtaining territory through attacks. He also expanded Russia's frontiers toward the Arctic and the Urals.

Meanwhile, after Ivan's first wife died, he married Sophia Palaeologus, the niece of a former Byzantine emperor. Historians disagree as to whether she influenced Ivan and shaped state policy. Some claim that at her insistence, Ivan signed his letters "tsar," considered himself "Tsar of All Rus," and left his modest wooden dwelling for a palace designed by Italian architects. Certainly, Ivan did these things and considered Moscow the "Third Rome," with the Russian city the true leader of Orthodox Christians. But he may have acted less from Sophia's influence and more from his increasing boldness after his victories against the Novgorodians and Tatars and his expanding contacts with the West. (Paradoxically, his stringent anti-Catholicism worked to close Russia to certain Western ideas.)

Domestically, Ivan initiated numerous changes. Western Europeans not only designed his palace, they came to Russia as artists and doctors. Ivan established a code of law written by Russian and Greek experts that sanctioned torture to obtain evidence and established the beginnings of serfdom. Furthermore, he expanded tax collections to finance the growing services of the state and the expenses associated with his territorial acquisitions.

Ivan died on 27 October 1505 in Moscow. Historians debate the extent of Ivan's courage, but he clearly seized opportunities and left an enormous legacy. Under Ivan, the Russian state was consolidated, Russian territory tripled in size, trade expanded, and Western contacts shaped society. Perhaps above all else, he ended Tartar rule and elevated Moscow from a principality to a sovereign nation. In this way he earned the title "Ivan the Great."

Reference: Fennell, J. L. I., *Ivan the Great of Moscow*, 1961.

Izetbegović, Alija
(b. 1925)
Bosnia-Herzegovina

Over the years, Alija Izetbegović spent time in prison as a victim of political persecution, watched his people suffer at the hands of ethnic cleansing, barely escaped death, and had his authority as Bosnian leader limited to little more than the territory surrounding the capital, Sarajevo, in which he lived.

Alija Izetbegović was born on 8 August 1925 in Bosanski Samac, a town in northeastern Bosnia. His homeland had long been subjected to instability resulting from intense ethnic and religious differences on the Balkan Peninsula. In his youth, Bosnia was a part of the Kingdom of Serbs, Croats, and Slovenes, which had emerged after the Habsburg Empire collapsed in World War I.

During World War II, the Nazis annexed Bosnia and terrorized the country. After the war, Communists led by Josip Broz Tito came to power, and Bosnia-Herzegovina became a member republic of Tito's Yugoslavia. Izetbegović, who, like Tito, had fought against the Nazis, now opposed the Communists and joined the Young Muslims to protect Islam. His dissent resulted in the government arresting him, and in March 1946 he was sentenced to five years at hard labor.

In 1951, Izetbegović studied law in Sarajevo and after receiving his degree became a legal advisor to a construction company. Around 1980, he retired from this position and began writing about Islam. In 1984, his book *Islam between East and West* promoted the religion as a bridge between modern Western Europe and traditional Eastern European culture. By this time, Tito had died, but Izetbegović's writing still raised government retribution, and in 1983 he and several other prominent Muslims were sentenced to prison for disloyalty.

When Izetbegović was released in 1989, conditions in Yugoslavia were changing dramatically. The age-old ethnic and religious tensions grew, expressed through nationalist and anti-Communist movements. In 1990, Izetbegović and other Muslim activists organized the Party of Democratic Action (SDA). They demanded a market economy, multiparty democracy, and a united Bosnia. In November, Bosnia held an open election, and Izetbegović ran as the SDA's candidate for the governing seven-member council. He got 37 percent of the vote and thus won a seat. In December, he was chosen president of the council, and this made him president of Bosnia. The question remained as to what Bosnia's relationship would be with the other Yugoslavian states.

In 1991, a civil war erupted in neighboring Croatia. The following year, amid this turmoil, Bosnian Serbs declared their independence from Bosnia, claiming more than half of that state's territory. While Croatia, meanwhile, issued a declaration of independence from Yugoslavia and thus hastened the fall of that nation, Bosnia decided to hold its own referendum on nationhood. Bosnians voted overwhelmingly to break from Yugoslavia. Serb extremists in the Serbian areas then joined with the Yugoslav army, surrounded Sarajevo with roadblocks, and bombarded it.

Izetbegović had hoped to avoid bloodshed. All during 1991 he had contained radicals within his own Muslim community and tried to reach a negotiated settlement with Yugoslavia. But after Croatia seceded, it was clear that continued membership in Yugoslavia would mean domination by Serbs, who were now the most powerful group in the Yugoslav nation.

In April 1992, the United States and the European Community recognized Bosnia's independence. The Serbs, however, continued to attack Bosnian cities as they began "ethnic cleansing," forcing Muslims and Croats out of areas by relocating or killing them. Izetbegović entered negotiations with the Serbs, but at one point, while on his way back to Bosnia from Portugal (the site of the talks), they captured and threatened to kill him. An international protest led to his release after one night in captivity.

Throughout 1992, the situation in Bosnia worsened. Izetbegović tried to get the West to intervene with military assistance, if necessary, to stop the ethnic cleansing, but he obtained only a limited and uncoordinated response. In 1993, the United States and Britain proposed a plan that would divide Bosnia into provinces, each of them autonomous and distributed among Muslims, Serbs, and Croats.Izetbegović did not like the plan because it would allow the Serbs to keep land they had captured from the Bosnians and thus reward aggression. Bosnia's position, however, was weak, so he reluctantly agreed to the proposal. The Bosnian Serbs, though, rejected it and demanded a completely independent state carved from Bosnia.

By 1994, Izetbegović was presiding over a desperate situation. Although the Bosnian Serbs had a falling out with the Yugoslavian Serbs who had supported them, they continued to battle Bosnia with great success. And although Western European nations and the United States condemned Serb aggression, they did little to stop it and restricted their military action to occasional air strikes against the Bosnian Serb army. Izetbegović was only able to exert his authority over a small portion of Bosnian territory, as the Serbs controlled most of it. Late in 1994 a precarious truce took hold in Bosnia, one that Izetbegović hoped could lead to a permanent peace plan. While negotiations among various parties continue, so too does the violence, particularly as a result of attacks by the Bosnian Serbs, who, in May 1995, captured and held hostage several hundred UN troops.

References: Kaplan, Robert D., *Balkan Ghosts: A Journey through History*, 1993; Magas, Branka, *The Destruction of Yugoslavia: Tracking the Breakup of 1980–1992*, 1993.

Jagan, Cheddi
(b. 1918)
Guyana

Cheddi Jagan steered a radical course in his campaign for independence. In so doing, he won the enmity of the United States and antagonized the British who, on two occasions, dissolved his government.

Cheddi Jagan was born on 22 March 1918 in Plantation Port Mourant. His parents, who had emigrated from India, were poor and labored in the sugarcane fields that dotted this country. At the time, Britain ruled the territory as a colony, called British Guiana.

As a child, Cheddi, like his parents, worked the land. Despite his poverty, he attended Port Mourant Primary School, run by the Anglican Church, and then transferred to Scots School at Rose Hall Village. In 1933, his parents sent him to the capital, Georgetown, where he attended Queen's College, a government secondary school for boys.

After completing his schooling, Jagan failed to get a civil service job, so he went to the United States, where he enrolled at Howard University in a two-year predental program. From there, he went to Northwestern University in Illinois and obtained his degree in dentistry. While his stay in America exposed him to cultural diversity and economic prosperity, it also exposed him to deep racial antagonism that he long remembered.

In October 1943, Jagan returned home and established a dental practice in Georgetown. He had married while in the United States, and soon his wife, Janet Rosenberg, joined him. Through the years, she exerted an important influence in Guyanan political circles.

"I am looking to the day when there will be a greater justice in Guyana."

Within a short time, Jagan entered politics, becoming treasurer in 1945 of the Manpower Citizens' Association (MPCA), an organization representing the colony's sugar workers. Here he came into contact with other Caribbean-area labor leaders. One year later, he quit the MPCA in a policy dispute. In 1947, he won a seat to the House of Assembly on the Labour Party ticket, but considered that organization too moderate. Consequently, he affiliated with the Political Affairs Committee, a group that advocated Guyanan independence and Marxism, and helped lead a protest by Indo-Guyanese sugar workers. This effort earned him much recognition, and in 1950 he founded the People's Progressive Party (PPP). He built a following among the two major racial groups in Guyana, the Indians and the Africans, partly by bringing FORBES BURNHAM, a prominent Afro-Guyanan, into the party. Jagan worked as leader of the PPP parliamentary group, and Burnham served as party chairman.

The PPP scored its first victory in 1950 when Janet Jagan won a seat on the Georgetown council. By this time, Cheddi Jagan had become an ardent nationalist and socialist, a position that made the British wary. Nevertheless, the colonial power allowed elections in 1953 that resulted in the PPP gaining most of the seats in the Assembly and Jagan becoming premier. Jagan's term, however, was brief. After he expanded the state's role in the economy and got the legislature to pass a law favorable to a pro-PPP labor union, Britain suspended the colonial constitution and removed him from office.

Jagan returned to his dentistry but continued his involvement in politics. In 1955, race proved a factor in dividing the PPP when Burnham formed a separate wing within the party. Hence, while each man largely agreed on socialist economic policies, Jagan appealed to the Indo-Guyanese and Burnham to the Afro-Guyanese. In 1957, Burnham merged his wing with another group to form a new political party, the People's National Congress (PNC). That same year, the PPP again won at the polls, and Jagan was named minister of trade and industry.

Jagan continued his ascendency with another election victory in 1961 that made him prime minister. He pushed hard for independence, but the British refused to set a date for nationhood. Jagan also allied himself with Communist regimes, especially Cuba, and pursued a socialist agenda. From 1961 to 1964, the PNC encouraged strikes and riots to oust Jagan. These attacks were part of a plan developed and financed by the Central Intelligence Agency in the United States. A change in legislative apportionment by the British damaged the PPP, and although the PNC finished behind the PPP in the 1964 elections, it joined with another party to form a coalition government and keep the PPP from power. Jagan declared the election fraudulent and tried to stay in office, but under American pressure the British intervened and removed him in favor of Burnham. Two years later, Guyana gained its independence from Britain.

Jagan became the leader of the opposition in the National Assembly, but through the 1970s his following weakened as Burnham gained most of the power. In 1992, however, the PPP won a majority in the legislature, and Jagan became prime minister. Although Jagan was not the leader of Guyana at the time of its independence, his early crusade made him one of the founders of his nation.

References: Burrowes, Reynold A., *The Wild Coast: An Account of Politics in Guyana*, 1984; Jagan, Cheddi, *The West on Trial: My Fight for Guyana's Freedom*, 1966.

Jawara, Dauda
(b. 1924)
The Gambia

As The Gambia proceeded toward independence in the 1960s, Dauda Jawara reflected his homeland's political process in two ways. First, he was the reluctant nationalist; second, he pursued moderate policies and thus avoided extreme measures.

David Jawara was born of Mandingo parents in 1924 in Barajally and gained a distinct advantage when his father, a wealthy Muslim farmer, chose him from among six sons to attend the Methodist Boys High School at Bathurst. After graduation, Jawara worked in the Government Medical Department as a nurse and in 1948 won a scholarship to Achimota College, which he attended for a year before beginning his studies in veterinary medicine at Glasgow University in Scotland. He earned a degree as a veterinary surgeon and then in the early 1950s continued his studies and became a specialist in tropical veterinary medicine. In 1953, he earned appointment to the Royal College of Veterinary Surgeons, a great honor.

When in 1954 Jawara returned to his home, he entered the government service as a veterinarian and rose rapidly to become principal veterinary officer—symbolic of British attempts to Africanize the civil service. In 1955, he converted to Christianity. At this time, he involved himself in Gambian politics, focusing on the differences between the colony centered at Bathurst and the protectorate governing the interior. By Jawara's era, universal suffrage existed in the colony while Britain followed a policy of indirect rule over the protectorate that caused the area to have only limited political rights and a secondary economic status.

In 1959, Jawara joined the Protectorate People's Society aimed at advancing protectorate concerns. Later that year, this organization became the People's Progressive party (PPP), and in 1960 after Britain extended suffrage to the protectorate, Jawara entered politics. He ran for a seat in the Gambian assembly and won amid a strong showing by the PPP. Jawara also accepted appointment as minister of education. From this position he broadened his political following and advocated more autonomy for Gambians, not through radicalism but through new constitutional arrangements with Britain. He also explored political union with Senegal.

Jawara had a brief tenure as education minister—in 1961 he and all the PPP cabinet members resigned when the governor appointed P. S. N'Jie of the opposing United Party as chief minister. N'Jie represented the old colony interests and the traditional chiefs in the protectorate. New elections in 1962, however, provided Jawara and the PPP an overwhelming victory and he became prime minister. As the British pushed for an exit from The Gambia, Jawara began extended negotiations with them for his homeland's full independence, finally obtained on 18 February 1965. That same year, Jawara embraced Islam and changed his name to Dauda. The British knighted him in 1966.

As prime minister, Jawara proposed that The Gambia revise its constitution to provide for a republic with a popularly elected president. Although the voters at first rejected this idea, in 1970 a new constitution won approval, and on 24 April, Jawara became the first president of the Republic of The Gambia.

Throughout the 1970s, Jawara enjoyed widespread support, and the PPP dominated the legislature, regularly obtaining 70 percent of the vote. Jawara steered a moderate course for his nation; he avoided the extreme Islamic movements and tried to keep expenditures within The Gambia's means. He became an outspoken advocate of environmental concerns, and he led relief efforts to the drought-ravaged Sahel, an action for which he received a medal from the United Nations. The drought, however, affected The Gambia through reduced agricultural output.

As economic problems mounted in the 1980s, including increased oil prices, Jawara initiated budget cuts that caused discontent. In July 1981, while he was in Britain, dissidents launched a coup attempt. Assisted by the Senegalese army, Jawara defeated the rebels, but over 600 people died and Banjul, the capital, was in ruins. Jawara refused demands to kill those who had supported the rebellion, and he instead insisted on fair trials. Most rebel leaders were eventually released, and the 21 sentenced to death for treason were never executed.

After the coup attempt Jawara moved toward forming a confederation with Senegal. But as Gambian suspicions and nationalist feelings resurfaced, little came of this. In 1992, Jawara won relection to his fifth term and the PPP captured 25 of 36 seats in the House of Representatives. Two years later, though, a military coup overthrew Jawara and declared the suspension of political parties.

References: Cohen, Robin, ed., *African Islands and Enclaves,* 1983; Gailey, Harry A., *A History of The Gambia,* 1963.

Jefferson, Thomas
(1743–1826)
United States

Tucked in the verdant Virginia hills west of Charlottesville, Monticello bespeaks the values of its designer and builder, Thomas Jefferson; the Romanesque features show a mix of reason and passion, the essential contradiction of Jefferson's life and central to his consistencies. He embraced planning and rationality and exuded love for Virginia, his home, and republicanism.

Thomas Jefferson was the third child of Peter Jefferson and Jane Randolph Jefferson. Born on 2 April 1743 at Tuckahoe, the family home in Virginia, he entered a distinguished societal standing, for in marrying Jane Randolph, Peter Jefferson had connected with a wealthy and powerful Virginia family. As a surveyor, Peter familiarized himself with the best lands and in 1735 had acquired Tuckahoe, at the time unimproved acreage on which he built a house.

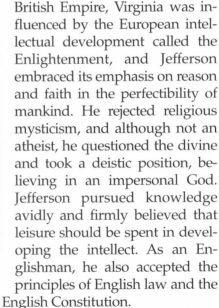

Even as a child, Jefferson pursued his studies with enthusiasm. He learned Latin, Greek, and some French from Reverend William Douglas and then, under Reverend James Maury, immersed himself in Greek and Roman classics, works he returned to throughout his life. In 1757, he unexpectedly obtained adult responsibilities when his father died. Peter left Thomas 2,750 acres of land, several slaves, and the responsibility of caring for his mother, brother, and four sisters. While this burdened Jefferson, it also provided him with the wealth that made possible his immersion in politics.

Jefferson made his own decisions in running the household and in 1760 entered William and Mary College, from which he graduated two years later. He subsequently pursued law under the guidance of the preeminent Virginia teacher, George Wythe. As a colony within the British Empire, Virginia was influenced by the European intellectual development called the Enlightenment, and Jefferson embraced its emphasis on reason and faith in the perfectibility of mankind. He rejected religious mysticism, and although not an atheist, he questioned the divine and took a deistic position, believing in an impersonal God. Jefferson pursued knowledge avidly and firmly believed that leisure should be spent in developing the intellect. As an Englishman, he also accepted the principles of English law and the English Constitution.

Jefferson gained admittance to the bar in 1767 and continued his law practice until the Revolution intruded. In 1772, he married Martha (Wayles) Skelton, and they lived at Monticello, then under construction. The marriage brought him additional land but did not ease his perennial indebtedness, not unusual in a plantation economy where many planters had outstanding accounts with British merchants. Meanwhile, he entered politics in 1769 when he won election to the House of Burgesses. In 1770, he was named lieutenant of Albermarle County and in 1773 became the surveyor.

By now, colonial relations with Britain had become strained over such issues as the Stamp Act, Townshend Acts, and the Boston Massacre. Jefferson sided with the radicals and in so doing reflected a consensus within the Virginia elite that something was seriously wrong with the British Empire. This stand partly reflected economics, for the colony's planters did not want their involvement in western land speculation hampered by regulations, and they disliked owing so much money to British merchants. While such economic concerns influenced Jefferson, so too did his conviction that British policies threatened local autonomy and liberty.

Unlike some other revolutionary leaders, such as his fellow Virginian Patrick Henry, Jefferson was not a good speaker; as a result, he worked mainly behind the scenes and used his impressive writing ability. By 1774, he emerged as the leading radical in Virginia and drafted a document too extreme for the Virginia Convention, then preparing to send delegates to the First Continental Congress. Yet, Jefferson's ideas were published in pamphlet form as *A Summary View of the Rights of British North America,* and widely read. In it, the Virginian denied Parliament's authority over the colonies, arguing that their attachment to Britain came only through their voluntary recognition of the king's sovereignty. As with most of his revolutionary writing, he displayed John Locke's view about laws of nature, and although he did not yet advocate separation, he set the foundation for it.

Jefferson sat in the Continental Congress in 1775 where, like SAMUEL ADAMS, he disagreed with John Dickinson and other moderates who wanted to pursue compromise with Britain. After helping Virginia compose its new constitution, he returned to Congress in 1776, influenced by *Common Sense,* an inflammatory pamphlet written by THOMAS PAINE, and more determined to pursue separation. Early in June, Congress chose him, JOHN ADAMS, BENJAMIN FRANKLIN, Roger Sherman, and Robert R. Livingston to draft a declaration of independence. Finished in July, the Declaration was largely his work and displayed the influence of John Locke; in fact, Jefferson admitted he had invented nothing

new. Nevertheless, when Jefferson asserted in eloquent language that "all men are created equal," he unleashed a revolutionary statement that thereafter influenced populist uprisings elsewhere in the world.

The Virginian did not believe in complete equality of all people, however, and this led critics to later accuse him of hypocrisy, particularly with respect to his negative statements regarding women and his continued ownership of slaves. (Interestingly, Jefferson included in the Declaration a condemnation of the slave trade that Congress ordered stricken.) Yet on numerous occasions he expressed his dislike for slavery and hoped for its abolishment. In fact, he believed in a continuing revolution that would not end with separation from Britain and would bring additional social and political changes. This view was evident in his comment more than a decade later that "the Earth belongs in usufruct to the living."

In the fall of 1776, Jefferson returned to Virginia and entered the House of Delegates. In June 1779, he won election to the governorship and vigorously pursued reform to lessen aristocratic privileges and firmly separate church and state. He and a special board proposed revisions to dozens of Virginia laws, and although the House did not pass most of them until after he left office, he clearly set changes in motion. In 1785, his proposal to end primogeniture took effect (which thus ended the requirement that all land go only to the eldest male heir), and the following year the legislature passed his Bill for Establishing Religious Freedom, one he considered an important libertarian statement for its assertion that religious opinions should not shape civil rights. His effort to establish gradual emancipation, however, failed.

Despite his many accomplishments, as governor Jefferson also experienced failure. He was unable to effectively meet the British military assaults against Virginia, in one instance displaying indecision in calling up the militia, and in another suffering disorganization in a botched defense of Richmond. Overall, his government lacked money and manpower, and in June 1781, as the Redcoats tightened their grip, he left the governorship. Days later (while technically still in office awaiting his successor), Jefferson fled Monticello to avoid capture by the invading British army. Later that year, the legislature investigated his conduct and

> *"The tree of liberty must be refreshed from time to time with the blood of patriots and tyrants."*

absolved him of any wrongdoing. Still, critics accused him of incompetence and even cowardice.

Back at his beloved Monticello, Jefferson supervised his farm and, in 1782, wrote his *Notes on the State of Virginia*, a masterful work that displayed his far-ranging knowledge. The *Notes* discussed Virginia geography, natural history, political and social customs, agriculture, and industry. He criticized slavery and offered observations that whites were superior to blacks in terms of intellect and inferior to them in terms of music—conclusions derided much later as racist.

Tragedy struck Jefferson in September 1782 when his wife died. He never fully recovered from this loss and never remarried. Perhaps to fill a void, he reentered politics and in 1783 was elected a delegate to the national Congress. He served on several important committees and made proposals that later became the Northwest Ordinance of 1787 and organized the Ohio Valley region, with slavery prohibited.

Jefferson traveled to Europe in 1784 to assist Benjamin Franklin and John Adams in negotiating commercial treaties. The following year, he was named minister to France. In that capacity, he reached a trade agreement with Prussia and gained concessions from the French on tariffs levied against American goods. During his stay in France, Sally Hemings, one of his slaves, tended to his household. Her presence added fuel to the accusations advanced in the 1790s that she was his concubine. To this very day, historians debate the assertion, recognizing that little evidence exists to prove the point.

The Virginian was thus in Europe when debate raged in America over whether to ratify the Constitution and end the Articles of Confederation. Jefferson sided with his fellow Virginian JAMES MADISON and supported the Constitution, although without enthusiasm. He returned to the United States in 1789 and accepted GEORGE WASHINGTON's request that he serve as secretary of state.

Jefferson had a tumultuous experience in Washington's cabinet as the new nation's politics intensified. He found himself constantly at odds with Secretary of the Treasury ALEXANDER HAMILTON, who pushed through Congress measures that strengthened the federal government at the expense of the states and provided financial programs and a national bank bill weighted toward commercial interests rather than the farmers'.

The French Revolution complicated the political scene when Hamilton and his followers considered the event a grave threat to order, and Jefferson and his followers praised it for advancing liberty. Hamilton soon emerged as leader of the Federalist Party, and Jefferson, along with Madison, organized the Jeffersonian Republicans, or Republican Party (no relation to the modern Republican Party). The Federalists sincerely believed that a Republican victory would unleash the masses and bring anarchy, while the Republicans believed that the Federalists intended to establish a monarchy.

As secretary of state, Jefferson supported a neutral policy toward the war then raging between England and France, although he sympathized with the French. In 1793, he agreed to the recall of the controversial French minister Edmund Genet, whose actions challenged Washington's authority. Jefferson resigned from the cabinet on 31 December and returned to Monticello.

His retirement proved short-lived as the fight between Federalists and Republicans polarized the nation. After Washington decided not to seek a third term, Jefferson entered the presidential contest for 1796. The electors chose John Adams over him, but Jefferson served as vice-president. During his term, he composed the Kentucky Resolutions of 1798 in reaction to the Alien and Sedition Acts, passed by the Federalist Congress to restrict foreigners and free speech. (Madison wrote the similarly worded Virginia Resolutions.) Jefferson portrayed the Constitution as a compact among the states and asserted that under certain circumstances the states could nullify federal legislation.

As the 1800 presidential election neared, Jefferson had a falling out with Adams, whom he considered too pro-British and too weak toward Hamilton. Although no longer in the federal cabinet, Hamilton exerted substantial influence in Adams's administration. Jefferson entered the presidential contest, and when the electors deadlocked between Jefferson and the New Yorker Aaron Burr, also a Republican, the House of Representatives chose the Virginian as president and Burr as vice-president.

Jefferson called his election the "Revolution of 1800." Although this phrase exaggerated his subsequent accomplishments, he initiated substantial changes to break with the previous Federalist administrations and build a Republican community that would protect and promote all the major segments of society: agriculture, banking, trade, and manufacturing.

He particularly sought to roll back Federalist programs that had favored aristocracy. For example, he determined to eliminate the national debt. Hamilton had considered the debt a positive good because it linked wealthy men, who purchased the securities issued by the treasury, to the national government and thus built loyalty to it. Jefferson considered the debt bad because it enriched the wealthy few and enhanced their power. Although the Virginian did not eliminate the debt, he reduced it considerably. He also lowered taxes, which he believed burdened the middle class. He accomplished these goals partly through a substantial reduction in defense spending.

No matter what the program, Jefferson feared that the Federalist-dominated courts would overturn Republican reforms. Hence, in 1803 he launched his War on the Judiciary to remove from the bench blatantly biased and vindictive Federalists. Although Congress impeached and convicted a few judges, the war ended after Jefferson failed at getting a Supreme Court justice removed.

In perhaps his most spectacular accomplishment, Jefferson purchased the Louisiana Territory from France in 1804. The acquisition, for about 4 cents per acre, doubled the size of the United States and extended its reach to the Rocky Mountains. Jefferson considered the new land an "Empire for Liberty," meaning a territory where small farmers could buy land and participate politically. The president, however, said little about the purchase, probably because its ratification required a loose interpretation of the Constitution, a position he had opposed in the past as too Hamiltonian.

In 1804, Jefferson won reelection. His second term, though, floundered on foreign policy. Britain and France, once again at war, attacked American shipping. The British did the most damage and impressed, or forced, American sailors into the Royal Navy. Jefferson retaliated in 1807 by having Congress enact an embargo, which took all American ships off the high seas. He thought this would force concessions from the British, who needed American foodstuffs. But the embargo wrecked the domestic economy and emboldened Jefferson's enemies. As Jefferson prepared to leave office in 1809, Congress partially lifted the embargo.

Jefferson lived his remaining years at Monticello, where he studied and conducted extensive correspondence with prominent Americans. At one point, he sold many of his books to the government and this became the basis for the Library of Congress. He promoted improvements in Virginia's schools and in 1814 developed plans for a university. In 1818, the state legislature agreed to found the University of Virginia, which was chartered the following year. Jefferson drew up the architectural plans and the program of courses, developed an innovational administrative structure, and promoted free inquiry.

In his later years, Jefferson received accolades from learned societies. His work in science broke new ground and his collection of paintings and statues signified his appreciation and support for the arts. Debt, however, threatened him, and he nearly lost Monticello (which later passed from his heirs). Jefferson died at Monticello on 4 July 1826, just hours before John Adams passed away at Quincy, Massachusetts; ironically, this occurred on the fiftieth anniversary of the Declaration of Independence, which along with the statute of religious freedom and the founding of the University of Virginia, Jefferson considered to be his greatest accomplishment.

References: Brodie, Fawn M., *Thomas Jefferson: An Intimate History*, 1974; Cunningham, Noble E., *In Pursuit of Reason: The Life of Thomas Jefferson*, 1987; Levy, Leonard, *Jefferson and Civil Liberties: The Darker Side*, 1972; Malone, Dumas, *Jefferson and His Time*, 6 volumes, 1948–1981; Miller, John C., *The Wolf by the Ears: Thomas Jefferson and Slavery*, 1980; Peterson, Merrill, *The Jefferson Image in the American Mind*, 1960; Peterson, Merrill, *Thomas Jefferson and the New Nation*, 1986; Randall, Willard Sterne, *Thomas Jefferson: A Life*, 1993; Smelser, Marshall, *The Democratic Republic, 1801–1815*, 1968.

Jinnah, Mohammed Ali
(1876–1948)
Pakistan

As Indian nationalists strived for independence after World War I, they confronted a major obstacle: the divisiveness between Muslims and Hindus. As a Muslim, Mohammed Ali Jinnah at first united with the Hindus in fighting British rule but then opted for a separate Muslim state, a decision that ultimately led to the creation of Pakistan.

Mohammed Ali Jinnah, born 25 December 1876, hailed from a prosperous family. His father, Jinnahbhai, was a merchant in Karachi. After being tutored at home, Mohammed attended Sind Madrasasah High School in 1887 and then Mission High School. In 1892, he traveled to London and studied at Lincoln's Inn, where he prepared for the bar. He became a keen student of British politics and involved himself in a successful effort to get an Indian nationalist, Dadabhai Naoroji, elected to Parliament. Naoroji, who had lived in London many years, was called the "Grand Old Man of India."

Jinnah returned to India in 1896 and began practicing law in Bombay, very much the Englishman in dress, manners, and speech. For the next decade, he concentrated on establishing his law firm, which became quite lucrative, and remained outside Indian politics. Yet political developments caused Jinnah to take a more public role. He did so when he participated in the 1906 session of the Indian National Congress (Congress), a Hindu-dominated nascent political party formed to advance Indian rights. At the meeting, he heard his friend Dadabhai Naoroji declare that Britain had inflicted suffering on Indians. This speech moved Jinnah and further convinced him to pursue reform. In 1910, he joined the colonial government's Imperial Legislative Council, established after British reforms the previous year provided for more elective offices and a widened, although still greatly limited, franchise for Indians. These reforms also met the demands of some Muslims in creating special electorates and representation for Muslims, hence fostering a separate Islamic identity that would thereafter permeate Indian politics.

In 1913, Jinnah joined the All-India Muslim League (the League), a Muslim-dominated organization that expressed loyalty to the Crown while calling for the advancement of Muslim rights. Despite this change in party loyalties, he remained committed to Hindu-Muslim cooperation and saw Indian nationalism as encompassing both religious groups.

During World War I, Jinnah played an instrumental role in formulating the Lucknow Pact that pledged Hindu-Muslim unity and was intended to forge a common effort against British rule. In 1918, he led a public demonstration against a retiring British governor and called for a democratic uprising against autocracy. The following year, he resigned from the Imperial Legislative Council as a protest against British policies.

Jinnah's cooperative position with the Hindus began shifting when MOHANDAS GANDHI gained the leadership of Congress in 1920. Gandhi converted Congress into a mass party and infused it with revolutionary ideas and tactics stressing civil disobedience. Jinnah considered Gandhi's approach too Hindu-oriented and too encouraging of popular political power, which he distrusted, and so he quit both Congress and the League and for a brief period removed himself from the main political currents. He still advocated Hindu-Muslim unity, however.

In the mid-1920s, Jinnah sat in India's legislature and led the faction in the League that advocated an alliance with the Hindus. He wanted to settle the religious conflict and, toward this end, in 1930 attended the first Round Table Conference in London. He sought separate electorates and reserved seats for Muslims in the various Indian legislatures; he failed to get these, however, and felt beleaguered when Congress leader JAWAHARLAL NEHRU opposed even minor concessions in this area.

Muslim separatism influenced Jinnah and other Indians in the 1930s. Sir Muhammed Iqbal, the foremost Muslim philosopher in South Asia, advocated communalism rather than national statehood as the basis for political entities. Thus, he believed India should be a confederation in which Muslims would have their own separate community. This was echoed by Rahmat Ali, who in a widely circulated pamphlet declared that India was not a single nation and that it should be divided into regions with the northwest as its own Muslim nation, to be called Pakistan.

After a period of disgust with Muslim divisiveness and in-fighting, during which Jinnah refused to return home and remained in England, he became the League's leader in 1934 and adopted the two-nation theory. Jinnah was not a devoutly religious man. In fact, he followed few of the traditional Islamic precepts, but he wanted to protect the Muslim community and considered the two-nation theory as a way to unite Muslims behind the League.

The final break with Congress and the Hindus came in 1937, when Congress won provincial elections and then rejected any League participation in forming the new governments. Jinnah feared Hindus would trample Muslim rights. When, in December 1939, the Congress provincial ministers resigned to protest British policy, Jinnah proclaimed that Muslims had been delivered from Hindu rule. Then on 23 March 1940, Jinnah and the League declared that Muslims should have a separate nation located in their strongholds of northwestern and northeastern India. Jinnah rejected any independence plan without this provision.

During World War II, Jinnah took a cooperative approach with Britain, while Congress became more confrontational and demanded that the British relinquish their rule over India. Despite his stance, Jinnah criticized a British proposal made in 1942 for Indian independence after the war as too vague with respect to a Muslim nation.

In 1946, rioting occurred between Muslims and Hindus, stirred in part by Jinnah's demands for direct action in getting a separate nation. Jinnah then worked within India's interim government to calm the violence. Many within Britain saw the unrest as an indication that Muslims and Hindus could not live together peacefully, and they thus became receptive to Jinnah's two-nation approach.

Finally, on 14 July 1947, the British House of Commons approved the India Independence Act that created two dominions, India and Pakistan. They would become nations after the various princely states in India decided to which entity they would accede their authority.

On 7 August, Jinnah arrived in Karachi, where throngs of people cheered him, and on 14 August, he became the first leader, officially the governor-general, of Pakistan. He faced enormous problems, including an economy torn from its Indian connections, enormous dislocations as Hindus left Pakistan for India and Muslims fled to Pakistan, and a dominion separated geographically between West and East Pakistan, with Indian territory intervening between them. Early on, Jinnah consolidated his power, becoming both legal advisor and president of the Constituent Assembly. He appointed as governors men loyal to him and began an economic policy reflecting his urban bias for industrialization. But before he could firmly establish a new government, age overtook him and he died on 11 September 1948.

Jinnah had been the architect of Pakistani independence, so much so that some observers claim he created the nation almost single-handedly. Pakistanis hailed him as Quaid-i-Azam (Great Leader). He was indeed the father of Pakistan and would have bemoaned the civil war in 1971 that resulted in East Pakistan seceding and forming a separate nation, Bangladesh.

References: Bolitho, Hector, *Jinnah: Creator of Pakistan,* 1954; Jalal, Ayesha, *The Sole Spokesman: Jinnah, the Muslim League, and the Demand for Pakistan,* 1985; Merriam, Allen Hayes, *Gandhi vs. Jinnah: The Debate over the Partition of India,* 1980; Wollper, Stanley, *Jinnah of Pakistan.*

John, Patrick
(b. 1938)
Dominica

An erratic leader, Patrick John guided Dominica to independence but also jeopardized its stability with his questionable financial dealings.

Patrick John was born on 7 January 1938 in Dominica, at that time a British colony. He attended Roseau Boys' School and St. Mary's Academy, both located in Roseau, the island's largest city. After graduating from St. Mary's, he taught there for four years. He then worked as a shipping clerk and in 1960 helped to organize the Waterfront and Allied Locals Union. His labor activity reflected the trend toward union development after World War II.

At that time, another change also occurred: Political parties developed after Britain made constitutional changes, including the expansion of suffrage. John's checkered public career began in 1965, when he ran as a member of the Dominica Labour Party (DLP) and won election as mayor of Roseau. Presently, scandal ensued when investigators reported that he had taken money from the city treasury to lend to a friend. The opposition Dominica Freedom Party (DFP) criticized him, and in 1968 he lost his bid for reelection.

In 1970, John resigned his post as union leader to run for a seat in Dominica's Parliament. An outgoing and friendly man, he developed a substantial following and advocated reforms to help Dominican workers. He won his seat and while in Parliament served in various ministerial positions, including minister of communications, home affairs, agriculture, and finance. When in 1974, the Labour Party leader resigned as premier, John was named to replace him. He immediately sponsored a bill to make illegal the radical black power movement that had surfaced on the island. Parliament passed the measure easily. He also took a strong stand in support of independence, and after he won election as premier in 1975, he formally announced his plan for Dominica to become a nation. The island gained this status in November 1978.

Although Dominicans as a whole supported the independence drive, John soon lost supporters with his controversial labor and financial programs. He proclaimed a "new socialism" that would benefit the entire nation, but he failed to abide by a government agreement to increase the pay of civil servants, and this led to strikes and demonstrations against him. Furthermore, in 1979 he reached a secret agreement with a disreputable financier to establish a zone in northern Dominica, some 45 square miles in size, which the developer would acquire under a long-term lease establishing a rental charge of only $100 per year. The "Freeport" deal compromised Dominican sovereignty, and after news of it was leaked, protests ensued.

Consequently, John had to cancel the deal. In 1979, he reacted to the controversy surrounding him by trying to censor the leading newspaper and make strikes illegal. When an antigovernment demonstration erupted in May, Dominican troops fired into the crowd, and John stood steadfastly behind the military's action.

In June 1979, the DFP joined in a coalition with dissident DLP members and others to deny John his majority in Parliament and oust him from office. Oliver Seraphin became the new prime minister. The crisis atmosphere intensified after Hurricane David devastated the island. A highly-charged political campaign in 1980 resulted in a DFP victory, and EUGENIA CHARLES became prime minister. John promised to end her administration, and in March 1981, Charles announced she had uncovered a plot by the former prime minister to overthrow the government. After a trial, John was sentenced to prison. In 1990, the government released him based on his good behavior while in jail, and he worked to rebuild his political following, winning appointment in 1991 as general-secretary of the National Workers' Union.

> *"Today we see law and order in Dominica! It is unfortunate that some have gone to the land of the beyond."*

Reference: Honychurch, Lennox, *The Dominica Story: A History of the Island*, 1984.

Jonathan, Leabua
(b. 1914)
Lesotho

A grandson of Mshweshwe, the Basuto chief and founder of the original Lesotho state, Leabua Jonathan advocated close relations with neighboring South Africa.

Leabua Jonathan was born on 30 October 1914. He obtained his education at a Protestant mission school in Leribe. In 1934, he worked in the gold mines in neighboring South Africa. Three years later, he returned to Lesotho and decided to enter public service. Britain governed Lesotho at the time as a Crown colony, and it was within this administrative structure that Jonathan gained valuable experience. He became president of the Basuto courts, served on the National Council (where he was named one of the ruling chiefs), and acted as advisor to the Paramount Regent, or ruler.

South Africa dominated Lesotho's economy (and territorially surrounded the colony), and in 1959 Jonathan organized the Basuto National Party (BNP) to promote cooperation with the neighboring nation—a controversial stand given the white supremacy there. The BNP did not do well in its first elections, but Jonathan gained a seat on the Legislative Council (a representative body created after a constitutional change).

In 1964, as Lesotho moved closer to independence, he advocated stronger economic ties with South Africa to develop industries and provide for the exportation of water. Although he criticized South Africa's white supremacy, he nonetheless considered his homeland's economic survival and growth crucial. He denounced communism, and for this received the support of the Catholic Church (which he had joined years earlier). He also journeyed to London as part of a delegation and joined in forcefully pressing his homeland's case for more autonomy. The British, who had been moving in this direction, agreed to new elections the following year, preparatory to independence.

Jonathan's proposals regarding South Africa stirred much opposition with accusations that he would be a mere puppet controlled by the neighboring nation. In the 1965 elections he lost his bid for a legislative seat, but the BNP won a narrow victory overall. Jonathan won a seat in a by-election and in July became prime minister. After Lesotho gained its independence on 4 October 1966, he continued as prime minister and served as minister of external affairs.

In 1970, though, the BNP lost in new elections, and when Jonathan thus faced ouster, he suspended the constitution and arrested the king, Moshoeshoe, who went into exile in the Netherlands. Jonathan justified his action as necessary to thwart communism, which he claimed his opponents embraced. His action produced turmoil, including riots. In December, he allowed the king to return, based upon the monarch's promise to serve only as a figurehead.

Despite his earlier warnings about communism, in the 1980s, Jonathan developed closer relations with China, North Korea, and the Soviet Union. At the same time, opposition to the BNP grew, and in January 1986 the military overthrew his government. Military rule continued until 1993, when a civilian prime minister gained power.

References: Helpern, Jack, *South Africa's Hostages*, 1965; Stevens, Richard P., *Lesotho, Botswana, and Swaziland*, 1967.

Joseph II
(1741–1790)
Austria

Following the rule of his mother, the Empress MARIA THERESA, Joseph II enthusiastically advanced reforms and further centralized the Austrian Empire. Yet he fell short of moving beyond a dynastic emphasis and creating a unifying nationalism; like many Austrians, he saw himself inextricably bound to German culture.

Joseph was born on 13 March 1741 in Vienna to Maria Theresa, the ruler of the Habsburg lands and empress of the Holy Roman Empire. His father, Francis Stephen of Lorraine, became Emperor Francis I. Joseph obtained an extensive education from tutors, studying the classics, ancient history, and religion, and at an early age developing a keen interest in politics. As a child, he displayed impulsive and often disrespectful behavior that worried his mother. As a young man, he suffered misfortune when his first two marriages ended in tragedy. In 1763, his wife of three years, Isabella of Parma, died during a miscarriage, and in 1767 his second wife, Maria Josepha of Bavaria, whom he had wed two years earlier, died from smallpox. As a result, Joseph became emotionally imbalanced. Amid this, Joseph's father died in 1765, an event that elevated the young man to Holy Roman Emperor. Joseph also became coregent with his mother of the Habsburg lands.

In his new position, Joseph inherited a difficult situation. For one, Maria Theresa had been at war with Frederick the Great, the Prussian ruler who successfully wrested from Austria the province of Silesia. For another, Maria Theresa allowed Joseph little independence, and her domineering manner left him little authority. This may have been a reason why he pressured her so greatly to join Prussia in partitioning Poland, a process that in 1772 led to Austria obtaining Galicia. He could rightfully label this gain as his own.

After Maria Theresa died in 1780, Joseph became the sole ruler and aimed at extending the absolutism developed by his mother, advancing reform, and establishing Austrian primacy as the leader of the Germans. Indeed, to him Austria was to be a German state.

Joseph's domestic reforms ranged widely and earned him the epithet "the enlightened despot." He plunged into applying what he had learned from the European Enlightenment philosophers (who advocated reason as a way to discover natural laws that could be studied and adapted to improve mankind). Working feverishly, during his reign he issued 6,000 decrees and 11,000 new laws. In trying to make the Habsburg domains a unified state rather than a collection of loosely affiliated entities, he centralized the administration well beyond what had been accomplished by his mother, by ending the remaining feudal governments and creating new administrative districts.

To make language uniform he declared German the official tongue, and to end Catholicism as the official religion he issued the Edict of Toleration. He also reformed finances to balance the treasury and recruited outstanding scholars and scientists for the University of Vienna. In trying to make life better for his subjects, he ended the death penalty for most crimes and abolished most forms of cruel punishment.

In addition to these, Joseph established two important measures: First, he ended serfdom and, in a remarkable action for that era, allowed the serfs to gain possession of their lands while at the same time prohibiting noblemen from purchasing those properties; second, he eliminated restrictions on the Jews, who subsequently played a vibrant and integral role in Austria's economic and cultural development.

Joseph also attacked the Catholic Church by limiting the authority of the bishops and closing some 700 monasteries. He was determined to protect the monarch's powers and change the way his subjects lived. Yet many Catholics resisted his efforts and held on to their traditional beliefs.

Indeed, many of Joseph's subjects did not appreciate his reforms—he often moved too quickly and tried to bring change through force rather than persuasion. In short, he believed he knew right and everyone else had to fall in line, regardless of the consequences.

The emperor encountered his greatest resistance in foreign affairs. After traveling to France and to Russia, where he met with that country's ruler, CATHERINE II, he decided to acquire Bavaria in a complex exchange of lands with a Bavarian prince. Frederick the Great, however, blocked this effort, at which point Joseph allied with Catherine. An agreement assured Austrian help in Catherine's plans to attack Turkey and acquire Constantinople and the Dardanelles. When Catherine launched her attack, however, Joseph's army proved poorly or-

ganized. Furthermore, his involvement with Turkey encouraged rebellious groups, long unhappy with his progressivism, to challenge his rule in the Austrian Netherlands and Hungary. The Netherlands even declared its independence, although Joseph's successor, Leopold II, ended the revolt. In Hungary, Joseph had to rescind most of his reforms.

Suffering poor health for several years, Joseph died amid this turmoil on 20 February 1790 in Vienna. Joseph never embraced republicanism; he never called the assembly, or Diet, into session, and he condemned the French Revolution. Yet his reforms advanced the general welfare and produced a unified bureaucracy, although a modern Austrian nation did not fully emerge until after World War I when KARL RENNER helped establish a republic.

Reference: Padover, Saul K., *The Revolutionary Emperor: Joseph the Second, 1741–1790,* 1934.

Juan Carlos
(b. 1938)
Spain

When Juan Carlos became king in 1975, he dramatically overhauled the government; for decades, it had been a right-wing dictatorship, but he established a democratic system within a constitutional monarchy.

Juan Carlos was born Juan Carlos Alfonso Victor Maria de Borbòn y Borbòn on 5 January 1938 in Rome. His parents and his grandfather, King Alfonso XIII, lived there in exile, having left Spain in 1931 following an antimonarchist upheaval. Juan Carlos's father, Don Juan, was the designated successor to Alphonso. His mother, Doña Maria de las Mercedes de Borbòn y Orléans was Countess of Barcelona and Princess of the Two Sicilies.

After residing in Italy and for a brief period in Switzerland, Juan Carlos went to Spain for the first time in 1947. In 1949, he entered a private preparatory school, the Instituto San Isidro. Five years later, Don Juan arranged for his son to obtain a mil-

itary education, and after tutoring by the Duke de la Toree, Juan Carlos entered the military academy at Sargossa. In 1957, he graduated as a lieutenant in the Spanish army. The following year, he studied at the Naval Academy, from which he also graduated as a lieutenant, and shortly thereafter attended the Spanish Air Academy at San Javier and the University of Madrid.

All during this time, Spain continued under the rule of Francisco Franco, a right-wing dictator who had come to power in 1939 with the backing of Adolph Hitler and Benito Mussolini. In 1945, Franco bristled at Don Juan's suggestion that he step down as leader, and by the time Juan Carlos began his military training, Franco had determined that the young man, and not Don Juan, would succeed him as Spain's ruler. Consequently, he oversaw the young man's education.

At first, Juan Carlos insisted he would never

assume the throne ahead of his father, but early in 1969 he told Franco otherwise, and on 22 July the dictator presented to the Cortes (the Spanish Parliament) a law proclaiming Juan Carlos as the next king. The Cortes readily agreed, and Juan Carlos swore loyalty to Franco's political organization, the National Movement.

When Franco died in 1975, Juan Carlos became king. After his coronation on 22 November, many assumed he would continue the fascist apparatus, but the monarch greatly altered the Spanish government. He granted amnesty to all political prisoners and announced that he would allow competing political parties. Adolfo Suárez González became his prime minister, with effective power. Under Juan Carlos, Spain had its first free elections in over 40 years, and on 15 June 1977, Suárez's coalition party, the Union of the Democratic Center, won the vote.

Juan Carlos had to deal with many challenges during his reign, including separatist movements in Catalonia and in the Basque region, an economic downturn, and polarization between conservatives and socialists. Perhaps his greatest challenge, how-

ever, came in 1981 when a splinter group from the military barged into the Cortes and held the legislators captive in an attempt to overthrow the constitutional monarchy. With the support of most of the military, Juan Carlos acted quickly and effectively and troops loyal to him surrounded the Cortes. Twenty-four hours later, the coup collapsed.

In 1982, Juan Carlos brought Spain into the North Atlantic Treaty Organization, the Western European military alliance. He also received the Charlemagne Award for major contributions toward a united Europe. For all his other work, Juan Carlos's major accomplishment was breaking with the fascist past and providing his countrymen with a largely democratic political setting. A competitive political system continues under his reign. Thus he can be ranked with Queen ISABELLA I and King FERDINAND V as a founder of his nation.

Reference: Carr, Raymond, and Juan P. Fusi, *Spain: Dictatorship to Democracy*, 1981.

Juárez, Benito
(1806–1872)
Mexico

As a boy, Benito Juárez lived in poverty, working his family's small corn plot. One day, he lost one of the sheep he was tending and, fearful that his uncle, who owned the animal, would punish him, he ran away to Oaxaca City. There a Franciscan lay brother introduced him to books and the ideas that stirred him to change Mexico.

Benito Juárez was born on 21 March 1806 in San Pablo Guelatao, Oaxaca State. His parents were peasants and full-blooded Zapotec Indians.

They died when Benito was three years old, and he subsequently lived with an uncle. Benito received little education until his journey to the city of Oaxaca, where the Franciscan befriended him.

At one time, the young man considered entering the priesthood, and toward this end, he studied theology and Latin. But in 1829, he began pursuing science and law at the Oaxaca Institute of Arts and Sciences. Two years later, he obtained his law degree and also won election to the municipal council. As a lawyer, he at first earned little money, representing mainly the impoverished. By 1843, however, he acquired sufficient finances to marry into a prominent family.

In the 37 years since his birth, Mexico had undergone substantial change. Up until 1821 it was a Spanish colony; in that year the efforts of JOSÉ MORELOS and AUGUSTÍN ITURBIDE led to independence. But after this, two organized groups, the Conservatives and Liberals, battled, and instability characterized politics. The Conservatives generally favored a strong central government and, supported by wealthy landowners and manufacturers, opposed social reform. The Liberals desired free trade and measures to reduce the huge gap between the wealthy and the impoverished. By the 1850s, political turmoil contributed to economic decay and the national debt mushroomed.

Juárez, meanwhile, advanced politically and attracted national attention. He became a judge and then governor of Oaxaca State. He criticized the aristocracy and the Catholic Church, with its massive hold on land, for stifling Mexico, and supported capitalist growth that would break monopolies and stimulate the economy. He also desired a federal political system that would give Mexico's states more authority.

By 1853, Antonio López de Santa Anna had developed a despotic regime, and in 1854 an uprising began in the nation's southern highlands. Led by Juan Álvarez, the rebels espoused liberal ideas and demanded a new constitution. Many middle-class mestizos (people of Spanish and Indian blood) supported the rebellion, particularly after the rebels rejected radicalism and issued a moderate declaration for change in 1854. Juárez's support for this uprising resulted in Santa Anna exiling him. For two years, beginning in 1853, he lived in New Orleans, where he plotted with fellow exiles. Late in 1855, Juárez returned home and joined the rebel force that captured Mexico City without a fight and toppled Santa Anna. Álvarez emerged as president and appointed Juárez minister of justice.

Álvarez soon resigned the presidency and Ignacio Comonfort succeeded him. Juárez and Comonfort differed on many issues, but the administration pursued a liberal program that Juárez helped shape. This included forcing the church to sell its lands with the intent of offering them at low prices to the landless. Unfortunately for the poor, although the church sold its holdings, the land was purchased mainly by wealthier Mexicans, and the peasants benefited little.

In yet another reform, a new constitution in 1857 established a federal political system. Elections that year resulted in a victory for Comonfort, and Juárez became vice-president and chief justice of the Supreme Court. Conservatives, however, rebelled against the Liberal victory and forced Comonfort to resign. This unleashed a civil war between the Conservative government and the Liberals, who, headquartered at Veracruz, named Juárez as Mexico's president.

At first the Conservative army gained the upper hand, partly due to funds supplied by the Catholic Church. In reaction to this, in 1859 Juárez ordered the confiscation of all church property not used for religious services. He also separated church and state and proclaimed religious liberty. As the civil war continued, Juárez established close ties with the United States that led to charges he was a tool of the Americans. By 1860, the Liberal army obtained the advantage, and in December it entered Mexico City. Victorious, Juárez presided over all of Mexico. He displayed leniency toward the Conservative rebels and allowed full freedom of speech. The Conservatives took advantage of this, severely criticized him, and through their control of Congress nearly removed him from office.

Juárez's greatest threat, though, entailed the national debt. The nation's treasury was empty, yet Mexico still owed money to foreign investors. In July 1861, Juárez ordered the suspension of payments on the debt. This brought an angry response from Europeans, including the severing of diplomatic relations. France went even further: With the United States preoccupied by its own Civil War, the French government under Napoleon III decided to install Archduke Maximilian of Austria as Mexico's emperor. Within a year after French troops invaded in 1862, Juárez was forced to flee Mexico City. The Conservatives hailed Maximilian's arrival, thinking they had a fellow believer, but Maximilian stunned them when he announced his support for Liberal reforms.

This position, however, proved his undoing, for the Conservatives deserted him and the Liberals distrusted him. Then, when the American Civil War ended, the United States informed France it would not allow Maximilian's government to continue. Once the French withdrew their troops, Juárez and the Liberals defeated Maximilian and in 1867 executed him. Despite the turmoil, the Maximilian affair boosted Mexican nationalism when large segments of the population united to expel the foreigners.

Unity did not, however, mark Juárez's return to power. He won reelection to the presidency in 1867 but ruled increasingly without consulting Congress. At the same time, his health deteriorated, and Mexico's financial situation remained bleak. Juárez angered many Liberals with his unilateral approach, his decision to grant amnesty to the Conservatives, and his unsuccessful attempt to alter the constitution and increase executive power.

Furthermore, he angered the army when he reduced it by two-thirds. In 1871, Juárez ignored Liberal requests that he step aside; he sought reelection and won in voting marred by fraud. One of the defeated candidates, Porfirio Díaz, led an armed revolt, but Juárez crushed it. The president's health, however, worsened, and on 18 July 1872 he died.

Elective government did not last much longer: In 1876, Díaz again mounted a revolt, this time a successful one. Despite the limited effectiveness of Juárez's reforms, he remained the hero of Mexican nationalism, a leader who weakened colonial practices and created a new Mexico. Additional revolutionary change occurred in the twentieth century under the leadership of FRANCISCO MADERO, EMILIANO ZAPATA, and LÁZARO CÁRDENAS.

References: Roeder, Ralph, *Juárez and His Mexico*, 2 volumes, 1947; Smart, Charles A., *Viva Juárez*, 1963.

Kabua, Amata
(b. 1928)
Marshall Islands

In developing the Marshall Islands, Amata Kabua represented a cross between tradition and modernity. A chief through inheritance, he also sought international investments.

Amata Kabua was born 17 November 1928 on Jaluit Atoll. At that time, Japan controlled the Marshall Islands under a League of Nations mandate to administer Micronesia. The Japanese, however, lost the islands at the end of World War II to the United States, which used Bikini Atoll in the north for testing atomic bombs.

This latter development occurred while Kabua was attending Maunaolo College in Hawaii. After he obtained his degree in 1955, he returned to the Marshall Islands and taught elementary school in Majuro, the main city. He became superintendent of the Marshall Island school system and then entered politics, serving in the Micronesia legislature and as president of the Senate.

Desirous of more autonomy for the Marshallese, Kabua, the son of a leading chief, served as a delegate to the constitutional convention held in 1979. He supported a democratic system that would also protect traditional rights. Hence, the constitution established a council of chiefs with limited powers and an elective legislature and presidency. In May, the legislature chose Kabua the nation's first president.

Kabua began programs to improve education, agriculture, housing, and health care. He also sought international investments that boosted a limited economy. He insisted that development and tradition could coexist. In 1986, he obtained membership for the Marshall Islands in the United Nations. Kabua won reelection in 1992 to his fourth term as president.

Reference: Bunge, Frederica, and Melinda W. Cooke, eds., *Oceania: A Regional Study*, 1984.

Karamanlis, Constantine
(b. 1907)
Greece

Known for his conservatism, Constantine Karamanlis led the Greek government not once, but twice. The second time, he established a democratic system that ended a military dictatorship.

Constantine Karamanlis was born 8 March 1907 to a poor family in Proti, Macedonia. Despite his poverty, he completed secondary school and attended the University of Athens, where he received a law degree in 1932. While in 1935 Greece was emerging from the strong-handed rule of ELEUTHERIOS VENIZELOS, Karamanlis entered politics, joining the Populist Party and winning a seat in Parliament as a delegate from Serres. Karamanlis was a committed royalist, meaning he supported the return to Greece of the monarchy that had ended in 1923. Many Greeks believed only a monarch could contain the army, which seemed to be out of control. In fact, an attempted coup occurred the year of Karamanlis's election, leading Parliament to abolish the republic and reestablish the monarchy under King George II.

Karamanlis won a second term to Parliament in 1936, although the Populists did not fare as well as they had the previous year. When it proved impossible to form a coalition government, King George appointed General Ioannis Metaxas as prime minister. Claiming that communists threatened to take over the nation, Metaxas quickly established a dictatorship, and although Karamanlis agreed with the prime minister's conservative royalist position, he disapproved of the dictatorial regime and refused to accept a position in the government.

Because the national legislature was suspended, and during World War II the Germans occupied Greece, Karamanlis did not hold office again until his election to Parliament in 1946. That year, on 24 November, Prime Minister Constantine Tsaldaris appointed Karamanlis minister of labor. He later held positions as minister of transport and minister of communications until, in 1948, he was appointed minister of welfare. In 1950, he briefly held the post of defense minister.

After Karamanlis won reelection in 1952, prime minister Alexandros Papagos made him minister of public works. In that post, he began irrigation projects and improved the nation's roads. When Papagos died in October 1955, King Paul appointed Karamanlis the prime minister. Backed by the United States, Karamanlis formed the National Radical Union (ERE), meant to focus on economic development to diffuse the expanding appeal of the communists. In 1961, he obtained associate membership status for Greece in the European Economic Community. This, in turn, stimulated economic growth and modernization through new markets and financial sources and proved to be a popular policy.

His decisions regarding Cyprus, however, caused controversy and threatened his election hopes. In 1960, to resolve a longstanding dispute with the Turks over control of Cyprus, Karamanlis agreed with Turkey and Britain to grant the island status as an independent republic, with a Greek Cypriot president and a Turkish Cypriot vice-president. As it turned out, the policy with its concession did not destroy Karamanlis's administration, and when he held new elections in 1961, the ERE won handily. Yet, in an ominous development, the army had engaged in vote manipulation to help Karamanlis.

The prime minister decried the fraud, but despite his disclaimer, the political opposition, especially the Center Union (CU) led by Georges Papandreou and his son ANDREAS PAPANDREOU, charged Karamanlis with leading an illegitimate government. As disputes and tension mounted, Karamanlis resigned in May 1963 and moved to Paris.

Four years later, after George Papandreou's short-lived prime ministry, the government once again shifted to a military dictatorship that became notorious for arrests, torture, and extensive censorship. When a naval mutiny occurred in 1973, the dictatorship blamed the king and deposed him. Economic problems and student protests brought down the government in 1974, and military and civilian leaders asked Karamanlis to restore democracy. On 24 July he became prime minister, replete with much goodwill and a conservative ideology.

With this second term, Karamanlis sponsored changes that produced a substantial restructuring of the Greek government, enough so that he can be considered a founder of the nation's modern political system. Karamanlis opened politics to wider participation: Left-wing parties that had been suppressed were now free to compete, including the Communist Party.

In preparing for elections in November, Karamanlis organized the New Democracy Party (ND), supported closer ties to the European Economic Community, and sought a stronger free enterprise system. The ND won an overwhelming victory in the election, and Karamanlis then grappled with the pressing issue on what to do with the monarchy—restore it or abolish it? After a plebiscite indicated that most Greeks supported the latter, Karamanlis agreed.

Following a failed coup in 1975, Karamanlis purged the military and promoted a new constitution that gave the executive greater power under a presidency. The president became commander in chief of the military and appointed, and could dismiss, the prime minister. Karamanlis's friend, Constantine Tsatsos, filled the new position and set the tone for future presidents by letting the prime minister remain the center of political activity.

The situation in Cyprus flared anew and Karamanlis faced another crisis with Turkey. In 1974, amid a political dispute, Turkish troops occupied the island's northern half. Karamanlis opened negotiations, and although they proved inconclusive, he avoided war.

The prime minister called for new elections in 1977, and the ND again won. The Panhellenic Socialist Movement (PASOK) under Andreas Papandreou, however, gained seats. This presaged the future, and amid declining public support Karamanlis gave up the prime ministry in 1980 to become president. In 1981, beset by economic stagnation and what voters perceived as a murky ideology, the ND lost to PASOK, thus beginning another era in Greek politics.

Karamanlis served as president until 1985, when he resigned in a dispute with Papandreou and PASOK. He returned to the presidency again, however, in 1990 after Papandreou lost his majority in the Parliament. Karamanlis, most noted for building and stabilizing a democratic system, continues in office.

References: Clogg, Richard, *Greece in the 1980s*, 1983; Clogg, Richard, *A Short History of Modern Greece*, 1979; Kousoulas, D. George, *Modern Greece: Profile of a Nation*, 1974.

Karimov, Islam
(b. 1938)
Uzbekistan

When the Soviet Union began to crumble, Islam Karimov transferred his loyalty from the Communist Party to nationalism and established an authoritarian nation.

In 1938, Islam Karimov was born in Samarkand. At that time, the Soviet Union ruled Uzbekistan as a Communist republic, and the Soviets radically altered Uzbek society by collectivizing agriculture and stressing cotton production. This created a one-crop economy and heavy environmental damage as water used for irrigation drained much of the Aral Sea.

For many young men, advancement in Uzbekistan came through the Communist Party, and Karimov was no exception. He graduated from the Central Asian Polytechnic Institute and the Tashkent Economic Institute and in 1964 joined the Uzbek Communist Party. At about the same time, he began working at the Tashkent aviation construction factory, a position he held until 1966, when he became a senior specialist in the party. From 1983 until 1986, he served as minister of finance and deputy chair for the Council of Ministers.

Meanwhile, the Soviet policy of centralizing power in Moscow and operating through Uzbek party officials located in the republic created corruption in Uzbekistan that led to a massive purge in the mid-1980s. Directed by Moscow, the purge itself, which resulted in the removal of Sharaf Rashidov as party first secretary, seemed indicative of Soviet interference. In 1989, the Communists named Karimov to take Rashidov's place, and he immediately advocated Uzbek sovereignty, although short of independence.

The years of Soviet oppression, along with a reform movement then under way in the Soviet Union to promote openness and political change, stirred riots that erupted in June 1989 in Uzbekistan's Farghona Valley as nationalist-minded Uzbeks attacked minority groups. Troops crushed the rioters, but Birlik, or "The Unity Movement," pushed for sovereignty.

In August 1991, when hard-line Communists tried to overthrow the reform government in Moscow, Karimov showed his conservatism by supporting the coup leaders. After the rebellion failed, he reorganized the Communist Party into the People's Democratic Party of Uzbekistan, a moderate alternative to Birlik and still beholden to the traditional Communist bureaucracy. Karimov advocated a revival of Uzbek culture and complete Uzbek independence. Many Communists within the Uzbek Supreme Soviet, or legislature, criticized his position as too reformist, and after Uzbekistan declared its independence in August 1991, he called a presidential election to bolster his power.

Karimov won the election in December with 85 percent of the vote, but only after Birlik had been prohibited from entering the contest. Karimov supported development of a market economy and economic diversification, but cautiously. He called for economics to take precedence over politics and promoted firm governmental rule that would protect order.

Uzbekistan still suffered from inadequate agricultural tools and methods and the loss of its fertile land from the chemically laden cotton farming. At the same time, Karimov failed to end state control over the economy—by 1993 some 96 percent of the farms and industries had not been privatized. Corruption within Karimov's government, meanwhile, spread and stimulated an exodus of Uzbekistani intellectuals.

While Karimov guided Uzbekistan into the United Nations in 1992, he also saw the nation's unity threatened by internal ethnic and religious animosities. He increasingly supported Islamic elements to the point that he took his presidential oath on the Koran, made a religious journey to Mecca, and endorsed the government-backed building of mosques.

Karimov supported and furthered an antidemocratic atmosphere in Uzbekistan. Birlik leaders were harassed and beaten and publications censored, and he sternly criticized those who disagreed with his policies. Karimov continues to suppress opposition politics and has increased the penalties for "antigovernment" activity.

Reference: Critchlow, James, *Nationalism in Uzbekistan: A Soviet Republic's Road to Sovereignty*, 1991.

Kasavubu, Joseph
(1910?–1969)
Zaire

As a leader in his homeland's nationalist movement, Joseph Kasavubu displayed two main characteristics evident in his upbringing: his origins as a member of the Kongo tribe and his status as an *évolué.* These greatly influenced his attempts to shape Zaire, formerly called the Congo.

Joseph Kasavubu was born in Tshela, probably in 1910. He obtained an education at Roman Catholic missionary schools and in 1942, after several years of teaching, entered the civil service and became a chief clerk, the highest position a Congolese could obtain within the Belgian administration.

Kasavubu's education, job experience, and adoption of European customs classified him as an *évolué,* one among a privileged group of Africans who had obtained a middle-class status. Kasavubu became active in the late 1940s in Congolese cultural societies, nascent political groups that sought from Belgium legal and educational reforms that would benefit *évolués* by eliminating their ranking as inferior to the Europeans. These societies represented a developing nationalist spirit in the Congo, a land controlled by Belgium since the late 1800s.

In 1955, Kasavubu became president of the Alliance of the Kongo People (ABAKO), which represented Kongo ethnic interests. In his fight for Congolese independence, Kasavubu was greatly influenced by this group and his Kongo origins. An independent Congo, he believed, had to have a federal structure providing substantial autonomy for the Kongo group. Meanwhile, PATRICE LUMUMBA headed the only truly national party, the National Congolese Movement (MNC).

ABAKO won the first municipal elections allowed by Belgium in 1957, and Kasavubu became the mayor of Dendale district. When, two years later, nationalist movements spread in the Congo, Kasavubu announced plans to address a mass audience in Kalamu. The Belgian authorities intervened to stop him, a move that ignited days of rioting and resulted in the imprisonment of Kasavubu and several other ABAKO leaders.

In 1960, Kasavubu led the 45 African delegates to the Round Table Conference in Brussels and demanded the setting of an exact date for independence. Later that year, in the first national elections, the MNC under Lumumba outpolled ABAKO, but a coalition government was necessary. Kasavubu and Lumumba subsequently formed an alliance whereby Lumumba became premier and Kasavubu became president. Within weeks, the Lumumba government faced enormous problems, including a secession effort by Katanga Province under MOISE TSHOMBE, an army mutiny, and intervention by Belgian troops. Lumumba reacted by trying to centralize authority and by appealing to the Soviet Union for help. His apparent radicalism and threat to provincial power led to his removal by Kasavubu, who secured the backing of the army led by MOBUTU SESE SEKO (JOSEPH MOBUTU).

Kasavubu then became a major influence in the Congo's evolving national government. He protested the presence of United Nations forces and sided with Katangans in backing a confederation form of government. Later he began a reconciliation with the UN and worked to end Katanga's secession movement.

When, in 1963, the legislature deadlocked and instability increased, Kasavubu directed the return of Tshombe from exile and his accession as premier. Kasavubu, however, soon criticized Tshombe's harsh actions in quelling domestic rioting, and when Tshombe began building an independent power base, Kasavubu dismissed his government. Tshombe, though, had a majority of delegates behind him in the legislature, and a deadlock arose between the two men. Political maneuvering resulted in Kasavubu's removal in 1965, and he then left politics, retiring to his farm at Boma in the Lower Congo. He died on 24 March 1969. The nation was renamed Zaire in 1971 as a national government consolidated under Mobutu.

References: Hoskyn, Catherine, *The Congo since Independence,* January, 1960–December, 1961, 1965; Young, Crawford, *Politics in the Congo: Decolonization and Independence,* 1965.

Kaunda, Kenneth David

(b. 1924)
Zambia

Church of Scotland missionaries developed a reputation in Zambia for extolling individualism and black pride. As a young man, Kenneth David Kaunda was immersed in this influence and carried it with him in his fight against British rule.

Kenneth David Kaunda was born on 28 April 1924 in Lubwa and learned from his father and mother the values of education, Christianity, and African culture. His father, David Julizgia, was a Presbyterian minister who worked as a missionary for the church and as a teacher. His mother, Hellen Kaunda, also worked as a teacher. When Kenneth's father died in 1932, the youngster helped with the family chores, carrying water from a well some two miles from home and laboring at the grinding stone to process millet.

After he decided to become a teacher, Kaunda attended Lubwa Training School for two years beginning in 1939, during which time he dug ditches and tended the local mission's garden. He pursued two more years of study at Mundi Secondary School, where he also played soccer.

In 1943, Kaunda taught at the Lubwa Training School and shortly thereafter became headmaster. In 1947, he worked as a teacher at a mission school in Salisbury, Southern Rhodesia. The following year, he became boarding master at Mufulira Upper School back home in Northern Rhodesia, a colony under British rule.

Kaunda then became politically involved, partly because his year in Southern Rhodesia had exposed him to racial degradation emanating from a white segregationist government. In 1949, he organized the Chinsali Young Man's Farming Association, an agricultural cooperative, and became interpreter for a white liberal member of Northern Rhodesia's racially mixed Legislative Council, from whom he learned important political skills. That same year, he helped found the Northern Rhodesia African National Congress (ANC), dedicated to expanding African political influence. In 1952, he became an organizing secretary for the party and one year later secretary-general, positions that gained him experience in mass politics.

> *"It is no good trying to lead my people to the land of their dreams if I get them killed along the way."*

In 1953, Kaunda protested when Britain formed the Federation of Rhodesia and Nyasaland, which brought together Northern and Southern Rhodesia with Nyasaland (the latter has become independent Malawi). Many Africans believed this amalgamation strengthened the white segregationists then ruling Southern Rhodesia and lessened any chance of future independence. Kaunda fell out with the ANC in 1958 when its president, Harry Nkumbula, refused to condemn a new constitution that granted Africans few additional political rights. Kaunda organized the Zambian African National Congress and announced his adherence to Gandhian principles of nonviolent resistance.

In 1959, the Federation government reacted to Kaunda's promotion of a boycott and the sometimes violent acts of his supporters by arresting him and banning his political organization. For nearly a year, Kaunda endured exile in Southern Rhodesia and confinement that worsened his tuberculosis, incurred during an earlier trip to India. But his imprisonment made him a hero among African nationalists.

On 9 January 1960, Kaunda was released and three weeks later won election as president of the United National Independence Party (UNIP), which had been organized several months earlier by a militant nationalist, Mainza Chona. Kaunda had a difficult chore stimulating black resistance while avoiding violence. He also had to appease tribal chiefs, who felt threatened by any reduction in favors they received from Britain. UNIP grew quickly, though, and by mid-1960 it claimed 300,000 members.

Kaunda received a warm welcome from African-Americans when he visited the United States in 1960 and participated in Harlem's African Freedom Day rally. Many observers considered 1960 "Africa Year" as Nigeria neared independence and several other colonies drew up new constitutions. In Northern Rhodesia, pressure built for more self-government, violence escalated with gasoline bombings, and UNIP guaranteed independence by October.

Independence did not come then, but Britain did promise changes, and Kaunda's prestige and his countrymen's expectations grew. In 1961, Kaunda represented UNIP at a conference in London that formulated a new constitution. Yet Britain hesitated about any move toward more African power in Northern Rhodesia, feeling the pressure from some 77,000 Europeans living there and fearing possible black violence.

Kaunda subsequently rejected the constitution for not allowing sufficient African suffrage. He continued his peaceful protests, but riots erupted in July. Britain then agreed to changes that made more likely an African legislative majority. After the October 1962 elections, UNIP and the ANC joined together, forming a coalition government under which Kaunda, who had won a seat in the legislature, became minister of local government and minister of social welfare. The coalition signaled a shift to African control of Northern Rhodesia's politics.

Kaunda continued working for an end to the Federation, and 1963 brought substantial change. A revised constitution in November began full internal self-government, and the Federation ended on 31 December, when Nyasaland withdrew from it. This left Northern Rhodesia and Southern Rhodesia separate (they never did reunite), and as complete independence for Northern Rhodesia neared, even white business leaders rallied behind Kaunda.

Another round of elections in January 1964 produced a landslide win for UNIP and Northern Rhodesia's first all-African cabinet, with Kaunda as prime minister. That August, he won the newly created presidency, and on 24 October, Northern Rhodesia became the republic of Zambia within the British Commonwealth, the ninth former British colony in Africa to gain independence.

As president, Kaunda steered a difficult course between support for African nationalism and Zambia's longstanding economic ties with white segregationist Southern Rhodesia and South Africa. Trade with those two areas continued, but when Rhodesian whites declared Rhodesia independent from Britain, Kaunda initiated economic sanctions against it. (Later, under African rule, Rhodesia became Zimbabwe.) He also had to deal with the use of Zambia as a base by guerrillas fighting for neighboring Angola's independence.

Faced with these pressures, with economic problems as copper prices declined, and with tribal strife, Kaunda banned all parties except UNIP in 1973. A new constitution that year provided for a stronger presidency and a unicameral legislature. He then tried diversifying and restructuring the economy; this entailed nationalizing many businesses such as hotels, breweries, and mills, and Zambia acquired majority interest in the nation's two major copper-mining companies. But economic mismanagement and then a severe drought took their toll, and the nation's economy collapsed. Kaunda, however, faced down attempted coups and rioting in urban areas. Unopposed, he won re-election as president through the 1980s.

As Zambia's economy continued its miserable performance, Kaunda's political position deteriorated. Inflation damaged incomes, and a huge national debt made it almost impossible for Zambia to secure loans. Kaunda reluctantly agreed to liberalize Zambia's politics, and in 1990 several political parties formed. Gradually, Kaunda's ministers broke with him, and early in 1991 the minister of state for power declared that Zambia stood on the brink of widespread starvation.

Elections for the presidency and the legislature on 31 October 1991 brought an overwhelming defeat for Kaunda and UNIP and ushered in a government headed by Frederick Chiluba of the Movement for Multi-Party Democracy that advocated privatization of businesses. Kaunda retired from office, his country facing enormous challenges and the popular admiration he enjoyed gone.

References: Burdette, Marcia, *Zambia*, 1986; Hall, Richard, *The High Price of Principles: Kaunda and the White South*, 1969; Hall, Richard, *Zambia*, 1965; Kaunda, Kenneth David, *The Riddle of Violence*, 1981.

Kayibanda, Grégoire
(1924–1976)
Rwanda

When Grégoire Kayibanda and his compatriots fought for a new Rwanda in the 1950s, they had two main goals: to end Belgian rule and to win for the Hutu majority its rightful place as Rwanda's ruling group.

Grégoire Kayibanda hailed from the Hutu tribe, which, although it constituted 80 percent of Rwanda's population, had for centuries been under Tutsi domination. Kayibanda was born at Gitarama in 1924, one year after Rwanda became a mandated territory under Belgian rule. He was brought up as a Catholic and received schooling at Kabgayi in central Rwanda.

He studied for the priesthood at the Grand Seminaire in Nyakibanda for two years, but his main interests became teaching and journalism. He subsequently left the seminary to pursue a career in education and became editor of a periodical, *Ami.* In the 1940s, he briefly edited a newspaper in Belgium, *La Cité,* and then returned to Rwanda, where he edited another newspaper, *Kimyamateka.*

In 1957, Kayibanda helped form the Hutu Social Movement, a group that demanded land reform and a restructured government. He believed these changes had to precede independence, or else the Tutsi would continue oppressing the Hutu. He expressed his ideology in "The Manifesto of the Bahutu," which he and other young Hutu intellectuals signed just weeks after the Tutsi declared support for nationhood—a move Kayibanda believed made his demands more urgent. Meanwhile, another Hutu organization emerged: the Association for the Betterment of the Masses (APROSOMA), headed by Joseph Habyarimana Gitera.

When, in 1959, Belgium announced impending independence for the Congo, Rwandans advanced their political activism. APROSOMA became a political party, and under Kayibanda's leadership, the Hutu Social Movement reorganized formally as the Party of the Hutu Emancipation Movement (PARMEHUTU). Other parties also appeared, including the Rwanda National Union Party (UNAR), a Tutsi-dominated group. Political tensions led to Hutu-Tutsi violence late in 1959.

Reacting against the oppression established by the Tutsi and recognizing that the Hutu majority would likely prevail, Belgium encouraged Hutu political power and on 26 October 1960 declared a provisional government in Rwanda with Gitera as president of the Legislative Council and Kayibanda as head of government. Gitera, Kayibanda, and a mass meeting of Hutu proceeded to declare an end to the Tutsi monarchy in January 1961, but when Belgium announced a recognition of this new government the United Nations objected, claiming the Belgians had abandoned their mandated role to guide Rwanda's development and had wrongfully allowed Rwanda's separation from neighboring Burundi. Belgium then renounced its recognition.

In September elections Rwandans voted overwhelmingly to dismantle the Tutsi monarchy, and PARMEHUTU gained a large legislative majority. In October, the legislatureabolished the monarchy and chose Kayibanda as president. Belgium granted Rwanda full internal autonomy in December 1961. At a meeting in April 1962, Kayibanda and delegates from Burundi agreed they should not federate their two countries. Rwanda gained complete independence on 1 July 1962..

Kayibanda had presided over a substantial change that included both Rwanda's independence and a massive shift in power from the Tutsi to the Hutu. He followed a balanced economic program with a mix of private and state development that stimulated growth. Yet a new Hutu elite used its privileges to dominate the peasants, and financial problems forced Kayibanda to undertake fiscal reform in 1966 and devalue Rwanda's currency.

When Tutsi exiles attacked Rwanda from camps in surrounding countries, their actions served only to rally support for Kayibanda and anger the

Hutu, who consequently went on a rampage against remaining Tutsi, hacking to death some 10,000 men, women, and children. Perhaps Kayibanda's greatest political challenge came from fellow Hutu. In the early 1970s, Rwanda became polarized regionally as northern Hutu protested party and government domination by Hutu from central and southern

Rwanda. On 5 July 1973 northern army officers overthrew Kayibanda's regime in a bloodless coup. The former president died on 22 December 1976.

References: Nyrop, Richard F., Lyle E. Brenneman, et al., eds., *Rwanda: A Country Study*, 1982; Pro Mundi Vita, *Rwanda: The Strength and Weakness of the Christian Center of Africa*, 1963.

Keita, Modibo
(1915–1977)
Mali

When Modibo Keita rose to power he embraced two goals that caused internal dissension: distancing his nation from France and building a Marxist state.

Modibo Keita was born in May 1915 in Bamako. Mali was then the French colony of Soudan. In 1930, Keita graduated from the William Ponty School in Dakar, Senegal, an institution attended by numerous African nationalists. He taught school and then entered politics. In 1946, he helped found the Rassemblement Démocratique Africain (RDA), a nationalist organization with chapters in several colonies, and the Union Soudanaise, his homeland's leading political party.

The French subsequently imprisoned him for a month, charging him with being a communist. Keita indeed embraced Marxism, but France may have worried more about his nationalism and its threat to the French Empire. His stature within French Soudan grew, and in 1948, as France allowed more African participation in colonial politics, he won election to the territorial assembly. In 1950, the French relegated him to teaching at an isolated school. But two years later, after the RDA broke all of its ties with the communists, he won reelection to the legislature and a seat in the French National Assembly. In 1954, he served in the French cabinet as secretary of state for France Overseas.

At the same time, Keita became president of Union Soudanaise and mayor of Bamako. In 1957, his party won 64 of 70 seats in the new colonial elections. The following year, the French allowed the African colonies to choose between becoming

members of the French Community, by which France would allow internal self-government while handling defense, or obtaining complete independence, without subsequent French economic assistance. Keita successfully led his countrymen in accepting the former.

He then strove to forge a union of West African states that had been French colonies. Only Senegal agreed, and in 1959 a Senegalese-Sudanese federation was formed with Keita as its leader. Much to his dismay, the two states separated in 1960. Keita continued in power as the president of his homeland, which became the independent republic of Mali.

Keita acted to distance Mali from France. He Africanized the civil service and developed close ties with Communist nations, especially China. He pursued socialist economic policies which, accompanied by a recession, provoked protests. A bad harvest in 1968 added to his problems, and on 19 November the army overthrew him in a bloodless coup. He died on 17 May 1977 in Bamako while still under government detention.

A military regime ruled until 1979, when civilian control returned, although limited by a political party system in which the army played an important role. In the 1990s, instability reigned with a military coup, followed by a prime minister who was forced to resign after large demonstrations erupted against his administration.

Reference: Evans, Lancelot, ed., *Emerging African Nations and Their Leaders*, 2 volumes, 1964.

Kenilorea, Peter
(b. 1943)
Solomon Islands

Peter Kenilorea not only led the Solomon Islands to independence but also defused a separatist movement.

Peter Kenilorea was born 23 May 1943 in the town of Takataka on Malaita. When he was a child, World War II ravaged the Solomon Islands, then a British protectorate, with the Japanese invading as far south as Guadalcanal. After the war, Britain reestablished its rule but faced resistance from a nationalist movement. Most people in the villages did not push for independence, but an educated elite favored it, and this included Kenilorea, who had graduated from Teachers' College in New Zealand. After a stint from 1968 to 1970 as schoolmaster at King George VI Secondary School, Kenilorea worked in the public service. This coincided with Britain placing more and more internal matters in the hands of Solomon Islanders. In 1970, a new constitution established a governing council that included elected representatives. Yet another constitution four years later created a legislature and cabinet system with a chief minister, in this case Solomon Mamaloni. Kenilorea served as Mamaloni's deputy secretary.

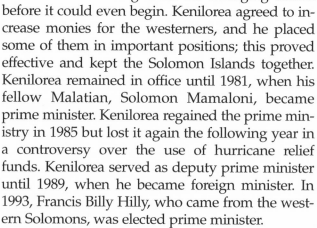

In mid-1976, as independence approached, the British held new elections in an attempt to create a clear mandate for Mamaloni. The mandate did not materialize, and to everyone's surprise, Kenilorea, an independent not attached to any political party, won election as chief minister. He faced internal turmoil after a political leader from the western Solomons died suddenly and rumors spread that the victim had been killed by Malatians, who came from the eastern islands. The rumors stimulated opposition to Kenilorea.

Nevertheless, in May 1977 he led a delegation to London and obtained a financial settlement from the British that included grants and loans for his nation's economic development. Opponents in the Solomon Islands legislature complained that they had not been consulted on the settlement, and considering it unfair, they nearly defeated it.

In September, Kenilorea and his advisors announced another agreement with Britain that provided the Solomon Islands with a liberal constitution that emphasized individual rights and a republican government. Solomon Islanders overwhelmingly supported the document, and the British felt grateful that they would soon be rid of the islands, which had become a financial drag. On 7 July 1978, the Solomon Islands gained their independence, and Kenilorea became prime minister.

During the move toward nationhood, Kenilorea faced another crisis as the western Solomons feared domination by the Malatians and considered seceding from the emerging nation before it could even begin. Kenilorea agreed to increase monies for the westerners, and he placed some of them in important positions; this proved effective and kept the Solomon Islands together. Kenilorea remained in office until 1981, when his fellow Malatian, Solomon Mamaloni, became prime minister. Kenilorea regained the prime ministry in 1985 but lost it again the following year in a controversy over the use of hurricane relief funds. Kenilorea served as deputy prime minister until 1989, when he became foreign minister. In 1993, Francis Billy Hilly, who came from the western Solomons, was elected prime minister.

Reference: Bennett, Judith A., *Wealth of the Solomons: A History of a Pacific Archipelago, 1800–1978*, 1987.

Kenyatta, Jomo
(1891?–1978)
Kenya

As a child, Jomo Kenyatta tended his family's flock in the interior pastureland of Kenya called the Highlands. What he saw awakened him early to the unfairness of the colonial system: Europeans, with assistance from Britain, the colonial power, dominating the most fertile areas and receiving the most economic benefits.

Near this time, probably in 1891, Kamau wa Ngengi—Kenyatta's original name—was born into the Kikuyu tribe, which long before the European era had been involved in extensive trade and agriculture. From his father, Kamau learned farming and herding, while from his mother he learned tribal customs. In 1909, he entered a mission school at Thogoto, where he studied both academic subjects and carpentry. He was baptized into Christianity in 1914 and took a new name: Johnstone Kamau. Then he worked in Nairobi, the capital, as a courier (from 1914 to 1917) and while there adopted his nickname Kenyatta as his own (later he Africanized Johnstone to make it Jomo).

As a young man, Kenyatta witnessed the return of African soldiers from World War I, men who had seen the vincibility of European armies. Their experience, coupled with land shortages among Africans—particularly galling as European settlers dominated the fertile tracts in the interior—produced protests among the Kikuyu, who in many instances had become workers on the Europeans' farms. In 1921, Harry Thuku formed the East African Association to represent Africans in Nairobi. The following year, colonial officials arrested Thuku for sedition. After his conviction, a demonstration in Nairobi turned violent as police fired into the crowd, killing 25 protestors. Thuku, considered Kenya's first nationalist, endured nine years of exile (from 1922 to 1931) in Somalia. Upon his return, Kenya's political movement had bypassed him and involved new, more radical participants, such as Kenyatta.

Kenyatta became politically involved while working as a meter reader for the public works department from 1922 to 1928 in Nairobi, Kenya's urban center. He joined the Kikuyu Central Association (KCA), which had evolved from Thuku's group and demanded tax reform, land rights, more schools, and African representation in the colonial legislature. He became general-secretary in 1928, a full-time position, and founded and edited the group's journal, *Muigwithania* (*Conciliator*), in which he called for tribal unity but refrained from attacking British authority. He journeyed to London in 1929 and again in 1931, petitioning the government for reforms but only obtaining the right of Kikuyus to form their own schools.

Kenyatta remained in Europe for 15 years, from 1931 to 1946, as a lobbyist for Kenyan interests. During this time, he visited the Soviet Union and attended an institute dedicated to Marxist ideology and revolutionary training at Moscow University. Although he wrote some militant articles in England in which he demanded independence for all Africa, he never totally embraced Marxism and remained wedded to his Kikuyu commercial heritage and European capitalism.

Before his return to Kenya, Kenyatta studied English at Quaker College in Birmingham for one year (1931 to 1932) and did graduate work in anthropology under Bronislaw Malinowski at the London School of Economics and Political Science. He wrote *Facing Mount Kenya: The Tribal Life of the Gikuyu* in 1938, which criticized colonialism and proclaimed Kikuyu culture as superior to European. He also adopted Pan-Africanism and in 1945 joined KWAME NKRUMAH, W. E. B. DuBois, and others in organizing the fifth Pan-African Congress in Manchester. Upon his return to Kenya in 1946, Kenyatta became vice-principal of the Independent Teachers' College at Githunguri and principal the next year. He also obtained election as president of the Kenya African Union (KAU), an intertribal political party, and embarked on building it into a major political force.

In 1948, landlessness and unemployment among Kikuyus sparked a violent uprising led by a secret society, the Mau-Mau. Europeans and their African supporters suffered attacks as sporadic waves of violence hit farms and police stations. The uprising ended in 1957, its death toll actually higher among African "British supporters" than among Europeans. While the Mau-Mau action stimulated some reforms, most notably more land for Africans, it led to recriminations—the British charged Kenyatta with having fomented the rebellion. Based on the testimony of one witness (who later recanted his story), Kenyatta was found guilty of being a Mau-Mau leader and in 1953 was sentenced to prison, where for six years he endured much hardship. His prison term ended in 1959, but the British then detained him in north Kenya.

"The hawk is in the sky, it is ready to descend on chickens who stray from the pathway."

In the meantime, constitutional changes in 1954 and 1958 allowed Africans on the Legislative Council in increasing numbers. In 1960, an African majority was allowed, and Britain made a surprise announcement of forthcoming independence. Two new political parties then formed. The Kenya African National Union (KANU), organized by Tom Mboya and Oginga Odinga and consisting largely of Kikuyu and Luo and former KAU members, acted in Kenyatta's name, while the Kenya African Democratic Union (KADU), consisting of Kamba and other ethnic groups, competed against the KANU.

In May 1960, KANU's leaders announced that, irrespective of British desires, Kenyatta would be KANU president should their party win in the upcoming elections; it did, and Britain gave in to pressure and released Kenyatta in February 1961. He returned home to an overwhelming reception and the KANU presidency.

In April 1962, the KANU won a close election to the Parliament and formed a coalition government with the KADU. After elections in May 1963, internal self-government began with Kenyatta as prime minister. Kenya gained full independence on 12 December.

Kenyatta had emerged as Kenya's dominant political figure. He established a government of highly personal rule that existed alongside the official bureaucracy. Early in his administration, he had to deal with ethnic Somalis who wanted northeastern Kenya to become a part of Somalia. His army put down rebel efforts there in the mid-1960s, after three years of fighting. With his capitalist preferences during the cold war, Kenyatta aligned Kenya with the West.

By 1964, the KADU had dissolved, and in November constitutional changes directed by Kenyatta produced a one-party state and created a strong presidency that Kenyatta filled. Kenyatta proclaimed African Socialism for Kenya, but he never strayed far from capitalist endeavors. By 1965, a dispute within his party intensified as Oginga Odinga, Kenyatta's vice-president, advocated a more leftist policy and charged Kenyatta with autocracy. Kenyatta subsequently expelled Odinga from the KANU. Odinga formed a new party in 1966, but within two years Kenyatta had harassed it into oblivion.

As president, Kenyatta portrayed himself as Father of the Nation and treated Kenya as his personal domain. In 1966, he sponsored constitutional changes transferring more power to the central government from the local councils, and he expanded government positions—over which he had full authority to make appointments—in an effort to provide employment and promote loyalty to him.

Then in 1969, Tom Mboya, who had gained a large intertribal following, was assassinated. This provoked riots between the Kikuyu and Mboya's tribe, the Luo. Kenyatta reacted by threatening to destroy all Luo, but after his guards fired into a crowd of Luo protestors and killed 78 of them, he moderated his position and initiated electoral reforms that allowed more competition within the KANU.

Land reform proved important for Kenyatta, and his program to help the landless achieved notable success. With British assistance, some 2,750 estates were purchased from Europeans in the Highlands, and by 1973 some 23 million acres of land in Kenya had been distributed to Africans. Many small farmers engaged in raising tea, tobacco, coffee, and pineapples. Although Kenyan agriculture suffered a disruption in production, it had by the mid-1970s diversified with small farms, state cooperatives, and large private plantations (the latter transferred from wealthy Europeans to wealthy Africans, many of them Kikuyu, thus creating another source of elite support for Kenyatta).

Yet Kenya suffered drought, higher oil prices, and rising unemployment, and protests expanded, led by J. M. Kariuki, a wealthy businessman who became an advocate for the poor and headed an opposition group in the National Assembly (which succeeded the old Parliament). As Kariuki's following grew in 1975, he was pulled from his Nairobi hotel room and killed. Protests erupted, and a government investigation never satisfactorily unraveled the murder. Kenyatta reacted to the crisis with power: He arrested several of his opponents as they sat in the National Assembly.

Kenyatta died on 22 August 1978 at Mombasa and left a legacy of strong personal governance that is still a part of Kenya today. His administration displayed corruption and extensive favoritism. His economic development, which heavily promoted multinational corporate investments, stimulated growth but also a high concentration of wealth, including an enormous amount for his inner circle. Yet Kenyatta also produced substantial political stability and important land reforms with a minimum of friction.

References: Cox, Richard, *Kenyatta's Country,* 1966; Miller, Norman N., *Kenya: The Quest for Prosperity,* 1988.

Khalifah ibn Hamad Al Thani
(b. 1932)
Qatar

Sheikh Khalifah ibn Hamad Al Thani gained his position as emir of Qatar only after much family intrigue. He presided over Qatar's independence from Britain—an event that did not display a strong nationalistic drive—and instituted moderate reforms that broadened political participation while protecting his power.

In 1932, Khalifah ibn Hamad Al Thani was born in al-Rayyan, a village near the Qatari capital, Doha. Like the other future emirs in this region, Sheikh Khalifah came from a leading family, in this case the Al Thani, which ruled Qatar.

In the early twentieth century, Qatar had fallen under the domination of Britain, and a treaty signed in 1916 prohibited the emirs from entering into any agreements with foreign governments unless Britain approved. Then in 1935, shortly after Sheikh Khalifah's birth, another action greatly affected the future emir's prospects: Britain gave its seal of approval to the accession of Sheikh Hamad ibn Abdallah Al Thani as emir, who was Sheikh Khalifah's father, and the decision positioned Sheikh Khalifah to eventually become emir himself. After Sheikh Hamad died in the late 1940s, however, his eldest son, Sheikh Ali, became the ruler. By this time, oil revenues had grown important to the Al Thani family, and there arose internal disputes as to the equity of their distribution under Sheikh Ali. While this tension intensified, Sheikh Khalifah gained political experience as a judge on the civil court and, in the late 1950s, director of education.

Although Sheikh Ali used the oil revenues to build schools and roads and make other improvements, by 1960 his excessive spending had nearly bankrupted Qatar. Backed by Britain, the Al Thani family deposed Sheikh Ali but bypassed Sheikh Khalifah in favor of Sheikh Ahmad. Nevertheless, Sheikh Khalifah and his supporters gained a concession: his appointment as deputy ruler. Sheikh Khalifah soon won so many other government positions that he, in effect, ruled Qatar. One of the positions he obtained in November 1960 put him in charge of financial and oil matters, a powerful responsibility. In 1966, he was appointed chairman of the board that directed the Monetary Commission of Qatar and Dubai. Three years later, he headed the Department of Foreign Affairs.

By then, Britain had announced its intention to

withdraw from the Persian Gulf. Sheikh Khalifah then began negotiations with Bahrain and the Trucial States (later the United Arab Emirates) to organize a federation, a concept he initially favored with enthusiasm. The talks broke down, however, over disputes involving the precise distribution of power among the emirates, and on 1 September 1971, Qatar decided to declare independence on its own.

Meanwhile, in April 1970 a constitution had created the office of prime minister and Sheikh Khalifah assumed the post, forming a cabinet in May. With independence, Sheikh Khalifah's powers expanded further, and Sheikh Ahmad became a mere figurehead. Then on 22 February 1972, Sheikh Khalifah deposed Sheikh Ahmad, who was away on a hunting trip in Iran.

As emir, Sheikh Khalifah protected the autocratic power of his office while instituting numerous liberal reforms. He changed the distribution of oil revenues so less money went to the Al Thani family and more to the state treasury; he called into session the Consultative Council to advise him; and he broadened the Council's membership to include representatives from several tribes and merchant families. His economic and development policies proved prudent, avoiding earlier wasteful expenditures. Despite these changes, power remained heavily concentrated in the emir.

Sheikh Khalifah has guided Qatar into nationhood and has produced a secure, reformist regime. His domestic actions and strong support of unity among the various Persian Gulf states have earned him a highly favorable reputation both within and outside the region. He remains embroiled in a territorial dispute with Bahrain over the Hawar Islands and continues to pursue close relations with the United States.

Reference: Sadik, Mohammed T., and William P. Snavely, *Bahrain, Qatar, and the United Arab Emirates: Colonial Past, Present Problems, and Future Prospects,* 1972.

Khama, Sir Seretse
(1921–1980)
Botswana

If he had not entered a controversial marriage, Seretse Khama might have become traditional chief of his people. As it turned out, he entered the modernizing political scene and emerged as his nation's first president.

Seretse Khama was born on 1 July 1921 in Serowe, a town in Botswana, which was then the British protectorate of Bechuanaland. His family's attachment to Britain went back many years: His grandfather, Khama III, had allied Bechuanaland with the British in the late 1800s to defend against encroachments by other tribes and Dutch settlers. At four years of age, Seretse ascended to the chieftainship of the Ngwato people, but his uncle, Tshekedi Khama, ruled as regent.

> *"[We] are situated in a part of Africa which is turbulent, a part of Africa which has various racial conflicts."*

In 1943, Seretse Khama graduated from Fort Hare College in South Africa and then continued his studies at the University of Witwatersrand. With a developing interest in law, he journeyed to England and in 1945 entered Oxford. Three years later, he obtained his law degree and stunned his uncle by announcing he would marry an Englishwoman, Ruth Williams. The decision caused an uproar among his people because, some claimed, a future ruler should marry within the tribe. Many in England protested, too, probably due to their dislike of interracial marriages. The British government may have had particularly strong concern in this regard because of its desire not to antagonize the white supremacist government in South Africa.

Whatever the case, Khama's tribe eventually approved the marriage, but Britain declared the young man unfit to rule as chief and in 1950 banned him from returning home. His exile ended six years later, but only after he agreed to renounce the chieftainship. Upon his return to Botswana, Khama entered politics and became a member of both the African Advisory Council and the Joint Advisory Council (consisting of whites and blacks). In this capacity, he pushed for more autonomy and criticized racial discrimination. In 1962, he founded the Bechuanaland (later Botswana) Democratic Party (BDP), and as Britain allowed more participation in the government by Africans the BDP obtained power. In 1965, the party won the legislative elections and Khama became prime minister. When his homeland finally gained complete independence in September 1966, he became president.

Khama promoted multiracial democracy and expanded education. He balanced his nation between white supremacist South Africa, whose economy was crucial to Botswana's economy, and his support for groups fighting racism. He rejected proposals to form an economic union with South Africa and instead, in 1980, entered an agreement with neighboring black nations to broaden Botswana's economic ties.

Khama gave refuge to guerrillas fighting against South Africa, and the latter nation's army frequently crossed the frontier to pursue them. He won reelection and held the presidency until his death in Gaborone on 13 July 1980. Knighted by the British government for his outstanding service, Khama had established a stable, democratic government that continued into the 1990s.

References: Gaabatshwane, S. M., *Seretse Khama and Botswana*, 1966; Stevens, Richard P., *Lesotho, Botswana, and Swaziland*, 1967.

Khomeini, Ayatollah Ruholla
(1902–1989)
Iran

One of the modern era's most exceptional revolutionary leaders, Ayatollah Ruholla Khomeini used his power in founding the Iranian republic to infuse the state with a fundamentalist Islamic crusade. In his insistence on ideological purity he abided by the Koran, but he also followed Plato in a career that captured the world's attention.

The name Ayatollah Ruholla Khomeini tells much about the man. Originally born Ruholla Hendi, Khomeini adopted a surname after his place of birth in 1902, Khomein, a medium-sized town south of Tehran. His first name, Ruholla, is a common one in Iran and means "soul of God." His title, Ayatollah, means "the sign of God," and signifies a scholarly religious standing, in fact the highest standing a person can attain among Shiite Muslim clerics. Only a few hundred Shiite leaders hold this status.

Khomeini's father was a leading cleric, an ayatollah, murdered under mysterious circumstances when Ruholla was only five months old. His mother thus raised him, as did an aunt, both of whom died when he was about 15 years old. Some analysts believe that these tragic losses produced in the youngster a harsh resolve.

As a boy, Ruholla underwent a thorough Islamic education at a Muslim school, reading Persian texts and the Koran. Although a serious student, he enjoyed playing soccer. About the time of his mother's death, Ruholla began learning Islamic jurisprudence from his older brother, an ayatollah. He experienced a great influence when

> *"... difficulties faced by the Iranian nation and the Muslim people are because of aliens, because of America."*

Ayatollah Abdul Karim Haeri, a devout and notable Islamic theologian, tutored him. When Haeri moved to Qom and started an Islamic school for advanced learning, Ruholla accompanied him and began teaching under his guidance. While Ruholla adopted a traditional belief in revelation, he also embraced reason, and at Qom he studied both Aristotle and Plato. The latter's *Republic* impressed him and served as a guide for his later efforts in establishing a new Islamic state.

From his teachers, Khomeini learned two contradictory aspects of his faith: the wisdom of political caution in separating religious from political concerns, and the effectiveness of political activism, of entering the secular arena when circumstances called for it.

As a religious scholar, Khomeini exhibited a prolific talent. Over the years he wrote 21 books, several of which were published, and nearly all of which dealt with Islamic theology. He trained many of his homeland's religious leaders and grew strident in his call for an Iran free from foreign domination and secular impurities—a state rigidly religious.

Khomeini had seen much foreign intervention in Iran and a monarchical state that, under REZA SHAH PAHLAVI, tied itself to Western influences. In 1941, Khomeini published a book condemning the shah for his dictatorial, irreligious rule. In the early 1950s, Reza Shah's successor, Mohammed Reza Pahlavi, owed his continuance in power to Britain and the United States after these two nations helped him in defeating a strong nationalist challenge from Mohammed Mosaddeq. Over the next few years, the shah developed an autocratic state wedded to U.S. military and economic assistance.

In the 1960s, Khomeini's following expanded when he took a prominent stance on several issues. He criticized the Local Council Elections decree issued by the shah's government for bypassing the Majilis (parliament). He opposed the shah's White Revolution intended to bring land reform—Khomeini and other Islamic leaders saw it as an assault on their own religious landholdings. Finally, he condemned the shah's granting of special diplomatic immunities, such as an exemption from Iranian court jurisdiction, to American military personnel stationed in Iran.

Khomeini's complaints provoked unrest. In 1963, students from Tehran University marched against the shah, and Khomeini supporters were killed in riots, causing the shah to invoke martial law. In 1964, after Khomeini criticized the diplo-matic immunities, he was exiled to Turkey and then expelled by the Turkish government when demonstrations erupted supporting him. He settled in southern Iraq where he headed a theological school and continued his denouncements of the shah. An Islamic republic, he asserted, should replace the shah's regime. During his exile, Khomeini maintained close ties with his supporters, including Hashemi Rafsanjani, who raised money and helped organize the movement in Iran.

Economic and political developments in Iran worked in Khomeini's favor. Prosperity tied to oil exports had spread, but unevenly. Many Iranians had been left out of the riches enjoyed by a few and, in any event, the wealth had brought more Western influences. As protests spread, the shah became more authoritarian and repressive, and his infamous secret police, SAVAK, arrested many dissidents. When, in 1977, Khomeini's oldest son was assassinated, the ayatollah accused SAVAK of the deed. In an open letter he condemned the shah. The shah answered back, and the war of words led to massive demonstrations supporting Khomeini. The shah pressured Iraq to expel Khomeini, and the ayatollah traveled to France, from where he continued to agitate for change in Iran.

In January 1979, as turmoil worsened (including mass demonstrations and strikes), the shah left Iran for Egypt, never to return. Khomeini announced formation of a Council of the Islamic Revolution and journeyed triumphantly to Iran. Millions turned out to greet him and fighting erupted between Khomeini's supporters and the Iranian military. On 11 February, the government that had been formed after the shah's departure collapsed, and on 1 April 1979, Khomeini and the Council of the Islamic Revolution proclaimed an Islamic republic headed by Khomeini serving as a "jurisprudent," a position that meant Khomeini had reached the highest level of religious and political development, a state of infallibility in which he could do no wrong.

Khomeini gained his power through shrewd political maneuvering. Early in the revolution he allied with the moderate secular and religious nationalists and even appointed a prime minister who reflected their views. But in November 1979, he grew more rigid, supporting the extreme Shiite fundamentalists. When on 6 November militant pro-Khomeini students seized the U.S. embassy and held hostages there, he praised the assault as the "second revolution" because it struck at the "evil" American influence. Khomeini issued laws requiring that women give up Western dress for the traditional Islamic *chador,* and he prohibited alcohol, coeducational classes in elementary and high schools, mixed swimming, and most Western entertainment, including movies and television shows. Khomeini censored publications, and his revolutionary groups arrested dissidents who were then imprisoned or shot.

The revolution enlarged the role of the state in economics. The government nationalized and expropriated much property, including banks, insurance companies, and large farms. An Islamic religious commitment to social justice motivated many of the reforms, attempting to make society more equitable.

Khomeini's success relied in part on the support of a fellow revolutionary cleric, Hojatolislam Ali Khamenei. When war erupted with Iraq in 1980, Khamenei, as deputy defense minister, organized the revolutionary guard and helped direct the strategy. Although Khomeini held the ultimate religious and political authority, Khamenei, backed in an election by the ayatollah, obtained the presidency in 1981 and from this position helped develop the rigid Islamic state Khomeini envisioned. Khamenei criticized American influence and Zionist plots and reached an economic and military agreement with Syria. He had difficulties addressing the huge unemployment and inflation in Iran, but in 1985 won reelection with 85 percent of the vote.

Criticism of Khamenei increased when it was revealed that the Iranian government was involved in a secret plan with the United States under which the American president, Ronald Reagan, agreed to exchange arms for Iran's help in getting American hostages released by terrorists who were holding them in Lebanon. But even greater attacks befell Ayatollah Hashemi Rafsanjani, who had been intimately involved in the contacts with the United States. Only Khomeini's personal intervention saved Rafsanjani politically.

When Khomeini died on 3 June 1989, Khamenei worked out an arrangement with Hashemi Rafsanjani under which Khamenei became the grand ayatollah (formerly Khomeini's position) and Rafsanjani stood for election as president. In the election, Rafsanjani defeated the one opponent the government allowed to run against him, and on 3 August he assumed the presidency. Rafsanjani had been the second most powerful man after Khomeini and a founder of the Islamic Republican Party, which had organized to support the revolution. He and all of Iran have to confront continuing high unemployment and widespread economic hardship and to struggle with Ayatollah Khomeini's legacy—that of an Islamic republic in an increasingly Westernized world.

References: Amir, Arjomand Said, *The Turban for the Crown: The Islamic Revolution in Iran,* 1988; Bakhash, Shaul, *The Reign of the Ayatollahs: Iran and the Islamic Revolution,* 1984; Ramazani, R. K., *Revolutionary Iran: Challenge and Response in the Middle East,* 1986.

Kim Il-Sŏng
(1912–1994)
Democratic People's Republic of Korea
(North Korea)

Driven by nationalism and communism, Kim Il-Sŏng rose to become leader of North Korea. After a decade in office, he consolidated his authority into an absolute dictatorship, one that countenanced no significant opposition.

Kim Il-Sŏng was born Kim Sŏng-ju on 15 April 1912 in Man Gin-dyu, a village near Pyonyang. His father was a schoolteacher who became involved in a struggle that would occupy much of Kim's life: the fight against Japanese rule. About 1925, Kim's father took his family to Manchuria to flee the Japanese, then returned to Korea, fought in the revolutionary militia against Japan, and died shortly thereafter. Greatly influenced by this sacrifice, Kim joined the Communist Youth League in 1931. Later, he served as the League's secretary. He attended the Whampoa Military Academy in Canton, China, known as a training center for revolutionaries.

There is much debate as to Kim's activities in the 1930s. He likely organized a small guerrilla group to oppose Japan after that country invaded Manchuria in 1931. Five years later, he fought in the Korean mountains at Kanggye, where he established a base for attacking the enemy troops. The Japanese nearly captured him, and in 1941 he fled to Siberia. While in the Soviet Union, he studied at a military academy and then joined the Soviet army. He fought against the Germans at Stalingrad, became a major, and then, after the Soviet army occupied northern Korea in 1945, shifted to the Far Eastern theater.

In 1946, Korea was formally divided in half at the thirty-eighth parallel between the Soviet-dominated North and the American-dominated South (where SYNGMAN RHEE was in power), and the Soviets sponsored the formation of Peoples' Committees at the local level. These, in turn, formed the Provisional Peoples' Committee for North Korea to run the country, and Kim was chosen its chairman. He also served as secretary-general of the Korean Communist Party that merged with another party to form the Workers' Party. Kim subsequently became head of the Politburo, the most powerful political position in North Korea.

Kim initiated land reform laws, the nationalization of industries, and the development of government economic planning. In 1947, he accused the United Nations of being a tool of American imperialism and urged South Korea to join the North in forming a unified Communist Korea. He portrayed Syngman Rhee's government in the South as a puppet of the United States. On 18 September 1948, Kim added to his offices when he became premier of the Democratic Peoples' Republic of Korea.

In 1950, he launched a suprise attack on South Korea. After United Nations forces repelled his army later that year and forced it to retreat toward the Chinese border, China sent in its own army to help Kim. The Chinese pushed the Americans back and a stalemate ensued, resulting in a truce signed in July 1953 that established a line of demarcation, once again at the thirty-eighth parallel.

After the war, Kim purged his political rivals and consolidated his power into an absolute dictatorship. When in 1956 his opponents moved against him at the plenary session of the Central Committee of the Workers' Party, he successfully isolated them as "anti-party reactionaries." When they tried to escape to China, he had them arrested; henceforth, Kim had complete political control.

Kim developed a strict militaristic society and a personality cult that encouraged North Koreans to worship him. He established close ties with the Soviet Union and Communist China and maintained an abiding hostility toward the United States and South Korea, which in the 1960s had its own dictatorial regime under CHUNG HEE PARK. In 1972, Kim gave up his premiership and became president while continuing to head the Communist Party. In March 1993, he withdrew North Korea from the international Nuclear Nonproliferation Pact, but after the UN threatened economic sanctions he suspended the withdrawal. His military buildup was widely believed to include attempts to develop nuclear weapons.

Tension mounted with the United States in 1994 after Kim refused international inspection of his nation's nuclear sites. The situation eased after Jimmy Carter, former president of the United States, convinced Kim to pursue a compromise. The Americans and North Koreans reached an interim agreement in August, shortly after Kim's death, which occurred on 8 July. Kim's son now leads North Korea, although it is uncertain whether he has consolidated his power, particularly on the scale of his father.

References: Dae-Sook Suh, *The Korean Communist Movement, 1918–1948*, 1967; Tai Sung An, *North Korea in Transition: From Dictatorship to Dynasty*, 1983.

Kohl, Helmut
(b. 1930)
Germany

A political moderate, Helmut Kohl did not lead a nationalist revolution. But as chancellor, he presided over one of the more momentous events in modern history: the reunification of Germany.

Helmut Kohl was born on 3 April 1930 into a strongly nationalist family in Ludwigshafen. His father, Hans Kohl, served in the German army during World War II, a conflict in which Helmut's older brother was killed. In 1945, Helmut was drafted into the German army, but the war ended before he entered combat. He then completed his secondary schooling in his hometown. From there he went on to the universities at Frankfurt and Heidelberg, where in 1958 he earned a doctorate in political science.

In the meantime, he involved himself in practical politics, joining the Christian Democratic Union (CDU) in 1947, a conservative to moderate political party that sought to lead postwar West Germany, that portion of Germany dominated by the Western powers. He helped form the CDU youth organization and criticized many trade union proposals. He won his first elective office in 1959, a seat in the Rhineland-Palatinate Landtag, or state legislature. He became floor leader in the Landtag in 1963 and continued in that position for six years.

Kohl's national prominence began in 1964 when he obtained an executive post in the CDU. On 19 May 1969, Kohl won election as president of Rhineland-Palatinate and became the youngest chief executive in a German state. He reformed the state administration and attracted numerous industries that diversified what had been almost an exclusively agricultural area. He also rose in the party ranks and became the CDU national deputy chairman in 1969 and, four years later, chairman.

In the 1976 federal elections Kohl ran for chancellor, but his party lost in a close vote. In 1982, the CDU joined with two other parties in passing a no-confidence vote against the sitting chancellor. The CDU won the 1983 election by continuing the coalition, and Kohl subsequently became chancellor. He proved popular and easily won reelection in 1987.

In the cold-war atmosphere, Kohl strongly supported the West, including the North Atlantic Treaty Organization (NATO), the military bulwark against the Soviet Union's army. As Soviet power in Eastern Europe declined, Kohl moved to the forefront in calling for reunifying Germany; that is, bringing West Germany together with heretofore Soviet-dominated East Germany. Throughout the 1980s, Kohl had expanded cultural ties between the West and East to ease political repression in the latter territory, while envisioning a day when the German nation would once again be united. Now the time had come.

Protests and demonstrations coupled with a Soviet withdrawal from Eastern Europe shattered the existing East German government, and in 1990 it agreed to hold elections. Before the vote, Kohl promised an even exchange rate for wages and savings in East Germany, a move intended to help the CDU-supported Alliance for Germany in the campaign. The Alliance won, and Kohl and the new East German government began discussions aimed at reunification, discussions coordinated with the old World War II occupation powers—Britain, France, the United States, and the Soviet Union.

Reunification posed enormous problems, particularly economic ones. East German industries were antiquated, and its economy neared collapse. Kohl eased West German concerns by insisting that modernization of the East German economy would not entail a tax increase. With this assurance, unification talks proceeded. Kohl removed another obstacle when he obtained from the Soviet Union a promise not to interfere with a united Germany joining NATO. To get this agreement, however, he had to commit Germany to reduce its troop strength and pay $8 billion for the complete withdrawal of the Soviet army. The last Soviet troops left the nation in 1994.

Unity came on 3 October 1990, and Kohl added East German ministers to his cabinet. Delegates from the East German legislature joined the lower house of the West German legislature, or Bundestag. After special elections, East Germans also joined the upper house, or Bundesrat.

Kohl's support slipped, though, as problems mounted. The eastern German economy spiralled downward, with industrial production in 1991 just one-third of what it had been two years earlier. This damaged the national economy and western Germans feared they would suffer as a result of the unification, a fear reinforced by the influx of east-

"I'm for more human policy and less bureaucracy."

ern German workers into the West, causing a labor glut. Kohl's insistence on no new taxes coupled with increased spending to help the East stimulated inflation and drove interest rates higher. This, in turn, provoked an economic recession.

Despite these problems, Kohl leads a difficult transition and remains committed to the full reintegration of East and West Germany. This is symbolized by his push to get the national capital moved from Bonn to Berlin, a process that will be completed near the year 2000.

Reference: Detwiler, Donald, *Germany: A Short History*, 1989.

Kravchuk, Leonid
(b. 1934)
Ukraine

Ukrainians often called Leonid Kravchuk "the crafty fox," for he underwent a quick political change from Communist Party ideologue in the 1980s to advocate of Ukraine's independence in 1991. "An opportunist," some said about him; "A reformed man," he said about himself.

Leonid Kravchuk experienced an impoverished childhood. He was born on 10 January 1934 in Zhytyn, a village in western Ukraine. His parents were peasants, and his father was killed during World War II. This left the family in difficult circumstances, made worse by a collectivization program that damaged the agricultural economy. At this time, Ukraine was a republic within the Soviet Union, having been forcefully annexed in 1921.

Kravchuk discovered his route out of poverty within the Communist Party, which he joined in 1958. That same year, he graduated from Taras Shevchenko State University in Kiev with an advanced degree in political economics. He took a position teaching at a university in Chernivtsi and then studied for his doctorate in economics, which he obtained from the Academy of Social Sciences in Moscow.

Kravchuk continued his loyalty to the Communist Party even as Ukrainian nationalists suffered persecution. Ever since the 1940s, the Soviet Union had intensified its campaign to Russify Ukrainian culture, and it considered nationalist sentiment treasonous. Kravchuk battled these nationalists as an official in the formulating ideology within the

Ukrainian Communist Party, a position he obtained in 1979 after serving as regional party leader. His main task was to counter nationalist arguments with propaganda, and in 1988 he obtained appointment as head of this program.

By this time, the Soviet Union faced collapse and nationalism in Ukraine grew, stimulated by economic distress and the disastrous failure a few years earlier of the Chernoybl nuclear power plant. In 1989, Ukrainian dissidents such as Ivan Drach and VYACHESLAV CHORNOVIL formed Rukh, or "The Movement," to obtain democracy, economic reform, and sovereignty (initially, short of complete independence). In March, Rukh captured one-third of the seats in the Ukrainian Supreme Soviet, the republic's legislature. The Communist Party sensed a change and adopted Rukh's call for national sovereignty.

Unlike other nationalists, Kravchuk did not relinquish his Communist Party membership, but he did address Rukh in 1989—the only senior Communist official to do so—and in 1990 supported the sovereignty stance. That year, he won election as chairman of the Supreme Soviet. Then in August 1991, conservative hard-liners attempted a coup in the Soviet Union in order to halt reform in the various republics. For awhile, it seemed they might succeed and reinstate firm Communist control. Kravchuk at first refused to condemn the coup and his posturing bespoke indecisiveness. When it became clear the coup had failed, he criticized it as unconstitutional and quit the Communist Party.

On 24 August 1991, Ukraine declared its independence and scheduled a referendum to confirm it. Rukh then split over strategy, with Vyacheslav Chornovil wanting quick development of a market economy and attacking Kravchuk as an opportunist, and Ivan Drach wanting slower economic reform and supporting Kravchuk as the man best able to defend Ukraine's independence. Ukrainians, voting on 1 December, approved nationhood and chose Kravchuk their president. He obtained over 60 percent of the tally in a multicandidate race, defeating, among others, Chornovil. The Soviet Union immediately recognized Ukraine's independence.

Kravchuk preempted Rukh by appointing

"We have to learn from the experience of other East European states. Ukraine will take its own path."

several of its members to his administration. He also steered a moderate course between the left, which supported socialism, and the right, which promoted an ethnically based nationalism. He faced an enormous economic challenge, with sharp declines in industrial output and food production. Ukraine also had limited oil reserves and needed to purchase fuel from Russia and Kazakhstan.

At first, Kravchuk appointed a liberal reformist as minister of economics, but in July 1992, after inflation increased, he fired him. Kravchuk struggled to follow a compromise path, initiating some privatization but retaining many state-controlled businesses. Observers doubted this strategy would work, and in 1993 production continued to fall while inflation hit 170 percent.

In foreign affairs, after the Soviet Union collapsed in December 1991, Kravchuk joined Ukraine with Russia and several other former Soviet republics in a loose confederation, the Commonwealth of Independent States. Despite this, he disputed control of the powerful Black Fleet with Russia. He reached an agreement in August 1992 whereby the fleet was placed under joint command, and then in June 1993 he agreed to split the fleet with the Russians. During this controversy, Kravchuk visited the United States and obtained most-favored-nation trading status for Ukraine. Yet another dispute erupted concerning what to do with nuclear weapons, formerly under Soviet control, that remained in Ukraine. In January 1994, Kravchuk reached an agreement with Russia and the United States whereby Ukraine promised to destroy its arsenal.

In addition to these challenges, Kravchuk faced a separatist movement in the Crimea. He supported substantial autonomy for the region, including full property rights and control over natural resources. In July 1994, as economic problems still beset Ukraine, voters elected Leonid Kuchma, a former Communist, as their nation's president. Kuchma promised closer ties to Russia and gained the approval of the Supreme Council (Parliament) to proceed with Kravchuk's agreement for dismantling Ukraine's nuclear weapons.

Reference: Solchanyk, Roman, ed., *Ukraine: From Chernoybl to Sovereignty: A Collection of Interviews*, 1992.

Kucan, Milan
(b. 1941)
Slovenia

In 1987, Slovene intellectuals issued a call for their homeland to secede from Yugoslavia and become an independent nation. Milan Kucan, a Communist politician, agreed and provided the leadership that brought Slovenian nationhood.

Milan Kucan was born on 14 January 1941 in Krizevci, a town in northeastern Slovenia. During his childhood, Slovenia joined five other Balkan states to form the Socialist Federal Republic of Yugoslavia. Josip Broz Tito emerged as its leader and established a Communist regime. His authoritarian rule held the ethnically disparate nation together. Young Milan attended school in Murska Sobota and went on to study law at the University of Ljubljana, from which he graduated in 1963. A few years earlier, he had joined the League of Slovenian Communists. He became a member of the Central Committee of the Slovenian Youth Association and served as president of the organization's commission dealing with education and ideology.

Kucan continued to rise in politics. In 1968, he was chosen president of the Youth Association and the following year was named to the Central Committee of the Slovene Communist Party, a prominent position. He served in that capacity for four years, during which time he supported reforms intended to decentralize economic development. From 1973 until 1978, he headed the Socialist Alliance of Working People, an organization developed to rally popular support for government programs. In 1978, he won election to the Slovenian legislature. Not long after this, Tito died and Yugoslavian politics changed. The nation resorted to a collective presidency, rotated among the various member states, but this arrangement pleased no one and proved unable to handle ethnic tensions.

In the 1980s, as reform movements affected East European nations, Slovenian nationalism grew. Many Slovenians felt exploited in the Yugoslav nation—for years their country had been the wealthiest member of the federation, only to have its money drained to the other states. Slovenians also supported progressive economic reforms, but found them blocked by Serbia. They especially disliked the Serbian opposition to developing a market economy at a time when an economic crisis gripped Yugoslavia.

When it was revealed in 1988 that the Yugoslav army intended to arrest Slovenian reformers, Slovenes pushed for greater autonomy and determined to follow their own path. By this time, Kucan had been elected president of the Slovenian League of Communists and won a large following when he agreed with the reformers, supported the development of a multiparty state, and fought to protect Slovene sovereignty. When, in January 1990, Serbia rejected Slovenia's reformist demands, Slovenians quit the Yugoslav legislature. Three months later, Kucan, running under a new banner, the Party of Democratic Renewal, won election as Slovenia's president with 58 percent of the vote.

"The only possible response to an ultimatum is an ultimatum."

In December 1990, Slovenes held a referendum and approved independence but also permitted a revised arrangement with the other Yugoslav states, if one could be worked out. Kucan wanted a loose confederation, and in this he was supported by Croatia. After an agreement with the Croatians was reached, Kucan announced that the Slovene military would handle all border-crossing points formerly handled by Yugoslavian officials. Yugoslavia reacted by calling this an unacceptable secessionist move. Kucan labeled Yugoslavia's position an ultimatum that would be resisted. Confident of victory, the Yugoslav army attacked Slovenia. Surprisingly, the Slovenes repelled the attack, and the Yugoslavian forces retreated. Slovenia officially declared its independence on 25 June 1991.

Kucan gained diplomatic recognition for Slovenia, including important support from Germany and, in 1992, from the United States. He faces enormous challenges as conversion to a market economy and an ongoing war between Bosnia and Serbia disrupt trade and imperil his nation's stability.

Reference: Magas, Branka, *The Destruction of Yugoslavia: Tracking the Break-Up, 1980–1992*, 1993.

al-Kuwatli, Shukri
(1891–1967)
Syria

When Syrians sought to gain their independence from France, disagreements appeared relating to strategy. Shukri al-Kuwatli gained an enormous following in steering a course between violent protest and acquiescent concessions.

Shukri al-Kuwatli was born in 1891 in Damascus, Syria's largest city. His family owned land and engaged in trade. He went to school in Damascus, and then attended college in Turkey, where he earned a degree in political science and associated with Arab nationalists. When he returned to Syria, he joined a secret nationalist organization, al-Fatah. The Turkish authorities who ruled Syria as part of the Ottoman Empire arrested him. Stories of his bravery under torture made him a nationalist hero. After World War I, Kuwatli helped organize the Arab Independence Party, a radical group seeking nationhood.

In 1920, the French demanded Syrian recognition of their mandate to rule, obtained after the Ottoman Empire collapsed. When the Syrians resisted, French troops landed and expelled the Syrian monarch. Amid French repression, Kuwatli was forced into exile and lived in Egypt. In 1922, France separated Lebanon from Syria and centralized its control. The French also built roads and schools, established the University of Damascus, and reformed agriculture. Yet their high-handed policies angered the nationalists and produced the Great Syrian Revolt of 1925 to 1927.

While living in exile, Kuwatli worked to gather money for the Arab nationalist movement and in so doing won French enmity. When France issued an amnesty in 1930, he returned to Syria and developed his landholdings into the Syrian Conserves Company that produced fruits and vegetables for export and raised money for the nationalists. Kuwatli even earned the title "the Apricot King."

In 1932, he joined the National Bloc, which had rejected armed conflict in favor of popular protests and negotiated concessions aimed at acquiring greater autonomy for Syria. Kuwatli was uncomfortable with this moderate approach but used his influence to make sure the Bloc did not agree to unfavorable terms. As the French dragged their heels, Kuwatli organized a 50-day general strike in 1936. This tactic led to negotiations and a French agreement to allow Syrian independence. In elections to establish a transitional government, Kuwatli won a seat in the legislature and served as minister of defense and finance. In 1938, however, he resigned to protest the Syrian government's acquiescence to changes in the independence treaty that made it more favorable to France. As it turned out, the French government did not ratify the treaty.

On 20 March 1941, Kuwatli demanded Syria's immediate independence. By now, amid World War II, food shortages and unemployment plagued Syria and nationalist riots had become widespread. On 27 September 1941, France formally recognized Syrian independence, although troops remained present and elections were delayed. Finally, in August 1943, Kuwatli was chosen president by Syria's new legislature, and after further riots in 1945 and Kuwatli's insistence that French troops remain in their barracks, France withdrew in April 1946, thus beginning Syria's complete independence.

Kuwatli embraced pan-Arabism and led Syria into joining the League of Arab States in 1945. He also attempted agricultural reforms, but his administration suffered from continued economic difficulties brought by the devaluation of the French franc, by misspending, and, in 1948, by Israel's defeat of the Syrian army. On 30 March 1949, Kuwatli was ousted in a bloodless coup and charged with corruption. He was held a prisoner in a hospital for a month and then left for exile, first in Switzerland, later in Egypt. The coup began a series of such upheavals. Two additional coups occurred in 1949 until a new constitution was adopted in 1950. The following year, the Nationalist Party, dominated by the business leaders in Damascus, sought Kuwatli's return, but another coup led to a military dictatorship, and he did not come back to Syria until 1954.

Kuwatli regained the presidency in 1955, but by this time the position had been weakened as power shifted to the military. Nevertheless, he did cooperate with Egypt and Saudi Arabia in resisting what Arabs claimed to be Israeli aggression, and he supported Egypt in the Suez Canal crisis of 1956.

When Egypt proposed merging with Syria to form the United Arab Republic (UAR), Kuwatli agreed, and in 1958 he resigned the presidency so that Egyptian leader GAMAL ABDEL NASSER could serve as president of the UAR. He retired from politics and died in Beirut on 30 June 1967. In the meantime, the UAR dissolved and a radical pan-Arab Baath Party obtained power.

References: Devlin, John F., *Syria: Modern State in an Ancient Land*, 1983; Tibawi, A. L., *A Modern History of Syria Including Lebanon and Palestine*, 1969.

Landsbergis, Vytautas
(b. 1932)
Lithuania

There developed within Vytautas Landsbergis not only a love for classical music, but also a desire to see Lithuania expel its Soviet oppressors. Thus emerged the political leader who gained his homeland's independence.

Vytautas Landsbergis was born on 18 October 1932 in Kaunas. His family had a history of involvement in Lithuania's nationalist movements. His father, for example, fought in the independence campaign after World War I, and against the Nazis during World War II. As a child, Vytautas saw Lithuania change from a nation—a status it had gained in 1932—to a republic within the Soviet Union, which came about in 1940 when the Russians forcibly annexed the area. Vytautas studied music and became a notable pianist and professor at the Lithuanian Conservatory in Vilnius, the school where he had earned his doctorate. He specialized in Lithuanian music and ran afoul of the Soviets who wanted to crush his country's culture and with it Lithuanian identity as a distinct ethnic group.

Landsbergis recorded albums and wrote articles. He did not display any substantial political orientation until 1988 when he joined other intellectuals to form Sajudis, or "The Movement." This group aimed to spread nationalism and challenge communism. In October, he won election as the group's president and also served as a Lithuanian delegate to the Soviet legislature in Moscow.

Landsbergis displayed invaluable political skills, crafting the statements issued by Sajudis and developing its strategy. He restrained the more radical members and pursued a carefully considered course toward autonomy, at first rejecting complete independence.

Conditions changed rapidly, however, as the Soviet Union entered an era of reform and began to disintegrate. In February 1989, Sajudis declared it would seek Lithuanian independence. Landsbergis organized protest rallies and gained some concessions from the Soviets that permitted the expression of formerly forbidden Lithuanian cultural practices. In March, Sajudis candidates captured the Lithuanian seats in the Soviet legislature. In September, the Lithuanian legislature declared the 1940 Soviet annexation void, and in December it allowed political parties to compete against the Communists.

Landsbergis continued to direct the nationalist

movement to additional success. In February 1990, he won election to the Lithuanian Parliament, and the following month this group elected him Lithuania's president. On 12 March, he presided over Parliament as it declared Lithuania independent. Landsbergis worried about the Soviet reaction; after all, the Soviets still had a formidable military, and the Lithuanian economy was linked to the U.S.S.R., particularly for its supplies of oil and gas. The Soviets did, indeed, impose an economic blockade on Lithuania and sent troops into the country.

Landsbergis sought to defuse the crisis, and when the Russians indicated they would end their restrictions if Lithuania would suspend its declaration of independence until negotiations could be concluded, Landsbergis agreed. Tension still continued and the situation worsened in January 1991 after the Soviets sent troops to capture the Lithuan-

"We are not making an omelet here; we are making Lithuanian history."

ian television headquarters and in the attack killed several unarmed people. In August, though, the conservatives within the Soviet Union lost their power, and the following month the Soviet Union recognized Lithuania as an independent nation.

Under Landsbergis's leadership, Lithuania joined the United Nations and participated in forming the Baltic Council with Estonia and Latvia, intended to improve economic relations. Landsbergis moved the nation toward privatization and a free market. Economic problems, however, caused a reaction against him, and in the 1992 elections former Communists won a majority in Parliament and ousted Landsbergis from the prime ministry.

Reference: Remeikis, Thomas, *Opposition to Soviet Rule in Lithuania, 1945–1980,* 1980.

Lauti, Toaripi
(b. 1928)
Tuvalu

Amid a controversy with the neighboring Gilbert Islands, Toaripi Lauti led Tuvaluans in forming their own nation.

Toaripi Lauti was born on 28 November 1928 in Papua (New Guinea). He attended Queen Victoria School in Fiji and then St. Andrew's College and Christchurch Teachers' College in Christchurch, New Zealand. From 1953 until 1962 he taught school in the Gilbert Islands.

During this time, Tuvalu was called the Ellice Islands and, joined with the Gilbert Islands, it formed a single colony under British rule. In the mid-1960s, a nationalist movement developed among the Gilbertese, and for the first time Britain allowed an elected legislature in the colony. This body, however, had only 4 Ellice members as opposed to 19 from the Gilbert Islands. As the Gilbertese pressed for independence, the Ellice people feared they would be dominated, and in 1969 they announced their intention to separate from the Gilbert Islands as soon as the British allowed the colony more self-government.

In 1974, elections resulted in Lauti winning a seat in the colonial legislature. He had appealed to the voters as a man of principle with an educated background who had experience in labor relations on nearby Nauru, where he had worked in the 1960s during the dispute with the Gilbert Islands. Lauti represented the island of Funafuti.

Lauti supported both separation and independence and preferred the latter materialize without a preliminary stage of internal self-government. In 1974, the Ellice people approved independence in a referendum, and the following year the islands formed the separate British colony of Tuvalu.

In 1976, the Tuvalu Assembly named Lauti the colony's chief minister. He then introduced a measure into the Assembly to study the writing of a constitution. Although many in Tuvalu expected nationhood, Lauti moved quicker than he had earlier planned, partly because he believed that Tuvalu's financial situation would be much better upon gaining independence.

In August 1977, Lauti won election to an enlarged House of Assembly and reelection as chief minister. He then changed his course and supported a self-government stage, believing that such a transitional interlude would allow him to strengthen the chief ministry. This he did, adding minister of finance to his duties.

Tuvalu gained its complete independence from Britain on 1 October 1978, and Lauti officially became prime minister. But he soon became embroiled in controversy. In 1979, he invested government funds with a real estate speculator from the United States, expecting to make substantial profits for Tuvalu. The deal fell through, and when Lauti failed to get the money back, the matter became a major political issue. In 1981, the voters rejected Lauti, and Tomasi Puapua became the new prime minister. Lauti's legacy remains, however, as the main architect of Tuvalu's independence.

References: Faaniu, Simati, et al., *Tuvalu: A History,* 1983; MacDonald, Barrie, *Cinderellas of the Empire: Towards a History of Kiribati and Tuvalu,* 1982.

Lee Kuan Yew
(b. 1923)
Singapore

Lee Kuan Yew grew up fully acculturated into the British culture that pervaded Singapore. Yet he emerged as an outspoken nationalist, a leader who saw Singapore's future tied to an independent Malaysia.

On 16 September 1923, Lee Kuan Yew was born into a moderately wealthy Chinese family in Singapore. His father was a lawyer, a counsel to a wealthy merchant. Lee turned out to be extremely brilliant. He obtained his secondary education at Raffles Institution, a preparatory school, and scored the highest grades in Malaya on his Cambridge School Certificate in 1939. He won a scholarship to Raffles College in Singapore and then studied law at Cambridge, where he earned honors.

When he returned to Singapore in 1950, he quickly became one of the best and highest-paid lawyers in his homeland. He also represented labor groups in their fight for better treatment and won a

> *"I cry with Nehru when I think I cannot speak my mother tongue as well as I speak English."*

pay raise for postal union employees. Since 1869, Singapore had been under British Crown control, and the Chinese who held government positions were wealthy Anglicized merchants who ignored the laboring and poor classes.

Lee initially supported this elite group, but in 1955 he broke away and formed the People's Action Party (PAP). Lee wanted Singapore free of British control and in a union with Malaya (the British territory on the Malayan Peninsula). He also advocated radical socialist reforms to address the island's dire poverty and willingly allied with the local Communist movement. Under Lee's leadership, the PAP grew rapidly and even won a few seats in the new legislature. Lee, however, often lost control of the party to rival factions, including the Marxists. Shrewdly, he used their persecution by the British to regain his leadership of the party.

The PAP subsequently won handily in elections under a new constitution in 1959. Lee campaigned as an anticolonialist and a non-Communist reformer, and the victory made him prime minister of a semiautonomous state still under British oversight. Yet by 1962, as radicals challenged him, Lee's following diminished and this threatened his rule. He reacted by pushing to achieve the PAP platform of a merger with an independent Malaya. This materialized in 1963 after Lee negotiated favorable terms for Singapore and after Malays, who feared Chinese domination, arranged to make Malay-dominated states on Borneo a part of the new nation. These changes brought about the Federation of Malaysia and boosted Lee's popularity.

Lee surrounded himself with Singapore's brightest elites and altered his course to develop Singapore along capitalist lines, with the government directing economic planning. New development boosted the island's economic growth and prosperity (creating the highest standard of living in Asia) while destroying old areas as high-rise buildings decimated historical districts. This growth, along with expanded education and public housing for many Singaporeans, made Lee even more popular. Yet his hold on power was also due to an increasing authoritarianism. While Lee portrayed Singapore as democratic, he had little patience with political dissidents, mainly leftists who objected to his dilution of socialism. They were fre-

quently harassed and imprisoned, and one dissident served a 23-year jail term.

In 1965, Lee's union with Malaysia unraveled when the national government under TENGKU ABDUL RAHMAN expelled Singapore from the union. The Malays had become frightened at Singapore's growing economic power and Lee's attempts to make the PAP a Malaysian-wide political party. Such developments were interpreted by Malays as examples of Chinese desires to dominate the country.

Lee ran into internal problems in the 1980s when a more educated populace desired greater political choices and an economic recession struck. The PAP lost some of its usually large voting percentage in legislative elections. Lee subsequently arrested over 20 opponents, participants in a supposedly Marxist conspiracy. In 1984, he announced his intention to retire as prime minister within several years and did so on 28 November 1990. His deputy prime minister, Goh Chok Tong, replaced him. Lee, however, remained the head of PAP and still wielded significant influence.

References: Josey, Alex, *Lee Kuan Yew and the Commonwealth*, 1969; Turnbull, C. M., *A History of Singapore, 1819–1975*, 1984.

Lin Piao
(1907–1971)
China

A master military strategist, Lin Piao rose among the Chinese Communists to become the heir apparent to the great ruler, MAO TSE-TUNG. But in 1971, he suddenly disappeared from office and died under mysterious circumstances.

Lin Piao hailed from Huang-kang located in Hupeh Province in central China. On 5 December 1907 he was born into a landholding family. He acquired his elementary education at the village school and transferred to middle school at

Wuchang. There the nationalist ideas that had been spreading through his country influenced him.

At this time, China was in tremendous turmoil. Earlier in the century the Ch'ing dynasty had come under severe attack as antiquated and backward-looking, conditions that, critics claimed, had allowed domination by foreign powers. Chinese reformers advocated a technological and political renaissance, including the adoption of Western approaches as a means to advance China and to restore its greatness. SUN YAT-SEN emerged as the foremost reformer who fought to overthrow the Ch'ing rulers, and WANG CHING-WEI became a prominent propagandist for the cause. In 1912, the dynasty collapsed and Sun's Kuomintang, or Nationalists, came to power. In a political arrangement, Sun agreed to let Yüan Shih-kai become president, but he soon tried to grab absolute powers and create his own dynasty. This brought opposition and with it more upheaval.

The May Fourth Movement of 1919 in particular affected Lin. In this instance, students at Peking University held a mass demonstration at Tiananmen Gate to protest the Treaty of Versailles that upheld Japan's intrusions into China and to

> *"The People's Liberation Army is the mighty pillar of the dictatorship of the proletariat. . . ."*

criticize the government headquartered in Peking. Lin agreed with the calls for modernization that came from this protest, and he began pursuing new ideas. A cousin and an older brother interested Lin in communism, and in 1925 he joined the Socialist Youth League. That same year he participated in a protest against the treatment of Chinese by foreigners in Shanghai.

About this time, Sun Yat-sen took the Nationalist movement into a new phase when he admitted Communists into the Kuomintang Party and turned to Russian revolutionaries for help in developing a strategy to unite all of China. Sun established the Whampoa Military Academy as a training school for a revolutionary army, and in 1925 Lin became a cadet there. When Sun died during that year, CHIANG KAI-SHEK gained leadership of the Nationalists and in 1926 launched an offensive into the north. Lin joined the fight and rose quickly in the ranks from deputy platoon leader to battalion commander.

The following year, however, Chiang turned on his Communist allies in the Kuomintang and purged them. Lin sided with the Communists, and in 1928 he joined Mao Tse-tung in the mountains of central China, where he became a commander in the Red Army. For several years, from 1928 to 1934, Lin successfully defended Kiangsi Province against Chiang's forces. But in the latter year, Chiang overran the area, and Lin's First Army Corps joined Mao and other Communists in the historic Long March to escape the Nationalists. In 1935, the Communists arrived in northern China, removed from Chiang's army, and Lin received accolades for his performance in the march. He became president of

the Red Army Academy and ranked among the highest commanders. As Mao consolidated his hold on the Chinese Communist Party (CCP), Lin displayed an intense loyalty to him that would last for years. He especially won Mao's favor in his fervent support for the guerrilla tactics controversial among the Communists.

In 1937, the fighting between the Nationalists and Communists came to a temporary end when the two sides joined in a united front against the Japanese who invaded China. Lin led an army division to an important victory, but in 1938 he was wounded in battle and sent to the Soviet Union for recuperation. While there, he studied military techniques. He returned to China in 1942 and served on the Communist liaison team to the Nationalists. In 1945, he won election to the CCP central committee.

After World War II came to a close, the Nationalists and Communists resumed their civil war, and Lin went to Manchuria, where he commanded the Fourth Field Army against Chiang's invading troops. He developed a strategy to retreat from the cities and base his defense in the countryside, a move that dumbfounded the Nationalists, who considered it a sign of weakness. The strategy allowed him and Mao, though, to build a strong following among the peasants and to use guerrilla tactics that gradually isolated the Nationalists in the cities and forced them to surrender. By 1948, Lin secured Manchuria and then moved his forces south in 1949 to help in Mao's capture of Peking, Wuhan, and Canton. The Nationalists fled the mainland to Taiwan, and in October Mao proclaimed the People's Republic of China.

Lin obtained numerous appointments in the new government. Until 1954, he served as administrative chief and party head in six provinces located in south-central China. Then he was made vice-premier in the cabinet and vice-chairman of the National Defense Council. In 1955, he advanced to the Central Committee's 13-man Politburo and in 1958 to the Politburo's select 7-man Standing Committee.

He continued to rise in prominence. In 1959, he became minister of defense and rebuilt the army along lines desired by Mao: political indoctrination to accompany improved military training. He ordered that the soldiers' thoughts be monitored closely and shaped into Maoist ideas. In 1965, he stressed egalitarianism by ordering all officers to serve time as privates and by ending all distinguishing insignias. The People's Liberation Army served as a model for society to follow, and the Communists implored Chinese to emulate its discipline and spirit. Lin's reputation soared, especially with Mao and his wife, CHIANG CH'ING, who had become a powerful promoter of Maoism, and he gave a major policy speech, claiming that the underdeveloped areas of the world would one day conquer the developed ones. Lin's work with the army encouraged Mao to promote the Great Cultural Revolution, which began in the mid-1960s. In it, Mao acted to rid China of bourgeois practices and moved to cleanse the CCP of leaders who had strayed from the Maoist line. He wanted the discipline and ideology Lin had instilled in the army, and he circumvented the party to use the army as his main basis of support. Well into the 1970s, in fact, the military remained dominant.

In 1966, Lin emerged as one of the CCP's top three leaders, and a new constitution in 1969 designated him as Mao's successor. This move was an additional attempt by Mao to contain the CCP and emphasize ideological purity. Then came the strange events of 1971, still clouded in mystery. On 13 September, after a dispute with CHOU EN-LAI,

China's premier, Lin died in a plane crash in Mongolia. The Chinese government reported he was fleeing the country because he had been discovered in a plot to overthrow Mao. Supposedly, Lin had even sponsored several assassination attempts on the aging Chinese leader.

Analysts are not sure how much truth there is to this story, or even if Lin actually died in the plane crash. There is evidence to indicate that a struggle erupted aboard the plane Lin was supposedly traveling on, a struggle between Lin and those loyal to Mao, that produced gunshots. Lin may have died at that point, with the plane then going into a free fall. There is also evidence that after turning to the army, Mao had come to regret giving it and Lin too much power, and that he saw them as a threat. Whatever the case, the Chinese government officially vilified Lin after his death, calling him a reactionary and a traitor. Yet his true legacy will be much broader than that: a military genius and an architect in building a new China.

References: Ebon, Martin, *Lin Piao: The Life and Writings of China's New Ruler*, 1970; Kau, Michael Y. M., *The Lin Piao Affair: Power Politics and Military Coup*, 1975; Robinson, Thomas W., *A Politico-Military Biography of Lin Piao, Part I, 1907–1949*, 1971.

Lini, Walter
(b. 1942)
Vanuatu

Within the Anglican Church, Father Walter Lini could see clearly the discrimination by Europeans toward the Melanesians. This stimulated his desire to gain independence for Vanuatu.

Walter Lini was born in 1942 at Agatoa, a village on Pentecost Island. At five years of age, he began attending a missionary school and from 1954 to 1960 attended Vureas High School on Aoba. He then moved to Lolowai, where he managed a bookshop and worked part time for the director of education. At first he thought about becoming a lawyer,

but then decided to enter the ministry and in 1962, to broaden his knowledge, enrolled at St. Peter's College in the Solomon Islands. Three years later, he began his studies at St. John's College in Auckland, New Zealand. While there, he joined other Pacific island students and formed the Western Pacific Students' Association, which published a newsletter and broadened the awareness of indigenous problems.

Lini graduated in 1968 and returned home. At the time, Vanuatu was called New Hebrides, and

Britain and France had joint control over it. Ever since the end of World War II, Melanesians had protested their mistreatment under these foreign rulers. In 1969, Lini was ordained a deacon in the Anglican Church and immediately noticed the prejudice shown by the European clergy toward himself and other Melanesians. He helped begin the *Kakamora Reporter* to express Melanesian opinions. In 1970, he published and edited a more prominent newspaper, *New Hebrides Viewpoints*.

The following year, Lini and his friend, Father John Bani, led demonstrations against British and French plans to subdivide additional land. In 1973, Lini helped found the New Hebrides National Party and built an effective organization on Aoba, North Pentecost, and Maewo. He won election in January 1974 to the party presidency and obtained a leave of absence from the Anglican Church to tend to his political duties. He declared his intention to see his homeland gain its independence by 1977.

Legislative elections were held in 1975, and the National Party, renamed the Vanua'aku Pati (VP), swept all the elected seats. The appointive seats in the legislature, however, were in French hands. This caused Lini and the VP to establish a separate government, and the crisis led to an agreement with the European nations to end colonial control.

Vanuatu became an independent nation on 29 July 1980, and Lini was elected prime minister. He faced an immediate crisis when Jimmy Stephens Nagriamel declared Espiritu Santo, the largest island in the chain, separate from Vanuatu. With the help of troops from Papua (New Guinea) and Australia, Lini crushed the rebellion in August and arrested Stephens. The rebel's trial revealed he had been supported by the Phoenix Foundation, a right-wing group in the United States.

Lini faced the substantial challenge of ameliorating the differences between three cultures: French, British, and Melanesian. He needed and

> *"God and custom must be the sail and the steering-paddle of our canoe."*

accepted French financial assistance for his nation's largely impoverished economy. Lini developed a widely popular administration, although not without its controversies and critics. Twice in the early 1980s, his opponents tried to secure a vote of no-confidence in him, partly based on his controversial dealings with a New Zealand businessman who contracted to build a *copra* (coconut meat) mill.

Lini boosted his political standing when he defied France and claimed Hunter and Matthew Islands, two uninhabited rock outcroppings, as Vanuatu territory (a move the French rebuffed). In other popular actions, he won land rights for Melanesians who had claims against Europeans in Vanuatu and established an airline and a central bank.

Lini twice won reelection in the 1980s and twice turned back efforts to oust him from the national and VP leadership—the first time in 1988 when he expelled Barak Tame Sope from the party secretary-generalship he had held for many years, and the second time in 1989 when he arrested Sope for colluding with the nation's president to oust him as prime minister.

In April 1991, some members at the VP National Congress criticized Lini for what they called increasing authoritarianism. He responded by dismissing several of his cabinet ministers who had joined in the attack. This, however, led to his ouster as prime minister in September. He then formed a new organization, the Vanuatu National Unity Party (VNUP). As a result, the VP vote was split, and a third party formed a coalition government with the VNUP. In August 1993, Lini withdrew the VNUP from the coalition. The prime minister, Maxime Carlot, consequently maintains a tenuous hold on power.

Reference: Lini, Walter, *Beyond Pandemonium: From the New Hebrides to Vanuatu*, 1980.

Louis XI
(1423–1483)
France

Louis XI acted secretively and used devious tactics; he commanded loyalty and functioned ruthlessly; he disliked his father and may have poisoned him; he crushed the power of the nobles and championed the bourgeoisie. Through this, he cobbled a French state that his successors were able to expand into a modern nation.

Louis was born at Bourges on 3 July 1423 to King Charles VII and Marie d'Anjou. As a child he lived in obscurity and seclusion at the Loches Castle in Tourraine, a bleak and foreboding structure that seemed to encourage his youthful rebelliousness. Supporters hid Louis there, afraid that enemies would kill him to prevent him from ever becoming king. A tutor taught Louis traditional courses in Latin, history, mathematics, and music. He also learned to use a sword and lance and became an excellent horseman.

At this time, foreigners controlled most of France, and Charles VII had little real authority. In the wake of the Hundred Years' War, the English possessed the west and a vast area in the north, and the Duke of Burgundy controlled large areas in the northeast, stretching through the Netherlands. This situation encouraged nationalist sentiment as the French experienced a common struggle against the foreigners. Joan of Arc helped Charles VII drive the English from Orléans in 1429. Charles established a national standing army in 1439 and a national tax to finance it—measures which fostered absolutism and a French identity—and he subsequently gained territories from the English, acquiring Normandy and Aquitaine in 1449 and 1451. Charles also ended the medieval system, but he did not complete national integration, and the Burgundians remained strong.

Meanwhile, as dauphin (heir to the throne), Louis had authority over the southeastern province of Dauphiné. In 1440, he joined several princes in rebelling against his father, but the effort failed. Charles VII pardoned Louis and the dauphin returned to his province. He then helped his father in the wars against England, but he did not get along with the king's advisors, and when he plotted against them his father sent him back to Dauphiné, this time in exile. Louis reformed Dauphiné, reducing the nobles to obedience, centralizing the administration, and establishing the University of Valence. In 1456, he had another dispute with his father, this time over foreign policy and his marriage to Charlotte, daughter of the Duke of Savoy, of which Charles disapproved. When Charles sent troops against his wayward son, Louis fled to the Netherlands and the court of Philip the Good, Duke of Burgundy, a man much hated by Charles VII.

From Philip, Louis learned the workings of the powerful Burgundian state. He also kept close watch on his father, who had become ill. He did this by using spies, and some analysts claim that through them he may have poisoned Charles (others insist the king's affliction came from a more mundane jaw infection). When Charles died in 1461, Louis became king of France and moved quickly against his father's advisors. He imprisoned them and built his power by allying with the lesser nobles and the middle class, or bourgeoisie, an increasingly influential group as Europe entered a commercial era.

Although Louis went to war several times, he preferred diplomatic intrigue to gain his ends, often using devious means, which earned him the sobriquet "the universal spider." From the outset he sought to expand his territories and centralize his administration, but opposing princes had other ideas. In 1465, they formed the League of the Public Weal and attacked Louis in a war that resulted in the king having to recognize the authority of the rebels in northern France, including Normandy.

Charles the Bold, Philip's son and successor as the Duke of Burgundy, became Louis's main enemy.

The duke, who also possessed Franche-Comté, Flanders, Artois, Picardy, and the Netherlands, sought to form a middle kingdom between France and the Holy Roman Empire. In 1468, Louis, who had recently regained Normandy, decided to resolve the Burgundian problem and journeyed to Peronne to negotiate with Charles. During the talks a rebellion broke out at Liège (located within the Duke's territory), sparked by Louis's agents. Charles suddenly broke off the negotiations, arrested Louis, and did not release him until he agreed to a treaty recognizing territorial concessions.

In 1471, Louis attacked Burgundy, but failed. Charles the Bold, however, soon met his end when, in 1477, he was killed in a battle against the Swiss. Louis then warred against Burgundy, and even though Austria defended the Burgundians, he obtained Burgundy, Picardy, and Artois and continued an ongoing dispute with Austria over the Netherlands.

Louis later acquired Roussillon, Provence, Anjou, and Maine, so that by the time of his death in 1483 Brittany remained as the only major territory in France outside his control. Louis used force and political leverage to crush the power of the nobles so successfully that some analysts claim his reign

"I am France."

marked the end of feudal France. He established a quid pro quo with the bourgeoisie, whereby in return for their support he appointed them as government ministers and initiated efforts to expand trade and industry. For example, he encouraged the building of ships, improved the harbors and river traffic, expanded mining, and introduced the silk industry.

Known for his distaste of royal trappings and for his conviviality with the middle class (he did not like courtiers), Louis, nevertheless, fostered much discontent. His efforts, both diplomatic and economic, led to high taxes on the peasants—an oppression so severe they despised his reign. Indeed, when Louis died on 30 August 1483 at Plessis-les-Tours, many French rejoiced. Still, this man of great talent and influence has been called "the founder of the national state in France," and although the making of France into a modern nation would take several more centuries and evolve through numerous stages, including the current Fifth Republic begun by CHARLES DE GAULLE, Louis greatly advanced the process.

References: Cleugh, James, *Chart Royal*, 1970; Kendall, Paul M., *Louis XI: The Universal Spider*, 1986.

Lumumba, Patrice
(1925–1961)
Zaire

While Patrice Lumumba's strong character brought him to the fore of Zaire's nationalist movement, it also brought him an early death. When he rejected compromise and pursued radical policies, his enemies killed him.

Patrice Lumumba was born in July 1925 in Ona Lua, a village in Kasai Province, and came from the small and politically weak Batetela tribe. This may have made him less attached to ethnic goals and more willing to pursue a nationalist course embracing all tribes.

When Lumumba was born, Zaire was under Belgian rule. After World War II, nationalism became a problem for Belgium as *évolulés* became numerous. These were Africans who had obtained substantial education and had adopted many European cultural practices, thus distancing themselves from traditional institutions. Lumumba was among them. He had attended a Protestant mission school, obtained Belgian citizenship, and spoke fluent French, Swahili, and Ngala. In the 1950s, while living in Kindu-Port-Empain, he began writing essays and poems for Congolese publications, and he joined an *évolué* club. These organizations emerged as the seedbeds of nationalist activities, and Belgium responded with compromise, eliminating some of the distinctions between middle-class Africans and Europeans.

Meanwhile, urbanization encouraged Africans to emphasize their ethnic identities, and ethnic clubs emerged, some *évolué* in character. These were a factor in shaping Congolese politics. In 1950, members of the Kongo tribe formed the Alliance of the Kongo People (ABAKO) and advanced their own ethnic agenda.

Around this time, Lumumba moved to Leopoldville (Kinshasa), where he became a postal clerk, and then to Kisangani, the capital of Orientale Province, where he became an accountant in the postal service and continued writing his articles. In 1955, he entered labor politics, winning the presidency of the Association of Native Personnel of the Colony (APIC), a Congolese trade union representing government employees and advocating African advancement and just pay.

Then, in 1956, events brought him into the nationalist fray. On 30 June, several African leaders published a manifesto calling for political change; never before had such a document been published in the Congo. ABAKO reacted by demanding even greater political rights, such as free speech and a free press. These actions, plus an economic downturn and Belgium's rejection of many *évolué* demands, stimulated political party formation.

Lumumba joined in founding the National Congolese Movement (MNC), begun in Kinshasa and dominated by *évolués*; he was made party president and became an energetic critic of Belgian policies. In 1956, Belgium invited him to Brussels to help develop a uniform code for regulating government employees. Upon his return to Kinshasa, he was arrested, charged with having embezzled post office monies, was found guilty, and served one year in prison.

Nationalism soon grew stronger when, in 1958, France allowed its colonies autonomy within a French Community, and Ghana hosted the first Pan-African conference. Upon his release from prison, Lumumba attended this meeting in Accra, met KWAME NKRUMAH, and adopted the idea of African solidarity. In Leopoldville, he made a bold address—the first public speech calling for Congolese independence.

After colonial elections late in 1958, Belgium announced a five-year plan to bring independence.

Most nationalists, however, objected to the delay as a plot to install pro-Belgian puppets in office, and they announced a boycott of the 1959 local elections. Belgium responded by repressing dissident activities, and riots flared in Kinshasa. Lumumba supported the election boycott, and the government imprisoned him, claiming he had incited the riots.

Lumumba's MNC then changed tactics and entered candidates in the 1959 elections, winning 90 percent of the votes in Stanleyville. In January 1960, Belgium called a Round Table Conference in Brussels, and 45 African delegates attended, including Lumumba. The conferees agreed on elections for May 1960, preparatory to independence the following month. In this atmosphere, the Congo's political situation became more confused as rival parties based largely on ethnic differences multiplied. Lumumba's MNC remained the most truly nationalist party, but it too split, and bloody ethnic fighting broke out in several locations, leaving a substantial death toll.

Lumumba's MNC prevailed over some hundred other parties, although it did not win a majority in the Chamber of Deputies. Lumumba subsequently formed a coalition government and became premier. He faced an immediate crisis when, under the leadership of MOISE TSHOMBE, Katanga Province seceded and the Congolese army rebelled. Belgium sent troops into the Congo to protect Belgian nationals, but the troops landed mainly in Katanga and appeared to support Tshombe. Lumumba then requested United Nations help, but when the UN troops arrived, they refused to crush the Katangan revolt.

Lumumba was beleaguered on all sides: an unstable army, a government bureaucracy filled with inexperienced workers, and an uncertain UN military presence. Amid these difficulties, he turned to the Soviet Union for help, a move many interpreted as a shift to radicalism and which, amid the prevailing cold-war atmosphere, the United States interpreted as hostile.

Lumumba also called for a more centralized government, and this alarmed many provincial politicians who favored local autonomy. Rather than compromise, he arrested several prominent opposition leaders and declared martial law. On 5 September 1960, in a tactic of dubious constitutional validity, President JOSEPH KASAVUBU removed Lumumba from office. Lumumba, however, still claimed he was the Congo's legitimate leader. Then, on 14 September, Army Chief of Staff

MOBUTU SESE SEKO (JOSEPH MOBUTU) seized power, with Kasavubu remaining as president.

In November, while traveling to Stanleyville, Lumumba was captured by Kasavubu's military and interned at Camp Hardy, Thysville. He was then transferred to Katanga and killed under mysterious circumstances in January 1961. News of his death led to violent riots. Lumumba left behind a message of national unity and Pan-Africanism.

References: Kaplan, Irving, ed., *Zaire: A Country Study,* 1979; Van Lierde, Jean, *Lumumba Speaks: The Speeches and Writings of Patrice Lumumba, 1958–1961,* 1972.

Macdonald, John Alexander
(1815–1891)
Canada

Convivial and outgoing, shrewd and abusive, John Alexander Macdonald's statesmanship and his vision of national unity made him the foremost Canadian leader, the man who forged disparate provinces into a dominion.

Born on 11 January 1815 in Glasgow, Scotland, John Alexander Macdonald emigrated with his family in 1820 to Kingston in what is now Ontario, Canada. As a young man he studied law and entered the bar in 1836, opening his office in Kingston.

British North America experienced great tension in the 1830s and 1840s. In each colony an oligarchy dominated power; closed and elitist, this oligarchy angered many. Furthermore, in Lower Canada, political and social conflict erupted between the French and English settlers in Québec and Montréal, and a short-lived armed uprising occurred there, one year after Macdonald began his law practice. On top of this, in Upper Canada, reformers seeking increased popular power staged their own revolt, one also quickly crushed. Macdonald, a social conservative, opposed the rebellions and worried about the viability of the existing political system.

These developments caused Britain to send Lord Durham to assess the situation. Durham reached a conclusion that influenced Macdonald and other Canadians: The entire area should have more self-government, and the two Canadas should be unified into a confederation. In 1840, the British Parliament approved the latter recommendation by passing the Union Act that created the Province of Canada.

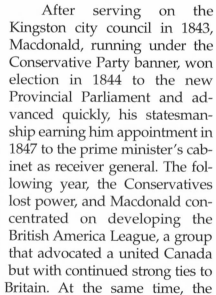

After serving on the Kingston city council in 1843, Macdonald, running under the Conservative Party banner, won election in 1844 to the new Provincial Parliament and advanced quickly, his statesmanship earning him appointment in 1847 to the prime minister's cabinet as receiver general. The following year, the Conservatives lost power, and Macdonald concentrated on developing the British America League, a group that advocated a united Canada but with continued strong ties to Britain. At the same time, the colonies gained greater internal self-government after Britain replaced its protectionist economic policies with free trade and instructed that the colonial assemblies should have additional power within a ministerial cabinet system.

By the early 1850s, Macdonald was leader of the Conservative Party in Canada West (formerly Upper Canada). In 1856, he was named attorney general and the following year won election as co-prime minister for the entire Province of Canada, a position held with GEORGE ÉTIENNE CARTIER, the French representative from Canada East (formerly Lower Canada).

Pressures continued to build toward a Canadian confederation. First, the existing system with its co-prime ministry and constant turmoil between English- and French-speaking areas produced disorder. Second, the colonies needed expanded railroads, which were too expensive for the Province of Canada or the Maritime Provinces to undertake separately. Third, the colonists desired westward expansion to boost the economy and thwart territorial desires by the United States, a concern intensified in 1858 after gold was discovered in the Pacific Northwest.

When, in the fall of 1864, the Maritime Provinces decided to meet at Charlottetown on Prince Edward Island to discuss unity among themselves, Macdonald obtained permission to lead a delegation to the meeting. Gathered at the colonial building, in the legislative council room with its great pillars and gold decor, were the men who became prominent leaders of Canadian union: Macdonald, Cartier, SAMUEL TILLEY, CHARLES TUPPER, and GEORGE BROWN. The delegates listened as Macdonald presented his case for a Canadian confederation. Following his appeal, they agreed to hold a conference in Québec that resulted in resolutions to form a union.

Opposition to confederation still existed: The French feared they would be dominated by the English, and the Maritime Provinces feared they would lose too much autonomy. But in New Brunswick, Charles Tupper convinced the legislature to support union. In December 1867, Macdonald and other delegates from the Province of Canada, New Brunswick, and Nova Scotia met in London, and from this came the British North America Act, modeled closely after the Québec Resolutions. The act outlined the union, which Macdonald wanted to be called the Kingdom of Canada. After Britain objected to this name, the colonists settled for the Dominion of Canada. The Dominion officially emerged on 1 July 1867 and, although still under British control, represented the unification of Canada. (This led several decades later, in the 1930s, to equal Commonwealth status with Britain.)

The Canadian governmental structure reflected Macdonald's preferences for a federal system with a parliamentary establishment, rather than the American system of a presidency. Macdonald became Canada's first prime minister and worked at expanding the confederation. In the early 1870s, Prince Edward Island joined the Dominion.

At the same time, Macdonald turned his attention to the West. After a rebellion erupted in the northwest, he negotiated a settlement that, in 1870, created the Province of Manitoba. The area more distant, which had few white settlers, was organized as the Northwest Territory.

Along the Pacific Coast, British Columbia remained questionable—would the colony join Canada? While many residents there wanted to, others contemplated joining the United States. At this juncture, Macdonald persuaded Britain to appoint a governor to British Columbia who favored the confederation, and in 1870 the colony's Legislative Council voted to unite with Canada. Macdonald and his cabinet secured the agreement after they promised British Columbia that Canada would build a railroad to connect the area with the East. In 1871, British Columbia officially became Canada's sixth province.

Early on, Macdonald exerted federal authority. Under his direction, a provision had been placed in the constitution allowing the central government to overrule any provincial legislation within one year of its passage. Macdonald used this power on several occasions, nullifying legislation he considered unconstitutional or injurious.

Railroad construction both united the nation and provided problems for Macdonald. In 1867, the government began building a system joining Halifax to Québec. Completed nine years later, it connected with several smaller lines to form the Intercolonial Railway. In the West, Macdonald intended the Canadian Pacific Railway to fulfill the promise made to British Columbia. The opposition Liberal Party criticized the plan as too expensive, but Macdonald's policy helped him win reelection in 1872.

Then the following year a scandal broke: Informers revealed that the contract for building the railroad had been given to a company headed by a major contributor to Macdonald's Conservatives. The controversy forced Macdonald to resign, and he lost the 1874 general election. Liberal leadership lasted only until 1878, at which time Macdonald regained the prime ministry. Under his direction, construction of the Pacific Railroad was transferred to a group of investors who completed it in 1885.

Macdonald worked tirelessly to develop nationalism in Canada. In this regard he was helped by George Cartier, the prominent French leader in Québec. The Washington Treaty, which had been signed by the United States and Britain in 1871, also helped Macdonald's effort: Its terms enraged Canadians by opening their fisheries to Americans while gaining no concessions in the American markets for Canadian goods. Macdonald, who had long distrusted the United States, subsequently pursued protectionism with his National Policy that promoted Canadian pride.

Macdonald stimulated controversy with some of his financial dealings and his reputation for prolonged drinking bouts. Yet his political talents far exceeded those of his opponents, and when he died on 6 June 1891 in Ottawa, Canadians felt a great loss: The man who had created the Dominion was gone.

References: Creighton, Donald, *John A. Macdonald: The Old Chieftain,* 1956; Creighton, Donald, *John A. Macdonald: The Young Politician,* 1952.

Machel, Samora
(1933–1986)
Mozambique

When, in the 1960s, the Mozambique Liberation Front became prominent in Mozambique's fight against Portuguese rule, Samora Machel joined his colleague EDUARDO MONDLANE in utilizing his familial anticolonial heritage. And, like Mondlane, he advocated a radical restructuring of his homeland's society.

Samora Machel came from a family that had long opposed Portuguese rule. In the late 1800s, his paternal grandfather had served as a commander in the Maguiguana Rebellion, and the Portuguese had exiled both his maternal grandparents for their political resistance. Samora Machel was born on 29 September 1933 in Chilembene, a village in the Limpopo Valley of southern Mozambique. As a boy, Samora attended missionary school, where he received not only an education in books but also an education in exploitation as the Catholic Church forced him to work in the fields raising crops for market. He displayed a strong rebellious streak that concerned his teachers, who decided he should go to a seminary where they hoped he could be better disciplined. Samora, however, refused, and instead went to high school and, at the same time, worked as a medical assistant at Miguel

"Marxism-Leninism did not appear in our country as an imported product."

Bambarda Hospital in Maputo, Mozambique's capital, to raise money for his education.

Portugal's influence in Mozambique had been recognized by other European nations in 1884, but prior to 1926 the Portuguese had only a loose hold on the area. Yet they began a system of forced labor that would last into the 1960s. Machel saw his father forced into cotton production and saw him lose his land in the early 1950s to a Portuguese immigrant. He also witnessed his brother being forced to work as a contract laborer in the mines of South Africa, where he died in an accident. These harsh experiences stirred Machel's political consciousness.

When, in 1961, the Mozambique Liberation Front (FRELIMO) was formed, Machel joined its ranks. In 1963, he received military training in Algeria and then obtained command of FRELIMO's first military camp. He become a strategist in planning FRELIMO's upcoming battles against Portuguese troops. In 1964, he directed the military campaign in Niassa that began the armed struggle, and two years later he became FRELIMO defense secretary.

In the 1960s, FRELIMO experienced several internal struggles over ideology. In each, Machel sided with Eduardo Mondlane in supporting radical reform within Mozambique. One year after Mondlane was assassinated in 1969, Machel became FRELIMO president and moved the organization into an open embrace of socialism. He adopted Marxism-Leninism but considered this ideology less an import and more an outgrowth of the Mozambiquan experience that had transformed it. By this time, FRELIMO dominated the country's interior, while Portuguese forces controlled the coast and several towns. Early in 1974, FRELIMO launched a new offensive that greatly damaged the Portuguese standing by destroying their plan to contain the rebels in the north.

When, later in 1974, a revolution occurred within Portugal, Machel stepped up FRELIMO attacks on Portuguese troops (now numbering over 70,000), including intensified efforts in the cities of Maputo and Beira. Most outside observers agreed that the Portuguese army had become dispirited and demoralized. In September, Portugal agreed to independence, and a provisional government was installed while Machel resided in Tanzania, distancing himself from any public cooperation with the outgoing colonial authorities. With independence on 25 June 1975, Machel became his nation's first president. This intense, articulate leader admitted he had only vague ideas, but he directed a campaign against oppression and exploitation and immediately announced the nationalization of all land, businesses, and public services.

Machel dedicated his administration to helping Africans rid themselves of white rule. This entailed support of liberationists in Zimbabwe, but produced a predicament respecting South Africa. Since Mozambique relied heavily on that country for trade and electricity, Machel found himself following a pragmatic course of cooperation with its white supremacist government.

He also developed a pragmatic approach to his socialist doctrine, partly because most Mozambicans—poorly educated, suffering from poverty, and used to tribalism—did not understand its intellectual content and the sacrifices demanded, and partly because Mozambique suffered from a shortage of trained workers resulting from the long years of Portuguese exploitation and a mass exodus of whites. In 1977, Machel ended his idea of FRELIMO as a mass movement encompassing all classes; it now became an ideological elite directing Mozambique. Because the Mozambican economy remained stagnant in the 1980s, Machel permitted private investments, and he initiated discussions with Portugal for a closer economic relationship. At the same time, he faced an armed insurgency that destroyed much industrial and agricultural production. On 19 October 1986, Machel died in a plane crash along the Mozambique-South Africa border. Three years later, FRELIMO ended its Marxist-Leninist commitment.

References: Isaacman, Allen, and Barbara Isaacman, *Mozambique: From Colonialism to Revolution, 1900–1982;* Munslow, Barry, *Mozambique: The Revolution and Its Origin,* 1983.

Macías Nguema, Francisco
(1924–1979)
Equatorial Guinea

In the 1970s, Equatorial Guinea's presidential palace near Bata loomed as an imposing edifice surrounded by thick walls topped with electric wire. Built by President Francisco Macías Nguema, it reflected his paranoia, his distrust, and his fortress mentality. Amnesty International once called the Macías regime "among the most brutal . . . in the world."

When Francisco Macías Nguema was born into the Fang tribe on 1 January 1924, he became part of an ethnic group numerically superior to all others but long oppressed. At the time, his homeland was called Spanish Guinea—the only equatorial African area under Spanish rule—and consisted of Fernando Póo, an island near Nigeria, and Río Muni, on the African mainland. Sharp ethnic differences existed, with the Bubi and Nigerian immigrants on Fernando Póo (today Bioko Island) dominating politically and economically, although the Fang of Río Muni outnumbered them.

As a young man, Macías felt inferior to foreigners, particularly Europeans, and changed his name from Masié to the more Spanish-sounding form. In 1944, he became a clerk in the colonial government at Bata and then entered the Forest Service and the Public Works Department. Between 1947 and 1951, he worked on his family's coffee plantations. Immediately after this, he served as an interpreter at the Racial Court in Mongomo and later became mayor. As Guineans pushed for autonomy, Spain changed its administration in 1963, making the territory a province and allowing a legislature and a council. This, however, did not please the nationalists and in particular the Fang, who believed Spain had long favored the Bubi.

Macías did not distinguish himself politically until 1963, when he joined the Popular Idea of Equatorial Guinea (IPGE)—a group banned by Spain when first founded in 1959 but legal by the time Macías joined it. In 1963, after the IPGE split apart over the issue of whether to merge with Cameroon, Macías joined the newly organized National Union Movement of Equatorial Guinea (MUNGE). This party was moderate and developed a nationwide appeal, although it remained strongest in Fang-dominated Río Muni. In 1964, Ondo Edu served as party president and developed a platform that supported independence, but with continued close ties to Spain.

Macías disliked this moderation, broke with MUNGE, and took a radical course. He joined the National Liberation Movement of Equatorial Guinea (MONALIGE) that condemned any transitional status and demanded immediate independence while threatening armed conflict. Macías served as a delegate to the Río Muni legislature in 1964 and as a member of the General Assembly, or Parliament. Four years later, he participated in a constitutional conference intended to prepare his homeland for independence. At this meeting, he exhibited a strong dislike for competing politicians. In the elections to form a national government, MUNGE finished first, and Macías defeated Ondo Edu for the presidency.

> *"I have not killed anybody. . . . I don't think I've committed any offense. I regard all Guineans as my sons."*

Macías's victory proved devastating as his Fang biases combined with a strong paranoia and megalomania to produce a brutal dictatorship. This became evident in 1969 when he lured Ondo Edu back to Equatorial Guinea from his exile in Gabon, promised him safety, and then had him assassinated. Macías engaged in nearly continuous purges aimed first at rival political leaders, but then at anyone who opposed him. Government officials, diplomats, doctors, teachers, police—all mysteriously disappeared in large numbers. Macías especially hated educated people and aimed his violence at them, even making it illegal to utter the word "intellectual."

Early in 1969, he became virulently anti-Spanish in his pronouncements, a move that produced intervention by Spanish troops and then a large withdrawal of Europeans. Macías declared a state of emergency and in March announced he had defeated a coup attempt. That same year, riots occurred involving disputes between Fernando Póo islanders and Río Muni province. After Macías claimed an attempt was made on his life in 1971, he ordered attacks on the Bubi, resulting in numerous deaths.

In 1970, Macías had begun building his presidential palace costing U.S.$12 million. He installed a bed that cost U.S.$4,400 and placed high walls around the building, topped with electric wire. He became more reclusive and spent much time at Mongomo in Río Muni protected by fortified military installations. He proclaimed himself president for life in 1972.

Meanwhile, his country's economy, which he had heavily nationalized, spiraled downward. Macías imported Cuban guards to protect him and in 1976 ordered that all people change their Christian names to African ones. Perceiving more and more enemies, he continued to purge and kill those near him to the point the government relied only on him and three close relatives. By this time, over 600 people had been eliminated by Macías, and his terror and the economic hardship had resulted in 120,000 exiles fleeing to neighboring countries. In October 1978, he ordered 32 new executions. Finally, an opposition to him coalesced around his nephew Obiang Nguema, who in 1979, led a successful coup.

Macías fled into the forest only to be captured by peasants. He subsequently faced a trial—

charged with genocide, murder, treason, and the misappropriation of public funds totalling millions. He was sentenced to death and executed in 1979, along with six former aides. Thus Macías provided a legacy of forging independence and establishing tyrannical rule that gained freedom from Spain but brutalized and impoverished his nation. Unfortunately for Guineans, his successor, Obiang Nguema, had participated in many of his uncle's executions and as president engaged in his own brutal policies, including overseeing torture sessions at Playa Negra prison.

Reference: Cronje, Suzanne, *Equatorial Guinea—The Forgotten Dictatorship: Forced Labor and Political Murder in Central Africa,* 1976.

Madero, Francisco
(1873–1913)
Mexico

In a fiery assault on Mexico City in 1913, rebels overthrew Francisco Madero and with him the democracy he sought. The collapse displayed his weakness: an inability to govern a polarized society.

Francisco Madero was born into a wealthy landowning family in Parras, Coahuila, on 30 October 1873. He grew up during a period when a dictator, Porfirio Díaz, ruled Mexico. Díaz advanced his nation's economy with highways, railroads, telegraph lines, and industries. But despite increased prosperity, Mexico suffered an enormously high concentration of wealth among its elite and widespread poverty; in addition, many believed Díaz had become too much of a strongman.

As these developments unfolded, young Francisco obtained his higher education in the United States at Mount Saint Mary's College in Emmitsburg, Maryland, which he attended from 1886 until 1888, and at the University of California at Berkeley, which he attended for one semester. He then studied for three years at a business school in Paris.

In 1904, Madero organized the BENITO JUÁREZ Democratic Club in Coahuila, an organization that supported democratic reform. By this time, discontent with Díaz had risen, and even many among the wealthy disliked the dictator's self-interest and corruption—and the disorder spreading through society. Díaz responded to his critics in 1908 by announcing he would not serve another term as president and would retire in 1910. Madero then gained prominence by issuing his book *The Presidential Succession in 1910,* which was widely read. It displayed his moderate nature by arguing that should Díaz decide to run, the people should be allowed to elect his vice-president. Since the vice-president would become president if the aging Díaz died, Madero was in effect asserting that the people should choose the president's successor.

> *"Effective Suffrage— No Reelection!"*

In 1909, Díaz indeed changed his mind and announced he would again seek the presidency the following year in an open election. Madero then announced his candidacy, proclaiming "Effective Suffrage—No Reelection!" In other words, he urged democracy and a vote against Díaz. The dictator then arrested him. Upon his release, Madero lived in Texas, and from his exile published *The Plan of San Luis Potosi,* in which he demanded that Díaz resign. The book ignited demonstrations in Mexico City, and neither the army nor hardly anyone else wanted to defend the dictator. In May 1911, Díaz fled the nation, and on 7 June, Madero entered the capital.

Many people had high expectations for Madero, but while he had an outstanding talent to foment protest and express democratic ideals, he lacked practical political abilities. A presidential election in October 1911 resulted in a huge victory for him, and he assumed office from an interim leader on 6 November. He found himself immediately besieged by conservatives who complained about assaults on their landed estates by impoverished rebels, some led by EMILIANO ZAPATA, whom Madero tried to crush; and by liberals, who wanted him to go much further in promoting democracy and lessening social inequality. Madero seemed unable to make decisions or to stop corruption that engulfed his administration. In addition to these factors, the American ambassador maneuvered to dislodge Madero.

In February 1913, an assault began on Mexico City, directed by conservative rebels. Within days, Madero's government fell, and on 22 February, Madero was murdered by guards who were taking him to prison. Victoriano Huerta assumed the presidency as a conservative dictator.

Mexico had been in much turmoil ever since the early 1800s when JOSÉ MORELOS led a radical rebellion and the controversial AUGUSTÍN DE ITURBIDE launched an independence movement. Madero obviously did not quell the disorder nor did he bring the radical reforms demanded by some, reforms that would finally come under LÁZARO CÁRDENAS. Yet he did assume a heroic role in the 1910 Revolution and reinforced democratic aspirations.

Reference: Ross, S. R., *Francisco I. Madero: Apostle of Mexican Democracy,* 1955.

Madison, James
(1750–1836)
United States

Throughout his life, James Madison was a frail and bookish man, hardly what an observer might expect to be a revolutionary. Yet he applied his ideas and considerable political acumen to create a constitution for the United States that produced an innovative republican government in a Western world dominated by monarchies.

When James Madison was born on 5 March 1750 in Port Conway, Virginia, he entered a family of comfortable wealth. His father, James Sr., had inherited a plantation of several thousand acres and over 20 slaves on the western frontier, then in Orange County, Virginia. His mother, Nelly Conway Madison, hailed from a merchant family.

Little information remains concerning James's boyhood. His father was well read and had a substantial library, thus the youngster may have received early instruction from his parents. His formal schooling began in 1762, when he studied under a prominent teacher, Donald Robertson. In 1767, James undertook two years of additional study under Reverend Thomas Martin and then entered the College of New Jersey (Princeton). By this time, tension had mounted between the American colonies and their mother country, Britain. James likely heard the debates of the day and was influenced in his position by his father, who strongly opposed Parliament's efforts at taxation, such as the Stamp Act.

At Princeton, James studied in an atmosphere where religious freedom was prized and students and teachers criticized British policy. The Virginian developed a great hunger for knowledge, spending many hours reading. After he graduated in 1771, he continued studying at Princeton for another year, focusing on Hebrew and ethics.

"Wisdom and good examples are necessary at this time to rescue the political machine from impending storm."

When he returned to Orange County, he expressed concern about his sickly condition and had, as yet, no idea as to a career.

He showed, however, a great interest in the clash with Britain and in public affairs overall. He studied some law and wrote about religious freedom, criticizing the Anglican establishment and championing the rights of dissenters. When, under the direction of SAMUEL ADAMS, the Boston Tea Party occurred in 1774, Madison cheered the protestors and criticized the moderates. Late that year, he and his father were elected to the Orange County Committee of Public Safety, an extralegal revolutionary body. The following year, as the colony suffered an attack by British troops and as THOMAS PAINE's pamphlet *Common Sense* inflamed public opinion, Madison won election to the Virginia convention that wrote a state constitution and declaration of rights. As a delegate, he presented the resolution on religious liberty.

Shortly thereafter, Madison was elected to the Virginia Assembly, but served only one term. In 1778, though, the Assembly named him to the Governor's Council and an important relationship began: Madison became close friends with THOMAS JEFFERSON. The two men read extensively and exchanged ideas; over the years, they worked hand-in-hand politically. In 1780, the Assembly appointed Madison as a delegate to the Continental Congress, and there he supported BENJAMIN FRANKLIN in his efforts to secure assistance from France and helped formulate plans to organize the lands in the Old Northwest, thus enabling additional states to enter the Union in the future.

He then returned to Virginia and his home, Montpelier, where he resumed studying law (although he never entered the profession) and criticized his reliance on slave labor. He was elected to the Virginia House of Delegates in 1784 and led in formulating progressive legislation, particularly to develop the economy. Like his countrymen Franklin and Jefferson, Madison engaged in scientific pursuits and in January obtained membership in the American Philosophical Society.

Madison despaired that the national government under the Articles of Confederation had become too weak, and when several states sent delegates to Annapolis in 1786 to consider improving commercial relations, Madison was one of them. He wanted the states to consider reforming the Union and rejoiced when the Annapolis convention agreed to issue such a call.

In 1787, Madison journeyed to Philadelphia to attend the Constitutional Convention. He went convinced that America needed a strong central government, one with a judiciary and a vigorous executive. He favored a legislature where representation from each state would be based on population, and he promoted powers for the federal government that would allow it to create a national bank—an ironic position in light of his later opposition to the bank as proposed by ALEXANDER HAMILTON. One of his most important acts was to successfully defend the concept of a lower house elected directly by the people. Madison kept copious records of the deliberations, and it is from them that we know much about what occurred at the convention. He exerted such a substantial influence that, although the delegates rejected many of his ideas, he became known as the "father of the Constitution."

After the convention, Madison took a prominent position in getting the Constitution ratified. He exerted considerable influence in Virginia and teamed with Hamilton and John Jay in writing a series of articles that later became known as *The Federalist Papers.* In them, he expanded on his assertion at the Constitutional Convention that a republic was better suited to a large nation since the inclusion of diverse interests would prevent oppression by a minority. In his views, Madison expressed his concern that property rights be protected, and many historians consider the Constitution as emphasizing that point. To him, human rights and property rights were inextricably linked. Madison served in the Virginia ratifying convention in 1788 and probably made the difference in getting the state to support the document.

He then won election to the House of Representatives and was the congressman responsible for getting the Constitution amended to include the Bill of Rights. He became increasingly discontent with the leadership provided by Hamilton, secretary of the treasury in GEORGE WASHINGTON's administration. Madison agreed with his fellow Virginian, Thomas Jefferson (Washington's secretary of state) that Hamilton's financial plans, including a national bank, created a too powerful national government and enriched an elite to the point of forming a dominating aristocracy. In fact, Madison and Jefferson feared Hamilton would lead the United States into monarchy.

As Hamilton organized his support in Congress, and got his measures passed, the Federalist Party emerged with him as its leader. In opposition to Hamilton, Jefferson and Madison organized the Jeffersonian Republicans, or the Republican Party (no relation to the modern Republican Party), which coalesced by 1795. Many consider Madison to have been the architect of the party.

At this time, the French Revolution generated enormous controversy. Hamilton condemned it for promoting disorder and irresponsible mass power. Madison and Jefferson supported the uprising for advancing republican ideals and considered Hamilton and Washington too pro-British in their policies. As the Federalists expanded their hold on the federal government, Madison retired from Congress in 1796. After having married Dolly Payne two years earlier, he contemplated a peaceful life on his plantation. Madison, however, reacted to Federalist policies, particularly the Alien and Sedition Acts intended to restrict immigrants and make illegal any statements "defaming" Congress. In 1798, he wrote the Virginia Resolutions, which asserted that the states could nullify congressional laws violating liberty.

In 1800, Madison believed America was saved by the election of Jefferson to the presidency. The two friends once again worked closely, and Jefferson named Madison secretary of state. In that capacity, Madison's greatest challenge came from the continuing warfare between Britain and France. Just as the situation had plagued Jefferson's predecessors, Washington and JOHN ADAMS, so too did it nearly ruin the Republicans. Britain caused the most problems with its attacks on American ships headed for Europe and its impressment of American sailors. Madison initially reacted with a series of written protests—but they did little good.

What to do beyond this puzzled many in the administration, for most believed that war would be disastrous for their fledgling nation. Finally, in 1807, Jefferson and Madison convinced Congress to pass the Embargo Act, which removed all American shipping from the high seas. The Republicans believed this would place pressure on the British, who needed American foodstuffs, and that they would then cease their attacks and recognize America's neutrality. The policy, however, crippled the domestic economy, and in March 1809 Congress replaced it with the Non-Intercourse Act, which allowed trade with all nations except Britain and France.

The previous year, Madison won the presidency, with Jefferson's backing, and in March 1809 assumed office. By far his most important and controversial policy was the nation's war with Britain. As American ships returned to the Atlantic, the British resumed their raids. Through sly diplomatic maneuvers, Napoleon convinced Madison that France had ended its restrictions on American trade, and the president reacted by proclaiming non-intercourse to be in effect only with Britain. This angered the British, and relations worsened when Britain encouraged Indian raids on the American frontier and Madison arbitrarily annexed West Florida, a Spanish territory, to Louisiana.

On 1 June 1812, the president requested Congress to declare war on Britain. This was done on 18 June, but Madison found his nation poorly prepared for war. The military leadership, mainly a holdover from the Revolution, lacked talent and vigor, the navy had few ships, and after an initial surge of volunteers, the army had difficulty finding recruits. In addition, New Englanders generally despised the war and radicals there even talked about secession. The Federalist Party, recently moribund, revived itself as the "peace party" and made dramatic gains. Most embarrassing for Madison, British troops raided Washington, burned the Capitol, and forced him to flee.

In August 1814, Britain and the United States began peace negotiations in Europe at Ghent. The ensuing treaty did not bring the country any concrete gains, and the war was really a standoff. Nevertheless, after Andrew Jackson's stunning victory at New Orleans—a battle that occurred after the Treaty of Ghent had been signed—Americans closed ranks in hailing the war as a victory.

With regard to domestic policy, Madison adopted many of the proposals made in the 1790s by the Federalists and derided by him, including tariff protection for industries and establishment of a national bank (in this case, the Second National

Bank). He left the presidency in March 1817 after his second term expired. Except for brief service in the state constitutional convention of 1829, the Virginian lived his remaining life in retirement at Montpelier. He wrote extensively and voiced his opinion that the Union should be maintained against sectional differences. Madison died on 28 June 1836 at Montpelier, remembered more for his work on the Constitution than for his service as secretary of state and president.

References: Brant, Irving, *The Fourth President: A Life of James Madison,* 1970; Ketcham, Ralph, *James Madison: A Biography,* 1990; Koch, Adrienne, *Jefferson and Madison: The Great Collaboration,* 1950; McCoy, D. R., *The Last of the Fathers,* 1989; Rutland, Robert A., *James Madison,* 1987; Rutland, Robert A., *The Presidency of James Madison,* 1990.

Maga, Hubert
(b. 1916)
Benin

As a French colony, Benin gained a reputation for its substantial number of intellectuals and its turbulent regional politics. Into this environment stepped Hubert Maga, who represented his homeland's northern interests.

Hubert Maga was born in 1916 in north Benin and obtained an education at the local Catholic mission schools and at the William Ponty School in Dakar. He returned to his homeland in 1935 and taught at a school in Natitingou, where he became director in 1945.

After World War II, France initiated changes in its colonial possessions that stimulated further reform. The French constitution of 1946 permitted assemblies in each territory along with a regional council for all of French West Africa. Maga represented north Dahomey in the first legislature, or Conseil Général, winning office in 1947 and serving until 1952. He joined the first political party, the Dahomean Progressive Union (UPD), but then left it in 1951 to form a regional organization in the north with whose support he won a seat in the French National Assembly. He held this position until 1958 and from 1957 to 1958 was the undersecretary of state for labor.

In 1958, prime minister SOUROU-MIGAN APITHY appointed him minister of labor in a new Dahomey administration that reflected recent reforms in France to provide its colonies with their own executives. One year later, when charges of corruption undermined Apithy, Maga became prime minister. In 1958, he merged his political party, the Dahomean Democratic Movement, with Apithy's party to form the Progressive Dahomean Party (PPD), but it collapsed when Apithy broke away to oppose a proposed confederation with other West African nations. Maga again allied with Apithy to defeat Justin Ahomadégbé, who vied for power after Dahomey gained independence in 1960. Maga and Apithy formed the Dahomean Unity Party and wielded their power to imprison Ahomadégbé. In the 1960 elections, Maga became president and Apithy vice-president. Maga soon eclipsed Apithy's power and sent his vice-president overseas as an ambassador.

Maga's presidency lasted until 1963, replete with extravagant expenditures and widespread corruption. A deteriorating economy and austerity measures brought a coup that overthrew Maga in 1963. He went into exile and did not return to Dahomey until 1970. In presidential elections that year he ran strongly, but the army annulled the results, and Maga retreated to the north, where he threatened to have the region secede. Later that year, he agreed to serve in a civilian regime with a rotating chairmanship. He became the first chairman with his opponents, Apithy and Ahomadégbé, serving as copresidents. But once again his rule suffered from corruption and, as a sign of more turmoil, two army mutinies erupted. In October 1972, another coup toppled Maga's regime, and the triumvirate and the army placed the fallen leader under house arrest (which lasted until 1981). His political career had come to an end.

The coup ushered in a long period of stability but also a Marxist-Leninist regime that controlled most economic and social activities. During this time, Dahomey changed its name to Benin. This radical regime continued in power until 1991. The current president supports the establishment of a multiparty system.

Reference: Decalo, Samuel, *Historical Dictionary of Benin*, 1987.

Makarios III
(1913–1977)
Cyprus

When he looked out upon Cyprus, his island home, Makarios III thought not about forming an independent nation, but about uniting his people with Greece. The island's Turkish minority, however, opposed this move, and reluctantly Makarios supported nationhood as the only alternative to continued British rule.

Makarios III was born as Mikhail Khristodolou Mouskos on 13 August 1913 in Pano Panayia, a town in the rugged Troodos Mountains. His father, a shepherd, was a Greek, thus making young Mouskos part of the majority community on Cyprus. At the time, Britain ruled the island and tried to maintain harmony between the Greeks and Turks. The British presence, however, antagonized many Greek Cypriots who wanted to unite their island with Greece, a movement they called *enosis*.

At age 13, Mouskos entered Kykko Monastery and from there pursued his education at the Pan-Cyprian Gymnasium, or secondary school, in Nicosia, and the University of Athens. At the latter, he studied theology and law. In 1946, he received ordination as a priest in the Greek Orthodox Church and adopted the name Makarios.

In 1948, while the Church of Cyprus expanded its influence among Greek Cypriots, Makarios became a bishop and two years later was elevated to

"We believe one ideology can be fought only by another . . . not by force."

archbishop. He took office as Makarios III—the youngest archbishop in the history of the Cypriot church. He pledged himself to *enosis* and in 1952 appeared before the United Nations and condemned the British occupation of his homeland. He also allied himself with George Grivas, a colonel in the Greek army who strongly supported *enosis*. While over the years Makarios and Grivas worked together, they had numerous differences, generally involving the use of armed force. Grivas preferred a military solution to the Cypriot problem; Makarios preferred diplomacy.

While Greek Cypriots pursued *enosis*, Turkish Cypriots had a different goal. Should British rule end, they wanted Turkey to take over the island. Some Turks even formed a guerrilla resistance group. The dispute invariably involved Greece and Turkey, and on more than one occasion the two sides approached war.

In 1955, Makarios and Grivas formed the National Organization of Cypriot Fighters (EOKA), and in April it began attacking police and military installations. The following year, Makarios entered negotiations with Britain, but when they faltered, the British arrested him and exiled him to the Seychelles. This only emboldened the rebels, and with Makarios's moderate voice gone, Grivas's fighters unleashed a tremendous wave of violence. Presently, the British allowed Makarios to leave the Seychelles (although they prohibited him from returning to Cyprus), and he arrived in Athens to a tremendous welcome. By now the Cypriot issue had become a major part of Greek politics, and administrations rose and fell in popularity based upon their handling of the situation.

In 1958, Britain proposed partitioning Cyprus between the Greek and Turkish communities, but Makarios adamantly refused any such division. He did, however, for the first time indicate his willingness to forego *enosis* in favor of independence, provided the partitioning plan was dropped. In February 1959, he signed an agreement to make Cyprus a nation and in December won election as president of the republic.

Many Greek Cypriots had mixed feelings about independence. On the one hand, they preferred *enosis*, and Makarios was widely criticized for abandoning it. On the other hand, they were relieved to have avoided partitioning.

Throughout his presidency, Makarios had to deal with worsening relations between Greek and Turkish Cypriots. For some time he used Grivas as commander of the national guard to maintain order, but in one prominent instance the military acted too harshly and, in 1967, Grivas was forced to resign. Makarios won reelection in 1968 by an overwhelming margin, showing his massive following in the Greek community. But despite his opposition to partitioning, by the early 1970s Cyprus was, in fact, two separate entities. The Turkish community refused to recognize Makarios as president or abide by the national legislature's actions.

Then in July 1974, the year after Makarios won a third term, the Greek government, suspicious of the president's ties to leftist groups for support and hoping to accomplish *enosis*, overthrew him. Makarios fled the island, but the Greek action led Turkey to invade Cyprus. The Turks defeated the Greek troops and proclaimed the northern portion of the island a separate state.

In December, Makarios returned to Cyprus and resumed his presidency while refusing to recognize the Turkish occupation and partition. He died on 3 August 1977 in Nicosia—a reluctant nation builder and a leader disappointed to see his homeland divided. In 1983, northern Cyprus declared itself independent, with its official name the Turkish Republic of Northern Cyprus. This state, however, has not received international recognition.

Reference: Mayes, Stanley, *Makarios: A Biography*, 1981.

Malespin, Francisco
(?—1846)
El Salvador

Francisco Malespin fought to defeat liberalism and establish independence for El Salvador under conservative rule.

In 1823, Salvadorans expelled the Mexicans, who had conquered their country after Spanish rule had ended, and joined with Guatemala, Honduras, Nicaragua, and Costa Rica in forming the United Provinces of Central America. This federation, however, began falling apart shortly after Liberals under FRANCISCO MORAZÁN gained power. Between 1829 and 1840, Morazán, who favored economic modernization, battled the Conservatives, led by Rafael Carrera of Guatemala. El Salvador proved to be a strong supporter of Morazán, but in 1840, Carrera defeated him. At this point, Malespin negotiated with the Guatemalans to arrange a treaty for El Salvador. The settlement placed Malespin in command of the Salvadoran army, while the following year El Salvador declared itself an independent republic.

Malespin acted to gain control of El Salvador. With Carrera's backing, he became president on 1 February 1844 and aligned himself with the Conservative Party. He restricted freedom of the press and undid the Liberal efforts to distance El Salvador from the Catholic Church. The monastic orders that had been expelled, for example, were allowed to return.

Guatemala distrusted Malespin and encouraged a rebellion against him. After the Salvadoran president crushed the uprising, the rebels fled to Nicaragua, and when that country refused to extradite them, Malespin declared war. On 24 January 1845, he captured the city of Léon in Nicaragua, but in February his rebel enemies reentered El Salvador and overthrew him. Malespin tried to regain the presidency and secured the backing of Honduras to do so. In 1845, this ignited a war between El Salvador and the Hondurans. A subsequent treaty forbade Malespin from returning to El Salvador, but he tried again by launching an invasion in 1846. His effort ended when he was murdered on 26 November.

Reference: Haggerty, Richard A., ed., *El Salvador: A Country Study*, 1990.

Mandela, Nelson
(b. 1918)
South Africa

In 1963, South African police raided the headquarters of Nelson Mandela's political organization. Then they threw him into prison, where he spent more than 27 years, never wavering in his commitment to a new nation devoid of racial segregation and white supremacy. Upon his spectacular return to politics he pursued this goal.

Nelson Mandela was born into a royal family on 18 July 1918 at Qunu in the Transkei Reserve. His father, Henry Gadla Mandela, was main councilor to the paramount chief of the Thembu. The elder Mandela also served on the Transkein Territories General Council, an organization of Africans and Europeans who advised the government in Pretoria. South Africa had been settled by the Dutch and English, and under British supervision in 1910 the Union of South Africa was formed, an independent nation consisting of four colonies merged into a federal

state. The government, led by JAN SMUTS and LOUIS BOTHA, established a system whereby the white minority ruled the large black population.

Young Nelson attended a mission school and quickly discovered the domination of the Europeans when he noticed that the history books he read depicted whites as heroes and blacks as savages. He continued his education at the Methodist high school in Healdtown and then enrolled at Fort Hare College in Alice, where he studied for two years until 1940, when he got into trouble for helping organize a student strike. He returned home, rejected his preparation for the chief's position, and headed for Johannesburg.

Once there, Mandela enrolled in a correspondence program and completed his bachelor's degree. He then began studying law part time at Witwatersrand University while working at a white-run law firm. In 1942, he joined the

African National Congress (ANC), an organization dedicated to uniting blacks and seeking social justice through removal of the color barrier. Although the ANC had led many nonviolent protests in the 1920s and 1930s, by the time Mandela joined the group it had weakened considerably.

In 1944 Mandela, who two years earlier had obtained his law degree from the University of South Africa, joined Walter Sisulu and Oliver Tambo to form the Congress Youth League within the ANC. They intended to develop a strong national liberation movement and establish democracy through racial equality. Mandela (and the ANC in general) allied with leftist groups and had contacts with the Communists, but never adopted Marxism. He disagreed with those who wanted to eliminate whites, and asserted that progress rested on racial harmony among the three main groups in South Africa: whites, blacks, and East Indians. He insisted, however, that white domination must end.

Much to his dismay, conditions worsened in 1948 when the National Party gained power. This group, largely Dutch, or Afrikaner, legalized racial segregation, formally establishing a system called apartheid. Mandela and the Youth League reacted by leading civil disobedience campaigns. In 1950, the police crushed a labor strike, and the government announced it would prosecute as a Communist anyone who used unlawful acts to bring about political change. This drove the Communists and the ANC into an alliance.

In June, Mandela experienced his first jail term when the police arrested him and several other demonstrators. He was soon released, but on 30 July the police raided his home and those of other ANC leaders and charged him with Communist activities. Mandela received a suspended sentence. In 1951, he was elected president of the Youth League, and the following year became president of the ANC Transvaal branch and deputy national president.

In 1952, Mandela organized and led a mass campaign against unjust laws. The government reacted by restricting him to Johannesburg and denying him the right to address any rallies. That year, he founded a law firm and continued working to gain civil rights. South Africa, however, tightened its segregationist policies.

Mandela addressed a gathering in 1955 after the restrictions against him had been lifted, and

"Our goal is the winning of national freedom for African people . . ."

helped unite the ANC with other organizations to form the Congress Alliance. The following year, the government pursued Mandela again after additional protests and demonstrations had erupted. Charged with promoting communism, Mandela endured a trial that continued until 1961. In the meantime, he divorced his first wife and married Winifred Nomzamo. Later, Winnie Mandela, as she was popularly called, gained recognition as a leader in the protest movement.

Meanwhile, tragedy struck in 1960 when police fired on unarmed Africans at Sharpeville, killing 69 of them. The Sharpeville Massacre resulted in the government banning demonstrations and detaining people without trial. That same year, the ANC was also banned. Mandela, still in the midst of his own trial, was one of the persons detained, and during this period his views shifted: He became convinced that nonviolent protest would not work. He now supported violent efforts to end oppression.

After his 1961 trial resulted in a verdict of not guilty, he was named secretary of the All-African National Action Council, committed to mass demonstrations and underground attacks, and headed the Spear of the Nation, a paramilitary group that sabotaged facilities. The government declared him a fugitive and hunted him. Mandela used a variety of disguises to avoid capture, but on 4 August 1962 the police arrested him.

At his trial, he presented a spirited condemnation of apartheid, but the court found him guilty and sentenced him to five years in prison. Mandela's travail had only begun; the authorities charged him a second time, and he stood trial for sabotage and Communist activities. In June 1964, the court ordered him imprisoned for life.

He remained incarcerated for 27 years, isolated but still committed to his cause. Despite petitions from governments and people overseas, South Africa refused to release Mandela. At first, he served his time at Robben Island, but when it appeared he was organizing the prisoners there, the government transferred him in 1982 to the Pollsmoor maximum security prison.

On the outside, protests by blacks continued and Winnie Mandela became a leader within the ANC. The organization engaged in sabotage and also developed diplomatic contacts with foreign governments, hoping they would put pressure on South Africa to change. Many nations imposed sanctions prohibiting trade with South Africa, and the economy there began deteriorating. Amid this turmoil, the South African government agreed in 1986 to modest reforms to lessen apartheid, such as an end to the bans on mixed-race marriages and interracial political organizations.

These measures, however, were too limited, and the protests escalated. Then in 1989, FREDERIK WILLEM DE KLERK became South Africa's president and stunned many whites by moving the nation rapidly toward substantial reform. In early February 1990, he lifted the ban on the ANC and later that month released Mandela from prison.

On 6 August, Mandela met with De Klerk, and the two men signed the Pretoria Minute, a document that moved South Africa toward a new constitution and in the process committed the ANC to suspending its attacks and the government to re-leasing political prisoners. The following month, De Klerk embraced the principle of one-man, one-vote. In 1991, Parliament repealed numerous apartheid laws, and two years later nonwhites entered the cabinet.

Elections were scheduled, and in 1994 Mandela won his campaign for president. When he was sworn in on 10 May, a new era began; at least politically, white supremacy crumbled and Mandela and the ANC were now responsible for South Africa's development. As president, Mandela promises a policy of conciliation toward whites. Critics within the black community, including Winnie Mandela, meanwhile, consider his economic policy to be too conservative.

References: Benson, Mary, *Nelson Mandela: The Man and the Movement*, 1986; Mandela, Nelson, *The Struggle Is My Life*, 1986.

Manley, Michael
(b. 1924)
Jamaica

During one campaign, Michael Manley held aloft the Rod of Joshua—his ebony cane, considered by Rastafarians to have great power. He intended to stir the masses and shake Jamaican complacency in order to build a radically new government.

Michael Manley was born on 10 December 1924 in Kingston. His father, Norman Manley, was a lawyer and prominent political leader who founded the People's National Party (PNP), a socialist organization. His mother, Edna (Swithenbank) Manley, was a sculptor who produced critically acclaimed works. Young Michael began his secondary education in 1935 at Jamaica

College, a school tailored for the elite. In 1943, he trained in Canada with the Royal Canadian Air Force and attended McGill University. At the end of World War II, he enrolled at the London School of Economics, from which he graduated four years later. While engaged in his studies, he became an admirer of the school's famous teacher, Harold Laski, and his democratic socialism. From 1948 to 1951, Manley helped lead the West Indian Students Union and, although light skinned, as a mulatto he experienced racial discrimination that stirred his desire to separate Jamaica from British colonialism.

After obtaining his degree, Manley cut an

impressive swath in journalism. He reviewed books for the British Broadcasting Company, appeared on a weekly television series called *Caribbean News,* and in 1952 returned to his homeland and joined the leftist newspaper *Public Opinion* as associate editor.

At the same time, he entered the labor movement, a particularly tense one in Jamaica where trade unions seldom cooperated with one another and often fought selfishly over limited economic rewards in a society marked by sharp class differences. He first became an organizer in the sugar industry for the National Workers' Union (NWU), a group tied closely to the PNP. He exuded a compelling speaking style and a charismatic personality as he traveled the countryside into the early 1960s and organized several regions.

> *"Gross maldistribution of the world's wealth and food is no longer a moral offense only."*

Manley won a substantial following when as a negotiator he obtained a wage increase for workers in the bauxite industry. As PNP leader, Norman Manley appointed his son to the Jamaican Senate in 1962, the year the country gained its full independence under WILLIAM BUSTAMANTE. The Manleys and the PNP supported independence, although in a federation with other West Indian islands. In 1964, Michael Manley experienced what he called a turning point in his life: a strike led by the NWU against the Jamaica Broadcasting Corporation (JBC). When he stood before the JBC building and declared "There are the walls of Jericho!" he won the nickname "Joshua" from his supporters.

The strike caused Manley to formulate an explicit democratic socialist program and promote it throughout the nation. He opposed any movement toward dictatorship (which he feared was happening under Bustamante) and supported laws to reduce social and economic inequality. In 1967, he ran for a seat in the House of Representatives, which he won by a narrow margin. Two years later, he succeeded his father as president of the PNP and became opposition leader in Parliament.

Manley supported the cooperation of the Caribbean states in a regional organization. He believed this would boost economic development by giving the area more weight in trade and investments, and he believed it would prevent the developing nations from engaging in damaging competition with one another. In the early 1970s, he expanded the power of the PNP in an attempt to make it the majority party. He toured the nation and met with farmers and workers and identified with their plight by attacking high unemployment and government corruption. He often rallied the masses behind him by appealing to the Rastafarian religion, which emphasizes that whites perverted black culture. The Rastafarians were thus receptive to Manley's criticism of inequality begun under a racist colonial system. His overall strategy propelled the PNP to the forefront, and in 1972 it won two-thirds of the seats in Parliament's lower house.

As prime minister, Manley immediately reformed the economy, at the time burdened by 20 percent unemployment. He engaged the government in public works projects, began programs to retrain the unemployed, started a free educational system to eliminate widespread illiteracy, and shifted tax levies from an emphasis on income to an emphasis on wealth. In 1974, he boosted the price of bauxite, a major export for his nation. This move was heavily criticized by the United States, the primary importer of the mineral. In a shift to the left, the government acquired utilities and a 50 percent interest in the bauxite mines, increased poor relief, and established a national minimum wage.

In 1976, the Jamaican Labor Party (JLP) severely criticized Manley's socialism and disrupted political meetings with protests. Manley called for an unarmed retaliation by the PNP and violence escalated. At one point, he was forced to declare a state of emergency. In elections that December, the PNP scored an impressive victory, capturing nearly 60 percent of the vote. Manley had successfully shifted the party to a mass-oriented organization, although at the cost of much middle-class support.

Manley's administration began unravelling in 1977. Economic problems amid a world oil crisis damaged him, and when he turned reluctantly to the International Monetary Fund (IMF) for help, he antagonized the left. Then when the IMF rejected Jamaica's application for assistance, he suffered embarrassment and was forced to devalue the Jamaican currency. A subsequent agreement with the IMF brought financial help, but also severe economic stringencies. In 1980, after breaking with the IMF, Manley called for new elections, which ignited political violence between the PLP and the JLP. He appealed for peace, and despite the attacks the elections were held in October. The prime minister, derided by the slogan "Joshua = Judas" and mired in economic problems, lost handily.

In 1983, the JLP captured all the seats in the lower house after Manley and the PNP boycotted the election in a dispute involving voter rolls. Inflation soared, unemployment remained high, and riots erupted early in 1985, enabling Manley to lead a PNP comeback. He oversaw a shift in party ideology to a more centrist position, and the PNP even eliminated the word "socialism" from its platform. After a severe illness, Manley campaigned again in 1986, and the PNP swept the local elections. In 1989, the voters returned Manley and the PNP to power in a landslide.

The new prime minister faced continuing economic woes, including a foreign debt exceeding $4 billion. Jamaicans confirmed their support for Manley in 1990, when in local elections the PNP captured all but one of the parish councils. Manley, however, suffered from his recurring illness and on 15 March 1992 resigned the prime ministry. He left behind a government more moderate than its predecessor in the 1970s, but still pursuing a radical course.

References: Kaufman, Michael, *Jamaica under Manley: Dilemmas of Socialism and Democracy*, 1985; Levi, Darrell E., *Michael Manley: The Making of a Leader*, 1989; Manley, Michael, *Jamaica: Struggle in the Periphery*, 1982; Manley, Michael, *The Politics of Change: A Jamaican Testament*, 1974.

Mao Tse-tung
(1893–1976)
China

One of the great revolutionaries of modern times, Mao Tse-tung forged a new order in China, determined against great odds to develop an independent Communist state that would restore Chinese dignity and improve the lot of the peasants. To do so, he looked to the past glories of Chinese culture and the promise offered in Marxism-Leninism, the one modern Western philosophy he considered most relevant to China.

Mao was born on 26 December 1893 in Shao-shan, a village in Hunan Province, a land dotted with hills, lakes, and fertile farms. His father Mao Jensheng had been a peasant who, by the time of Mao's birth, had gained success as a grain dealer. Mao's father valued education only as a means for his son to be successful in business, and he

placed great emphasis on directing Mao's life. Indeed, Mao later portrayed him as bigoted and a bully.

Mao attended a village primary school, where he studied the Confucian classics and tilled the family farm. But at age 13 his father required him to work longer hours and this interrupted his education. Mao frequently rebelled against his father's dictates and in one instance, after his father accused him of being lazy, he ran away from home only to be brought back by his mother, a gentle and generous woman. Soon he left home again to continue his education at the Tung-shan Primary School. There he heard about an event that deeply impressed him. Hungry peasants had recently protested their plight only to be arrested by the government and decapitated, their heads displayed on poles as a warning to others.

Mao also learned of the nationalist ideas held by the Chinese patriot SUN YAT-SEN, then fighting for China's unity and freedom from foreign domination. By that time, the Ch'ing dynasty had deteriorated and several nations had carved China into spheres of influence. Mao listened to those who claimed China had to be modernized politically and technologically to regain its power and dignity. He did not yet oppose the dynasty, but he was convinced that reform must come.

"A revolution is an insurrection, an act of violence by which one class overthrows another."

About the time Mao began secondary school in Ch'ang-sha, a major rebellion erupted on 10 October 1911 as rebels in Wu-ch'ang fought the Ch'ing. The rebellion spread, and Mao joined a revolutionary army unit in Hunan. In 1912, the Ch'ing dynasty fell, and a new Chinese republic was proclaimed. This government, however, lacked the leadership and unity to stabilize China's politics. While the republic continued a precarious existence, Mao drifted, going to a police school, a law school, and a business school. He also read extensively; much of his education after secondary school came through his reading, which he once claimed he took to as voraciously as an ox to a vegetable garden. In 1918, he graduated from the Hunan Normal School in Ch'ang-sha, a training school for teachers, and traveled to Peking—his first trip outside Hunan Province—where he lived in a small apartment with seven other people and attended Peking University and worked under Li Ta-chao, the head librarian, who taught Mao much about Marxism. Mao soon wrote an article in which he stressed the importance of social class in society, a Marxist view.

Once again Mao found himself amid an explosive situation when on 4 May 1919 an infamous student rebellion occurred. The May Fourth Movement, as it was called, protested the ineffectual central government and Japanese incursions into China, and in its strong anti-imperialism the movement developed an affinity for the Marxism-Leninism then emanating from the Russian Revolution. Mao reacted by calling upon his generation to take charge and be the main actors in shaping a new China.

By 1921, Mao embraced communism, and as a school principal and magazine editor he recruited workers and students to the cause. That year he helped found the Chinese Communist Party (CCP), which challenged the major political party begun by Sun Yat-sen, the Kuomintang (KMT, or Nationalists). In the early 1920s, the KMT forged an alliance with the CCP in an attempt to create a national government that would overcome the increasingly chaotic politics in China, a time when various warlords ruled over their own domains. Mao had the duty of coordinating the KMT and CCP, an enormously difficult task given the competing factions, and one he did not apparently do well, since he was sent to Hunan in 1924 to reconsider his tactics.

At Hunan, Mao lived among the peasants and developed a crucial ideological position: He believed the peasants should be at the vanguard of a revolution. This contradicted many Marxist-Leninists who stressed the crucial role of the urban proletariat (although Lenin himself had recognized the importance of peasants in underdeveloped areas). While Mao still believed the proletariat to be an important element in revolution, he now placed it in a secondary position and shaped his views to fit the preindustrial society found in China. Mao also developed his effective means of communicating with the peasants: his appealing writings and sermons that combined Confucian and biblical-style aphorisms and avoided complex intellectualism. Mao did not believe in articulating specific objectives. His philosophy remained amorphous and reliant on rebelliousness bringing a good result, one he often left undefined. His vagueness and contradictions confused many Chinese but also provided an idealism behind which they could rally.

When the military governor of Hunan pursued him, Mao fled to Canton. He headed the KMT propaganda department and edited *Political Weekly*, a party organ. He also served on the staff at the recently established Peasant Movement Training Institute.

In 1926, the KMT-CCP alliance shattered. One year earlier Sun Yat-sen had died, and his chief lieutenant, CHIANG KAI-SHEK, emerged as the leader of the Nationalists. Chiang considered the Communists a threat to his power, and he realized that the army officers who supported him were tied to the landlords and thus opposed to any radical ideas to help the peasants. Chiang also concluded that the Communists had made the interests of an international Communist movement paramount to those of China. So in 1926 he began purging Communists from the KMT, and in April 1927 he ruthlessly killed several hundred of them in Shanghai. Shortly after this, another important Nationalist, WANG CHING-WEI, also broke with the Communists. The CCP thus stood isolated and suffered almost total devastation. Mao returned to Hunan, leading a bedraggled band of peasants and miners, which he called the First Division of the First Peasants' and Workers' Army. He attacked the Nationalist troops, but suffered a disastrous defeat and retreated into the mountains that straddled Hunan and Kiangsi Provinces. There he built a base and other Communists soon joined him, including LIN PIAO. Mao's failure brought him dismissal from the Politburo, the governing body of the CCP. Mao continued his struggle, though, and concentrated on learning guerrilla tactics and teaching his soldiers to treat the peasants with respect. He prohibited them from stealing anything—in this they would be scrupulous and avoid the degradations usually administered by the warlord armies, including those allied with the Nationalists. Early in 1929, Mao declared a soviet, or Communist governing council, in southern Kiangsi Province.

Chiang reacted by attacking Mao. The Nationalist leader's "scorched earth policy" resulted in 2 million peasant deaths, alienating the countryside but nearly obliterating Mao's forces. Nearing collapse, Mao and his Communist colleagues took their armies on the infamous Long March in October 1934 to break through the Nationalist lines. The odyssey lasted nearly a year as Mao's men journeyed 6,000 miles across rivers and snow-capped mountain ranges to make their way from south China to Shensi Province in the north. At one point they reached the Dadu River, where the only suspension bridge had been rendered unusable by the Nationalists, who had removed its planks. Mao ordered 20 men to climb along the bridge's ropes and cross the river to a blockhouse. The men moved quickly, dangling precariously above the water. They reached the blockhouse and, firing their machine guns, they defeated the garrison stationed there, retrieved the missing planks, and repaired the bridge to allow Mao's troops across. The Communists had started the Long March with 90,000 men and completed it with considerably fewer. The losses came from starvation, desertion, and battles with the enemy that seemed interminable. Mao, however, had brought his forces to safety in an area bordering Soviet Russia, a supportive ally,

and earned a remarkable reputation, which made him a hero to his fellow Communists. In January 1935, he took over the CCP as chairman of its Politburo, a victory signifying his ascendency over the faction that had earlier removed him, although he had not yet consolidated his power.

In 1936, military leaders in northeastern China kidnapped Chiang Kai-shek. They realized Japan would soon attack, and they wanted Chiang to redirect his efforts from fighting the Communists to fighting the Japanese. Chiang agreed and entered into a united front with the CCP. Mao gained a reputation, soon advanced further by war, as the man who, more than Chiang, committed himself foremost to fighting Japan.

For China, World War II began in 1937 when Japan launched its offensive from Manchuko. The Japanese quickly captured China's main cities, with Peking and Nanking falling by December. The countryside, however, never came under complete Japanese control, and here Mao planned his resistance and the change in his fortunes.

The Communists broke into small units and operated as guerrillas. In the countryside they gained a vast following, partly because they stirred nationalist sentiment against Japan, partly because they helped the peasants by undertaking land reform in the areas they controlled. With these tactics, Mao positioned himself for defeating Chiang after the war.

In the late 1930s, Mao did much reflecting and writing. He wrote poetry and a book about his military tactics against Japan, entitled *On Protracted War*. He also advised his followers to prepare for a socialist struggle after the war. In 1939, following a divorce, he married a movie actress from Shanghai, CHIANG CH'ING.

By 1941, the KMT-CCP coalition unraveled as clashes occurred between the troops from each side. At this time, Mao consolidated his party leadership with the Rectification Campaign of 1942–1943, in which he moved to eliminate what he called "foreign dogmatism," meaning unquestioning devotion to the Soviet Russian experience and acceptance of Soviet Russian direction. The training of party members, he insisted, should reflect the Chinese experience. Thus Mao broke with the Soviet Russian faction in the CCP, and in 1943 he purged disloyal elements. He also widened his powers to become not only chairman of the Politburo but also chairman of the Secretariat, in effect giving him full command of the CCP. Around his concept of communism Mao developed a cult of his own personality, which with each passing year intensified.

Meanwhile, serious problems plagued the Nationalists under Chiang Kai-shek. Many in the Nationalist army sympathized with Mao and, in the areas where they ruled, the Nationalists engaged in much corruption. Inflation swept the country and Chiang allied himself with the right-wing, which opposed land reform. His armies suffered enormous defeats, including the loss of 700,000 men to the Japanese in the summer of 1944.

After World War II, the Nationalists collapsed quickly. In April 1949, Mao's People's Liberation Army, as he called it, captured Nanking. By the end of the year the Nationalists had lost the mainland, retreating to Taiwan, an island off the southeast coast where Chiang had fled several months earlier. In October, Mao proclaimed the People's Republic of China with himself as chairman and CHOU EN-LAI as premier. In December, Mao traveled to Russia, where he met Joseph Stalin and signed a mutual assistance pact providing China with a limited amount of economic aid.

Under Mao, all power centered in the CCP and, as party chairman, he had the greatest power in China. He envisioned a nation devoid of materialistic selfishness. This, he believed, required economic reform and a radical transformation in mentalities. In the 1950s, Mao extended Communist power and its revolutionary ideal by liquidating more than one million landlords—this meant not just confiscating their land but imprisoning or even killing them. The redistribution of land to the peasants attached them to the Communists. The process included establishing collectives, which Mao believed would conquer selfishness. Mao also engaged in thought reform, which entailed a wholesale indoctrination into Maoist-Communist ideology, erasing bourgeois ideas, and dedicating oneself to society at large. Frequently, Mao circumvented the CCP apparatus and announced policies without consulting the party.

In 1956, Mao made his "hundred flowers speech" in which he encouraged Chinese to openly discuss their ideological differences, akin to "letting a hundred flowers bloom." Mao believed that any differences would prove to be minor, necessary to make slight course adjustments in the Revolution. But the discussions resulted in many Chinese questioning CCP policies, and Mao halted the open exchange with a severe repression of speech, particularly among intellectuals.

Two years later, Mao's desires to move the economy forward, to eliminate the divisiveness he had found in 1956, and to replicate the high morality of some earlier Chinese dynasties caused him to launch the Great Leap Forward. It relied on people working not to fill their own pocketbooks but to improve society. For example, to boost steel production, peasants were encouraged to construct their own backyard foundries and make steel in small quantities that, once collected, would result in a massive increase in overall production. To boost agricultural output, the peasants, who had earlier been organized into cooperatives and collectives, were now made a part of huge communes where all private property was disallowed.

These efforts met with widespread failures that damaged Mao's reputation. The steel produced from the small furnaces was inferior in quality and often unusable. While farm harvests expanded, many peasants resisted the larger communes. In all, the economy took a great leap backward with production gains from the early 1950s undone and poverty resurgent. By 1959, Mao was making adjustments, such as allowing the peasants their own private plots, yet he severely punished anyone who condemned his overall program.

Early in the 1960s, Mao broke with the Soviet Union. He disliked those in the CCP who looked to Soviet Russia for the path China should follow, and he disliked the Soviet criticism of his Great Leap Forward. For their part, the Soviets ridiculed Mao's economic policies, worried about Chinese power threatening their security, and subsequently withdrew their technical assistance.

Natural disasters and poor economic policies contributed to widespread famine that killed millions of Chinese. Mao at first accepted and then rejected plans to help the economy by introducing material incentives. He railed against those who, he said, were selling out to capitalism, and condemned the CCP bureaucracy for becoming too self-centered and unwieldy. Actually, Mao felt severe constraints on his power as CCP leaders, in the wake of the failures stemming from the Great Leap Forward, organized to isolate him.

To get around the bureaucracy, to protect Mao's power, and to purify society, the Cultural Revolution emerged. In the fall of 1965 Mao's wife, Chiang Ch'ing, wrote an article criticizing those who resisted Mao's ideology. Suddenly, student demonstrations erupted in Peking, partly spontaneous, partly encouraged by Mao, protesting revisionists and "bourgeois administrators." These students wore red arm bands and called themselves the Red Guards. They insisted on ideological conformity and loyalty to Mao. In this, Mao urged them on, and they had the support of the People's Liberation Army, which Mao's heir apparent Lin Piao had molded into a "school of Maoist thought." The "cleansing" resulted in many CCP leaders having to publicly admit their deviations and suffer disgrace. Some were imprisoned and tortured and others executed.

The Cultural Revolution threatened to run amok and Mao worried lest it become anarchistic. At that point, in 1967, he ordered that revolutionary committees be established to bring it under control and govern the provinces. These committees consisted of Red Guards, former members of the CCP who had been purified, and representatives of the People's Liberation Army. This extended an apparatus external to the CCP and responsible to Mao, and reined in the Cultural Revolution's decentralization. In this arrangement, the army exerted enormous influence.

In 1971, Lin Piao died mysteriously in a plane crash as he tried to flee China for the Soviet Union. Accounts indicated he had been accused by Mao of plotting to overthrow him. As Mao suffered from cancer and grew physically weak, Premier Chou En-lai assumed many duties, moderating the differences between the revolutionary committees and the CCP and rehabilitating several party leaders, such as Teng Hsiao-p'ing, who had been purged during the Cultural Revolution. He also loosened economic restrictions, and the economy grew impressively in the mid-1970s.

For China, 1976 proved to be a historic year. In January, Chou died from cancer. Then on 9 September Mao died, also from cancer. He left a mixed legacy, resonating powerfully through Chinese history. Mao had liberated China from foreign domination, unified the country, and made the peasantry a vanguard in revolutionary change. He had fused China's past with a forward-looking Marxist ideology, and in the process had created a new doctrine, Maoism, that influenced oppressed agricultural societies elsewhere in the world. His excesses brought economic disasters, ideological restrictions, mass imprisonments, and millions of deaths from internal fighting involving political disputes. Mao built a new China and left an indelible imprint on world history.

References: Karnow, Stanley, *Mao and China: Inside China's Cultural Revolution,* 1972; Schram, Stuart R., ed., *Chairman Mao Talks to the People,* 1975; Snow, Edgar, *Red Star over China,* 1974; Starr, John Bryan, *Continuing the Revolution: The Political Thought of Mao,* 1979; Terrill, Ross, *Mao,* 1981; Wylie, Raymond, *The Emergence of Maoism,* 1980.

Mara, Ratu Kamisese
(b. 1920)
Fiji

A tall man physically, a prominent man politically, Ratu Kamisese Mara organized one of Fiji's first modern political parties and then led his homeland to independence.

Ratu Kamisese Mara was born on 13 May 1920 and over the years obtained a broad education, attending the Queen Victoria School, Sacred Heart College, Oxford University, and the London School of Economics. In 1950, he joined the British colonial government that ruled Fiji. From 1951 until 1961, he held numerous civil service positions and served on the Fiji Legislative Council.

In 1963, Mara took the Fijian Association, which had been established in 1954 by Ratu Sukuna to gain administrative reforms, and changed it into a modern political party. By this time, Britain had enlarged the elective Legislative Council and expanded the franchise. In 1964, the National Federation Party (NFP), which appealed strongly to Fiji's Indian community, emerged and called for increased Indian influence in the government. Two years later, in reaction to this, Mara linked his Fijian

Association with the National Congress of Fiji and several smaller groups to form the Alliance Party (AP). This unified indigenous Fijians, who belonged to the Association, with reform-minded Indians, who belonged to the Congress, and thus crossed the societal ethnic lines.

In 1965, Mara led the Fijian delegation to London for a constitutional conference preparatory to independence. The constitution eventually adopted provided for a parliamentary system with a two-house legislature and a council of ministers.

In 1967, Mara, by then one of his homeland's paramount chiefs, won election as chief minister. After Fiji gained its independence on 10 October 1970, in a move propelled strongly by Britain in its desire to relinquish itself of the colony, Mara became prime minister and, having been knighted, was referred to formally as Ratu Sir Kamisese Mara.

Mara continued as prime minster for 17 years, during which time he fought challenges not only from the NFP but also the Fijian Nationalist Party, which promoted "Fiji for the Fijians" and advocated deporting all Indians. By the mid-1980s, polarization characterized the nation's politics, with the AP appealing mainly to indigenous Fijians and the NFP having almost an exclusive Indian following. While some political leaders advocated that Mara form a coalition with the NFP to weaken the Nationalists, he did not do so, fearing he would lose too much support among indigenous Fijians.

In the economic area, Mara sponsored a government takeover of the Colonial Sugar Refining Corporation, an important company. The Fiji Sugar Corporation (FSC) consequently monopolized sugar production. Throughout the 1980s, the FSC suffered production shortfalls and required subsidies. Mara maintained close trading ties with Australia and New Zealand, and he joined the South Pacific Area Regional Trade and Economic Cooperation Agreement, which boosted the economy.

Mara changed political course in 1985 and formed a coalition with the Indian-based Fiji Labour Party (FLP). As feared, this angered many indigenous Fijians, and in April, Mara lost his reelection bid. Timoci Bavadra, who headed the new FLP, became prime minister. At this point, public demonstrations erupted as indigenous Fijians believed the FLP leadership would result in domination by Indians. SITIVENI RABUKA, a lieutenant colonel, then stormed the Parliament building and arrested Bavadra. Rabuka formed a governing council that included Mara as foreign minister. In September, Rabuka abrogated the 1970 constitution, withdrew Fiji from the British Commonwealth, and proclaimed a republic. The following month, Mara returned as prime minister, although Rabuka exerted considerable influence as home minister. In 1992, Rabuka won election as prime minister. Two years later, Mara filled the largely ceremonial position of president.

Reference: Scarr, Deryck, *Fiji: A Short History*, 1984.

Margai, Sir Albert
(1910–1980)
Sierra Leone

Sierra Leone moved toward independence with little turmoil—a gradual, controlled movement. Yet differences did occur, and Sir Albert Margai found himself at odds with his brother.

Albert Michael Margai was born in Gbangatok in October 1910, the grandson of a local chief and son of a merchant. He obtained an education at a Roman Catholic school in Bonthe, followed by St. Edwards School in Freetown, and subsequently trained to become a pharmacist. After working as a nurse from 1932 to 1944, Albert decided to study law in London and passed his bar exams in 1947. The next year, he returned to Sierra Leone and entered politics.

Margai's older half-brother, Milton (later SIR MILTON MARGAI), had already become involved in a spreading but cautious nationalist movement against British rule. Milton wanted increased power for the interior adjacent to the Freetown Colony, an area known as the Protectorate, and wanted to reduce the influence of the Creoles, former slaves whom the British had settled in the area in the late 1700s. In 1946, Milton had helped form the Sierra Leone Organization Society (SLOS) to push for a more democratic legislature.

Albert Margai joined the SLOS and held a seat on the Moyamba District Council. In 1949, he became a member of the Protectorate Assembly and two years later helped his brother organize a new political party, the Sierra Leone People's Party (SLPP), that proved successful in elections held under a new constitution. The SLPP victory weakened Creole power. After this, the road to independence proved relatively smooth, with verbal exchanges far outdistancing violent ones.

But not all was harmonious, and a split developed between Albert and Milton shortly after the former became minister of education and local government in 1951. Milton emphasized cautious diplomatic dealings with Britain; Albert, however, wanted to quicken the pace toward independence. Like his brother, though, he wanted to contain populist energies and maintain an elite grip on the nationalist movement.

In 1957, the SLPP won overwhelming victories in the legislative elections, including Albert Margai's own huge win in Moyamba South. Albert used this power base to directly challenge Milton's leadership in the SLPP. He won an important procedural vote, but only by a close margin, and decided to withdraw and begin his own organization called the People's National Party (PNP). He advocated a quicker end to British rule.

Albert suffered a setback, however, when in the October 1959 election his party suffered defeat, winning only 33 of 324 District Council seats. He then agreed to link the PNP with the SLPP to help form the United National Front (UNF) that participated in constitutional discussions with Britain. After traveling to London to take part in those talks, he participated in forming a coalition government led by his brother. Albert became the minister of natural resources, and Sierra Leone gained its independence on 27 April 1961.

After Sir Milton died in April 1964, Albert Margai, recently knighted by the British, formed a new government as prime minister. Unlike his brother, however, he alienated numerous supporters, partly because he tried to establish a one-party state. Several tribes in Sierra Leone believed he was attempting to consolidate power in his own tribal group, the Mende. Hence, in 1967, Margai's SLPP lost many seats to the All People's Conference (APC), led by Siaka Stevens. After a conflict erupted over whether Margai could continue as prime minister, the army intervened and installed an interim government. In April 1968, the military relinquished its command, the APC leaders returned from exile, and Stevens became prime minister. Margai died in December 1980.

References: Cartwright, John R., *Politics in Sierra Leone, 1947–1967*, 1970; Kilson, M., *Political Change in a West African State*, 1966.

Margai, Milton
(1895–1964)
Sierra Leone

One observer has called the independence movement in Sierra Leone "an almost apologetic nationalism." Yet conflict existed, and it included a family clash between conservative elements led by Sir Milton Margai and more liberal elements led by his brother, SIR ALBERT MARGAI.

In December 1895, Sir Milton Margai was born Augustus Milton Margai in Gbangatok, an interior town that was part of the Sierra Leone Protectorate, then under British rule. He came from an important family—his grandfather served as a leading, or paramount, chief. He received advance schooling and in 1926 became the first physician from the Protectorate. He then began working in the government medical service.

Milton Margai lived in a land separated by class antagonisms and territorial differences that intensified in the late 1700s after British abolitionists settled several hundred former slaves from England. These settlers, called Creoles, objected to both Britain's restrictions on their power—restrictions that had increased in the early twentieth century—and any attempts to enhance the power of the black masses. Furthermore, they agitated against the domination of the Protectorate Assembly by the traditional chiefs. In this setting, Milton helped begin the Sierra Leone Organization Society (SLOS) in 1946. It opposed the Creole elite and wanted a more democratic assembly—but within well-defined limits that contained the power of the masses. After Britain resisted change, riots occurred between 1946 and 1951, which may have been organized in part by Milton Margai.

Milton labeled the Creoles "foreigners" who stood against the Protectorate that, after all, produced most of Sierra Leone's wealth. When, in 1951, Britain formulated a new constitution allowing a countrywide representative government, Margai convinced the Protectorate chiefs to join his SLOS and form a new political party, the Sierra Leone People's Party (SLPP). Under Milton's leadership the SLPP won the general election. From that moment on, Creole power dwindled quickly (although the Creoles petitioned Britain to grant the Old Colony separate independence), and Sierra Leone's move toward nationhood exhibited more verbal competition than violence.

Milton relied on a conservative strategy of gaining more power for his country through gradual constitutional changes. As majority leader in the Legislative Council and later member of the Executive Council, he served as minister of health and in 1953 became chief minister as well as minister of agriculture and forests. Three years later, he obtained the title of premier, although the British maintained authority over finances.

Milton soon had an unexpected challenge: His younger half-brother Albert accused him of being too cautious. In 1958, Albert broke with the SLPP and along with Siaka Stevens formed a new organization, the People's National Party (PNP). This group, however, suffered defeat in the 1959 district elections. That same year, Milton Margai was knighted.

Milton did not push forcefully for independence; indeed, the British initiated talks to hold a constitutional meeting in 1960. As this conference approached, he linked his SLPP with rival parties, including his brother's PNP, to form the United National Front (UNF). After the conference, Milton formed a coalition government in preparation for independence and elections. Yet opposition appeared when Siaka Stevens criticized Milton's conservatism and demanded elections before independence. Stevens broke with the PNP and UNF and organized the All People's Conference (APC), which gained much support from urban workers and won two of the three seats on the Freetown City Council.

Early in 1961, Milton Margai arrested Stevens and other APC leaders. Sierra Leone gained its independence on 27 April 1961, and as head of government Milton ordered elections for May 1962, which took place in a peaceful and fair atmosphere. His SLPP won a majority in the House of Representatives, although the APC captured a solid minority.

His administration included many opposition party members, and his consummate skills at negotiation produced a smooth-running leadership. Mineral resources brought in considerable money and contributed to improvements, especially in education, including the founding of Njala University College. Milton Margai served as prime minister until his death in Freetown on 28 April 1964, when Sir Albert Margai, succeeded him.

References: Cartwright, John R., *Politics in Sierra Leone, 1947–1967*, 1970; Kilson, M., *Political Change in a West African State*, 1966.

Maria Theresa

(1717–1780)

Austria

Constantly hounded by Frederick the Great, Maria Theresa fought to protect her Habsburg domain while centralizing and reforming its administration.

Maria Theresa was born 13 May 1717 in Vienna to the Holy Roman Emperor Charles VI, a Habsburg, and his wife, Elizabeth-Christina of Brunswick-Wolfenbüttel. Because Charles was the last Habsburg prince, the dynastic rule seemed headed for disruption, but in the Pragmatic Sanction, a special agreement with several surrounding countries made in 1713, Charles was permitted to pass his crown to a female heir. In 1736, Maria Theresa married Francis Stephen of Lorraine, who fathered her 16 children. In 1740, Charles VI died, and Maria Theresa asserted her right to the throne.

This, however, conflicted with the ambitious Frederick the Great, ruler of neighboring Prussia. His family, the Hohenzollerens, long claimed Silesia, and with Charles's death Frederick invaded the province. The attack totally surprised Maria Theresa, and the ill-prepared Austrian army retreated. Frederick's invasion sparked the War of the Austrian Succession, which lasted from 1740 to 1748. At first, the Austrian army seemed doomed, but Maria Theresa rallied it to victories over France (a Prussian ally), and the war ended with the peace of Aix-la-Chapelle that confirmed Maria Theresa as the rightful ruler of the Habsburg lands but also recognized the Prussian conquest of Silesia. Maria Theresa then stunned Europe by concluding an alliance with her former enemy, France. The next time, she believed, Austria would be ready for Frederick.

Maria Theresa initiated numerous domestic reforms that created an absolutist monarchy and a more unified Austrian state. She did not, however, develop Austrian nationalism; she remained primarily a dynastic ruler who saw her Habsburg lands as personal possessions, while on their part most Austrians identified with German culture. Indeed, the majority of high government officials in Vienna were German. Yet Maria Theresa did found the Austrian Empire and in the process created a standing army (under the advice of Count Friedrich Wilhelm Haugwitz) and contained the powerful nobles.

She also reformed the government bureaucracy (a move that largely unified Austria with Bohemia), created a separate judiciary in 1749, and reorganized the treasury. Influenced by Gerhard van Swieten, she backed substantial educational reform at the universities, such as the use of textbooks. And although a Catholic, she worked to keep the church subordinate to her.

The loss of Silesia still disturbed her, and encouraged by her advisor Wentzel Anton von Kaunitz, she decided to reconquer the province. Her preparation was preempted by Frederick the Great, who attacked first. This conflict, mixed with other international complications, ignited the Seven Years' War in 1756. The war proved inconclusive in Europe, and Frederick retained Silesia.

Maria Theresa continued her domestic reforms, producing a penal code and humanitarian laws to help the poor. She also began a compulsory primary education system. Under the pressure of her son, JOSEPH II, she cooperated with Frederick in partitioning Poland, and in 1772, Austria thus obtained Galicia. In her later years, she had increasing differences with Joseph, who upon her husband's death in 1765 had become emperor. When she died on 29 November 1780, she left behind a unified Habsburg monarchy that Joseph further centralized and reformed, although the emergence of a fully modern Austrian nation awaited the fall of the Habsburgs and the emergence of a republic in 1918 under KARL RENNER.

References: Bright, J. F., *Maria Theresa*, 1897; McCartney, C. A., *The Habsburg Empire, 1790–1918*, 1968; Pick, Robert, *Empress Maria Theresa*, 1966; Roider, Karl Jr., ed., *Maria Theresa*, 1973.

Martí, José
(1853–1895)
Cuba

As a writer who bore a strong social conscience while in high school, José Martí protested Spanish rule in Cuba and, as a result, was arrested. Resolute and determined, he eventually organized and led the War for Independence that cost him his life.

José Martí, the son of a Spanish army sergeant, was born on 28 January 1853 in Havana. As a boy, he showed a talent for writing, and at age 15 he had several of his poems published. One year later, he began his own newspaper, *La patria libre*, or "The Free Fatherland." He aimed his pen against Spain, which had possessed Cuba as a colony ever since the first voyage of Christopher Columbus.

While Martí was still in his youth, nationalist uprisings rocked Cuba. In 1868, several planters in Oriente Province declared the island independent. Meanwhile, Martí ran afoul of the Spanish authorities: When he expressed support for the revolutionaries in the 1868 uprising, the government sentenced him to hard labor, and he spent six months on a chain gang. Then, in 1871, he was deported to Spain. He continued to write and pursue his education and obtained a law degree in 1874 from the University of Zaragoza. He next traveled to France and Mexico, where he worked as a journalist, and to Guatemala, where he taught college before returning to Cuba in 1878. That year, he supported the revolutionaries in their renewed fight, and once again the government deported him to Spain. He arrived there in 1879, then went to New York and Venezuela, where he got into trouble with the military dictatorship. In 1881, he traveled back to New York.

Despite a decision by Spain to end slavery in 1886, turmoil continued in Cuba. Substantial American investments boosted the economy, but in 1895 a downturn hurt many Cubans, as did higher taxes. In New York, Martí organized Cuban exiles and wrote poems and essays that encompassed, among other themes, political issues. Although expressing a disdain for socialism, he championed the oppressed and believed that political revolution had to be accompanied by substantial social reform to create a more equitable society. Martí's prose earned him acclaim, especially his writing of the first Spanish novel in modernist form. His poems included "Guantanamera," later set to music and widely listened to as a popular song in the 1960s and later.

On the political front, Martí formed a school for Cuban exiles in 1890, and two years later, after meeting with exile leaders, he presented them his "Fundamentals and Secret Guidelines of the Cuban Revolutionary Party." In it, he called for the end to foreign domination of Cuba, establishment of a democratic government, and full equality for all Cubans—a social upheaval that would bring all classes and races together. That same year, he began publishing a revolutionary newspaper. His efforts focused substantially on organization because he believed that, more than anything else, disarray had doomed the previous revolutionary efforts. He also desired a quick war to prevent an American takeover, which he feared would end any chance at independence. In short, he wanted complete freedom from both Spain and the United States.

"The Cubans ask no more of the world than the recognition of and respect for their sacrifices."

In 1893, Martí selected Máximo Gómez to be the movement's military leader and revolutionary bands were organized in Cuba. In his efforts, Martí displayed a keen ability to rally the Cuban people. In February 1895, the revolutionaries began their attacks against the Spanish forces and suffered immediate defeats. On 25 March 1895, Martí issued the Proclamation of Montecristi that expressed the goal of organizing whites and blacks alike and attacking the properties of those who opposed the revolution. On 11 April, Martí and his men landed at Playitas, and five days later he was named major general of the liberation army. But in little more than a month, on 19 May, Martí was killed at Dos Rios in his first combat with the Spaniards.

He left behind a tremendous influence—his ideas and spirit continued to propel the revolution, which with American assistance and intervention ended Spanish rule in 1898. His nationalism affected Cubans decades later as they struggled against American domination; indeed, Martí was a strong influence on the prominent Cuban revolutionary FIDEL CASTRO.

References: Kirk, John M., *José Martí, Mentor of the Cuban Nation*, 1983; Martí, José, *On Education*, 1979 (translated and edited by Philip Foner); Martí, José, *Our America: Writings on Latin America and the Cuban Struggle for Independence*, 1978 (translated and edited by Philip Foner).

◆

Massamba-Debat, Alphonse
(1921–1977)
Congo

Within a revolving-door leadership, Alphonse Massamba-Debat not only provided guidance in his nation's formative years, he also promoted a socialist program.

Alphonse Massamba-Debat was born near Boko in 1921 at a time when France controlled the Congo. Although exploitation occurred, such as during the building of the Congo-Ocean Railway that cost 20,000 African lives, several factors worked against a strong nationalist movement, primarily low population density, poor communications, and restricted schooling. Despite this, in the late 1920s André Maswa used passive resistance to protest French rule. Although he died in 1942, he became a hero.

Massamba-Debat heard about Maswa, who came from the Lari tribe, the very same tribe into which Alphonse was born in 1921. The young man received training in education and began teaching at a primary school in Chad.

In the 1940s, he participated in the Chadian Progressive Party led by Gabriel Lisette, a radical West Indian. This raised his nationalistic consciousness and his desire to end French rule. From 1945 to 1947, he served as general-secretary of the Association for the Development of Chad. Presently, he returned to the Congo and served as headmaster at primary schools in Mossendjo and Brazzaville. In the early 1950s, he joined the reformist Congolese Progressive Party at a time when France was making constitutional changes allowing more self-rule in the territory. Unlike in the strongly nationalistic colonies, political parties did not develop in the Congo until after France made these changes.

In 1956, Massamba-Debat joined the first major political party in his homeland, the Democratic Union for the Defense of African Interests (UDDIA) founded by Abbé Fulbert Youlou, a Catholic priest and a Lari. The UDDIA soon had opposition when the African Socialist Movement (MSA) emerged. Already the territory's politics split along ethnic lines as the latter group represented the northern Vili in opposition to the southern Lari. When, in 1956, the French allowed Africans to hold major governmental positions, Massamba-Debat obtained appointment as assistant to the minister of education. Three years later he won election to the legislature.

By the time the Congo obtained its independence on 15 August 1960, the UDDIA had gained dominance, and the following year Youlou, who had served as premier, won election to the presidency. Many Congolese, however, soon protested Youlou's government as corrupt and incompetent, and demonstrations broke out when he tried to form a one-party system, a move particularly opposed by the Vili. The critics, though, included fellow Lari, among them Massamba-Debat, who considered Youlou too conservative, even reactionary. Amid turmoil and rioting in 1963, Youlou resigned and Massamba-Debat formed a provisional government.

In elections late in 1963, Massamba-Debat won the presidency. He accomplished what Youlou had failed to do: He founded a single-party system, built around the National Revolutionary Movement (MNR). Massamba-Debat pulled the Congo to the left, beginning state-run businesses, obtaining help from the Soviet Union and China, and offering sanctuary for the Popular Movement for the Liberation of Angola. Yet economic problems mounted, and in 1968 the army overthrew Massamba-Debat and replaced him with a military leader who continued the socialist policies. Poverty remained widespread, however, and French economic control substantial. An official Marxist program announced in the late 1970s was ended in 1990. In the meantime, Massamba-Debat died in 1977.

References: Allen, Chris, and Michael Raduin, *Benin and the Congo: Politics, Economics, and Society*, 1987; Gauze, René, *The Politics of Congo-Brazzaville*, 1973.

Massey, William
(1856–1925)
New Zealand

A supporter of the British monarch as the sovereign over all Commonwealth nations, William Massey hardly qualified as a nationalist. But he exemplified the independence movement in New Zealand: It lacked strong nationalism and a prominent leader—it simply evolved, gradually and without emotion.

Like many persons in nineteenth-century New Zealand, then a British colony, William Massey had emigrated from Europe. He was born on 26 March 1856 in Limavady, Ireland, and at age 14 traversed the oceans and settled with his family near Auckland. He became a farmer and reflected the tendency of men with modest backgrounds to participate and advance in politics. He joined the farmers' movement that sought a plan to make it easier for those who leased state land to purchase the land for farming. More importantly, as a conservative he feared that the dominant

Liberal Party would begin nationalizing landholdings; this he worked to prevent.

In 1894, Massey won a seat in the New Zealand Parliament and nine years later became leader of the conservative opposition. He organized this group into the Reform Party. A noted speaker and debater, he led Reform to victory in the 1911 elections and in 1912 became prime minister. Although he wielded much power, during World War I he formed a coalition with the Liberals, thus providing them considerable say in the government. As a conservative, he took a firm stand against labor strikes and promoted private business.

Several years earlier, in 1907, New Zealand had achieved status as a dominion within the British Commonwealth, a status that maintained considerable British influence in the country's politics—especially in foreign affairs—and recognized the British monarch as the sovereign. Massey did not seek to disturb this arrangement, and his conservatism in this area reflected the strong attachment New Zealanders held toward their mother country.

Nevertheless, after World War I, as New Zealanders returned from European battlefields, they developed a greater sense of national identity, distinct from Britain. Massey furthered this feeling when he engaged in international politics. In 1919, he signed the Treaty of Versailles and made New Zealand a founding member of the League of Nations. For the first time, New Zealand exerted itself as a sovereign state.

Domestically, after the war Massey struggled with inflation that caused discontent in both rural and urban areas. He continued as prime minister until his death in Wellington on 10 May 1925. New Zealand still had not obtained its full independence, and would not until 1947, when it did so without fanfare. Despite his strong support for the British Commonwealth, Massey helped forge a national consciousness.

References: Oliver, W. H., ed., *The Oxford History of New Zealand*, 1981; Sullivan, Keith A., *A History of New Zealand*, 1986.

Mata'afa, Fiame Faumunia Mulinu'u II
(1921–1975)
Western Samoa

Fiame Mata'afa demanded self-government for his people with a system that would recognize and codify rules and regulations from Somoa's traditions and also provide democratic change.

In 1921, Fiame Mata'afa was born into a royal family. He attended the Marist Brothers School in Western Samoa's main town, Apia. During these years, New Zealand ruled Western Samoa as a United Nations Trust Territory. Most Somoans disliked this arrangement, particularly since they had not been consulted about it. Mata'afa was among the critics. As a conservative, he strongly supported his homeland's traditional practices and believed they could best be protected through independence.

Mata'afa entered the political scene in 1954 when he attended a constitutional convention and argued that the leading families should occupy the highest positions in an independent nation, but that there should also be universal suffrage. The latter did not materialize, but Mata'afa won the respect of many Samoans as a talented and principled leader who recognized the needs of his extended family (an important part of the Samoan social structure).

In 1957, Mata'afa was named minister of agriculture and in 1959 won election as the colony's prime minister after New Zealand permitted a cabinet form of government. The following year, he traveled to UN headquarters in New York, where he talked about independence. In 1961, Western Samoans voted overwhelmingly for nationhood, and it was obtained on 1 January 1962. The constitution contained traditionalism and modern democracy with a limited franchise, a parliament, and recognition of family hierarchies.

Mata'afa served as his nation's first prime minister and promoted economic progress, maintained commercial ties with New Zealand, and increased involvement in international affairs. Changes occurred in Samoan politics as the system became more competitive. In 1970, Mata'afa lost his position as prime minister but returned to office three years later. Mata'afa died in May 1975, and shortly thereafter a constitutional crisis shook the nation that resulted in the establishment of universal suffrage, Mata'afa's original proposal.

Reference: Meleisea, Malama, *The Making of Western Samoa: Traditional Authority and Colonial Administration in the History of Western Samoa*, 1987.

Mazzini, Giuseppe
(1805–1872)
Italy

Giuseppe Mazzini epitomized the fervent idealistic nationalism that challenged traditional order in nineteenth-century Europe. Freedom, he believed, could come only when national boundaries corresponded with cultural ones, and only when the masses obtained dignity.

Giuseppe Mazzini grew up in a tumultuous time. Born on 22 June 1805 in Genoa, he was a sickly child who required much care by his mother. She taught him Italian culture and encouraged a strong belief in God. At age 14 he attended the University of Genoa and in 1827 began practicing law in his hometown. All during this time nationalism and liberalism grew stronger and challenged Europe's monarchies.

In 1820, when Mazzini was 15, Austria, which had long exerted dominance over the disparate Italian states, crushed a popular uprising in the Kingdom of the Two Sicilies. Metternich, the Austrian foreign minister, considered nationalism and liberalism diseases that had to be eradicated. In the late 1820s, Mazzini joined the nationalist effort when he became a member of the Carbonari, a secret society dedicated to a united Italy. The authorities, however, discovered his activity and in 1830 arrested him. He served six months in prison and while confined grew dissatisfied with the secret Carbonari rules and the group's tactic of soliciting French help for the unification of Italy. He began formulating ideas for a new organization, and after his release and exile to France, where he lived in Marseille, he formed Young Italy.

This group reflected romantic idealism in its belief that nationalism could best be forged by the masses bonded together by mystic attachments, and stood for a united Italy under constitutional republicanism. True to his upbringing, Mazzini advocated a strong religious attachment for the purpose of inspiration. In fact, he developed the motto: "God and the People."

Mazzini published a newspaper and issued propaganda that stimulated the formation of two similar groups, Young Germany and Young Poland. By 1833, Young Italy had 60,000 members. *Risorgimento* became the byword; it meant resurgence—in this case, a resurgence of Italy, united and strong, particularly against Austria. Mazzini's nationalism was wrapped in republicanism and considered monarchy destructive of free institutions. Dynastic interests, he believed, inevitably conflicted with the wishes of the people. Furthermore, monarchy made equality before the law impossible.

In the early 1830s, Mazzini had hoped for support from the King of Sardinia-Piedmont, perhaps the most repressive government among the Italian states (until reforms in the next decade). But when the king learned of a Young Italy conspiracy in 1834 to gain control of his army, he retaliated severely, including jailing and torturing Young Italy members. Unexpectedly, his reaction attracted more protestors to the organization.

In the middle and late 1830s, Mazzini fomented rebellion in Sardinia-Piedmont and other areas of Italy but met only with defeat as the Austrians and others crushed the uprisings. Yet he remained an activist, always believing the mere preaching of ideas was not enough. In 1844, seven years after he had moved to London, Mazzini accused the British of having betrayed Young Italy members in Naples to the King of Naples. Mazzini's charge had validity, since it was revealed that the British government had opened letters sent by the Italian leader to his nationalist colleagues elsewhere. The controversy gained Mazzini a wider audience for his ideas, expressed in his notable "Letter to Sir James Graham" that pleaded for an Italian nation.

Technological and economic change, however, worked against Mazzini. The building of railroads in Italy connected the Italian states economically and strengthened a middle class concerned about disruptions in the economy. Moderates, especially in Piedmont, emerged and expressed disgust with the failures of revolts inspired by Mazzini. They wanted unification, but only through the leadership of the pope or Sardinia-Piedmont.

Mazzini continued plotting, but events moved past him. Revolutionary fervor swept across Europe in 1848 and brought a new era of war and change. Although nationalism gained as an organizing principle, Mazzini's romanticism seemed outmoded, and realistic military alliances and diplomatic pursuits seemed more valuable than vague attachments to God and populist appeals. In short, tactics changed as the continent buckled under the conservatism of Metternich and the monarchies that supported him.

In 1849, a rebellion in the Papal States led to a democratic Roman Republic headed by Mazzini. But he tasted only brief victory: Within a few months French troops besieged the Republic and destroyed it. In the 1850s, Mazzini kept trying to foment revolts while moderates such as CAMILLO DI CAVOUR stressed progress through statecraft. As the decade ended, it was Cavour and GIUSEPPE GARIBALDI who gained the lead in promoting nationalism. Throughout the 1860s, a unified Italy emerged, but neither republican as Mazzini desired, nor built through federation as he preferred. Mazzini died on 10 March 1872 in Pisa. In many ways he failed, but observers believe that his constant agitation pushed Europeans into recognizing the importance of resolving the Italian situation. In this way, Mazzini may have been the most instrumental of Italy's modern founders.

References: Barr, Stringfellow, *Mazzini: Portrait of an Exile,* 1971; Griffith, Gwilym O., *Mazzini: Prophet of Modern Europe,* 1970; Salvemini, Gaetano, *Mazzini,* 1957.

M'ba, Léon
(1902–1967)
Gabon

Léon M'ba was accused by the French authorities of ritualistic murder. Yet he overcame this to become his country's founder in a society that lacked strong nationalist development.

Born in Libreville on 9 February 1902, the son of a Fang village chief, Léon M'ba attended Catholic schools and later held various low-level civil service jobs, including interpreter. As a young man he witnessed the harshness of forced-labor conditions imposed on his homeland under French rule. M'ba became politically active in the 1920s when he joined a Libreville chapter of the Rights of Man League and Young Gabonese. He presented Fang grievances to the colonial government, and many French administrators considered him a troublemaker; increasingly, however, they turned to him as a liaison with the Fang.

Serious troubles occurred for M'ba after he promoted Bwiti, a cult of the Fang. Some Bwiti ceremonies used human flesh. In the early 1930s, French officials charged M'ba with the ritual murder of two young women whose flesh had been sold in Libreville. The evidence against him proved contradictory; nevertheless, in 1933 he was found guilty and sentenced to three years in prison and then exiled to Oubangui-Chari.

French reforms in 1946 allowed Gabon a territorial legislature, and Jean-Hilaire Abume, a Fang who had worked in the colonial administration, organized the Union Démocratique et Sociale Gabonaise (UDSG), a moderate political party. Upon his return that year from exile, M'ba and the southern Fang organized a more radical, anticolonial party, the Comité Mixte Gabonais.

In 1947, France called a special Fang congress to discuss problems. M'ba represented Fang interests so effectively that his reputation as a leader spread. In 1951, M'ba joined with Paul Gondjout, from the rival Myéné people, to defeat the UDSG, which they accused of listening only to northern Fang interests. In 1952 Abume, Gondjout, and M'ba all won seats to the legislature, and two years later Gondjout organized the Bloc Démocratique Gabonais (BDG), of which M'ba became secretary.

M'ba failed to unseat Abume in the 1956 legislative election, but he did win office as mayor of Libreville, an important power base. That same year, France established another reform, the loi-cadre, which gave the territorial legislature substantive powers and established an Executive Council with African officers. While the UDSG won a majority of the popular vote in the 1957 legislative election, the BDG and a group of independents won most of the seats, and M'ba became head of the Council. As Gabon's leader, he opposed uniting his homeland with other French-speaking territories in West Africa, a move promoted by some in the region.

The BDG and the UDSG both supported Gabon's membership in the French Community in 1958 when France offered this status for its African colonies (a status that allowed France to maintain some control over foreign affairs). Gabon became a self-governing republic, and M'ba became prime minister. As Gabon approached full independence in 1960, a dispute arose between M'ba and the legislature, producing a falling out with Gondjout. Most members of both the BDG and the UDSG, including Gondjout, wanted a strong legislature, but M'ba desired a strong executive. Gondjout's stand temporarily prevailed when Gabon developed a new constitution and gained its independence on 17 August 1960.

Tension between M'ba and the legislature then grew worse as critics accused him of being too pro-French. He retaliated by imprisoning opponents and ordering new elections. M'ba obtained a new constitution in February 1961, creating a strong presidency. Then, in 1963, he called for all opposing parties to merge with the BDG into a one-party system. This provoked protests and a military coup in 1964. The army briefly held M'ba a prisoner, but France, recognizing M'ba's support of French economic interests, intervened militarily on his side and restored him to power.

Behind this French backing, M'ba became more autocratic and repressive. But a terminal illness struck him down. As he neared death in 1966, M'ba hand-picked his successor, Albert-Bernard Bongo, who won election as vice-president in 1967. M'ba died that year at a hospital in Paris on 27 November.

Reference: Lusignan, Guy de, *French-Speaking Africa since Independence*, 1969.

Meciar, Vladimir
(b. 1942)
Slovakia

Prior to the 1980s, Slovaks never really had an independent nation, but they had pride and a strong ethnic identity. Vladimir Meciar embraced this pride and amid rapid changes in East Europe led his people in creating Slovakia.

At the time Vladimir Meciar was born, on 26 July 1942 in Zvolen, World War II raged across Europe. Soon after the fighting ended, his homeland fell to the Soviet Union, which established a totalitarian Communist regime throughout Slovakia and the neighboring Czech lands, ruled together as Czechoslovakia, a country that had been formed in 1918 by the great nationalist, Tomas Masaryk, but disappeared under Adolph Hilter's aggression.

Meciar obtained his higher education at Komensky University in Bratislava and then served in various positions connected with the Communist Party. In 1967, he worked with the Slovakia Union of Youth and in 1969 became vice-chair of the People's Control and Auditing Committee. His nationalist views and criticism of Soviet policy brought retribution, however, and in 1970, during a general purge, the Communist Party expelled him.

In the 1970s, he worked first as a clerk and then as a lawyer for a Slovak company. In the mid-1980s, changes in Eastern Europe affected Czechoslovakia. Nationalist movements grew stronger, demanding an end to Russian domination, and within the Soviet Union reformers sought to make the Communist system more open. Meciar joined the nationalist voices in Czechoslovakia. He helped found Public Against Violence, the Slovak branch of Civic Forum, a reform group organized by the Czech writer VÁCLAV HAVEL.

In 1989, thousands of demonstrators marched in Prague, demanding democracy, and in November the Communist leadership collapsed. The following month a new cabinet took office, and Havel was chosen president of Czechoslovakia. Immediately, friction emerged between the Czechs and Slovaks, the latter feeling discriminated against in what had long been a Prague-dominated country. Havel committed his administration to competitive politics and economic reform. Despite this, Slovak nationalists pushed for autonomy while criticizing Havel's move toward a free market as damaging to Slovakia's heavy industry and charging that most

of the Western assistance to Czechoslovakia had been funnelled to the Czechs. Amid this controversy, Meciar became interior minister for Slovakia in 1990.

In 1991, Public Against Violence split between opponents and supporters of a Slovak nation. Meciar led the secessionists, and in March he and his followers broke with Public Against Violence. Two months later, the Czechoslovakian Parliament removed Meciar as prime minister. He then formed the Movement for a Democratic Slovakia, and in June 1992 his party, although short of a majority, finished first in elections to the Slovak legislature. During the campaign Meciar called for Slovakian sovereignty (but with continued commercial and defense links to the Czechs) and a referendum on the issue of complete independence. The election victory resulted in his becoming Slovakia's prime minister.

In July, Meciar and the Slovaks in the Czechoslovakian Parliament maneuvered successfully to oust Havel from the presidency. That same month, the Slovak legislature proclaimed its homeland's sovereignty, explaining that the proclamation was not establishing independence but enabling a referendum on the issue.

In the fall of 1992, Meciar began meeting with the Czechoslovakian prime minister, Václav Klaus, to seek changes in Slovakia's relations with the federal government. Much to Meciar's surprise, Klaus rejected all of Slovakia's demands and suggested the Czechs were ready to let secession proceed. (Klaus may have been anxious to break with Slovakia because of its impoverished economy.) Denied any concessions, Meciar brushed aside earlier talk of holding a referendum and arranged with Klaus an agreement for the peaceful dismemberment of Czechoslovakia. On 1 January 1993, Slovakia became an independent nation.

For several reasons, Meciar's rule in Slovakia became controversial and opposition increased. First, many Slovaks disagreed with the decision for independence. Second, Meciar's go-slow approach toward economic reform did not alleviate the nation's high unemployment. Third, he appointed many former Communists to the central government. And fourth, he used authoritarian tactics, such as censoring newspapers.

In addition to this, Meciar had to deal with increasing discontent among the nation's minority Hungarians, who disliked the attacks against their heritage displayed in some Slovak nationalist demonstrations. In 1994, the Hungarian leadership demanded autonomy; this, and more substantially, continued economic problems caused Meciar to lose a parliamentary vote of confidence in March 1994. In the fall, however, his Movement for a Democratic Slovakia finished first in elections. Meciar had difficulty forming a new government but in December arranged a coalition with two smaller parties.

Earlier in the year, Meciar had opposed the privatization projects undertaken by the outgoing prime minister, Jozef Moravcik, and allied with other parties to get them cancelled in the National council (a parliament). He now promises to reevaluate the continuing demands by Western finanical institutions for an end to state-controlled businesses. Complaints continue, however, that he is slowing privatization so as to redirect it to benefit his supporters. In the wake of his removing the directors of the state radio and television networks, critics complain that he is still trying to silence opponents through authoritarian measures.

Reference: Leff, Carol, *National Conflict in Czechoslovakia: The Making and Remaking of the State, 1918–1987*, 1988.

Meiji
(1852–1912)
Japan

Meiji presided over a profound change: Japan's development from a secluded, traditional country to a modern nation.

Meiji Tenno was born on 3 November 1852 at Kyoto, the imperial capital, the second son of the emperor Komei. On 10 July 1860, he was declared crown prince and heir apparent and later that year adopted the personal name Mutsuhito.

Two years after Mutsuhito's birth, a dramatic event shook Japanese society when Commodore Perry of the United States Navy used his powerful squadron in a show of force that compelled Japan to open its doors to American trade, and subsequently widen contacts with other nations as well. Up to that time, few foreigners were allowed to enter Japan, a medieval society, and the shoguns (military leaders who ruled

in the emperor's name) suppressed Western influences such as Christianity.

With Perry's arrival, long-simmering discontent erupted against the shoguns, and what is today called the Meiji Restoration began under Mutsuhito. In 1866, Emperor Komei died, and on 9 January 1867 Mutsuhito became the new monarch. At the end of that year, political leaders who supported Japanese nationalism overthrew Shogun Yoshinobu Tokugawa and restored authority to the emperor. Mutsuhito's coronation ceremony occurred in 1868, at which time he assumed the name Meiji.

The emperor showed his break with the past when in April 1868 he issued the Charter Oath, which deviated from his father's policies by committing himself to Japan's modernization and Westernization. The emperor did not write this document; rather, it was written by advisors who desired a constitutional government. Indeed, an upper-class elite exerted enormous power, especially early in Meiji's reign when he was little more than a figurehead. Although Meiji did not initiate the ensuing reforms, putting the weight of the emperor's position behind them made it possible to change Japan. To be legitimate, any reforms had to be issued as imperial decrees. In the 1870s and 1880s, Meiji approved the end to the feudal land system; the creation of a new educational system; the development of a cabinet in the government; the writing of a new constitution (the Meiji constitution of 1889); and establishment of the Diet, a two-house national assembly which had to approve any tax bills.

The image of Meiji became enormously important in leading Japan's modernization, and to a certain extent he took the initiative in this. For example, the emperor rejected the seclusion that characterized his predecessors, and he left the Imperial Palace to make numerous public appearances and tour the outlying provinces. After the 1889 constitution gave Meiji almost all of the state's legal powers, the nation's political leaders promoted the emperor as a man to venerate. Millions of Japanese closely followed his every move.

By and large, the ruling elites used the emperor as a way to protect their power and advance their agenda. Several political leaders promoted modernization under Meiji and served crucial roles during his reign. Toshimichi Okubo helped plan the coup that ended the shogunate, and he promoted the end to the feudal system. As Meiji's minister of home affairs from 1873 to 1878, and the most powerful man in the government, he encouraged the use of Western technology and developed government-built factories. Tomomi Iwakura also helped depose the shogunate and under Meiji served as an important statesman, who in 1872 headed a diplomatic mission to several Western nations that gathered information about technology and economic programs. ITO HIROBUMI supervised the constitutional reform that produced a more centralized and authoritarian system.

Meiji presided over the Japanese attack on China in 1894 and the war against Russia in 1904. In 1910, he formally proclaimed the annexation of Korea.

Meiji became seriously ill in 1912 and died on 30 July. With his death ended "Meiji Japan." Numerous changes had occurred, including industrial and military growth that placed the country among the world's economic powers. The importance Meiji obtained was exemplified in the official memorial built for him and in the continuing prestige of the emperor in Japanese society, although in the years leading up to World War II and in the rebuilding after the war under YOSHIDA SHIGERU, political changes eclipsed the emperor's power.

References: Beckmann, George M., *The Making of the Meiji Constitution: The Oligarchs and the Constitutional Development of Japan, 1868–1891*, 1957; McLaren, Walter W., *A Political History during the Meiji Era, 1867–1912*, 1965.

Meir, Golda
(1898–1978)
Israel

Golda Meir had a varied and challenging life as an impoverished child, a pioneer in Jewish Palestine, a caring mother, and a political leader. She is fondly remembered by Jews as Israel's matriarch.

On 3 May 1898, Golda Meir was born Goldie Mabovitz in Kiev, Ukraine. Her parents, Moshe and Bluma (Neiditz) Mabovitz, were poor, and in 1903 her father took the family to Pinsk and decided they would emigrate to the United States. He went to America first and prepared for his family to follow. In the meantime, pogroms affected the Jews in Pinsk, and Golda remembered these attacks against the Jewish community—they influenced her for years to come. In 1908, Golda, her mother, and her two sisters arrived in America and joined Moshe in Milwaukee. There she went to elementary school and attended high school, until she ran away from home after her mother tried to marry her off. She lived with her sister in Denver, where she met anarchist and Zionist intellectuals and liked the democratic socialist ideology promoted by the American Eugene V. Debs. In 1915, she joined Poale Zion, a Zionist group, and began making speeches to promote Jewish settlements in Palestine. She also fell in love with a Lithuanian immigrant, Morris Meyerson. She soon returned to Milwaukee and in 1916 completed high school.

In 1917, Golda organized demonstrations against the pogroms in Russia, the same year she graduated from Teachers' Training College. Rather than teach, however, she worked full-time for Poale Zion. In December, she married Morris Meyerson yet worried he would not agree to her desire: emigrating to Palestine. At about that time Britain, which controlled Palestine under a League of Nations mandate, issued the Balfour Declaration, supporting a home for Jews in the Holy Land. This and Golda's persuasiveness convinced Morris to leave for Palestine.

In 1921, Golda and Morris joined the Kibbutz Merhavia near Nazareth, a poor commune where they raised chickens. Two years later Morris decided he could not endure living on the kibbutz, and he and Golda moved to Tel Aviv. She worked in the office of the Histradut (Israel Labor Federation) and took in laundry to help make ends meet. Golda worked hard to raise her two children under dire economic circumstances and within a marriage that neared collapse.

In 1930, one year after Meir had been elected a delegate to the World Zionist Congress, she assumed an important role in Mapai (Labor Party). In the 1930s, she spent much time in Europe and the United States raising money for Zionism. In 1945, she separated from her husband (who died in 1951).

After World War II, the Jewish struggle for a homeland intensified, and Meir sided with DAVID BEN-GURION, who advocated an activist approach to circumvent British restrictions in Palestine and end British rule there. On 14 May 1948, she, along with Ben-Gurion and other prominent Zionists, was a signer of the Israeli Declaration of Independence and was chosen the only female member of the provisional council of state. Under prime minister Ben-Gurion and president CHAIM WEIZMANN she served as Israel's first minister to the Soviet Union and then in 1949 won election to the Knesset (parliament) under the Mapai banner. She also served as minister of labor, a position she held for seven years. In this capacity, she substantially improved housing and jobs for immigrants.

In 1956, she became foreign minister and changed her last name to Meir. She promoted the acquisition of arms for the military as a means to offset recent weapons modernization by Egypt and Syria, a move that proved invaluable for Israel in the Suez War later that year. Ill health forced her to resign from the cabinet in 1966, but she served as general-secretary of Mapai and closely advised Prime Minister Levi Eshkol. Meir resigned as general-secretary in 1968, owing to political differences with other party leaders, but not until after she had merged Mapai with several other parties to form a restructured Labor Party.

Shortly after Eshkol died in February 1969, Labor leaders bypassed MOSHE DAYAN, hero of the 1967 Six Days War, and chose Golda Meir as the new prime minister. She took the oath of office on 17 March 1969. Meir supported new Jewish settlements in the West Bank and peace initiatives with Egypt. At the same time, she underestimated Arab military strength, a mistake that likely contributed to Israel being poorly prepared when the Egyptians and Syrians launched a surprise attack in 1973. As Meir's popularity dropped, her Labor Party lost seats, and early in 1974 she resigned as prime minister. Meanwhile, a special committee investigating the 1973 war effort cleared her and defense minister Dayan of any wrongdoing. Her ardent Zionism, determination, and belief that Israel stood alone all contributed to the realization of a Jewish homeland. She died on 8 December 1978.

References: Meir, Golda, *My Life,* 1975; Safran, Nadav, *Israel the Embattled Ally,* 1981.

Menelik II
(1844–1913)
Ethiopia

In the early nineteenth century, traditionalism and disunity characterized Ethiopia. Emperor Menelik II decided he would bring his country into the community of modern nation-states.

Menelik was born Sahle Mariam at Angolala in 1844 among the Shewan people, son of Haile Malakof, Shewa king. At this time, Ethiopia consisted of several kingdoms and there existed competition among various princes for the emperorship. While Sahle Mariam was yet a boy, Emperor Tewodros, a reformer king, made war on two kingdoms he believed threatened his power: Gallos and Shewa. After Haile Malakof died from dysentery during this conflict, Sahle, as prince and apparent successor to his father as king, surrendered to Tewodros and the victorious emperor ordered the boy be held captive. Sahle spent ten years, 1855–1865, in that status. During his captivity he married one of Tewodros's daughters, but later he deserted her and made his escape, carefully sneaking through valleys where Tewodros's soldiers were stationed.

Tewodros brought Ethiopia's heartland under his rule and introduced modernization to his country. Yet some observers claimed that in his later years he was mad; whatever the case, he lost an important battle to British forces who invaded in 1868 (as they tried to free Britain's consul whom Tewodros had detained in a dispute), and he killed himself.

Meanwhile, that same year Sahle Mariam secured his position as King Menelik of Shewa, but only after he had captured his cousin, who had emerged as an opposing claimant to the throne, and ordered him to be bound in wax-soaked bandages and burned to death. As a tributary king under Tewodros's successor, Emperor Yohannes IV, Menelik had much power. With Yohannes's approval, Menelik used force and negotiations to expand his realm further southward, more than doubling its size. He sought a greater share of the lucrative trade in coffee, ivory, gold, and gum.

> *"I shall endeavor if God gives me life and strength to reestablish the ancient frontiers of Ethiopia."*

Profits from this, he believed, could be used to modernize society.

In 1889, Yohannes died from wounds received in battle and Menelik succeeded him as emperor. As with his rule of Shewa, Menelik sought modernization, including a well-armed military and protection of his borders. Menelik wanted agreements with Britain, France, and Italy protecting Ethiopian sovereignty, and he wanted to secure Ethiopia's ports on the Red Sea. The ambitious European nations at first resisted him. In 1889, Menelik signed the Treaty of Wuchale with Italy to define the boundary between Ethiopia and Italy's possessions along the Red Sea coast. Italy then declared that an article in the treaty gave it power over Ethiopia's foreign affairs and hence had established an Italian protectorate over Menelik's kingdom. Menelik, however, denied this—a view substantiated by the Ethiopian language text. Unable to reach agreement with Italy, he renounced the treaty in 1893.

Menelik met Italy in battle in 1896, and his army defeated the Italians at Adwa. Although he did not launch an attack against Italy's formidable posts in Eritrea, his victory facilitated boundary agreements with Britain over the Sudan in 1902 and with Italy over Italian Somaliland in 1908, and a recognition that Ethiopia was, according to European standards, independent. Indeed, many historians believe Menelik's victory at Adwa signaled Ethiopia's emergence as a modern nation.

A stroke paralyzed Emperor Menelik II in 1908, and in 1913 he died. In an ensuing palace intrigue, the empress and her supporters kept Menelik's death secret for months, even using impersonators at ceremonies. Menelik left a legacy of restored order, an expanded commercial base, and European recognition. His modernization program was later continued by Emperor HAILE SELASSIE.

Reference: Marcus, Harold G., *The Life and Times of Menelik II: Ethiopia, 1844–1913*, 1975.

Meri, Lennart

(b. 1929)
Estonia

An intellectual and a writer, Lennart Meri promoted Estonian language and culture to keep his homeland's nationalism alive against Soviet oppression. The forces he helped unleash led him into politics and Estonia's presidency.

When Lennart Meri was born in Tallinn on 29 March 1929, Estonia was experiencing a brief respite from foreign domination. In 1945, though, the Soviets returned, and Lennart's father, Georg Meri, a diplomat and writer who had served independent Estonia as an ambassador overseas, was imprisoned and his family exiled to Siberia as punishment for his nationalist beliefs.

During this exile, Lennart lived with his mother and brother in a small village. He had obtained his early education in Paris and Berlin and now continued to attend school while working to help his family survive its deprivation. He returned to Tallinn in 1946 and seven years later graduated from Tartu University with a degree in history. His travels and his studies made him fluent in several languages: Estonian, Russian, German, English, and French.

After graduation, Meri became head of the literature department at Vanemuine Theatre in Tartu. He remained there until 1955, when he joined Estonian Radio as an editor. From 1963 until 1971, he shifted his editorial work to the Tallinn film studio and also wrote several books and directed films. He emphasized preserving and promoting Estonian culture, which the Soviets tried to crush through oppressive regulations.

In the late 1980s, conditions changed dramatically within the Soviet Union and for Estonia. The Soviets decided to liberalize society and allow dissenting views to be openly discussed. Estonian dissidents formed the Popular Front of Estonia in 1988, and the Estonian legislature began questioning Soviet authority. At this time, Meri served as a senior official in the Estonian Writers' Union and helped lead the efforts to reform the political system. Prominent in the Popular Front, he advocated Estonian independence.

In March 1990, Meri won election to the Estonian Council in the country's first free elections since well before World War II. In open defiance to Soviet rule, he accepted appointment in April as minister of foreign relations. On 20 August 1991, amid political turmoil within the Soviet Union, Estonia officially declared its independence. In September, the Russians recognized Estonia, and near the end of the year the Soviet Union collapsed. Meri soon followed in his father's footsteps as a diplomat: In 1992, he was named ambassador to Finland.

> *"In . . . days [past] it was nearly hopeless to interest any foreigner in the Baltic states."*

In September, Meri, running under the Pro Patria party label, received 29 percent of the vote for president, compared to 43 percent for another leading nationalist, Arnold Rütel, and 23 percent for a third candidate. This close race—with no candidate receiving a majority—went to the parliament for resolution, and in a coalition with right-wing parties Meri won the presidency.

Meri acted quickly to privatize the economy and develop a free market. He sold state-run industries to corporations and cut taxes, joined Estonia with Lithuania and Latvia in forming the Baltic Council to facilitate economic relations among the three countries, and obtained membership in the United Nations. Meri continues to face enormous problems in moving Estonia beyond its Soviet-era economy.

Reference: Raun, Toivo U., *Estonia and the Estonians*, 1987.

Michelsen, Christian
(1857–1925)
Norway

As Norway and Sweden prepared for war in 1905, Christian Michelsen, a lawyer and a businessman, let his moderate instincts hold sway. He avoided combat and led Norway's peaceful separation from Sweden.

Christian Michelsen was born on 15 March 1857 in Bergen. After he obtained his jurisprudence degree, he worked several years as a lawyer. He then began a shipping firm, which in short time ranked among the largest in Norway.

Michelsen's country was linked to Sweden, as it had been since 1814. In 1884, the Storthing, Norway's Parliament, reduced the Swedish king's authority, resulting in the first truly parliamentary political system in Scandinavia. Shortly after this, in 1894, Michelsen won election to the Storthing for a two-year tenure. He represented a liberal political party called the Left and voiced strong criticism of the continuing union with Sweden. His domestic agenda, however, was less radical than his leftist colleagues', and he split with the party.

Michelsen lost reelection in 1894 but returned to the Storthing in 1903, this time as part of the Coalition Party, a moderate-to-conservative group. He served as finance minister in the government headed by G. Francis Hagerup and participated in efforts to obtain for Norway an independent consular service. Many Norwegians, including Michelsen, considered this an important expression of their independence and a step toward separating from Sweden. Negotiations with the Swedes to obtain the service, however, failed.

On 11 March 1903 Michelsen took over as prime minister to lead the strengthening movement for separation. He put together a cabinet encompassing conservatives and liberals united behind Norwegian independence. The Storthing then acted to defy the Swedes and intensify the crisis, and with Michelsen's backing passed a bill establishing the consular service. At the same time, the Storthing approved a resolution supporting separation in principle. When the Swedish king refused to approve the bill, Michelsen and his government resigned, producing a major crisis: The king could find no one to form a new government. In this situation, the Storthing met and on 7 June 1905 declared the union with Sweden over, thus ending more than 500 years of subjugation to, first, Denmark, and then Sweden.

Michelsen did not support a totally republican government, and he and his more conservative colleagues worked to maintain a monarch to oversee the parliamentary system. In August 1905, Michelsen called for an election to confirm the choice of a king and a plebiscite to gain public approval for the actions taken by the government toward Sweden. In November, the plebiscite results overwhelmingly supported the prime minister and the Storthing. The Norwegians chose Prince Charles of Denmark to serve as their king, and he reigned as Haakon VII. Michelsen hailed the outcome as a new work day, a new beginning.

Meanwhile, Sweden did not accept these developments without opposition. The two nations mobilized, and as tensions mounted it appeared war would occur. After Michelsen calmed the militants in Norway, both sides agreed to discussions, which began on 31 August at Karlstad. Michelsen led the Norwegian delegation, and the talks resulted in Norway agreeing to minor concessions on trade and military forts in return for Sweden agreeing to end the union.

Michelsen continued as prime minister in 1905 and served until 1907, at which time, suffering from an illness and stung by criticism that he had not done enough to control capital investments by foreigners, he left the government and returned to his shipping business. In 1909, he organized a new moderate party called the Liberal Left but did not serve as its leader, and the following year he retired completely from politics.

Michelsen died in Fjøsanger on 28 June 1925. He had carved his nation's independence and shaped the governmental structure that continues today.

Reference: Lindgren, Raymond E., *Norway–Sweden: Union, Disunion, and Scandinavian Integration*, 1959.

Micombero, Michel
(1940–1983)
Burundi

Michel Micombero's homeland has had a long history of ethnic violence: Tutsis versus Hutus. As revolutionary leader and president, Micombero deepened that violence, presiding over a Tutsi assault on Hutus nothing short of genocide.

Michel Micombero grew up as Burundi entered a new phase of post–World War II nationalism. He was born a Tutsi at Rutovu in 1940. Michel received a primary education at the Catholic mission located there and then obtained a degree in humanities at the Collège de Saint-Esprit at Bujumbura.

Micombero obtained important military experience after he was inducted into the Burundian army in 1960 and sent to the Belgian Military Academy at Brussels. The Belgians had high hopes for him; they believed he would become an officer opposed to the newly organized nationalist party, Union for National Progress (UPRONA). This group had been established in 1958 by Prince LOUIS RWAGASORE who wanted to unite Tutsi and Hutu in a movement for autonomy. UPRONA became an independence movement after Belgium announced in 1960 that the Congo would be allowed nationhood. Micombero obtained a commission as a captain in 1962 and early the following year surprised the Belgian authorities by joining UPRONA. He was appointed secretary of state for defense under the *mwami*, or tribal chieftain, and in 1965 became minister of defense. At this time, he grew more leftist in his politics—more anti-West and pro-Communist China.

Then, in 1965, he launched an attack on Hutu rebels fighting against the Tutsi-dominated government. These rebels had killed thousands of Tutsi, and Micombero retaliated by severely repressing the rebellion and massacring the Hutu—some 5,000 died.

In 1966, Micombero led a revolutionary coup that drastically altered Burundi's government and founded a new political system. He deposed the mwami and declared his nation a republic with himself as president and UPRONA as the only legal party. Then, in 1969, at the urging of Tutsi extremists, he purged most Hutus from power. But he also purged many Tutsi—those who did not agree with his policies. Many of them were imprisoned, tortured, and even killed.

Micombero next engaged in a plot to eliminate a key rival. In 1972, he invited the deposed Mwami Ntare V to return to Burundi. On 29 April 1972, under Micombero's orders, assassins killed Ntare V at Gitega. That same day, a Hutu revolt exploded, and Micombero had to get military supplies from Tanzania and troops from Zaire to defeat the rebels. Another bloody assault on the Hutu ensued, a slaughter so vast the United Nations condemned it. By 1973, over 100,000 Hutus had fled Burundi and some 150,000 had been killed, including nearly every educated Hutu.

Micombero buttressed his power by placing his relatives in leading positions in the military, the government, and in various businesses. Nevertheless, in 1976, Lieutenant Colonel Jean-Baptiste Bagaza overthrew Micombero's government, sending the president into exile. Micombero died in July 1983 from a heart attack while living in Mogadishu, Somalia, one year after he graduated from the University of Somalia with an economics degree.

In 1993, the first democratic presidential election in Burundi led to a Hutu president. Shortly thereafter, ethnic violence flared anew and, with it, more bloodshed. Hutus went on a rampage, massacring tens of thousands of Tutsis. Rebel forces under Tutsi control overthrew the government and a precarious truce exists between the ethnic groups.

Under Micombero, Burundi had continued as one of the poorest nations in the world with high unemployment, the greatest population density on the African mainland, and a debilitating AIDS epidemic. A man of excess, Micombero had ushered in a new form of government—he had destroyed the monarchy, although in the process he had destroyed stability and promoted genocide.

References: Melady, Thomas Patrick, *Burundi: The Tragic Years*, 1974; Weinstein, Warren, and Robert Schire, *Political Conflcit and Ethnic Strategies: A Case Study of Burundi*, 1976.

Milosevic, Slobodan
(b. 1941)
Yugoslavia

After Yugoslavia began disintegrating in the late 1980s, Slobodan Milosevic, stirred by Serbian crowds in Kosovo who hailed him as their leader, emerged as the most powerful man in the restructured nation. He waged an aggressive war of conquest and genocide and refuses to accept a Bosnian declaration of independence.

Slobodan Milosevic was born on 29 August 1941 in Pozarveac, a town in Serbia. Slobodan attended college, graduating with a law degree from the University of Belgrade in 1964. At this time, the Communist Party dominated Yugoslavia, and Milosevic entered its bureaucracy, holding a succession of economic posts. In 1968, he worked as an executive for a state-owned gas company and was in charge of it by 1973. Then in 1978, he became president of the United Bank. From this position, he entered politics and led the Communist Party organization in Belgrade.

During his rise, Milosevic proved a faithful, even ardent supporter of Marxism. He also displayed a strong Serbian nationalism, believing Yugoslavia should be led by the Serbs. The Yugoslav nation was a curious and complex collection of different peoples, languages, religions, cultures, and political persuasions. It was not a tightly knit nation, but rather a loose confederation of republics and provinces led by a collective presidency chosen by the republics. Serbia was one republic; the others were Croatia, Bosnia, Slovenia, Macedonia, and Montenegro, each with a substantial degree of autonomy. By the 1980s, as communism crumbled in Eastern Europe, it also weakened in Yugoslavia. The loss of this unifying organization (along with the death of the powerful Yugoslavian leader, Josip Broz Tito) accelerated nationalist feelings and the tendency of the various Yugoslav republics to pull apart from one another.

"We will win the battle for Kosovo. We are not afraid of anything."

Milosevic soon emerged as the overall Communist leader in Serbia after he intervened on behalf of Serbs in Kosovo, a province within Serbia that in 1974 had been granted substantial political and economic autonomy. In Kosovo, Serbs constituted a minority, with most of the population Muslim Albanians. In 1987, the Serbs sought to overrun the town hall in Kosovo Polje to demand restitution for what they claimed to be mistreatment by the Albanians. The Kosovo police, however, refused them entry and beat them back. The Serbs then called on Milosevic for help, and he convinced the authorities to allow the Serbs into the building. There, he listened to the complaints and developed a rapport with the Serbs. As he heard them tell their grievances, his Serbian nationalism grew stronger and may have steeled his determination to advance Serbian domination in Yugoslavia.

In any event, by late 1987, Milosevic had solidified his position as Serbian leader by purging his opponents, including the president of Serbia. He exploited the issue of Serbian mistreatment by the Albanians to gain not only Serb support but also support from Montenegrens who were traditionally anti-Albanian. Milosevic agitated with the aim of grabbing complete power in Kosovo, and his strategy brought progress: By September 1988, the Politburo of the Yugoslav Communist Party agreed to end Kosovo's autonomy. Although anti-Milosevic politicians remained in the province's cabinet, Milosevic now had more authority to move against them.

At about the same time, large demonstrations erupted in Montenegro, Kosovo, and the province of Vojvodina, propelled by Yugoslavia's deteriorating economy. Milosevic acted to use this situation, too, pressing for his Serbian supporters to gain the upper hand in Vojvodina. Serbians there began a strike, but this time Milosevic ran into difficulties: Opposing ethnic groups disbanded the Serbs, and leaders in Slovenia and Croatia strongly criticized Milosevic. They claimed that Serbian aggression had gone too far and that Milosevic sought to disobey Yugoslavia's collective government and rule the nation like a dictator.

Undaunted, the Serb leader continued to press for his supporters to hold offices in the contested provinces. In November, huge Serb crowds marched in Belgrade chanting their support for Milosevic. As the leaders in Kosovo and Vojvodina felt pressure from the deteriorating economy and Milosevic's expanding authority, they resigned their offices, and Milosevic appointed his own Serb politicians to take their places. In March 1989, after Albanian delegates had quit the Kosovo legislature, the pro-Milosevic faction voted to turn Kosovo's government over to Serbia. The same result occurred in Vojvodina. Rioting erupted in Kosovo as Albanians protested the change, but the fate of the province had been sealed.

On 8 May 1989, Milosevic was chosen president of Serbia and immediately moved to make sure a multiparty political system did not emerge. This angered two of Yugoslavia's republics, Croatia and Slovenia, which had scheduled competitive elections for 1990 and supported that approach for Yugoslavia as a whole. The Slovenes threatened to secede from Yugoslavia, and Milosevic reacted by trying to organize a Serb rally in Slovenia. After the Slovene government banned it, Milosevic announced a boycott of Slovene goods. Slovenia re-taliated with its own trade embargo against Serbia, and Yugoslavia crumbled further.

In November 1989, voters in Serbia ratified Milosevic's elevation to the presidency. Milosevic allowed little opposition in the election, but in any event had gained enormous popularity among the Serbs. In February 1990, the Slovenia Communist Party broke with the Serbian party, and in July, the Serbian Communists merged with the Socialist Alliance to form the Serbian Socialist Party. This ran into conflict with Slovenia and Croatia, where anti-Communist nationalist governments were elected.

In June 1991, both Slovenia and Croatia declared their secession from Yugoslavia (Macedonia followed in September), whereupon Milosevic openly proclaimed his determination to expand Serbia's borders to include Serbs living in any lands formerly a part of Yugoslavia. Fighting occurred between the Croatian and Serbian armies. But the fiercest fighting erupted early in 1992 between Milosevic's Serbian forces and those of Bosnia-Herzegovina after the Bosnians declared their independence from Yugoslavia. The clash reflected deep, long-held ethnic and religious differences, with the Bosnians mainly Muslim and the Serbians mainly Orthodox Christian.

Milosevic, in unison with Serbs who lived in Bosnia, launched an offensive against Bosnia intended not only to capture most, if not all, of Bosnia's territories but also to "ethnically cleanse" the area—meaning eliminate the Muslim Bosnians through relocation and mass killings. The Serb forces and the Bosnian Serb forces gained large areas of Bosnia and by the summer of 1992 laid siege to Sarajevo, Bosnia's capital. The United Nations, meanwhile, ordered a blockade of Yugoslavia.

On 17 April 1992, Serbia and Montenegro, at Milosevic's direction, declared a new Federal Republic of Yugoslavia, with a presidency chosen by the two republics. In December, Milosevic won reelection as president of Serbia but had effective opposition from Milan Panic, who blamed Milosevic for the war with Bosnia. Milosevic also had to contend with street demonstrations against him.

The war situation became more complex when Croats and Serbs attacked each other and Croats and Bosnians also battled. It was not always clear how much influence Milosevic had over his Bosnian Serb allies, and as the United States and Western European nations pushed for an end to the war, there were frequent differences between the Serbian president and the Bosnian Serbs over peace proposals.

Nevertheless, most outside observers held Milosevic at least partly accountable for the atrocities that occurred against the Muslim Bosnians. In June 1993, Milosevic protected his power when he convinced the Yugoslav legislature to remove Dobrica Cosic from the nation's presidency. Milosevic disparaged Cosic for supporting an international peace plan.

In 1994, the fighting continued, with Milosevic still in power as Serbia's president, waging war against Bosnia and denying the claims of Albanians in Kosovo to their independence. In promoting Serbian nationalism and pursuing what some analysts called "brinkmanship," he encouraged the dissolution of the former Yugoslavia. Although Yugoslavia continues, it is quite different from the nation that existed before Milosevic gained control of Serbia and is referred to by some observers as an unrepresentative or "rump" Yugoslavia. It now consists of only two republics, Serbia and Montenegro; and although it has a presidency chosen by both, it is overwhelmingly dominated by Serbia. Yugoslavia's future and that of the other former Yugoslav republics remains extremely uncertain, embedded in religious, ethnic, and territorial rivalries.

References: Curtis, Glenn E., *Yugoslavia: A Country Study,* 1992; Kaplan, Robert D., *Balkan Ghosts: A Journey through History,* 1993; Magas, Branka, *The Destruction of Yugoslavia: Tracing the Break-Up, 1980–1992,* 1993.

Mintoff, Dom
(b. 1916)
Malta

Although Malta gained its nationhood before Dom Mintoff became prime minister, he played a leading role in the effort to end British control, and importantly, he pursued a radical political agenda attached to a socialist world view and the desire for a demilitarized Mediterranean.

Dom Mintoff came from a modest background. He was born on 6 August 1916 in Cospicua to Lawrence Mintoff, a cook with the Royal Navy, and Concetta Farrugia Mintoff. After obtaining a bachelor's degree in science at the University of Malta in 1937 and a second degree in engineering and architecture in 1939, Mintoff studied at Oxford University under a Rhodes scholarship. As a student, he wrote letters to the press and expressed his belief that Malta had a medieval social system in dire need of reform. By this time, World War II had erupted, and after obtaining his master's degree in 1941, Mintoff worked as a civil engineer in the British War Office.

When Mintoff returned to Malta in 1944 he found it devastated by the war. He worked as an architect and engineer in helping to rebuild his homeland, and in 1945 entered politics when he served on the executive council of the Malta Labour Party. He proclaimed himself a socialist and liked to portray Labour as a radical organization.

In 1947, Britain allowed Malta internal self-rule, and Mintoff won election to the legislature in a major triumph for Labour. The party leaders named him deputy prime minister and minister of works and reconstruction. He resigned these posts two years later, however, in a dispute over aid from Britain, the amount of which he considered insufficient. Amid the controversy, the Labour Party chose Mintoff as its leader.

In 1955, Mintoff won the prime ministry and worked to get Malta accepted as part of the United Kingdom. When this failed, he resigned as prime minister in 1958 and advocated complete independence, thus agreeing with the opposition Nationalist Party on this issue.

In the 1960s, Mintoff had a falling out with the

> *"Now Malta is a republic. Everything has changed, nothing is British anymore. . . ."*

Catholic Church, a significant development given Malta's overwhelmingly Catholic population. He considered the church an opponent to progressive reform and publicly procalimed his dislike for its hierarchy. The church's opposition resulted in his losing two elections. In 1964, Britain granted Malta its independence under Prime Minister Giorgio Borg Olivier, who led the Nationalist Party, a more conservative organization than Labour on social and economic issues. Malta was designated a member of the British Commonwealth. Mintoff criticized the independence arrangement, claiming Malta was not truly free because Britain controlled the economy, the banking system, and maintained military bases and troops.

By 1970, Mintoff began mending his relations with the Catholics, and in 1971 he returned to the prime ministry. He then undertook his program to increase Maltese control of the economy and declared a nonaligned foreign policy. In the former area, he nationalized businesses, especially banking; in the latter area, he forbade the United States naval fleet from stopping at Malta and called the money paid his nation for military access "wages of sin." In 1974, Malta became a republic, thus ending the presence of a British governor-general. In 1979, the Maltese-Anglo defense agreement expired, and after a long, acriminous dispute over payments for bases, Britain withdrew its last military forces.

To gain financial assistance, Mintoff turned to Italy and China, both of whom provided grants and loans. After the Soviet Union recognized Malta's neutrality, he allowed that nation to store naval fuel at the former bases. He also entered into closer relations with Libya. Mintoff, who had won reelection in 1976, won the prime ministry again in 1981 amid charges of election irregularities. The controversy led to strikes and demonstrations promoted by the Nationalist Party, and Mintoff eventually agreed to election reforms, which were incorporated into the constitution. Mintoff's domestic policies brought further radical change when he socialized medicine and, in order to fund education, confiscated assets of the Maltese Catholic Church. He moved to replace private schools with public ones, and as a result of his initiative, free education was introduced.

Mintoff did not seek reelection in 1984, but the Labour Party remained in power until three years later, when the Nationalists captured the prime ministry. They reversed some of Mintoff's economic policies by initiating privatization. Many Maltese considered the tempestuous Mintoff a hero in exerting their nation's authority and fostering nationalist sentiment.

References: Austin, Dennis, *Malta and the End of Empire*, 1971; Dobie, Edith, *Malta's Road to Independence*,

Miranda, Francisco de
(1750–1816)
Venezuela

Francisco de Miranda plied the European political scene with skill. He variously gained support from England, ingratiated himself with Catherine the Great of Russia, and fought in the French Revolutionary army. Yet he remained loyal to his goal of liberating South America and, late in his life, returned to Venezuela, where he led the fight against Spain.

Francisco de Miranda was born in Caracas on 28 March 1750. His father, a wealthy Spaniard, had emigrated to Venezuela from the Canary Islands. As a young man, Miranda joined the Spanish army and in 1772 journeyed to Madrid. With letters of introduction, he purchased the rank of captain but was later charged with neglect of duty. After clearing himself, he was sent to Cuba—where he fought against the British—and again got into trouble: This time he was accused of misusing funds. Miranda claimed his innocence and then, in 1783, fled to the

United States, where he became a prominent figure in the new nation's political circles, socializing with GEORGE WASHINGTON and ALEXANDER HAMILTON, among others. He began developing plans for a revolution that would end Spanish rule in his homeland and throughout South and Central America.

In 1785, Miranda sailed for London, where he intended to get Britain's help with his plan for liberation. The British prime minister, William Pitt, handled Miranda cautiously—providing him money to live comfortably, but refusing to jump into a plan that might bring war with Spain. Miranda advocated that a single nation be created in South America and that it have a legislature and be ruled by a prince from the Inca Indian line. He founded a society, the Gran Reunión Americana, that brought together many Spanish-American dissidents.

As he pursued this grandiose scheme, the French Revolution erupted, and the adventuresome Spaniard joined the radical cause. He served briefly as a French Revolutionary general, but in the rapidly changing currents he soon found his political faction in disfavor and was imprisoned for treason. Ingenious as ever, Miranda maneuvered his way to freedom and returned to England and the good graces of the British government.

In 1806, Miranda set his liberation plan in motion and with a ship and a few volunteers—mainly adventurers from the United States—he invaded Venezuela. He found little popular support for his effort, and after the Spanish quickly defeated him, he escaped to England where he continued his lobbying.

Opportunity struck for Miranda in 1810 when a rebellion broke out in Venezuela. The revolutionaries sent SIMÓN BOLÍVAR to England to gain support, and although Bolívar did not get British assistance, he did convince Miranda to return home as leader of the revolution. Miranda, by then 60 years old, entered Venezuela as commander of the army and, shortly after the rebels declared Venezuela's independence on 5 July 1811, he was named dictator by the revolutionary legislature, although Spain still controlled most of the country.

Miranda encountered numerous problems: Venezuelans were not united behind him, the rebel army was disorganized, and the Spanish still possessed a formidable force. Miranda's men suffered several defeats in battle and, as the situation deteriorated, the revolutionary leader signed an armistice with Spain that conceded the struggle. Bolívar and other revolutionaries were so incensed they turned Miranda over to the Spanish, who, in turn, placed him in chains and sent him to prison in Spain. In the dark Cadiz fortress called Four Towers, he died from typhus on 14 July 1816. Thus Miranda did not live to see Venezuelan independence, but he had, in his controversial actions, promoted the cause that saw success under Bolívar and his outstanding general, ANTONIO JOSÉ DE SUCRE. Bolívar made Venezuela part of Gran Colombia, but in 1830 the country became a separate republic led by JOSÉ ANTONIO PÁEZ.

References: Robertson, William S., *The Life of Miranda*, 1929; Thorning, Joseph F., *Miranda: World Citizen*, 1952.

Mobutu Sese Seko
(b. 1930)
Zaire

In 1960, the Congo gained its independence from Belgium and slipped immediately into near anarchy. For five years it lacked an effective governing authority. Mobutu Sese Seko became its savior, using his military support to establish authoritarian rule.

Mobutu Sese Seko was born Joseph Mobutu on 14 October 1930 in Lisala. After obtaining an education at various missionary schools, Mobutu entered the Belgian Congolese army in 1949. He served as a clerk and then reached the highest rank allowed Africans, that of sergeant major. While still in the army, he began writing articles for newspapers and, after his discharge in 1956, he became a reporter for *The Future*, a daily. Shortly thereafter he became editor of *African Actualities*, a weekly. In 1959, he lived in Brussels, where he studied public relations.

With his education and knowledge of the French language, Mobutu became an *évolué*, one in a group of privileged middle-class Africans who had adopted European practices. By the mid-1950s, many *évolués* had become discontent with the legal barriers still separating them from Europeans. Like other *évolués*, Mobutu joined a political organization, in this case the National Congolese Movement (MNC), which had as its head PATRICE LUMUMBA. Mobutu won important recognition in 1960 when, during Lumumba's imprisonment for political activities, he represented the MNC at the Brussels Round Table Conference, which had been called to discuss the Congo's colonial status. Mobutu sided with Lumumba in calling for an independent Congo with a strong central government.

After the Congo obtained nationhood on 30 June 1960, the nation's leaders, Lumumba and JOSEPH KASAVUBU, appointed Mobutu secretary of state for national defense. The Congolese government, however, suffered immediate chaos. Under MOISE TSHOMBE, Katanga province rebelled and declared its secession. The army mutinied against the government, and Prime Minister Kasavubu antagonized numerous groups by arresting several political opponents. Amid this maelstrom, Mobutu squelched the army uprising by providing favors to the mutineers. With the army behind him, he became a strong influence within the government.

As Kasavubu and Lumumba engaged in a power struggle, Mobutu criticized Lumumba's turn to the Soviet Union for support and backed Kasavubu. In September 1960, he seized control of the government and commanded it until February 1961, when he turned power over to Kasavubu. In the meantime, he may have been involved in arranging the murder of Lumumba, who was killed under mysterious circumstances in Katanga early in 1961.

Mobutu next focused his efforts on modernizing the army, but when in 1965 a power struggle intensified between President Kasavubu and the new premier, Moise Tshombe, Mobutu staged a coup and became president, replacing Kasavubu. He installed Colonel Leonard Mulamba as prime

minister. Mobutu claimed he would stay in office for five years while establishing order in the Congo, but his term lasted longer than that.

Mobutu consolidated power around himself and established a highly personalized regime under which all office holders were loyal to or dependent on him. He eliminated his political rivals by banning all opposition parties and imprisoning or executing his competitors, and he filled his regime not with army officers but with civilians through an extensive spoils system.

In March 1966, Mobutu began ruling by decree; he prorogued the legislature and in October dismissed the prime minister, thus ending all separation of powers. He also reduced the authority of the provinces. Mobutu formed the Popular Movement of the Revolution (MPR), a politcal party fully subservient to him. By 1970, he established an autocracy and also a cult labeled "Mobutuism" under which Mobutu's words and actions were worshipped and the government officially referred to him as "Messiah." Mobutu ordered the Africanization of the Congo that required a change in place names including, in 1971, a new national name, Zaire. That year, he changed his own name to Mobutu Sese Seko, meaning "the Caesar."

Mobutu began nationalizing large sectors of the economy in 1973, a move that transferred ownership of firms from foreigners to Zairians. This action so disrupted production that the economy suffered immensely. Mobutu at first reacted with an even more radical nationalization program, but as Zaire's debt mounted in 1976, he moderated his strategy by allowing some foreign management.

In 1977, Mobutu faced an invasion by rebel forces backed by Angola and repulsed them only with the help of France and Morocco, which provided troops. Another invasion occurred the following year, which required Franco-Belgian assistance and thus showed limitations to Mobutu's rule.

Under Mobutu's personalized regime, corruption has run rampant. Few other governments have reached the heights of Zairian graft where 60 percent of the annual national budget makes its way into the governing elite's pockets. Mobutu himself has benefited tremendously, amassing one of the largest personal fortunes in the world. While Mobutu has brought national government to a nation that suffered nonrule and disorder, to this day he presides over extensive political abuses and economic failures.

Reference: Young, Crawford, and Thomas E. Turner, *The Rise and Decline of the Zairian State*, 1985.

Mohammed V

(1909–1961)

Morocco

For both Mohammed V and Morocco, independence was a long, gradual process and a surprising transition. What was once a seemingly compliant monarch grew into a bold nationalist leader who rejected French domination.

Mohammed Ben Yosuf, born in 1909, was the third son of Moulay Yosuf who, in turn, was the brother of the ruling Moroccan sultan, Moulay Hafid. In 1912, Moulay Yosuf became sultan after Moulay Hafid was deposed for refusing to call in French troops to put down an uprising, and Mohammed, born in Fez, was raised in the Royal Palace at Rabat. He received a traditional Islamic education and showed no real indications of attaining the throne. In a surprise move upon the sultan's death in 1927, however, France, the colonial power, opted to have Mohammed, rather than one of his older brothers, serve as sultan. The reason for this is unclear but probably included the belief that Mohammed would be a pliable ruler.

Mohammed saw to it that his children received a Western education, and he formed the College Imperial so they and the children from other elite families could obtain modern schooling. Hence a pattern emerged in Mohammed's life, a mixture of Islamic with French culture, the latter of which he embraced enthusiastically.

In 1930, Mohammed appeared to be doing what the French wanted, and he earned the enmity of many Moroccans, including the nationalist AL-LAL AL-FASI, when he agreed to the French edict granting Berber law supremacy over Islamic law among the Berber people. The law was considered an assault on Islam and an example of foreign oppression. The subsequent protests awakened Mohammed to the importance of political issues and the limits to which French rule should proceed. Several nationalists decided they would try to win Mohammed to their cause.

The transition, however, would not be immediate, and Mohammed particularly displayed a strong resistance to any violent protest. Thus he offered no objection when, in 1937, the French exiled two nationalist leaders, including Allal al-Fasi.

When, in World War II, Mohammed helped the United States and the Allies, the sultan expected American assistance in gaining more autonomy. But this did not materialize. Meanwhile, the nationalist movement reorganized and formed the Istiqlal, or Independence Party, which called for nationhood under Mohammed's rule. When the French repressed nationalist demonstrations, Mohammed remained silent.

But, in 1945, Mohammed began openly expressing sympathy for the nationalist aspirations of his people, and he convinced France to allow Allal al-Fasi and other nationalist leaders to return to Morocco. Two years later, he stunned the French when, at a public rally, he spoke of the "legitimate rights of the Moroccan people," and to journalists he proclaimed Morocco's closeness to the Arab states and their common drive to end foreign rule.

In the 1950s, nationalist protests intensified, and the French encouraged the sultan's opponents to attack him. When, in January 1951, Mohammed refused orders from France that he condemn the Istiqlal, the French governor-general had tanks surround the Royal Palace. Under duress, Mohammed gave in and agreed with the French demand. More strife emerged, however, and in 1953 the French finally deposed Mohammed, sending him into exile. For three years he and his family lived in Madagascar. This French action, however, only served to make Mohammed a nationalist hero, and he won the hearts of many Moroccans.

In Mohammed's absence, the Istiqlal organized economic boycotts and armed resistance. A harsh French repression followed but did not last long. France had other concerns, most especially a nationalist uprising in Algeria. To focus on that situation, the French opted for negotiations in Morocco. These talks began in 1955 and resulted in the return of Mohammed on 17 November. Huge crowds turned out to greet and hail him. Then on 2 March 1956, Morocco obtained its independence, and Mohammed became the nation's king (a title that superseded that of sultan). While some Moroccan politicians still expected Mohammed to be a figurehead, he exerted himself, balancing political groups and even assuming the prime ministry.

"I cannot forbid my people to think."

Mohammed V died on 26 February 1961 from complications during an operation. He left Morocco a more modern nation but one still uncertain about how to handle political competition. In 1972, King Hassan II (Mohammed's son) proposed a new constitution and its adoption limited the role of the national legislature.

References: Barbour, Nevill, *Morocco*, 1965; Landau, Rom, *Mohammed V, King of Morocco*, 1957.

Mondlane, Eduardo
(1920–1969)
Mozambique

As a young boy, Eduardo Mondlane learned early about colonial oppression, for his father protested Portuguese rule in Mozambique and his mother complained bitterly about its damaging effects. Their examples became his inspiration.

When Eduardo Mondlane was born in 1920, the son of a Tsonga chief, the Portuguese had just begun consolidating their rule in Mozambique. As a child, he had heard stories from his parents and other relatives of African resistance to Portugal. Strikes and work stoppages had occurred in urban areas, and rural peasants had engaged in work slowdowns and sometimes violent actions, as when the infamous rebel Mapondera operated on the Mozambican frontier in the 1890s, protesting hut taxes, raiding European property, and declaring death to all white men. The Portuguese captured and executed him in 1904.

Mondlane went to missionary schools in Mozambique and, later, South Africa, where he received a scholarship to Witwatersrand University in 1947. In college he became friends with students who opposed racial segregation. Before he could complete his college education, the South African government deported him in 1949 for his political activities.

Back in Mozambique, Mondlane organized the Mozambican student movement, known as NESAM, and stressed the oppression of Portuguese rule and the worthiness of Mozambican culture.

"I was interested in the nationalist struggle against the Portuguese for many, many years back."

Portuguese officials harassed him, placed him under police surveillance, and then decided to get rid of him by sending him to Portugal to continue his education. This, however, only brought Mondlane into contact with other militant students, including Marcelino dos Santos, who became an important ally in Mondlane's political struggle. As Portugal's Salazar dictatorship further harassed Mondlane, he fled to the United States, where he studied at Oberlin College in the late 1950s and obtained a doctorate at Northwestern University in 1960. He then taught at Syracuse University and served with the United Nations Secretariat.

In 1961, Mondlane used his diplomatic immunity as a UN employee to return to Mozambique, where he met secretly with dissidents who wanted him to form a nationalist movement. He subsequently began building a broad-based insurgency organization, the Mozambique Liberation Front (FRELIMO), founded in 1962, and served as its president. In September, its members compiled a platform appealing to a diverse membership. Mondlane and his colleague dos Santos stressed not only national independence but also internal reform through a socialist restructuring of society. The following year, Mondlane moved to Tanzania.

On 25 September 1964, FRELIMO soldiers attacked a Portuguese administrative post at Chai, thus beginning an armed struggle. Portuguese soldiers retaliated by beating FRELIMO sympathizers and indiscriminately killing peasants. By 1968, Mondlane had guided FRELIMO's capture of northern Mozambique, despite substantial military assistance provided Portugal by the United States. He worked unceasingly for his cause, raising funds for weapons (many of which he obtained through the Soviet Union), training his guerrilla fighters, and stressing education for FRELIMO members. In his efforts he received invaluable assistance from his American-born wife, Janet Mondlane, who, despite some African complaints about her being white, codirected FRELIMO with him.

As FRELIMO entered areas, Mondlane, believing that Mozambicans had to be liberated from the destructive myths created by their Portuguese rulers, established schools that stressed Mozambican history and culture. He also began establishing agricultural cooperatives where the peasants shared profits and produce equally, and peoples' shops that offered farmers short-term credit and barter arrangements.

In 1968, Mondlane won reelection as FRELIMO president on a platform of revolutionary ideology that emphasized analyzing historical change according to class dynamics, and creating a primary role for peasants and workers, rather than an educated elite. His victory and ideology antagonized some in FRELIMO, particularly Lazaro Nkvandame, a party secretary in Cabo Delgado Province who had been accused by many peasants of exploiting them. Nkvandame broke from FRELIMO and tried to organize his own group but failed. In February 1969, Mondlane opened a letter and it exploded, killing him. Evidence indicates Nkvandame planned this assassination with the help of the Portuguese secret police. The Mozambican Revolution for nationhood and socialism continued, now led by SAMORA MACHEL, who became president of Mozambique upon independence in 1975.

References: Isaacman, Allen, and Barbara Isaacman, *Mozambique: From Colonialism to Revolution, 1900–1982*, 1983; Mondlane, Eduardo, *The Struggle for Mozambique*, 1969; Munslow, Barry, *Mozambique: The Revolution and Its Origin*, 1983.

Mongkut
(1804–1868)
Thailand

Mongkut (Phra Chom Klao) underwent a stunning transformation as a young man: He rejected his riches as a royal prince and chose to live as a Buddhist monk, with few possessions. In so doing, he embraced his land's traditions and gained strength and wisdom for yet another change: As king, he embraced modern Western customs to protect Thailand.

Mongkut was born 18 October 1804 in Bangkok, the eldest son of King Rama II and his queen, Sri Suriyendra. Forty years earlier, Thailand (at that time called Siam) had been defeated in war by Burma. The great military leader Taksin reunited the Thai kingdom

> *"The only weapons that will be of real use to us in the future will be our mouths and our hearts . . ."*

by 1776 and became ruler; despite his delusional behavior, he is today considered a national hero. Under a new dynasty, founded in 1782, Thailand emerged even stronger.

Mongkut's father obtained the throne in 1809 and since Mongkut's mother was the chief queen, the young prince received an extensive education. Mongkut studied literature, Siamese history, and the art of war. He also learned Buddhism, and in 1817 passed the traditional tonsure, or religious rite—an official recognition that his childhood had ended. At age 20, Mongkut entered a Buddhist monastery, intending to stay only a few months. At that time, however, his father died and for reasons unclear, but dealing with political manipulation, he was passed over for the kingship and his half brother became ruler.

Mongkut then decided to enter the Buddhist priesthood. As a Buddhist teacher, he strived to reform the church, cleansing it of numerous superstitions that had arisen, while teaching the importance of the Buddha's initial moral lessons. He also studied intensively, learning several Asian languages, astronomy, and history.

In 1837, Mongkut became abbot of Wat Pawaraniwesa (a monastery), which he made into the leading religious and scholarly center in Thailand. From American missionaries he learned Western history and began to read and converse in English. He grew enchanted with Western culture and saw in it features that could benefit his own country. Mongkut's reform Buddhist movement eventually developed into a new order, the Thammayut, which is still known for its intellectualism.

When the reigning king, Mongkut's half brother, died in 1851, Mongkut ascended to the throne with the backing of those who supported his pro-Western outlook. With the help of his prime minister, Somdet Chao Phraya Si Suriyawong, Mongkut initiated many reforms, including treaties with Britain and the United States. He was convinced that for Thailand to maintain its independence and avoid the tragedies that had befallen Burma and China at the hands of Western aggression, his homeland must change. He sought to synthesize traditional Buddhist teachings with certain Western customs.

In doing this, Mongkut broke sharply with the usual tendencies in Southeast Asia to isolate kingdoms from foreigners. He reduced import duties to encourage foreign trade, permitted the exportation of rice, ended economic monopolies (a bold move that challenged the authority of numerous noblemen), completely reorganized his kingdom's monetary system to reflect a Western financial system (even establishing a royal mint to coin money), and encouraged road and waterway construction.

Mongkut employed westerners to serve as administrators and to spread Western ideas. His laws enhanced the rights of women and children and brought greater equality to the judicial system.

He even allowed his subjects to look at him—which might seem a minor change, but tradition held that the common people should not gaze upon their king, nor should the monarch travel. Such actions would, it was claimed, reduce the ruler's divine status. Mongkut's predecessors had left the Royal Palace only once a year to journey to Bangkok's temples. But Mongkut traveled frequently and sometimes unconventionally, as when he rode a steamer up and down the river several miles above his palace.

Mongkut's efforts stimulated economic growth and may have prevented a Western conquest—Thailand was the only Southeast Asian country to escape European colonization (although French and British desires to maintain a buffer zone between their territories may have had as much to do with Thailand's independent status). Despite the changes, Mongkut maintained many conservative ways, including the slave system and political domination by a few great families. More substantial reforms came under his son and successor, CHULALONGKORN, who abolished slavery and developed a cabinet form of government.

When on 15 October 1868 Mongkut died from malaria, he left behind a legacy of bringing his country into the modern world. His predicament seemed so challenging and his efforts so bold that Westerners popularized him in productions such as the fictionalized musical *The King and I.* Thailand's government underwent substantial changes in the twentieth century that diminished the monarchy, and its political system has been more unstable with numerous coups and military interventions. No single recent figure has emerged equal in stature to Mongkut, who is remembered as the progenitor of Thailand's modern era.

Reference: Moffat, Abbot L., *Mongkut, the King of Siam,* 1961.

Morazán, Francisco
(1792–1842)
Costa Rica, El Salvador,
Guatemala, Honduras, Nicaragua

Francisco Morazán did not bring independence to each of the Central American states; rather, he envisioned a united Central America free from external control. As a man with natural military abilities, he fought hard to bring his idea to fruition but lost to his Conservative opponents.

Francisco Morazán was born on 3 October 1792 in Tegucigalpa, a city that had a longstanding rivalry with another Honduran settlement, Comayagua. This conflict helped shape Morazán's life. In 1821, the Central American provinces declared their independence, a move Morazán supported. When leaders in Tegucigalpa called for a unified Central American state, Morazán sided with them against Comayagua, which favored unification with Mexico.

In 1822, the Central American provinces agreed to join Mexico, but the merger did not last long, and in 1823 they formed the United Provinces of Central America. Morazán served as secretary-general in the late 1820s, and in 1828 ably defended the federation against a Guatemalan uprising. Morazán achieved his victory without the benefit of military schooling; rather, he displayed what many observers believed to be a natural talent in handling battlefield strategy.

In 1829, Morazán led the organized Liberal forces that overthrew the Conservative regime headed by Manuel Arce and the following year was elected president of the United Provinces. He faced a continuing split between Liberals and Conservatives. As a Liberal, he wanted to restrict the power of the Catholic Church, develop political institutions like those in the United States, and diversify the economy. The Conservatives supported the church and preferred a more elitist government. The unstable situation exposed Morazán's government to uprisings as the various provinces each tried to gain a dominant position and advance either the Liberal or Conservative cause.

Morazán began programs to improve economic development and restrict the church. At one point he had the friars of the three leading brotherhoods seized, forced aboard a ship, and sent to

"I am alive!"

Havana. Morazán's liberalism created so much opposition that in 1833 he lost the presidency in an election to JOSÉ CECILIO DEL VALLE, a Conservative. The president-elect, however, died before he could take office, and in March 1834 Morazán was again chosen president.

He continued his reforms to found a new government—which earned him the nickname "the George Washington of Central America"—including an expanded educational system. Yet unrest still disrupted the federation, and with church support, a Conservative rebellion occurred in Guatemala in 1837, led by Rafael Carrera. In 1839, Honduras and Nicaragua decided to leave the federation, restricting Morazán's power base to El Salvador, long a Liberal stronghold.

General FRANCISCO FERRERA of Honduras then invaded El Salvador, but Morazán determined to fight back and save the federation. He defeated Ferrera in 1839 at the battle of San Pedro Perulapán. Morazán followed this with an attack on Guatemala and briefly held Guatemala City until Carrera drove him back. He then tried to stop the fighting by leaving El Salvador and between 1840 and 1842 lived first in Costa Rica and then Panama and Peru.

Morazán returned to Central America when the ruler of Nicaragua appealed for help against an attack led by Costa Rica. A treaty led to Morazán entering Costa Rica in July 1842 and becoming its president. In September, a rebellion erupted when Conservatives learned that Morazán intended to use Costa Rica as a base from which he could conquer Central America and reunite it. The Conservatives captured Morazán, and on 15 September he was placed before a firing squad. He survived the first volley and proclaimed, "I am alive!" The second round, however, killed him. With his death also expired the hopes of a Central American union.

Reference: Chamberlain, Robert S., *Francisco Morazán: Champion of Central American Federation*, 1950.

Morelos, José Maria
(1765–1815)
Mexico

As a young man, José Maria Morelos, the great Mexican revolutionary, lived in poverty and personally experienced the injustices of Spanish colonial rule.

José Maria Morelos was born on 30 September 1765 in Valladolid (today's Morelia) to poor parents of mixed blood—a heritage liklely Spanish, Indian, and Negro. As a boy, he received little education and survived by leading mule trains in southern Mexico. At the relatively late age of 25, he decided to advance his education and enter the priesthood. He attended the Colegio de San Nicolás in Valladolid and then continued his studies at Tridentine Seminary and, in Mexico City, the Royal and Pontifical University, from where he obtained a bachelor's degree. His reading exposed him to liberal European ideas and likely fueled his desire for revolutionary change. In 1797, he was ordained as a priest.

Morelos continued to live in poverty with his mother and sister in Valladolid. At this time, Spain ruled Mexico and political power was held first and foremost by persons born in the mother country and secondly by Creoles, those born in Mexico of Spanish parents. Mestizos—persons of mixed blood, such as Morelos—counted little and generally suffered economic oppression. Change, however, approached: Spain's power in Europe had weakened considerably, and the Spanish Empire neared collapse.

From 1796 to 1798, Morelos taught school in Uruapan and then was assigned to the parish at Carácuaro. He was working there in 1810 when the first phase in Mexico's war for independence erupted, led by Father Miguel Hidalgo. He seemed to represent Mexico's impoverished, and they supported him; yet some wealthy Creoles also backed him, and it was never quite certain what he sought beyond Mexican independence.

Hidalgo had been the rector at Colegio de San Nicolás when Morelos studied there, but they likely had little contact. On the other hand, some correspondence probably occurred between the two men as early as 1808, when Hidalgo first evolved his revolutionary plan, and he quickly made Morelos his chief lieutenant in the revolt. Hidalgo ordered Morelos to organize an army and capture Acapulco.

Meanwhile, in 1810 and 1811, Hidalgo's forces scored victories in central Mexico and the revolutionary likely could have captured Mexico City, but he inexplicably retreated, a fateful decision that led to his capture and execution. Morelos then assumed the revolutionary leadership in 1811 and continued his attacks in the south. His army grew larger and larger—a determined force of Indians, mestizos, and blacks. In the summer, he captured Chichihualco and in the fall defeated the Royalist forces at Izúcar and captured Tenancingo. In the spring of 1812, he repulsed the Royalist forces that had laid siege to Cuauhtla.

Morelos developed a reputation for instilling discipline in his men, and his passion and heroism earned him tremendous loyalty. Historians debate the extent of his military acumen, but with 8,000 men he effectively fought an enemy whose army exceeded 80,000, and at one point he controlled a vast area from the Isthmus of Tehuantepec in the east to Valladolid in the west (the states of Oaxaca, Valladolid, and part of Guadalajara). In January 1813, he attacked Acapulco and captured it after a long battle. Unfortunately for Morelos, the prolonged engagement allowed Royalist forces elsewhere to regroup.

In August 1813, Morelos and his revolutionaries assembled a congress at Chilpancingo. Here they proclaimed Mexico's independence and displayed their radical program. The revolutionaries intended to end slavery, abolish castes and special privileges, and establish a republican government (with a strong executive). A constitution written in 1814 gave substantial power to the masses. Morelos's own commitment to help the impoverished was evident in his instructions that the wealth of Spanish landowners and mine owners be redistributed to the poor.

Despite his widespread appeal, in 1814 Morelos suffered a defeat that ended his revolution. At Tezmalaca the Royalist forces, which included Colonel AUGUSTÍN DE ITURBIDE, defeated and captured him. The Spaniards imprisoned Morelos in Mexico City, defrocked him, and on 22 December 1815 executed him by firing squad. Although independence did not come from

Morelos's effort, he had contributed to the turmoil that resulted in nationhood a few years later (indeed, Mexicans consider 1810 their independence year), and more importantly, he laid out the radical program that infused later reformers such as BENITO JUÁREZ in the mid-1800s, and the Mexican Revolution of 1910 under FRANCISCO MADERO and EMILIANO ZAPATA, with its second stage in the 1930s under LÁZARO CÁRDENAS.

References: Magner, James A., *Men of Mexico*, 1942; Timmons, Wilbert H., *Morelos: Priest, Soldier, Statesman of Mexico*, 1970.

Moreno, Mariano
(1778–1811)
Argentina

One observer called Mariano Moreno "the soul of the revolution." Moreno's tenure as Argentine leader was short, but his proposals were radical as he sought not only independence but also social change.

Mariano Moreno was born on 23 September 1778 in Buenos Aires. His homeland, then under Spanish rule, had just been reorganized into a new political unit, called the Viceroyalty of the Río de la Plata. It encompassed present-day Argentina, Uruguay, Paraguay, and part of Bolivia. Mariano's father, who came from a noble family, and his mother, the daughter of a government official, had emigrated from Spain. His father served in several official positions with the viceregal government.

In 1790, Mariano entered Colegio de San Carlos, a secondary school in Buenos Aires. There he avidly read Enlightenment literature and admired Rousseau. While at first he lacked the funds to continue his education, he eventually obtained help from a wealthy priest and in 1799 went on to college, attending the university at Chuquisaca in Upper Peru. As a student, he identified with the Creoles—persons of Spanish blood born in America—and with the poor Indians. He wrote a thesis detailing the oppression of the Indians, and he came to consider the Creoles as suffering from economic hardship under Spain. He began advocating freedom of expression and freedom of trade—political and economic rights linked.

"I go, but the tail which I leave is very long."

In 1809, Moreno, known for his fiery personality, issued his "Landowners' Petition" in which he argued the end to commercial restrictions. The viceroy reacted by granting concessions. Later that year, after Napoleon had invaded Spain and overthrown the monarchy, Moreno emerged as a leading proponent of greater autonomy, although still unwilling to break with the deposed king. He and other radicals began meeting at the Café de Marcos, where they discussed republican ideas. As the turmoil amid Napoleon's victory continued, the Buenos Aires city council, or *cabildo*, held public meetings in May 1810, which led to the May Revolution. A junta replaced the Spanish viceroy, although it moved cautiously, still professing loyalty to the king and refusing to announce complete independence.

The revolutionary leaders named Moreno secretary for government and war, and he immediately exerted an important influence. He ordered military campaigns, led by MANUEL BELGRANO, to put down rebellions and extend the revolution into the provinces. He also deterred threats from Peru, convinced the British to lift their blockade of Buenos Aires, and supported the execution of several antirevolutionary conspirators in Córdoba.

In October 1810, while possessing near dictatorial power, he issued a manifesto in which he declared for popular sovereignty. By the next month, he was supporting complete independence. Yet conservatives criticized his radicalism and claimed he had become too dominant. In December, Moreno issued decrees weakening the standing of the Spanish-born elite, and this increased the opposition. On 18 December, the provincial deputies met and voted to dilute Moreno's power. He then resigned and undertook a diplomatic mission to London. He left Argentina on 24 January 1811 and died aboard ship on 8 March. Meanwhile, the junta fell to a triumvirate dominated by BERNARDINO RIVADAVIA. Complete independence was achieved several years later under JOSÉ DE SAN MARTÍN.

Reference: Bagú, Sergio, *Mariano Moreno*, 1939.

Mugabe, Robert
(b. 1924)
Zimbabwe

Where others in Zimbabwe's African community compromised, Robert Mugabe did not. He firmly believed white minority rule should be torn down and a black-led socialist polity erected in its stead.

Robert Mugabe came from Kutama, born the son of a village carpenter on 21 February 1924. Like many young Africans during colonial rule, he obtained an education at Roman Catholic mission schools, first at Kutama and then at Empenden. At this time, the British ruled Zimbabwe, then called the colony of Southern Rhodesia.

"Genuine independence can only come out the barrel of a gun."

Mugabe became a teacher, beginning at the Kutama mission in 1942, and then, a year later, at the Dadaya mission. Then, in 1950, Mugabe left Southern Rhodesia to gain a higher education at the University of Fort Hare in South Africa. This brought him into contact with African nationalists and radicals who had congregated there, and his interest in politics developed.

He returned to Southern Rhodesia in 1952 and again entered teaching, this time at the Drifontein mission school in Umvuma. Other teaching positions followed, including one at the Chipembe Teacher Training College; then from 1956 until 1960, Mugabe lived in Ghana, where he taught at the St. Mary Teacher Training College, got married, and absorbed the political ideas of Ghanaian president KWAME NKRUMAH, who advocated mass organizations to advance black nationalism and a socialist state to bring economic fairness. Mugabe became firmly committed to an independent homeland free of white oppression.

During these developments, back in 1955, several educated young blacks formed the City Youth League in Salisbury that praised nationalism and criticized what it called "black stooges." Its members formed the Southern Rhodesia National Congress in 1957 and chose JOSHUA NKOMO as their president. Whites reacted by rejecting any substantial participation by blacks in the political system.

In 1961, Mugabe entered the nationalist fight when he worked as information minister for Nkomo's National Democratic Party (NDP), which wanted an end to white supremacy and a democratic polity to be accomplished through civil disobedience and a propaganda campaign. He initiated a new course when he convinced the NDP to recruit uneducated rural residents for the nationalist effort. Later that year, he played another influential role that displayed his hardening stance: He convinced an NDP congress to reject a new constitution that would have given blacks 15 of 65 seats in the legislature while reserving the remainder for whites, who comprised one-twentieth of Southern Rhodesia's population.

After this development, and as black protests continued, the British banned the NDP. Mugabe then became acting secretary-general of the Zimbabwe African People's Union (ZAPU), which Nkomo founded. It soon met the NDP fate when the government banned it in 1962. Colonial officials arrested Mugabe in September, released him in December, and then, when he made a fiery speech, arrested him again. Mugabe, however, escaped and fled to Tanzania. In 1962, the Rhodesian Front won decisively in that year's elections and demanded that Southern Rhodesia be granted its independence under a white government. Britain, however, refused, saying additional political power should be granted to blacks. The Rhodesian Front subsequently declared an independent nation of Rhodesia under white rule.

Mugabe reacted to white intransigence by calling for radical action. When Nkomo refused, Mugabe and Ndabaningi Sithole broke with him and formed the Zimbabwe African National Union (ZANU). Mugabe served as secretary-general, second in command to Sithole, and called for a one-man, one-vote society and immediate change through armed struggle. He returned to Rhodesia in 1962, but two years later the government arrested him. He spent ten years either in jail or under restricted movement. During this time, he adopted Marxism and vowed a socialist future for his homeland. He also earned a law degree through correspondence school and degrees in administration and economics.

Meanwhile, differences developed between Mugabe and Sithole, whom Mugabe accused of being too soft on the white regime. In 1975, Mugabe organized a guerrilla force in Mozambique, called the Zimbabwe African National Liberation Army, and directed several guerrilla raids into Rhodesia. In October 1976, Mugabe met with Nkomo and formed an alliance for upcoming negotiations, called the Patriotic Front. With this, Mugabe usurped Sithole as ZANU leader. The negotiations did not conclude until 1979, but British-supervised elections the following year led to a sweeping ZANU victory, and Mugabe became prime minister of Zimbabwe.

He then initiated a moderate course for his new nation. He formed an alliance with ZAPU, bringing Nkomo into his cabinet, and permitted whites a substantial role in the House of Assembly. He undertook programs to increase wages among blacks and improve social services.

Nevertheless, Zimbabwe suffered from a worsening economy and intensifying ethnic conflict. Mugabe forced Nkomo from the cabinet in 1982 and embarked on creating a one-party socialist state. In 1984, his party, its name changed to the Zimbabwe African National Union–Popular Front, chose him as its leader and developed a new structure whereby a Central Committee and Politburo under Mugabe's control ruled both the party and the nation. In 1987, he merged his party with Nkomo's, effectively establishing one-party rule, and the constitution was changed to create a presidency. On 31 December 1987, Mugabe became Zimbabwe's first president (while maintaining control over the party), a position he continues to hold. He has, however, abandoned his Marxist ideas while being challenged by those who want a free-market economy.

References: Barber, James, *Rhodesia: The Road to Rebellion*, 1967; Nelson, Harold D., ed., *Zimbabwe: A Country Study*, 1983; Smith, David, and Colin Simpson, *Mugabe*, 1981.

Nabiyev, Rakhman
(1930–1992)
Tajikistan

Rakhman Nabiyev had no desire to end communism and little enthusiasm for the breakup of the Soviet Union. Yet for several months he led Tajikistan in its move toward nationhood, a process so tumultuous that the country lacks any prominent founder.

On 5 October 1930, Rakhman Nabiyev was born in the Tajik capital, Dushanbe. The previous year, authorities in the Soviet Union had separated the area from Uzbekistan and proclaimed it the Tajik Soviet Socialist Republic. This was done to provide the Tajiks with a greater sense of ethnic distinctiveness, part of the Soviet policy toward the Turkic peoples of divide and conquer.

During Nabiyev's childhood, the Soviets established an authoritarian Communist state that built the republic along lines deemed desirable by Moscow. The Communists developed cotton agriculture at a ruinous rate, destroying both water tables and land fertility. They invested little money in Tajikistan, leaving its infrastructure poor.

Nabiyev, however, grew up a loyal Communist. He obtained a degree from the Tashkent Institute of Irrigation and Agricultural Mechanization and from 1954 to 1958 worked there as an engineer. In 1960, he joined the Tajik Communist Party and entered government service as head of the agriculture department. From 1961 until 1971, he served on the party's Central Committee and in 1973 became minister of foreign affairs for the republic, a position he held until 1983. That year, Nabiyev emerged as overall leader of the Tajik Republic when he became the Communist Party's first secretary.

In 1985, however, MIKHAIL GORBACHEV, president of the Soviet Union, dismissed Nabiyev amid charges of corruption. Nabiyev's primary political opponent, Kakahar Makhkamov, became first secretary. He guardedly supported Gorbachev's reform program while maintaining a totalitarian system in Tajik. When, in 1990, economic problems and ethnic tensions led to an uprising in Dushanbe, Makhkamov called in Soviet troops whose violent crackdown helped ignite a nationalist revolt. Rastokhez, or "Renewal," emerged as a popular front that sought to reform communism and gain autonomy.

Makhkamov erred again in August 1991 when he supported an attempted coup against the Soviet government launched by Communist hardliners in Moscow. After the rebels failed, Makhkamov found himself in a difficult position. Demonstrators demanded his resignation, and on 31 August the Tajik Supreme Soviet, or legislature, obtained it. The Supreme Soviet then declared the republic independent, calling it Tajikistan, and scheduled an election for the presidency.

Nabiyev entered the contest and finished with 58 percent of the vote, although reform opponents charged fraud. In fact, many of them supported Davlat Khudonazarov, who endorsed democracy. Nabiyev won under the Tajik Socialist Party label, little more than a renaming of the Communist Party, and committed himself to moderate change. After Islamic protestors took members of the Majlis (parliament) hostage, he tried to forestall additional civil unrest and co-opt the nationalist groups by naming to his administration leaders from the reform organizations. In his "government of national reconciliation," he assigned a third of the ministerial positions to such persons. His actions, however, pleased few: Reformers remained dissatisfied and conservatives felt he had gone too far.

In May 1992, civil war erupted between pro- and anti-Nabiyev forces in southern Tajikistan. On 1 September, the anti-Nabiyev militia seized the Majlis, and six days later they captured Nabiyev. He appeared on television and at gunpoint announced his resignation. After his captors released him, he tried to regain power. In October, his army captured Dushanbe but was soon forced back, and in November he announced his retirement from politics. In 1992, he died in Dushanbe from natural causes while Tajikistan remained gripped by turmoil and war as reformers and Communists battled, caught in a web of ethnic and religious differences. Nabiyev's successor as Tajikistan's leader, Emomali Rakhmonov, steadfastly refused

> *"It was . . . a coup. I had no choice but to sign the resignation statement. . . . If I hadn't, dozens would have died."*

any agreement with Islamic extremists and requested military assistance from the confederation of former Soviet republics, the Commonwealth of Independent States. He was succeeded in 1993 by Abdujhalil Samadov. The nation continues on an uncertain course, with both the press and political parties restricted.

Reference: Fierman, William, ed., *Soviet Central Asia: The Failed Transformation*, 1991.

Nakamura, Kuniwo
(b. 1943)
Palau

Kuniwo Nakamura became president of Palau amid a deep controversy: the continuing efforts of the United States to get his homeland to abandon its nuclear-free status.

Kuniwo Nakamura was born on 24 November 1943 in Peleliu State at a time when, during World War II, Japan controlled Palau, an island chain within Micronesia. The United States captured the main island of Babeldaob in 1944, and after the war administered Palau as part of the Trust Territory of the Pacific Islands under United Nations auspices. Over the years, the American presence exerted a tremendous influence on Palau.

After attending Peleliu Elementary School and Palau Intermediate School, young Nakamura journeyed to Guam in the early 1960s, where he enrolled in Tumon High School. After graduation, he attended the University of Hawaii and in 1967 obtained his bachelor's degree in economics and business administration. He then taught at Palau High School and worked as an economic advisor to the Trust Territory.

By the 1970s, Palauans desired change in their relationship with the United States to obtain more autonomy. Nakamura supported this drive, while also recognizing the important economic links between Palau and the Americans. From 1975 to 1978, he served as a member of the House of Representatives in the Congress of Micronesia. He then served in the Palau legislature and at the same time, in 1978, represented Koror State at the Palau constitutional convention. As floor leader, he helped shape the document that gave Palau self-government within the trusteeship. The constitution included a bill of rights and also protection of traditional culture. Most importantly, and perhaps most radically, the constitution established Palau as a nuclear-free zone—the only such provision in the world. The article conflicted with American desires to use the islands as a transport point for naval vessels that might carry nuclear weapons and perhaps as a storage area for nuclear materials. As a result, the United States placed pressure upon the Palauans to void the constitutional article and sign a compact of free association that would allow America to operate nuclear-capable and nuclear-propelled vessels while providing Palau economic assistance.

Palauans voted several times in the 1980s on referendums to overturn the constitutional article. Each time, the United States and its supporters in Palau lost the vote. This occurred in an atmosphere of distrust as assassins killed President HARUO REMELIIK in 1985, and three years later President Lazarus Salii committed suicide. Salii's death appeared mysterious, and some believed Remeliik was killed under orders from the U.S. government, since he seemed to oppose any change in the constitution (although he wavered on the issue).

In 1989, Nakamura became vice-president and chaired the commission on future Palau-U.S. relations, a body intended to ease tensions. In November 1993, Palauans finally agreed to the compact for free association, with the United States expressing assurances it would not use Palau as a military training ground.

Nakamura, who also served as minister of justice from 1990 to 1992, was elected president of Palau in 1993 and thus headed the new nation when it became completely independent on 1 October 1994. The United States provided Palau a 15-year, $500 million aid package which Nakamura promised he would use to stimulate a weak economy. The president operated his nation's major port

services firm, a position that provided him much knowledge of business practices, and observers believe he will focus on tourist development (including scuba diving adventures) to boost an economy reliant on tuna exports.

References: Aldridge, Bob, and Ched Myers, *Resisting the Serpent: Palau's Struggle for Self-Determination*, 1990; Robie, David, *Blood on Their Banner: Nationalist Struggles in the Pacific*, 1989.

Nasir, Ibrahim
(b. 1926)
Maldives

Ibrahim Nasir led his nation from an autocratic sultanate to a republican government.

Ibrahim Nasir was born on 2 September 1926 in Male, the main city and capital of Maldives. Not long after completing his schooling in Ceylon (today's Sri Lanka), he entered politics. In 1954, he became undersecretary of state to the minister of finance and to the minister of public safety. This occurred while his homeland was a protectorate under Britain, an arrangement that allowed considerable power for the sultans, who traditionally ruled the islands. Despite his attachment to the sultanate, Nasir worked to reform the government and introduce a more representative system. He may have been influenced in part by Maldives' brief experiment in 1953 with a republican government under Muhammad Amin Didi.

Nasir rose rapidly within the political structure: In 1956, he became minister of public safety, the following year was appointed minister of home affairs, and within weeks of that was chosen prime minster. In the latter capacity, he confronted a separatist movement in 1959 by the southern atolls. The rebels proclaimed the United Suvadivan Republic, but Nasir and the sultan crushed the uprising.

Maldives gained its complete independence on 26 July 1965, but the autocratic sultanate contin-

ued. In 1968, however, Nasir finally achieved his change in the political system, and a republic was proclaimed. The legislature elected him president, and he in turn appointed a prime minister. He won reelection in 1972 and shortly thereafter the British decided to abandon their military base on Gan, an island in the south. This move adversely affected the local economy, but Nasir rejected a request by the Soviet Union to establish a base there and announced that the island would not be leased to any superpower.

In 1975, the prime minister was arrested after his increasing influence threatened Nasir. Just three years later, though, Nasir retired from office for reasons unclear, although he claimed poor health. He later fled the country after his opponents accused him of corruption while president. The legislature confiscated his property and tried to get him extradited from Singapore, but failed. In 1980, the Maldives government defeated a coup attempt, one which it accused Nasir of planning. The former president denied the charge. A political system based on factional and personal alliances prevailes in Maldives.

Reference: Bunge, Frederica M., ed., *Indian Ocean: Five Island Countries*, 1983.

Nasser, Gamal Abdel
(1918–1970)
Egypt

When in 1954 Gamal Abdel Nasser wrote his 40-page pamphlet *The Philosophy of Revolution,* he told of expecting a revolutionary fervor led by the masses that would wipe clean years of British rule and slovenly habits. Instead, he found lingering British influences and a populace mired in tradition. Nasser realized that his overthrow of the British two years earlier had signaled only the beginning of a long reform process.

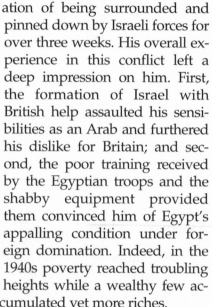

Gamal Abdel Nasser was born on 15 January 1918 in his parents' mud-brick house, typical of lower-middle-class dwellings in Alexandria. His father, Abdul Nasser Hussein, worked in the government bureaucracy as head of the local post office. Later he was transferred to al-Khatatibah, a poor village in the Egyptian delta. Gamal first attended school here before being sent to live with an uncle in Cairo.

At this time, Egypt, headed by a monarchy, was only nominally independent. The British army and government officials occupied the country and basically ran it. In 1934, Gamal led student protests at Al Nahda Al Misria, his school in Cairo, against British rule. This action displayed his already keen organizational abilities and strident nationalism.

Upon graduation, Nasser attended the Royal Military Academy where, once again, he openly condemned colonialism. After joining the Egyptian Third Rifle Brigade and becoming a platoon commander, his discontent showed when he complained of the incompetency of his senior officers and even led some junior officers in a protest.

He saw duty as a lieutenant in Alexandria and then served in the Sudan. Shortly after, he returned to the Royal Military Academy as a teacher. While in the Sudan, Nasser made friends with three other officers, and they began a secret organization called Free Officers. This group had as its goal a revolutionary overthrow of British rule and the Egyptian monarchy that supported it. Nasser so structured Free Officers that only he knew its full membership. Furthermore, he was able to keep the group's existence hidden from the British.

In 1948, the Egyptian army participated with other Arab armies in a war against the new nation of Israel. As an officer, Nasser suffered the humiliation of being surrounded and pinned down by Israeli forces for over three weeks. His overall experience in this conflict left a deep impression on him. First, the formation of Israel with British help assaulted his sensibilities as an Arab and furthered his dislike for Britain; and second, the poor training received by the Egyptian troops and the shabby equipment provided them convinced him of Egypt's appalling condition under foreign domination. Indeed, in the 1940s poverty reached troubling heights while a wealthy few accumulated yet more riches.

For the next four years Nasser carefully planned his overthrow of Egypt's existing government. Members of the Free Officers—perhaps numbering 700—infiltrated the government and worked against King Farouk. They soon gained hold of the military high command, and on 23 July 1952 a coup occurred. Nasser's Revolutionary Council grabbed control of the nation. Nasser, however, did not publicly emerge as Egypt's leader—because he and other members of the Free Officers believed that their youth and inexperience would be rejected by the Egyptian people, he selected Major General Mohammad Naguib, a respected war hero, as head of state, and made himself deputy prime minister. In 1954, however, Nasser deposed Naguib—whom he suspected of plotting against him—and became prime minister. (By this time, as a part of the upheaval, the monarchy had been ended.)

In *The Philosophy of Revolution*, Nasser wrote that his country faced the challenge of undergoing two revolutions at the same time: a political one and a social one. This complicated process shaped Nasser's rule; so too did his experience from the

Free Officers that included a paucity of revolutionary and reform ideology and a heavy reliance on secretive planning. Hence, his governance often lacked consistent direction, and his policies were issued with little public discussion. He met political opposition with repression, particularly when it came from Muslim groups and communists. Early in 1953, his government dissolved all opposing political parties, and only the Liberation Rally, a group supportive of Nasser, could function legally. Nasser filled scores of government positions with military officers he felt he could trust and imprisoned large numbers of trade unionists, intellectuals, and students who criticized him.

Nasser's initial foreign-policy accomplishments won him the adoration of many Egyptians, for he seemed finally to have restored the dignity of his nation. In 1954, he reached an agreement with Britain for the removal of British forces two years later, thus ending foreign occupation. He voiced support for the Algerian revolution against France, signed a major Czech-Russian arms deal in 1955, and, the next year, nationalized the Suez Canal. This last move provoked retaliation from the British, who conspired with France and Israel to attack Egypt. The Israelis marched into the Sinai Peninsula, and the Egyptian air force was destroyed. Yet diplomatic pressure brought the invaders' withdrawal and victory for Nasser in successfully portraying his enemies as aggressors grasping for imperialistic power.

Nasser considered himself the leader of the Pan-Arabic movement and sought to place Egypt in the forefront of advancing Arab unity. He viewed Egypt as the epicenter of three great circles enclosing Arabs, Muslims, and Africans, and envisioned the day of leading all Arabs and Muslims. Toward this end, he signed a pact in 1958 that brought Syria and Egypt together as the United Arab Republic (later the union briefly included Yemen). In 1961, though, the UAR collapsed when Syria withdrew, primarily because of economic policies that angered Syrian interests and Nasser's attempt to dominate the union.

Within Egypt Nasser remained a popular hero, buoyed by the widespread approval of his domestic policies. He tried to help the poor in his country, and early in his regime had broken the power of the landed oligarchy with a land reform law. While this law recognized the right to private property, it limited the size of landholdings to 208 acres (later modified downward). Also, Nasser's government constructed the Aswan High Dam, completed in 1968 with the help of the Soviet Union. The dam aided agriculture through irrigation and generated hydroelectric power for industry.

Under Nasser, industry became the fastest growing part of the Egyptian economy (while agricultural production increased a significant 2 percent per year). Yet Egypt had its problems with his emphasis on state-owned businesses. In 1961, he nationalized banks, insurance companies, and other firms, and companies handling light industry had to turn over 50 percent of their capital to the government. Industrial growth, however, did not reach the levels envisioned by Nasser, the peasants received few economic benefits, and by 1967 the economy hit bottom as the nation's hard currency reserves nearly evaporated. Despite his mixed economic performance, the Egyptian masses largely supported Nasser as their friend, partly because he promoted the peoples' interests.

Nasser's penchant for secrecy and absolute rule grew. He distrusted those around him and interfered in their work, actions that caused friction between himself and his colleagues. Nasser and his associates picked the candidates for public office, and he sent his political enemies to prison. All of this intimidated many officials and produced a closed political system.

Partly because of domestic pressures, Nasser challenged Israel in 1967 when he ordered United Nations troops removed from the Gaza Strip and Sharm ash-Shaykh, where they had been placed after the 1955 conflict. He also announced the closing of the Gulf of Aquaba to Israeli shipping. In the process, he worked the Egyptian people into a frenzy of anti-Israeli vehemence and instilled in them the belief that war with Israel would not only result in a quick military victory for Egypt but also a full restoration of the nation's position as leader of the Arab world. At the same time, Israel looked favorably toward a decisive showdown with Egypt.

The ensuing 1967 war proved a disaster for the Egyptians. Within six days of battle the Israelis destroyed Egypt's air force and routed the army. Poor planning, inept leadership, and overconfidence had doomed the Egyptians. Nasser accepted full responsibility for the fiasco of the Six Days War and on 9 June resigned as premier. But at that point massive street demonstrations broke out as the Egyptian people pleaded with their leader to remain in office. Crowds shouted "Nasser do not leave us, we need you!" and he responded by resuming his rule. The event amounted to an incredible political recovery, and from the flames of disaster Nasser emerged an even greater hero.

Now that Israel had military superiority over Egypt and had gained Egyptian lands (the Gaza Strip and Sinai Peninsula), Nasser turned to the Soviet Union for help. The Soviets replaced all of his destroyed military hardware and even placed surface-to-air missiles along the Suez Canal.

Nasser unexpectedly took a new course in 1970 when he advocated improved relations with the United States—broken since the Six Days War—and accepted a plan initiated by Washington that would begin peace talks with Israel. By then, however, the Egyptian leader had lost much of his health and suffered from the strains of office. Diabetes took its toll along with circulatory problems and a bad heart condition, and on 28 September 1970, while at his villa outside of Cairo, he died from a heart attack.

Nasser's revolution proved limited. He never held a clear ideology, and his goal of gaining independence and breaking the power of the landed elite oftentimes took contradictory turns. In fact, his reliance on conservative military officers for ad-

vice probably prevented a more radical socialist revolution. Furthermore, he left Egypt economically weak and beholden to the Soviet Union for assistance. Still, Nasser went well beyond the efforts of SAAD ZAGHLUL earlier in the century and expelled Egypt's British rulers, established a policy of nonalignment respecting the United States and the Soviet Union, redistributed landholdings, and nationalized important segments of the economy. Importantly, despite the Six Days War, he restored a substantial amount of Egyptian pride. His twin elements of nationalism and socialism as projected against the Western world made an enormous impression on other Arab nations, which subsequently emulated many of his policies. At his death, millions of Egyptians thronged to his funeral and wept as they considered, and still consider, Nasser a great hero in the struggle for Egyptian independence.

References: McDermott, Anthony, *Egypt from Nasser to Mubarak: A Flawed Revolution*, 1988; St. John, Robert, *The Boss*, 1961; Wheelock, Keith, *Nasser's New Egypt*, 1960.

Nazarbayev, Nursultan
(b. 1940)
Kazakhstan

Amid a collapsing Soviet Union, Nursultan Nazarbayev proved reluctant to push for Kazakhstan's independence. While his conservatism encouraged this stand, so too did his belief that his homeland needed more time to stabilize itself.

Nursultan Nazarbayev grew up in a land under Communist control, which was, since the 1930s, a republic in the Soviet Union. He was born in 1940 to a Kazakh shepherd. His

> *"Kazakhs were deprived of their native language, alienated from their own country."*

schooling included college, and in 1960, after working in a steel mill, he became an economist at the Karaaganda Metallurgical Combine. While there, in 1962 he joined the Communist Party. His political career began in 1969 when he began advancing in the party hierarchy. From 1973 to 1979, he served as second secretary in the Kazakh Communist Party and in 1984 won appointment as the republic's prime minister. Throughout, Nazarbayev proved a loyal party leader, firmly believing in authoritarian rule. Yet he also had concern for his homeland's economy and supported reforms.

In 1986, riots rocked Kazakhstan when the Soviet leader MIKHAIL GORBACHEV selected an ethnic Russian, Genadii Kolbin, as first secretary of the Kazakh Communist Party. This powerful position had previously been occupied by a Kazakh, and the switch to a Russian seemed to underscore the shabby political and economic treatment given Kazakhstan. The Russians crushed the riots, and some Kazakhs believed that Nazarbayev supported this reaction. Whatever the case, Gorbachev appointed him in 1989 to replace Kolbin as first secretary.

Meanwhile, nationalism spread, demonstrators chanted "Kazakhstan for the Kazakhs!," and groups appeared criticizing everything from cultural oppression to the environmental devastation forced on the republic by Soviet nuclear facilities and the overuse of the Aral Sea in irrigation projects. The Kazakh Communist Party joined in the call for cultural programs, such as bilingualism. At the same time, reform movements appeared in the Soviet Union, and Nazarbayev supported the general spirit of change.

Nazarbayev presented a peculiar mix: He resisted efforts to make Kazakhstan independent but promoted substantial economic reform and criticized government corruption. In April 1990, the Kazakhstan legislature elected Nazarbayev to the newly created office of president. After hard-line Communists failed in their attempt to overthrow the Soviet government in August 1991, Kazakhstan declared its independence. In the same month, Nazarbayev displayed his increasing commitment to change by quitting the Kazakh Communist Party and overseeing its dismantlement. In October, he formed a new party, the People's Congress of Kazakhstan.

At the end of the year, the Soviet Union collapsed, but ever-reluctant to see Kazakhstan venture on its own, Nazarbayev helped the Russians form a loose confederation of former Soviet republics, the Commonwealth of Independent States, which Kazakhstan joined. On the domestic front, Nazarbayev jailed several political opponents and refused to permit open elections. He relied for his support on many former Communists and kept the Soviet-era bureaucracy intact. Yet he appointed a market-oriented reformer as chief economist, pursued Western investments, and set in motion a plan to sell government-owned housing and businesses.

In 1993, Nazarbayev joined Russia and Uzbekistan in forming a single currency zone, and Kazakhstan agreed to sign the international nuclear nonproliferation treaty. Although cautious in his nationalism—a position resulting partly from Kazakhstan's ethnic diversity that made independence precarious—Nazarbayev continues to hold his homeland together and pursue reforms needed for economic growth.

References: Fierman, William, ed., *Soviet Central Asia: The Failed Transformation*, 1991; Nazarbayev, Nursultan, *Without Left or Right*, 1991; Olcott, Martha Brill, *The Kazakhs*, 1987.

Nehru, Jawaharlal

(1889–1964)

India

As an ardent supporter and follower of MOHAN-DAS KARAMCHAND GANDHI, Jawaharlal Nehru embraced the Indian nationalist movement. More political than Gandhi, he strove to build a democratic and socialist society for his countrymen.

Jawaharlal Nehru was born 14 November 1889 into a wealthy family at Allahabad. His father, Motilal Nehru, was a member of the top Brahmin caste and practiced law. He and Jawaharlal's mother, Swarup Rani Nehru, determined that Jawaharlal would become a lawyer. The young man obtained his initial schooling from a tutor and then in 1905 entered the exclusive Harrow school in England. In 1907, he entered Trinity College, Cambridge, and three years later graduated with honors. Jawaharlal then studied law at London's Inner Temple, and when he returned to India in 1912 he joined the High Court.

Attracted to politics, Nehru gravitated to the Indian National Congress. This organization had formed to gain concessions from the British who ruled India. In the early twentieth century, Indians were largely prevented from holding positions within the colonial government and were segregated racially from white Europeans, a discriminatory arrangement the British had followed for decades, ever since their rule began in the mid-eighteenth century, first under the British East India Company and then, beginning in the mid-nineteenth century, under direct Crown control. As a political party, Congress consisted of wealthy elites (primarily Indians but with a few Britons) who wanted home rule within the British Empire.

Near the end of World War I, Gandhi began reshaping Congress into a mass party, more activist and committed to principles of nonviolent protest. This attracted Nehru and stimulated his own political activism. He was always, however, more the internationalist and more the modernist than Gandhi, who focused on Indian self-reliance,

Hindu religious principles, and the glory of his homeland's ancient past.

Nehru traveled throughout India protesting British policies, such as the regressive salt tax, and defying restrictions that forbade him from entering certain areas. His activities landed him in prison for several months beginning late in 1921. Two years later, he became secretary of Congress, but in 1925 he began a 20-month stay in Switzerland, trying to help his wife regain her health. He resumed his position as secretary in 1927.

In 1929, Gandhi promoted Nehru for the Congress presidency. Nehru won the election, but in 1930 the British imprisoned him again for his continued protests. Upon his release the following year, he led Congress in developing a socialist political platform. Arrested again in 1932, he spent another two years in prison, reading Marx and Chinese philosophy. In the mid-1930s, he objected to British constitutional reforms as too limited and oppressive, and later in the decade he toured India in an extensive campaign to promote Congress legislative candidates, who were generally successful in the elections. By this time he had become extremely close to Gandhi, and many in India believed he would be Gandhi's successor.

When in 1939, without consulting any Indians, Britain declared India to be on its side in the war with Germany, Congress, angered by this snub, led a widespread protest. Nehru supported Gandhi's decision to seek Indian independence even amid the war. In the ensuing civil disobedience campaign of 1940, Nehru was arrested, but the British released him, Gandhi, and other Congress leaders in 1941. Nehru's continuing protests against British rule resulted in yet another arrest (Gandhi and other Congress leaders were arrested too), and he served a prison term from 1942 to 1945.

Upon his release, Nehru intensified his agitation, sometimes contributing to the increasingly violent nature of the protests. A change in the British government helped him and the other nationalists. The Labor Party, which came to power in 1945, announced its desire to grant India independence. Unlike Gandhi, Nehru accepted the plan to create two nations, a predominantly Hindu India and a predominantly Muslim Pakistan. Yet he did so reluctantly and considered this development merely an expedient to gain nationhood. He always believed that in time Pakistan would opt for reunification with India. When India became an independent nation in August 1947, Nehru became both prime minister and foreign minister.

Nehru strongly supported a democratic government. He toured his nation, educating people in the issues facing India and urging them to vote. He declared full respect for Parliament and an independent judiciary, built a strong following for Congress, and, through the party machinery, skillfully influenced legislation.

As prime minister, Nehru headed a nation facing enormous development problems, including capital shortages and a burgeoning population. His reforms encompassed expanding women's rights and reforming land ownership so as to reduce tenancy. He advocated what he called a "socialist pattern of society" to increase fairness and decrease the communist threat.

His mixed economic policy involved investing public funds in the infrastructure, such as roads and transportation facilities, and developing state dominance in heavy industries while encouraging private investments. He initiated several five-year plans to set economic goals and develop hydroelectric power. With much faith in technology, he promoted scientific research, which he believed would produce a more widespread and efficient use of natural resources. Under Nehru, industrial production rose about 7 percent per year from 1951 to 1965, an attractive performance. But agricultural production lagged behind the enormous population increase of 2.3 percent annually.

In foreign affairs, Nehru supported nonalignment amid the cold war. He obtained considerable foreign aid from both the Soviet Union and the United States. He tried to build peaceful relations with China, whose own internal reforms he often respected, and felt betrayed by the Chinese when, in 1962, they invaded India's northeastern border area. The Chinese eventually withdrew, but the Indian army's defeat revealed an embarrassing military weakness, and the Chinese intrusion shattered Nehru's faith in his plan for peaceful coexistence. In January 1964, Nehru suffered a stroke, and on 27 May he died. He left behind many books that he had authored, including *Toward Freedom*, published in 1941.

Nehru had overseen Indian independence and had led his nation through its crucial early political development. In the process, he laid the groundwork for the prime ministry of his daughter, INDIRA GANDHI.

References: Akbar, M. J., *Nehru: The Making of India*, 1989; Brecher, Michael, *Nehru: A Political Biography*, 1959; Dutt, Vishnu, *Gandhi, Nehru, and the Challenge*, 1979; Gopal, Sarvepalli, *Jawaharlal Nehru: An Anthology*, 1980; Singh, Akhileshwar, *Political Leadership: Jawaharlal Nehru*, 1986.

Neto, Agostinho
(1922–1979)
Angola

Agostinho Neto won the attention of his countrymen when he wrote a volume of poems focusing on indigenous Angolan culture. His subsequent fight for national independence entailed not only overcoming Portuguese domination but also surmounting a fractious Angolan society.

Agostinho Neto was born on 17 September 1922 in Icolo e Bengo. He attended high school in

Luanda and then became a secretary to the Methodist bishop residing in that city. In the 1940s, when Viriato da Cruz formed the Movement of Young Intellectuals, which promoted Angolan culture, and published poetry criticizing Portuguese rule and expressing Angolan nationalism, Neto became attracted to the cause. In 1948, he published his own volume of poems and shortly thereafter received a Methodist scholarship to study medicine in Portugal. While a student in the 1950s, he maintained his interest in politics, and Portugal's Salazar dictatorship imprisoned him several times for his political activities. He earned his medical degree in 1959 and then returned to Angola.

By now his homeland's political climate had become more heated and the nationalist movement more complex. In 1956, the Popular Movement for the Liberation of Angola (MPLA) had formed, headed by Mario de Andrade as president and Viriato da Cruz as secretary-general. The People of Northern Angola (UPNA) had also organized, tied to the traditional Kongo power structure and led by Manuel Nekaka, Eduardo Pinock, and Holden Roberto. One year later, it dropped "Northern" from its name and became the UPA. The MPLA had a leftist orientation, and the UPA criticized it as a "communist" group.

Portugal reacted to these organizations by arresting their members or forcing them into exile. As a political activist for the MPLA, Neto was arrested on 8 June 1960, expelled from Angola, and exiled to Portugal; this sparked a peasant demonstration in Catete during which Portuguese soldiers fired into a crowd, killing 30. Neto escaped his exile in 1962 and arrived at the MPLA headquarters at Leopoldville, where later that year he won election as the organization's president. Meanwhile, a protest at Malanje in 1961 included attacks on government facilities. Violence spread into other areas, resulting in hundreds of Europeans being killed. The Portuguese retaliated, and 40,000 Africans died. The uprising in Luanda on 4 February 1961, in which the MPLA had a role, is today celebrated as the beginning of Angola's fight for liberation.

In 1962, a serious rift occurred within the MPLA between Neto and Viriato da Cruz that resulted in the latter's expulsion. This dispute greatly damaged the standing of the MPLA within Angola and internationally. Yet Neto tightened his organization's structure, and in 1964 his meeting with Che Guevara, a leader of the Cuban Revolution, resulted

"The People's Republic of Angola will . . . gradually advance toward a people's democracy state . . ."

in Cuba extending aid to the MPLA. In 1965, Neto opened a new military front in eastern Angola, and both Zambia and Tanzania supported him. A more formal ideology emerged, declaring support for economic nationalization, democratic government, and a general Marxist-Leninist strategy.

Neto's opposition continued to evolve. In 1962, Holden Roberto changed the UPA to the National Front for the Liberation of Angola (FNLA), which he ruled autocratically. And another major group organized: the National Union for the Total Independence of Angola (UNITA), headed by Jonas Savimbi, who had broken with the FNLA.

On 25 April 1974, a revolution occurred in Portugal that, in June, resulted in the Portuguese government declaring its support for independence in Africa. At the same time, Neto announced his group's determination to continue fighting, irrespective of the upheaval in Portugal. Consequently, the MPLA, UNITA, and FNLA signed the Alvor agreement of 15 January 1975 providing for a provisional coalition government, but it did not hold together and fighting flared between the MPLA and FNLA. Neto's position vis-à-vis the other organizations became stronger when Cuba agreed to send troops to help him, although factional fighting characterized by personality clashes within the MPLA hampered Neto.

When independence came on 11 November 1975, the MPLA forces had firm control of central Angola, including the capital of Luanda, and Neto was proclaimed president. By January 1976, the presence of some 18,000 Cuban troops had greatly weakened both the FNLA and UNITA. Meanwhile, Neto faced enormous obstacles: an economy in tatters, an infrastructure weak and hobbled by destroyed bridges and roads, and continued guerrilla activity, primarily by UNITA. Neto promulgated a Marxist-Leninist policy and converted the MPLA into the MPLA-Party of Workers. He restricted the press and churches, directed state intervention in private companies, and collectivized agriculture while still permitting foreign investments, particularly in the petroleum industry, where Gulf Oil resumed production. Continued high unemployment contributed to a coup attempt in May 1977, which Neto turned back.

Neto announced an amnesty for political exiles in September 1978, but he also purged the MPLA of his critics (including many from the left who thought him too authoritarian or too moderate) and arrested protestors. He increased his presidential powers by abolishing the prime minister's office, reorganized the MPLA to provide a more ethnically diverse leadership, and cooperated more extensively with private companies in economic endeavors, thus softening his Marxist policy. These moves brought more stability to the MPLA. Yet UNITA continued its military attacks, backed by South Africa with United States support.

Neto died on 10 September 1979 in a Moscow hospital. José Eduardo dos Santos succeeded him as president and faced continuing hostilities with UNITA.

References: Henderson, Lawrence W., *Angola: Five Centuries of Conflict*, 1979; Somerville, Keith, *Angola: Politics, Economics, and Society*, 1986.

Ngawang Namgyel
(1594–1651)
Bhutan

Ngawang Namgyel used his heritage as a Buddhist abbot to unite several political entities into the country of Bhutan.

In 1594, Ngawang Namgyel was born into a princely family, the Gya, and became the eighteenth abbot of a prominent Buddhist monastery in Tibet, called Ralung. He eventually took the honorary title of Shabdrung, meaning "at whose feet one submits." His distinguished lineage included his great-great-grandfather, a founder of monasteries in Bhutan's Thimphu and Paro Valleys.

Buddhism had spread across Bhutan in the eighth century A.D., and monasteries appeared throughout the countryside. At the same time, migrations occurred from Tibet, and Bhutan became linked to that region's developments. When turmoil swept Tibet in the ninth century, Buddhism declined in Bhutan. But it revived in the eleventh century, and different schools or sects of Buddhist beliefs appeared, including the Drupka, the Shabdrung's school. Religion and politics fused together, and monks built fortified monasteries, or *dzongs*, from which they extended power over territories and struggled with one another for control.

It was from such a monastery that the Shabdrung expanded his authority. In 1616, he arrived in western Bhutan after fleeing Tibet, where the head of a province had challenged his authority. In 1619, he founded the monastery of Cheri and in 1629 founded Simtokha, a *dzong*.

In his new home, Shabdrung encountered opponents both foreign and domestic. Several times in the 1600s, Tibetan forces attacked Bhutan, and on two occasions, in 1645 and 1647, the Tibetans were assisted by the Mongol army. In each instance, the Shabdrung repelled them. Within Bhutan the five groups of llamas, or religious schools in alliance, opposed him. His victory over these made him the spiritual and political leader of Bhutan, which he called Drukyul, meaning "Land of the Thunder Dragon."

The Shabdrung united several leaders of powerful families and brought local lords under a centralized system. In the process, he built many *dzongs* in each valley, and these protected Bhutan from outside invaders. He established a theocratic political system, under which a monk or lay person elected by a monastic council headed the civil government. A state council, which was the major adiminstrative unit, included regional rulers (the kingdom had three regions), but the Shabdrung held ultimate civil and religious authority. He also established a legal code reflecting Buddhist religious law.

In 1651, the Shabdrung began a spiritual retreat at Punakha *dzong* and died while there. Yet his death was kept secret for over 50 years. In order to prevent Bhutan from splintering, the authorities announced that the Shabdrung was still in his retreat. (Extended retreats by rulers were not uncommon.) Officials were still appointed in the Shabdrung's name, and food was even left outside the locked door behind which the Shabdrung supposedly still lived.

Reference: Savada, Andrea Matles, ed., *Nepal and Bhutan: Country Studies*, 1993.

Niyazov, Saparmurad
(b. 1940)
Turkmenistan

When hard-line Communists staged a coup in 1991 to oust the reformist leader of the Soviet Union, Saparmurad Niyazov hedged his bets: He did not condemn the illegal rebellion until it failed. This move bespoke his conservatism as a reluctant nationalist and an even more reluctant reformer.

In 1940, Saparmurad Niyazov was born in Ashkhabad, the capital city of Turkmenistan. While still a child, he lost both his parents in a terrible earthquake. At that time, the Soviet Union controlled the area, which was officially a republic within the Communist nation. Niyazov, an ethnic Turkmen, obtained a degree in electrical engineering from the Leningrad Polytechnic Institute, in 1959 became an instructor with the Trade Union Organization of Mineral Prospecting in Turkmenistan, and in 1962 joined the Communist Party. Five years later, he became a foreman and then senior foreman of a shop in a heat and power plant. In 1970, he began working full time in the Communist Party.

From 1970 until 1979, Niyazov served as a deputy head within the Central Committee of the Turkmen Communist Party. He then became first secretary of the Ashkhabad City Committee within the party, a position he held until 1984. The following year, he became chairman of the Turkmen Council of Ministers, in effect making him the second most powerful man in the republic. Changes in the Soviet Union further advanced his career after the Soviet leader MIKHAIL GORBACHEV launched a re-

> *"I understand democracy to mean the will of the majority, not the promotion of discord."*

form program. In December, Gorbachev removed the longtime Turkmen party boss, Muhamednazar Gapurov, from power and replaced him with Niyazov who, although lacking a spectacular record in his oversight of Turkmen industries, had a competent background and supported change.

As a full member of the Central Committee of the Soviet Communist Party, Niyazov addressed the party congress in 1986 and requested aid to develop his homeland's economy. His commitment to political reform, however, was minimal as he rejected democracy and favored an authoritarian system. In 1990, he became chair of the Turkmen Supreme Soviet, or legislature, and called for his republic to obtain additional autonomy.

Turkmenistan, however, did not march toward independence—it stumbled, swept along by events in the Soviet Union. In August 1991, some Communists tried to topple Gorbachev. Not until their effort failed did Niyazov condemn the move. Then, as the government in Moscow lost its grip on the various republics, Turkmenistan declared its independence on 27 October, after a referendum controlled tightly by Niyazov approved the move. Under Niyazov's guidance, the Supreme Soviet arranged a quick presidential election. Niyazov, running unopposed, received 99 percent of the vote. He remained in the Turkmen Communist Party as first secretary, while the Soviet Union disintegrated in December.

Niyazov did not want the turmoil unfolding in the other former Central Asian Soviet republics to overtake Turkmenistan—thus, he decried the ethnic and religious warfare that had erupted elsewhere, and he worked to establish a strong rule. The limit to his political reform was evident in his refusal to dismantle the Turkmen Communist Party. He simply renamed it the Democratic Party and continued with the same structure. His belief in political pluralism extended only to his support for competing socialist parties. He harassed political opponents, frequently imprisoning them, and censored newspapers.

On the economic front, Niyazov supported only minimal privatization. The economy remained heavily under state control and limits were imposed on the amount of wealth a person could accrue. In January 1994, Niyazov won 99.99 percent of the vote in a referendum that extended his rule until the year 2002. He worked to avoid any reassertion of Russian control and to contain Islamic extremists. By 1994, he had developed a cult of personality, with numerous buildings, monuments, and streets named after him and a new currency displaying his likeness. He also courted foreign investments, the results of which remain uncertain.

Reference: Fierman, William, ed., *Soviet Central Asia: The Failed Transformation,* 1991.

Nkomo, Joshua
(b. 1917)
Zimbabwe

Of all the leaders in Zimbabwe's independence movement, Joshua Nkomo was perhaps the most popular. He also exerted a moderate restraint on a progressively radical struggle.

Joshua Nkomo was born on 19 June 1917 to a rural family. His father owned more than a thousand head of cattle, thus making him a substantial rancher as well a lay preacher. The Nkomos came from the Karanga tribe. By this time, Nkomo's homeland had come under British rule as the colony of Southern Rhodesia, and Africans had minimal economic opportunities, no real political authority, and no chance at social equality with whites.

Nkomo obtained his primary schooling in this environment, attending a white-run mission school. He worked as a carpenter and

truck driver to earn money for his schooling and received his diploma from Tjolotjo Government School in South Africa. He then enrolled in the Jan Hofmeyer School of Social Work and in 1945 returned to Southern Rhodesia, where he became the first black social welfare worker for Rhodesian Railways. He earned a bachelor's degree in social science at the University of South Africa through correspondence courses.

After World War II, blacks began protesting white domination in Southern Rhodesia, partly by forming unions and engaging in strikes. In 1951, Nkomo became general-secretary of the Rhodesian African Employees' Association, a major black organization. In this position, he increased the number of branches and members, and enhanced his political role. In 1952, he attended a conference in London and protested a proposal—one that later took effect—to separate Southern Rhodesia from Northern Rhodesia (these two colonies had been joined together in a federation) and allow continued white domination in his homeland. He subsequently was chosen president of the African National Congress (ANC), the colony's leading nationalist organization.

In the late 1950s, as ANC president, Nkomo fought against the Native Land Husbandry Act that forced Africans from their farms and into the cities, where they worked as cheap labor. In 1959, the government banned the ANC, and for two years Nkomo lived in exile. The next year, blacks formed the National Democratic Party to replace the ANC, and Nkomo was chosen its leader. He always hoped for a negotiated constitutional change to bring black rule, but as white intransigence hardened, he veered from his moderate stand to a more militant one. When, late in 1961, the government banned his party, he formed yet another one, the Zimbabwe African People's Union (ZAPU), which took its name from the African term for Rhodesia and thus sent a clear message to whites as to the independence blacks expected.

In 1962, Nkomo traveled to the United Nations and requested an investigation of conditions in Southern Rhodesia. As a result, the UN demanded constitutional changes, but Rhodesian officials reacted by banning the ZAPU and restricting Nkomo's movements. Then, in 1963, the ZAPU faced an internal crisis when radicals accused Nkomo of moving too slowly. This wing, led by Ndabaningi Sithole, expelled Nkomo and reorganized as the Zimbabwe African National Union (ZANU). Nkomo continued heading ZAPU. Two years later, white reactionaries, proclaiming no compromise with black nationalists, imprisoned Nkomo and other opposition leaders. Nkomo served ten years in confinement. In the meantime,

the white party declared the colony's independence in 1965, calling it Rhodesia and maintaining white supremacy.

But when African nationalists gained power in several surrounding colonies, South Africa pressured Rhodesia's leaders to compromise. In December 1974, the government announced discussions with the African National Council, the only black group that it recognized, and Nkomo and other nationalist leaders were released. He subsequently joined his followers within the Council to participate in the negotiations. These talks, however, failed, and Nkomo found himself at odds again with the radicals, particularly ROBERT MUGABE, who advocated an armed struggle. Mugabe had already begun guerrilla actions under ZANU and refused to end the fighting as a precursor to negotiations. Nkomo and ZAPU also participated in guerrilla activity, but on a smaller scale and, importantly, Nkomo offered to suspend fighting to begin negotiations.

In 1976, Nkomo joined Mugabe in an alliance to form a united front for future talks—the Patriotic Front. A new conference in London produced a settlement in 1979; in British-supervised elections the next year, Mugabe swept to victory and became prime minister of independent Zimbabwe. Mugabe formed a coalition with ZAPU, and Nkomo entered the government.

In 1982, Mugabe ejected Nkomo from the cabinet, a move that encouraged ethnic strife, since the two men came from different tribes. Then, in 1987, they agreed to merge their parties and heal the fighting. A constitutional change created a presidency and vice-presidency, and Nkomo served under Mugabe in the latter position. He continues today as Zimbabwe's vice-president.

References: Nelson, Harold D., ed., *Zimbabwe: A Country Study*, 1983; Mlambo, Eshmael E. M., *Rhodesia: The Struggle for a Birthright*, 1972; Nkomo, Joshua, *Nkomo, The Story of My Life*, 1984.

Nkrumah, Kwame
(1909–1972)
Ghana

When Ghana obtained independence in 1957, it continued on a course begun several years earlier by Kwame Nkrumah, one of the most strident and controversial African leaders. Nkrumah, called "the deliverer" by Ghanaians, advocated strong executive power in advancing his concept of African socialism.

Kwame Nkrumah was born on 21 September 1909 into the Nzima tribe. At that time, Ghana was under British rule and called the Gold Coast. Kwame's father worked as a goldsmith in Nkroful, a small village in the Western Province. Kwame went to mission schools for his elementary education and after high school matriculated at Prince of Wales College at Achimota, where he received training as a teacher. He graduated in 1930 and taught for several years while thinking seriously about becoming a priest.

In 1935, he traveled to the United States and studied at Lincoln University in Pennsylvania, where he majored in economics and sociology. He completed the program in 1939 and then received master's degrees from Lincoln and the University of Pennsylvania. While in college, he served aboard ships as a steward to earn money for his education; he also preached in black churches in Pennsylvania and New York.

Nkrumah studied revolutionaries such as Lenin, Gandhi, and Marcus Garvey, and became particularly impressed with the latter's Pan-African ideology. Nkrumah served on the faculty at Lincoln University, where he taught philosophy, black history, and Greek. Yet he exhibited much restlessness, an ambitious striving that in 1945 brought him to England to pursue a law degree. When this proved unsuccessful, he tried earning a doctorate in philosophy—but he abandoned that course, too.

Nkrumah's political interests deepened, and in England he served as general-secretary of the West African Secretariat (from 1945 to 1947), an organization committed to establishing a united Africa. He also served as secretary to the Pan-African Congress; edited the official publication of the West African Students' Union, an organization in which he served as vice-president; led "The Circle," a group experimenting in revolutionary activism; helped prepare a pamphlet distributed in the Gold Coast, entitled *New Africa;* and wrote *Towards Colonial Freedom,* which promoted an anticolonial struggle.

Nkrumah committed himself to exerting Africa's black identity, which had been subjugated by white Europeans, a process evident in his homeland where Britain governed the Gold Coast by dividing it into a "colony" along the littoral, and a "protectorate" inland. In the former, the residents possessed British citizenship; in the latter, they did not. There existed a Legislative Council composed mainly of senior colonial officials with a few elected Africans who had little power. The colonial governor exercised the most authority.

By the time Nkrumah reached adulthood, new political organizations had emerged. J. B. Danquah began the Gold Coast Youth Conference that criticized foreign exploitation, calling it "dangerous to the economic stability and permanence of the people of this country." Shortly thereafter, he formed the United Gold Coast Convention (UGCC), which advocated gaining self-government through constitutional procedures.

Nkrumah became general-secretary of the UGCC when he returned to the Gold Coast in 1947, but he disliked the largely conservative, elitist nature of the organization. In 1948, he founded the *Accra Evening News* to promote his radical ideology, and in 1949, breaking with the UGCC, he founded the Convention People's Party (CPP), which appealed to younger, poorer educated persons and that quickly gained a mass following.

Many strikes and even a few riots—mainly linked to harsh economic conditions—disrupted the Gold Coast in 1948. The British subsequently arrested and detained several leaders, including Nkrumah. In 1950, he promoted what he called "positive action," meaning nonviolent strikes and protests directed against British rule. Nkrumah's strategy brought the Gold Coast to an economic standstill and stirred crowds to chant "Self-government now!" After more rioting and violence, the British again arrested Nkrumah, along with other CPP leaders. This, however, merely created a "cult of martyrdom," as it was called, and in the 1951 general elections the CPP won 35 of 38 legislative seats, a landslide victory that meant it would direct the struggle for independence, now recognized as virtually certain to occur.

Released from jail so he could serve in the legislature, Nkrumah made sweeping promises that expanded support for the CPP. He pledged jobs for all, industrialization, free primary education, a national health service, and even free public transportation under a socialist state. He called for power to be given to the masses and for immediate self-government. On 5 March 1952 Nkrumah became prime minister, although much power remained with the British government and its colonial governor. Nkrumah promoted a review of the existing constitution and in July 1953 introduced his "Motion of Destiny" in the legislature, calling for the British to grant independence; it carried unanimously, and the following year Britain approved a constitutional change allowing the Gold Coast internal self-government but stopping short of complete independence.

Thus in the remarkably short time of three years since the CPP had come to power, Nkrumah had led his homeland to the brink of nationhood. This resulted partly from the nature of Gold Coast society, with its relative homogeneity and mature economic development. But it also resulted from the attributes that made Nkrumah a strong leader: his near total commitment to politics, his appeal to youth, his activation of women as a political force, and his knowledge of the Gold Coast's traditional authority structures and how to use them.

Yet in 1954, Nkrumah faced serious challenges to his power from emerging sectional, ethnic, and religious parties, particularly the National Liberation Movement (NLM), an Ashanti-based group. The NLM advocated more Ashanti power before nationhood, and it resorted to violence, which

"We had succeeded because we had talked with the people and by so doing knew their feelings and grievances."

caused Britain to hesitate in proceeding toward independence.

After a series of conferences, Nkrumah accepted the British recommendation of establishing regional assemblies alongside a central government, hence providing for some Ashanti autonomy. The NLM, however, rejected this proposal, whereupon Britain, to Nkrumah's chagrin, insisted on elections in 1956 to determine popular support for both the proposal and nationhood. The CPP won the vote handily, and the legislature again called for independence. In September 1956, Britain agreed, and on 6 March 1957 the Gold Coast became the nation of Ghana.

Nkrumah moved quickly to consolidate his power. He pushed constitutional changes that discontinued the regional assemblies and established a deportation act, allowing the exiling of those persons threatening public welfare. Thereafter, political opposition was increasingly risky. On 1 July 1960, Ghana became a republic under a new constitution, and in a rigged election, the enormously popular Nkrumah became president. The 1960 constitution consolidated his power over the legislature, the judiciary, and the CPP.

Nkrumah reorganized the CPP to establish his African socialism and a welfare state. After massive labor unrest and a general strike in 1961, he further harassed his remaining political opponents, frightening people into silence. His repression resulted in two assassination attempts against him, one in 1962, the other in 1964. After the first attempt, he allied with Marxist extremists, became more reclusive, and encouraged a personality cult labeled "Nkrumaism." After the second attempt, he officially made Ghana a one-party state through a plebiscite, with himself president for life. Despite his socialist policies and affinity for Marxism, the Soviet Union did not offer Nkrumah the support he desired, and in practice he actually cooperated with businessmen and remained economically dependent on Western nations.

Nkrumah stridently supported Pan-Africanism and pushed for a union with other nearby states to avoid what he feared would be the Balkanization of Africa. But the other African nations had just won their independence and wanted to preserve it; furthermore, Nkrumah's goals and procedures suffered from poor planning and nebulous ideas. Soon most African leaders began deriding his union plan. Only a few radical states, such as Tanzania, supported him, and in 1964 even this backing evaporated.

As Ghana's economy deteriorated with shortages of foodstuffs and other items, and as Nkrumah moved to break relations with Britain over the failure of the former colonial power to act forcefully against the white supremacist government in Rhodesia, Ghana's army launched a coup on 24 February 1966, while the president was in Beijing as part of a peace mission concerning Vietnam. Nkrumah subsequently lived in exile, residing in Guinea. While there, he continued to advocate black nationalism and claimed that an important link existed between Africa's revolutionary struggle and Marxism. He wrote books and articles describing oppression in Africa and advocating activation of the masses in a class struggle. While in a Bucharest hospital on 27 April 1972, Nkrumah died from cancer.

Although Nkrumah left Ghana with enormous debts totalling billions of dollars, he also left many improvments in his nation's infrastructure, a rich political literature, and a revolutionary consciousness. Furthermore, his legacy of black nationalism and black pride stirred sub-Saharan Africa toward new accomplishments.

References: Austin, Dennis, *Politics in Ghana: 1946–1960*, 1964; Nkrumah, Kwame, *Ghana*, 1957; Omari, T. Peter, *Kwame Nkrumah: The Anatomy of an African Dictatorship*, 1971.

Norodom Sihanouk, Samdech
(b. 1922)
Kampuchea

As Kampuchea's nationalist leader, Norodom Sihanouk was known for his erratic changes. At various points he abruptly abdicated his kingship, rejected American aid, and joined and then broke with his Communist supporters.

Norodom Sihanouk was born on 31 October 1922 in Phnom Penh, the son of Prince Norodom Suramarit and Princess Kossamak Nearirath. At that time, this land was called Cambodia and France controlled it. As a boy, Prince Sihanouk attended a day school in Phnom Penh, where he studied a French curriculum. For his secondary schooling he went to Lycée Chasseloup Laubat in Saigon and compiled a solid, although not exceptional record. He never obtained his diploma because his education was interrupted when the French decided he should become king. Another contender for the crown, Prince Monireth, could also have filled this role, but the French disliked his demands for reforms in the political system. Prince Sihanouk seemed more pliable and, indeed, he did not initially disappoint France.

On 26 April 1941 Prince Sihanouk became king. By this time, World War II had begun and Cambodia fell to Japanese control. Japan allowed the French administrators to remain and Sihanouk to be installed. The new king did little during the Japanese occupation, but when the French promoted an anti-Japanese uprising in March 1945, and as the defeat of Japan approached, the occupiers encouraged Sihanouk to declare Cambodia independent—and he did.

When the French returned in 1946, however, they rejected Sihanouk's declaration and reached an agreement with him whereby French officials regained control in exchange for a vague recognition of Cambodian desires for eventual independence. Many in Cambodia criticized the king, but Sihanouk wanted a gradual movement toward nationhood, one that would protect him from extremists, especially Communists, within Cambodia and avoid the turmoil then under way in Laos and Vietnam.

As the French suffered military defeats at the hands of the Communists in Vietnam, Sihanouk took the position that the Europeans could either offer him concessions or risk a Communist victory in Cambodia. At the 1954 Geneva conference, where France entered into negotiations to determine the political future of French Indochina (Cambodia, Laos, and Vietnam), it was agreed that Cambodia would gain its complete independence, effective near year's end.

Sihanouk's insistence that his homeland gain full autonomy boosted his popularity. Consequently, he founded the Sangkum Reastr Niyum (People's Socialist Community), a political party, but when he proposed constitutional changes in 1955 that would disfranchise large numbers of people in parliamentary elections, an outcry caused him to suddenly abdicate the throne on 2 March. His father then became king and he became prime minister. While some saw his abdication as a hasty act in a pique of anger, it was likely a coy move to enhance his power, for he now controlled the three pillars of Cambodia: the prime ministry, the socialist party, and the monarchy.

In fact, the national assembly became a mere shadow, meeting only occasionally; real policies emanated from the Sangkum Reastr Niyum, and, although it had opposition, under Sihanouk's leadership it swept Cambodian elections. When in 1960 Sihanouk's father died, the prime minister declared himself head of state, further consolidating his power.

Sihanouk took a neutralist stand in foreign policy, and after the North Vietnamese agreed not to back the Communists in Cambodia, he let them operate covertly from bases inside his nation, and these became launching points for attacks on American forces in South Vietnam. Later, when anti-Vietnamese feelings increased, he tried to get the intruders to abandon their bases, but failed.

With largely foreign help, Sihanouk made many improvements, including building an airport, constructing highways, hospitals, and schools, and developing a seaport called Sihanoukville. In 1963, he nationalized all banks and import-export businesses and abruptly terminated American economic assistance, complaining about capitalist exploiters and imperialist plots within the country, including an alleged plan by the Americans to assassinate him.

Sihanouk struggled to keep political radicals at bay and bring economic growth to Cambodia, and for 15 years he generally succeeded. But in 1970, General Lon Nol deposed him in a coup sponsored by the United States. The Americans were discontent with his neutral stand in the Vietnam War; and so the plotting he feared, and long suspected, turned out to be real. Unfortunately for Cambodia, the American action destabilized the nation for years to come.

After his overthrow, Sihanouk moved to Peking and worked to help the Khmer Rouge Communists in Cambodia. When they overthrew Lon Nol, Sihanouk returned home as head of state, but the Khmer Rouge distrusted him and arrested him in 1976. Under the rule of Pol Pot, the Khmer Rouge imprisoned many political opponents, and a reign of terror prevailed during which millions of people died. After Pol Pot fell in 1979, Sihanouk was released, and he became an outspoken critic of the Vietnamese invasion of Cambodia, which was then under way. He also broke with the Khmer Rouge, still in power under Heng Samrin, Pol Pot's successor. Samrin changed Cambodia's name to the People's Republic of Kampuchea and relied on Vietnamese troops to remain in power.

In 1982, Sihanouk headed a coalition government-in-exile consisting of Khmer Rouge elements at odds with Heng Samrin, an anti-Communist liberation front, and Sihanouk's own neutralist followers. International discussions to replace the Heng Samrin regime faltered, but in 1990 the United States, the Soviet Union, and China convinced the various factions involved in Cambodia to reach an agreement, and in 1992 a Supreme National Council headed by Sihanouk began ruling Kampuchea (officially the State of Kampuchea). A shaky cease-fire began, and elections were held in a political situation most observers considered unstable. A new constitution restored the monarchy and Sihanouk became king. Sihanouk thus continues his role of trying to balance Cambodia's polarized political factions, but the challenge remains great as discontent Khmer Rouge forces battle the government.

References: Chandler, David, *A History of Cambodia*, 1983; Hanna, Willard A., *Eight Nation Makers: Southeast Asia's Charismatic Statesmen*, 1964.

Nujoma, Sam
(b. 1929)
Namibia

In the complex and bloody fight that won Namibia its independence, Sam Nujoma served as an organizer of his people, the Ovambo, and a strong advocate of meeting South African violence with violence.

At the time of Sam Nujoma's birth, South Africa controlled Namibia, and discontent with this arrangement developed strongest in the north, near the Angolan border, among the Ovambo. Sam Nujoma hailed from this area, born into a poor peasant family in Ongandjera on 12 May 1929. As a youth, he tended his family's cattle and enrolled in night school, where he received a primary education. At age 16, he left school and became a dining-car steward and later worked in Windhoek, the capital city, as a janitor and messenger. By now, political change had emerged as Africans began organizing. In the early 1950s, the South West Africa Progressive Association united many nonwhites in the territory, and Ja Toivo, an Ovambo who had moved to Cape Town, founded the Ovambo People's Organization (or OPO, initially called the Congress) to attack the oppressive contract labor system.

Participating in this change, Nujoma first attempted to organize the railway workers, but for this he was fired and forced to work as a clerk in a store. Nujoma then helped Ja Toivo, holding meetings under the trees in the northern territory and recruiting workers in the factories and mines. In April 1959, Nujoma became the OPO leader and established several new OPO units.

Then, after the government announced a forced removal of many blacks from Windhoek to a different township, African discontent mounted and Nujoma addressed a mass rally. The government rejected the protest, however, and when several days later Africans began picketing, the police fired into a crowd, killing 11. The government ordered Nujoma's movements restricted, but he escaped into Tanzania. He then reorganized the OPO, forming and becoming president of the South West African People's Organization (SWAPO), which called for national unity and

"Let us open a new chapter based on love, peace, human rights, patriotism, respect for one another. . . ."

independence. Meanwhile, more refugees fled the territory and several exile groups organized in addition to SWAPO.

Under Nujoma, SWAPO made a balanced appeal during the cold war to both East and West and built widespread support in the United Nations. In 1961, he submitted a petition to the UN, but the world organization's ineffectiveness to do anything about South Africa's rule and violent behavior convinced Nujoma to pursue a radical course. In 1962, SWAPO began a military training wing; soon guerrillas infiltrated northern Namibia, and by 1966 the armed struggle had begun. Four years later, the UN called for South Africa's withdrawal from the occupied territory.

As SWAPO began its military attacks, Ja Toivo initially criticized the tactic but then agreed to help. After South African forces assaulted a guerrilla base in 1966, he was arrested, placed in solitary confinement, tortured, and sentenced to 20 years in prison. His endurance elevated him to heroic status among Africans. SWAPO continued to grow, sponsoring strikes and demonstrations, launching military attacks, gaining widespread ethnic support in Namibia, and in 1975, even winning UN recognition as the sole legitimate representative of the Namibian people. Nujoma, still in exile, orchestrated cooperative agreements with Angola, China, and the Soviet Union. He also attracted other exile organizations into the SWAPO structure. Then, in 1978, Nujoma and South Africa agreed to a cease-fire in the guerrilla war and to UN-sponsored elections. The plan collapsed, however, when South Africa refused to allow Walvis Bay, an important port area, to become part of an independent Namibia.

Meanwhile, Nujoma continued a leftward tilt and welcomed Cuban troops to help SWAPO. As the bloody conflict continued, so did negotiations. These foundered, however, over South African demands that all Cuban troops be withdrawn before any elections, a demand Nujoma refused. Nujoma found himself in a difficult position in the late 1980s as several African nations experienced economic difficulties and, since they were tied to South Africa's economy, pressured him into new negotiations. By now, neighboring Angola desired a resolution to the problem, and South African influence proved strong in Togo, Senegal, and elsewhere. Furthermore, the Soviet Union reduced its support for anticolonial rebellions.

In 1988, South Africa agreed to give up Namibia, and Nujoma agreed to withdraw the Cuban troops. Finally, in 1989, UN-supervised elections were scheduled and in September, after nearly 30 years in exile, Nujoma returned to Namibia to head SWAPO's campaign. SWAPO scored an overwhelming victory, and on 21 March 1990 Nujoma became his nation's first president.

Nujoma subsequently followed a moderate policy. He negotiated a new settlement with a British-American company to gain more money from his nation's diamond mines, gained sovereignty over Walvis Bay, and welcomed expansion by white-controlled businesses. In 1994, Nujoma led SWAPO to a landslide election victory and won a second term as president. He continues to express his commitment to attracting foreign investors.

References: Schoeman, Stanley, and Elna Schoeman, *Namibia*, 1985; Soggot, David, *Namibia: The Violent Heritage*, 1986.

Nyerere, Julius Kambarage
(b. 1922?)
Tanzania

In the mid-1950s, Julius Nyerere battled with his conscience and made a decision that influenced Tanzania's future: He gave up his teaching position and devoted himself to building a career in politics and an ideology able to guide his homeland. Across Tanzania's dusty roads he traveled in a battered Land Rover, developing a new political party and a mass following while spreading a message of nationalism and reform.

"I am a trouble maker because I believe in human rights strong enough to be one."

Tanzania stems from a merger of two formerly separate, and in certain ways quite different, colonial entities: Tanganyika on the African mainland and Zanzibar, with a substantial Arabic presence, immediately offshore in the Indian Ocean. After Germany's defeat in World War I, Britain, already in control of Zanzibar, gained most of German East Africa, which became a League of Nations mandate in 1922, and renamed it Tanganyika. As in Nigeria and other of its holdings, Britain established a policy of indirect rule that relied on cooperative tribal chiefs. Meanwhile, British authority over Zanzibar tightened.

By the 1930s, while Nyerere was still a child, a racially stratified economic system had emerged in Tanganyika. Europeans and Asian settlers (largely Indian) controlled the processing industries and retail trade while Africans engaged in small-scale commercial agriculture or subsistence activities. Tanganyika's commercial agricultural areas harbored the most discontent with European domination. Here, cooperative organizations of farmers formed and Tanganyikans became acquainted with modern organizational techniques.

Julius Kambarage Nyerere, born about 1922, came from the eastern shore of Lake Victoria and was one of 26 children of a Zanaki tribal chief who had several wives. Julius grew up herding sheep and had no contact with whites until age 12, when he entered a school at Musoma. At age 15, he began his secondary education, attending a Roman Catholic mission school at Tabora. From there, he pursued a career in teaching. In 1943, the same year he was baptized into the Catholic Church, he entered Makerere

College in Uganda, where he began the Tanganyika Students' Association and a branch of the Tanganyika African Association (TAA) that had been formed in Dar es Salaam, Tanganyika's main seaport, to unite Africans and protect their interests.

He earned his teaching diploma in 1945 and returned to Tanganyika, where he taught briefly at Tabora. In 1949, he began graduate work in economics and history at the University of Edinburgh in Scotland, received his M.A. in 1952, and subsequently taught at a Catholic secondary school near Dar es Salaam.

After World War II, the United Nations and Britain agreed to make Tanganyika a trust territory under British rule with stipulations that Britain further develop the area. Britain began building more schools and developing the production of foodstuffs, but modernization proceeded unevenly and raised expectations that produced tension. At the same time, Tanganyikans became more politically assertive, and in 1954 Nyerere formed the Tanganyika African National Union (TANU) as an outgrowth of the TAA. TANU demanded educational and labor reforms while challenging British authority. Britain appointed Nyerere to a temporary seat on the Tanganyika Legislative Council, from where he advocated making all Council seats elective.

The next year, he made his fateful decision to give up his teaching position and concentrate on promoting TANU and developing ideas for Tanganyika's future. Throughout the countryside and in the cities he gained recruits, some 250,000 by 1956. For Nyerere and Tanganyika as a whole, party development and nation building evolved more smoothly than in other African colonies because the country had a minimum of tribal rivalries and a uniform dialect, Swahili. While Nyerere eschewed violence, he called for independence, and in 1957 Britain banned his public speaking as inflammatory.

The following year, Britain allowed elections to the Legislative Council but restricted voting to only 60,000 people and reserved most seats for European and Asian representatives. Nyerere criticized this procedure but agreed to run candidates from the TANU. His party won overwhelmingly, although British officials had him tried and convicted for libel. As unrest threatened, Britain sent a new governor, who defused the situation by ordering elections in 1959 and by changing the rules to permit both an African voting majority and an African majority on the Legislative Council. Nyerere's TANU won this election and another one in 1960, resulting in his becoming chief minister and thus head of government under a new, liberalized constitution.

As Nyerere gained prominence in Tanganyika, changes were occurring in nearby Zanzibar. In 1954, Arabs, having decided independence would allow them to lead and dominate an African majority, had begun pushing for self-government, and in this maelstrom several political parties had formed. The Zanzibar Nationalist Party (ZNP) promoted a Marxist program while, in 1957, the Afro-Shirazi Union (ASU) was started by Shirazis, persons of mixed African and Persian blood. Two years later, another group of Shirazis from Zanzibar and nearby Pemba founded the Zanzibar and Pemba Peoples' Party (ZPPP). When Britain scheduled elections for 1961, the ZNP and ZPPP formed an alliance, winning a narrow margin in the legislature. Riots then broke out as dissatisfied Africans attacked Arabs, killing 65 of them.

That same year, Tanganyika gained independence ahead of Zanzibar when it became a nation within the British Commonwealth on 9 December 1961. Nyerere led his homeland as prime minister but then resigned unexpectedly in January 1962 amid rumors he had been forced out by party radicals. Nyerere, however, insisted he was leaving to develop a new direction for the TANU. After a constitutional change, elections later that year resulted in Nyerere winning the presidency, which had replaced the prime ministry.

Nyerere advocated democratic socialism, a program he outlined in his *Democracy and the Party System*, published in 1963. He insisted that a Western multiparty system would destroy Tanganyika because it would encourage confrontation. Thus he desired and established a one-party system in which open debate occurred within the party and policies developed from consensus. He also strived for a socialist economy based on moral foundations of equality and community.

As Nyerere governed Tanganyika, Zanzibar, still under British control, gained its independence on 10 December 1963 with a government formed by the ZNP-ZPPP alliance loyal to the sultan, the traditional Arab ruler of Zanzibar who had been allowed to continue his office under British supervision. Many Africans on Zanzibar considered this arrangement as independence for Arabs only. Hence, on 12 January 1964 a revolution broke out, and the sultan barely escaped to Britain. The movement, led by John Okello, resulted in 5,000 Arabs killed and the establishment of a Zanzibari Revolutionary Council.

Factional infighting quickly forced Okello's departure, and Abeid Karume, head of the Afro-Shirazi Party (ASP), a renamed ASU, became president. Instability continued, however, and Karume requested a meeting with Nyerere in Tanganyika. He thought an alliance with Tanganyika would provide political stability and economic support, particularly since Nyerere and the ASP both desired socialist development. In April 1964, the two leaders agreed to merge their countries, forming the United Republic of Tanganyika and Zanzibar. Late that year, it was renamed Tanzania. The arrangement maintained substantial autonomy for Zanzibar, including its own foreign policy, and tension between the two formerly separate nations became acute.

Nyerere withstood an attempted army coup in 1964, although he had to flee Dar es Salaam. Afterward, he arrested the army mutineers and leading critics of the TANU. In foreign affairs, when the British failed to end a white rebellion in Rhodesia that created an independent segregationist nation, he broke relations with his former colonial rulers. Nyerere also allowed exiled groups fighting against racist governments in Angola, Southwest Africa, and Rhodesia to use Dar es Salaam as a base.

When, in 1972, Tanzania's economy faltered and failed to develop egalitarianism, Nyerere issued the Arusha Declaration, which called for developing labor-intensive agriculture and nationalizing banks, insurance companies, agricultural processing firms, and export trade businesses. He also ordered peasants to live in villages and develop communal land practices. Problems ensued as poor government management badly damaged sisal production (a fibrous plant used in making rope) and, all in all, Arusha failed to stimulate the economy. But Nyerere's Arusha program did achieve success in reducing the concentration of wealth, enrolling more students in schools, and opening more health clinics.

Meanwhile, relations with Zanzibar underwent further change. Aboud Jumbe became president in 1972 after Karume was assassinated. Where Karume had distrusted Nyerere, Jumbe moved to develop close relations and agreed to a merger of the ASP with the TANU, forming Chama Cha Mapinduzi (CCM). They agreed that the president of Tanzania would also serve as chair of CCM. A constitutional change stipulated that the presidency and vice-presidency of Tanzania had to be shared by a mainlander and a Zanzibari. Jumbe subsequently served as vice-president under Nyerere.

In the 1980s, Nyerere supported economic privatization in some areas as Tanzania reeled from Arusha's failures, a severe drought, floods, and higher oil prices. Despite changes, Tanzania suffered from conflict and confusion between the TANU and the government bureaucracy, a burgeoning civil service grew burdensome, and living standards slid downward. Nyerere uncovered a plot to overthrow him in 1983, then launched a crusade against government corruption, encouraged increased private investment, and ordered state farms to operate commercially.

Nyerere supported a constitutional amendment in 1984 that separated the presidency from the CCM chairmanship. In 1985, he resigned as president while continuing as chairman. As leader of Tanzania, Nyerere infused African politics with a strong moral quality. He believed in no compromise with racist or cruel regimes, as evident in his fight against Idi Amin in Uganda, a war that brought Amin down but at a great financial cost to Tanzania (and suspicion from neighboring nations when Tanzanian troops remained in Uganda for several years after). He sincerely believed in democratic socialism, in fighting excessive concentrations of wealth, and in maintaining popular influence within a one-party system. His successes and failures never lacked an ideological commitment or a will to guide his nation toward a better future. Nyerere resigned as party chairman in August 1990 and retired from politics.

References: MacDonald, Alexander, *Tanzania: Young Nation in a Hurry*, 1966; Nyerere, Julius K., *Uhuru na Maendeleo (Freedom and Development)*, 1973; Nyerere, Julius K., *Uhuru na Umoja (Freedom and Unity)*, 1967; Yeager, Rodger, *Tanzania: An African Experiment*, 1989.

Obote, Milton

(b. 1926)

Uganda

Upon its emergence as a modern nation, Uganda, not unlike other African states, presented its founders with an enormous problem: sharp cleavages along sectional, religious, and ethnic lines. As prime minister and later president, Milton Obote tried surmounting this obstacle to national development.

Milton Obote was born in 1926 and grew up in northern Uganda, a member of an elite ruling family in Maruzi County. He attended Lira Protestant Mission School in Lango, Gully High School, Busoga College, and Makarere College in Kampala. He eventually obtained a degree through correspondence courses. As a northerner, Obote was cognizant of the power and influence of Buganda, a kingdom in southern Uganda. In fact, of the several kingdoms and districts that constituted Uganda under British rule, Buganda was the strongest.

Obote spent much of the 1950s in Kenya, where he associated with nationalist movements. In 1957, he returned to Uganda and joined the Uganda National Congress (UNC), formed in 1952 under Ignatius Musozi to promote greater Ugandan autonomy. The UNC had enormous difficulties building a national base; Gandans (persons from Buganda) dominated it, as did Protestants in a nation with a Catholic majority. Yet the UNC appealed successfully to northern interests, and Obote became leader of its Lango branch. Then, in 1958, he won election to the Legislative Council, part of the governing system for the Uganda Protectorate.

When the UNC split into two factions in 1959, Obote's group merged with the Uganda Peoples' Union, a Bantu-supported southern-based party that had a substantial following outside Buganda, and formed the Uganda Peoples' Congress (UPC). Obote became its leader. Another party, the Kebaka Yekka (KY), had its base in Buganda and reflected that kingdom's interests.

In 1960, Obote became part of the Uganda constitutional delegation that negotiated in London with the British government to end the protectorate and gain independence. Obote opposed all talk of Buganda exisiting as a separate nation, but agreed that it could maintain wide leeway in its procedures for electing delegates to a national legislature. In effect, the Uganda constitution, drafted in June 1962, created a federation of kingdoms in which Buganda had substantial local autonomy and a dominant influence.

Obote, who had become a strong voice for the northern districts opposed to Buganda's power, nevertheless linked his UPC with the KY in a strange union of disparate parties for the sole purpose of gaining political power. Unusual coalitions such as this became prominent features of Ugandan politics and generally did little to lessen separatist tendencies.

With independence scheduled for autumn 1962, the UPC-KY alliance won the national legislative elections and Obote became prime minister. Uganda became independent on 9 October 1962.

Obote operated from a position of weakness. The UPC had not developed an effective national organization, and the party had several strong local leaders who challenged the prime minister. Religious antagonisms between Catholics and Protestants continued, as did friction between Buganda and the other Ugandan states.

In 1964, Obote repulsed a coup with the help of British troops sent in from Kenya. Two years later, he acted to strengthen his hand by arresting several KY leaders, forcing through the legislature a new constitution that stripped Buganda of its special status, launching an attack on the Buganda palace—an attack that drove the kingdom's ruler into exile—and assuming far-reaching presidential powers. His rule depended on the support of Uganda's army; thus he gained a tenuous unity through force instead of coalition building and compromise. In 1967, a new constitution established a presidency, filled by Obote, that placed nearly all state and military power under presidential control.

Although Obote's political maneuvers helped shape an independent Uganda, he failed at creating a stable unified government. In relying on the army for support, he emboldened generals such as Idi Amin, who on 25 January 1971 led a coup that overthrew him. Amin began his own regime—one of the more ruthless in modern history, characterized by mass executions.

In the late 1970s, Obote encouraged a Tanzanian invasion of Uganda, and Amin's regime was toppled in 1980. Obote returned home and with the support of the military ran for president. He won the office in an election of dubious validity and subsequently closed the opposition press and harassed his critics. In 1985, an army coup deposed him.

References: Jorgensen, Jan Jelmert, *Uganda: A Modern History,* 1981; Karugire, Samwiri Rubaraza, *A Political History of Uganda,* 1980.

O'Connell, Daniel
(1775–1847)
Ireland

At a meeting of fellow Irishmen in 1846, Daniel O'Connell urged that his homeland's struggle for independence be peaceful. With that, radical Young Irelanders in the audience responded with a fiery retort, advocating violence against their British rulers, and stormed out of the meeting.

Daniel O'Connell, who was born into a wealthy Catholic family on 6 August 1775, attended Lincoln's Inn (London), where he studied law in the 1790s. By the early 1800s, he had become a successful lawyer in Dublin. Only gradually did he come to oppose British power in Ireland. He developed two goals: the emancipation of Ireland's Catholics through expanded political rights and the repeal of Britain's Act of Union that had forced Ireland into the United Kingdom.

O'Connell formed the Catholic Association in 1823 to advance emancipation and in 1828 won a seat in Parliament, where he voiced his demands. By 1829, the British leadership, having undergone a change and fearing violence by Irish dissidents, approved the Relief Act. With it, Catholics gained some political rights. O'Connell then moved ahead with his drive for Irish independence and formed the National Repeal Association that rallied poor tenant farmers behind promises of Irish freedom and tenant rights. He indicated to the British that failure to repeal the Act of Union would result in violent insurrection. Britain, however, did not react as it had toward emancipation; instead, it placed

"My struggle has begun, and I will terminate it only in death or repeal."

troops in Ireland and threatened severe reprisals against any uprising.

In 1831, the British arrested O'Connell for antigovernment activities, but he continued his political struggle from a new platform when, ten years later, he became Dublin's first Catholic Lord Mayor.

As O'Connell grew older he became more conservative, opposing all violence and rejecting government assistance programs for the poor.

Then the repeal movement underwent further changes. O'Connell's Association grew bigger, and he led demonstrations that attracted so many people they were called "monster rallies." To his dismay, however, the Association's new members included Young Irelanders—idealistic nationalists tired of old approaches and favoring violent protest.

When these Young Irelanders left the meeting at which O'Connell spoke in 1846, an important split occurred. O'Connell, growing old and exhausted by a recent three-month prison term, saw his leadership slip away. On 15 May 1847, he died in Genoa, Italy—triumphant in gaining Catholic emancipation but frustrated by his inability to obtain Irish independence. Nevertheless, he represented the nationalist fight that others also advanced, including MICHAEL COLLINS, EAMON DE VALERA, CHARLES STEWART PARNELL, and PATRICK PEARSE.

Reference: O'Faolain, Sean, *King of the Beggars: A Life of Daniel O'Connell, the Irish Liberator,* 1938.

O'Higgins, Bernardo
(1778–1842)
Chile

Bernardo O'Higgins joined JOSÉ DE SAN MARTÍN in traversing the high Andean mountains and launching an assault that ended Spanish rule in Chile. As the new country's leader, he antagonized powerful elites with his call for a more equitable society.

On 20 August 1778, Bernardo O'Higgins was born in Chillán, a small town in Chile, which was a Spanish colony and part of an administrative unit called the Viceroyalty of Peru. Bernardo's father, Ambrosio O'Higgins, had been born in Ireland and later achieved high office as viceroy of Peru. His mother, Isabel Riquelme, was the daughter of a wealthy Chilean landowner. Bernardo was an illegitimate child, and his father rejected him, leaving him to be raised by foster parents. Bernardo attended San Carlos College in Lima and was then sent to England. While there, he studied liberal reform and embraced the independence movement for Spanish America as advocated by FRANCISCO DE MIRANDA.

"I detest aristocracy, such is my nature; beloved equality is my idol."

O'Higgins returned to Chile in 1802, after his dying father reconciled with him and granted him an estate. Once back home, the ideas of Juan Martinez de Rozas influenced him. Rozas promoted Chilean independence and liberal reforms, including a federal political system. Events encouraged O'Higgins and other nationalists when in 1808 Napoleon overthrew Spain's monarchy, prompting colonials throughout Spanish America to organize their own governments distinct from Napoleon's rule, although still loyal to the deposed king. Such was the case in Chile in 1810. The more radical nationalists, however, soon took advantage of the situation and gained the upper hand. José Miguel Carrera, a young aristocrat, rejected any loyalty to Spain, and in 1811 he seized power as dictator.

Carrera's heavy-handed approach produced a rebellion by several leading families who backed O'Higgins. He organized his own army, but in October 1814 the Spanish defeated his men and those of Carrera at Rancagua. O'Higgins fled to Argentina, while the royalists reasserted their control in Chile. Their three-year rule produced enormous discontent and enflamed many Chileans. In 1817, San Martín assembled his army in Argentina and planned to defeat the Spanish in Chile, gain reinforcements, and march into Peru. In choosing his second-in-command, he bypassed Carrera and appointed O'Higgins. In February 1817, the two revolutionaries triumphed, with the army defeating the Spaniards at Chacabuco. Three days later, the Chileans named O'Higgins supreme director after San Martín refused the position. On 12 February 1818, Chile formally declared its independence.

As Chile's leader, O'Higgins supported the continued fight to evict Spain from South America. He formed a navy under a Briton, Lord Thomas Cochran, and it raided Spanish shipping along the Pacific coast. In 1820, he helped organize an expeditionary force, commanded by San Martín, that sailed north and invaded Peru. After some setbacks, San Martín's invasion, along with the efforts of the great South American liberator SIMÓN BOLÍVAR, led to Peru's independence.

On the domestic front, O'Higgins initiated numerous controversial reforms. Ruling by decree, he abolished all titles of nobility, weakened the patronage power held by the Catholic Church, enlarged the National Library, established primary schools, and recruited teachers from England. Additionally, he improved the roads and sanitation services. To pay for these changes, he increased taxes on the wealthy. O'Higgins also proposed reforms that would dilute the elite domination of landholdings. These measures, and in particular the last proposal, angered the wealthy landed class. At the same time, his Irish background brought criticism, and a disastrous drought and severe earthquake in 1822 encouraged more opposition.

Later that year, O'Higgins was chosen to succeed himself as president for a ten-year term, but an uprising occurred, and in February 1823 he resigned. An investigation cleared him of any wrongdoing during his administration, at which point he emigrated to Peru, where he lived his remaining days in retirement. He died on 24 October 1842, and Chileans later hailed him as the father of their country.

Reference: Clissold, Stephen, *Bernardo O'Higgins and the Independence of Chile,* 1969.

Olter, Bailey
(b. 1932)
Micronesia

In 1991, Bailey Olter became the third president of the Federated States of Micronesia but the first such leader to serve after his nation gained complete independence.

Bailey Olter was born on 27 March 1932 in Mwoakilloa on the island of Pohnpei (Ponape). While he was still a child, American troops occupied Micronesia during World War II and evicted the Japanese. In 1947, the United States began administering the islands under United Nations oversight as part of a trust territory. Shortly after this date, Olter obtained his higher education at the University of Hawaii.

Upon his return home, he entered teaching, business, and politics. In the early 1960s, he represented Pohnpei on the Advisory Board to the High Commissioner and served on the Council of Micronesia. In 1965, he served as the Micronesian advisor to the U.S. delegation to the United Nations Trusteeship Council. That same year, the United States allowed the Micronesians to elect a Congress and Olter won office. He became Senate vice-president in this first Congress and was chairman of the External Affairs Committee in both the first and second Congresses. In this capacity, he established an important working relationship with American officials and helped guide the islands toward increased autonomy.

In 1978, Micronesia adopted a constitution and four years later approved a Compact of Free Association with the United States. This did not bring complete independence, since the Americans still handled defense, and the islands remained under the UN-mandated trusteeship. During the political change, Olter served as vice-chairman of the Commission on Future Political Status and Transition and chairman of the Status Committee.

Micronesia's autonomy continued to evolve in the mid-1980s, while Olter served as vice-president. In 1986, the United States announced its intention to end the trusteeship after Olter and other Micronesians declared their desire to see this change. Olter, meanwhile, served in the fourth Congress and chaired the Ways and Means Committee in the Senate. His efforts to gain nationhood moved forward and reached fruition in 1991. After the United States assured the Soviet Union in the previous year that it would not construct additional military bases on the islands, the last barrier to UN dismantlement of the trusteeship was eliminated.

Olter became president on 11 May 1991 and presided over the official admission of Micronesia into the United Nations on 17 September. This formalized Micronesia's status as a completely independent nation.

Reference: Bunge, Frederica, and Melinda W. Cooke, eds., *Oceania: A Regional Study*, 1984.

Olympio, Sylvanus Epiphanio
(1902–1963)
Togo

When Sylvanus Olympio pressed for an independent nation to unite all Ewe peoples, he confronted an obstacle that had divided many Africans: territorial boundaries made by Europeans. He fought hard, but unsuccessfully, to surmount this situation.

Sylvanus Olympio came from a prominent Brazilian family. Born in Lomé on 6 September 1902, he obtained an education locally and then studied at the University of Vienna and the London School of Economics. Upon his return to Lomé in 1926, he joined the United Africa Company, a major business. After stints in Nigeria and the Gold Coast (Ghana), he became the company's general manager for Togo in 1928, a position he held for ten years and that brought him considerable wealth.

Such economic activity reflected the strong European presence in the area. After Germany established a protectorate over Togo in the 1880s, it developed Lomé as a capital and modern town with railroad transportation. After World War I, France and Britain, which now administered the eastern part and western part respectively, continued this economic development.

Turmoil occurred during World War II when many Togolese resisted Vichy authority (the French government that collaborated with Adolph Hitler). At this time, Olympio, who helped found the Circle of French Friends, opposed Vichy France and sided with CHARLES DE GAULLE's government. For this stand, Vichy officials imprisoned him in 1942. Olympio returned to Togo after World War II and in 1946 won election to the first territorial legislature, leading his Committee for a United Togolese (CUT, later the Togolese National Union Party) to victory.

Olympio became a strong proponent of uniting all Ewe peoples into one nation. This proposal, however, encountered a major obstacle: In drawing up territorial boundaries, the British and French had divided the Ewe, many of whom lived in British Togoland and in the Gold Coast. Olympio allied himself with the All-Ewe Conference and at the same time complained to the United Nations about French rule. This produced conflict between him and the French and in 1954 led to his prosecution for violating currency regulations. He was convicted and prohibited from seeking office. France then engaged in harassing CUT leaders and forming political parties that would be more amenable to its wishes.

The CUT reacted by boycotting elections (a policy followed until 1958), and this strategy allowed Nicolas Grunitzky to win office in 1951 as representative to the French National Assembly (Olympio did not hold any office from 1952 to 1958). Grunitzky won the support of many pro-French elements, including évolués, Africans who had adopted European practices.

In May 1956, Olympio's hopes for a united Ewe entity ended when, in a United Nations–supervised election, British Togoland opted to become a part of the Gold Coast, later renamed Ghana. Several months later, after French Togo became an autonomous nation within the French Union, Grunitzky became premier. In 1958, however, Grunitzky was rejected when his Togolese Progress Party lost to Olympio's CUT. This made Olympio prime minister and committed Togo to withdrawal from the French Union and obtaining complete independence, which was finalized on 27 April 1960. In the meantime, Olympio also won election in 1959 as mayor of Lomé.

When Togo adopted a new constitution in 1961, Olympio became president. He instituted an authoritarian rule under a one-party system and followed a conservative financial program to balance his country's budget. He also had a falling out with Ghana's ruler, KWAME NKRUMAH, as Ghanians applied pressure to merge Togo with their nation. Soon, opposition to Olympio began to build. Northerners felt left out of his government, many Western-educated Togolese disliked his strongman tactics, and soldiers and veterans disliked his opposition to enlarging the army. At the same time, CUT's youth wing became a separate group, JUVENTO, and attacked Olympio for being too pro-French.

By 1963, Olympio arrested several JUVENTO leaders, while others fled the nation. Finally, later that year, disgruntled army officers launched a coup and laid siege to Olympio's house—the first coup in any West African nation. Olympio fled his residence and, desperately seeking asylum, tried to scale the wall to the U.S. embassy. Before he could finish his climb, Togolese soldiers spotted him and killed him.

Soon thereafter, opposition leaders returned to Lomé and political prisoners were released.

Grunitzky became president, but he remained in office only four years—removed in yet another coup.

Reference: Hargreaves, John D., *West Africa: The Former French States,* 1967.

Onn, Dato
(1895–1962)
Malaysia

He did not seem like a nationalist, nor did he seem much like other Malays. Dato Onn liked socializing with British administrators and at one point criticized the independence drive as moving too quickly. Yet he initiated the most substantial protest against British rule in his homeland's history.

Born in Johore, a sultanate north of Singapore, in 1895, Dato Onn came from a wealthy, prominent family and obtained his education in England. When he returned to Johore, he worked briefly in the government service, where he got to know many British administrators.

As British expansion occurred in the region before World War II, Onn left government service to become a journalist, and he edited two Malay newspapers, *Lembaga Melayu* and *Warta Malaya.* With World War II, Malaysia temporarily fell to the Japanese. After the war, Britain determined to reclaim Malaysia, but found a land whose nationalism had been stirred, partly by the damage to British prestige from the Japanese conquest.

By this time, Onn had grown critical of British control. He especially disliked Britain's plan for a Malayan Union that centralized power in the Crown. In 1946, he organized the United Malay Nationalist Organization (UMNO) to oppose this plan. His obstinacy and that of the various sultans he rallied to his support effectively blocked Britain from reimposing the prewar colonial system. Instead, a plan for a Federation of Malay emerged that left substantial power with the sultans. In 1947, the sultan of Johore appointed Onn as prime minister in his government, and he also became member for home affairs for the Federation of Malaya.

Onn followed a confusing policy regarding Malaysia's ethnic tension. The area had long been torn between Malays and Chinese, and violence between these groups flared sporadically. In the 1940s, Onn spoke out against the dangers of Malays becoming overwhelmed by the economic wealth in Chinese hands. Yet in 1951, he tried to bring the Chinese into the UMNO to diversify an organization hitherto exclusively Malay. When his colleagues opposed him, he quit the party and was replaced as leader by TENGKU ABDUL RAHMAN.

Onn pushed for full independence from Britain, yet often criticized Rahman and others for moving too fast. Between 1951 and 1955, he formed two political groups to oppose UMNO: the Independence of Malaya Party and the National Party. Onn, however, had organizational problems, and his political views vacillated so much that Rahman soon eclipsed him.

When Onn died on 19 January 1962, he was more a picturesque man than a power. Nevertheless, Onn had stirred nationalism and the drive toward independence that provided the foundation for Malaysian nationhood. He is today considered Malaysia's first great nationalist.

References: Hanna, Willard A., *Eight Nation Makers: Southeast Asia's Charismatic Statesmen,* 1964; Turnbull, C. Mary, *A History of Malaysia, Singapore, and Brunei,* 1989.

Onofri, Antonio
(1759–1825)
San Marino

An outstanding statesman, Antonio Onofri defended tiny San Marino's independence and its republican government against the powerful challenges of Napoleon and the prominent nations that later arranged the peace at Vienna.

Antonio Onofri was born in San Marino in 1759, a member of a leading family. By the time he reached 30 years of age, tumultuous developments shook Europe with the outbreak of the French Revolution. Onofri's homeland, perched around and atop Mount Titano in north-central Italy, watched anxiously as the Revolution led to Napoleon's rise and the expansion of French power that could threaten the republican government San Marino had established hundreds of years earlier.

In 1797, Napoleon's army approached Mount Titano, and the French general indicated he wanted to make San Marino a place where his relatives or supporters could hold power, much as he was doing with a series of small republics he was establishing in Italy. He also indicated his desire to expand San Marino's borders. Onofri, by then the regent or leader of San Marino, stood firm, rejecting any territorial expansion, and asked only that his homeland be left alone. Napoleon agreed, perhaps out of respect for Onofri's elegant request, perhaps out of concern that seizing San Marino would display too blatant a contradiction between his republican pronouncements and actual practices. He even extended San Marino an exemption from taxes and established special commercial relations.

Over the ensuing years, Onofri time and time again displayed his statesmanship. He headed the San Marino delegation to the Congress of Vienna in 1815 and got the powerful European nations to recognize his homeland's independence. Then in the 1820s, when a few people in San Marino sought annexation by the Papal States, Onofri led the opposition and diplomatically sent a note to Pope Leo XII, welcoming the Catholic's ascension while denying any desire by his countrymen to lose their independence. When some San Marinese demanded Onofri expose those who had sought annexation, he destroyed all documents that might reveal their names, thus emphasizing national unity over recrimination.

Hence, although Onofri neither created his nation nor crafted its constitution, his diplomatic skill maintained independence for a small, militarily weak state in trying times. His importance proved so essential that after his death on 25 February 1825, the San Marinese erected a monument to Onofri bearing the inscription "Father of His Country."

References: Bent, J. Theodore, *A Freak of Freedom, or the Republic of San Marino*, 1879; Matteini, Nevio, *The Republic of San Marino: Historical and Artistic Guide*, 1981.

Ortega Saavedra, Daniel
(b. 1945)
Nicaragua

Born while a harsh dictatorship ruled Nicaragua, Daniel Ortega embraced the nationalism of Augusto César Sandino and the revolutionary ideology of pragmatic socialism. Nicaraguans, he determined, would have a nation free from foreign control and elite oppression.

Daniel Ortega Saavedra was born on 11 November 1945 in La Libertad. His father, a peasant, had fought in Sandino's guerrilla army in the 1930s when it ranged the hills and valleys, battling the conservative dictatorships that were supported by U.S. money, arms, and troops. Sandino's nationalist and anti-imperialist ideology was passed on to young Daniel. After completing secondary school, he enrolled at the Central American University in Managua but dropped out, politicized and ready to fight the Somoza regime, yet another American-backed government considered by many analysts as among the most brutal Latin American dictatorships.

In 1963, Ortega joined the Sandinista National Liberation Front (FSLN), which had been formed in 1961 by Carlos Fonseca Amador, Silvio Mayorga, and Tómas Borge Martinez. The Sandinistas had as their goal the overthrow of Somoza and the establishment of a revolutionary government committed to ending poverty and building an equitable society.

The FSLN, however, was divided into factions, most notably between Marxist ideologues and pragmatic socialists. Ortega sided with the latter, called the Terceristas (Third Party). He climbed rapidly within the FSLN and soon headed its urban resistance campaign. But in 1967, after he led a bank robbery, Somoza's infamous National Guard captured him and threw him in jail. There he remained until 1974, when he was released in a prisoner exchange and exiled to Cuba.

By this time, the anti-Somoza effort had acquired renewed support. After an earthquake devastated Managua in 1972, Somoza stole the foreign aid intended for the victims and, in rebuilding the city, moved slowly and favored a few large property owners linked to his regime. His actions angered not only the poor and the already-revolutionized Sandinistas, but many middle-class professionals and businessmen who, sometimes reluctantly, sided with the FSLN. Then, early in 1978, a prominent and popular newspaper editor, Pedro Joaquín Chamorro, was assassinated, perhaps with Somoza's involvement.

Concurrently, the Sandinistas healed their factional rift and established a unified command. Ortega moved to the forefront, and the FSLN launched an offensive in 1979, which Somoza reacted to, as he had on previous occasions, by unleashing the National Guard. The soldiers swept through villages, burned buildings, and killed young men of fighting age. The desperate tactic backfired, and even the United States withdrew its support from Somoza. In July, the dictator fled to Miami (one year later he was assassinated in Paraguay), and Ortega and the other FSLN leaders entered Managua triumphant.

Ortega headed a five-person civilian junta that governed Nicaragua. The Government of National Reconstruction followed Ortega's pragmatic course, promoting a mixed economy with limited nationalization, mainly of banks and insurance companies. In a bold move, he initiated reforms for farmers that brought a substantial redistribution of land ownership. Ortega cooperated closely with the Catholic Church, which had become an FSLN supporter.

The Sandinistas included Marxists, whose ideology worried many middle-class Nicaraguans. This caused problems for Ortega's leadership, as did a change in the United States that in 1981 brought Ronald Reagan to the presidency. Reagan resolutely opposed the FSLN that, he claimed, was an extension of Fidel Castro's Communist Cuba. He immediately ended loans to Nicaragua, announced a 90 percent reduction in American sugar imports, and directed the Central Intelligence Agency (CIA) to mine Nicaragua's harbors and train former Somoza National Guardsmen, called Contras, for attacks against the Sandinista government.

Amid this foreign assault and a worsening economic situation, Ortega still directed a practical, conciliatory course. In 1983, he announced he would no longer buy arms from overseas, and he ordered Cuban advisors to leave Nicaragua. He further announced an amnesty for all political exiles and the scheduling of elections for the following year. Yet none of this placated Reagan, who was determined that he would bring down the Sandinistas.

In the 1984 election, Ortega won an overwhelming victory in what foreign analysts considered a fair campaign. The United States, however, called the election a farce after the CIA-backed candidate had withdrawn from the race. In January 1985, Ortega became president.

Reagan reacted with a complete embargo of Nicaraguan trade and increased support for the Contras, even to the point of using illegal money transfers (a move linked to Reagan's secretive attempt to sell arms to Iran in exchange for release of Americans held hostage in the Middle East). Ortega faced a plummeting economy with an annual inflation rate exceeding 33,000 percent. The Contras had not gained popular support, but they harassed Ortega's government and increased their attacks as a new election approached in 1990.

Many of even the strongest Sandinista supporters tired of the economic ruination and the continued fighting. Confident now that the vote would turn in its favor, the United States endorsed the election and funneled millions of dollars to the Sandinista opponents, an eclectic assortment of largely conservatives but also disaffected Communists and other leftists, organized as the National Opposition Union (UNO) and led by VIOLETA CHAMORRO, wife of the slain journalist.

Ortega lost the election by a popular vote margin of 55 to 41 percent and then announced he would recognize the outcome and support Chamorro's inauguration. In a political arrangement, the Sandinistas retained command of the army, and Chamorro agreed to abide by the recent agrarian reforms. Yet many Sandinistas disagreed with Ortega and accused him of selling out to the United States and the Chamorro conservatives.

An uneasy political situation continued with Ortega leading the opposition. Despite the reversion to a more conservative government, Ortega had guided his countrymen to a substantial break with its Somoza past.

References: Collins, Joseph, *Nicaragua: What Difference Could a Revolution Make?*, 1986; Walker, Thomas, *Nicaragua: The First Five Years*, 1985; Walker, Thomas, *Nicaragua: The Land of Sandino*, 1991; Zwerling, Philip, and Connie Martin, *Nicaragua: A New Kind of Revolution*, 1985.

Páez, José Antonio
(1790–1873)
Venezuela

José Antonio Páez ousted the great South American liberator SIMÓN BOLÍVAR from Venezuela and established both an independent nation and a line of rule by *caudillos*, or strongmen.

José Antonio Páez was born on 13 June 1790 in Aricagua. He grew up on the Venezuelan plains and became a horseman, or *llanero*. By age 20, he owned considerable land and cattle and in 1810 joined the revolutionary uprising against Spanish rule led by Simón Bolívar. Páez contributed greatly to the rebel victory; in fact, he took the leading role in persuading many horsemen to desert their pro-Spanish position. Bolívar appointed Páez as Venezuelan commander, and the *llanero* helped win crucial victories at Carabobo, in 1821, and Puerto Cabello, in 1823. Throughout the war, Páez proved to be a master tactician of guerrilla strategy and fought ruthlessly against those *llaneros* who opposed the revolutionary cause.

Bolívar envisioned a united South America, and so he joined Venezuela with Colombia and Ecuador to form Gran Colombia. This plan, however, did not sit well with Venezuelan nationalists, including Páez. He developed plans for an independent nation with himself at the forefront, and beginning in 1826 led the movement to secede from Gran Colombia. Venezuelan separatism triumphed in 1829, and two years later Páez was elected president of the new nation.

He established an authoritarian but enlightened administration, building schools, developing industry, and generally respecting civil rights. He approached the controversial issue of church-and-state relations with moderation. Although he reduced the power of Catholics by abolishing tithes and special ecclesiastical courts, he provided support for the clergy and defended the church from Liberals, who wanted severe restrictions to lessen institutionalized Catholic power. Turmoil existed during Páz's rule, and the president had to put down five uprisings, but in all he brought substantial stability to an uncertain setting.

In 1846, Páez agreed to a moderate successor as president, José Tadeo Monagas. For awhile, Páez retained power behind the scenes, but in 1848 Monagas booted all Conservatives from his administration and sent Páez into exile. In 1858, Venezuela deteriorated as chaos reigned. On more than one occasion, Páez tried to reestablish his presidency but did not succeed until 1861 when, at the head of armed *llaneros,* he became dictator. Unlike his earlier reign, he ruled oppressively and acted forcefully against political opponents and censored the press. He backed the Catholic Church and expanded its power, a move that angered Liberals. Finally, in 1863, a Liberal rebellion ousted him from office, and he went once again into exile. Páez lived in New York City, where he wrote his memoirs, which were published between 1867 and 1869. He died on 7 May 1873 at age 84. In Venezuela, he ranks second only to Bolívar as a great national hero.

Reference: Gilmore, Robert L., *Caudilloism and Militarism in Venezuela, 1810–1910,* 1964.

Paine, Thomas
(1737–1809)
United States

As Thomas Paine set sail for England in 1787, a European storm lingered on the horizon: a revolution in France that would revivify his promotion of Reason and his commitment to eradicating tyranny. After having helped precipitate America's Revolution, his entry into the French adventure clearly confirmed his radicalism as one that transcended national boundaries.

Thomas Paine was not a man of privilege; born into a poor family in Thetford, England, on 29 January 1737, he received little formal education, and

"These are the times that try men's souls."

his father, Joseph Paine, a stay maker (one who fashioned whalebone used in corsets), struggled to earn a modest living. Consequently, young Thomas was forced at age 13 to work as an apprentice in his father's trade.

For 12 years, Paine thus labored, interrupted only by a brief stint in 1756 as a privateer. After opening his own stay-making shop, he married in 1759, but his wife died within a year. In 1762, Paine became an excise officer and collected taxes, but three years later was dismissed in a controversy involving his job performance.

From 1766 to 1768, he taught school in London, and then obtained reappointment as an excise officer.

He again ran into trouble, though, this time when he organized his fellow workers to demand higher wages. During this dispute he wrote his first pamphlet, *The Case of the Officers of Excise*, in which he expressed ideas he would repeat in later writings, especially discontent with the poverty in England and dislike for the wealthy. Paine remarried in 1771 and ran a tobacconist shop that had been owned by his recently deceased father-in-law. He had little interest in business, however, and spent considerable time reading and attending lectures. Three years later, tragedy struck when the shop folded, he and his wife separated, and he lost his government job.

In 1774, Paine decided to sail for America. In London, he had met BENJAMIN FRANKLIN, then an agent for several of the British North American colonies, and the Pennsylvanian provided him with letters of introduction. Paine arrived in Philadelphia on 30 November and began writing for the *Pennsylvania Magazine*, which he soon edited. By this time, differences between the colonies and Britain had reached a critical point. The colonists rejected Parliament's attempts to tax them, and the Boston Tea Party, led by the radical SAMUEL ADAMS, pushed events closer to revolution.

Then, after the first revolutionary shots rang out in 1775 at Lexington and Concord, Paine issued a work that had an enormous impact on the colonists, removing their last restraints. This was his pamphlet *Common Sense*; it changed the political debate and went through 25 editions within one year, perhaps reaching a circulation of 500,000. In this work, Paine argued not only that the colonies should be independent, but also that a republican government was superior to a monarchy. He insisted that power should reside largely in the people, and in this he took the most radical position among the emerging nation's founders. The stir caused by his pamphlet impressed GEORGE WASHINGTON, THOMAS JEFFERSON, JAMES MADISON, and ALEXANDER HAMILTON, but to varying degrees they worried that he had gone too far in advocating popular power.

Paine provided crucial leadership in guiding Pennsylvania to support independence and adopt the most democratic constitution of all the states. Indeed, he desired more than separation from Britain; he wanted radical political change. This occurred when the Pennsylvania convention adopted a state constitution that largely followed the ideas Paine had outlined in *Common Sense*. The document provided for a one-house legislature with no executive branch, annual elections, no property qualifications for holding office, and nearly universal male suffrage. Although conservatives dismantled this constitution in 1787 (enacting changes even Paine considered necessary), the document nevertheless signified the radical stream of the Revolution, one that distrusted elites and challenged the traditional power structure by advancing popular power.

In 1776, while the Pennsylvania convention met, Paine enlisted in the army and, as aide-de-camp to General Nathanael Greene, retreated with the Continental troops when the British advanced across New Jersey. During this time, he wrote *The American Crisis*, with its famous lines about "the times that try men's souls," and summer soldiers and sunshine patriots. With the recommendation of Massachusetts leader JOHN ADAMS, the following year Congress appointed Paine as secretary to its foreign affairs committee. He resigned, however, in 1779 after a messy controversy in which he publicly revealed that the French had sent supplies to the United States at a time when France and Britain were at peace—a transaction the French government did not want disclosed to the British.

In November, the Pennsylvania Assembly appointed Paine as its clerk, and he continued to write his *Crisis* pamphlets while diverting part of his salary to support the Revolution. After the British surrender in 1783, Paine obtained a small farm in New York, where he lived until 1787. He largely avoided politics, although he did speak out in 1785 to voice his support for the Bank of North America, the first "national" bank, which he considered important to stabilize America's currency and provide capital for economic expansion.

Paine sailed for England in 1787, seeking to get his innovative plan for an iron bridge accepted. Financiers eventually built the bridge, but by then the French Revolution had erupted. In 1789, he journeyed to Paris, convinced his help was needed to spread revolutionary ideals. Two years later, he wrote his *The Rights of Man*, a reply to *Reflections on the Revolution in France*, written by the English conservative Edmund Burke, who attacked the upheaval as destroying the wisdom of the past and promoting riotous disorder. Paine supported the radical break with tradition, insisting that each generation must reinvent institutions or else be tyrannized by the past.

In 1792, he issued his *The Rights of Man, Part Second*, in which he condemned monarchy and promoted the concept of democracy, at the time considered a dangerous ideology. He also insisted that each individual possessed natural rights and that a bill of rights should exist to protect them. He hoped that his works would lead to the end of the monarchy in England, but the British government censored him and in 1792 convicted him, in absentia, of treason.

Paine was by then in Paris and in September won election to the French Assembly. After the moderate group, or Girondins, with which he associated fell from power in June 1793, Paine no longer attended the Assembly. In December, radical revolutionaries arrested him, and he was imprisoned in Luxembourg. During this confinement, he completed writing *The Age of Reason*. In it, he presented his deism, or belief in an impersonal God, and pil-

loried churches, the Bible, and the Revelation of Saint John for representing or promoting superstition. He believed that a rational, reasoned world would best promote man's welfare, and he presented Christianity and deism as incompatible. The clergy in Europe and America widely attacked him. In July 1795, he returned to his seat in the French Assembly.

The following year, Paine wrote *Agrarian Justice*, in which he advocated the regulation of private property for society's welfare. He stressed the urgency of ameliorating the worsening poverty in Europe but did not advocate the end to private holdings.

Paine returned to America in 1802 and lived part of the time in New York and part of the time in New Jersey. He had little money and most of his revolutionary colleagues ignored him as too radical, particularly since stories circulated—quite inaccurately—that he was an atheist. He died in New York on 8 June 1809, largely forgotten, with his funeral attended by only six mourners. So passed the man who helped create the United States and pursued Reason in his revolutionary activities.

References: Aldridge, A. Owen, *Tom Paine's American Ideology*, 1984; Ayer, A. J., *Thomas Paine*, 1989; Foner, Eric, *Tom Paine and Revolutionary America*, 1976; Keane, John, *Tom Paine: A Political Life*, 1995.

Papandreou, Andreas
(b. 1919)
Greece

After Andreas Papandreou left Greece for the United States, he became a noted college professor and an American citizen. He changed course, however, and entered Greek politics to bring radical change.

On 5 February 1919, Andreas Papandreou was born into a prominent family on Chios, one of the Aegean Islands. His father, Georges Papandreou, was governor-general of the area. At age five his

parents divorced, and Andreas lived with his mother in Athens, although he remained close to his father. After secondary school, he attended American College in Athens and then the University of Athens Law School, which he entered in 1937. At the same time, his father fell into disfavor with General Ioannis Metaxas, leader of the Greek military dictatorship, and was exiled. While in law school, Andreas joined a Marxist group, and in 1939 the government arrested and tortured him. Upon his release, he obtained his law degree in 1940 and then emigrated to the United States.

In America, Andreas excelled as a scholar. He graduated from Harvard with an M.A. degree in 1942 and a doctorate in economics the following year. In 1944, he became a U.S. citizen and joined the navy. After World War II, he became a lecturer in economics at Harvard and in 1947 an associate professor at the University of Minnesota. In 1950, he went to Northwestern University and the following year returned to the University of Minnesota as a full professor. There he stayed until 1955, when he began teaching and serving as chair of the Economics Department at the University of California at Berkeley. His advance in academia coincided with his substantial publications, including three books.

In 1959, Andreas journeyed to Greece under a Fulbright scholar program, and his father, Georges, encouraged him to return permanently to his homeland. He did so in 1963 when he left Berkeley and became director of the Center of Economic Research in Athens. He wrote two more books and came to believe he could change the Greek political and economic system. He renounced his U.S. citizenship in order to run for parliament as a member of the Union of the Center Party, which his father led. In 1964, he won election, and at the same time his father became prime minister. Georges then appointed Andreas as his chief aide and also made him deputy minister of economic coordination.

Andreas criticized the Greek military and its habit of intervening in politics, and he attacked the United States for its support of such activity. These criticisms won him and his father the enmity of the right wing, and Andreas lost his administrative post when King Constantine dismissed the Papandreous government in July 1965. The right-wing attacks emboldened rather than discouraged Andreas, and they boosted his popularity with the left.

When it appeared Georges and Andreas would triumph in the 1967 elections, the military staged a coup, began a dictatorship, and arrested the two men. Andreas spent eight months in solitary confinement. After his release, he went into exile and taught at the University of Stockholm in 1968 (the year his father died), and York University in Toronto from 1969 to 1974. While teaching, he organized the Panhellenic Liberation Movement to oppose the Greek dictatorship. He traveled extensively and condemned the United States for supporting the regime. (In fact, his charges were accurate: America had backed the Greek military and the nation's right-wing movements for years.)

In 1974, a crisis with Turkey over Cyprus embarrassed the dictatorship and it collapsed. The military and civilian leaders turned to CONSTANTINE KARAMANLIS to form a new government. Although conservative in his politics, Karamanlis restored democracy in Greece and allowed party competition. Andreas subsequently returned home and organized the Panhellenic Socialist Movement (PASOK). In elections that year, PASOK fared poorly, but Andreas determined to build the party from the grass roots, and in 1977 it won 25 percent of the vote.

Andreas criticized the government for allowing American military bases in Greece and for promoting an economic policy injurious to workers. He also condemned Turkey for stationing troops on Cyprus and insisted Greece needed change. In 1981, PASOK won a majority in Parliament, and Andreas became prime minister.

His election began the first socialist government in Greek history and established policies that substantially changed society. Although once in office Andreas tempered his anti-American stand and his radical proposals, numerous reforms ensued while he expressed his commitment to national prestige, popular sovereignty, and social liberation. He lowered the voting age from 20 to 18, legalized civil marriages, and established supervisory councils that gave workers more say in the development of industries. PASOK won important local elections held in 1982, although many socialists criticized the prime minister's moderation, and the Communists made political gains.

In 1983, Andreas reached an agreement with the United States that allowed American military bases to remain in Greece for an increased payment, and the United States also promised not to transfer any of the bases to Turkey. Two years later,

PASOK scored another election victory, and Andreas continued as prime minster.

Then in the late 1980s, his government fell during a serious scandal involving cabinet members who had participated in illegal financial deals and bribery. Andreas lost the 1989 parliamentary election. After he left the prime ministry, he was himself charged with corruption, primarily the use of illegal wiretaps, but in 1992 he was acquitted. The following year, Andreas again won election to the prime ministry.

Andreas Papandreou protected the Greek government from its tendency in modern times toward military rule and established a new economic and political direction. His reform programs placed him with ELEUTHERIOS VENIZELOS and Constantine Karamanlis as founders of modern Greece. He faces increased tensions with Albania over the status of ethnic Albanians within Greece.

Reference: Clogg, Richard, ed., *Greece in the 1980s*, 1983.

Park Chung Hee
(1917–1979)
Republic of Korea (South Korea)

Park Chung Hee is best known for substantially altering the South Korean government. He toppled the Second Republic and, after installing a strict military regime, began the Third Republic.

Park Chung Hee was born Pak Chŏng-hŭi on 30 September 1917. His family worked as farmers in Sangmo, a poor village located in southeastern Korea. He went to normal school in Taegu, where he trained to become a grammar school teacher. After he graduated in 1937, he began teaching in Kyŏngsang-pukdo, a small town that he found stifling.

In 1939, he enrolled in the military academy at Manchukuo, a state established in China by Japan after its military conquest of Manchuria. He entered the Japanese Officer Corps in 1944, but the surrender of Japan in World War II interrupted his military career. Upon his discharge, Park returned home, and in 1946, after the efforts of SYNGMAN RHEE and other nationalists resulted in Korean independence, he entered the Korean Military Academy.

During the Korean War, Park rose rapidly in the military ranks, becoming a brigadier general in 1953. He then journeyed to the United States, where he received advanced artillery training at Fort Sill in Oklahoma. He returned to Korea and headed the army's artillery school and then won appointment as commanding general of the 5th Infantry Division. In 1957, he enrolled in the Korean army's Command and General Staff College.

In 1960, President Syngman Rhee, who in establishing the Second Republic had ruled dictatorially, encountered enormous opposition. Student demonstrations and violence exploded, and when he lost military support, he resigned. Unknown to Rhee, Park had been planning a military coup, only to have it interrupted by the student outburst. Chang Myŏn now headed the government and Park decided to bide his time.

Korea remained in political and economic turmoil, and on 16 May 1961, Park at last staged his coup. With Myŏn overthrown, the entire Second Republic collapsed. Park established the Supreme Council for National Reconstruction (SCNR), with executive and legislative powers combined, and assumed its leadership. Democratic procedures, which had been expressed in the Second Republic's constitution and largely bypassed by Rhee, totally collapsed, and Park formed a tight military regime centered around himself, which from the standpoint of its authoritarianism resembled the rule by KIM IL-SŎNG in North Korea.

On 16 March 1962, Park banned most political dissent. Also that month, he formally assumed the presidency, vacated after President Yun Po-sŏn protested the deepening militarism by resigning. When Park reorganized the government, he founded the Korean Central Intelligence Agency (KCIA). He claimed the nation needed it to fight communism, but he used it to terrorize all political opponents.

A national legislature and political party competition did exist under Park, but were greatly proscribed. When he announced he would continue his military regime until 1967, riots erupted and the violence forced him to hold an election. In 1963, he won election to the presidency and ended direct military rule. This began the Third Republic, although Park still held enormous powers. Park allied South Korea closely with the United States and encouraged American investments and corporate growth. The economy expanded and prosperity increased substantially. Many Koreans, though, disliked his political repression, and in 1972 he imposed martial law after renewed student demonstrations. In November 1972, a new constitution gave Park even greater power, and he cracked down harshly against political dissidents. Severe riots occurred in 1979 after he arbitrarily removed a popular opposition leader from the national legislature. Amid this turmoil, on 26 October 1979, Kim Jae Kyu, an old friend and head of the KCIA, assassinated Park.

Reference: McKenzie, Frederick A., *The Tragedy of Korea*, 1969.

Parnell, Charles Stewart
(1846–1891)
Ireland

He could not have been further removed from the ordinary people of Ireland: On his family estate at Avondale he frequently traversed the green hills, hunting and riding with his hounds. Yet Charles Stewart Parnell eventually turned his back on such aristocratic preoccupations and became an oddity in Irish politics as a wealthy Protestant nationalist activist fighting for the rights of the largely Catholic peasants and for eventual Irish independence from Britain.

> **"No man has a right to set a boundary to the march of a nation."**

The Parnell lineage originally hailed from England, but the family had been in Ireland a long time. Charles's father inherited large amounts of land and became an Irish landlord, while his mother was an American and strongly anti-English. As a young boy, Charles, who was born on 27 June 1846, heard stories of Theobald Wolfe Tone's daring attempts in the eighteenth century at winning Irish freedom from Britain and the stirring formation of an idealistic, nationalistic movement: Young Ireland.

Parnell developed Anglophobia, a distaste for England and its culture, but at first had no political ambitions. After graduating from Cambridge University, he lived a leisurely life. Two developments intervened, however: First, the British executed three Irish radicals for their part in a jailbreak that had accidentally resulted in the death of a policeman; then the Irish economy slipped, and hardship worsened with three years of catastrophic harvests beginning in 1877. These developments convinced Parnell of Ireland's dire straits.

In 1875, he had entered the British Parliament as one of the Irish Party delegates—a tall, handsome man, who sat quietly and looked grave. Now in 1877, he began speaking out and developed a strategy aimed at getting a greater audience in Parliament for Ireland's problems. He used obstructionism to take advantage of Parliament's rules: He and his colleagues spoke on the floor for days on end, filibustering legislation and blocking its passage.

When Michael Davitt, an Irish nationalist, formed the Land League to help the peasantry in 1879, Parnell agreed to become the group's president. The League wanted to unite Ireland's peasants into a group that could force lower rents. Parnell rejected violence and argued for change within constitutional boundaries, yet many in England considered him dangerous when he stridently advocated home rule. This, and his frequent criticism of the British government, landed him in jail briefly in the early 1880s.

After Parliament passed some modest land reforms, Parnell organized the National League in 1882. Home rule became the group's focus with Parnell demanding repeal of the Act of Union, enacted in 1800, which had made Ireland a part of the United Kingdom. With the election of additional Irish delegates to Parliament in 1885, Parnell effectively used political alliances to gain influence. Indeed, the ruling Liberal government depended upon the Irish Party, which Parnell led, for a working majority against the Conservatives and, consequently, supported a Home Rule bill. A split within the Irish Party, however, coupled with the continuing Conservative opposition, defeated it in 1886.

Despite this failure, Parnell's actions had immense appeal in Ireland and awakened many Irishmen to the possibility of gaining independence. He kept working for Irish liberty, but a controversy destroyed his enormous influence. He had lived for years with Katherine O'Shea. Many people knew about this arrangement and knew that she was still married. In 1890, however, her husband sued for divorce and details of the affair saturated the newspapers. The imbroglio conflicted with Victorian principles, and the court proceedings particularly sullied Parnell. The Liberal Party announced that it could no longer work with the Irish Party as long as Parnell remained its head, and Ireland's Catholic bishops severely criticized him.

The Irish Party consequently deposed Parnell as leader. He fought back, though, and became more radical, appealing to the secret societies that supported violent actions for peasant welfare and home rule. Many Irishmen, however, disliked these groups and supported the Catholic Church's condemnation of Parnell. When he appeared, crowds sometimes pelted him with rocks and threw lime into his eyes. On 27 September 1891, he spoke in Galway. A pouring rain drenched him, he did not change his clothes, and he thus became seriously ill. On 6 October, he died in the arms of Katherine O'Shea, whom he had earlier married. Despite his death, his clarion call for independence lived on and helped stimulate the new upheavals of the twentieth century. Together with Wolfe Tone, MICHAEL COLLINS, DANIEL O'CONNELL, EAMON DE VALERA, and PATRICK PEARSE, the Irish consider Parnell a hero in their ongoing nationalist movement.

References: Abels, Jules, *The Parnell Tragedy*, 1968; Lyons, Francis Stewart, *The Fall of Parnell*, 1960; McCaffey, Lawrence, *Irish Federalism in the 1870s: A Study in Conservative Nationalism*, 1962; O'Brien, Richard Barry, *The Life of Charles Stewart Parnell*, 2 volumes, 1968.

Pearse, Patrick
(1879–1916)
Ireland

Myths danced in the mind of Patrick Pearse, myths of ancient lordly heroes battling demonic hosts. The myth of Cuchulainn was a powerful influence, and Pearse attached himself to the hero of the story. Brave and noble Cuchulainn, while suffering a mortal wound, declared: "I care not though I were to live but one day and night, if only my fame and my deeds live after me."

Patrick Pearse was born in Dublin on 10 November 1879. His father, James Pearse, an Englishman, sculpted Gothic figures, and his work appeared on many of the Dublin churches built after 1850.

In the late 1800s, as nationalism in Ireland intensified, a new movement promoted the revival of Gaelic culture and the Irish language. Many of the movement's adherents later entered Ireland's fight for independence, including EAMON DE VALERA. The Gaelic Revival enraptured Patrick Pearse, and at age 16 he became perhaps the most mystical member of its formal organization, the Gaelic League. Pearse attended secondary school at Westland Row, which he considered an ordeal filled with rote memorization to prepare for standardized exams, and graduated from Royal University in 1908. He practiced law but soon derided it as "the most wicked of professions." He then changed his career and founded an experimental secondary school for boys, St. Enda's College.

"One man can free the people as one man redeemed the world."

Pearse's school reflected his ardent devotion to Gaelic culture and its legends. He had words from the myth of Cuchulainn chiseled into a prominent wall and insisted his students re-create the ancient Irish tradition of knightly standards. He talked about the Fianna, a prehistoric Irish army, and told them that a short life devoted to honor was better than a long one dishonored. At St. Enda's, Irish prevailed as the official language.

By 1913, Pearse had grown frustrated with the Gaelic League as too nonpolitical. Within a year, he joined the Irish Republican Brotherhood (IRB) and committed himself to a violent overthrow of British rule. After the IRB split in October 1914 over the issue of whether to support the British fight against Germany in World War I, Pearse led the militant wing that opposed helping Britain. The mystic nationalist served on the IRB's military council.

Pearse's rousing oratory helped rally support for the Irish independence movement. He convinced himself that an insurrection would soon come, and he helped bring it to fruition. Pearse and several fellow conspirators maneuvered the leader of the Irish Volunteers (the IRB's military wing, later called the Irish Republican Army) into calling a general mobilization scheduled in 1916 for Easter Sunday. Few people heeded the call; nevertheless, he and his followers proceeded with an uprising that day in Dublin.

They had little hope of military success but wanted to stir the Irish masses into sympathy for their cause. Pearse also likely considered the uprising a mystical redemption for Ireland's sin of having succumbed to years of British rule. About 1,000 rebels occupied the post office and several buildings in Dublin's center and proclaimed an independent Irish republic. As supreme commander, Pearse directed the military effort, but after one week it became apparent that further fighting against the numerically superior British forces would be futile. Pearse and his contingent then surrendered.

Many Irishmen considered the Easter Rising foolish; after all, Dubliners had recently enjoyed some economic gains and, furthermore, they opposed efforts that might result in helping Germany during World War I. When the British marched Pearse and the other captured rebels through Dublin's streets, crowds jeered them. But the jeers quieted when in the weeks ahead the British government imprisoned dozens of rebel leaders and executed 15 by firing squad. Martyrs had been created—among them Patrick Pearse, who was executed on 3 May 1916, and whose legacy resembled his mythical hero, Cuchulainn, and paralleled the lives of De Valera, MICHAEL COLLINS, DANIEL O'CONNELL, and CHARLES STEWART PARNELL.

References: *Collected Works of Patrick H. Pearse: Political Writings and Speeches*, 3 vols., 1917–1922; Le Roux, Lois, *Patrick H. Pearse*, translated by Desmond Ryan, 1932.

Pedro I
(1798–1834)
Brazil

Near the Ipiranga River, Dom Pedro unsheathed his sword and proclaimed "Independence or Death!" With that, he ended Brazil's status as a Portuguese colony.

Dom Pedro was born Antonio Pedro de Alcantara in Lisbon, Portugal, on 12 October 1798. He had a privileged beginning: He was the son of Dom João, who acted as regent of Portugal during the mental illness suffered by his mother, the queen. When Napoleon conquered Portugal in 1807, João and the rest of the royal family sailed to the Portuguese colony of Brazil. Their presence greatly affected Brazilians, making them feel as if their country had attained enormous importance, equal to Portugal—a perception reinforced in 1815 when Brazil was declared a partner in the United Kingdom of Portugal, Brazil, and Algarve. This feeling later stimulated the rise of nationalism and the gaining of independence.

Dom Pedro grew up with little formal education but had common sense and energy. International events again affected him when, in 1816, Dom João's mother died. The once regent, now King João VI, returned to Portugal, but left Dom Pedro behind as prince with authority over internal affairs. In 1821, a new Portuguese Cortes, or Parliament, expressed its desire to make Brazil, once again, a colony. Toward this end, it ordered Dom Pedro back to Portugal. In January 1822, members of Brazil's elite requested that Dom Pedro remain, and he agreed. He reorganized his government and made JOSE BONIFÁCIO his minister of the kingdom. Bonifácio thus became the most powerful official in the government, and as a strong nationalist he pushed for Brazilian independence.

Several additional factors caused Brazil to break with Portugal. For one, Enlightenment ideas stirred an emphasis on individual rights, ideas reinforced by the examples of the United States obtaining its independence from Britain, and Latin American colonies gaining theirs from Spain; second, economic restrictions angered many Brazilians; and third, Britain worked to weaken the Portuguese Empire, a move that would increase British trade with Brazil. The final break occurred in September 1822 when Dom Pedro, angered by the Cortes' attempts to restrict him, and sincerely believing that Portuguese actions threatened Brazil's welfare, declared an end to his country's colonial status. On 1 December 1822, he was crowned emperor of Brazil.

Although during the move toward independence Portuguese troops battled the Brazilian army, the conflicts were short, and for the most part the transition to nationhood was peaceful. Dom Pedro created a strong monarchy—he had little use for republicanism. Although he called a constituent assembly together in May 1823, he quickly dissolved it (and exiled Bonifácio, whose views opposed his) after the delegates acted to restrict his power. This move and his tendency to surround himself with Portuguese advisors stirred opposition to him. However, he protected Brazil's independence when he refused his father's request to reunite the country with Portugal.

In 1824, Dom Pedro oversaw the writing of a new constitution, conservative and with a strong monarchy. This, along with complaints of high taxes, stirred a rebellion in Pernambuco. Although the emperor crushed the revolt, his popularity continued to decline. After he involved Brazil in a war with Argentina over Uruguay in 1828, and the nation's finances continued to deteriorate, he was pressured to resign. On 7 April 1831, Dom Pedro abdicated in favor of his son, who soon ruled as PEDRO II.

Dom Pedro then returned to Portugal and worked successfully to get his daughter declared Queen Maria II. He died in Lisbon on 24 September 1834. In 1889, the Brazilian monarchy collapsed and MANUEL DEODORO DA FONSECA established a republic.

References: Correa da Costa, Sergio, *Every Inch a King: A Biography of Dom Pedro I,* 1964; Macaulay, Neill, *Dom Pedro,* 1986.

Pedro II
(1825–1891)
Brazil

Pedro II traveled extensively among his subjects, visiting schools, hospitals, and museums. A moderate man with a modern outlook, he stabilized the new nation, supported political balance and scientific advancement, and promoted abolition to the extent that many Brazilians still hail his enlightened rule as the greatest in their nation's history. Nevertheless, his involvement in a controversial war and his attacks against slavery helped undermine the monarchy.

Pedro II was born Dom Pedro de Alcantara in Rio de Janeiro on 2 December 1825. His father, PEDRO I, was emperor of Brazil and along with his chief minister, JOSE BONIFÁCIO, had led the nation in gaining its independence from Portugal. When the younger Pedro reached age five, his father abdicated and a regency assumed power. For ten years, while Dom Pedro obtained an education and waited to rule, turmoil engulfed Brazil as separatist movements threatened to destroy the new nation. When the crisis worsened, the country's political leaders decided to advance the designated maturity date for Dom Pedro, and on 18 July 1841 they crowned him Emperor Pedro II.

Throughout his rule, Dom Pedro exhibited intelligence and a strong concern for the masses. His steadying hand likely saved Brazil from disintegration. His regime, however, was not democratic: The franchise was highly restricted and he dissolved the legislature at will.

Dom Pedro acted immediately to end Brazil's civil wars. In 1841, he suppressed a revolt in Maranhão, and the following year he did so in Minas Gerais and São Paulo. In 1845, he ended a decade-long revolt in Rio Grande do Sul.

Meanwhile, the economy expanded. Irineu Evangelista de Souza, the Baron of Mauá, developed the nation industrially, and his banking empire helped finance the government. Railroads, roads, ports, and canals emerged, textile mills appeared, and telegraph lines linked the countryside.

Sugar and cotton exports grew and coffee boomed, earning half of Brazil's export income. Dom Pedro supported and encouraged these advances, enthusiastically backing scientific societies. The expansion had its limits—Rio de Janeiro had no sewers and slums appeared in huge swaths—but most praised the emperor for an era of prosperity.

Dom Pedro involved Brazil in several foreign policy controversies. The slave trade produced tensions with Britain, an abolitionist nation, until 1850, when Brazil finally renounced the trafficking. In 1864, Dom Pedro intervened in Uruguay, where he installed a pro-Brazilian government. But this unleashed a bloody conflict, the War of the Triple Alliance. Brazil blamed Paraguay for inciting this war, claiming that its ruler, Francisco Solano López, had built a mighty army with the goal to conquer Uruguay. Contrary to this, Paraguay claimed it had no such intentions and with its military expansion sought only to counterbalance the enormous power of Brazil and Argentina by protecting Uruguayan independence. Hence, when Brazil installed its government there, Paraguay criticized the action as violating Uruguay's sovereignty and threatening regional security.

Indeed, Dom Pedro reached an agreement in 1865 with the ruler Brazil had installed in Uruguay and with Argentina. The ensuing Triple Alliance provided for Argentina and Brazil to conquer Paraguayan territory and divide it between them. By this time, López had attacked Brazil, and Dom Pedro countered with a vengeance. He demanded that López resign, but the Paraguayan leader refused. Subsequently, Brazil captured Asuncíon, and the war ended in 1870. Although Dom Pedro defeated Paraguay, the war drained the treasury and strengthened the role of the military in Brazilian society. Furthermore, numerous battlefield defeats during the conflict hurt his standing domestically, and the international community criticized what it called Dom Pedro's aggression.

The emperor's demise came over issues involving religion and slavery. In the 1870s, Dom Pedro opposed a papal edict that prohibited Catholics from joining Masonic lodges. When two bishops sought to enforce the edict, the emperor had them imprisoned, an action that alienated many Catholics. A more substantial issue was abolition. Dom Pedro sought to end slavery, and a law in 1871 freed the newborn children of slaves. Finally, in 1888 the "Golden Law" abolished slavery, and some 700,000 slaves were freed without compensation to their owners. Many wealthy planters never forgave Dom Pedro, and they refused to support him in his time of troubles.

That difficulty came in 1889 when Dom Pedro's prime minister proposed liberal reforms, such as complete religious freedom, and tried to restrain the power of the army. On 14 November a military uprising occurred led by MANUEL DEODORO DA FONSECA who, on the following day, declared a republic. He insisted that Dom Pedro leave the country, and the emperor and his family departed on 17 November. Subsequently, the man who had saved newly independent Brazil from collapse settled in Paris, where he lived the rest of his life in exile. Dom Pedro died on 5 December 1891.

References: Williams, Mary W., *Dom Pedro the Magnanimous*, 1966; Worcester, Donald, *Brazil: From Colony to World Power*, 1973.

Pereira, Aristides
(b. 1924)
Cape Verde

Like other Cape Verdean nationalists, Aristides Pereira tied his homeland to the anticolonial movement in nearby Guinea-Bissau. But when in 1980 a coup overthrew the mainland government, he successfully led Cape Verde on its own path.

Aristides Pereira was born in 1924 on Boa Vista Island, part of Cape Verde, where he attended school and trained as a radio-telegraph technician. At that time, Portugal ruled Cape Verde, as it did the nearby African mainland area of Guinea-Bissau. In 1954, the nationalist leader AMILCAR CABRAL began his efforts to liberate Guinea-Bissau and two years later extended his campaign to Cape Verde, when he formed the African Party for the Independence of Guinea-Bissau and Cape Verde (PAIGC).

Pereira joined the PAIGC and traveled to the mainland, where he helped organize the infamous Pijiguiti strike of dockworkers that led to Portuguese soldiers and armed settlers firing into a crowd of protestors, killing 50 and wounding many more. The Portuguese acted to repress the PAIGC, and Pereira fled with Cabral to Conakry in neighboring Guinea. From there he wrote propaganda demanding a peaceful end to colonial rule, served on the political bureau of the party's Central Committee, and organized workers in the city of Bissau and other urban areas.

In 1961, Cabral and Pereira concluded that only armed insurrection would bring independence, and in 1963 the PAIGC launched attacks in Guinea-Bissau's southern region. Portugal used Cape Verde as a base from which to fight against the rebels. In 1964, Pereira became the joint secretary-general of the PAIGC and, in 1965, a member of its War Council. Throughout 1969 and 1970 the Portuguese suffered major military defeats. In November 1970, Portuguese troops raided the PAIGC headquarters at Conakry and tried to kill Pereira, but failed in their mission. That same year, the Cape Verdean joined Cabral as a member of the PAIGC Permanent Commission of the Executive Committee for the Struggle, where he handled security matters and foreign affairs.

When on 20 January 1973 dissidents within the PAIGC backed by Portugal assassinated Cabral, Pereira became the party's leader, winning formal election as secretary-general in July. In September, the PAIGC sponsored the First Peoples' National

Assembly, and it formally declared independence, naming Luís Cabral, Amilcar Cabral's brother, as president.

In September 1974, Portugal recognized the Republic of Guinea-Bissau, and on 19 October Pereira and Luís Cabral officially entered Bissau as nationalist heroes. The situation in Cape Verde, however, remained unsettled. Although the PAIGC prevailed there and many Cape Verdeans supported unity with Guinea-Bissau, others expressed desires for a separate nation and, in any event, the PAIGC showed no enthusiasm for unification. On 5 July 1975, the islands became the independent Republic of Cape Verde, yet closely linked to the mainland by several official agreements. Pereira returned home and became president of Cape Verde, governing under the PAIGC banner. He also still served as secretary-general of the PAIGC while Luís Cabral, the president of Guinea-Bissau, served as his deputy.

The close relationship between Cape Verde and Guinea-Bissau shattered in 1980 when a coup on the mainland drove Luís Cabral from power. Pereira disagreed with the overthrow and early in 1981 reorganized the Cape Verdean PAIGC to form the African Party for the Independence of Cape Verde. In February, Pereira won reelection as president and continued ruling in a one-party political system. He promoted Cape Verde's economic development by encouraging water conservation, reforestation, and agricultural research, and developing fishing and light industries, such as textiles and ceramics. Furthermore, he involved himself directly in attempts to resolve the racial strife in South Africa. In 1990, Pereira agreed to open the Cape Verde political system to multiparty competition. He then relinquished his position as secretary-general to be, as he put it, "above party politics." The following year, Pereira lost the presidential election to Antonio Mascarenhas Monteiro, head of the Supreme Court.

Reference: Andrade, Elisa, *The Cape Verde Islands: From Slavery to Modern Times*, 1974.

Peter I
(1672–1725)
Russia

In 1703, there arose in Russia a new city, Western in appearance, grand in its architecture, the epitome of tsarist absolutism. Peter I, known as Peter the Great, a tall dominating figure who once traveled Europe incognito, ordered the city be built. Nothing so clearly symbolized his grandeur and his renascent vision than this massive feat, the construction of St. Petersburg. In contrast to this, Peter dispensed cruelties on those around him—the loyal and disloyal—subjecting them to his drunken excesses, his infatuation with freakish behavior, and his torture chambers, where death by flogging and burning awaited unfortunate victims.

Some 60 years after the Romanov Dynasty began in Russia, Peter was born in Moscow on 30 May 1672. His father, Tsar Alexis, had ruled Russia since 1645 and had several children by his first wife, as well as Peter by his second wife, Natalia Naryshkin. In 1676, Tsar Alexis died and Fyodor III ascended to the throne. Fyodor assigned Nikita Zotov to be Peter's tutor, but Zotov preferred drinking wine and taught the youngster only the basics of reading and writing. This was the extent of Peter's formal schooling.

When Fyodor died in 1682, a struggle ensued over his successor. Fyodor had two brothers: Ivan, a half-wit, and Peter. The *boyars*, or nobility, named Peter the tsar, but the relatives of Alexis's first wife stirred the *streltsy*, or royal guard, to oppose the *boyars*, and chaos erupted in the Kremlin. Peter witnessed the bloodshed as those allied with his mother were murdered, including a *boyar* and advisor to the tsar, who, in front of Peter's eyes, was impaled on pikes. The episode had an enormous psychological impact on Peter: He developed a nervous facial twitch and could never again sleep alone—it may also have made him dislike traditional Russian culture, although he later pursued his own abuses.

After the turmoil subsided, Ivan emerged as co-tsar with his sister, Sophia, as regent. She wielded the real power, and Peter and his mother were relegated to the royal estate in Preobrazhenskoe, a village near Moscow. As a child, Peter was uncontrollable, attracted to military games, during which he inflicted real injuries on his playmates. He particularly liked fireworks and setting off cannon. On the more serious side, he developed his play troops, some 600 of them, into a trained fighting unit and learned military tactics and artillery from a Dutchman.

At age 16, Peter's mother arranged her son's marriage, but he grew bored with his wife and returned to his military games, particularly attracted to boats and formulating plans for a great navy. In 1689, Sophia's rule ended after Peter gained the support of the *streltsy*, banished her from the Kremlin, and sentenced her to a convent. This left Ivan and Peter as co-tsars, but given Ivan's condition, Peter commanded the nation. (Ivan died in 1696, leaving Peter the sole tsar.)

At first, Peter showed little inclination for serious rule. He formed the "Drunken Council of Fools" that consumed vodka in enormous quantities and entertained itself by engaging in impaling, flogging, and beard burning. He went sailing on the White Sea, and although he captured Azov from the Turks in 1696, he left most affairs of state to relatives who governed incompetently and robbed the treasury.

In 1697, he developed a wild scheme to launch a crusade against the Turks. To broaden his knowledge and gain the help of other nations, he decided to tour Europe. During part of this journey he traveled incognito. His disguises—which he intended his hosts to see through—proved ludicrous. Peter was a huge man—nearly seven feet tall—and thus easily recognizable. Furthermore, he traveled with a large entourage, including jesters and dwarfs, whom he considered amusing.

The tour displayed Peter's wild excesses as well as his seriousness. He visited with monarchs and worked on the docks, where he learned navigation and shipbuilding. In Amsterdam, during a four-month stay, he studied mathematics, astronomy, architecture, and fortification. He asked questions constantly, inquiring as to what things were used for and how they worked. Attracted by Amsterdam's museums, he decided to start one in Russia and toward this end learned how to mount swordfish and embalm human freaks.

In 1698, Peter arrived in London, where he visited Parliament, viewed the shipyards, and learned various crafts. He also wrecked the ornate house in which he stayed, his drunken revelries destroying everything. Much to Peter's dismay, none of the European nations agreed to support his crusade against the Turks.

The journey had an important ramification for Russia: Peter determined that Western societal practices must shape his nation. Soon he imported European experts in large numbers, sent Russians abroad for schooling, and promoted European clothing— even wielding a barber's razor, grabbing *boyars* to shave off their beards, and levying a tax on any nobleman who wore one. Sometimes his reforms were trivial, but in all, Peter believed that his nation was backward and that if it did not Westernize it would fall victim to European expansion. Importantly, he supported those aspects of Western society that expanded his power and complemented Russian political practices; most notably, he liked Prussian absolutism, with its central government direction of the economy, because it contained the masses, a time-honored approach in Russia.

Peter also crushed challenges to his power and used torture to extract information and retaliate against treason. When the *streltsy* revolted late in 1698 and forced him to cut short his European tour, he punished the rebel regiments with great cruelty. He constructed chambers where the *streltsy* and their families were flogged, roasted, and even buried alive. In between bouts of drinking and feasting, the tsar personally oversaw the tortures and brandished an axe that he used to behead several prisoners.

Although often haphazard in action, Peter did

most everything with a central goal in mind: expanding Russia. This is why he wanted internal reform and why he involved himself in European diplomacy. In 1699, he arranged a secret treaty with Poland and Denmark to attack Sweden. Four years later, amid the ensuing war, Peter began building St. Petersburg (which he named after his patron saint) on marshy territory still claimed by the Swedes. In 1707, Peter, whose armies had not been impressive against Sweden, tried to arrange a peace, but the enemy refused. Reinforced by additional men and new techniques, Peter attacked the Swedes in 1709 at Poltava and scored an enormous victory. By 1710, the Russians controlled the Baltic shoreline from Riga to Vyborg, and for the first time, Peter's success stimulated modern nationalism in his country.

Emboldened, Peter attacked the Turks, but in 1711 suffered defeat and had to relinquish Azov. Other attacks followed against Finland and two Swedish-owned ports and further expanded Russian territory, making Peter's nation the primary power in northern Europe. In 1721, after additional battles against Sweden, Russia obtained Livonia, Ingria, and the Karelian Isthmus.

Meanwhile, Peter pursued greater internal reform, trying to advance Westernization. Among other political measures, he restructured the government, dividing Russia into eight provinces, each with its own governor appointed by him. To stifle and crush dissent, he developed a secret police. In the military area, Peter modernized and enlarged the Russian forces. He required that all landowners serve some time in the army and stipulated that peasants conscripted complete a 25-year term. He imported weapons from Europe and by 1725 had a standing army of 200,000. True to his infatuation with the sea, he founded the Russian navy and developed a Baltic fleet, built largely at the St. Petersburg shipyards.

While expanding the military, which consumed some 80 percent of the national budget, Peter sought additional taxes. At first, he increased the tax on each household. In 1718, after this proved insufficient, he initiated the "soul tax"—a levy on each adult male. Since the gentry, clergy, and merchants were excluded from the tax, its burden fell almost exclusively on the peasants. Their condition worsened in 1722, when Peter solidified serfdom by forbidding any serf from leaving the estate on which he worked, unless he had his master's permission.

To foster economic growth, Peter copied from the Royal Mint in England and began coining money—gold and silver pieces that replaced the older kopeks (small silver ovals) and the ever-present foreign money. Peter expanded industry, in part by importing Western craftsmen to teach Russians new skills. Much of this industrial expansion related directly to the military. Russian factories produced armaments, including muskets and bayonets, and to support this Peter developed an iron industry in the Urals. He also turned to consumer production, and glassware, china, linens, and other goods were manufactured. The merchants who developed the industries received tax breaks and the benefit of forced labor. Peter ordered serfs, criminals, and orphans to work in the factories.

The tsar also expanded foreign trade, especially linked to St. Petersburg. Determined to make his new city a thriving port, he provided lower shipping fees and ordered that certain goods be transported only from there. By 1725, St. Petersburg's shipping superseded that of Archangel.

In an attmept to modernize Russia, Peter tried to improve Russian education, but obtained mixed results. An elementary school system began in 1714; soon after Peter's death, however, it collapsed. He founded the Russian Academy of Sciences that offered courses to students from the gentry, but it did not achieve respectability until the nineteenth century. In another modernization effort, Peter diluted the power of the nobility by opening it to newcomers. Persons who served in the civil service and obtained high rank, or sailors and soldiers who became officers, automatically gained the standing and privileges of a hereditary noble.

Peter closely supervised the construction of St. Petersburg, determined to make it different from Moscow in both form and function. He ordered that many buildings be constructed of stone to avoid the crude appearance of Moscow and its frequent fires, and European architects designed baroque buildings surrounded by Western-style gardens. With its architecture, its great Winter Palace, and its imposing fortress, the city did not look "Russian," and the emerging beauty led many to call it the Venice of the North. Peter loved St. Petersburg for its Western modernity. In 1712, he began transferring the government to his new city, which became the capital.

Many Russians disliked Peter and his policies. Traditionalists opposed his Westernization efforts and peasants buckled under his oppressive taxes. There appeared widespread discontent with Peter's violence, a cruelty that seemed epitomized by the treatment of his eldest son and heir to the throne, Alexis. Unlike Peter, Alexis disliked government and the military. He had no desire to rule Russia, and when his father ordered him to either renounce his succession or enter a monastery, he fled to Europe. After a long search, Peter's agents found him and convinced him to return home, promising he would not be punished. Alexis went back to Russia and in 1718 dutifully renounced his succession. Peter, however, was convinced that his son's flight was part of a plot to erase his Westernization program. He subsequently ordered Alexis to reveal those who helped him run away. To get more names, he ordered that his son be tortured, and he watched the gruesome procedure. After one such session, Alexis died.

In the early 1720s, Peter led an assault against Persia that, in 1723, resulted in obtaining the western and southern coasts of the Caspian Sea. In 1724, his health deteriorated rapidly from a urinary-tract infection, and on 25 January 1725, suffering complications from a cold, he died.

Peter left a stunning legacy; he had consolidated the Russian state and greatly expanded it, making it a powerful nation founded on absolutism. Historians dispute the extent to which Peter revolutionized Russia, with most agreeing he did not invent the nation's Westernization; rather, the process had begun years before under previous tsars, particularly IVAN III. Nevertheless, he reshaped Russia—hastening the developments that accelerated under CATHERINE II—and in the end created a paradox: a European power on the one hand, internal tensions on the other—tensions so substantial that years later, in 1917, they pulled the nation apart in a great upheaval, the Communist Revolution, itself undone in the 1980s under MIKHAIL GORBACHEV and BORIS YELTSIN.

References: Grey, Ian, *Peter the Great, Emperor of All Russia*, 1960; Massie, Robert K., *Peter the Great: His Life and World*, 1980.

Pilsudski, Józef
(1867–1935)
Poland

After Józef Pilsudski led an armed band that stole money from a Russian mail train, he organized an army to pursue his ambition—an ambition encouraged by his mother while he was still in his boyhood: an independent Poland liberated from Russian control.

Józef Pilsudski was born on 5 December 1867 in Zulowto to Józef Pilsudski and Maria Billewicz Pilsudski. At an early age, he learned to hate the Russians who controlled Poland, including Lithuania, then federated with Poland. Their harsh treatment of the Poles in the wake of an aborted Polish uprising in 1863 and three successive partitions of Poland influenced Józef, as did his father, who participated in the uprising, and his mother, who vividly recounted for

"Romanticism of ideals, realism in their pursuit."

him the cruelty of the occupiers. Józef attended secondary school in Lithuania at Vilnius (then called Wilno), and in 1885 entered the university at Kharkov with plans to study medicine. The authorities, though, soon suspended him for anti-Russian political activities after he edited a journal in which he criticized the oppression in Lithuania. In 1887, they exiled him for five years to Siberia under the contrived charge that he had conspired with his brother and others to assassinate Czar Alexander III. (His brother had indeed helped the conspirators).

When Pilsudski returned to Poland in 1892, he joined the Polish Socialist Party (PPS). This group saw Poland's liberation as requiring two developments: independence from foreign control and formation of a Marxist state. In 1894, the PPS chose Pilsudski as its leader, and he edited a party newspaper, *The Workman*, declared illegal by the authorities. He and others then packed the editions in suitcases and smuggled them to the subscribers. In 1900, Pilsudski was arrested, but after pretending to go insane by going into tirades and refusing food, he gained transfer to a hospital in St. Petersburg, from which he later escaped with the help of a Polish doctor who took him from the prison by passing him off as a newly hired orderly. Pilsudski made his way to Cracow in 1901 (at that time part of Austrian Poland).

Three years later, he traveled to Japan to try to take advantage of a war then under way between that nation and Russia. He asked the Japanese for help in waging a battle with Russia that would bring Poland its independence, but they rejected his proposal. Following this, he entered Russian Poland surreptitiously to help in fomenting revolutionary activity then under way. After the czarist government crushed the 1905 revolution in Russia, the PPS was torn by a clash between Pilsudski, who promoted Polish independence and a distinct Polish nationalism, and an internationalist left that advocated a revolt in cooperation with the Marxists in Russia.

Pilsudski proceeded to de-emphasize socialism and stress military action. He believed that the Russian Empire was nearing collapse and that a general war might soon erupt in Europe. To address this possibility, he formed the secret League of Military Action in Austrian Poland in 1908. He obtained money for this organization by leading a daring raid on a train traveling from Russia to Warsaw. The bandits stopped the train at Bezdany, took jewels and money from the passengers—only the Russian ones—and raided the lucrative mailbags containing securities and banknotes. Two years later, the Austrian government provided him funds, hoping he would cause problems for Russia.

As Pilsudski had predicted, war engulfed Europe. During World War I, he commanded the First Brigade of the Polish Legion against the Russians. Germany and Austria-Hungary backed this effort as a way to tie down Russian troops and allow German forces to reinforce the western front. Unknown to them, however, Pilsudski continued to maintain his own underground intelligence group.

He demanded that in return for Polish assistance, the Germans and Austrians (the Central Powers) recognize Poland's right to independence. On 5 November 1916 they agreed, and Pilsudski and several other moderates and conservatives—not "tainted" by Marxism—were appointed to the Polish State Council. Shortly thereafter, the Central Powers rejected Pilsudski's demand that his army be recognized as an official part of Poland, and they placed the Polish Legion under German supervision. Pilsudski refused to cooperate with this, and the Germans arrested him in July 1917. Meanwhile, the Russian Revolution had toppled the czarist regime, a development with great implications for Poland's, and Pilsudski's, future.

In 1918, after the Central Powers lost the war, Pilsudski entered Warsaw as a hero. He went immediately to work: Earlier in the year, the Allied governments had proclaimed their support for an independent Poland, and he now began forming a government. In November, Pilsudski was made provisional president and commander in chief. He named Roman Dmowski, a conservative nationalist, as his representative to the Paris Peace Conference. In 1919, the Polish Parliament proclaimed Pilsudski as chief of state, and at his urging it elected Ignace Jan Paderewski as prime minister, a moderate whom Pilsudski hoped would appeal to all of Poland's political factions.

Pilsudski then turned his attention to Russia. The Communist army threatened Poland, seeking to push through the Poles and into Germany. Pilsudski worked to drive the Russians back and create a Polish-Lithuanian Commonwealth and an independent Ukraine that could block Russian and Communist expansion. In April 1920, he allied Poland's army with Ukrainian forces, and together they entered Kiev and declared the Ukraine independent. Soviet forces counterattacked, however, and forced the Poles all the way back to Warsaw. As the city neared collapse, Pilsudski launched a successful assault, but was unable to advance into Russia. A peace treaty in 1921 recognized Poland's border with the Soviet Union to the east of Pinsk.

Pilsudski resigned the presidency in 1921 when a new constitution reduced his power and shifted it to the prime ministry. He continued as army chief of staff, but resigned this position on 29 May 1923 when a conservative government gained power. Despite his opposition to Marxism, Pilsudski preferred a moderate socialist approach and a federated government, whereas the right wing favored a strong central government and expressed hostility to Ukrainians and Jews.

As Poland's government wallowed in chaos and excluded all leftists from participation, Pilsudski staged a coup on 12 May 1926. He refused the presidency but ran the country as a dictatorship and from 1926 to 1928, and again in 1930, served as prime minister. Although at first he received substantial support from the left, Pilsudski eschewed a radical agenda in favor of developing a more efficient and orderly government under the leadership of specialized technocrats. The government stimulated economic recovery by developing industries and establishing a state monopoly of transportation.

When political opponents campaigned to end Pilsudski's dictatorship in 1930, he had them arrested and imprisoned. In 1932, he reached a nonaggression pact with Russia and two years later reached another one with Germany, although he personally considered Hitler untrustworthy and had earlier suggested to the French a military alliance to overthrow the German dictator, a suggestion France rejected. In his last months, Pilsudski refused to meet with Hitler and pushed to improve Poland's military. Death from cancer ended his effort on 12 May 1935, and four years later Poland fell to the invading German army, an event that began World War II. Shortly after the war, Poland lost most of its autonomy to the Soviet Union and complete independence did not come again until 1989 under the nationalist workers' movement led by LECH WALESA.

References: Jedrzejewicz, Waclaw, *Pilsudski: A Life for Poland*, 1982; Reddaway, W. F., *Marshal Pilsudski*, 1939.

Pindling, Lyndon Oscar
(b. 1930)
Bahamas

On a memorable Tuesday in 1965, Lyndon Oscar Pindling entered the halls of the Bahamian Parliament, took the ceremonial mace, and heaved it out the window. His action proclaimed that white society must change, and that blacks must gain their equality and independence.

On 22 March 1930, Lyndon Oscar Pindling was born into a black family of modest means in Nassau. His father was an immigrant from Jamaica, a former schoolteacher and a policeman who, four years after Lyndon's birth, quit his position to open a grocery store, a move that provided the family with enough money to support Lyndon's education. The youngster attended Western Senior School and then Government High School in Nassau.

The pronounced dichotomy in Bahamian society greatly influenced Lyndon. The islands, a British colony, had a dominant white elite that controlled everything. Most blacks had little money and no effective political power. Society was strictly segregated along racial lines (and would remain so until reforms in the 1950s). Lyndon could see the inequality in the contrast between the white-owned mansions on Nassau's Bay Street—the Bahamas of tourist ads—and the squalor in which most Bahamians lived. The "Bay Street Boys," as they were called, ruled the islands imperiously.

Pindling determined to advance his education, and in 1948 he enrolled at the University of London, studied law at Middle Temple (also in London), and in 1953 entered the English bar. He later said that his years in England awakened him politically and intensified his desire for reform. He returned to the Bahamas, began to practice law, and in 1954 joined the Progressive Liberal Party (PLP), formed to challenge Bay Street and advance black nationalism and civil rights. Two years later, Pindling won a seat to the House of Assembly, and in 1958 he helped lead a strike by black taxi drivers that resulted in limited political reform. The white elite reacted by organizing the United Bahamian Party (UBP).

Pindling continued to criticize the social inequities that suppressed blacks and the political regulations that created a malapportioned legislature and protected white power. In 1959, his efforts resulted in the end to property qualifications for voting, and in 1962 women were granted the right to vote. Pindling was reelected to the House that year, although the PLP won only 8 of 33 seats. In 1963, Pindling became chairman of the PLP, and his and the party's pressure for greater Bahamian autonomy convinced the British that they should expand home rule while maintaining full authority over foreign relations.

Pindling intensified his attacks against the white minority, accusing it of illegalities in issuing government contracts and harboring criminal connections in the gambling industry. Then on 27 April 1965, he reacted to the expulsion of a PLP member from the House by throwing the ceremonial mace out the window, proclaiming he was returning it to the people. A PLP colleague took the legislature's hourglass and tossed it too, causing it to smash in pieces. The two men then left the House and entered the street, where blacks gathered and began singing "We Shall Overcome."

As elections approached in 1967, Pindling called on Bahamians to remain peaceful and follow the tactics developed in the United States by Martin Luther King Jr. Most took his advice and flocked to the polls, producing enormous gains for the PLP. On 16 January 1967, Pindling succeeded Roland Symonette, a shipping magnate and the UBP leader, to become prime minister.

"We shall win with a mighty meekness."

Pindling undertook immediate reforms. He appointed the first all-black cabinet in Bahamian history, announced increases in the casino taxes, and began efforts to establish free high schools. Elections in 1968, forced by a breakup of the PLP ruling coalition, resulted in a landslide victory for Pindling and his party. After this, he advocated a new constitution to gain the Bahamas yet more internal authority, and in 1969 Britain allowed a status just short of nationhood. He also brought under closer supervision the white-dominated corporations that developed and largely owned the island of Freeport. Pindling opened the island's tourist and industrial complex (especially the oil refining industry) to investments by black Bahamians.

In 1972, Pindling ran for reelection on a pro-independence platform, partly to deflect attention from a moribund economy. He easily defeated the opposition, and on 9 July 1973 the Bahamas obtained its complete independence as a member nation of the British Commonwealth.

In foreign affairs, Pindling established diplomatic relations with Communist Cuba, but advocated a balanced approach with continued close ties to the United States (particularly needed for defense purposes). Pindling built new schools and clinics, developed low-cost housing, and improved the utilities. His encouragement of foreign investments opened new opportunities for Bahamians, and black businessmen formed consortiums.

In the 1982 election the PLP won 32 of 43 seats, and a similar result occurred in 1987, despite allegations that Pindling and other government officials were involved in drug trafficking. No evidence directly linked the prime minister to the illicit activity, but it did reveal an administration rife with corruption. The PLP lost the 1992 elections to the Free National Movement, although the outcome was likely little influenced by the scandal. Lyndon Pindling left office after having created a new status for the Bahamas, both internationally and with respect to the nation's society.

References: Albury, Paul, *The Story of the Bahamas*, 1975; Craton, Michael, *A History of the Bahamas*, 1986.

Pinto da Costa, Manuel
(b. 1937)
São Tomé and Príncipe

Manuel Pinto da Costa not only won his homeland's independence but also envisioned a radical leftist future. Economic pressures, however, caused him to abandon his socialist commitment.

Manuel Pinto da Costa was born on 5 August 1937 in Agua Grande, the son of an official in charge of plantations. In the late 1950s, he graduated from the University of London and traveled to France, Cuba, and then East Germany, where he began his graduate studies and obtained a doctorate in economics. Pinto da Costa joined the São Tomé nationalist movement in its early stage, when in 1960 he helped organize the Committee for the Liberation of São Tomé and Príncipe (CLSTP), both islands located in Africa's Gulf of Guinea. At that time, Portugal controlled the two islands with a regime that relied on political oppression and an exploitive contract labor system on the plantations, and it kept the CLSTP well contained. In 1965, the CLSTP called for agrarian reform to help the many landless workers. The organization, however, succumbed to factional fighting and weakened greatly. Seven years later, the CLSTP reorganized as the Movement for the Liberation of São Tomé and Príncipe (MLSTP), and at a meeting in Guinea the members chose Pinto da Costa as general-secretary.

Hope for independence increased after a coup occurred in Portugal that established a provisional government there in April 1974. Pinto da Costa and the MLSTP, still classified as an illegal organization, remained underground, but they formed the Civic Association as a legal political arm under the leadership of a popular poet and nationalist, Alda do Espirito Santo, who was Pinto da Costa's sister-in-law. Pinto da Costa rejected Portuguese attempts to hold a referendum concerning nationhood and demanded immediate independence. In August, Portugal agreed to self-determination for São Tomé and Príncipe. Yet violence occurred during an MLSTP demonstration in September, when government troops fired into a crowd.

In October, Miguel Trovoada, the MLSTP secretary for foreign relations, led a delegation that opened talks with Portugal. The Portuguese recognized the MLSTP as the representative for the people of São Tomé and Príncipe, and the two sides agreed to an interim government and elections for an assembly. São Tomé and Príncipe gained its independence on 12 July 1975.

Amid this shift to a national government, Pinto da Costa and the moderates within the MLSTP purged its extreme left wing. After Pinto da Costa was named president in 1975, he appointed his associate and fellow founder of the CLSTP, Miguel Trovoada, as prime minister. In foreign relations, Pinto da Costa established ties to the Soviet Union and Communist China. He also opened the Conference of Nationalist Organizations of the ex-Portuguese Colonies at São Tomé and called for economic cooperation to rebuild the new nations. At the end of 1975, he directed the state acquisition of most plantations, made necessary when many Portuguese fled the islands at independence.

Pinto da Costa built a strong following as president and won reelection in 1980 and again in 1985 in an atmosphere that did not permit multiparty competition. In the 1980s, he moderated his policies, encouraging Western investment in order to diversify his nation's economy, which was heavily reliant on cocoa, and moving closer to the European Economic Community. In 1986, Pinto da Costa returned some of the state-run plantations to private investors and promoted tourism. And although he developed a close relationship with the revolutionary movement in Angola, he improved his diplomatic contacts with the West. He withdrew from the 1991 presidential election, and Miguel Trovoada became the nation's new leader.

Reference: Hodges, Tony, and Malyn Newitt, *Sao Tome and Principe*, 1988.

Price, George Cadle
(b. 1919)
Belize

A political leader who couched his ideology in religious terms, George Price dominated Belizean politics for over four decades, successfully broadening his support to include radical nationalists. His impassioned leadership guided Belize to its independence from Britain and protected its sovereignty against threats from Guatemala.

George Cadle Price was born on 15 January 1919 in Belize City. He came from a large family of 11 children, and his father earned a middle-class living as an auctioneer. Of Scottish and Mayan Indian ancestry, George attended Holy Redeemer primary school and later enrolled at St. John's College in Belize City. At this point he considered becoming a Catholic priest and studied briefly at the St. Augustine Seminary in the United States at Bay St. Louis, Mississippi. In 1942, though, his father became ill, and the young man returned home. He then returned to St. John's and after graduation became a private secretary to a local businessman.

In the 1940s, several political groups vied for power in Belize, then a colony called British Honduras, and Price joined the General Workers Union (GWU), which emphasized labor issues. Another group, the Peoples' National Committee, meanwhile, advocated independence from Britain. In 1944, Price ran for the Belize City Council but lost. He tried again in 1947 and won the seat he would hold for 17 years. That same year he was elected president of the GWU. Despite his position in support of the workers, he won backing from many middle-class businessmen and those favoring close ties to the United States. He appealed strongly to his country's Indian heritage, advocating that its name be changed to Belize because it derived from a Mayan word.

A major event in 1949 encouraged Price to form a new political party. That year, Britain devalued the British Honduran dollar, a move that angered Price and others because it was done arbitrarily and damaged the workers' purchasing power. Price organized the People's United Party (PUP) and called for complete independence. From 1950 to 1956, he served as party secretary, during which time he allied the PUP with the GWU and won election to the colonial legislature. In 1956, he became party leader, and two years later was elected mayor of Belize City. An opposing group, the National Party (NP), charged Price and the PUP with religious prejudice and communist leanings. Largely consisting of professionals and the wealthy elite, the NP opposed independence.

While offering vague promises of "cooperativism" and "wise capitalism," Price more clearly continued to call for an end to colonialism. In 1957, he led a delegation to London to open talks about his homeland's status, but the discussions collapsed after it was revealed he had met secretly with Guatemalan leaders to discuss a possible union with their nation. In 1958, the British tried him for sedition, but he was acquitted.

Britain soon agreed to a new constitution that would prepare the colony for independence, and in 1961 Price's PUP swept the legislative elections. Two years later, Price headed another delegation to London. This time he acquired a grant of internal self-government and on 1 January 1964 became prime minister.

He faced many problems, including a depressed economy and devastation from a recent hurricane. Externally, he had to deal with the Guatemalans, who had long considered British Honduras their territory and in an ominous move stationed troops along the border separating the two states.

In 1965, Price and the PUP won national elections, and he promised independence by 1967. That, however, did not occur, primarily because the Guatemalan threat proved disruptive. In 1973, British Honduras officially changed its name to

Belize, and Price continued to press for nationhood. Talks bogged down as Belize and Britain tried to reach an agreement with Guatemala that would guarantee Belizean territorial integrity. After these discussions failed, Price and the British agreed to move ahead with independence, and on 21 September 1981 Belize became a nation within the British Commonwealth.

In the early 1980s, Price and the PUP experienced a stronger political opposition from the United Democratic Party (UDP). This group won all the seats to the Belize City Council in 1984, and Price subsequently shifted his policies to emphasize liberal reforms. In legislative elections later that year, he lost his seat in the House of Representatives, and the UDP finished ahead of the PUP. Price then led a move that expelled the right-wingers from his party.

The indefatigable Price mounted a comeback and in 1989 regained the prime ministry. Two years later, he reached an agreement with Guatemala whereby that nation recognized Belize's sovereignty. Despite this accomplishment, in 1991 Price lost his reelection bid.

Reference: Bolland, O. Nigel, *Belize: A New Nation in Central America*, 1986.

Prithvinarayan Shah
(1722–1775)
Nepal

Prithvinarayan Shah combined practicality in his military pursuits with a vision: to unite the disparate Nepalese states into one kingdom.

On 27 December 1722, Prithvinarayan Shah was born into the royal House of Gorkha. A small hill state founded in 1559, Gorkha did not expand until the seventeenth and eighteenth centuries, when it began to ally with various surounding states. Nar Bhupal Shah, Prithvinarayan's father, acquired territory to the north and east, but failed at other attempts at conquest. His successes, though, served as a model for his son, who adopted his father's determination. Prithvinarayan's foster mother, Chandraprabha, also served as an important influence, since for a time she ran Gorkha's affairs and taught Prithvinarayan leadership duties. Late in her life, she assisted Prithvinarayan after he became king.

In Prithvinarayan's childhood, Nepal was not a unified state but a collection of small kingdoms similar in social and political structure, but each retaining its own autonomy. Political alliances and wars punctuated the scene, but generally speaking, the masses and their rulers had no desire to build a large state. In the Kathmandu Valley three kingdoms dominated, formidable obstacles to any Gorkhian desires to expand.

Analysts believe Prithvinarayan's leadership made a crucial difference in Gorkha's development. Crowned king of Gorkha on 3 April 1743, Prithvinarayan claimed he had a vision to conquer the Kathmandu Valley. He certainly had ambition, and almost immediately began planning his assault. While the valley kingdoms were wealthier and bigger than Gorkha, he knew they suffered from disputes among themselves; and although huge mountains, towering above 9,000 feet, surrounded the valley and acted as protective barriers, Prithvinarayan believed his military tactics would succeed based on surprise. He quietly acquired loans and bought weapons, including new European-made muskets. In an assault on Nuwakot, he had his troops move cautiously, proceeding down the Trisuli Ganxa River disguised as farm workers, digging irrigation ditches and preparing fields. Then he gathered them on boats and amid darkness crossed the river, attacking and conquering the city in September 1744.

Prithvinarayan knew many failures, particularly his defeats in trying to capture Kirtipur, a key settlement in any movement into Kathmandu Valley. In one assault on the town he was almost killed. Yet his vision and determination remained fixed, and after adjusting his tactics, in 1767 he finally captured Kirtipur, with the help of collaborators inside the settlement who threw open the gates to allow the invaders to enter. As usual, Prithvinarayan punished those who had resisted, cutting off the tips of the enemy's noses.

From Kirtipur, Prithvinarayan proceeded to conquer the important cities of Kathmandu and Patan. In September 1768, his troops sneaked into Kathmandu during a religious festival and the city fell without a fight. Patan fell without a struggle, too, and he subsequently moved into eastern Nepal, where nobles who had been bribed allowed his troops within the walls of Bhadgaon. Here resistance occurred as defenders set fires and burned houses to impede the invaders. The palace, however, fell and in 1769, after 26 years of conquest, the entire Kathmandu Valley had been united under a single ruler. Throughout, Prithvinarayan had kept his followers united, linked to his vision.

With his victory, Prithvinarayan protected Gorkha power by isolating Nepal. He expelled all foreigners, including Roman Catholic missionaries, and banned unacceptable music. By the time Prithvinarayan died in 1775, he had established a foundation for further expansion, which continued until 1790.

There have been many changes in Nepal since Prithvinarayan ruled. He, however, is remembered as the father of modern Nepal.

Reference: Stiller, Ludwig, *The Rise of the House of Gorkha*, 1973.

Qābūs ibn Sa'īd
(b. 1940)
Oman

The Dhofar rebellion, which began in 1965, emerged as the greatest modern challenge to Oman's unity. Qābūs staged a palace coup that turned the tide against the rebels.

As a child in a ruling family, Qābūs ibn Sa'īd was educated in England at Bury St. Edmunds in Suffolk and at the Royal Military Academy in Berkshire. For a brief period, he served as an officer with the British army in Germany. When he returned home in 1965, his father, the Sultan Sa'īd ibn Taymūr, worried that his son would usurp him and so held him as a prisoner. Sultan Sa'īd also grew isolated and suspicious of outside influences, which he considered more threatening as oil revenues enriched the sultanate.

As Qābūs languished, a great threat spread: a rebellion in Dhofar (south Oman). This area had been largely ignored in Oman's development and many people there had close ties to neighboring Yemen. The rebels, who by 1971 called themselves the Popular Front for the Liberation of Oman—a largely Marxist group—captured nearly all of Dhofar, excepting Salalah. As conditions deteriorated, Qābūs staged a successful palace coup in 1970, pledged himself to ending the revolt, and in a visit to Muscat, promised an end to his father's isolationist policies.

Qābūs subsequently undertook a modernization program. He changed his country's name from "Muscat and Oman" to Oman—not just a linguistic maneuver, but a change that indicated an end to an old compartmentalization and a beginning of a more unified state. He built roads, hospitals, schools, harbors, and industrial facilities. Furthermore, he ended many medieval laws and political practices his father had supported; for example, he introduced a modern cabinet system and municipal councils. He also ended Oman's isolation by joining the Arab League and the United Nations. On the other hand, he continued traditional tribal structures and avoided democratization.

With regard to the Dhofar rebellion, his army won several important battles and largely crushed the opposition by 1976, although some operations continued into the early 1980s. Qābūs accomplished this with Iranian military help and a few Jordanian troops. He then acted to more closely integrate Dhofar with Oman through a development program.

Qābūs resolved a border dispute with Yemen in 1992 and the following year announced his intent to establish a free-trade zone with the Yemenis. Although Qābūs has modernized his homeland, Oman remains crtiical of democratic institutions and committed to rule under a sultan.

Reference: Graz, Liesl, *The Omanis: Sentinels of the Gulf,* 1982.

al-Qaddafi, Muammar
(b. 1942)
Libya

Muammar Qaddafi's critics have censured him as "100 percent sick and possessed of the demon." But he has long considered himself a crusader striving for a Pan-Arabia that would stretch from the Persian Gulf to the Atlantic Ocean, a utopian Islamic state.

As a boy, Muammar al-Qaddafi listened to Radio Cairo and heard Egyptian leader GAMAL ABDEL NASSER advocate Pan-Arabism, Arabic unity, and self-determination. Muammar thought about conditions in Libya where, under King Idris I, foreigners dominated, and he thought about his own humble beginnings.

Muammar was born in 1942 in a tent on the desert; his father was a Bedouin, or nomadic herder, who owned no modern conveniences and who lived much as his ancestors had centuries before. In Muammar's youth, Libya was under Italian control, and the dictator Benito Mussolini settled 150,000 Italians in the colony. After World War II, Libya emerged impoverished. Then, in 1949, the United Nations decided that Libya should become an autonomous kingdom, a move emanating not largely from Libyan demands but from Western strategic considerations. On 24 December 1951, King Idris I declared Libya independent. But he can hardly be considered a founder—both his regime and his nation remained under European domination.

Amid these developments, Muammar gained an education. He went to elementary school at Sirte and devoutly attended the local mosque. In 1956, he began his secondary education at Sebha in southwestern Libya and earned a reputation as an outspoken proponent of Nasser's Pan-Arabism. School authorities expelled him after he led several demonstrations against Western domination. He completed his secondary education at a school in Misurata, graduating in 1963. He had already developed a plan to overthrow King Idris, whom he considered a puppet of the West: He would enter the Royal Libyan Military Academy and gain a following within the army.

By this time, oil, a lucrative revenue source, had been found in Libya. Yet corruption overwhelmed the monarchy and intensified dissatisfaction with the king. Numerous groups emerged to challenge the government, among them Qaddafi's Free Officers' Movement, founded in 1964. On 1 September 1969, Qaddafi headed a military coup that overthrew King Idris. He declared himself commander in chief of the armed forces and chair of the new governing body, the Revolutionary Command Council. His coup signified a truly independent nation—he had deposed the Western-dominated monarchy.

Qaddafi immediately pursued his Pan-Arab ideals wth a combination of conviction and a desire to become the new Nasser. Qaddafi considered the Arab world bound by a common language, religion, and history. He desired unity, a reinvigorated Islam, and a reformed society. In 1972, he initiated an alliance with Egypt and Syria to form the Federation of Arab Republics, but nothing substantive came of it. One year later, he undertook a closer economic relationship with Egypt, but it soon collapsed.

> *"I believe that the Arab nation can become a paradise."*

This latter dissolution revealed Qaddafi's erratic side, his unpredictable lurches that to many made him dangerous: While approaching Egypt, Qaddafi urged Libyans to march on Cairo and ignite a revolution to advance Arab unity. Thousands gathered, but Egypt turned them away at the border. Relations deteriorated further after Qaddafi condemned Egypt's negotiations with Israel. Indeed, Qaddafi denounced anyone he considered soft on Pan-Arabism. He called Yassir Arafat, the leader of the Palestine Liberation Organization, weak and treasonous and expelled many PLO militants; he advocated the assassination of Jordan's King Hussein; and he called the pro-Western Saudis the "pigs of the Arabian peninsula."

In 1973, Qaddafi invaded Chad and occupied the Aouzou Strip, an area with uranium deposits. His troops, however, suffered a severe defeat in 1987 and had to retreat. He may have sponsored coup attempts in Egypt and Syria, and there is evidence to indicate he envisioned creating a Greater Saharan Islamic republic that would unite black Muslims by overthrowing governments in Niger, Burkina Faso, Ghana, Senegal, Mali, Somalia, and The Gambia.

When Qaddafi infiltrated Tunisia with hundreds of spies, that nation broke diplomatic relations in 1985. As relations with Algeria and Morocco also worsened, Qaddafi reacted to his isolation by forging an alliance with Iran. He also vilified both capitalism and communism and insisted that the United States and the Soviet Union were equally imperialist, with communism being a godless blasphemy.

Qaddafi backed terrorist groups as a way to destroy Israel. This reflected his belief in radicalized masses and his disgust with "weak" Arab governments. He ordered Libyan political opponents overseas assassinated and likely supported Black September (a terrorist group that killed Israeli athletes at the 1972 Olympics in Germany), the Revolutionary Council, and the Irish Republican Army, among others. There are also strong indications—but no hard evidence—that he was involved in the 1986 bombing of a discotheque in Berlin that killed an American soldier, to which the United States retaliated by launching air attacks on Libya in an attempt to kill Qaddafi. The assault, however, missed the Libyan leader and killed or wounded several of his children. In another affront to the West, Qaddafi refused to turn over two Libyans suspected of carrying out the bombing of Pan Am flight 103, which exploded over Scotland in 1988 and took 270 lives.

Within Libya, Qaddafi has made the government a major shareholder in all oil companies, has nationalized banks and insurance companies, and established government cooperatives. He considers Western capitalist influences morally damaging and has promoted Islamic fundamentalism and his own socialist scheme called the "third universal theory." While economic changes have disrupted oil and agricultural production, new housing, schools, and hospitals have helped the masses and, coupled with measures to more equally distribute wealth, have won him a widespread following.

In the late 1980s, Qaddafi moderated his foreign policy and ended his isolation with his Arab neighbors. Relations with Chad, Jordan, Tunisia, Morocco, Algeria, and Egypt greatly improved, and he even visited Cairo in 1989.

Qaddafi's governing style involves closed meetings with his Revolutionary Command Council, edicts issued without consultation, and policy pronouncements in speeches—pronouncements that immediately become law. He remains a curious combination of idealist and opportunist, a man with plans, yet a man unpredictable.

References: Blundy, David, and Andrew Lycett, *Qaddafi and the Libyan Revolution*, 1987; First, Ruth, *Libya: The Elusive Revolution*, 1974; Qaddafi, Muammar, *The Green Book*, 2 volumes, 1976 and 1980; Sicker, Martin, *The Making of a Pariah State: The Adventure Politics of Muammar Qaddafi*, 1987.

Qassem, Abdul Karim
(1914–1963)
Iraq

Ever since the end of World War I, Iraq had seethed with nationalism. In the 1950s, Abdul Karim Qassem formed a secret group and led a tumultuous, bloody revolution that swept away British influences.

Abdul Karim Qassem was born on 21 November 1914 in a poor section of Baghdad. His father raised corn along the Tigris River and the young boy experienced much poverty, an episode that likely influenced him in his later efforts at social reform. Abdul attended school in Baghdad and at age 17, after a brief stint teaching in elementary school, he enrolled in the Iraqi Military College. Two years later, in 1934, he graduated as a second lieutenant. Shortly thereafter, he attended the General Staff College and in 1941 became a staff officer. That same year, he gained command of a battalion and during World War II fought against rebellious Kurdish tribesmen in northern Iraq, a campaign that earned him the highest Iraqi military decoration.

In 1942, while stationed in Basra near the Persian Gulf, he developed a friendship with Abdul Salim Arif. These two men circulated antigovernment leaflets and developed a mutual desire to overthrow the Iraqi monarch, King Faisal II (successor to the nationalist FAISAL I), who was under heavy Western influence. In 1948, Qassem commanded a battalion in Palestine as the Iraqi army battled against Israel in the Arab-Israeli War of 1948–1949. He fought bravely but grew embittered over what he considered to be incompetent leadership in the Arab loss. He then attended a senior officers' school in Britain for six months. When he returned to Iraq, he was elevated to the rank of colonel and one year later became a brigadier general. During the Suez Crisis of 1956, he commanded Iraqi troops in Jordan. His schooling and his combat experience brought him respect and prominence.

During these years, Qassem maintained his desire to overthrow the government. In 1956, he helped organize the Free Officers, a clandestine association whose central organization he headed. He and Abdul Salim Arif worked closely together and awaited the right moment to launch a revolu-

"I will not hang traitors just because you or some other group demands it!"

tion. That came in 1958 when an anti-Western revolt broke out in Lebanon. The pro-Western Iraqi monarchy feared that the upheaval might spread to neighboring nations and then Iraq, so it ordered Iraqi troops into Jordan. When Arif's battalion entered Baghdad on 13 July, however, it did not move on. Instead, the next day Arif's troops occupied the radio broadcasting studio, and he went on the air to proclaim a revolution. Surprisingly, King Faisal II, perhaps thinking of the best way to save his life, did not resist the assault. If that was his plan, it did not work, for on 14 July the king, the crown prince, and the rest of the royal family were gunned down and killed as they left their palace. Only later in the day, around noon, did Qassem arrive in Baghdad with his troops. Some attribute this delay to his desire to let Arif take all the risk in the initial assault. Whatever the case, Qassem soon gained the upper hand on Arif in a political struggle that continued throughout the revolution.

Qassem assumed the leading role as prime minister in the new government, and Arif became his deputy, while also serving as minister of the interior. A dispute soon occurred over the direction of the revolution. Arif favored a Pan-Arabist stance that sought unity with Egypt and inclusion in the United Arab Republic founded by GAMAL ABDEL NASSER, while Qassem supported a more independent Iraqi nationalism and leftist internal reform. Later in 1958, Qassem accused Arif of plotting to assassinate him. Arif was removed from office and, after a trial, sent to jail.

Qassem then began promoting himself as the sole architect of the revolution. His political hold was tenuous, though, and became even more so after he formed an alliance with the Communists in Iraq. Their uncompromising attacks on opponents resulted in atrocities and a negative popular reaction. Two incidents in particular angered people: First, in March 1959, after Qassem crushed a revolt by army units in Mosul, his Communist allies went on a rampage, killing anti-Communist supporters of the rebellion. Second, later that summer Communist elements encouraged massacres in Kirkuk.

In his foreign relations Qassem announced a nonalignment policy, but his actions tilted Iraq strongly toward the Soviet Union and included substantial arms purchases from Communist bloc nations. At the same time, contacts with Egypt deteriorated as Qassem condemned the Nasserists, and they in turn plotted to overthrow him.

In October 1959, the Pan-Arabist Ba'ath Party concluded that Qassem's antagonism toward Egypt and alliance with the Communists necessitated his elimination. Young Ba'athists developed a plot to kill him as he passed along a street in Baghdad. On 7 October they attacked but succeeded only in wounding their target. Several of the conspirators fled Iraq, including SADDAM HUSSEIN.

The following year Qassem allowed political parties to form—but only if they did not threaten national unity. In practice, this meant no independent party could last long and, in any event, by late 1960 Qassem moved to suppress all parties—both right wing and left wing. Qassem found his only support among segments of the military, and after the assassination attempt he lived an increasingly isolated existence barricaded in the office of the defense ministry.

Qassem did undertake several domestic reforms. First, he lessened the maldistribution of land by limiting the size of holdings. Second, he expanded women's rights in the areas of marriage, divorce, and inheritance. Third, in a highly successful move he reduced the influence of oil companies by confiscating large amounts of land held by the foreign-owned Iraq Petroleum Company. This step prepared the way for full nationalization in 1973.

Qassem's unpopularity increased when he failed to quell a Kurdish rebellion in northern Iraq. He also caused discontent by boggling an attempt to capture Kuwait: In 1961, he announced that this neighboring nation was part of an Iraqi province, but when British, and later Arab League troops, landed there to guard against an invasion, Qassem backed down.

As the economy declined and Communist influence became destructive, and foreign policy mistakes and Qassem's own isolation increased, the army—Qassem's last solid support—grew restless. On 8 February 1963, a military coup led by Ba'athists toppled Qassem. After a bloody street battle, he was captured and executed. Qassem left behind many failed policies but also substantial reforms and an Iraqi government freed from foreign control.

References: Dann, Uriel, *Iraq under Qassem: A Political History, 1958–1963*, 1969; Marr, Phebe, *The Modern History of Iraq*, 1985.

Rabuka, Sitiveni
(b. 1949)
Fiji

After a controversial election in 1985, Sitiveni Rabuka stormed Parliament and arrested the prime minister. For the next decade Rabuka stood as a symbol of Fijian nationalism and dramatically altered the government while pursuing an erratic course.

Sitiveni Rabuka was born in September 1949 in Cakaudrone Province. Fiji was, at the time, a British colony, as it had been since 1874. The young Rabuka attended Queen Victoria School and then obtained military training at the Army Staff College in Waiouru, New Zealand. In 1979, he attended the Indian Armed Forces Staff College and two years later the Joint Staff College in Australia. In 1984, he commanded a battalion in the Sinai as part of an international peace-keeping force.

By this time Fiji had gained its independence, which was granted in 1970, and became a member of the British Commonwealth. Although RATU KAMISESE MARA was influential in guiding Fiji to nationhood, the break with Britain came more from British initiative than from the Fijians. Mara was Fiji's first prime minister, and he held the position into the 1980s. In that decade, though, Fijian politics grew bitter as the nation polarized between indigenous Fijians and the East Indian minority. (Indians were brought into Fiji in the late nineteenth and early twentieth centuries to work on plantations as indentured laborers.) Elections in April 1985 resulted in a coalition government dominated by Indians. Fijians demonstrated against this development, and at this point Rabuka assaulted the Parliament building and arrested the prime minister, Timoci Bavadra. Rabuka then formed a temporary government with Mara as foreign minister.

Rabuka tried to govern as prime minister, but political maneuvering by various factions prevented him from doing so. He did, however, gain appointment as commander in chief of the Fijian military. As political confusion continued, Rabuka staged a second coup on 25 September 1985. He forced the government to annul the 1970 constitution, and on 7 October 1987 he proclaimed Fiji a republic fully removed from the British Commonwealth. Rabuka,

> *"[I will strive to] promote dialogue and consensus as a basis [for] resolving our national problems."*

who was promoted to brigadier general, served as home minister in the new government and Mara served as prime minister.

In 1990, Fiji returned to full civilian rule after Rabuka resigned his government post, and a new constitution prepared the nation for parliamentary elections. After his resignation, Rabuka acted erratically. In July 1991, he resigned his military commission and again became home minister. In October, he defeated two prominent Fijian chiefs and won election as head of the new Fijian Political Party (FPP). Consequently, he resigned as home minister. The following year, the FPP finished first in elections to the House of Representatives. Largely a Fijian party, the FPP surprised many by forming a coalition government with the Fiji Labour Party, an Indian-based organization. After the victory, Rabuka became prime minister.

Although long identified as the most prominent Fijian nationalist, one who feared Indian ascendancy, Rabuka seems committed in the 1990s to easing his nation's ethnic strife. In February 1994, the voters elected him to a second term as prime minister.

Reference: Scarr, Deryck, *Fiji: A Short History*, 1984.

Rahman, Mujibur
(1920–1975)
Bangladesh

Mujibur Rahman had the distinction of being involved in not one, but two independence movements. First he participated in the efforts to create Pakistan, free from British control; then he led the fight to form Bangladesh, free from Pakistani control.

Mujibur Rahman—popularly known as Mujib—was born into a moderately wealthy landholding family on 17 March 1920 in Tungipara, then a part of India. As a student he showed more interest in sports than in studies. He attended a mission school in Gopalganj, where he obtained a secondary education, interrupted by a serious health problem when he developed glaucoma. In 1942, he entered Islamia College in Calcutta and became general-secretary of the Islamia College Student Union and a member of the All-India Muslim League, which called for the advancement of Muslim political rights.

Rahman's home district, Faridpur, and Bengal in which it was located were overwhelmingly Islamic, and Mujib himself was of this religion, hence his joining the League and his attachment to MOHAMMED ALI JINNAH, the great leader who by the 1940s had broken with the effort to keep Hindus and Muslims together in the Congress Party and instead advocated a separate Muslim state to be called Pakistan.

In 1946, Mujib won election to the Bengal legislature and tried to calm the rioting that had broken out between Hindus and Muslims, unleashed on a greater scale after Britain had agreed to allow India its independence within two years. At the same time, Mujib continued his studies, and in 1947, he graduated from Islamia College with a B.A. in history and political science. Then he entered law school at the University of Decca in East Bengal.

Mujib supported the British decision to create from India two nations: India as a primarily Hindu state and Pakistan as a primarily Muslim one. When Pakistan emerged as an independent nation in 1947, it had a curious configuration: West and East Pakistan were separated from each other by 1,000 miles of Indian territory. The West, carved out of Punjab, and the East, carved out of Bengal, seemed united based on a common religion, but they had serious ethnic differences, and to Mujib and other Bengalis it became clear that the Punjabis intended to dominate the new nation (even though Bengal had a majority of the population).

Mujib took a momentous step in 1947 when he quit the Muslim League and formed the East Pakistan Muslim Students' League which opposed the attempt by Mohammed Jinnah, now Pakistan's ruler, to make Urdu, a dialect spoken in the Punjab, the new nation's official language. In 1949, Mujib helped found Pakistan's first opposition political party, the Awami League, initially headed by Hussein Shaheed Suhrawardy. Mujib's political positions and his campaign to organize the menial workers at the University of Decca brought him expulsion from law school.

In 1954, Mujib won election to the East Pakistan legislature under the United Front banner, a coalition of the Awami League and other opposition parties. He was imprisoned by the Pakistani government, however, as a threat to national security. After 14 months in jail he won election in 1955 to Pakistan's national legislature, where he became a greater thorn in the central government's side. He demanded more autonomy for East Pakistan and protested when constitutional reforms in 1956 did not bring this about.

A military coup in 1958 brought Mohammed Ayub Khan to power in Pakistan, and he immediately criticized Mujib as a national threat. Mujib defied Khan's nationwide ban on political campaigning and was imprisoned again. After his release in 1959, he continued his efforts for East Pakistan autonomy, winning a widespread following among Bengalis. He gained a reputation for sincerity concerning the plight of most Bengalis, who lived in great poverty.

When in 1965 Pakistan failed to adequately defend East Pakistan in the Pakistani-Indian War, Mujib became convinced that the nation should be converted into a confederation of East and West, under which the central government would control only defense and foreign policy. Khan rejected this proposal and in 1966 arrested Mujib for what he called secessionist activities.

Another crisis arose in 1970 when a cyclone and tidal wave ravaged Bengal, killing one million people. When the Pakistani government failed to provide enough relief, Mujib warned of civil war should national elections not be held soon. Those elections, scheduled prior to the disaster, occurred in December, and Mujib's Awami League swept the districts in East Pakistan, gaining a majority in the national legislature. When the government, now headed by Yahya Khan and Zulfikar Ali Bhutto, refused to convene the legislature, Mujib issued a declaration of independence on 23 March 1971.

Two days later, Pakistani troops entered Dacca and began slaughtering largely unarmed Bengalis, causing over a million deaths and producing a mass exodus of Bengalis to India. Yahya Khan outlawed the Awami League and arrested Mujib.

The turmoil in East Pakistan, and particularly the pressure felt by India from the millions of Bengali immigrants, led the Indian government to enter the Pakistani conflict. On 3 December 1971, war broke out between Pakistan and India. On 6 December, India extended its recognition to an independent Bangladesh, and by 16 December Pakistan was defeated. On 8 January 1972, Pakistan released Mujib, and he returned to Bangladesh a hero.

Mujib created a parliamentary system and served as prime minister. He favored a moderate socialist policy and nationalized major industries while gaining foreign assistance for the widespread poverty and starvation in Bangladesh. In January 1975, Mujib gained greater political control as reforms created a powerful presidency, which he assumed. His regime became a dictatorship and as famine and inflation ravaged the country, opposition to him grew. On 15 August 1975 a military coup overthrew Mujib, and he and most of his family were killed. The army leaders came from the right wing and there were indications the United States backed the coup. Mujib had led in creating Bangladesh, but the nation still faced massive problems from an explosive population growth and a declining economy.

References: Bhattacharjee, G. P., *Renaissance and Freedom Movement in Bangladesh,* 1973; Maniruzzaman, Talukder, *The Bangladesh Revolution and Its Aftermath,* 1980.

Rahman, Tengku Abdul
(1903–1990)
Malaysia

The man whom Malaysian nationalists rallied around, Tengku Abdul Rahman, was in many ways a reluctant leader. He valued his own leisurely pursuits, but in the end his organizational acumen and his charisma made him highly successful.

Tengku (Prince) Abdul Rahman was born 8 February 1903 in Alor Star, the capital of Kedah, a northwestern Malay state, which his family had ruled for centuries. He was one of 45 children of Sultan Abdul Hamid Halim Shah, who had eight wives in his harem and who suffered from mental illness and lived for many years as a recluse. His mother, Makche Menjelara, a Siamese commoner, wielded considerable influence in Malaya, since she shrewdly amassed her own fortune, separate from the sheikh's. At this time Britain dominated Malaya, although the local sultans were allowed to retain some power.

As a young man, Abdul Rahman obtained an education often against his desires, for he preferred sports to anything academic and thought more of swimming and fishing than his studies. Nevertheless, he attended an English-run school in Alor Star and then a Siamese school in Bangkok. In 1915, he returned to Malay to complete his secondary education. He sailed for England in 1920, planning to continue his education, but first underwent extensive tutoring to compensate for his weak academic background, after which he enrolled in St. Catherine's College at Cambridge. He obtained his bachelor's degree in 1925 and then began a long, intermittent pursuit of a law degree (which he did not complete until 1949). While at Cambridge, he earned a reputation as a friendly socializer known for driving fancy cars at high speeds and avidly following horse racing.

In 1931, Abdul Rahman entered the Kedah Civil Service, in which he applied himself vigorously. The following year, he obtained the rank of district officer, a major civil service position. He worked in Kuala Nerang, a small town, before being transferred to the Langkawi Islands and, later, Sungei Patani. He frequently criticized the way the bureaucracy functioned and, as a result, was forcibly transferred to other districts.

With World War II, however, Malaysia temporarily fell to Japanese control. Abdul Rahman remained at his government post throughout the Japanese occupation and protected Malayan interests, although for years afterward he had to endure accusations of collaboration with the enemy. Once the war ended, Britain sought to rule Malaysia as it had before, but found a land whose nationalism

> *"There is nothing very remarkable about me. I am an ordinary, simple man . . ."*

had been stirred, partly by the damage done British prestige in the Japanese conquest. Many Malays disliked Britain's plans for a Malayan Union that would centralize power in the Crown, and DATO ONN formed the United Malay Nationalist Organization (UMNO) in 1946 to oppose this plan, thus stimulating Malayan nationalism and earning for himself the reputation as Malaya's first nationalist leader.

In 1949, Abdul Rahman left Kedah and became deputy public prosecutor in Kuala Lumpur. At this time, friends encouraged him to enter national politics. He had been a leader in the north for the UMNO in 1946, but quit in a disagreement over policy issues. In the meantime, the UMNO had been successful in getting the British to modify their plans for a Malayan Union, but the party organization splintered when Dato Onn advocated that it admit Chinese and other non-Malayans as members. After Onn left the party, the UMNO asked Abdul Rahman to become its leader, and he agreed.

In this prominent role, Abdul Rahman had to not only deal with Chinese-Malayan friction, but also with local Communists, who had taken up arms to end British rule and establish an independent Marxist state. The British, wanting to defeat this faction, realized they would have to cooperate with Abdul Rahman and his brand of nationalism. Abdul Rahman strengthened his position by advocating a cooperationist approach toward Malaya's Chinese and East Indians (a policy close to the one proposed by Onn). He linked the UMNO with the Malayan Chinese Association and the Malayan Indian Congress to form a group called the Alliance. It promoted a reconciliation of internal Malayan differences while pronouncing a stridently nationalistic program aimed at gaining independence. The Alliance did well in municipal elections held in 1952.

When Britain appeared reluctant to grant Malaya its nationhood in 1954, Abdul Rahman led a peaceful protest that included widespread resignations from government positions. This jeopardized British-Malayan cooperation and threatened to encourage moderate nationalists to join the Communists. With this, Britain changed its stand. Elections for a national legislature in 1955 produced a sweep for the Alliance, and the British promised Abdul Rahman, who had become chief minister, that independence would be granted. On 31 August 1957, the independent Federation of Malaya emerged, consisting of nine states on the Malay Peninsula, plus Malacca and Penang. Abdul Rahman became the first prime minister.

As his nation's leader, Abdul Rahman achieved numerous successes. He effectively suppressed the Communist uprising and presided over territorial expansion when, in 1963, the Federation of Malaya became the Federation of Malaysia consisting of 11 states on the Malay Peninsula and 2 states on Borneo (although Singapore was evicted from the federation in 1965 for its Chinese influence and became an independent nation).

But Abdul Rahman was not able to end ethnic tensions. In 1969, widespread rioting exploded between Malays and Chinese, the immediate cause being gains made by the latter in recent elections. One year later, Abdul Rahman resigned as prime minister when his powers were usurped by a special national council formed to handle the ethnic emergency. It was headed by Abdul Razak, who became prime minister. Abdul Rahman died on 6 December 1990, having skillfully guided an ethnically disparate land to its independence.

References: Hanna, Willard A., *Eight Nation Makers: Southeast Asia's Charismatic Statesmen*, 1964; Turnbull, C. Mary, *A History of Malaysia, Singapore, and Brunei*, 1989.

Ramgoolam, Seewoosagur

(1900–1985)

Mauritius

Although hailing from the Indo-Mauritian elite, Seewoosagur Ramgoolam distinguished himself by maintaining close ties with those less privileged. Many remember him as *chacha*, meaning "uncle," a term of respect and endearment.

Seewoosagur Ramgoolam exemplified Mauritius's educated Indian class under British rule. Born on 18 September 1900 in Belle Rive, as a young man he studied in England, where he became a Royal College laureate and earned a degree in medicine. After he returned to his homeland in 1932, he faced the rampant discrimination that relegated most Indo-Mauritians to menial positions. When middle-class Creoles formed the short-lived Action Liberale in 1907 to get more autonomy for Mauritius, they stirred nationalist sentiment that influenced Ramgoolam. He was also affected by the teachings of MOHANDAS KARAMCHAND GANDHI and in the mid-1930s began writing literary and social criticism. In 1940, he helped found *Advance*, a newspaper that stressed philosophical views.

Amid World War II, Ramgoolam protested what he considered Creole dictatorial methods in controlling the Port Louis city council. He became an outspoken advocate for Indo-Mauritians, common workers, and small planters, and believed that social and economic reform would come only after a change in the constitution. Some constitutional revisions occurred in 1947 and provided greater power for Indo-Mauritians, but within strict limits.

Around this time, Ramgoolam served in the Council of Government, and in 1950 led the Labour Party, an alliance of East Indians and Creoles. (The party was founded in 1936 by Maurice Curé, who first appealed to the common workers.) Opponents fearing Indian, and particularly Hindu, domination attacked Ramgoolam as a communist, but in 1955, Labour won 13 of 19 council seats, and with constitutional changes in 1957, Ramgoolam became prime minister (originally called chief minister), a position he held into the postindependence era.

Between 1959 and 1967, Ramgoolam and his Labour colleagues moved toward gaining Mauritian independence. In this they not only had to contend with British authority but also with competing ethnic and class groups. Ramgoolam accused Britain of moving too slowly. In the 1963 elections, he helped Labour defeat serious challenges from competing parties, and maneuvered it into a prominent position for postindependence leadership. By 1965, however, Ramgoolam's Labour government faced widespread dissatisfaction as sugar prices fell and taxes rose. In the 1967 elections, Ramgoolam convinced Labour to support independence. He asserted that with autonomy the Franco-Mauritian influence would lessen, and Mauritius would get American economic help.

Labour, in alliance with several other parties as the Independence Party, swept the elections, and on 22 August 1967 Ramgoolam oversaw the Mauritian Assembly's approval to separate from Britain. In October, serious ethnic and religious rioting occurred, and Ramgoolam had to call in British troops to restore order. But Mauritius moved toward finalizing its independence, gained in March 1968.

As prime minister, Ramgoolam began efforts to diversify the economy by stressing industrial development and increased tourism. Per capita income rose in the early 1970s, as did the gross national product. Ramgoolam became president of the Organization of African Unity, and it held its annual meeting on Mauritius in 1974.

Many younger Mauritians, however, believed Ramgoolam had become too old and too attached to an entrenched ruling class, and that Labour had become too corrupt—they wanted change, and so they organized the Militant Mauritian Movement (MMM). In the late 1970s, a sharp economic downturn strengthened the MMM while weakening Ramgoolam. The prime minister tried scaring voters by portraying the MMM as communist and he arrested its leaders, but his appeal had clearly declined, and in the 1976 and 1977 elections the MMM finished first. Ramgoolam remained in power through a coalition arrangement, but in 1982 the MMM swept the balloting and Ramgoolam's prime ministry came to an end. Shortly thereafter, in 1983, he filled the largely ceremonial role of governor-general. He died at Port Louis, the capital, in December 1985.

Reference: Simmons, Adele Smith, *Modern Mauritius: The Politics of Decolonization*, 1982.

Rashid bin Said al-Maktum
(1912–1990)
United Arab Emirates

The seven emirates comprising the United Arab Emirates (UAE) never experienced a nationalist movement. Yet bringing these entities together took skill and determination, and in this Rashid bin Said al-Maktum provided crucial leadership.

Along the Persian Gulf, in a dry climate zone nearly devoid of all vegetation, lies the emirate of Dubai, home of Rashid Bin Said al-Maktum. As with the other emirates in the area, Dubai's rulers have come from the most powerful tribal grouping, in this case Al bu Falasah, a subtribe within the larger Bani Yas tribe. In 1912, Rashid was born into this setting while his father, Said, ruled Dubai. Rashid received little formal schooling, but as a young man educated himself at the Dubai customs house. He developed a business mentality that reflected the commercial orientation of his tribe and of Dubai in general.

As he matured, Rashid displayed his father's shyness but also the forceful personality of his mother, Hussah, considered by some the real power behind the throne. Beginning in 1939, Rashid as regent (a status he would hold until 1958, when he became emir) exerted most of the power in Dubai, with the help of Hussah. At one point, they invited several political opponents to Rashid's wedding, men who had been plotting to overthrow the regency. When these guests arrived, Rashid's armed guards acted according to plan and attacked and killed them. This ended all significant challenge to Rashid's rule.

With his business mentality, Rashid focused on building Dubai commercially and modernizing his society. Dubai is essentially a commercial city-state whose financial and trade strategies have brought great wealth. Early in his regency, Rashid encouraged Indian and Iranian merchants to settle in Dubai, resulting in a vibrant business community. In the 1950s, he developed Port Rashid, which today includes the Gulf's biggest shipyard, the Dubai dry dock. During the next decade, Rashid oversaw the development of Dubai's oil reserves, which brought lucrative earnings. Amid much criticism about extravagance, he constructed the Dubai International Trade Center in the 1980s, the tallest building in any Arab state, to provide office and exhibition space. It has been a financial success.

Concurrent with his economic programs in the 1960s and 1970s, Rashid provided important political leadership in forming the UAE. In 1968, Britain, faced with severe financial difficulties at home, announced its intention to withdraw from the lower Persian Gulf area, which it had dominated for over a century. Neither Dubai nor any of the other emirates, which Britain called the Trucial States, favored this loss of protection, partly because Iran and Saudi Arabia coveted territory in the area.

The British encouraged Dubai, Abu Dhabi, the five other Trucial States, and Qatar and Bahrain to join together in a federation. Rashid worried lest Dubai lose its autonomy, particularly to Abu Dhabi, long a rival in the gulf. Nevertheless, he put aside his objections and in February 1968 agreed to join Abu Dhabi in a federation and invite the other states to do likewise. Qatar and Bahrain never joined—they went their own separate ways—but the Trucial States agreed, and in late 1971 the UAE was created. Rashid became its vice-president and, in 1979, its prime minister.

Throughout the negotiations to form the federation, Rashid proved cooperative, but he also strongly defended Dubai's interests, and as such his homeland gained political parity with Abu Dhabi, the wealthiest emirate. He obtained an equal number of votes with Abu Dhabi in the Federal National Council (the UAE advisory body.) He also secured an agreement requiring that Dubai and Abu Dhabi concur before any decision by the Supreme Federal Council, the ruling organization comprised of the leaders from all seven emirates, could take effect. And he won important positions for his three sons in the new federation government, one of whom became defense minister.

Within the UAE, Rashid staunchly defended Dubai's business enterprises from excessive regulation by the UAE. His overall protective stand hampered the development of an effective federation military, and since Rahsid did not meet his emirate's revenue quota, most funding for the UAE was left to Abu Dhabi. These actions promoted friction with Abu Dhabi's emir, ZAYED BIN SULTAN AL-NUHAYYAN.

Thus while Rashid displayed boldness in helping to form the UAE, his actions in protecting Dubai created a weak federal government. Rashid died on 7 October 1990, leaving a legacy of a wealthy business state always prepared to follow its own interests.

References: Abdullah, Mohammed Morsy, *The United Arab Emirates: A Modern History*, 1978; Peck, Malcolm C., *The United Arab Emirates: A Venture in Unity*, 1986.

Ratieta, Naboua
(b. 1938)
Kiribati

Naboua Ratieta prepared his people for independence but lost his leadership to those who considered him attached to colonial practices.

Naboua Ratieta, the son of Bauro Ratieta, was born in 1938 at Banaba, one of the Gilbert Islands then under British control. He grew up, however, on Nonouti, where he lived with the family that adopted him. He attended Bairiki Primary School and then continued his education at King George V School.

In 1957, Ratieta joined the government in a civil service position, eventually working in the medical department. At this time, Gilbertese nationalism began stirring. In 1961, Reuben Uatioa formed the Tungaru, a group dedicated to protecting Gilbertese culture. Four years later, Uatioa joined Ratieta and several others in founding the Gilbertese National Party, the colony's first political party. The group's platform advocated greater autonomy, improved education, Gilbertese unity, and the promotion of Gilbertese culture.

Several political changes soon occurred. In 1967, the British permitted an elected House of Representatives and Ratieta won a seat representing Marakei. A new constitution in 1971 gave power to elected members of the Executive Council to conduct government business. Ratieta became the member for communications, works, and utilities and developed policy proposals. Under this arrangement, the British governor still held ultimate authority.

Another constitutional change in 1974, however, gave the Gilbertese internal self-government with a House of Assembly, Council of Ministers, and a chief minister. Ratieta, who led the National Progressive Party, was chosen to fill the latter position.

Ratieta supported independence, and as the colony moved toward that goal a separatist movement appeared on the Ellice Islands, where the people disliked the prospect of a Gilbertese-dominated government that would likely ignore their economic concerns. After the Ellice people approved independence in a referendum, Ratieta agreed that separation should occur. Following a transition period, the Ellice people formed their own nation of Tuvalu in 1978. Ratieta opposed another separatist movement by Banaba, which subsequently did not separate from the Gilberts.

The chief minister soon lost his support among many Gilbertese who considered him too representative of the elite colonial power structure and unresponsive to the general electorate. In 1978, the House of Representatives met to compile a list of candidates for the upcoming presidential election that would prepare for independence. They bypassed Ratieta and chose four other candidates. Ieremia Tabai, the 27-year-old nationalist and leader of the Democratic Labour Party, won the presidency. He waged a populist campaign that urged the voters to rise above island and village loyalties and consider public issues.

Thus when Kiribati emerged as a fully independent nation on 12 July 1979, Tabai was its first president (a position he held for 12 years). Nevertheless, Ratieta had led in promoting Gilbertese nationalism and directing his homeland toward nationhood.

References: MacDonald, Barrie, *Cinderellas of the Empire: Towards a History of Kiribati and Tuvalu*, 1982; Talu, Alaima, et al., *Kiribati*, 1979.

Ratsiraka, Didier

(b. 1936)

Madagascar

Tensions swept across Madagascar in the early 1970s. The nation reeled under years of French economic domination, and class divisions became more acute. The cautious socialist president PHILIBERT TSIRANANA rejected reform and crushed a student protest. Then political assassination struck. In this maelstrom, Didier Ratsiraka founded the Democratic Republic of Madagascar and led his countrymen on a tumultuous revolutionary course.

Ratsiraka was born on 4 November 1936 in Tamatave Province on Madagascar's eastern coast. As a *côtier*, or coastal resident, he came from an area that had for years been denied many of the benefits and economic rewards obtained by the Merina people of the interior and the recent French rulers. This societal division became a significant influence in Ratsiraka's life. After attending the lycée in Tananarive, he received a scholarship to study at the École Navale in France. He served with the French navy as an engineer officer, attended the École Superieure de Guerre Navale, and became a lieutenant commander.

In 1972, Ratsiraka became a prominent leader in the protests against President Tsiranana. Despite having led the Malagasy in forming the First Malagasy Republic within the French Commonwealth in 1958, and two years later overseeing the acquisition of full independence, Tsiranana suffered domestic criticism from a foreign policy that aligned Madagascar with conservative black African governments and white South Africa. His economic policy permitted the French to control three-fourths of Madagascar's exports and over half of its commercial agriculture, important in a land where farming dominated. With all of this, the gap between wealthy and poor widened. The protestors of 1972 demanded nationalization of foreign industries and a lessening of wealth disparities.

In October 1972, Tsiranana resigned the presidency and Major General Gabriel Ramanantsoa became ruler. He initiated drastic changes that included removing French military forces. Ratsiraka was prominent in these actions. He served as for-

> *"If Communism means struggling against social inequalities . . . then we are all Communists."*

eign minister, negotiated the French evacuation of the naval base at Diego Suarez, and after a visit to Peking in 1972, became an enthusiastic admirer of Marxist China.

Despite Ramanantsoa's reforms, political unrest continued, stimulated by high unemployment and inflation. In 1975, Ramanantsoa resigned, but a new president was assassinated just six days into his term. On 15 June 1975, a military directorate appointed Ratsiraka president. The Malagasy confirmed this appointment in a referendum that established the Democratic Republic of Madagascar, an affirmation of Ratsiraka's readable and popular *Charter for the Malagasy Revolution* (his "Red Book," patterned after that of Communist Chinese Chairman MAO TSE-TUNG).

Ratsiraka proclaimed a true revolution under way. He immediately nationalized banks and insurance companies and moved Madagascar away from the West and into a close alliance with Communist nations. He received aid from China and closed the United States space-tracking station. In 1976, he furthered his power by forming the National Front for the Defense of the Revolution, a coalition of several political parties, and banned multiparty politics. After winning reelection in 1983, he at first continued to expand the government's role in the economy, but economic conditions worsened, and as a result, Ratsiraka did an about-face—in 1986 new laws established a free-market economy.

France subsequently forgave Madagascar its huge debt and, sensing a profitable market, increased its investments there. Ratsiraka moved Madagascar back into cooperation with South Africa and even met with South African President FREDERIK WILLEM DE KLERK. In 1991, opponents forced Ratsiraka to accept multiparty competition and appoint a new prime minister. Elections two years later ended Ratsiraka's presidency.

Reference: Stevens, Rita, *Madagascar*, 1988.

Remeliik, Haruo
(1934–1985)
Palau

Haruo Remeliik helped draft perhaps the most radical modern constitution among all the world nations: It provided for a nuclear-free zone. His participation in this controversy led to his death.

Haruo Remeliik was born in 1934 while Palau was under Japanese control as part of the Micronesian islands. During World War II, the United States evicted Japan, and in 1947 the area was made an American trust territory under United Nations oversight.

In the 1950s, Remeliik worked in the judicial system and in the 1960s became Palau's deputy district administrator. By this time a strong nationalist movement had emerged in Palau, accompanied by charges that the United States had neglected the area's development. In 1979, Remeliik served as president of Palau's constitutional convention and gained his reputation as "father of the constitution." This document reflected Remeliik's views as leader of the Peoples' Committee for a Nuclear-Free Constitution. Palauans worried that the United States would make their homeland a site for storing nuclear materials, and they opposed the incursion into their waters of nuclear-powered and nuclear-capable ships. Hence, the constitution declared a nuclear-free zone while it established a representative government with a president and national legislature.

The United States reacted strongly against the constitution and refused to grant Palau complete independence until the nuclear-free zone article was eliminated. Remeliik initially defended the constitution and won election as Palau's president in 1981, with the island republic still operating as a U.S. Trust Territory.

Palauan politics then took a tumultuous turn. The United States pressured Palau to hold several referendums in an attempt to get the 75 percent vote required to amend the constitution. American representatives used propaganda and promises of financial assistance to influence the outcome. In each instance, however, Palauans rejected any change.

At the same time, labor strife shook Remeliik's administration when government workers went on strike, and violence erupted when dissidents bombed the president's office. To many, the strike appeared confusing and inexplicable, and some observers wondered if outside agitators had not been a factor. Remeliik eventually issued an executive order granting amnesty to those accused of violence.

"Let's forget this [violence] and work for the betterment of our new nation."

The president won reelection in 1984 and shifted his position on amending the constitution. This may have been caused by his longstanding support of close relations with the United States (despite his disagreement with the Americans over the nuclear issue) and by Palau's increased need for financial aid. Indeed, the United States held out the promise of several hundred million dollars in funds.

Still, Remeliik wavered and in his final days seemed to be renewing his support for the constitution as written. Then on 30 June 1985, President Remeliik was shot and killed near his home in Koror. The police arrested four men who were later released after evidence against them proved faulty. The assassination continued to be controversial, with charges that before the killing mysterious outsiders from the United States had infiltrated the islands. In any event, some Palauans had wanted a more stable presidency that could correct the republic's weak financial condition and more effectively promote the constitutional change necessary for independence and stable relations with the United States.

Although Remeliik did not bring nationhood, he authored the constitution that established Palau's republican government under a radical principle. In 1993, Palauans finally agreed to enter a compact of free association with the United States that overrode the nuclear-free zone provision of the constitution, with America providing economic assistance and promising not to use Palau as a military training ground. Palau thus became completely independent on 1 October 1994 under President KUNIWO NAKAMURA.

References: Aldridge, Bob, and Ched Myers, *Resisting the Serpent: Palau's Struggle for Self-Determination,* 1990; Robie, David, *Blood on Their Banner: Nationalist Struggles in the Pacific,* 1989.

René, France Albert

(b. 1935)
Seychelles

Early on a June morning, 60 Seychellois men disguised in camouflage outfits disembarked from a Tanzanian ship and, armed with rifles, captured two police stations on Mahé along with the office used by the Seychelles president, who was away on a trip. This assault, known as "the coup of 60 rifles," led to the attackers installing France Albert René as their nation's leader.

Unlike the man who preceded him as president, France Albert René came from a modest background. He was born on 16 November 1935 on the island of Farquhar, where his father managed a plantation. In his schooling, he proved to be an outstanding student and earned scholarships to St. Joseph's Convent School, St. Louis Primary School, and Seychelles College Secondary School, all located on the island of Mahé.

He then traveled to Switzerland in the mid-1950s, where he studied for the priesthood. After two years, however, he left and attended St. Mary's College in England and the University of London, where he studied law and in 1957 obtained his degree. He lived in the Seychelles from 1958 until 1961, when he returned to England to study at the London School of Economics. During his stay, which lasted until 1964, he joined the Labour Party and became politically active.

All during these years, the Seychelles were under British control. Shortly after René returned home for the second time, in the mid-1960s, universal adult suffrage led to the formation of political parties. James Mancham organized the Seychelles Democratic Party (SDP). René founded the Seychelles People's United Party (SPUP) and, unlike Mancham, called for independence.

Although the SDP outpolled the SPUP in the 1967 elections, René's party captured three of the eight elective seats in the Upper Council. From this base of support, René continued his push for nationhood. He also rallied many workers behind him by sponsoring the first trade union strike on the islands and particularly appealed to the black Creole population by using race in his campaigns; he criticized Mancham's Asian heritage and talked about removing all East Indians from the Seychelles.

René's position was so popular that Mancham eventually supported Seychelles independence. In 1974, the SDP won most of the seats in the legislature, but Mancham included René in a coalition government, and the SPUP leader served as prime minister (a largely powerless position). When Seychelles gained its independence on 29 June 1976, Mancham became the nation's first president.

Mancham and René had substantial political differences. Mancham favored capitalist development, although under Seychellois direction. René, on the other hand, desired a socialist society to deal with the nation's dire poverty. Mancham did not remain in the presidency long; his profligate ways and high-profile partying angered many Seychellois, as did substantial inflation. Then came "the coup of 60 rifles," and with it René's presidency, which he declared to be the beginning of the Second Republic.

> *"As a child I was poor. I was always against the system and I always wanted to change it."*

An ambitious and idealistic man, the new ruler quickly outlawed all competing political parties. He reorganized the SPUP into the Seychelles People's Progressive Front (SPPF), which a national constitution in 1979 recognized as the only legitimate party. Elections continued to be held, but competing candidates came from within the SPPF. Furthermore, René made the legislature subservient to the party. He also restricted basic rights, such as freedom of association and the press, a move he claimed was necessary to eliminate factional strife and foster unity and development.

René's administration ushered in a dedicated and hard-working government. He proclaimed: "We are not communists—just Indian Ocean socialists," and then proceeded to nationalize the medical service, establish a National Youth Service dedicated to improving communities and indoctrinating young people in socialism, and founded a government-operated commodities market that brought price controls. René also emphasized the development of tourism. His economic results

337

proved mixed, while many who opposed his socialist approach fled the country after he began arresting dissidents.

Throughout the 1980s, René increased government involvement in the economy, creating public corporations and even smaller state businesses. Many Seychellois benefited from the public medical care and education along with a new social security system. Without fully competitive elections, however, the degree of René's popularity was difficult to measure. In 1981, mercenaries from South Africa attempted a coup that failed. In 1993, he agreed to a constiutional convention that produced a new governing document providing for a multiparty system. René won that year's presidential election and continues to preside over Seychelles.

Reference: Franda, Marcus, *The Seychelles: Unquiet Islands*, 1982.

Renner, Karl
(1870–1950)
Austria

Karl Renner, who was born into an impoverished family, became a lawyer, and then emerged as a prominent politician in his country's most trying time: its devastation resulting from World War I. He helped to build the first Austrian republic and became president of the second one.

Born on 14 December 1870 into a peasant family in Unter-Tanowitz, Bavaria, Karl Renner studied law at the University of Vienna, where he embraced a modified Marxism that sought socialism through peaceful rather than violent means. Along with other reforms, he advocated a social security system and an easing of the taxes levied on the lower class. He soon joined the Social Democratic Party, a socialist organization that represented the urban workers. Renner obtained his law degree in 1896 and then worked in the library of the Reichsrat, or Austrian Parliament. In 1907, he won election to the Reichsrat as a Social Democrat.

Renner wrote numerous treatises in which he expressed a desire for a democratic political system. In so doing he displayed a strident nationalism and strongly opposed the existing Habsburg monarchy, which for centuries up until World War I had ruled Austria and achieved a degree of centralization under MARIA THERESA and JOSEPH II. When, during the war, rivalries among nationalities, economic collapse, hunger, and military defeat forced the Habsburg emperor to resign, the Austrian National Council declared Austria an independent republic on 12 November 1918 and made Renner its chancellor. He encountered domestic pressure to make Austria part of the newly Marxist Soviet Union, but successfully opposed this movement. Continuing his writing, he expressed his nationalism in *The Nation's Right to Self-Determination*, which was published in 1918.

While chancellor, Renner faced the loss of Austrian territory to other nations, as Poland and Italy, for example, sought land. Although he headed the Austrian delegation to the Paris Peace Conference, he proved unable to prevent a substantial dismemberment, confirmed in the Treaty of Saint-Germain, which he signed on 10 September 1919. Austria lost three-fourths of its territory. In that year, Renner won reelection as chancellor, heading a coalition government. He promoted Austria's entry into the League of Nations and developed a neutral foreign policy. In 1920, Renner and the Social Democrats lost control of the government when elections were won by conservatives.

Renner continued to serve in the Reichsrat and was Speaker of the House from 1930 to 1933, when he resigned in a dispute with the chancellor. Back in 1918, Renner had supported an Austrian merger with Germany, a move many in Austria still desired. By now, however, the Nazis had gained power in Germany, and this changed Renner's position, for the Marxist socialism he represented was at odds with the German Social Democratic Party. In 1934, the Austrian government outlawed the Social Democrats and briefly jailed Renner. Then in 1938 he changed his position again and endorsed the German annexation, or *Anschluss,* of his country. Some historians assert he did so in order to protect his Jewish son-in-law, Hans Deutch, who had been arrested by the Gestapo. Indeed, after Renner voiced his approval,

the Nazis released Deutch. Whatever the case, Renner soon resigned from Parliament when his disenchantment with Hitler grew.

Near the end of World War II, the Russian army liberated Austria, and the Soviet Union approved a provisional government established on 27 April 1945 and headed by Renner, who was handpicked for the position by Joseph Stalin. Renner served as chancellor until his Socialist Party lost to the conservative Austrian People's Party in elections that November. Renner's socialists had a substantial minority in the new Parliament, however, and they reached an agreement with the conservatives whereby Renner would serve as Austria's president, a largely ceremonial position. On 20 December, the Parliament subsequently elected Renner president of the Second Republic, an office he held until his death on 31 December 1950 at Doebling. Austria went on to regain its full sovereignty in 1955 after the Allied occupation ended.

References: Rickett, Richard A., *A Brief Survey of Austrian History,* 1977; Stadler, Karl R., *Austria,* 1971.

Reza Shah Pahlavi
(1878–1944)
Iran

An ardent modernist and nationalist, Reza Shah Pahlavi ended foreign control in his homeland and then worked to contain the power of the Islamic clergy and encourage Western influences.

Reza Shah Pahlavi was born Reza Khan on 16 March 1878 in Alasht, a town in Mazanderan Province. When he was 14 his father, Abbas Ali Khan, a colonel in a Persian Cossack brigade, died and his mother took him to Tehran. At this young age, Reza joined the military. Although he did not obtain formal schooling, he proved himself intelligent and talented, and advanced through the military ranks.

At this time, Russian officers headed the army in which Reza Khan served and, with their pres-

ence, reinforced his dislike for the foreign domination of his country, which he blamed partly on Iran's traditional society. In addition to Russia, Britain exerted influence over Iran, and at the end of World War I the Iranian prime minister signed an agreement that would make his nation a British protectorate. This unleashed a nationalist reaction within Iran, and the legislature, or Majlis, rejected the deal.

As nationalism intensified, and as revolution engulfed Russia, Reza Khan allied with several officers in 1920 to evict the Russians. Then on 21 February 1921, he joined Sayyed Ziya al-Din Tabatabai, a prominent journalist, and overthrew the tainted Iranian government. In the new administration

Tabatabai ruled as prime minister and Rezha Khan served as minister of war.

Within a short period, Reza Khan consolidated his power, largely by gaining control of the army. Soon after he forced Tabatabai to resign, he convinced the monarch, Ahmed Shah, to appoint him prime minister and to leave the country. In 1925, the Majlis officially deposed Ahmed Shah and named Reza Khan the new monarch, officially titled Reza Shah Pahlavi.

Having successfully expelled the foreign rulers, Reza Shah acted to strengthen Iran by modernizing it. For this, he looked to the Western nations as his role model. Even before his coronation, he solidified his authority by ending the power of Shaykh Khazal, who had established a nearly independent regime in Khuzestan. In the late 1920s and 1930s he enacted numerous reforms, including secularizing the educational system, building roads, establishing state-operated industries, and completing the trans-Iranian railroad. In 1931, he reached a new agreement with the Anglo-Persian Oil Company, intended to provide Iran with more profits, although it brought only marginal change. Three years later, he founded the first university (located in Tehran). He also worked to emancipate women by ordering them in 1935 not to wear veils, opening the schools to them, and bringing them into the work force.

His policies raised the opposition of many traditional Islamic clerics, particularly in 1936 when his troops raided a shrine in order to break up a rally against him. Others grew disenchanted with

> *"The duty of carrying out the fundamental reform of the country . . . leaves no time for contemplation and laxity. . . ."*

Reza Shah when his regime became more autocratic. He restricted the press and arrested opponents, including religious leaders. Furthermore, his tax policies hit the peasants and lower urban class the hardest, the army often abused people, and Reza Shah displayed greed in his personal acquisition of valuable real estate.

As World War II approached, Reza Shah invited German investments to offset the British and Russian economic influence in his nation. Then when the war erupted, he proclaimed Iran neutral. This displeased Britain and Russia, which as allies against Nazi Germany needed to cross Iranian territory to transport supplies. In August 1941, these two nations invaded Iran and quickly defeated the Iranian army. Reza Shah realized that the occupiers would not allow him to remain in power, and so in September he abdicated in favor of his son, who ruled as Mohammad Reza Shah Pahlavi.

Reza Shah went into exile and lived in South Africa. He died in Johannesburg on 26 July 1944. In a turn of events, the state he founded came under attack. First, in the early 1950s Mohammed Mosaddeq tried to end the monarchy but failed. Then in 1979, AYATOLLAH RUHOLLA KHOMEINI led a successful revolution that aimed to dismantle the Westernized society and establish a fundamentalist Islamic state in Iran.

References: Lenczowski, George, ed., *Iran under the Pahlavis*, 1978; Upton, Joseph M., *The History of Modern Iran: An Interpretation*, 1960.

Rhee, Syngman
(1875–1965)
Republic of Korea (South Korea)

As a nationalist, Syngman Rhee became the leading spokesman for Korean independence; as a president, he assumed dictatorial powers in presiding over a society facing Communist challenges.

Syngman Rhee was born Yi Sŭng-man on 26 April 1875 in Pyŏng-san, a village located in Hwanghae Province. His father was part of the local gentry. Shortly after Syngman's birth, the family moved to Seoul. Syngman obtained a Confucian education until he enrolled in 1894 at Paejae Haktang Academy, a Methodist school. There he learned English and studied Western political theorists whose ideas convinced him that the Korean monarchy had become corrupt and antiquated. He combined this outlook with the Confucionists who criticized the encroachment of foreign powers on Korea.

At this time, Korea had only nominal independence. Britain, France, the United States and, paramountly, Russia and Japan had all established spheres of influence that robbed the Korean emperor of his powers. In 1896, the Independence Society emerged, headed by Kyŏng-su. It sought economic and political modernization, promoted Korean culture, and advocated the end to foreign interference. Rhee joined this group, but the organization collapsed in 1898, destroyed by internal conflicts. Around this time Rhee founded and edited *Independence*, Korea's first daily newspaper. In 1897, Rhee's public denunciation of the emperor, which included organizing a student demonstration, landed him in jail, where he remained until 1904. He later testified that this experience converted him to Christianity. While in prison, he wrote an extremely influential book, *Spirit of Independence*, widely read in Korea.

In 1904, he traveled to the United States, hoping to meet with President Theodore Roosevelt and get American support to defend Korea against a recently begun Japanese invasion. That year, Japan stationed several military battalions in Korea and gradually conquered the country through numerous concessions forced on the Korean government: the expropriation of land, control over transportation, stationing of additional troops, and the appointment of a powerful resident-general. Rhee did not get his audience with Roosevelt, and it would not have mattered, anyway. The United States desired close ties with Japan to counteract Russian influence in the Far East.

In 1905, Rhee enrolled at George Washington University, from which he graduated two years later. He continued his studies at Princeton, earning a Ph.D. in political science in 1910, a crucial year for Korea, when Japan formally annexed the country. Rhee returned to Korea, bearing his Westernized ways. He worked in a YMCA and promoted Christianity among young people while serving as a missionary teacher for the Methodist Mission Board. In 1912, he returned to the United States as a lay delegate to a Methodist conference. He then founded and headed the Korean Christian Institute in Honolulu and began *Korean Pacific Magazine*.

> *"The American people . . . as well as the people of the other democracies are . . . responsible for Korea's plight."*

On 1 March 1919, after several anti-Japanese demonstrations had erupted in Korea, nationalists issued a declaration of independence. Rhee, who had remained in contact with his Korean compatriots, was chosen by the protestors as president of a provisional government, and he represented the independence movement in Washington, D.C. The Japanese, however, ruthlessly crushed the uprising.

The provisional government continued to function outside of Korea, and in 1920, Rhee journeyed to Shanghai to direct it. A liberation army operated in the 1920s and helped the Chinese after Japan invaded Manchuria. Rhee returned to the United States, where he continued his efforts to get recognition for a free Korea. In 1933, he went to Geneva and tried to get help from the League of Nations. The major powers, however, had no desire to antagonize Japan. Meanwhile, many nationalists in Korea joined with the Communists there to form a united front.

During World War II, Japan forced Korean laborers from their homes to work in Sakahalin and Southeast Asia. They also recruited Koreans into the army and tightened their prohibition against political protest. After Pearl Harbor, Rhee made progress in gaining cooperation from the United States. In 1943, China, Britain, and the United States agreed to support Korean independence, and with the defeat of Japan in 1945, Rhee returned to Korea, which he had not seen in over 30 years. Koreans greeted him wildly, and he moved to the forefront of the right-wing groups. Rhee was disappointed by the partitioning of Korea at war's end into a Soviet-dominated North and an American-dominated South and the establishment of a trusteeship under the United States, the U.S.S.R., Britain, and China. This seemed to be a continuation of colonial rule.

Rhee organized a political party in the South, the Association for the Rapid Realization of Independence, and with police support and the use of political assassinations, won a plurality of votes in the 1948 election for the national legislature. Later that year, a new constitution establishing the Republic of Korea made Rhee president. The United States ended its military government and withdrew its troops.

Rhee faced much instability, primarily from Communists whose uprisings challenged the government. Then on 25 June 1950, North Korean ruler KIM IL-SŎNG had his Communist army invade South Korea, beginning the Korean War. Under the auspices of the United Nations, the United States sent troops to help Rhee. When American forces pushed the Communists back to the Chinese border, China intervened, and its army in turn sent the Americans reeling. In March 1951, a stalemate prevailed, with North and South Korea divided as they had been before the war, at the thirty-eighth parallel.

Rhee decided to consolidate his power into an authoritarian regime. In 1952, the National Assembly amended the constitution to allow him to run again. He won reelection under his Liberal Party banner and then won a third time in 1956. The much narrower margin of victory in the latter year seemed to reflect popular discontent with his dictatorial policies, which included outlawing the opposition Progressive Party and executing its leader. Virulently anti-Communist, Rhee had even hindered the 1953 talks to end the Korean War.

In 1960, Rhee won reelection to the presidency in balloting that he and his party rigged. This ignited student demonstrations, and pitched battles between the protestors and the police produced bloodshed. Rhee blamed the Communists for the riots and imposed martial law. He called troops into Seoul to restore order, but the army under Lieutenant General Song Yo-ch'an remained neutral in the showdown between Rhee and the students. Without military support, Rhee's regime tottered, and on 25 April 1960 he resigned the presidency and went to Hawaii, where he lived in exile. He had led the nationalist movement and rallied South Koreans against the Communist incursion, but in the end had fallen victim to his strident right-wing intolerance. In 1961, the government was overthrown and the Third Republic was established by CHUNG HEE PARK. Rhee died of an illness on 19 July 1965.

References: Allen, Richard C., *Korea's Syngman Rhee: An Unauthorized Portrait*, 1960; Oh, John Kie-chiang, *Korea: Democracy on Trial*, 1968.

Richelieu, Cardinal de
(1585–1642)
France

Committed to making France a truly national entity, Richelieu made everything subordinate to his famous dictum, *raison d'état*—reason of state.

Cardinal de Richelieu was born François du Plessis in Paris on 9 September 1585. His father was a nobleman, and young François decided to pursue a military career. He forsook this, however, in 1602 to study theology. Four years later, he became bishop of Lucon.

France was, at this time, but an ill-formed state, one that had, in the fifteenth century, begun developing a national structure and consciousness under King LOUIS XI. François determined to strengthen the crown and make France a fully integrated nation. To do this, he entered politics and in 1616 was named secretary for foreign affairs. A change in his political fortunes forced him from office the following year. In 1622, he became a cardinal, and two years later King Louis XIII appointed him to the Royal Council, where he wielded enormous influence and soon emerged as its leader.

Louis XIII wanted a strong minister and Richelieu obliged him with a forceful personality and a definite plan of action. He intended to parry the Habsburg threat as that royal family sought to surround and contain France. He also wanted to make the nobles in France clearly subservient to the king, build a great navy, and make everyone and everything function in agreement with his *raison d'état*. On these counts, he was highly successful. He had, however, to defeat an attempt to remove him from office. This occurred in 1630, when advisors to Louis XIII convinced the king to dismiss Richelieu. The wily cardinal, however, surprised the plotters by sneaking along hidden corridors in the Royal Palace and barging into a room where a closed meeting was under way. After this confrontation, in which Richelieu defused the charges against him, the king retained him, and from then on the cardinal's power went almost unchallenged.

In the 1630s, Richelieu built a powerful navy consisting of some 38 warships. He promoted French culture to develop national attachments, and toward this end founded the French Academy in 1635 to put together a French-language dictionary and set cultural standards. That same year, he involved France directly in the ongoing Thirty Years' War. His effort, after numerous battlefield setbacks, resulted in defeat for the Habsburgs. This, however, had its domestic problems, foremost among them economic distress that caused several rebellions—and a ruthless reaction on the cardinal's part to crush them.

Richelieu's genius was in political manipulation and, through this, building a centralized state that resembled more a modern nation than any that had existed in France until that time. In the process of achieving his goals, Richelieu exhausted himself and, always a man of frail health, on 4 December 1642 he died. Just a few months later, Louis XIII also passed away. The monarchical state that Richelieu supported did not, of course, last through succeeding centuries. But while the Fifth Republic founded by CHARLES DE GAULLE after World War II represented a markedly different political system from Richelieu's, the cardinal had built the territorial structure and the attachment to nation that largely continued throughout the twentieth century.

References: Bergin, Joseph, *Cardinal Richelieu: Power and the Pursuit of Wealth*, 1985; Burckhardt, Carl J., *Richelieu and His Age*, 3 volumes, 1972; Church, William F., *Richelieu and Reason of State*, 1972.

Rivadavia, Bernardino
(1780–1845)
Argentina

Bernardino Rivadavia carried with him a grand vision: He would remake Argentina along radical lines and produce a truly free society.

On 20 May 1780, Bernardino Rivadavia was born in Buenos Aires. His father was a wealthy lawyer who served in the city government. Bernardino attended the Colegio Real de San Carlos in Buenos Aires, where he especially liked philosophy and read the Enlightenment writers. After completing his education, he engaged in several different business endeavors. In 1806, he took up arms and helped defend Buenos Aires from a British invasion.

At the time, his homeland was a Spanish colony within the Viceroyalty of the Río de la Plata. Rivadavia and other liberal thinkers criticized Spain for its onerous restrictions on trade. In 1810, after Napoleon had disrupted relations between Spain and its overseas colonies by overthrowing the Spanish monarchy, Buenos Aireans deposed the viceroy and formed a junta. By this time, Rivadavia had been influenced by MANUEL BELGRANO, one of the great revolutionary intellectuals. He supported the junta, which declared greater autonomy but did not formally announce independence. The junta was dominated by MARIANO MORENO, who assumed near dictatorial power.

Turmoil ensued as a struggle erupted between liberal revolutionaries and Royalists (who supported Spain), and between Buenos Aireans and other provinces. In 1811, the junta gave way to a triumvirate, and Rivadavia was named its secretary. He exerted great influence and reorganized the army, ended the slave trade, protected freedom of the press, established the National Library, and began many schools. In 1813, however, Rivadavia left politics after JOSÉ DE SAN MARTÍN gained control of the revolution.

Rivadavia reentered public service in 1814 when he journeyed with Belgrano to England and Spain on a diplomatic mission. Although a republican, he believed that Argentina needed a monarchy to stabilize the country. He sought to find a prince in Europe, but failed.

In 1816, the revolutionaries officially declared their independence from Spain as the United Provinces of La Plata. Yet civil war swept the nation as the outlying provinces continued to resist the power of Buenos Aires. In 1821, Rivadavia returned home and became a minister of state in the new government. In this position he achieved much, including establishing new legislative procedures, expanding suffrage, restricting the clergy, and developing the University of Buenos Aires. European utopian ideas influenced him, and he gravitated toward radical reform. He tried to make landholding more egalitarian, but his program to accomplish this failed, particularly because of opposition from wealthy cattle ranchers who did not want to see their lands reduced.

"I am reason and I do not wish to be force."

Rivadavia also involved the United Provinces in a war as he tried to evict Brazil from Uruguay, which it had recently conquered. The battles resulted in many setbacks for Rivadavia, and in 1828 Britain arranged a peace settlement with Brazil.

Meanwhile, in 1826 the national legislature elected Rivadavia president. He supported a centralized government and proposed that Buenos Aires be made a federalized city with a status different from the surrounding provinces. The ensuing political controversy weakened Rivadavia, and the city kept its federal status only until the president left office. In addition to this, many disliked Rivadavia's inability to defeat Brazil in the war over Uruguay. Amid the ensuing political crisis, Rivadavia resigned in 1827 and sailed to Europe. He returned in 1834 but the government sent him into exile. He departed for Brazil and then back to Europe, where on 2 September 1845 he died in Cádiz, Spain.

Reference: Levene, Ricardo, *A History of Argentina*, 1937.

Rizal, José
(1861–1896)
Philippines

José Rizal is considered to be the first Asian nationalist. As a writer, he revealed injustices in the Philippines and so angered colonial officials that they banned his leading work and severely persecuted him.

Born on 19 June 1861 in Calamba, Luzon, José Rizal grew up in a comfortably wealthy Philippine family. His mother, Teodora Alonso, was highly educated. At an early age, José displayed brilliance and a creative bent. In his secondary education at Jesuit Ateneo Municipal School in Manila, he won literary honors. For a time, he attended the University of Santo Tomás, then traveled overseas and completed his studies in medicine and the liberal arts at the University of Madrid, where he received a doctorate in philosophy and letters.

While in Spain, Rizal wrote *Noli me tangero* in 1886 (*The Social Cancer*), a sociological and historical novel that detailed the oppression Filipinos suffered at the hands of the Catholic friars. This established the main theme in his writing, which emphasized Philippine culture, class oppression, and the corrupting character of the Catholic Church as then structured in the islands. In 1891, Rizal's *El filibusterismo* (*The Reign of Greed*) was published, and it pushed him to the forefront of the Filipino reform movement.

Rizal was reacting to the history of the Philippines under Spanish rule and to his family's own experiences. In 1887, colonial injustices struck him directly. His family and many others in Calamba, his hometown, were tenants on an estate owned by the Dominicans. These tenants petitioned the government, complaining about abuses by the Catholic order. After a long court trial, the tenants lost their case, and the Spanish governor had them evicted from the estate. The authorities deported Rizal's father and his three sisters. In *El filibusterismo*, Rizal attacked the entire economic system as bourgeois and exploitive and predicted a mass revolution.

Rizal became leader of the Propaganda Movement, which advocated reforms. At no time did he call for Philippine independence, but he did raise national consciousness and glorified the Filipino culture that had existed long before Europeans arrived on the islands. Spanish officials reacted to his books by banning them and setting them afire, and they punished anyone caught reading them. Rizal retaliated by writing more books and by writing for *La Solidaridad*, a newspaper produced by Filipino intellectuals in Spain. He formalized his political platform that consisted of making the Philippines a province of Spain, replacing the Spanish friars with Filipino priests, protecting freedom of expression, and establishing the equality of Filipinos and Spaniards before the law.

> "*. . . I have unmasked hypocrisy which, under the guise of religion, came to impoverish and brutalize us.*"

Rizal moved to Hong Kong in 1890, where he planned a colony in British North Borneo for dispossessed Filipinos. He returned to the Philippines in 1892 and founded Liga Filipina, a nationalist organization that reflected his platform. Although this group lasted only a short time, it stimulated other young nationalists into action, including ANDRES BONIFACIO and EMILIO AGUINALDO, who became revolutionaries.

Spanish authorities reacted to Liga Filipina by arresting Rizal on 2 July 1892, four days after he had formed the organization. They deported him to Mindinao in the southern Philippines. At Dapitan, he spent his exile practicing ophthalmology. Along with his writing, he had been an accomplished doctor who had performed the first cataract operation in the Philippines.

Rizal also began town improvements and founded a school. He then requested placement as a surgeon in the Spanish army, the government agreed, and in 1896, he headed for Spain. On his way there, however, the Philippine Revolution began, and the Spaniards suddenly arrested him for masterminding the rebellion, a completely false charge since he had no direct connection with the revolutionary uprising. Rizal was placed on trial and with the help of church officials was convicted of treason. On 30 December 1896, he was executed in Manila by a firing squad, in full public view.

The execution created a martyr and stimulated the revolutionaries to expand their fight.

They did not succeed in gaining independence, at least not immediately. In 1898, the United States replaced Spain as the colonial ruler. But the patriotism inspired by Rizal finally brought nationhood after World War II, and MANUAL ROXAS became the first president. Rizal became a great figure in Philippine history and his influence even produced a Rizalist cult that still worships him as a Filipino Christ.

References: Coates, Austin, *Rizal*, 1969; Osias, Camillio, *José Rizal: His Life and Times*, 1949; Zaide, Gregorio, *José Rizal*, 1970.

Roberts, Joseph Jenkins
(1809–1876)
Liberia

When Joseph Jenkins Roberts emigrated to Liberia in 1829, he entered one of the most unusual settlements in Africa. On the inland plateau and within the vast rain forests, tribes lived as they had for years previously, while along the coast—spotted with lagoons, marshlands, and white sandy beaches—recently arrived blacks from the United States bargained with tribal chiefs, gained land, and carved out a new country, a place of hope where former slaves could live in freedom.

Joseph Jenkins Roberts was born on 15 March 1809 to a mulatto family in Virginia; they were part of the small free black community that existed in the antebellum American South. He and other freedmen experienced severe restrictions in the United States as laws of segregation became increasingly harsh, pushing free blacks closer to the conditions of slaves. These laws reflected white fears about liberated blacks and complemented the perplexity faced by many white abolitionists: Slavery, they believed, was evil and should be ended, but free blacks and whites could never live together peacefully.

Out of this quandary came the American Colonization Society. The ACS advocated ending slavery and sending freedmen to Africa. In 1820, an ACS ship, the *Elizabeth*, left America and arrived on Africa's western Grain Coast with 88 free blacks. While aboard ship, the settlers wrote and signed the Elizabeth Compact, which outlined their government. More settlers arrived in 1821; many died from disease, but the survivors began building a community called Liberia—the Home of the Free.

Liberia, however, nearly collapsed, and when Roberts arrived and began a merchant trade, the settlement still seemed a tenuous undertaking. Perhaps Liberia's salvation came back in 1822 when Jehudi Ashmun, a white Methodist missionary sent by the ACS as director of the colony, tackled its mounting problems. He helped organize a militia, prodded the colonists to farm rather than rely on trade for food, laid out a town called Christopolis (later renamed Monrovia after James Monroe, president of the United States), purchased additional lands, and reduced the African slave trade.

"Liberia has been established upon principles recognized by the whole civilized world . . ."

In the late 1820s, other American colonization groups acquired lands near the ACS project. In 1838, most of them merged into the Commonwealth of Liberia under a white governor appointed by the ACS. At this time, the ACS chose Roberts as vice-governor, and he became renowned for his use of force and negotiation in subduing indigenous tribes. When in 1841 the governor died, Roberts succeeded him and became Liberia's first black leader.

Roberts faced a great challenge as governor when differences within the country's population caused substantial tensions. Conflicts broke out between Americo-Liberians and Africans. The latter neither understood the concept of land sales nor supported the often illegal actions of their chiefs in transferring land to the intruders. Furthermore, the settlers always considered Liberia a nation for black American immigrants; they patterned their emerging government after that of the United States and many social customs after those of the antebellum South. They excluded indigenous people from any substantive political participation, and many Africans thus considered the immigrants interlopers akin to white Europeans.

As a result, political clashes occurred among Americo-Liberians. Several lines of dispute emerged: between mulattos and nearly pure blacks; between farmers and merchants; and between city and rural dwellers. Additionally, Roberts faced substantial economic difficulties and the cumbersome arrangement of ACS control.

Under Roberts, Liberia moved toward independence and recognition as a nation. After Britain rejected Liberian sovereignty under ACS rule and British agents refused all Liberian taxes levied on their trade, Roberts insisted that Liberia needed nationhood. The ACS agreed, and on 29 July 1847 the Americo-Liberians adopted a declaration of independence and a constitution. Roberts became Liberia's first president.

As a prominent merchant, Roberts applied his financial acumen to the government. He reformed policies on customs tariffs and restricted foreign traders to six designated ports where duties could be collected. In 1849, he signed a commercial agreement with Britain.

Roberts exerted his leadership in other areas. In the 1850s, he visited Prussia, Holland, and Belgium, as well as France, where he obtained an audience with Napoleon III. These visits earned diplomatic recognition for Liberia. He supported the final elimination of the local slave trade and in 1856 personally led an armed force that quelled a tribal uprising. He also organized the True Liberian or Republican Party, which retained power until 1869. This party reflected mainly merchant interests and the power of mulattos, who as an educated elite within the Americo-Liberian community had formed a governing clique.

Roberts supported the establishment of the Masons (an international secret fraternity) in 1851, and within Masonic lodges he and other Liberian leaders often worked out political policies before presenting them publicly. This network became an important part of the young nation's elite power structure.

After five terms as president, Roberts was defeated for reelection in 1856. He subsequently became president of the new College of Liberia, a position he held until his death. In the late 1860s, a diplomatic dispute erupted with Britain over an outstanding loan, the perennial economic crisis worsened, and the legislature removed the president. Facing this severe emergency, Liberia's legislators chose Roberts to again serve as president. He held office from 1872 to 1876, during which time he rejected a transfer of territory to Britain. His term was one of the last exertions of mulatto political domination. On 24 February 1876, one month after leaving office, he died in Monrovia. Roberts is today considered the "Father of Liberia."

References: Buell, Raymond L., *The Native Problem in Africa*, 2 volumes, 1928, reprint 1965; Marinelli, Lawrence, *The New Liberia: A Historical and Political Survey*, 1964; Nelson, Harold D., ed., *Liberia: A Country Study*, 1985.

Rogier, Charles Latour
(1800–1885)
Belgium

As a nationalist and a liberal, Charles Latour Rogier epitomized the elitist nature of Belgium's revolution. The new state would be the most democratic in Europe, but dominated by the nobility and wealthy businessmen.

Charles Latour Rogier was born 17 August 1800. His father fought with the Napoleonic army against Russia and died in the campaign. In the 1820s, Rogier became a lawyer in Liège, beginning a journal in 1824 called *Mathieu Laensbergh,* which attacked his homeland's Dutch rulers.

The Dutch domination had begun after Napoleon's empire collapsed, and the Congress of Vienna in 1815 decided to link Belgium with the Dutch territories to form the United Netherlands under King William of Orange, a Catholic of moderate persuasion. Many Belgians accepted this arrangement as practicable. Liberals, in particular, saw it as a way to prevent a harsher Catholic rule and to develop their businesses.

King William, however, managed to antagonize Belgians and bring the Liberals and their long-standing opponents, the Catholics, together. He did this in the late 1820s by pursuing reform in the secondary schools, where many of the nobility and middle class studied, and insisting that a secularized Dutch education prevail. Catholics feared an attempt to destroy their religion, and the middle class, especially in the Walloon provinces, feared the loss of their French language.

Rogier's nationalism, already evident in his journalistic activity, surged, and others joined him to protest William's actions. As a Liberal, Rogier advocated freedom of religion and education, freedom of the press and association, and a more democratic polity. In 1828, he helped organize the Union of Opposition to join leading Liberals and Catholics together in seeking constitutional reforms. This effort was aided by the support of another leading nationalist, Étienne-Constantin Gerlache, a Conservative pro-Catholic statesman. Unlike many in the movement, Rogier took an extreme position in seeking Belgian independence.

The Belgian nationalist movement thus began as an elitist effort, although Rogier recruited a popular following. In 1830, the movement took a turn that threatened to wrest it from elite control, and

Rogier both used and directed the turbulent populism. The economy had turned sharply downward, stirring public demonstrations that turned violent at an opera in Brussels on 25 August 1830. The performance depicted a patriotic revolution in Naples, which so stirred the audience that it ran into the streets shouting "Down with the Dutch! Down with the Ministers!" and began rioting against Dutch rule. Unemployed industrial workers joined the revolutionaries, and by the end of September Dutch troops had been forced from Brussels.

For his part, Rogier led an armed group from Liège under a banner proclaiming "Win or Die for Brussels!" and engaged in the fighting. On 25 September, he and other Liberals gained control of the revolt and formed a provisional government that on 4 October declared Belgium independent. He arranged an armistice with the Dutch and supported the establishment of a constitutional monarchy under Leopold of Saxe-Coburg, who was chosen king of the Belgians and assumed the throne on 21 July 1831. In this arrangement the monarch had limited powers with a bicameral parliament and a prime minister holding most authority. Rogier favored this as fostering the modern business-oriented state he preferred.

From 1831 until the following year, Rogier was governor of Antwerp and then served as minister of the interior. In the latter position he sponsored a bill for building a national railway system, crucial to his nation's economic recovery. In 1834, he left his post at interior and for several years was blocked by Catholic opponents from holding office. They believed, quite accurately, that he wanted to limit clerical power in building an industrial economy. In 1847, a Liberal victory enabled Rogier to become prime minister, and the next year he enacted an electoral reform law that lowered property qualifications and thus broadened the suffrage to include most of the middle class.

Rogier sought to contain the public influence of the Roman Catholic Church, and in 1850 his education reform created schools that were an alternative to the Catholic system and that were secular (although in 1854 the government agreed to two hours per week of religious instruction for school children). Shortly thereafter, Rogier left the prime ministry but returned for a ten-year term beginning in 1857. During this period he reached an important agreement with the Dutch under which the Schedt River was opened to commerce, allowing Antwerp to become a major European port.

Rogier left the prime ministry in 1867 but remained an influential political force through the 1870s. He died on 27 May 1885.

References: Kossmann, E. H., *The Low Countries, 1780–1940*, 1978; Lijphart, Arend, ed., *Conflict and Coexistence in Belgium: The Dynamics of a Culturally Divided Society*, 1981.

Roxas, Manuel
(1892–1948)
Philippines

Although a nationalist, Manuel Roxas did not embrace radicalism. In striving for Philippine independence, he supported American institutions and represented the elite.

Manuel Roxas was born on 1 January 1892 at Capiz, Panay, in the central Philippines. At an early age he was influenced by Philippine nationalism, when his father supported the rebellion against Spanish rule and was killed by Spanish soldiers. This Philippine Revolution had been stimulated not only by Spanish oppression but by the patriotic writings of JOSÉ RIZAL and the organizational activities of ANDRES BONIFACIO. By the time Manuel began to attend school, the Philippines had passed from Spain to the United States after the Spanish-American War of 1898. Manuel went to a public high school established by the United States in Manila.

In 1909, he entered law school at the University of the Philippines, where he earned first honors and graduated in 1913. Two years later, he became a law professor at National University in Hong Kong. He returned to the Philippines in 1916 to practice law and entered politics in 1919 when he ran for governor of his province. He won that election, and in 1921, after his term expired, he won election to the House of Representatives from Capiz.

There he grew close to Manuel Quezon, the Senate president who headed the Nationalista-

> *"I am truly a product of the American system of education."*

Colectivista coalition as a nationalist seeking independence from the United States. With Quezon's support, Roxas became Speaker of the House and did much to build his mentor's power in that legislative body.

In the 1920s, Roxas formed Bagong Katipunan, a patriotic group dedicated to ending American rule; but despite this move he declared himself loyal to American institutions. Roxas served as a delegate to several conferences in Washington intended to arrange Philippine independence. The session in 1932–1933 produced a document acceptable to him, but it was rejected by Quezon. The dispute involving it turned into a fight for political power, and Quezon removed Roxas from the speakership. Roxas subsequently organized his own political party. In 1934, Quezon accepted a renegotiated agreement with the United States and received the credit for gaining Philippine independence. The agreement provided for a temporary commonwealth status to be followed in a few years by nationhood.

Despite his quarrel with Quezon, Roxas won election to the constitutional convention of 1934. There he led the anti-Quezon faction, but the constitution, which Roxas largely shaped, reflected most of Quezon's goals. Roxas then won a seat in the commonwealth legislature but soon retired to practice law. As Roxas and Quezon healed their rift,

Roxas was appointed by Quezon, now president, to the National Economic Council and chair of the National Development Council, formed to oversee economic development. In 1938, Quezon appointed Roxas to his cabinet as secretary of finance.

During World War II, Roxas served as a lieutenant in the Philippine Army Reserve and became an aide to General Douglas MacArthur. The Japanese captured Roxas early in 1942, and this began a controversial part of his career. He served in the government set up under Japanese control and critics accused him of collaborating with the enemy, a charge also leveled against an older Philippine nationalist, EMILIO AGUINALDO. Roxas later claimed that he used his official positions in the government to spy on the Japanese and sabotage their efforts. MacArthur and several other observers confirmed this account, while some Filipinos rejected it.

In 1945, Roxas campaigned for the presidency of what was the following year to become an independent Philippines. He ran against another nationalist leader, Sergio Osmeña, who had succeeded to the presidency upon Quezon's death in 1944. When the ballots were counted in April 1946, Roxas emerged the winner and became president of the commonwealth and president-elect of the Republic of the Philippines, which officially became independent on 4 July. Roxas had to deal with a peasant uprising north of Manila and an economy devastated by the war, but before he could establish many policies he died in 1948.

References: Recto, Claro M., *Three Years of Enemy Occupation: The Issue of Political Collaboration in the Philippines*, 1946; Steinberg, David Joel, *Philippine Collaboration in World War II*, 1967; Tubangui, Helen R., ed., *The Filipino Nation: A Concise History of the Philippines*, 1982.

Rwagasore, Louis
(1932–1961)
Burundi

The son of a Burundian king, Louis Rwagasore was destined to become ruler of his homeland under Belgian control. But in the 1950s, he adopted a strong nationalist stance and changed the course of his country's development.

Louis Rwagasore was born on 10 January 1932 at Gitega, the son of Mwami Mwambutsa ("mwami" meaning king) and Thérèse Kanyonga. Since 1916, Burundi had been under Belgian rule as the result of a mandate from the League of Nations (which, in 1946, became a mandate from the United Nations). The mwami, who came from the politically dominant Tutsi ethnic group, had imposed on him a Westernized administration and substantial restrictions on his power.

Louis attended Catholic mission schools in Bukeye, Kanyinya, and Gitega, and in 1945 he began six years of study at the Groupe Scolaire D'Astrida (GSA), which had been created to train the sons of Tutsi chiefs to become future chiefs and top-level administrators. Most of Burundi's administrative elite graduated from the GSA. In 1956, Louis traveled to Belgium and attended college there, but he did poorly in his studies and returned home later that year. He then decided to enter politics, particularly to challenge Belgian authority. He formed cooperatives under complete African control, but Belgium declared them illegal in 1958.

He took an even bolder step in 1959 when he organized the Union for National Progress (UPRONA). Initially, Rwagasore sought to maintain Burundi's traditional institutions, especially the mwami, while also striving for autonomy within the Belgian system. By 1960, two events altered Rwagasore's position: growing differences with his father and Belgium's announcement that the Congo would soon receive independence. Rwagasore consequently questioned the institution of the mwami, moderated UPRONA's defense of it, and called for Burundi's nationhood.

Both the mwami and Belgium opposed UPRONA in legislative elections held in 1960. Amid charges of widespread fraud, Rwagasore and UPRONA lost. Supported by nationalist leaders in Africa, such as JULIUS NYERERE of Tanganyika, Rwagasore complained to the United Nations that, in this instance, Belgium had violated its responsibilities in handling Burundi as a mandate. The UN agreed and ordered new elections, which resulted in an UPRONA victory. Rwagasore subsequently became prime minister.

Then after a cabinet meeting on 13 October 1961, Rwagasore went to a restaurant to dine with several of his government ministers. While eating, he was assassinated. The government arrested several leaders of an opposing political party, the Christian Democratic Party (PDC). This group had formed to promote greater political autonomy for Burundians, but under Belgian rule; it supported the mwami as an institution, although with powers limited by elective offices. The PDC had received substantial financial support from Belgium and evidence implicated, but never definitely proved, Belgian involvement in the assassination. In any event, in 1973, after the case was reopened following a long delay, five men were found guilty, sentenced to death, and, on 15 January, executed.

Despite his brief tenure as prime minister, Rwagasore is remembered as an important figure in furthering Burundi nationalism. His formation of UPRONA was a major move toward nationhood, as was well recognized by Belgium, which strongly opposed Rwagasore. When Burundi obtained its independence on 1 July 1962, Rwagasore's imprint was indelibly present. The end of the mwami and the introduction of radicalized politics that contributed to tragic developments in Burundi occurred under MICHEL MICOMBERO.

References: Webster, John, *The Political Development of Rwanda and Burundi*, 1966; Weinstein, Warren, and Robert Schrire, *Political Conflict and Ethnic Strategies: A Case Study of Burundi*, 1976.

Saleh, Ali Abdullah
(b. 1942)
Yemen

Yemen had undergone decades of traditional rule followed by a revolutionary upheaval when Ali Abdullah Saleh emerged as its leader. He determined to solidify the revolution and bring his country into the twentieth century.

In 1942, Ali Abdullah Saleh was born in the village of Bayt al-Ahmar. At that time, this land, called North Yemen, was ruled by YAHYA, a religious traditionalist from the Zayid Islamic sect. Yahya believed in preventing modern influences from entering North Yemen, and under him the Yemenis built few schools and hospitals and had few telephones or other recent technologies.

Saleh, like Yahya, belonged to the Zaydis and at his village school obtained an Islamic education. As a young man, he joined the military forces of Yahya's son and successor, Ahmad, in 1958. He attended noncommissioned officers' school in 1960 but then found his military career altered by an internal convulsion when, in 1962, revolutionaries overthrew the government, one week after Ahmad had died. Abdullah al-Sallal led this revolt, but his regime depended heavily on Egyptian troops for survival and collapsed in 1967.

Indeed, the revolt precipitated fierce fighting within North Yemen between traditional forces supporting an Islamic autocracy as established by Yahya and Ahmad, and republican forces seeking modernization and supported by Egypt. Saleh sided with the latter, which had declared the Yemen Arab Republic as the new government. The ensuing civil war brought not only Egyptian but also Saudi intervention. Egypt favored a modern government attuned to its leadership in the Arab world, and Saudi Arabia worried lest modernizing antimonarchical forces spread north.

This civil war ended in 1970 when moderates gained command and a republican government agreed to participation by conservatives. Yet tensions continued into the advent of Saleh's regime. On 24 June 1978, assassins killed President Ahmad Hussein al-Ghashmi. At that time, Saleh was military governor of Taiz Province. He outmaneuvered several contenders, and on 17 July the Peoples' Constituent Assembly elected him president and commander of the armed forces.

Saleh had to constantly balance Egyptian and Saudi influences, tribal disagreements, and efforts by two groups to overthrow him: the National Democratic Front (NDF), founded in the mid-1970s in Yemen, and the Marxist People's Democratic Republic of Yemen (PDRY), founded in South Yemen (formerly Aden). The leftist NDF attempted a coup in October 1978, but it failed. Saleh then began intermittent negotiations with the NDF and brought into his regime both leftists and conservatives, while maintaining an even-handed approach in dealings with Egypt, Saudi Arabia, and other Arab states.

In 1979, Saleh entered into negotiations with the PDRY, seeking to unite the two Yemens. At the same time, he effectively fought NDF forces, defeating them in an important battle in 1982. In foreign relations, Saleh wanted to avoid aligning his country with either the pro-Western Saudis or the radical South Yemen Marxists. Going too far to either side, he believed, would tear Yemen apart. He firmly supported Arab positions, including Iraq in its war with Iran and the Palestine Liberation Organization in its fight against Israel.

Internally, he convened the General Peoples Congress that encouraged mass political participation, although under his watchful supervision. He also supported modern economic development, and the discovery of oil in 1984 soon pumped money into Yemen for agricultural and industrial growth.

Finally, on 22 May 1990, Saleh merged his nation with the PDRY, which had developed a Marxist regime under SALIM RUBAY ALI and ABD AL-FATTAH ISMAIL. He did so only after South Yemen had moderated its Marxist policies, a move crucial in allaying Saudi fears.

Saleh held the presidency, the most powerful position in the new nation, and Ali Salem al-Baidh of South Yemen's Socialist Party became the vice-president. The country formally adopted the name of the Yemeni Republic. Although Saleh did not initiate the revolutionary overthrow of the Islamic monarchy, he was an important participant in its early stages, a founder who provided the leadership to stabilize the republican revolution and the Yemeni government.

References: Bidwell, Robin, *The Two Yemens*, 1982; Burrowes, Robert, *The Yemen Arab Republic*, 1987.

San Martín, José de
(1778–1850)
Argentina, Chile, Peru

José de San Martín led the rebellion against Spain that liberated Argentina, Chile, and Peru. This came after he made an abrupt change in 1812 from commanding Spanish forces to allying with nationalist rebels.

José de San Martín was born on 25 February 1778 in a small village called Yapeyú, located on the northern frontier of Argentina. His father served as an official in the Spanish colonial government that controlled the area. In 1785, his parents returned to Spain, where they had both been born, and took young José with them. He attended an aristocratic school, the Nobles' Seminary, in Madrid and began his military career when he entered the Royal Academy and became a cadet in the Murica infantry regiment. He subsequently fought in battles against the British and the Portuguese and by 1804 advanced to the rank of captain. Following this, he fought in the war between Spain and Napoleonic France.

After Napoleon occupied Spain, San Martín continued to fight for the Spanish crown, earning promotion to lieutenant colonel and in 1811 commanding the Sagunto Dragoons. The following year, he made his puzzling and unexpected transformation, quitting the Spanish military in 1812 and returning to Argentina where he allied with the rebels in Buenos Aires who demanded independence from Spain. To this day, historians are uncertain as to why San Martín switched his loyalty; he may have been influenced by a British agent who sought to undermine Spain, or he may have become disgusted with the prejudice he encountered from Spaniards who looked down upon him as an inferior Creole, a person of Spanish blood born in the Americas.

Whatever the case, in 1812 he helped found the Lautaro Lodge, a secret organization committed to independence. He organized Argentine troops against the pro-Spanish royalist forces and in 1813 won an important battle at San Lorenzo, which secured supply lines with Montevideo. The following year, he was appointed general and ordered to attack Upper Peru (today, Bolivia). He publicly balked at the impossibility of this mission, while privately he concluded that independence from Spain could not be secured without a victory in Peru, which had become a royalist stronghold. In a skillful maneuver, he resigned his command—claiming ill health—and requested and obtained appointment as governor of Cuyo Province, located near the Andes, where he could supposedly recuperate. He actually used this move to gather his forces in western Argentina and develop a plan to cross the Andes into Chile, acquire reinforcements, and attack Peru.

With little support from Buenos Aires, San Martín gathered his men over a three-year period and joined with the Chilean liberator, BERNARDO O'HIGGINS. Early in 1817, San Martín led his men over the Andes, scaling incredible heights and fighting Spanish forces in a campaign that enhanced his reputation as a great general. About this feat, he observed: "The difficulty that had to be overcome in the crossing of the mountains can only be imagined by those who have actually gone through it." In February, he captured Santiago and was offered the Chilean governorship. He refused, however, so that his friend O'Higgins could rule, a move that also allowed him to secure Chile militarily and prepare for his attack on Peru. In 1818, he defeated the last Royalist troops in Chile.

San Martín then aimed at Peru. After gathering his force, he departed aboard a ramshackle naval fleet in 1820 and landed at Pisco. Rather than directly assault the heavily fortified capital, Lima, San Martín waited out his enemy. The Royalist troops failed to get supplies and reinforcements. When they retreated into the mountains in 1821, San Martín entered Lima. On 28 July, the revolutionaries declared Peru independent and San Martín their nation's protector.

Trouble soon arose, however, for Spanish troops remained in Peru and many Peruvians feared San Martín's intentions—perhaps he would make himself dictator, weaken the Catholic Church, or destroy the large landholdings. As disorder threatened, San Martín indeed became dictator, and to defeat the Royalists he decided to form an alliance with SIMÓN BOLÍVAR, the great South American liberator. Bolívar had recently defeated the Spanish in Venezuela, Colombia, and Ecuador.

In July 1822, the two leaders met at Guayaquil in Ecuador. Little is known about what transpired, but after two days of talks, San Martín unexpectedly returned to his ship and, under the cover of darkness, set sail for Peru. He likely believed it impossible to reconcile his differences with Bolívar, who did not offer him an adequate number of reinforcements and opposed the idea of San Martín serving under him in the final assault against the Spaniards. The two men may also have disagreed over territory, with San Martín opposing Bolívar's having declared Guayaquil a part of Colombia.

In any event, San Martín apparently believed his presence would bring discord and disrupt the war. In September 1822 he resigned as protector and, while suffering from illness, he traveled to Chile. After his wife died in 1824, he sailed for England with his daughter and settled in Belgium. In 1829, he decided to return to Buenos Aires, but when he received news aboard ship that political strife had intensified, he headed back to Europe without having entered Argentina. He lived in Paris and then Boulogne, where he died on 17 August 1850. The "Liberator of the South" eventually returned home: In 1880, his remains were moved to Buenos Aires.

References: Metford, John C. J., *San Martín: The Liberator*, 1950; Mitre, Bartolomé, *The Emancipation of South America*, 1969; Rojas, Ricardo, *San Martín: Knight of the Andes*, 1945.

Santander, Francisco de Paula
(1792–1840)
Colombia

Francisco de Paula Santander disagreed so severely with the great South American Liberator SIMÓN BOLÍVAR that many believe he tried to kill him. But Santander is most remembered for his stunning accomplishments on the battlefield in the revolutionary war and for his firmness in promoting a constitutional government.

Like so many of his fellow revolutionary leaders, Francisco de Paula Santander, who was born on 2 April 1792, came from a wealthy Creole family—persons of Spanish blood born in the colonies. He grew up in Cúcuta, located in Spain's colony of New Grenada (now Colombia), where he engaged in horseback riding on his father's huge estate and obtained his initial schooling from a tutor.

At age 13, Francisco was sent to Bogotá to live with his uncle and attend the Colegio de San Bartolomé. At a later date, Francisco claimed that from his uncle he learned about the injustices of Spanish rule. After this schooling, he went on to study law, but revolution soon interrupted after the French, in 1810, deposed Spain's king, and the Spanish colonies formed juntas to establish self-government. Young Francisco joined a revolutionary regiment, mainly volunteers from Bogotá's leading families.

The rebels immediately bickered about the form of government in New Grenada—whether it should be centralized or a federated union of the provinces. Santander sided with the federalists and in 1812 fought with the army that defeated the opposition. At this time, Simón Bolívar entered New Grenada and recruited men to help him evict the Spanish from neighboring Venezuela. Santander served as a captain under Bolívar and, after disagreeing with his plan to attack Venezuela without first securing New Grenada, fell in line and remained loyal to "the Liberator" for over a decade.

As it turned out, the Spanish defeated Bolívar in Venezuela and forced him to flee. While the Liberator went to Jamaica, Santander retreated to the Apure Valley. There he conflicted with the great *llanero*, or horseman, JOSÉ ANTONIO PÁEZ (a founder of Venezuela), who forced him to relinquish his command. Nevertheless, Santander played a cru-

cial role in ensuing battles in the valley, battles notable for their daring attacks against the Spaniards.

After Bolívar returned to Venezuela in 1817, Santander was named commander of the New Grenadian forces, and when the Liberator attacked New Grenada, Santander fought in the important victory at Calabozo in March 1818. When Bolívar launched his infamous journey across the Andes in 1819 to surprise Spanish forces in New Grenada, Santander's men opened a strategic mountain pass that enabled the rebels to gain a key victory at Boyacá in August.

> **"[Colombia is] the only daughter of the immortal Bolívar."**

That same year, Bolívar organized Venezuela, Ecuador, and New Grenada into Gran Colombia. Santander worked as an able administrator, and when a congress at Cúcuta wrote a constitution in 1821, Bolívar became president and Santander vice-president. Bolívar, however, continued to fight the Spanish forces still located to the south in Peru, and in his absence Santander acted as president.

Santander faced enormous challenges, not the least of which involved trying to hold Gran Colombia together amid nationalist demands for three separate countries. Yet he moved effectively to begin numerous reforms, particularly in education. In 1820, he ordered that schools be established in every town, and he began four colleges. Often against Bolívar's wishes, he insisted that the government function within the constitution, and for this he was called the "man of laws."

In 1825, Santander won reelection as vice-president, but the nationalist pressures intensified, and the following year a revolt erupted in Venezuela. When Bolívar settled the rebellion by making concessions to Páez that kept Venezuela in Gran Colombia, Santander objected. This strained relations with the Liberator, and the situation deteriorated further when Bolívar suspected Santander of fomenting a rebellion in Peru (a charge unfounded).

In 1827, Bolívar reacted to the turmoil in Gran Colombia by establishing a dictatorship, and Santander and his supporters opposed him. To get rid of Santander, the Liberator appointed him minister to the United States. But before Santander could leave, the September Conspiracy of 1828 unfolded and assassins tried to kill Bolívar. Santander's role in this assault remains murky, and there is evidence to indicate he actually tried to halt the plot, but, in any event, he was arrested and sentenced to death. Bolívar, however, intervened and saved him. Santander then went into exile and lived in Paris.

Gran Colombia collapsed in 1830, and a convention met in New Grenada that elected Santander president of the new republic. In 1832, Santander returned home and began his presidency. Fairness and orderliness marked his administration, and he settled several disputes with

Venezuela while putting down separatist rebellions. In 1833, he defeated an effort by some conservatives to overthrow him. Santander worked hard to place the government on a stable footing and to expand education.

In 1836, Santander's term ended, and he was unsuccessful in getting his handpicked candidate elected president. The "man of laws" continued in politics, serving as a representative in the legislature. Santander died in Bogotá on 6 May 1840, hailed as the "true founder" of Colombia.

Reference: Forero, José Maria, *Santander,* 1937.

Sayiid 'Abdille Hassan, Mohammed
(1864–1920)
Somalia

Amid the dusty backcountry of Somalia, infused with a powerful Islamic faith and angered by foreign intrusion, Mohammed 'Abdille Hassan led a holy war that stimulated Somali nationalism. His legacy became a cornerstone in Somalia's independence movement after World War II.

Mohammed 'Abdille Hassan was born on 7 April 1864 at a watering place in the dry Dulbahante country. Mohammed learned the Koran as a boy and by age 15 became a teacher of Islam. His learning proved so extensive and wise and his piety so great that four years later he earned the title of "sheikh." He then traveled to Harar, Mogadishu, the Sudan, and Nairobi in search of more knowledge. In 1891, he returned home and married the first of his several wives.

By this time, Britain, France, Italy, and Ethiopia had begun carving Somalia into territories; this once-homogeneous land of shifting clan rivalries and alliances had imposed on it foreign rulers

"Now choose for yourselves. If you want war we accept it; but if you want peace, pay the fine."

and connections to a European economy that enriched only a few coastal merchants. Many Somalis concluded that Christianity and materialism posed a threat to Islam. Sheikh Mohammed denounced assaults on Islamic tradition, condemning excessive indulgence and luxury, and he insisted that Somalis must unite in a common war against foreign domination. Otherwise, he warned, Christian colonizers would destroy Islam.

In the late 1890s, Sheikh Mohammed preached his message, served as a mediator between warring clans, and called for interclan unity. He also became a prolific poet; his words carried a message of hope and vision. Sheikh Mohammed's supporters came mainly from the interior of the country. He organized them into military units and by 1900 had command of 5,000 men. He then declared a "jihad," or holy war, aimed primarily at the British and Ethiopians. The latter had particularly antagonized inland clans by raiding herds and religious establishments in the Ogaadeen region.

Sheikh Mohammed now called himself Sayiid, a title of respect accorded Islamic leaders. His followers became known as the Dervishes, meaning persons dedicated to God and community. For 20 years they fought against Somalia's foreign invaders. In 1900, Sayiid led 6,000 men in attacking an Ethiopian post at Jigjiga. The Dervishes suffered heavy losses (about 170 dead), but recovered the livestock previously stolen from them and made a considerable show of force. Sayiid's militarism, his poems, and his continued calls for clan unity made him a national figure.

In 1910, Britain decided to withdraw its forces from the interior part of Somalia. This enhanced Sayiid's prestige but also unleashed interclan fighting; the resulting chaos produced impoverishment and starvation—referred to by Somalis as the "Time of Eating Filth." British policy changed in 1913, and a Camel Constabulary entered Somalia's interior, where it contained the Dervishes. Sayiid, however, followed guerrilla tactics that often succeeded against much superior numbers.

In 1915, Sayiid suffered a serious setback when British forces captured the Dervish fort at Shimberberis and a coastal blockade reduced his armaments. Then, early in 1920, Britain launched a major assault employing a new technology from World War I: fighter aircraft. As ground forces advanced against the Dervishes, British bombers leveled Sayiid's fortress at Taleh. He fled into the Ogaadeen, where he reorganized his remaining forces and refused surrender. But new attacks occurred—this time from rival clans—and they inflicted a heavy defeat on Sayiid, driving him into Ethiopia. On 21 December 1920, Sayiid died from influenza. He left behind a legacy of devotion to Islam and a united Somali cause against foreign oppression. When nationalist sentiment surged again in the 1940s, many Somalis felt stirred by Sayiid, whom they called "the man who had fought great odds."

References: Laitin, David D., and Said S. Samatar, *Somalia: Nation in Search of a State*, 1987; Lewis, I. M., *The Modern History of Somalia*, 1980.

Sayiid Barre, Mohammed
(1920?–1995)
Somalia

Given the dissolution of an effective national government in the 1990s and the country's uncertain future, a case can be made that modern Somalia really lacks any founder. Yet Major General Mohammed Sayiid Barre held power for 22 years and brought together a divided country with policies and programs that have left their mark on a young nation still struggling for unity.

"A Soviet socialist cannot tell me about Somalian problems which must be put in an African context."

Sayiid Barre's origins were humble. He was born around 1920, the son of a desert herdsman near Shiilaabo in Ethiopia, and came from the Mareehaan clan. He joined the Italian Somaliland police force and became chief inspector in the 1950s and then commander in chief of the Somalia armed forces.

In the meantime, nationalist protest stirred, partly a result of the unsuccessful rebellion against foreign rule led decades earlier by MOHAMMED SAYIID 'ABDILLE HASSAN, and partly because of weakening European power after World War II. In the 1950s, the nationalist Somali Youth League (SYL) joined with two political parties, the Somalia National League and the National United Front, and built a mass following to become Somalia's leading political organization. In 1960, the year when Italy would have to grant Italian Somaliland its independence based on a United Nations mandate, Britain issued a surprise announcement granting British Somaliland its freedom. Amid this unexpectedly tumultuous scene, negotiations between the SYL and several leaders from northern Somalia, particularly Michael Mariano, a former administrative employee in British Somaliland and a firm nationalist, produced a merger of North and South into the independent Somali Republic, declared on 1 July 1960.

Somalia's new government proved ineffective, however, and this power vacuum facilitated the rise of Mohammed Sayiid Barre. As political, economic, and social stagnation gripped the nation, Sayiid Barre led a military coup in October 1969 that renounced the existing constitution. He disbanded Somalia's national legislature and replaced it with a Supreme Revolutionary Council (SRC) headed by him. He also established himself as president with widespread powers.

As a strong proponent of Somalian unity, Sayiid Barre insisted on a merit-based civil service that deemphasized clan alliances, and he included on his SRC not only military and police officers but also a large number of civilians. At the beginning of his regime, Sayiid Barre launched a strong attack against official corruption and thus developed a populist image. He also followed a strident anti-American policy as he considered the United States an enemy of Islam and an opponent of Somali unification. He ejected the Peace Corps, claiming that its youthful workers had undermined Somalian values, and cultivated strong ties with the Soviet Union, which built naval bases and provided arms.

In April 1970, Sayiid Barre repulsed a military coup. He then acquired additional power and launched a vitriolic attack against the United States. He accelerated his pursuit of national unity—still an illusive goal as clan alliances continued to shift. His unification program included some far-reaching policies: He established a National Security Service that kept a careful watch on dissidents, and he founded the Victory Pioneers, a youth group dedicated to community help and ideological indoctrination.

Most notably, Sayiid Barre began his "scientific socialism," which he proclaimed would end poverty, disease, and ignorance. In the early 1970s, scientific socialism produced several results that temporarily lessened internal problems. For example, his program ordered a uniform official language and official script that ended a crucial difference between the English-speaking North and the Italian-speaking South. Furthermore, under the program he channeled more aid to nomads to reduce the inequality in wealth between rural and urban areas, curtailed extravagant bureaucratic spending, and strove to reduce sexual inequality in education by enrolling more girls in schools. He also tried to ameliorate an imbalance in economic development between the North, which under British rule had received little economic help, and the South, which under Italian rule had reaped considerable economic benefits.

Yet by 1975 Sayiid Barre's scientific socialism had stagnated. The economy did not expand significantly and discontent with his authoritarian manner increased. Sayiid Barre attempted rallying his unification drive with two new efforts. First, he formed the Somali Revolutionary Socialist Party (SRSP) in 1976, the only legal political party in the nation. Second, he decided to wrest the Ogaadeen region from Ethiopia. Encouraged by the recent overthrow of Ethiopia's monarchy, Sayiid's army invaded the Ogaadeen in 1977. But to Sayiid's surprise, the Soviets criticized his attack and, in attempting to develop a new client state, sided with Ethiopia. In 1978, the Ethiopians rallied and with help from Soviet arms and 11,000 Cuban troops, they drove Somali forces from the Ogaadeen.

Sayiid Barre's military adventure cost him dearly. Over 1.5 million refugees flooded Somalia, the nation's economy suffered, and he lost his Soviet ally. Sayiid Barre reacted by turning to the United States for support and jettisoning scientific socialism for capitalist investments. This about-face, however, bewildered Somalis.

Then as his power waned, Sayiid Barre turned to various clans for support. This ruined his effort at fostering unity; it actually produced a rise in tribal antagonisms and encouraged interclan feuds over who would receive government favors (a situation that exploded in the 1990s).

In 1979, Sayiid Barre's SRSP drafted a new constitution that revived Somalia's legislature. But it left enormous powers for the president and his revolutionary council and stipulated that his SRSP would choose all the candidates for seats in the legislature. Sayiid Barre's destabilized government suffered attacks from revolutionaries based in Ethiopia. He reacted by arming several clans, particularly opponents of the ones involved with the guerrillas, and by 1988 a full-scale civil war had erupted, causing his government to disintegrate further. In January 1991, he fled Mogadishu as chaos grew. Once again order proved elusive and Somalia entered its current period of internal warfare. Sayiid Barre died on 2 January 1995 while living in exile in Lagos, Nigeria.

References: Laitin, David D., and Said S. Samatar, *Somalia: Nation in Search of a State*, 1987; Lewis, I. M., *The Modern History of Somalia*, 1980.

◆

Senghor, Léopold Sédar
(b. 1906)
Senegal

Léopold Sédar Senghor and Senegal complement one another in a peculiar way: They both possess qualities unusual in the history of French West Africa. For Senghor, it is the experience of an intellectual poet turned calculating politician; for Senegal, it is a heritage of black political participation from almost the beginning of French rule.

Born into a middle-class family on 9 October 1906, Léopold Sédar Senghor grew up in Joal, a farming village. His father was a planter and merchant, and his mother, a Catholic, had Léopold baptized into Catholicism and sent him to a missionary school in Dakar, where he completed his secondary education. Léopold attended the University of Paris in 1928 and during his years of study there discovered that African culture had an enormous impact on modern art.

Senghor became a brilliant essayist, philosopher, and poet and advanced the concept of "négritude." By this he meant the literary, artistic,

"Let us listen to the voice of our Forebears . . . In the smoky cabin, souls that wish us well are murmuring."

and social expression of the black African experience. He believed that blacks possessed two unique qualities: intuitive judgment and harmony with nature. These attributes, he insisted, should become a part of human knowledge; indeed, social perfection required combining the contributions of all races. Senghor displayed his mix of assimilated French culture and black heritage in his approach toward Senegal's political status. He advocated African independence but within a framework of cooperation with Europe.

In 1935, Senghor achieved the highest teaching rank in France—the first black African to do so. He taught first at a school in Tours then at a lycée near Paris. He served in the French army during World War II and was captured by German forces, who held him in a concentration camp. After his release, he joined the French Resistance and when the war concluded returned to Senegal.

By then, his homeland was experiencing a drive to advance black power. In 1936, LAMINE GUÈYE had organized a political party linked to the French socialists, and Senghor, who had joined this party before the war, won election to the French National Assembly in 1945, along with Guèye.

Senghor soon broke with Guèye, though. He objected to the party's control by a black elite and desired more independence from the French socialist organization. He also forcefully criticized the *loi-cadre* reform passed by the French National Assembly that gave the individual colonial territories additional power but weakened French West Africa, the federation of which Senegal was a part. Senghor believed this measure would divide western Africa into a multitude of ineffective states.

To offset these developments, Senghor undertook two actions. First, he and several other African leaders organized an interterritorial political party in 1946, the Rassemblement Démocratique Africain (RDA), or African Democratic Rally, aimed at fostering regional unity. Then in 1948 he formed the Senegalese Democratic Block (BDS) to compete in his homeland with Guèye's party. This urban, intellectual Catholic toured the rural areas of Senegal where Muslim religious leaders and a low level of schooling held sway. In an amazing display of skill, he rallied the countryside to his cause, and in 1951 the BDS won the territorial assembly elections.

Guèye then merged his party in 1958 with the BDS, forming a new Senegalese Progressive Union (UPS). Meanwhile, after the *loi-cadre* of 1956 eroded the power of French West Africa, Senghor pushed for a union of republics. Within the RDA, many supported his concept. Yet his stand was opposed by FÉLIX HOUPHOUËT-BOIGNY, the leader of Côte d'Ivoire (one of the wealthier nations in western Africa), who effectively killed Senghor's idea.

In 1956, Senghor won election as mayor of Thies, a major city and railroad center. The voters also returned him as deputy in the French National Assembly.

An admirer of CHARLES DE GAULLE, Senghor endorsed the French leader's idea to join France and its colonies together in a French Community, and he served on the Consultation Committee that studied this proposal. The UPS rallied support, and in 1958 Senegal became a Community member with its own constitution and wide authority over domestic matters, while retaining important economic links to France and allowing continued French control of foreign affairs. A small group of young radicals within the UPS, some of whom embraced Marxism, wanted no attachment to France. They demanded a declaration of complete independence and broke with the party.

In the late 1950s, nationalism continued fueling politics in Senegal and throughout Africa. Senghor worried that disruption of the French Community would hurt his nation, particularly since it relied heavily on a one-crop economy: groundnuts. In preparation for independence, he organized the Mali Federation with Senegal, French Sudan (Mali), Dahomey (Benin), and Upper Volta (Burkina Faso) as members. Yet under pressure from France and Côte d'Ivoire, all except Senegal and French Sudan soon left the nebulous grouping. Then in 1959, he appealed to de Gaulle for African independence. Amid the rising calls for nationhood in several colonies, France allowed complete autonomy for its Community members in 1960, and on 20 August, Senegal declared independence. That month, the Mali Federation completely dissolved.

Senghor became Senegal's president in 1960 and shared power with a prime minister, Mamadou Dia. When Dia attempted a coup in 1962, the Senegalese legislature removed him and made Senghor interim head of the nation. A new constitution enlarged the president's powers, and the Senegalese elected Senghor to that position in February 1963.

Senghor proved an adept and effective leader, who shrewdly consolidated his powers. His form of governing resembled a monarchy in which various groups obtained audiences, and he dispensed judgments. Senghor maintained power through effective alliances with the Muslim religious leaders, who wielded substantial power in the rural areas. He also organized agricultural cooperatives whose leaders became economically linked to his regime. Within Dakar, he allowed considerable political expression, thus avoiding widespread alienation of urban intellectuals. From 1963 until 1976, a one-party system existed, with Senghor's UPS (after 1976 called the Socialist Party) the only legal party. Furthermore, Senghor had the exclusive right to introduce legislation into the legislature and to make appeals to the Supreme Court on constitutional matters.

Then in 1976, Senghor undertook a liberalization program that allowed four political parties to compete for office. Senghor won reelection overwhelmingly in 1978, but on 31 December 1980, midway through his fifth term, he resigned from office.

As president, Senghor had helped direct Senegal's difficult transition toward independence. Although the nation's economy did not expand substantially under his rule, the government continued a top-heavy bureaucracy, and French businessmen and officials still held enormous influence, he nevertheless brought intellectual leadership, maintained cooperation with France, developed a sense of black pride, and strongly defended the interests of Third World nations in the international arena. As a poet and essayist, he wrote several highly acclaimed works, including *Black Offerings* and *Songs of Shadow*, and overall, his political and literary renown extended well beyond the borders of Senegal.

References: Hymans, Jacques L., *Léopold Sédar Senghor: An Intellectual Biography*, 1971; Vaillant, Janet G., *Black, French, and African: A Life of Léopold Sédar Senghor*, 1990.

Shevardnadze, Eduard
(b. 1928)
Georgia

Eduard Shevardnadze stood amid the smoldering ruins of Sukhumi, a city attacked by rebels seeking to overthrow him. As he did so, he thought about his Communist past in support of the Soviet Union and how, at this point, he wanted above all else to maintain Georgian independence.

Eduard Shevardnadze was born on 25 January 1928 in Mamati, a village in Georgia near the Black Sea. Since 1801, Georgia had been a part of Russia, and since the 1920s, it had been a republic within the Soviet Union. Eduard's father was a teacher who rose within the ranks of the Communist Party and was later appointed to the Georgian Supreme Court.

While in his teens, Eduard joined the Komsomol, or Communist Youth League, and in 1948 he joined the Communist Party. This was the traditional route to success for ambitious young men in the Soviet Union, and by the 1950s Shevardnadze served in numerous party positions, including secretary of the regional Komsomol committee and first secretary of the Central Committee of the Komsomol in Georgia. In 1959, he earned a degree in history from the Kutaisi Pedagogical Institute and became a member of the Supreme Soviet of Georgia, the republic's legislature. He also served in the

"I want only that my destiny be the same as Georgia's."

KGB, the Soviet secret police, and eventually became its chief in Georgia.

More party and government positions followed, and in 1965 Shevardnadze gained appointment as head of Georgia's Ministry of Internal Affairs. This made him the chief law enforcement officer in the republic, and in that capacity he earned a reputation as a vigilant and energetic fighter against corruption. The Georgian government had been rife with graft, and Shevardnadze arrested hundreds of officials, recovered money stolen from the treasury, and forced Communist Party officials to give up their luxurious cars and mansions. At the same time, he imprisoned political dissidents.

In 1976, the Communist Party named Shevardnadze to its Central Committee in Moscow. He also served as a nonvoting member of the Politburo and as a delegate to the Supreme Soviet of the U.S.S.R. Then in 1985, the Soviet premier, MIKHAIL GORBACHEV, surprised many observers by naming Shevardnadze his foreign minister. The Georgian lacked diplomatic experience, but Gorbachev, who had long been friends with Shevardnadze, was impressed by his dedication and commitment to reform. Shevardnadze adjusted Soviet policy to reduce foreign entanglement (such as the occupation of Afghanistan) for the sake of cutting military expenditures and making possible needed changes within the Soviet Union.

By this time, though, the U.S.S.R. neared collapse, torn asunder by economic problems and ethnic nationalism within the various republics, including Georgia. Whereas Gorbachev sought moderate reforms to save the Communist Party, Shevardnadze supported a more drastic approach. Conservatives attacked him for this, and in December 1990 he resigned as foreign minister.

In August 1991, after a coup attempt by conservatives against the Soviet government failed, Gorbachev asked Shevardnadze to resume his post. At first he refused, but in November he changed his mind and once again became foreign minister, partly as a last-ditch attempt to save the dissolving Soviet Union. This effort failed, however, and in December the U.S.S.R. collapsed. Back in Georgia, the Communist Party had become discredited after Soviet troops massacred 20 nationalist demonstrators in 1989. Zvid Gamsakhurdia emerged as charismatic leader of a political coalition determined to end Communist rule and gain Georgian independence. In 1990, Gamsakhurdia won election as chairman of the Georgia Supreme Soviet. He acted quickly to close opposition newspapers and intimidate other politicians. He also pushed for nationhood and sponsored a referendum in March 1991 that resulted in a resounding vote for independence. On 9 April the new legislature declared Georgia independent, and in May Gamsakhurdia won election as president in a fraud-ridden campaign. In September, he used National Guard troops to fire on demonstrators engaged in a peaceful protest against him.

In December 1991, as the Soviet Union collapsed, Georgian troops toppled Gamsakhurdia, and in March 1992 the provisional government installed Shevardnadze as chairman of the governing State Council. Many in Georgia distrusted him; he had not initially supported Georgian independence. In fact, he had tried to hold the old Soviet Union together. Furthermore, his past membership in the Communist Party and role in the KGB disturbed many.

Nevertheless, Shevardnadze declared his commitment to Georgian independence, and both democrats and local warlords supported him as the man best able to save the nation. In October 1992, he won election to the presidency. To maintain his nation's complete sovereignty he declared his opposition to the propopsal that Georgia join the other former Soviet republics in a confederation with Russia, called the Commonwealth of Independent States (CIS). This decision, however, encouraged Russia to support rebels in Georgia, primarily a group in Abkhazia, situated along the Black Sea coast, associated with Gamsakhurdia.

Shevardnadze sent troops into Abkhazia, but the situation worsened when they exceeded their orders and went on a rampage, destroying historical sites and killing tourists. When the rebels retaliated and attacked Sukhumi, a city in Abkhazia, Shevardnadze flew there to help defend it, ready if necessary to die in the conflict. The rebels destroyed the city, but Shevardnadze lived, taking the last plane out to Russia, where he hoped to obtain support for ending the war. His appeal worked, although Russia agreed to provide him with military help only after he agreed to join the CIS. While Shevardnadze worried that his decision would weaken his position as a nationalist, Georgians largely supported him. Shevardnadze successfully launched some reforms, such as the privatization of landholdings. Peace, however, remains elusive as the Abkhazi rebels continue their fight. The question remains as to whether Shevardnadze can maintain Georgia's independence and unity.

Reference: Suny, Ronald, *The Making of the Georgian Nation*, 1989.

Shushkevich, Stanislau
(b. 1934)
Belarus

In the collapse of the Soviet Union, which pitted reformers against the Communists, Stanislau Shushkevich took a centrist position, supported in his leadership role by the emerging nationalist movement.

At the time Stanislau Shushkevich was born in 1934, his homeland was a republic within the Soviet Union. During his youth, he witnessed the Soviet program to crush Belarus nationalism and culture through Russification. In fact, it affected him firsthand when his father, a Belarus poet, was sent to prison for his beliefs.

Shushkevich obtained an advanced education at the Belorussian State University in Minsk, where he studied nuclear physics, earned his doctorate, and became a professor. He did not show any inclination to enter politics but rather focused on his scientific career, achieving distinction and gaining membership in the Belorussian Academy of Sciences. Like many prominent men in the republic, he joined the Communist Party.

In the 1980s, two major developments stirred Shushkevich's nationalism. For one, a reform movement in the Soviet Union encouraged openness and criticism, and in Belarus a popular front emerged whose ideas attracted Shushkevich. For another, the explosion at the Chernoybl nuclear power plant in 1986 revealed the exploitive nature of the Soviet system and brought criticism from Shushkevich, who sought to reveal official negligence. Although Chernoybl was located in Ukraine, it was near the Belorussian border and, in fact, Belarus suffered the most devastation. The subsequent popular outrage stimulated protests against Moscow.

Yet Belarus was a conservative area and in 1991, as the Soviet Union began to unravel, voters participating in a referendum chose to stay within the Soviet system. Shortly after this, however, workers began strikes and demonstrations to obtain wage increases and a change in political leaders. Then in August, Soviet conservatives tried to overthrow the reform government in Moscow. When the coup attempt failed, Belarus declared its independence and in September officially became the Republic of Belarus. The Supreme Soviet, or legislature, turned to Shushkevich to lead the nation as its first president. He was a newcomer, having been elected to the Supreme Soviet little more than a year before, but the Belarussian Popular Front backed him, and many Communists considered him an acceptable moderate. Near the time of his election, he quit the Communist Party, which soon dissolved.

Shushkevich indeed initiated moderate policies. While moving toward democracy, he kept intact much of the Communist bureaucracy. At the same time, the Supreme Soviet continued to be dominated by former Communist Party leaders. Shushkevich's moderation brought criticism from Zyanon Paznyak, head of the Belarussian Popular Front, and more radical than Shushkevich.

Late in 1991, Shushkevich guided Belarus into joining the Commonwealth of Independent States, a confederation with Russia and other former Soviet republics. Yet he balanced this conservative move with a government takeover of all Communist Party property.

Like the leaders of the other former Soviet republics, Shushkevich faced great economic challenges as stagnation and inflation beset Belarus. The disaster wrought by Chernoybl only made the situation more difficult—over two million people lived in areas heavily contaminated by nuclear radiation. For his part, Shushkevich seemed committed to a go-slow approach in developing a market economy. The former Communists contributed to this by blocking reform proposals and keeping intact the Soviet-era secret police and the information ministry that still produced pro-government propaganda. In January 1994, the parliament again displayed its conservatism when it removed Shushkevich from office in reaction to his market economics.

Reference: Kipel, Vitaut, ed., *Byelorussian Statehood: Reader and Bibliography,* 1988.

Sigurdsson, Jón
(1811–1879)
Iceland

Iceland's ancient sagas came alive in Jón Sigurdsson's writings, and his nationalism found intellectual expression in his political journal. In the end, he stirred Icelanders into gaining their independence from Denmark.

Jón Sigurdsson was born on 17 June 1811 in Rafnseyri, a town in western Iceland. After completing secondary school, he obtained a classical education at the University of Copenhagen. While in Denmark, he began to take keen interest in Icelandic history and became secretary of the Arnamagnaean Foundation (a cultural and historical society), where he collected and edited Icelandic manuscripts. In 1843, he started to publish them in a multivolume work, not completed until 1857.

Sigurdsson was greatly influenced by Iceland's romantic movement that longed for the country to gain its independence from Denmark (which had ruled Iceland since 1381). Sigurdsson wanted Iceland's ancient assembly, or Althing, to be revived, although in modernized form; and he wanted the city of Rekjavik to be the meeting site for the Althing. The assembly, he believed, would develop Iceland politically and facilitate independence. Along with this, he advocated economic development through vocational, agricultural, and medical schools, and the formation of cooperatives. His educational plan was blocked, however, by its expense (although a medical school was established in 1876, shortly before his death).

At about the time he first started to publish the Icelandic manuscripts, Sigurdsson founded *Ný Félagsrit*, a political journal dedicated to liberal reform. He used historical argument and idealistic appeals to deal with his fellow Icelanders and with the Danes. Other writers also expressed a growing Icelandic nationalism, such as Bjarni Thorarensen and Jonas Hallgrimsson. Sigurdsson, however, was the leader of Icelandic studies and encouraged many scholars and writers.

Sigurdsson's efforts brought results. In 1843, he participated in the discussion that caused Denmark to revive the Althing, although only as an advisory body. He then won election to the assembly's first session in 1845 and became its speaker. He headed the Patriotic Party, through which he promoted his economic program, and in 1854 got Denmark to lift the regulations that had prevented his country from engaging in direct trade with other nations.

Most analysts believe that Sigurdsson's agitation led directly to another Danish concession. In 1874, Iceland was allowed a constitution providing for a semiautonomous status under which it obtained increased legislative power and control over its finances, although Denmark retained its supervisory role and ultimate sovereignty.

Sigurdsson died in Copenhagen on 7 December 1879, well before Iceland achieved its independence. His effort was most immediately continued by Benedikt Sveinsson. In 1918, Denmark recognized Iceland as a separate state, although still nominally under the Danish king. Full independence came on 17 June 1944 after Icelanders voted in a referendum to break completely with Denmark. Thus Sigurdsson's dream and that of his countrymen came true. Today, Icelanders look fondly on Sigurdsson as the architect of their nationhood.

References: Gjerset, Knut, *History of Iceland*, 1924; Stefansson, Vilhjalmur, *Iceland: The First American Republic*, 1943.

Simmonds, Kennedy
(b. 1936)
St. Kitts and Nevis

Beset by numerous political defeats early in his career, Kennedy Simmonds recovered to direct St. Kitts and Nevis to independence under a moderate coalition government.

Kennedy Simmonds was born on 12 April 1936 on St. Kitts, which, along with the small island of Nevis, was under British control. He began his education at the Basseterre Boys' School and then in 1945 earned a scholarship to the St.Kitts-Nevis Grammar School. In 1954, he began pursuing a degree in medicine at the University of the West Indies. He served his internship at a hospital in Jamaica and then returned to St. Kitts, where he opened his own practice.

Simmonds favored independence for St. Kitts and in 1965 helped found the Peoples' Action Movement (PAM) to advance toward that goal. In 1966, he lost a race for a seat in the legislature and shortly after this decided to pursue postgraduate studies in the Bahamas and the United States. When he returned to St. Kitts three years later, he resumed his medical practice and once again pursued political office. Twice more, in 1971 and 1975, he lost elections, yet in 1976 he became president of the PAM.

In 1979, Simmonds's political fortunes changed when he won the seat left vacant by the death of Premier Robert Bradshaw. Overall, the PAM was successful in the elections, defeating the socialist St. Kitts Labour Party, and Simmonds became premier in a coalition government with the Nevis Reform Party. In July 1982, he issued a proposal for a new constitution that would govern St. Kitts and Nevis as a nation, and in December he began negotiating with Britain for independence. The British Parliament approved the terms of nationhood and independence took effect on 19 September 1983, with Simmonds becoming the nation's first prime minister. The following year, he won reelection and in addition to the prime ministry served as minister of finance and minister of foreign affairs.

Simmonds gained admission for St. Kitts and Nevis into the United Nations and the Organization of American States, and followed a foreign policy aligned closely with the United States. In 1983, he supported the American invasion of Grenada. He urged the developed nations to help meet the needs of small states, such as St. Kitts and Nevis, and championed the cause of blacks in South Africa.

Domestically, he pursued improvements in the country's infrastructure and school system. In the late 1980s, he promoted tourism by opening the southeastern portion of St. Kitts to development and worked to revive the sugar industry, which had been heavily damaged by a hurricane. In 1989, he was again reelected, and three years later a referendum went against the Nevis secessionists and halted their effort. Simmonds continues to hold on to his parliamentary margin and govern as prime minister.

References: Dyde, Brian, *St. Kitts: Cradle of the Caribbean*, 1993; Gordon, J., *Nevis: Queen of the Caribees*, 1993.

Smuts, Jan
(1870–1950)
South Africa

As a shy and reserved young man, Jan Smuts discovered in war the courage that made him successful in politics. Using it, he helped forge an independent South Africa founded on white supremacy.

Jan Smuts was born on 24 May 1870 in the Malmesbury district of Cape Colony, then one of the British possessions that eventually became part of South Africa. His father, Abraham Smuts, was a wealthy farmer and prominent political leader. In 1882, young Jan entered a boarding school. Later, he attended Victoria College, from which he graduated in 1891. He studied law at Christ's College, Cambridge, and compiled a brilliant record. In 1895, he returned home and practiced law at Cape Town.

His shyness seemed to hamper his work as a lawyer, but in 1898 he was named state attorney for the Transvaal Republic. Transvaal and the Orange Free State were two Dutch settlements in South Africa, and at this time tensions were high between the Dutch, or Afrikaners, and the English after the British government tried and failed to conquer Transvaal. The differences resulted in the Boer War, which lasted from 1899 to 1902. During this conflict, Smuts discovered his fortitude as leader of the Boer (another name for Afrikaner) troops against the British.

Britain defeated the Boers, and Transvaal and the Orange Free State fell under its control. Smuts participated in the peace conference that ended the war. In 1904, he and LOUIS BOTHA formed Het Volk (The People), an organization dedicated to obtaining autonomy. Smuts entered negotiations with Britain, and in 1906 and 1907, Parliament allowed the two colonies internal self-government.

He and Botha then pursued unifying the colonies with Natal and Cape Colony to form one republic. In 1908, they headed a convention for this purpose, and in 1910, after Parliament granted its approval, the Union of South Africa emerged as an independent nation. Smuts was instrumental in getting South Africans to approve a unitary constitution with a strong central parliament, and he ad-

> *"To us, Union means more than the Native question, and it will be the only means of handling the vexed question."*

vocated delaying any consideration of the problem of black representation until after a national government had been created.

The constitutional convention did grapple with the race issue, but only insofar as it affected voting and representation, and the delegates opted, in general, for a status quo under which blacks in Cape Colony maintained the suffrage they had possessed for years, while they were denied it, as they traditionally had been, in the other territories. In the long run, the government extended republican politics only to the white minority, and as Smuts likely realized, the black franchise stood doomed. Overall, segregationist practices restricted blacks and other nonwhites to secondary positions in the new nation.

For ten years, from 1910 to 1919, Smuts served as minister of defense in a cabinet headed by Prime Minister Botha. During World War I, he commanded the South African army on the Allied side and captured South West Africa from Germany. In 1916, he commanded the Allied forces in East Africa, and the following year served in the British Imperial War Cabinet. He helped reorganize the Royal Flying Corps, making it into the Royal Air Force. He also gained prominence as a leader in advancing the League of Nations and represented South Africa at the Paris Peace Conference.

In 1919, Botha died and Smuts became prime minister. Amid labor agitation, however, he lost his bid in 1924 for another term, and the National Party under James Hertzog gained power. Smuts became leader of the opposition and during this time, in 1926, published his philosophical treatise, *Holism and Evolution*. In 1933, Smuts and Hertzog joined to form a coalition government, with the former as deputy prime minister and minister of justice, and the latter as prime minister. They promoted legislation to combat an economic depression and advance racial restrictions, the latter accepted grudgingly by Smuts to maintain the coalition.

When World War II erupted, Smuts broke with Hertzog over foreign policy. Hertzog wanted

South Africa to take a neutral stand, and Smuts wanted to side with the Allies against Germany. Smuts became prime minister in 1939 and commanded the South African military. In 1941, the British named him a field marshal in their army. Two years later, Smuts won reelection and soundly defeated the recently formed National Party, which advocated Afrikaner nationalism and strict racial segregation. When the war ended in 1945, Smuts attended the international conference in San Francisco and helped put together the charter for the United Nations.

In May 1948, Smuts lost the prime ministry to the National Party and resumed his previous role as leader of the opposition. He suffered a heart attack on 11 September 1950 and died on his farm in Irene. Some historians argue that for all his greatness in creating the Union of South Africa, Smuts failed to provide a dynamic vision for his nation and thus allowed the segregationists to gain the upper hand. Whatever the case, white supremacy prevailed in South Africa until the 1990s, when FREDERIK WILLEM DE KLERK and, more notably, NELSON MANDELA, created a new democratic republic.

References: Friedman, Bernard, *Smuts: A Reappraisal*, 1976; Haarhoff, Theodore, *Smuts, the Humanist*, 1970; Ingham, Kenneth, *Jan Christiaan Smuts*, 1986.

Snegur, Mircea
(b. 1940)
Moldova

Committed to reform, Mircea Snegur promoted Moldovan independence and then balanced the ethnic differences that threatened to tear his new nation apart.

Mircea Snegur was born on 17 January 1940 in the Floresti District of Moldova. His homeland was then a republic within the Soviet Union, and he obtained his advanced education at the Kishinev Institute of Agriculture and at age 24 joined the Communist Party. Snegur worked as an agronomist and from 1967 until 1971 managed state and collective farms. In the 1970s, he worked in the Ministry of Agriculture. His activities with the Communist Party expanded, and from 1981 to 1985 he served as secretary for the Central Committee in the Yedinetsky District. In 1985, he became secretary for the republic's Central Committee, a position he held for four years.

By this time, Snegur's homeland was experiencing substantial change. In trying to unify Moldova, the Soviets declared Russian the official language for the republic's ethnic groups. This policy, however, antagonized the majority of Moldovans and stirred their nationalism. When at the same time a reform movement emerged within the Soviet Union, the language issue and other grievances led to the formation of political organizations. The Alexe Mateevici Literary and Musical Group, named after a Moldovan poet, promoted the indigenous culture, while the Democratic Movement called for democracy, economic privatization, and autonomy. In 1989, the Democratic Movement and several other reform organizations joined together to form the Moldovan Popular Front (MPF). Although a longstanding Communist, Snegur supported reform and clashed with the Moldovan leader, Semen Grossu, who opposed nearly all concessions to the nationalists.

Grossu harassed his opponents, but his position weakened as the Soviet Union began to unravel. In November 1989, after public demonstrations spread, Moscow removed Grossu from office. Five months later, elections to Moldova's Supreme Soviet, or legislature, resulted in the MPF winning 40 percent of the seats and other reform groups winning an additional 30 percent. Snegur was named the Supreme Soviet's chair.

In June 1990, the Supreme Soviet declared

Moldova a sovereign republic, and when the Soviet Union advocated avoiding secession through a compromise, Snegur rejected the proposal. In September, he became Moldova's first president. He clearly sided with the nationalists, and in May 1991 Moldova changed its name to officially become the Republic of Moldova. In August, after hard-line Communists in the Soviet Union failed in their attempt to overthrow the reform-minded Soviet government, Snegur outlawed the Moldovan Communist Party. In the same month, Moldova officially proclaimed its independence. The Soviet Union officially dissolved in December.

Snegur then worked to get diplomatic recognition for Moldova, obtained admission into the United Nations, and began building an army. He faced daunting problems: For one, Slavs (including many ethnic Russians) in the Trans-Dniester region, an important industrial area, declared their independence from Moldova, and in June 1992 Russian troops assisted them. Snegur engaged in ongoing discussions with Russia, Romania, and Ukraine to resolve the crisis, but in 1994 Russian troops remained stationed in the region. Second, Gagauz and Bulgarian minorities located in southern Moldova demanded autonomy. Snegur made concessions to prevent secession, guaranteeing the minorities their own schools and language. Third, economic and ecological problems worsened as inflation spread and years of heavy pesticide use caused enormous soil pollution.

Responding to the situation, Snegur proclaimed in 1994 his desire to see Moldova form an economic union with Russia. He also began privatizing businesses and distributing farmland to the peasants. That same year, many former Communists won election to Parliament. With more than 20 political parties in Moldova, stability remains Snegur's primary challenge.

Reference: Nedelcvic, Vasile, *The Republic of Moldova*, 1992.

Sobhuza II
(1899–1982)
Swaziland

A strident defender of traditional Swazi practices, at one point in his reign Sobhuza II dismantled the political system established by the British.

Sobhuza II was born on 22 July 1899 in Swaziland. His father, Ngwane V, king of the Swazi, died when Sobhuza was a young child. A regent then ruled while Sobhuza obtained an education at the Zombodze National School and Lovedale College in South Africa. Britain controlled Swaziland at this time as a British High Commission Territory, an arrangement under which the Swazi had lost large amounts of land and grazing and mineral rights.

On 22 December 1921, Sobhuza gained full power as ruler of the Swazi, but was still under British authority. In 1963, Britain allowed limited self-government, and four years later a new constitution established the Kingdom of Swaziland, with Britain retaining control of external affairs. Sobhuza proclaimed that if whites wanted to have a role in the region's development they would have to become Swazis and thus drop their European practices. The following year, the British granted Swaziland complete independence with a popularly elected legislature.

Sobhuza, though, desired the restoration of traditional Swazi political practices. Extremely powerful as a result of his more than 70 marriages that established a supporting clan system, he solidified his rule by building an army loyal to him, and in 1973 voided the constitution. He assumed nearly all power, dissolving the legislature and banning political parties. This consolidation in the hands of the king accompanied by a village governance system reflected the political practices that predated British rule.

Under Sobhuza, the economy expanded considerably and stability prevailed. He allied Swaziland with the West and maintained good relations with both South Africa and Marxist Mozambique, a not inconsiderable achievement given the pressure from many blacks to support guerrilla armies then attacking South Africa's white supremacist regime.

Sobhuza died on 21 August 1982 at Lobzilla near Mbabane. After a power struggle, his son, Prince Makhosetive, ruled as King Mswati III.

References: Booth, A. R., *Swaziland*, 1984; Davies, R. H., et al., *The Kingdom of Swaziland*, 1986.

Somare, Michael
(b. 1936)
Papua New Guinea

Facing a people divided on the issue of independence, Michael Somare toured his homeland's mountain region in 1972 and so skillfully built support that nationhood became a reality.

Michael Somare, the son of a policeman, was born on 9 April 1936 in Karau, a village on the northern coast of the main island, New Guinea. In 1951, young Somare, who had attended primary school at Wewak, continued his education at Finschhagen, and five years later completed teacher training at Sogeri Secondary School. He then taught at the high school level from 1956 to 1962. Following that, he became a journalist with the territorial information department. In 1965, he studied at the Administrative College in Port Moresby, where he socialized with others among his homeland's small, educated elite. He increasingly criticized Australia's rule and favored independence.

In 1967, Somare joined with several Papua New Guinean civil servants and two Australians to form Pangu Pati, a political party committed to home rule. Somare told a visiting United Nations delegation that it was important for his people to gain local control through a stronger House of Assembly. In 1968, he ran for a seat in the House from the East Sepik Region. He emerged victorious and continued to push for greater autonomy, a position that caused debate in Papua New Guinea as many in the territory either feared losing Australian assis-

"There will be frustrations, but we will not have much trouble. Those who have no faith can go . . ."

tance or did not believe the entire territory should exist as one nation. Some in the interior highlands, for example, wanted their own entity, and a strong separatist movement existed on Bougainville, an island important for its copper mine.

After his election victory, Somare became the leader in the House and served on several committees, where he earned a reputation for expertise and persuasiveness. A big man, he once broke up a fight between two representatives by bear-hugging one of them into submission.

Pangu Pati entered the 1972 elections with the conservative United Party (UP) as its main competitor. The UP won the most seats, but Somare skillfully formed a coalition with several smaller parties to become Papua New Guinea's chief minister, forming what many observers considered to be the first indigenous government. Then he toured the highlands to promote unity, and so ably built alliances that his main political opponent there supported him on most issues.

Australia backed Somare's push for independence, and the chief minister formed a constitutional planning committee. In late 1973, Papua New Guinea obtained internal self-government, but a continuing wrangle over the constitution delayed complete independence until September 1975. Under the new government, Somare served as prime minister. Unity became a great challenge as he governed a nation consisting of 1,000 separate tribes speaking 500 distinct languages. Perhaps his finest moment came when he ended the secessionist drive in Bougainville through peaceful measures. In 1976, the Bougainvilleans decided to rebel against the national government. Many in Port Moresby, Papua New Guinea's capital, urged Somare to react with force. Instead, he flew to Bougainville with his advisors and negotiated a settlement that granted concessions on taxes and kept the region within Papua New Guinea.

Somare won reelection in 1977, but opponents grew stronger by charging him with ineffectiveness in bringing law and order to the Highlands, an area where crime and resistance to the government had become rampant. In 1980, Somare lost the prime ministry after a new coalition formed in the House. Two years later, however, his revived Pangu Pati scored a huge victory, and he returned as prime minister. Then in November 1985 he lost a parliamentary vote of confidence on the budget, and he was replaced by a new prime minister.

In 1988, Somare returned to government as foreign minister. One year later, trouble again erupted in Bougainville when a separatist revolutionary army attacked several plantations. Somare arranged a cease-fire in March 1990, but after negotiations collapsed the government blockaded the island. The rebels then declared Bougainville independent. After diplomatic intervention by New Zealand, Somare and the rebels reached an agreement in January 1991, but the two sides did not completely adhere to it, and tensions remained substantial. The following year, the Pangu Pati lost its reelection bid, and Somare was no longer foreign minister. Nevertheless, he left a reputation for skillful leadership and a commitment to democracy and national unity.

References: Somare, Michael, *Sana*, 1975; Woolford, Don, *Papua New Guinea: Initiation and Independence*, 1976.

Souphanouvong
(1909–1995)
Laos

Souphanouvong became known as the "Red Prince." In the confusing factional battles that characterized Laotian politics, he adopted a Communist position and, although sometimes more a follower than a leader, he symbolized the country's revolution.

Souphanouvong, the son of Viceroy Boun Khong, was born a prince on 13 July 1909 at Luang Prabang. His half-brother was Prince Souvanna Phouma, who also played a leading part in Laotian politics. Souphanouvong went to school at the Lycée Albert Saurraut in Hanoi and then journeyed to France, where he obtained training as a civil engineer and, according to legend, worked on the docks at Bordeaux as a day laborer and learned about life among the workers. In 1938, he returned to Southeast Asia and joined the French Indochina bureaucracy, where he applied his engineering skills in building bridges and dams in Vietnam. When Souphanouvong worked for the French, he developed a dislike for their imperious manner and their treatment of him and other Laotians as second-class citizens.

During World War II, after the Japanese had ended French control of Indochina, Souphanouvong was transferred to Vientiane in Laos. As the war drew to a close, Souphanouvong and other leading Laotians opposed a French reconquest. In March 1945, under Japanese auspices, Laos declared its independence with Sisavong Vong as king and Prince Petsarath as premier. Souphanouvong held the post of defense minister. France, however, did not recognize this independence and determined to once again control Laos.

In 1946, as the French returned, Souphanouvong was wounded in a battle against the foreigners.

Shortly thereafter, he left his homeland and in 1947 served as foreign minister of Free Laos, a government-in-exile located in Bangkok. The following year, he broke with this group and allied with the Viet Minh, the Communist-nationalist movement centered in Vietnam. With Viet Minh backing, he organized the Pathet Lao (Lao Nation) in 1950, a guerrilla group dedicated to an independent, Marxist Laos. Meanwhile, France had granted Laos greater autonomy as a nation within the French Union. The struggle continued, however, both for full independence and to determine which political figures and ideology would prevail.

Souphanouvong headquartered the Pathet Lao government and army in northern Laos at the Plain of Jars, where he had a substantial following. In 1953, France agreed to full independence for Laos, and at the international conference on French Indochina held at Geneva in 1954, an arrangement was reached concerning Laos' internal government. Souphanouvong attended this meeting and represented the Pathet Lao, and sat opposite his half-brother Souvanna Phouma, who represented the neutralist royal Lao government. The conference recognized Souphanouvong's control over two northern provinces and thus assured him a crucial role in any new central government.

In 1957, Souphanouvong disappointed many of his Communist supporters when he decided to join Souvanna Phouma in a cooperationist government. He was appointed minister of planning and economic development and as such controlled the foreign aid pouring into Laos, especially that from the United States. But Souphanouvong's plan to integrate the Pathet Lao with the government raised opposition from both radical Communists and the conservative military. The latter provoked a battle with the Pathet Lao and in July 1959 imprisoned Souphanouvong. In May 1960, he escaped into the jungle.

In 1962, Souphanouvong again joined a coalition government established by Souvanna Phouma after another international conference. All sides proved uncooperative, however, and the coalition collapsed in 1963. Souphanouvong and the Pathet Lao resumed their fighting. Souvanna Phouma, who had relied heavily on American aid, saw his situation worsen in the early 1970s when the United States withdrew from Vietnam, and the Pathet Lao gained control over most of Laos. The warring sides reached an armistice in February 1973, and in April 1974 they formed a new coalition government, but one clearly under Communist domination with Souphanouvong as premier.

In December 1975, Laos became the People's Democratic Republic of Laos, the figurehead monarchy was abolished, and in a political reshuffling Souphanouvong was relegated to a ceremonial role as president. He still served on the Politburo of the Laotian Communist Party, but resigned the presidency and largely retired from politics in 1986. In the 1990s, the Communist government relaxed its economic regulations and allowed a market economy but resisted multiparty elections. Souphanouvong died from heart disease on 9 January 1995.

References: Gunn, Geoffrey C., *Rebellion in Laos: Peasant and Politics in a Colonial Backwater,* 1990; Halpern, Joel M., *Laos Profiles,* 1990.

Spinola, Antonio de
(b. 1910)
Portugal

Antonio de Spinola appeared an unlikely revolutionary: He had been a military man his entire adult life, and in Africa he upheld his nation's colonial system. But in 1974, he decided the system must fall—Portugal had suffered enough.

On 11 April 1910, Antonio Sebastião de Spinola was born into an aristocratic family that lived in Estremoz. It was an eventful year: The longstanding monarchy that traced its roots back to the twelfth century and King AFONSO I fell to a republican government.

In 1930, Spinola, after attending a preparatory school, entered the Escola Militar, Portugal's national military academy. While he studied there, the national government underwent yet another change when, in 1933, Antonio de Oliveira Salazar replaced the republican government with a right-wing dictatorship. In November, Spinola graduated as a second lieutenant in the cavalry. Four years later, he earned promotion to lieutenant and in the Spanish Civil War commanded Portuguese volunteers, who sided with Francisco Franco's fascist movement. During World War II, Portugal remained neutral, but the government sent Spinola to observe Hitler's military and learn German combat techniques.

After his promotion to captain in 1944, Spinola served in the Azores and then continued a steady climb in the military ranks, becoming a major in 1955. Six years later, a crisis erupted when African revolutionaries in the Portuguese colonies rebelled. Portugal sent Spinola to Angola as a lieutenant colonel, and he soon earned a reputation for daring and heroism while commanding a cavalry battalion. The army promoted him to colonel in 1963, and he returned to Portugal the following year. He then headed the National Republican Guard, a police force, and in 1966 was made a brigadier general.

Spinola went back to Africa in 1968 to command the military and serve as governor in Guinea-Bissau (then called Portuguese Guinea). He did more than fight the revolutionaries on the battlefield: He initiated reforms, such as building roads and schools and organized an indigenous army to weaken the revolutionaries. The rebellion continued, however, led first by AMICAR CABRAL

and then his brother, Luís Cabral. The Portuguese presence had obviously become tenuous, and Spinola began reassessing his own position toward the colonial crisis. He returned home in 1973 to accolades and Portugal's highest military honor.

Once back in Lisbon as deputy chairman of the Joint Chiefs of Staff, Spinola grew troubled over conditions in his homeland. Portugal had struggled for years as the poorest nation in Western Europe, and now the colonial war was making conditions worse. The government had passed from Salazar to Marcello Caetano, who wanted to reform the political system but ran into opposition from conservatives. The nation stagnated.

Then in 1974, Spinola released his book, *Portugal and the Future,* and it shook the entire country. In it, he criticized Portugal's involvement in the colonial wars as draining the economy, and he called his nation's role as a civilizing nation overseas a myth. He did not advocate granting the colonies their independence, but did believe they should have equal status with Portugal through what he called a federal union. He struck a responsive chord among many military men and the masses as widespread discontent had been simmering over the loss of money, as well as lives, in Africa. That a distinguished man, a leader within the establishment, could take such a position emboldened others to speak out. The government dismissed Spinola, further enraging popular opinion.

On 16 March 1974, 200 soldiers loyal to Spinola staged a coup, but it failed. There followed another attempt in April, led by the Armed Forces Movement (MFA), and this time it succeeded. Although Spinola had not planned the operation, he apparently had given it his approval, and in any event, as a symbol of reform, the rebels immediately turned to him for leadership. On 26 April, he became head of a seven-man Junta of National Salvation chosen by the military.

Spinola did not envision a massive social upheaval; he desired moderate reform rather than revolution. But massive crowds began parading through the streets, and the old regime's enforcement devices, including the secret police, fell apart. Leftists began manipulating the demonstrations and radical labor and peasant leaders emerged.

Spinola made some substantial changes, including an end to press censorship and permitting freedom of speech and open political parties. Some called this the "flower revolution," a largely bloodless upheaval.

On 15 May, Spinola became provisional president of a left-oriented government, but promised he would leave politics the next year, after elections for a national legislature. The government continued in turmoil, with Spinola forced to form a second provisional government in July. At the same time, Portugal recognized Guinea-Bissau's independence and moved to grant the same to its other colonies.

At home, the revolution intensified, and although Spinola drifted further to the left, he worried that events had outpaced his actions. The masses began confiscating farms, shops, and industries. In September, another political dispute rocked the nation when the MFA pressed for radical economic change. Spinola, however, resisted the radicals; he feared a Communist takeover and desired more moderate measures, including a modernized financial system and membership in the European Community. As the dispute intensi-

fied, he tried to seize full power and was ousted from office. He then complained that anarchy threatened to engulf the nation. Another provisional leadership emerged, and as the Portuguese Communist Party grew more influential, the government turned increasingly to the left.

In 1975, Spinola tried to regain power in a coup, but failed. He then went into political retirement. His attempt, though, unleashed a virulent reaction by the left and brought a wave of nationalizations. Presently, the government owned almost all of Portugal's newspapers, insurance companies, hotels, and many other businesses.

The revolution soon moderated, and elections held in 1976 stabilized what was called the Second Republic. As prime minister in the 1980s, Cavaco Silva directed modest economic growth, and the emergence of an ongoing parliamentary system seemed to signify a democratic political environment. The impetus for reform, however, came first from Spinola.

References: Porch, Douglas, *The Portuguese Armed Forces and the Revolution*, 1977; Robinson, Richard Alan Hodgson, *Contemporary Portugal: A History*, 1979.

Sucre, Antonio José de
(1795–1830)
Bolivia, Colombia, Ecuador, Venezuela

A brilliant military leader, Antonio José de Sucre served SIMÓN BOLÍVAR as a general and helped liberate large areas of South America from Spanish rule. His spectacular victory at Ayacucho was the last major battle against Spain.

Like many leaders in the South American struggle for independence, Antonio José de Sucre hailed from a wealthy family. He was born on 3 February 1795 in Cumaná, Venezuela, at that time a Spanish colony. In 1808, he went to Caracas to continue his schooling and soon became involved in a revolutionary uprising. Venezuelan rebels struck against Spain in 1810, and the young Sucre joined the patriot army in its fight. FRANCISCO DE MIRANDA

commanded the rebels and in 1811 was named ruler of Venezuela, but the revolutionaries were disorganized and controlled only a limited territory. Furthermore, Spain fought back, resulting in a defeat for Sucre and the other patriots. In 1814, he fled to the Antilles. He returned, however, to fight again in 1815 and, after another defeat, retreated to Haiti.

Sucre's tactical brilliance amid renewed fighting in 1816 earned him the attention of Simón Bolívar, the great South American liberator. So, too, did his loyalty to Bolívar in a power struggle with General Santiago Moriño. Bolívar chose Sucre to lead the fight in freeing southern Gran Colombia (today, Ecuador) from Spanish rule. Sucre commanded a daring invasion, landing on the Pacific coast at Guayaquil and then taking his army into the mountains, where he climbed the 9,200-foot terrain into Quito and, on 21 May 1822, routed the Spanish on the slopes of Pichincha. Bolívar then arrived to augment Sucre's force and secure the area.

At the head of a 5,800-man army, Sucre proceeded into Colombia, where in August 1824 he and Bolívar crushed the Spanish at the Battle of Jurin, an event that signaled the beginning of the end in the revolutionary war. Bolívar was determined to liberate Peru, and after he triumphantly entered Lima, he chose Sucre to deliver the final major blow. Once again, the young general proved brilliant: On 9 December 1824, he met the Spanish soldiers on the high plateau near Ayacucho and routed them. This ended Spain's rule in all but Upper Peru, and Sucre evicted the royalists there in 1825.

After his victory, Sucre, motivated by fears Upper Peru might become a bloody area of conflict between Peru and Argentina, both of which coveted it, called a representative assembly that on 6 August 1825 declared independence. The assembly then named the country Bolivia, in honor of Bolívar. Nevertheless, Bolívar was angry, for he had desired that Upper Peru and Peru be united as one nation. After Bolívar entered La Paz and ruled Bolivia for five months, Sucre repaired his relations with "the Liberator" by allowing him to write the Bolivian constitution. Upon its adoption, early in 1826, Sucre was elected president for life.

While in office, Sucre reformed the tax structure and weakened the power of the Catholic Church by confiscating its wealth and closing its monasteries. Many conservatives opposed him and political factions formed. A substantial uprising in 1828 against his government, coupled with an invasion by Peru and an assassination attempt, caused him to leave Bolivia in disgust for Ecuador. Andrés de Santa Cruz then served as Bolivia's first native-born president.

Sucre ended his political retirement when, in 1829, Peru attacked Gran Colombia. He led an army that defeated the Peruvians at Tarqui on 27 February 1829. The following year, he served as president of a constitutional convention whose representatives came from the three states comprising Gran Colombia: Ecuador, Venezuela, and Colombia. The meeting was intended to resolve worsening differences among the states and keep Gran Colombia together. This effort proved fruitless, and as Sucre headed back home to Quito on 4 June 1830, assassins attacked and killed him at Berruecos. Three months later, Gran Colombia dissolved. Sucre was later hailed as the father of Bolivian independence.

Reference: Sherwell, Guillermo Antonio, *Antonio José de Sucre: Hero and Martyr of American Independence*, 1924.

Sukarno
(1901–1970)
Indonesia

In his youth, mysticism intrigued Sukarno. In his adulthood, he applied it to Indonesian independence and the authoritarian state he created.

Sukarno was born 6 June 1901 in Surabaja on Java, of what was then the Dutch East Indies. His father, Raden Sukemi, was a Javanese teacher, and his mother, Ida Njoman Rai, a Hindu, came from Bali. Sukarno's father had only a modest income, and so he frequently sent Sukarno out to live with other families. For example, Sukarno spent several years with his paternal grandparents in Tulungagung. There he liked to watch the Hindu puppet shadow plays and was enthralled by the mysticism they embodied. Some analysts claim that later in his life Sukarno treated his politics as theater wrapped around mystical, unfathomable performances by a great leader.

Even as a child Sukarno appeared bright, forceful, and confident, and he obtained the nickname "Djago," meaning champion. Sukarno attended the same secondary school where his father taught, Europe Lagere School in eastern Java; he excelled as a student, and learned both Dutch and French. He completed his secondary education at a Dutch school in Surabaja, where he lived with a patron, H. O. S. Tjokroaminoto, a political activist who had a big influence on him. Tjokroaminoto's friends included nationalist businessmen and intellectuals who spent much time at his home, where Sukarno imbibed the discussions and the broad spectrum of ideologies these men represented, from Islamic Fundamentalism to Marxism. Sukarno often engaged in these conversations, honing his speaking and persuasive skills, and even contributed articles to Tjokroaminoto's newspaper.

In his late teens, he attended a Dutch technical school in Bandung, where he met several bright young men recently returned from colleges in Europe. Their ideas stimulated his nationalism. Sukarno earned an engineering degree in 1925 while also mastering German, English, Japanese, and Indonesian.

He then turned to politics, and with his charismatic, even hypnotic, speaking style he became a favorite of Bandung's young nationalists. Many believed he would become a great national hero, and Sukarno agreed. He encouraged the nickname "Bung," meaning elder brother, and later the names "Bung Besar" (The Big Bung) and "Bung Besar-Besar" (The Big, Big Bung).

In his political actions, Sukarno aimed his nationalism at the Dutch, who controlled Indonesia. In July 1927, he began the Indonesian Nationalist Union, which the following year became the Indonesian Nationalist Party (PNI). In response to his efforts, the Dutch colonial authorities imprisoned him from 1929 to 1931 and then sent him into an eight-year exile, beginning in 1933.

While Sukarno thus lived as an outcast, a major change swept Indonesia: the expulsion of the Dutch by Japan during World War II. The Japanese returned Sukarno and other nationalists to their homes. Sukarno saw the Japanese as liberators, and they in turn made him their chief propagandist. He also recruited tens of thousands of young Indonesians to defend the archipelago from Allied attack and others to work as laborers in Burma, Thailand, and the various Pacific islands. He and his colleague Mohammed Hatta, who as a dedicated nationalist advised him and often tried to keep his flamboyance in line, pressured Japan to grant Indonesia its independence.

In 1945, Sukarno announced the Five Principles that under his leadership became official state ideology: Nationalism (independence and love of country), Internationalism (a leading role for Indonesia in the Third World), Democracy, Social Prosperity, and Belief in God. As Japan neared surrender in the war, Sukarno and Hatta considered whether to push more quickly for independence. As they pondered, an incredible situation unfolded when a radical nationalist law student kidnapped them. Persuaded, perhaps intimidated, by this radical and his colleagues, Sukarno declared Indonesia independent on 17 August 1945.

A legislature chose Sukarno to be president and Hatta to be vice-president, but Dutch forces invaded in 1948 and captured the two leaders. This, however, brought severe criticism from the United States and other countries, and the United Nations intervened to arrange a conference. On 27 December 1949, the Netherlands officially agreed to Indonesia's independence.

Sukarno then resumed his presidency, moving into the huge palace once occupied by the Dutch governor-general in Jakarta. Here began the main features of Sukarno's rule: extravagance, cronies, and a reliance on generalities rather than specific policies. While he surrounded himself with opportunists and self-centered officials, Sukarno won mass support through his powerful speeches and his ability to evoke Indonesian pride. His attacks on imperialists as an external enemy were also well received. Furthermore, despite inefficiencies and inequitable development, Indonesia's economy experienced a postwar boom.

In 1956, Sukarno claimed he had experienced a mystical dream in which he was advised to end political factionalism. He subsequently dissolved the legislature and initiated programs he called the

Guided Democracy and Guided Economy. He veered more and more to a Marxist ideology, although he lacked a consistent approach. In a highly popular move with Indonesians, the government seized Dutch enterprises, including the giant shipping line KLM. Meanwhile, dissidents tried on several occasions to assassinate Sukarno, the first attempt occurring in 1957.

After Sukarno's reforms, the economy spiraled downward, with inflation reaching staggering levels and making basic foodstuffs such as rice difficult to obtain. Sukarno tried diverting attention with attacks on what he perceived to be external enemies. In 1962, he called the formation of Malaysia an imperialist plot to encircle Indonesia and even withdrew from the UN to protest its opposition to him in the controversy. He also told the United States to keep its foreign aid and moved closer to the Soviet Union and China. Soon the Soviets, however, grew discontent with his belligerency and erratic behavior.

Suddenly, on 30 September 1965, a coup attempt led by the Communists and dissident military units rocked the nation. Many believed that Sukarno had actually supported the attack to turn Indonesia more to the left and crush the increasing criticism of his regime. If he did, the plan backfired. The army under General Suharto rallied to crush the Communists, but the fighting caused carnage with some 300,000 Communists and alleged Communists killed. The disorder and Suharto's increasing power led Sukarno to resign his presidency on 11 March 1966. In 1967, Suharto became president and Bung Besar faded from politics.

On 21 June 1970, Sukarno died from a kidney ailment. Many people considered him to have been disgraced, yet 500,000 mourners turned out for what was scheduled to be a quiet funeral. The crowd stood as testament to Sukarno's continuing influence as his image, the power of his words, and his national heroism extended beyond his life.

References: Hanna, Willard, *Eight Nation Makers: Southeast Asia's Charismatic Statesmen*, 1964; Hughes, John, *Indonesian Upheaval*, 1967.

Sukhebator, Damdiny
(1893–1923)
Mongolia

Damdiny Sukhebator became the dashing military hero, galloping on his horse as he led his Mongolian revolutionaries into battle. His bravery and patriotism propelled him to the forefront of Mongolia's founders.

Damdiny Sukhebator was born in 1893 in eastern Mongolia. His father lived an impoverished existence, a wanderer looking for work, often unsuccessfully. At 14, Sukhebator, like many nomadic Mongols an accomplished horseman, rode the courier routes, bringing back horses after they had been used. He obtained little education (Mongolia had no regular schools) but nevertheless learned to read and write.

As a young man, Sukhebator witnessed a Mongolia undergoing many changes. For years the area had been under foreign rule, with the Russians and Chinese especially struggling for control. In 1912, Sukhebator was drafted into a newly organized Mongolian army, which received training from tsarist Russia. He served until 1919, when Chinese troops forced the army to disband. By this time Sukhebator had won a loyal following among his men, and later they supported him politically.

Sukhebator apparently was not attached to any ideology until he met HORLOYN CHOIBALSANG, who promoted the Marxism of the emerging Russian Revolution. Shortly after leaving the army, Sukhebator organized a military group to resist the Chinese. In 1920, under direction of the Communist International, he merged his group with another one formed by Choibalsang. The two men found themselves compatible and cooperated in building their radical organization dedicated to ending foreign rule and transforming Mongolian society. As a result, Sukhebator became head of the Mongolian People's Party and advanced its Marxist ideology. He met Lenin in 1921, at which time the Communist leader advised the Mongolian to form "islands of socialism" in his country's economy.

Sukhebator led the Mongolian Partisan Army, established early in 1921 when it numbered some 400 men, and gave it combat training. In one battle he charged the middle of 100 soldiers and killed one of them with a striking blow from the butt of his rifle. In February, the army captured Kiakhta, a Mongolian city the revolutionaries declared to be the capital of a provisional government. On 11 July, a new People's Government of Mongolia replaced the existing government, and Sukhebator became commander in chief of the army and minister of war under premier Dogsomyn Bodoo. Soviet troops backed the new government and assisted Sukhebator's army. By January 1922, the last enemy forces, the anti-Soviet White Russians, were defeated.

When a dispute erupted that same year within the Mongolian People's Party between those who supported a close alliance with Soviet Russia and those who opposed it, Sukhebator sided with the former and helped lead the purge of the opposing faction that included Bodoo, who was summarily executed. Shortly after this, on 22 February 1923, Sukhebator died under mysterious circumstances, one accusation being that he was poisoned by anti-Communist political enemies. He is remembered, however, as a hero of the revolution and a brave fighter for Mongolian independence.

References: Lattimore, Owen, *Nationalism and Revolution in Mongolia,* 1955; Lattimore, Owen, *Nomads and Commissars, Mongolia Revisited,* 1962.

Sun Yat-sen
(1866–1925)
China

For years, Sun Yat-sen's revolutionary efforts seemed doomed. Failed plots hatched more failed plots as Sun had to travel widely and struggle mightily to get even modest financial support; he had to form unstable alliances with local warlords, and he never presided over a unified country. Yet he became the father of the republic, of modern China, hailed by conservatives and leftists alike.

Western influences had an enormous impact on Sun Yat-sen's life. He was born into a poor peasant family on 12 November 1866 at Hsiang-shan in Kwangtung Province, near Canton. At first he obtained a traditional Confucian Chinese education, but in 1879 his brother, Sun Mei, who had earlier emigrated to Hawaii, brought him to Honolulu. There he attended a British missionary school and, for one year, the American-run Oahu College. Western science and philosophy attracted him, as did Christianity.

In 1883, Sun returned to Hsiang-shan where he was heavily criticized for his Westernization. He then moved to Hong Kong where Western influences again proved strong, mixing with Chinese culture. In 1884, he began studying at the Diocesan Home before transferring the next year to the Government Central School. Around this time an American missionary baptized him, and he married Lu Mu-chen, who had been chosen by his parents to be his wife. He made another trip to Hawaii, but left in 1886 and enrolled in the Canton Hospital Medical School, followed by the College of Medicine for Chinese, located in

> *". . . capitalism makes profit its sole aim, while the Principle of Livelihood makes the nurture of the people its aim."*

Hong Kong. He graduated in 1892 and tried to begin his medical practice at Macao, then run by Portugal. The Portuguese, however, denied him a license, and Sun returned to Hong Kong where he began a brief career as a doctor.

Sun had grown enormously discontent with the Chinese government, then under the conservative Ch'ing Dynasty. Along with many Chinese, especially the younger, higher-educated groups, Sun condemned his country's technological backwardness, which allowed outside powers to dominate. He criticized the foreign nations that had humiliated the dynasty and the nation by carving China into spheres of influence. He tried to get the Chinese authorities to listen to his pleas for reform, but when he got only rejection he gave up his medical practice and dedicated himself to radical revolutionary change. In 1894, he went back to Hawaii and formed the Hsing-Chung hui (Revive China Society), a secret revolutionary organization. After China suffered more humiliation with its loss to Japan in the Sino-Japanese War of 1894–1895, Sun journeyed to Hong Kong, where he plotted an uprising to be staged in Canton. The Chinese government uncovered his revolutionary group, however, and executed several of its members. Sun fled to Japan where he found new stimuli, for many Chinese exiles gathered there to discuss and plan great changes.

Sun traveled extensively, spreading his belief that revolution must ensue and seeking monetary contributions from Chinese living overseas. He visited the United States and then Britain, where in London he fell into a dramatic episode. As he walked along a street, several men jumped him and dragged him into China's legation. They then chartered a ship to send him back to China for execution. At the last minute Dr. James Cantlie, Sun's former medical professor in Hong Kong, obtained news of the kidnapping and gave the story to the London *Times.* This ignited a furor, the British government intervened, and the Chinese released Sun. The adventure made Sun a hero in China, an image promoted by him in a book he wrote about the incident, *Kidnapped in London.*

In July 1897, Sun arrived back in Japan and obtained financial assistance from several influential Japanese. While there, he developed his Three People's Principles, his main political platform. The principles were People's Nationalism, People's Democracy, and People's Livelihood. By the first he meant striking against both foreign imperialism and the Ch'ing Dynasty; the second meant establishing a constitutional government of the people, by the people, for the people; the third meant pursuing substantial economic reforms to help the masses. He left this last point vague, but apparently meant land redistribution and an end to what he called the "evil capitalistic system."

Sun's ideology never assumed the importance of his actions, which he himself considered the marrow of revolutionary activity. In 1900, he sponsored an uprising in Hui-chou, but it collapsed after just 12 days. Then Sun received assistance from Liang Ch'i-ch'ao, who had fled to Japan and begun a Chinese press attacking the various Ch'ing practices and praising Sun. This widely read publication boosted Sun's following. In 1905, he and several other radicals formed the T'ung-meng hui (United League) in Tokyo. Sun then went to Hanoi, where he put together several uprisings in South China. These revolts also failed, and Sun lost supporters and financial backing. Many areas even banned him, such as Japan, Hong Kong, and French Indochina.

But the Ch'ing Dynasty receded further, initiating reforms in 1901 that pleased nobody. On 10 October 1911, what Chinese call the Double Tenth, a rebellion broke out in Wu-han and the rebels, led by army units sympathetic to the T'ung-meng hui, overthrew the provincial government. Several provinces in central, south, and northwest China declared their independence from the Ch'ing. At the time, Sun was traveling in the United States raising money. He departed quickly for China, and revolutionary delegates gathered in Nanking elected him president of a provisional government. On 1 January 1912 Sun proclaimed a new nation: the Republic of China. He also formed a new political party, the Kuomintang (KMT or National People's Party).

Sun, however, lacked the military support he needed to extend his power throughout China. In Peking, Yüan Shih-kai, an official in the Ch'ing government and a political boss in northern China who had military backing, stepped in and expressed his support for Sun and his desire to mediate a settlement between Sun and the Ch'ing government. In February 1912, the dynasty agreed to abdicate and as part of the arrangement, Sun relinquished his presidency in favor of Yüan, who was inaugurated at Peking, the new capital of the provisional government. Sun became director of railroad development and formulated plans to modernize China's transportation. At the same time, Yüan amassed power for himself, making the legislature, dominated by the KMT, totally ineffectual.

Sun benefited from events during World War I when Japanese actions spurred Chinese nationalism. Japan took over several Chinese ports and presented the weak Chinese government with demands, including the stationing of Japanese police in certain areas of China. The latter stipulation would have meant a complete loss of sovereignty, and under pressure from the Western powers, Japan dropped it. But the Japanese efforts left most Chinese seething. Amid this insulting development, Sun rebelled against Yüan, but he was forced to flee in failure to Japan. Sun then alienated many revolutionaries by promising concessions to the Japanese in a fruitless attempt to get their backing, by requiring his supporters to take an oath of allegiance to him personally, and by marrying his secretary without officially divorcing his first wife. Meanwhile, Yüan declared himself president for life and planned to start a new dynasty. Army units rebelled, though, and Yüan died in June 1916 from an illness.

China sank into more turmoil, often called the "warlord period," and in 1917 Sun formed a military government in Canton allied with a southern warlord. This government collapsed in 1918. One year later, another factor further complicated Chinese politics: Students held a mass demonstration at the Tiananmen Gate in Peking to protest Japan's intrusions. This movement stirred an intellectual ferment that persuaded some scholars to embrace Marxism.

Sun supported the student movement and continued his fight for power. In 1921, he headed a new regime based in Canton. Once again, however, he was frustrated. When he allied with northern Chinese warlords to expand his power, he met resistance from his major military supporter in the south, Ch'en Chiung-ming. Sun then took his struggle into a new phase: getting help from the Russian Communists. Sun admired the Russians for having led a successful revolution in their own country, and he joined with a Russian agent, Adolf Joffe, to collaborate in China. In 1923, Sun sent his chief lieutenant and brother-in-law, CHIANG KAI-SHEK, to Moscow for training. Later that year and into 1924, the KMT allied itself with the Chinese Communist Party, and Sun and the Russians developed a tighter party organization, centralizing it, and putting it in control of all civilian and military activities. Sun gained a lifetime appointment as party director (with the appelation *Tsung-li*). Needless to say, Sun's actions alienated conservatives within the KMT.

Sun had also maneuvered himself during 1923 to gain control of a military government in Canton and renewed his drive to link with the north and unite China. In 1924, he went to Peking and met with the warlord who controlled that city, but the negotiations failed. While still in Peking, cancer overtook Sun, and on 12 March 1925 he died.

The fight for Chinese reunification would take many more curious twists and include a struggle between the Nationalists Chiang Kai-shek and WANG CHING-WEI and a full-scale civil war between Chiang's right wing and the Communists led by MAO TSE-TUNG (who with his wife CHIANG CH'ING developed a Maoist revolutionary ideology), CHOU EN-LAI, and LIN PIAO. All factions, however, looked to Sun Yat-sen as their national hero.

References: Schiffrin, Harold Z., *Sun Yat-sen and the Origins of the Chinese Revolution*, 1968; Shao Chuan Leng, and Norman D. Palmer, *Sun Yat-sen and Communism*, 1960; Sharman, Lyon, *Sun Yat-sen: His Life and Its Meaning*, 1934.

Svinhufvud, Pehr Evind
(1861–1944)
Finland

Pehr Evind Svinhufvud led the Finnish opposition to Russian rule. But he wanted more than independence; a firm and resolute leader, he sought a rightist state that would contain the Communist movement.

Pehr Evind Svinhufvud was born on 15 December 1861 in Sääksmäki. In 1894, he was elected to the Diet (which in 1906 became the Eduskunta, or Finnish Parliament). At this time, Russia controlled Finland as it had since 1814 when, during the Napoleonic Wars, it conquered the area from Sweden. Technically speaking, Finland retained some autonomy under the Russians with its status as a grand duchy under the personal possession of the czar. Nevertheless, nationalism stirred in the Finnish- and Swedish-language movements. The former was a reaction against the dominant Swedish language in Finland's culture, and Johan Vilhelm Snellman led the movement, advocating the use of Finnish literature to fight Russian assimilation. The Swedes reacted with a countermovement to protect their linguistic dominance and cultural leadership. A Russian edict in 1863 elevated the Finnish language to legal parity with the Swedish one.

Notwithstanding this, in the 1890s the Russians began an autocratic Russification campaign in Finland. In reacting, Svinhufvud took a strong anti-Russian position, siding with the Constitutionalists, or Young Finns, who advocated an outspoken defense of Finnish institutions. This burgeoning nationalism grew into a mass movement when in 1901 Russia decreed the merging of the Finnish and Russian armies. Then in 1914 Finns learned that Russia intended to completely absorb Finland. Consequently, Svinhufvud decided to support Germany in World War I as the only possible means to stop this Russian policy. The Russians arrested him and sent him to Siberia, where he lived in exile from 1914 to 1917.

Svinhufvud's return coincided with the outbreak of the Russian Revolution, an event that triggered a complex response in Finland: a drive for independence combined with a civil war. The two major factions in Finland developed their own armies with the Civil Guard (later called the Whites) representing the middle class, or bourgeoisie, and the Red Guard (or the Reds) representing the workers. In this tumultuous situation, the Social Democratic Party (SDP) and its Red Guards moved to form a new revolutionary government. Later in 1917, the SDP called for revolutionary action, and a workers' strike in November placed them on the brink of seizing full power, but emboldened by an arms shipment from Germany intended to help the Whites, Svinhufvud urged his fellow bourgeoisie not to compromise. He and his conservative supporters then formed an independence senate that on 6 December declared Finland an autonomus nation and made Svinhufvud prime minister. Many Finns expected Russia to react negatively to the news, but Svinhufvud and several senators traveled to Petrograd, and in late December Lenin told them he would recognize Finland's independence.

In 1918, civil war gripped Finland, and Svinhufvud led the White government to victory. He refused any concessions to the socialists and declared he would rule without them. On 9 January he authorized the Civil Guard to enforce state security, a move that encouraged the workers to begin a general uprising. Effective military leadership under Carl Gustav Emil Mannerheim and the influx of German weapons, and even men, soon gave Svinhufvud's government the upper hand. Both sides engaged in terrorist attacks that produced much bloodshed. On 16 May 1918, the Whites emerged victorious, and sitting in Parliament, they elected Svinhufvud "possessor of supreme authority," while they searched for a monarch to head the state.

Svinhufvud supported offering the crown to a German nobleman, but in November Germany surrendered in World War I, and this discredited Svinhufvud's right-wing policy. Meanwhile, the SDP, which had refused to officially endorse the

Red uprising in the civil war, reorganized and in 1919 gained a majority in Parliament, thus ending Svinhufvud's rule. The SDP rejected a monarchy and established a republican government with a strong presidency. Svinhufvud then joined the conservative National Coalition Party (KOK).

Out of office, Svinhufvud fought the Communists, who had formed their own party. He was a leader in the Lapua movement, named after a conservative town, and sought to eradicate the Communist threat. Beatings and kidnappings, including the capture of a former president accused of being soft on communism, discredited the Lapua. Still the Lapuans successfully backed Svin-

hufvud for the presidency, which he won as the KOK candidate in 1931. He held the position until 28 February 1937. Svinhufvud broke with the Lapuans when they called for a Finnish Hitler and attempted a coup. He crushed the rebellion to protect the Finnish constitution, and the Lapuans were subsequently outlawed. Thus Svinhufvud added to his accomplishments of Finnish independence and conservative leadership the protection of parliamentary democracy. Svinhufvud died in Luumaki on 29 February 1944.

References: Räikkönen, Erik, *Svinhufvud, the Builder of Finland: An Adventure in Statecraft,* 1938; Solsten, Eric, ed., *Finland: A Country Study,* 1990.

Ter-Petrosyan, Levon
(b. 1945)
Armenia

Highly educated, moderate, and willing to compromise, Levon Ter-Petrosyan rejected guerrilla gangs and guided Armenia along a legal path toward independence.

At the time of Levon Ter-Petrosyan's birth on 9 January 1945, Armenia was part of the Soviet Union, as it had been since 1921. Ter-Petrosyan, born in Aleppo, Syria, was taken to Armenia by his family in 1946. As a young man, he attended Leningrad University and Yerevan State University. He became an outstanding expert in Oriental studies and wrote numerous scholarly articles.

As the Soviet Union crumbled in the late 1980s, Ter-Petrosyan joined the struggle to make Armenia independent. The Soviet government imprisoned him for six months because of his participation with the Karabakh Committee, a nationalist group that organized demonstrations. Upon his release in 1989, he won election as a deputy to the Armenian Supreme Soviet. In 1990, elections were held to create a new legislature, and after these ended in August, the delegates chose Ter-Petrosyan president of Armenia.

> *"The very idea of the Soviet Union is unthinkable in any other form but a partnership like the European community."*

Ter-Petrosyan supported independence but sought to accomplish it through legal and peaceful means rather than through the violence advocated by nationalist guerrilla groups. Toward this end, he insisted that Armenia follow the rules for secession stipulated in the Soviet constitution. They entailed a six-month advance notice to Moscow and holding a plebiscite on the issue. In September 1991, Armenian voters made an overwhelming decision for nationhood, and within days the legislature issued a declaration of independence. In October, Armenia held its first direct presidential vote, and Ter-Petrosyan won as the candidate of the Armenian National Movement.

As president, Ter-Petrosyan favored cooperation with the other former Soviet republics and development of a free-market economy. In November 1991, he visited the United States and in December obtained diplomatic recognition from Washington. Shortly thereafter, he obtained an important foreign aid package from the United States.

Meanwhile, he played a leading role in defusing

a tense dispute between the Soviet Union and Lithuania, and after the U.S.S.R. collapsed, he signed several treaties with the former Communist republics, including Russia. He faced a daunting problem, however, in his relations with Azerbaijan when war erupted in Nagorno-Karabakh. This territory, situated within Azerbaijan, consisted largely of ethnic Armenians who demanded autonomy. Violence between them and the Azerbejanis had increased since 1988. In 1991, Ter-Petrosyan signed an agreement with Azerbaijan to end the violence, but within weeks it collapsed when the opposing forces broke the imposed truce. Refugees fled the conflict in large numbers and burdened Armenia with additional economic problems. Fighting escalated in 1992 and continued into 1993 while Armenian leaders requested international mediation. Despite this crisis, Ter-Petrosyan improved relations with Iran and Turkey and acted to boost the domestic economy by ending price restrictions. Although Ter-Petrosyan continues to pursue his course of gradual reform for Armenia, the war has brought economic devastation.

References: Demirchian, K. S., *Soviet Armenia*, 1984; Suny, Ronald G., *Looking toward Ararat: Armenia in Modern History*, 1993.

Tilley, Samuel
(1818–1896)
Canada

In many ways Samuel Tilley seemed quite the pragmatist—a man who stressed finances and calculated his political moves. But he had an idealistic streak that perhaps influenced his reformist nature: He advocated temperance, and did so zealously.

Samuel Tilley was born on 8 May 1818 in Gagetown, New Brunswick. His family had migrated from New York shortly after the American Revolution. As a prosperous farmer, his father had been a Loyalist in the conflict and sought refuge in New Brunswick, a British colony. In 1831, young Samuel became an apothecary's clerk in a dispensary. Seven years later, he entered into a merchant partnership, applied his financial acumen, and gathered considerable wealth.

At the same time, Tilley began his crusade against alcohol. A confirmed teetotaler, he preached total abstinence and demanded prohibition. In a hard-drinking, frontier society his message won few converts. Nevertheless, he took his position with him into politics, heading a group referred to as "The Smashers." In 1850, he won election to the New Brunswick legislature but resigned the following year in a political dispute. He won election again in 1854 and in 1855 was named provincial secretary. In this position he convinced the legislature to enact prohibition. The move proved extremely unpopular, and in 1856 he lost his legislative seat. From that time on he placed prohibition in the political background, although in his private life he continued to promote abstinence.

Tilley skillfully repaired his public career and in 1857 returned to the legislature. Four years later, he became New Brunswick's premier, allied to the Liberal Party. Tilley saw the wisdom of a greater union and advocated a federation of New Brunswick with the Maritime Provinces of Nova Scotia and Prince Edward Island, a view he shared with the Nova Scotian leader, CHARLES TUPPER. In 1864, Tilley led a delegation to meet with the other Maritime Provinces at Charlottetown on Prince Edward Island. The delegates then heard from JOHN MACDONALD, the premier of the Province of Canada (today's Ontario and Québec). He appealed for a union of all Canada, and the delegates agreed to hold a great conference in Québec to pursue a confederation. At that conference in September, Tilley and the other delegates, among them Canada's leaders in the nationalist movement, such as Macdonald, Tupper, GEORGE ÉTIENNE CARTIER, and GEORGE BROWN, approved resolutions creating a union. Despite this, it was far from certain New Brunswick would ratify the resolutions. In fact, the following year Tilley was defeated in his reelection bid by an anti-union candidate.

The situation, however, continued to be unstable, and in 1866 Tilley won election to the legislature and served in a pro-union cabinet. When the union plan still floundered in the provinces, Tilley agreed to head a delegation to London where Macdonald, Tupper, and others from the Québec conference met and ended the impasse. The British North America Act, based closely on the Québec resolutions, provided for a Dominion of Canada consisting of the Province of Canada, New Brunswick, and Nova Scotia (Prince Edward Island joined in the 1870s). The Dominion officially came into existence on 1 July 1867.

Tilley won election to Canada's first Parliament and represented Saint John City. Although the prime minister, Macdonald, was from the Conservative Party, he chose Tilley, a Liberal, to serve in his cabinet and give it balance. Tilley undertook the important though unappealing job of organizing the national government bureaucracy. In 1873, Macdonald appointed him minister of finance, but within weeks the prime minister was removed from office, and Tilley returned to New Brunswick, where he served as lieutenant governor.

In 1878, Tilley again ran for Parliament and won, whereupon Macdonald, recently elected prime minister, appointed him to the cabinet's finance post. Tilley supported Macdonald's National Policy, a protectionist program meant to boost the Canadian economy and promote nationalism.

Tilley returned to New Brunswick as lieutenant governor in 1885 and retired from politics eight years later. On 25 June 1896 he died in Saint John. Tilley is considered by Canadians to be one of the "fathers of confederation."

References: Hardy, William George, *From Sea unto Sea: Canada, 1850 to 1910—The Road to Nationhood*, 1960; Morton, William L., *The Critical Years: The Union of British North America, 1857–1873*, 1964.

Tombalbaye, Francois
(1918–1975)
Chad

Young men gathered for the *yondo*, painful and prolonged initiation rites that had for generations been a part of Sara society in southern Chad. This time, however, the rites meant something more. President Francois Tombalbaye had decreed them in the early 1970s as requirements for entering the civil service, a move that reflected his desperation in a declining presidency rent by inconsistent policies and ethnic divisions.

Born into a Protestant trading family in southern Chad, Francois Tombalbaye became a teacher, took a leading role as an activist in the teachers' union in the early 1950s, and joined the nationalist Chadian Progressive Party (PPT). The French-dominated government soon removed him from his teaching position because of his activism, and he was forced to become a brickmaker to survive.

In 1956, under the *loi-cadre* (reform legislation passed by the French National Assembly), France permitted Chad to have an executive chosen by its territorial legislature. After the PPT won most of the legislature seats in 1957, Gabriel Lisette, a Marxist, became prime minister. But because the PPT lost the next election, his term lasted only one year.

After the defeat, Tombalbaye replaced Lisette as head of the PPT. Meanwhile, France organized the French Community and Chad became a republic within it. When the PPT won the 1959 legislative election, Tombalbaye became prime minister. As leader of Chad, he headed a society with little modern technology, an impoverished economy, and serious disagreements between North and South and among various ethnic groups. Tombalbaye expressed his support for modernization. When Chad became a fully independent nation on 11 August 1960, Tombalbaye became president.

At that point he quickly developed a dictatorship. He purged Lisette from the PPT and in 1962 banned all other political parties. He established a criminal court that sentenced his political enemies to prison. By 1964, he fully controlled the National legislature and reduced the number of French officials under a policy of Africanization.

Tombalbaye's measures produced numerous problems. Africanization brought a decline in services as inexperienced bureaucrats exhibited little expertise. Southerners dominated Tombalbaye's administration, producing resentment in the North, long a predominantly Muslim and largely Arab region in contrast to the South, with its Christianity, traditional African religions, and largely black population. Riots broke out in 1963 and 1965 protesting the arbitrary arrest of several Muslim leaders and the enactment of higher taxes. In addition, neighboring Libya and the Sudan supported rebel groups within Chad.

These troubles, particularly intervention by Libya, forced Tombalbaye to get help from France. The French provided military assistance but required that the embattled president enact reforms. He did so reluctantly; they included reducing corruption in the civil service and giving more regional authority to various sultans. Tombalbaye's reforms continued as he led a liberalization movement. He released hundreds of political prisoners, confessed his mistakes to the PPT in 1971, and brought more Muslims and Northerners into his administration.

But after a failed coup attempt and the discovery in 1972 of a sabotage team within Chad backed by Libyan leader MUAMMAR AL-QADDAFI, Tombalbaye changed course again. He crushed student strikes and arrested political opponents. He shifted his foreign policy as he tried to gain support from Arab nations and ended relations with Israel while obtaining financial assistance from the man he had recently accused of disrupting his regime, Qaddafi.

Internal discontent continued, though, and protests in the South indicated Tombalbaye was losing his main regional base of support. In 1973, he arrested opponents there, whom he accused of engaging in political sorcery through animal sacrifices. He tried rebuilding his domestic support by announcing "Chaditude," the elimination of foreign practices and the Africanization of names. He then proclaimed his support of the *yondo* as an initiation rite that should be used as a prerequisite to obtaining civil service positions. This policy, however, antagonized many Southerners who did not participate in a rite peculiar to one ethnic group and who opposed its extension.

By 1974, a serious drought further damaged Chad's economy and Tombalbaye began losing military support with his frequent shuffling and purging of officers. In March 1975, he ordered the arrest of several leading officers whom he considered enemies. On 13 April 1975, a military coup overthrew his administration and the attackers killed him.

References: Kelley, Michael P., *A State in Disarray: Conditions of Chad's Survival*, 1986; Thompson, Virginia M., and Richard Adloff, *Conflict in Chad*, 1981.

Torrijos Herrera, Omar
(1929–1981)
Panama

Although to many outside observers Omar Torrijos Herrera appeared to be just another in a long line of Panamanian dictators, he actually began a new era in his nation's politics: His rise to power represented a break in the dominant role played by the traditional oligarchy.

Omar Torrijos Herrera was born on 13 February 1929 in Santiago de Veragua to parents who were schoolteachers. Omar did not follow in their footsteps; instead, he pursued a military career. He attended a military school in El Salvador and in 1952 earned a commission in the Panama National Guard. He received additional military training at schools in the United States, Venezuela, and the Canal Zone.

At the time, in the 1950s, an oligarchy of wealthy white families controlled Panama, as it had since independence in 1903. By the mid-1960s, however, this oligarchy faced increased pressure from an expanding middle class to relinquish some power. In a national election held on 12 May 1968, Arnulfo Arias Madrid won the presidency and promised radical reforms. He initiated moves to obtain Panamanian control of the Canal Zone from the United States and also tried to lessen the threat of a coup by removing two senior officers in the National Guard. This latter strategy backfired, and on 11 October guardsmen overthrew Arias's presidency. By January 1969, Torrijos emerged as commander of the National Guard, and in early March he assumed leadership of the country with the title Chief of Government and Supreme Leader of the Panamanian Revolution.

Torrijos purged the National University of what he called dangerous elements and appointed several prominent leftists to government positions. On 15 December 1969, disgruntled National Guard officers staged a coup while Torrijos was traveling in Mexico. Torrijos counterattacked quickly: He flew back to Panama, where he landed in the town of David, and then drove with his supporters to Panama City, which he entered as some 10,000 people cheered him. Officers loyal to Torrijos joined the counterassault, and on 16 December he thwarted the coup.

Stronger than ever, Torrijos moved to gain full control and reorient Panamanian politics, making it less elitist and more attuned to the rural and urban lower classes. He appointed additional leftists to the government and toured the backcountry, where he met with peasants—an almost unheard-of practice in Panamanian politics. Torrijos praised socialist developments in Bolivia and Peru and announced a land redistribution program. Thousands of poor families received land, and he began state-owned commercial farms. Torrijos initiated educational reforms to focus on technical training and expanded schools in the countryside. He improved health care, including an unprecedented building of hospitals in the rural areas, and launched a public works program to construct roads and bridges.

Torrijos got money for these projects by levying higher personal and corporate taxes. He made it a point to expand his appeal into the cities by supporting labor unions and making collective bargaining mandatory. Although he had to repeal the latter reform and several others in 1976 due to economic problems, his program remained largely intact.

Nationalism proved to be both Torrijos's strength and his undoing. He called for the United States to relinquish its control over the Panama Canal, and in 1971 began negotiations with the American government. Talks, however, stalled until 1977, when the new American president, Jimmy Carter, agreed to changes. In September, Torrijos flew to Washington, D.C., where he and Carter signed a treaty that gave Panama immediate legal jurisdiction in the Canal Zone and provided for a gradual end to the American operation of the facility (scheduled to be finalized in the year 2000).

While the treaty boosted Torrijos's support, it also unleashed a wave of criticism from opponents who had said little so as not to disrupt the negotiations, but now felt free to speak out. Many Panamanians disliked a side agreement to the treaty that seemed to allow unilateral American intervention in Panama. Furthermore, they criticized their nation's continuing economic difficulties.

Torrijos weakened his grip on Panamanian politics when he agreed in 1978 to elections. He resigned as head of government, although he continued as leader of the National Guard and still wielded the most power. Torrijos's party lost several legislative seats in 1980, but he remained dominant by controlling two-thirds of the National Assembly. Then on 31 July 1981, Torrijos was killed in an airplane crash in western Panama. While as ruler he had continued Panama's reliance on dictators (a pattern followed after his death with the rise of Manuel Antonio Noriega Moreno), he had broken the oligarchy and shifted the political system to include radical reform. Whether his reforms prove to be fleeting remains to be seen.

Reference: Ropp, Steve C., *Panamanian Politics: From Guarded Nation to National Guard*, 1982.

Touré, Ahmed Sékou
(1922–1984)
Guinea

Ahmed Sékou Touré led one of the most dramatic changes in Africa: the transformation of Guinea from a relatively quiescent land under French control to a radically independent nation. He began this odyssey by taking trade unionism and molding it into an instrument of power.

When Sékou Touré was born at Faranah on 9 January 1922, he came into a land that as a French colony experienced extensive impoverishment. Most Guineans engaged in subsistence agriculture and lived in small villages. Nevertheless, an urban elite emerged that adopted the French language and many French cultural practices.

Touré had an ambiguous relationship with this elite. He never completed his secondary education, and thus had limited formal schooling, but he developed into an urban trade unionist with attachment to French influences, particularly French Communist officials. In the late 1930s and 1940s, he served as a clerk, first with a French commercial business, then with the colonial post office, and later with the colonial Treasury Department. In 1946, he helped organize the interterritorial African Democratic Rally (RDA) in his homeland, forming the Democratic Party of Guinea (PDG) as a branch. He then became a full-time trade union official and quickly gained prominence not only within Guinea but also throughout West Africa. Touré considered trade unionism crucially important as a route to substantial social and economic change. He combined this view with his Marxist ideology to advance a truly revolutionary cause.

In a development that worked in Touré's favor, Guinea underwent an industrial economic boom in the early 1950s that made an expanded labor force receptive to union efforts. In 1953, as secretary-general of a local chapter of the General Confederation of Workers (CGT), Touré led a two-month strike in Conakry that resulted in wage hikes for the poorest workers. At this point, Touré became a hero throughout West Africa.

Touré won election to the Guinea Territorial Assembly in 1953 and became vice-president of the Government Council in 1957 and mayor of Conakry in 1958. He also claimed election to the French National Assembly in 1954, but the French refused seating him until 1956, citing irregularities in the vote while actually acting from concern about Touré's radicalism. During this time Touré built a larger following through five appeals. First, his union victories gained more worker support. Second, his radical attacks on the privileges possessed by traditional tribal chiefs won a wide urban audience. Third, his appeal to community and harmony attracted many Guineans tired of intertribal strife. Fourth, his Islamic faith earned him the backing of religious leaders. Finally, he seemed to represent the anti-European appeal of the nineteenth-century nationalist hero Almamy Samory Touré. He also prepared Guinea for a new political structure by using his position on the Government Council to weaken the power of the tribal chiefs.

When France offered its colonies a choice in 1957 between full independence without continued

French financial help or more limited autonomy within a French Community, Touré took the radical position of supporting a total break with the imperial power. He campaigned hard for this policy, and in the 1958 referendum Guineans supported him. It was an unusual move because the other French colonies opted for Community membership.

Touré's successful effort resulted in the French removing their technicians and administrators from Guinea, ending all financial aid, and eliminating Guinea's access to French markets. As president of an independent Guinea, Touré turned to Communist nations for help, and his stridency in standing up to France won him widespread fame in Africa, although it brought considerable economic hardship to Guinea. He called for Africans to gain not only their political independence but also their cultural and social separation from European domination.

Touré rapidly developed a one-party state and a highly personal and disciplined regime. He argued that Guinea was not ready for a multiparty system and that PDG rule was democratic since he had built the party on a popular mass following. He established state control over most of the economy and, in the process, presided over a substantial economic downturn (although bauxite production did enjoy some expansion). Many Guineans fled their homeland for Senegal or the Côte d'Ivoire, and intellectuals complained about dictatorial policies and spreading corruption.

Throughout the 1960s and 1970s, Touré purged the PDG on an annual basis, expelling what he called bourgeois elements and arresting political enemies. He put together a people's militia—young men, mainly—to keep watch on impurities of thought. At this time, Touré suffered two major attacks on his rule. First, he narrowly escaped assassination on 24 June 1969 while attending a ceremony for the visiting president of Zambia. Then, on 2 November 1970, Guinean exiles backed by Portugal attacked Conakry. Touré repulsed this raid and had 92 traitors sentenced to death.

Amid this turmoil, many Guineans expressed their support for Touré, and he continued his rule into the 1980s. Then Touré died unexpectedly on 26 March 1984 while at the Cleveland Clinic Foundation in the United States. A military coup occurred in April, and a new constitution in 1991 proclaimed a republic with promises of full democracy by 1996.

Touré left behind more than a controversial political legacy. He had published a huge collection of his works—over 20 volumes encompassing his speeches and essays on African freedom—and developed a stirring influence on African nationalism.

References: Adamolekun, Ladipo, *Sékou Touré's Guinea: An Experiment in Nation Building*, 1976; Riviére, Claude, *The Mobilization of a People*, translated by Richard Adloff and Viriginia Thompson, 1977.

Toussaint L'Ouverture
(1743?–1803)
Haiti

While some criticized Toussaint L'Ouverture as duplicitous, others saw his behavior as diplomatic skill. Indeed, his sobriquet, *L'Ouverture*, meant the man who could make an opening anywhere—and gain the advantage. Whatever the case, he navigated around competing black leaders and French colonialists to advance a bloody revolution that, shortly after his death, enabled Haiti to gain its status as Latin America's first independent nation.

Around 1743, Toussaint L'Ouverture was born a slave on a sugar plantation in Bréda, an impoverished town in Haiti (then called Saint-Dominque). Toussaint's birth name was Francois Dominque Toussaint. His father, Gaou-Guinou, was the son of an African king and an educated slave who encouraged Toussaint to obtain his own education. Under the guidance of the Jesuits, Toussaint learned French, Latin, and geometry. As a young man, he was withdrawn, solitary, and physically small. But he overcame his shyness and diminutive size by engaging in challenging activities, such as horseback riding, which he excelled in by age 12. His French master allowed him numerous opportunities, and over the years he worked as a livestock dealer, coachman, and steward. He accumulated some wealth and in 1777 was legally freed.

After the French Revolution proclaimed liberty and equality for all, rebellions erupted in Haiti. In 1791, mulattos rose up under Vincent Ogé; after this, black slaves rebelled. As the violence spread, Toussaint feared for his former master's family and helped them to safety. Then he joined the rebels.

It was a risky move in a racially and economically divided society, the complexity of which exceeded white-versus-black. The Haitian African-American community was itself split between blacks and mulattos, who frequently attacked each other. Class differences also complicated the situation, with disputes between upper- and lower-class whites, slaveholding and non-slaveholding blacks, and freedmen and slaves.

When Toussaint joined the slave revolt led by Boukman Dutty, he joined a black uprising. The rebels burned plantations and attacked whites and mulattos, killing 1,000 whites at Plaine du Nord. Toussaint, however, considered the rebel leaders incompetent, so he formed his own group and trained it as a guerrilla army. Intending to end French rule, he aligned his followers with Spain in 1793, after that country went to war against France. With his army he traversed the mountains and valleys, and although his men were poorly equipped, he displayed brilliant strategy and scored several victories against the French. In the process, he attracted talented rebels, including JEAN-JACQUES DESSALINES.

By August 1793, the situation in Haiti looked bleak for the French after the British joined the fray to assist Toussaint and the Spaniards. The French commissioner in Haiti reacted by formally abolishing slavery and providing the freedmen arms. Surprising many people, Toussaint then switched to the French side, claiming that the end to slavery and his own republican preferences amid the French Revolution convinced him to make the change. He quickly slaughtered hundreds of Spaniards and gained the military advantage. His decision reversed the situation in Haiti, causing Spain to retreat. The French governor, Étienne Laveux, appointed Toussaint lieutenant governor.

In 1795, Spain ceded Santo Domingo (today called the Dominican Republic) to France, and Toussaint led his men through the area, battling whites and mulattos, and expanding his rule. In 1798 and 1799, he negotiated with the British and obtained their withdrawal, and in the latter year he crushed a rival mulatto state that had formed under André Rigaud, massacring thousands of Rigaud's followers and sending him fleeing to France. By 1801, he controlled nearly all of Hispaniola, the island that encompasses Haiti and Santo Domingo. Although France still possessed the region, it had only nominal authority.

> *"With my overthrow, one has merely cut down the trunk of the tree of black freedom."*

Under Touissant, the economy revived and many whites, surprised by his magnanimity toward them, initially supported the order he imposed as he built a dictatorship. Touissant issued a new constitution in 1801 and established often-contradictory policies. He freed the slaves in Santo Domingo, and the freedmen now shared in the profits from the plantations. On the other hand, because he believed people would not work without coercion, he began a forced-labor system.

The new constitution made Toussaint governor for life and established Catholicism as the state religion. He had to constantly balance French, black, and mulatto interests. Napoleon, who disliked blacks and once proclaimed about Toussaint, "Never again will I leave an epaulette on the shoulder of a Negro," publicly recognized the Haitian's rule, but privately planned to restore French authority and return slavery. Some blacks disparaged what they called Toussaint's atrocities; more radical blacks, however, criticized Toussaint's moderation and wanted to get rid of all whites and divide the plantation lands. Mulattos, on the other hand, desired a return to white rule.

Amid this turmoil, Napoleon ordered General Charles Leclerc to Haiti with a force of 54 ships and 23,000 men. When the invasion began in January 1802, most whites and mulattos joined the French side and even numerous blacks, disgusted with Toussaint and promised amnesty, deserted, including Jean-Jacques Dessalines. Despite this, the

French had a difficult time subduing Toussaint, partly because yellow fever ravaged their army.

Before the year ended, Leclerc invited Toussaint to a meeting to discuss the Haitian's surrender, promising him sincerity and friendship. Toussaint agreed, but when he arrived the French betrayed him: He was seized, chained, and forced to board a ship that took him to a French prison in the Jura Mountains, where he died on 7 April 1803.

Although Toussaint did not obtain complete Haitian independence, he did move his countrymen toward that goal. After his death, the fighting continued, and the French suffered a devastating defeat. Haiti gained its independence under Jean-Jacques Dessalines. More than this, the dictatorial form of government begun by Toussaint and continued by Dessalines remained the dominant type in Haiti's history. This pattern may be altered in the 1990s if Jean-Bertrand Arisitide establishes the democratic system he has promised.

References: Bellgarde-Smith, Patrick, *Haiti: The Breached Citadel*, 1990; James, C. L. R., *The Black Jacobins: Toussaint L'Ouverture and the Santo Domingo Revolution*, 1963; Korngold, Ralph, *Citizen Toussaint*, 1979; Parkinson, Wenda, *This Gilded African: Toussaint L'Ouverture*, 1978.

Tshombe, Moise
(1919–1969)
Zaire

Shortly after the Congo gained its independence, Moise Tshombe challenged the first government and produced a national crisis. Later, however, he became premier and continued his tumultuous role in helping shape the Congo's early development.

Born on 10 November 1919, Moise Tshombe came from a privileged background. His father owned several businesses in Katanga Province—the Congo's wealthiest region, dominated by the Lunda tribes and the place of Tshombe's birth. In 1951, Tshombe's father died and the young man, who had attended an American Methodist mission school and completed a correspondence course in accounting, took over the family businesses. Under his leadership, however, they failed, and he declared bankruptcy.

Meanwhile, Tshombe took a greater interest in politics. As an *évolué*, or member of the Congo's elite African community, he praised the Belgian monarchy and served as president of the African Chamber of Commerce. Subsequently, he became one of only eight Congolese Africans appointed to the Council of Katanga, on which he served for three years. In

> *"I have no inferiority complex toward the white man as do some of my Congolese colleagues."*

1956, he became president of the Mutual Associations of the Lunda Empire, originally formed as a debating society. Three years later, this group evolved into a political party called the Confederation of the Tribal Associations, or Conakat, and formed a close alliance with Katanga's Belgian-run mining monopoly, thus strengthening the link between Tshombe and the Congo's colonial business rulers.

As talk of Congolese independence widened in the late 1950s, Tshombe and Conakat insisted Katanga should become a separate state. They argued that the rest of the Congo drained wealth from their copper-rich region. All the whites and most blacks in Katanga supported Tshombe, but many others in the Congo opposed his idea, and even Belgium refused to endorse it. Tshombe then moderated his views and called for an independent Congo with a loose provincial federation. He presented this concept early in 1960, when he attended the roundtable meeting in Brussels meant to prepare the Congo for nationhood. Tshombe, however, found himself overruled and the delegates, led by

PATRICE LUMUMBA, opted for a strong central government.

In the first elections to the Congolese legislature, in May 1960, Conakat won only 8 of 137 seats. The Congo's independence came on 30 June 1960, with Lumumba as premier. His government, however, lasted only two months, and in this demise Tshombe was important. Two weeks after independence, he declared Katanga's secession. He received support from leaders in other provinces who opposed Lumumba and obtained financial and military aid from Belgium. On 8 August, the Katangan legislature elected Tshombe president, although leaders of the rival Balubakat tribe opposed him.

Tshombe accused Lumumba of having started the Congo down a radical path and advocated strict neutrality in the cold war. After Lumumba was deposed in September, Tshombe began negotiations with the Congo's president, JOSEPH KASAVUBU. Meanwhile, Lumumba was taken prisoner and then transferred to Katanga, where he was killed. Many observers believe Tshombe ordered the murder to eliminate his rival.

Tshombe participated in several discussions to determine the Congo's future, but at one such meeting in April 1961 he refused to cooperate with other Congolese leaders and walked out. The central government then arrested him, accused him of treason, and held him for two months. He was released only after he promised not to try removing Katanga from the Congo. Tshombe, however, claimed he had made this agreement under unfair pressure, and so he broke his promise. United Nations forces entered Katanga in the summer of 1961 to end the sectional strife.

After Katanga suffered battlefield reverses in 1963, Tshombe fled to Spain, but his integral involvement in shaping the Congo did not end. President Kasavubu recalled him from exile in 1964 and appointed him premier to end a rebellion in the eastern Congo. Tshombe had at his disposal Katangan troops stationed in neighboring Angola. The fighting, especially battles in and around Stanleyville, a rebel stronghold, became brutal, and Tshombe's methods, including reliance on Belgian and American military direction, made him increasingly unpopular. When he organized a new political party and challenged Kasavubu, the president removed him.

In this turmoil, MOBUTU SESE SEKO (Joseph Mobutu) staged a coup and gained power. Tshombe returned to Spain in 1965, and two years later, after rumors circulated that he intended to return to the Congo, kidnappers grabbed him and took him to Algeria. The Algerian government refused Congolese requests to execute Tshombe, and he subsequently lived his remaining years in exile and died in Algiers on 29 June 1969.

While Tshombe often followed a route damaging to the Congo's nationhood, his influence in Congolese politics was substantial and his commitment to a Congolese nation, albeit one united loosely and with much power for Katanga, helped shape a future distanced from Belgian rule. In 1971, the Congo was renamed Zaire while a national government consolidated under Joseph Mobutu.

References: Hoskyn, Catherine, *The Congo since Independence, January, 1960–December, 1961*, 1965; Young, Crawford, *Politics in the Congo: Decolonization and Independence*, 1965.

Tsiranana, Philibert
(1910–1978)
Madagascar

When Philibert Tsiranana emerged as the prominent political leader of Madagascar, his strategy recognized two major social influences in his homeland's history: sectional divisions and French occupation. Hence, in the 1950s Tsiranana advocated both provincial autonomy within the territory so that *côtiers*—coastal residents—could have local authority over institutions long dominated by the interior and centralized governance so that Madagascar could exert greater self-determination without Balkanization.

Philibert Tsiranana was born in 1910 and came from a peasant family in Majunga. He was considered a *côtier* and attended a leadership training school at Tananarive, which was almost exclusively populated by people from the Merina tribe, who inhabited Madagascar's interior. During a widespread but unsuccessful revolt in 1947 against French rule, he was studying at the University of Montpellier, located in France. He returned to Madagascar in 1950 and became a teacher. In 1952, he entered politics and won a seat in the territorial legislature.

Tsiranana realized that most *côtiers* accepted the political status quo with France so as to avoid any confrontations that might strengthen the Merinas, many of whom supported nationalism. He, however, advocated a more aggressive pursuit of Malagasy interests. In 1956, he was elected to the French National Assembly. That same year, France enacted reform legislation called the *loi-cadre* that provided for an executive Council of Government elected by the territorial legislature, and Tsiranana was chosen in 1957 to head it.

The French considered the *loi-cadre* a substitute for independence. Concerned about Merina power and the growing support of communists for Malagasy nationhood, they rejected repeal of the 1896 law that had confirmed their annexation of Madagascar. At the same time, the *loi-cadre* had an important impact on Madagascar's internal politics by establishing substantial powers for local and provincial councils, a move Tsiranana supported as allowing more authority for the *côtiers*.

"The extremists want independence, but we moderates favor the golden mean."

The decentralization encouraged a proliferation of political parties, in which Tsiranana took part. With assistance from French socialists, he formed the Social Democratic Party (PSD) that became Madagascar's leading political group and furthered the power of the *côtiers* while diluting that of the Merinas. As nationalism intensified, Tsiranana and the PSD by late 1957 supported repeal of the 1896 annexation law. Yet, cautious about Merina power, he opposed a rump congress's call for full independence and instead advocated a new constitution that would allow more Malagasy authority while permitting French roles in defense and diplomacy.

Then, in 1958, France agreed that its overseas territories could choose membership in a new French Community, whereby France would determine foreign policy but provide economic assistance, or they could choose full independence devoid of economic help. On 28 September 1958, the Malagasy voted for a republic within the Community, and on 14 October the Malagasy Republic came into existence.

Tsiranana established a quick timetable for writing a constitution, and the PSD pushed his proposals through the legislature. Tsiranana was elected president on 1 May 1959, and in response to calls for a more complete severing of relations with France that would remove Madagascar from the Community, he took a conservative approach, for he believed that as an isolated nation Madagascar needed its French alliance.

Amid the tensions of the cold war, Tsiranana moved Madagascar into close cooperation with Western powers, the more conservative black African countries, and South Africa. When France allowed her former colonies complete autonomy, he oversaw Madagascar's gaining of independence on 26 June 1960.

Tsiranana developed an indigenous socialism that rejected communism, the nationalization of important industries, and any changes in landholding practices. His highly diluted brand of socialism did, however, proclaim government supervision of private investments and promoted the formation of companies that used both public and private funds.

The Malagasy reelected Tsiranana president in 1965 and again in 1972, but by the latter date his health had deteriorated. Furthermore, the PSD became more intolerant of dissenters, friction between *côtiers* and Merinas increased, and labor unrest spread. More than 100,000 university students went on strike in protest of continued foreign economic exploitation. Indeed, under Tsiranana the French dominated exports and commercial agriculture while thousands of French nationals held important positions. Although the government suppressed the student strikes, Tsiranana's position had become untenable, and he resigned

the presidency on 11 October 1972. He died six years later.

Tsiranana avoided rigid ideological stands. Caution characterized his approach, and he usually took positions only after determining that he had wide popular support. Yet he broke the lassitude of the *côtiers* toward France, built the first national political party, steered Madagascar toward membership in the French Community, and formed the first Malagasy Republic. More radical developments would await the presidency of DIDIER RATSIRAKA.

References: Kent, Raymond K., *From Madagascar to the Malagasy Republic*, 1976; Kottak, Conrad, ed., *Madagascar: Society and History*, 1986; Thompson, Virginia, and Richard Adloff, *The Malagasy Republic*, 1965.

Tudjman, Franjo
(b. 1922)
Croatia

As a young man, Franjo Tudjman joined the Communist resistance and fought against the Nazis. But in the 1970s, he deserted the Communists, criticized their transgressions, and embraced Croatian nationalism.

Franjo Tudjman was born in Veliko-Tgroviste on 14 May 1922. Educated at the Higher Military Academy, he fought in World War II alongside Josip Broz Tito and the Partisans against the Nazis. After the war, Tito included Croatia as a member state in Yugoslavia, a Communist nation that he kept together despite deep ethnic and religious differences on the Balkan Peninsula. As a dedicated Communist, Tudjman, who had a background in political science, held numerous positions in the Yugoslav government. In the 1940s and 1950s, he served in the Defense

Department and as head of the general staff. In 1961, he became director of the Institute of the History of the Croatian Workers' Movement, a post he held until 1967. At the same time, he was professor of political science at Zagreb University and edited several journals.

Tudjman mixed his communism with a strong nationalist strain and in 1967 resigned from all of his official positions to protest restrictions on the Croatian language. The government twice imprisoned him for his nationalist activities, and in the early 1970s he broke with the Communist Party.

In 1980, Tito died and his strong rule was replaced by a weak collective presidency. This, along with reform movements in Eastern Europe, unleashed a Balkan nationalism that mixed with the region's religious and ethnic differences. By 1990, Yugoslavia was collapsing as its member states moved toward independence.

In April 1990, Tudjman led the Croatian Democratic Union (HDZ) to a huge victory in elections for the state's legislature—the first free vote in Croatia since World War II. The Communist Party won only 13 seats. Tudjman and the HDZ advocated secession from Yugoslavia, and on 25 June 1991 Croatia declared its independence. This ignited an attack by the Yugoslav federal army, dominated by the Serbs. They waged a total war against Croatia, seeking to destroy its cities and its entire infrastructure. In October, Tudjman indicated his willingness to agree to a settlement brokered by the European Community, provided Serbian forces relinquished the Croatian territory they had captured.

As Croatia struggled, critics accused Tudjman of political conservatism and ethnic intolerance. His government was loaded with former Communists and in a controversial work entitled *Bespuca— Povjesne Zbiljnosti*, or *Wastelands—Historical Truth*, written in the 1980s, he minimized the Croatian role in the Nazi Holocaust during World War II that resulted in the deaths of thousands of Croatian Jews and Serbs. Even though Tudjman had fought against the Nazis, his book indicated an authoritarian approach to rewriting history and a failure to offer a forgiving approach to the region's ethnic hostilities.

> *"It is we, the Croatian people, who have risked our lives to put forward a democratic party and to vote our conscience."*

Despite this attitude, Tudjman positioned himself against the more extremist Croatians who opposed all negotiations with the Serbs. In February 1992, one month after Germany and other European Community nations recognized Croatia, he expressed his support for a new peace plan proposed by the United Nations. A fragile cease-fire soon prevailed; by July, however, Tudjman engaged in his own territorial grab when Croatian troops seized land from neighboring Bosnia, another former Yugoslav state. At the same time, he attacked ethnic Serb villages within Croatia and suppressed his political opposition by censoring newspapers.

In August 1992, Tudjman won reelection as president by a wide margin after he supported a new peace plan that placed UN troops on Croatian soil. In November, he proceeded to extend his censorship of newspapers and broadcast stations while calling for a more forceful UN presence in the Balkans to end the fighting between Serbia and Bosnia. Meanwhile, Tudjman faced a declining economy with high unemployment and inflation. Today, as the turmoil in the Balkans continues, Tudjman's survival, indeed Croatia's survival, as that of all the former Yugoslav states, remains uncertain.

References: Kaplan, Robert D., *Balkan Ghosts: A Journey through History*, 1993; Magas, Branka, *The Destruction of Yugoslavia: Tracking the Break-Up, 1980–1992*, 1993; Tudjman, Franjo, *Wastelands—Historical Truth*, 1988.

Tupou IV, Taufa'ahau
(b. 1918)
Tonga

A political conservative, King Taufa'ahau Tupou IV maneuvered his Pacific homeland to its independence but rejected democracy.

Since the tenth century A.D. and the rule of Tonga's first king, Tu'i Tonga, the monarchy devolved to several different lines. In 1831, the present dynasty began with King George Tupou I. Taufa'ahau Tupou IV, descended from this line, was born on 4 July 1918, the son of Uiliami Tungi, Tonga's premier, and Queen Salote Tupou III, a social and economic progressive who greatly improved the island's educational system. The future king became the first college-educated Tongan, receiving his degree from Sydney University in Australia. He gained experience in government by working in his mother's administration and served as minister of education in 1943 and minister of health from 1944 to 1949. In the latter year, he became premier while also engaging in scholarship, studying traditional Tongan culture and reviving the Tongan alphabet.

In 1965, Queen Salote died, and the premier ascended to the throne as King Taufa'ahau Tupou IV. He soon determined to gain independence for Tonga, which had been a British protectorate since 1901, a status that meant Britain handled foreign affairs and reviewed all governmental appointments. King Tupou concluded negotiations with the British in 1970, and on 4 June Tonga became independent.

King Tupou presided over a nation that in the 1970s and 1980s underwent enormous change. Most prominently, many Tongans moved from the outlying islands to the main island, Tongaputu, and its principal city, Nuku'alofa. They sought jobs in Tonga's modernizing economy, but unemployment increased substantially. King Tupou sponsored programs to expand tourism and improve telecommunications. The export of copra (dried coconut meat) at higher prices became an important revenue source.

The increased population on Tongaputu resulted in King Tupou supporting family planning. Still, demographic and social pressures threatened the stability of his rule. As land became in short supply, many young Tongans protested its domination by the royal family and nobles. In 1992, for the first time in Tongan history, a political party contested the hereditary nobility. In 1993, this pro-democracy party won six out of nine seats open to commoners in the Legislative Assembly. Under the Tongan constitution, however, the legislature had little authority apart from what the king permitted, and the pro-democracy movement remains frustrated as King Tupou refuses to make substantial governmental reforms.

Reference: Rutherford, Noel, *Friendly Islands: A History of Tonga*, 1977.

Tupper, Charles
(1821–1915)
Canada

In 1866, Charles Tupper maneuvered adroitly around the substantial opposition in Nova Scotia to form a confederation. As the province's premier, he got the legislature to support union in principle, and soon Nova Scotia found itself meeting in London with other Canadians to form a united nation.

Charles Tupper hailed from a traditional Puritan family. Born on 2 July 1821 in Amherst, Nova Scotia—then a British colony—he pursued his higher education in Edinburgh, Scotland, where in 1843 he obtained a medical degree. He returned to Nova Scotia and practiced medicine. In 1855, he entered politics and won a seat in the legislature from Cumberland County. The following year, he became Nova Scotia's provincial secretary and in 1860 won election as the province's premier.

He focused on education and union. In the first area, he formed the Council of Public Instruction to bring reform. In the second, he joined SAMUEL TILLEY in promoting the unfication of Nova Scotia with the other Maritime Provinces of New Brunswick and Prince Edward Island. Then he expanded his vision: When in 1864 the Maritime Provinces decided to meet at Charlottetown on Prince Edward Island to discuss unity, JOHN ALEXANDER MACDONALD, who was then the prime minister of the Province of Canada (today Ontario and Québec), urged the delegates to work for a Canadian confederation, and Tupper, known for his domineering personality, reacted with vigorous support. Indeed, his efforts helped persuade the Maritimers to attend another meeting at Québec. There, during deliberations, he advanced a proposal that, along with one by Macdonald, shaped the form of the upper house, or Senate. He also helped save a provision that reserved to the federal government powers not granted to the local governments. In October, the Québec conference produced resolutions to create a Canadian confederation.

Yet Tupper faced substantial opposition in Nova Scotia to any ratification of the resolutions as the Maritimers feared domination by the Province of Canada. In reaction to this, on 17 August 1866 Tupper completed a bold move to further confederation by getting the provincial legislature to support union in principle without any specific reference to the resolutions formulated in Québec. Just weeks later, elections in Nova Scotia supported Tupper and other pro-unionists. At the same time, he promoted the union through his newspaper, *The British Colonialist.*

Late in 1866, Tupper, Macdonald, and other British North American delegates met in London to advance the union plan, a meeting that resulted in the British North America Act. Modeled closely after the Québec resolutions, it created the Dominion of Canada, which officially came into existence on 1 July 1867. (Although a nation, Canada did not gain full parity with Britain in the Commonwealth until 1931.) Tupper won election to the new Canadian Parliament as a Conservative Party candidate and served in the House of Commons.

Macdonald, chosen as Canada's first prime minister, relied on Tupper as his main advisor. Tupper had been expected to serve immediately in Macdonald's cabinet, but in a selfless act he relinquished his claim to a ministerial position so the

prime minister could arrange the appointments to meet demands for representation made by the French in Québec. Three years later, in 1870, Tupper at last joined the cabinet. He supported Macdonald's vigorous efforts to develop nationalism within Canada and both expand and connect the nation through territorial acquisitions and the building of railroads, programs completed successfully by Macdonald with the entry of British Columbia and Prince Edward Island into the confederation and railway construction in both the East and the West.

After opposition from the Liberal Party forced Macdonald's government to resign in 1873, Tupper returned to Nova Scotia. The Conservative Party victory of 1878 brought him back into Macdonald's cabinet, where he supervised completion of the Canadian Pacific Railway to British Columbia. Critics disgruntled with the way he handled the project forced his resignation from the cabinet, and from 1884 until 1896, except for a one-year interlude, he served as ambassador to Britain.

In the latter year, the Conservatives chose Tupper to govern as prime minister. Weeks later, however, he lost the general election and served as leader of the opposition in the House of Commons until 1900, when he lost reelection and retired from politics. He remained active in numerous business ventures until his death in Bexleyheath, Kent, England, on 30 October 1915. Canadians remember Tupper, along with Macdonald, Tilley, GEORGE ÉTIENNE CARTIER, and GEORGE BROWN as one of the "fathers of confederation."

References: Longley, James W., *Sir Charles Tupper,* 1917; Tupper, Charles, *Recollections of Sixty Years in Canada,* 1914.

U Nu

(b. 1907)

Myanmar

UNu presented a curious combination of qualities: a politicized nationalist, he often retreated into Buddhism to find peace; a statesmen caught in the uncertainty surrounding a new nation, he often appeared the picture of serenity.

U Nu was born in 1907 at Walema, Burma, a small village of bamboo structures, to U San Hum and his wife, Daw Saw Khin. As a boy, he lived wantonly, indulging in alcohol and, as he later described it, by age 12 becoming a drunk. But in his late teens, he underwent a drastic change, partly influenced by Buddhism, and ended his drinking and concentrated on his studies. U Nu obtained his higher education at the University of Rangoon, where he received his B.A. in 1929. A devout Buddhist, he was often seen washing the floor at the Shwedagon Pagoda before starting his day. After graduation, he served as headmaster at the National High School in Pantanaw before returning to the university in 1934, where he entered law school and made contact with student groups that advocated Burma's independence from British rule.

U Nu became president of the Student Union of Rangoon, and his criticism of the university administration resulted in his expulsion, along with that of a fellow nationalist, AUNG SAN. U Nu used fiery rhetoric against the British, denouncing them as slave masters, and in one instance he set the Union Jack afire. He joined Aung San in leading 700 students on a strike in 1936 that ignited the nationalist outbreak. The next year, he joined the Dobams Asiayone (We Burmans), more popularly called the Thakin (Master). They advocated full equality with the British and even eventual nationhood. Toward these ends, they stirred student and labor protests.

U Nu and the other Thakins decided to seek outside help in their fight against Britain. For this they turned to Japan, with Aung San taking the lead in recruiting a corps of followers, later called the Thirty Companions, which received military training from the Japanese. U Nu was not among this group; in 1940, he had been arrested by the British for sedition, and he languished in prison. As World War II spread to Asia, he could only wait while the Thirty Companions returned home, formed a Burmese army, and with Japanese help expelled the British.

This development resulted in U Nu's release from prison, and in 1943 he served as foreign minister in the Ba Maw government, established under Japanese control. Like other Thakins, U Nu soon grew disenchanted with Japan and supported the British in their successful return to Burma after World War II. Negotiations for independence began in 1946, and early in 1947 the British agreed to relinquish Burma, effective in one year. Aung San, then serving as Burma's provisional leader, fully expected to head this new government, but tragedy struck on 19 July 1947 when an assassin killed him and several members of his cabinet.

U Nu was then asked to head the government and complete the transition to nationhood. He accepted and also became leader of Burma's most prominent political party, the Anti-Fascist People's Freedom League (AFPFL). When Burma became independent in January 1948, U Nu became the first prime minister, a position he held for ten years, except for a one-year hiatus.

U Nu faced a declining economy with extensive urban poverty in Rangoon and heavy damage from the war. He earned widespread respect for the way he conducted politics, particularly in his distancing himself from the military. He appeared serene and calm in the face of great challenges and led an austere life, rejecting meat, drink, and tobacco, and frequently retreating to a Buddhist monastery for spiritual rejuvenation.

In the mid-1950s, U Nu seemed unable to handle the increased challenges from communists, charges of administrative corruption, and a worsening policy drift. His land nationalization act reduced the power of wealthy landlords, but the economy suffered as rice exports declined. The military in particular grew restless, and in 1958, after army units had surrounded the capital, U Nu turned to his fellow Thakin, General Ne Win, to "temporarily" take over the government until elections could be held. U Nu then retired to a monastery but returned as prime minister in 1960 after a parliamentary government was restored and his AFPFL swept recent elections. His prime ministry, however, did not last long: In March 1962,

Ne Win led a coup that deposed him. He was placed in prison, where he remained until 1966.

That year, U Nu left for India and then Thailand, where he organized a resistance movement against Ne Win. This effort failed, and he lived in India until 1980, when Ne Win invited him back to his homeland. U Nu returned in July and became a Buddhist monk. His nation underwent a change in name in 1989, from Burma to Myanmar.

Reference: Butwell, Richard, *U Nu of Burma,* 1969.

Venizelos, Eleutherios
(1864–1936)
Greece

Greece obtained its modern territorial shape and secured its independence through the leadership of a dedicated irredentist and fiery reformer, Eleutherios Venizelos.

Eleutherios Venizelos was born on 23 August 1864 in Mournies, a town on the island of Crete. In 1866, his family took him to Siros, one of the Aegean Islands. Eleutherios's father was sent there by the Turks for his participation in a revolt to end Turkish rule over Crete. As a young man, Eleutherios attended the Law School at the University of Athens, from which he graduated in 1887. While at the university, he organized and led the Cretan students.

Law degree in hand, Venizelos returned to Crete and worked as a lawyer and journalist. He also entered politics and won election to the Cretan National Assembly as a member of the Liberal Party. Venizelos remained opposed to the Turkish rule that continued over the island. His nationalism complemented that of mainland Greeks who protested the continued intervention of foreign powers in Greek affairs—a notable limitation on the independence allowed Greece in 1831—and the restricted size of the Greek nation. Macedonia, Crete, the Aegean Islands, Smyrna, and Thrace remained to be "redeemed," and irredentism became a powerful force: the desire to regain those lands considered culturally and historically a part of Greece. Venizelos fervently embraced this irredentism.

When war erupted between Greece and Turkey in 1897, Venizelos led an unsuccessful rebellion to link Crete to Greece. Although the defeat embarrassed most Greeks, some gains were made when the European powers intervened to assure Crete a semiautonomous status under Turkish supervision. In this setting, Venizelos was appointed minister of justice in 1899, a position he held until 1901. In 1905, he rebelled against the absolutist rule of the Greek Prince George, Crete's high commissioner, and declared Crete united with Greece. Venizelos lost this battle, but he did force the prince to resign in 1906.

Meanwhile, a reform movement called the Military League emerged on the mainland in reaction against Parliament's internal bickering. In August 1909, the League sponsored an uprising by army units, during which Parliament was surrounded and held hostage. In December, the League recruited Venizelos, and he advised it and King George to write a new constitution aimed at creating a more effective legislature. This was done, and in August 1910, Venizelos won a seat in the new body. Two months later he was appointed prime minister.

Supported by the urban middle class, Venizelos moved rapidly to advance irredentism. First, he reorganized the Greek army; then he formed an alliance with Bulgaria. In 1912, the First Balkan War erupted as the Greeks and Bulgarians tried to push the Ottoman Turks out of the Balkan Peninsula. The effort proved successful, and in May 1913 Turkey surrendered the Balkans.

This, however, led to the Second Balkan War, after Greece and Bulgaria had a falling out over how to divide the spoils. Greece, Serbia, Turkey, and Romania allied against Bulgaria, and when the war ended later in 1913, Greece obtained Crete, the Aegean Islands, and Macedonia. Venizelos had scored a stunning victory for his irredentist policy: Greece's size increased nearly 70 percent, and its population surged from 2.8 million to 4.8 million.

His enormous popularity allowed him to continue reforms he had begun in 1910; indeed, an economic and social revolution weakened the traditional oligarchy and strengthened the urban professionals and small businessmen. He guaranteed civil rights, reformed the tax system, and reduced bureaucratic waste.

When World War I broke out, Venizelos promoted an alliance with Britain as the means to further pursue irredentism and gain Thrace and areas in Anatolia. King Constantine, however, favored Germany in the war and committed Greece to a neutral course. In 1915, Venizelos resigned, and a political battle raged between the king and Venizelos's enormously popular Liberal Party. In 1916, Venizelos led an uprising in Thessaloniki against the king and established his own provisional government there. As the conflict between the king and Venizelos intensified, conservatives rallied around the monarch while republicans supported Venizelos.

With French and British help, Venizelos forced the king to flee in 1917 and then returned to Athens as prime minister. He brought Greece into the war on the side of the Allies and later participated in the Paris Peace Conference from which Greece obtained additional territory, most notably eastern and western Thrace. Venizelos, however, returned home diminished in popularity, probably because it was realized that the territorial gains could not be held without a war against Turkey. In 1920, he resigned as prime minister after elections produced a coalition of parties opposed to him and supportive of the monarchy.

Greece went to war against Turkey in 1922 and lost its territory in Anatolia. After the defeat, two military coups resulted in the return of Venizelos to power in 1924, but he quickly had a falling-out with other political leaders and left Athens later that year.

He soon resumed his leadership of the Liberal Party, however, and after it scored an impressive victory in the 1928 elections, he became prime minister. Venizelos began his administration by promoting economic reform but later changed and protected the entrenched interests. In foreign relations, he signed a treaty of friendship with Turkey in 1930.

The Great Depression encouraged opposition to Venizelos, and in the 1932 elections the Liberal Party's margin of victory was too narrow for him to form a government. In 1935, he retired from politics and moved to Paris, where he died on 18 March 1936.

Venizelos was crucial in founding modern Greece. Although the government succumbed to several military coups over the succeeding years, Venizelos had enlarged Greece beyond its restricted borders and set an example for reform later revived by CONSTANTINE KARAMANLIS and ANDREAS PAPANDREOU.

References: Kerofilas, C., *Eleutherios Venizelos: His Life and Work*, 1915; Shinn, Rinn S., *Greece: A Country Study*, 1986.

Victor Emmanuel II
(1820–1878)
Italy

When Victor Emmanuel marched triumphantly into Rome in 1871, he completed *risorgimento,* or the unification of Italy, and he did so by having stood up to Europe's most influential powers: Austria and the pope.

Victor Emmanuel was born in Turin on 14 March 1820, the son of Charles Albert, who was prince of Savoy-Carignano. In this illustrious family, young Victor developed a preference for studying military strategy. His first major battlefield test came in 1848. By this time, Charles Albert had become king of Sardinia-Piedmont, one of several Italian states. He supported a liberal constitution (after years of absolutist rule) and sided with the nationalists in a challenge to Austrian power over the divided Italian region. When, amid revolutionary fervor on the European continent and the nationalist appeals of GIUSEPPE MAZZINI, war erupted between Sardinia-Piedmont and Austria, Victor Emmanuel commanded a division. He fought well, but was overpowered by the Austrians. As Sardinia-Piedmont faced humbling peace terms in 1849, Charles Albert abdicated, and his son became king as Victor Emmanuel II.

Controversy gripped Sardinia-Piedmont as some in the kingdom argued over the peace terms with Austria. That victorious nation had offered Victor Emmanuel a choice: The kingdom could have increased territory if it repudiated its liberal constitution, or lose territory if it kept the constitution. Several delegates in the kingdom's Parliament argued that the loss of Parma, Modena, Lombardia, and Veneto meant a desertion of the nationalist cause.

Victor Emmanuel, however, believed the constitution should be maintained, and elections to a new Parliament showed that most in the kingdom agreed with him. Historians debate the extent to which Victor Emmanuel embraced liberal reform. Many believe that he supported the constitution not from any endearment to republican ideals, but from a recognition that to rule autocratically would likely have caused a popular upheaval and cost him the monarchy. In any event, his decision,

> *"Public opinion has approved the principle that each nation has an incontestable right to govern itself as it believes best."*

coupled with his getting Austria to agree to an amnesty for all those in Lombardy who had fought in the war, made him a hero not only in the kingdom but beyond, where Italians looked to him as a possible leader of *risorgimento.*

In 1850, the king appointed CAMILLO DI CAVOUR to his cabinet. Cavour exhibited outstanding ability, and two years later became prime minister. At this time, Sardinia-Piedmont felt increasingly threatened by the absolutist powers surrounding it. After Louis Napoleon declared himself emperor in France as Napoleon III, Cavour worked to use the ruler's desire for grandeur to the advantage of Sardinia-Piedmont.

In 1859, Cavour convinced France to join the kingdom in a war against Austria. As part of the arrangement, Victor Emmanuel agreed to give France territory, namely Nice and Savoy. The king turned to the adventurer-soldier GIUSEPPE GARIBALDI to lead the kingdom's army. Initially, the war went in Victor Emmanuel's favor, but then Napoleon III signed a secret agreement with Austria and withdrew from the fight. Late in the year, Victor Emmanuel signed a treaty with the Austrians under which his kingdom obtained Lombardy but recognized Austria's rule in Venetia.

Despite this setback, Victor Emmanuel believed events would soon work in the direction of *risorgimento.* He secretly provided assistance to Garibaldi, who invaded Sicily. When Garibaldi marched on Naples, Cavour, who was by now back in office, urged Victor Emmanuel to openly join the effort, partly as a way to further unification, partly as a way to control Garibaldi. The king did and conquered the Papal States. In return, he was excommunicated by the pope. In October 1860, Garibaldi agreed to turn over his conquests to Victor Emmanuel, and in March 1861 the Kingdom of Italy was proclaimed.

As ruler of the unified state, Victor Emmanuel worked to remove the remaining obstacles to fulfillment of *risorgimento:* the foreign control of Venetia and the pope's control of Rome. The king lost Cavour, who died in 1861, but displayed his own expertise. First, in 1866, he acquired Venetia after allying with Prussia. Then in 1870, the French withdrew their garrison from Rome, and despite the pope's protest, Victor Emmanuel acquired the city, although recognizing the autonomy of the Vatican. The king entered Rome in 1871, and the city became Italy's capital. Victor Emmanuel died on 9 January 1878—his role in Italian unification less crucial than that of Cavour, Garibaldi, and Mazzini, but nonetheless notable.

Reference: Forester, Cecil S., *Victor Emmanuel II and the Union of Italy,* 1927.

Walesa, Lech
(b. 1943)
Poland

In fighting for Polish autonomy, Lech Walesa navigated carefully to advance workers' rights while avoiding a Soviet invasion. His heroic union activism brought Polish independence and contributed to the demise of the Soviet Empire.

When Lech Walesa was born in Popowo on 29 September 1943, Poland was under Nazi occupation. The Germans had decided that Poland would be nothing more than a labor camp, and in their oppressive rule they forcibly relocated, imprisoned, and killed millions of Poles. Their actions complemented those of the Russians who, prior to the German invasion, had occupied portions of the country. Shortly after World War II ended, Poland emerged a weak and devastated nation, and the Soviet Union quickly planted a Communist government there, one that would recognize Soviet domination and permit Soviet troops.

Walesa grew up in this environment and despised the occupiers, who had been barbaric in their treatment. Young Lech was raised in a large family. Lech attended a vocational school in Lipno, near his hometown, and after completing his courses moved to Gdansk, where he obtained a job as an electrician. As a port, Gdansk housed huge shipping facilities, and Walesa worked at the Lenin Shipyard. This industry, like most in Soviet Poland, was under state control. In fact, the Soviets nationalized all banks and credit and insurance companies, as well as major industries.

For most workers, the economy proved disastrous. Over the years, numerous protests occurred, most notably a workers' uprising in Poznan in 1956. But conditions did not improve, and in 1970 violent protests erupted in Gdansk after the government raised food prices. Walesa participated in the protest. Six years later, food shortages stirred additional demonstrations and strikes. By this time, Walesa had become more prominent, and in April 1976 the government fired him for his role in presenting a list of grievances from the workers at the Lenin Shipyard.

A more liberal Soviet policy stirred further protests. To show the world their desire for better relations with the West, the Soviets decided not to crush dissent in Poland. As strikes spread across the nation in 1978, Walesa organized the Baltic Free Trade Unions Movement. The following year, he and several other protestors signed a charter of workers' rights in which they demanded an eight-hour day, higher wages, an end to censorship, the right to strike, and the right to form independent trade unions, an important demand given the Communist Party's desire to control all labor activity.

In 1980, workers at the Lenin Shipyard took over the facility. Walesa climbed the locked fence that surrounded it and became the workers' leader. In August, the government agreed to meet with Walesa and, at month's end, he and the Polish premier signed the Gdansk Agreement, granting the workers the right to strike and form independent unions. Walesa, in turn, acknowledged the supremacy of the Communist Party. He had scored an enormous triumph—the first time ever that an East European Communist government had accepted a prominent labor organization independent of its control.

Under Walesa's leadership, the various Polish unions joined together as the Solidarity movement, which, despite initial government obstruction, obtained legal sanction in November. The Soviet Union then signaled a change in its policy with a military buildup on Poland's border, and a new Polish premier began imprisoning some dissidents. Throughout 1981, strikes and demonstrations occurred over the arrests and food shortages. In August, Walesa demanded free elections.

Then in 1982 the government cracked down: It imposed martial law, declared Solidarity dissolved, and arrested Walesa. Amid international criticism for the arrest, the authorities released Walesa in November, and in 1983 he won the Nobel Peace Prize. By 1988, economic collapse forced the government to grant Walesa and Solidarity a major role in rebuilding the economy. Only Walesa, it seemed, could get the workers' cooperation and contain the strikes. The government officially recognized Solidarity and agreed to elections that would provide the organization with seats in the legislature. At the same time, events in the Soviet Union favored Walesa's cause as that nation's grip on Eastern Europe weakened— partly because of the Polish protests. In fact, the entire Soviet Union neared collapse.

> **"Those who brought us to the present situation . . . are anti-socialist. We in the unions are the upholders of socialism."**

In June 1989, Solidarity swept the legislative elections, soundly defeating the Communists. Walesa refused to serve as premier, but in 1990 he ran for the presidency, which he won. He then resigned as the leader of Solidarity. Upon gaining office, Walesa supported the privatization of Poland's economy in order to develop a free market. Antiquated factories, poor investments, and the workers' reluctance to depart with job security made difficult the bringing of prosperity to Poland. Economic dislocations produced inflation and widespread unemployment. Critics accused Walesa of being too dictatorial; they claimed his true talent lay in opposing government authority, not in becoming a part of it—that is, in agitating rather than in mediating.

In 1994, Walesa announced he would seek reelection as president in upcoming elections. But he had lost nearly all of his popular support, with many voters saying they would rather see Wojciech Jaruzelski, Poland's former Communist leader, serve as president. Even Solidarity deserted its former crusader, claiming he had not fulfilled his promises. Others in Poland feared Walesa would form his own dictatorship as the economic crisis continued. Walesa, however, maintains he will retain the presidency and continue to fight for a better Poland.

Irrespective of these later developments, Walesa's role in reestablishing his nation's independence cannot be understated. What he began as a worker's movement expanded into a call for a new government, a future free of Soviet control— Polish autonomy as envisioned by an earlier patriot, JÓZEF PILSUDSKI: not just in name but in reality.

References: Ascherson, Neal, *The Polish August: The Self-Limiting Revolution*, 1981; Ash, Timothy Garton, *The Magic Lantern: The Revolution of '89 Witnessed in Warsaw, Budapest, Berlin, and Prague*, 1990; Ash, Timothy Garton, *The Polish Revolution: Solidarity*, 1985.

Wang Ching-wei
(1883–1944)
China

An ardent nationalist early in his political career, Wang Ching-wei urged cooperation with Japan during World War II after it invaded China.

Wang Ching-wei was born on 4 May 1883 in Canton to wealthy parents. As a young man, he was a brilliant student and in 1903 won a government scholarship to Japan, where he obtained a degree at Tokyo Law College. While there he socialized with other Chinese students, many of whom believed China needed reform. At this time, the Chinese government was weak, and China was dominated by foreign powers. Chinese reformers blamed the situation on the ruling Ch'ing Dynasty, and some wanted to overthrow it and establish a modern, Western-oriented government. Wang helped found the T'ung Meng hui (United League) revolutionary association and became a propagandist. In 1910, he tried to assassinate the prince regent. The government arrested him and sentenced him to a life term, but he won his release in 1911 when the Ch'ing Dynasty fell and the Kuomintang, or Nationalists, under SUN YAT-SEN proclaimed a republic.

The new government soon came under the control of Yüan Shih-kai, who sought to establish his own dynasty. This led Sun Yat-sen to renew the Nationalist fight for a united, republican government, and in 1917 Wang joined the effort. When Sun died in 1925, Wang became head of the Kuomintang, but CHIANG KAI-SHEK effectively controlled the Nationalist army, and in 1926 he wrested the leadership away from Wang. Presently, Chiang began purging Communists from the Nationalist organization. Sun had opened the Kuomintang to these leftists, but Chiang considered them a threat to his power and to the right-wing interests supporting him. Such Communists as MAO TSE-TUNG (who later with his fourth wife, CHIANG CH'ING, would develop Maoism as an enormous influence in China), CHOU EN-LAI, and LIN PIAO now organized their own fight for a unified nation. Wang initially supported continuing the Communist alliance, and indeed the Nationalist left wing backed Wang in establishing a government in Wuhan, a city in central China. But Wang found the Communists opposed to his proposals, and in July 1927 he purged them.

Between 1929 and 1932 Wang concentrated on toppling Chiang Kai-shek, but in the latter year Japan threatened China, and the two men reached an agreement whereby Wang became head of the Kuomintang government and Chiang continued as head of the army. In 1935, an assassin wounded Wang, and he temporarily retired from his Kuomintang position. When Japan invaded China in 1937, Wang called on the Chinese government to reach a peaceful settlement with the Japanese. On 30 March 1940, Japan chose him to head the occupation government centered in Nanking. Apparently, Wang believed the Japanese would allow him much autonomy, and he saw the arrangement as a way to build a truly Chinese government, minus both Chiang and the Communists. Japan, however, allowed Wang little real power. He died on 10 November 1944 in Nagoya, Japan, from complications related to his gunshot wound.

Reference: T'ang Leang-li, *Wang Ching-wei: A Poltical Biography*, 1931.

Washington, George
(1732–1799)
United States

Perhaps George Washington's experience during his long trek into the Ohio country in 1754 revealed his unusual nature; or maybe it was his battle against the French in 1756 that did so. In the first incident, he nearly drowned and nearly froze to death; in the second, four bullets pierced his clothing. Time and time again, Washington survived close encounters with his life intact, and many persons then and since wondered if, indeed, destiny shaped the man.

George Washington was born on 11 February 1732 in Westmoreland County, Virginia. Little is known about George's father, Augustine Washington, or his mother, Mary Ball. Augustine Washington died in 1743 and left most of his considerable property to George's two half-brothers.

From 1743 to 1750, George lived with relatives, including his older half-brother Lawrence, who resided at Mount Vernon. During these years, the young man obtained his education from Lawrence (he had previously received some from his father) and proved especially adept at mathematics and map making. He read widely, although not extensively, and since Virginia was a British colony, adopted the English social graces then prevalent. Also, Lawrence married Ann Fairfax, which brought George into intimate contact with an extremely prominent English family and the customs practiced by the elite.

In 1748, Washington gained invaluable experience when he accompanied the surveyor for Prince William County on a month-long assignment. The following year, he was named surveyor for Culpeper County and just months later, at age 18, purchased 1,459 acres of land. In 1752, Lawrence Washington died, and George soon inherited Mount Vernon. By this time, military adventure attracted him, and in 1753 Lieutenant Governor Robert Dinwiddie sent him to the Ohio country, where Britain and France were competing for influence.

Dinwiddie instructed Washington to present the French with an ultimatum, warning them to withdraw. The Virginian, accompanied by six companions, completed his task with great hardship; he did not meet up with the French until nearly reaching Lake Erie, where they rebuffed him; on his return, his horse gave out—forcing him to walk part of the way—an Indian attacked him, his raft capsized in the Allegheny River, and the cold weather nearly killed him.

In April 1754, Dinwiddie made Washington a lieutenant colonel and put him in charge of 150 men. The governor ordered Washington back to the Ohio country, and at Great Meadows, Pennsylvania, he built Fort Necessity. In May, he attacked and defeated a French regiment. The enemy, however, soon counterattacked and forced Washington to retreat. After a standoff, the two sides reached an agreement, but Washington was embarrassed when the French included in the document a clause overlooked by him and his translator whereby he took full blame for having started the shooting.

In 1755, Major General Edward Braddock arrived in Virginia and appointed Washington as his aide. From this position Washington gained extensive military experience, but the slights that the British displayed toward the colonists also encouraged in him a desire to reform the relationship between the colonies and the mother country. In a battle along the Monongahela River, the French shot two horses out from under Washington, and four bullets pierced his coat. The stately Virginian, over six feet tall, had been an attractive target, but he survived, although he and Braddock lost this fight. Later, a British inquiry blamed the colonials for the defeat (a gross inaccuracy), and thus worsened relations between Virginians and their rulers.

Later in the year, Dinwiddie named Washington commander of all the Virginia forces, with the rank of colonel. He had under him only 300 men to guard a huge frontier. In this situation, he gained experience in planning military operations and learned the difficulties of supplying soldiers. Furthermore, British arrogance again reared its head, as when Washington saw his supplies commandeered by an officer in the "regular" army; this intensified the Virginian's discontent. With these obstacles and his own inexperience, Washington committed many errors in trying to defend against the Indians. Yet he kept his army in the field under trying circumstances, won the praise of many Virginians, and displayed a quality that proved crucial in his career: the ability to gain the devotion of his men.

Washington resigned his commission in 1758 and on 6 January 1759 married Martha Dandridge Custis, widow of Daniel Parke Custis. The couple lived at Mount Vernon, where Washington tended to his duties as a planter. The Virginian entered politics when, in the same year of his marriage, he took a seat in the House of Burgesses. For 15 years the people of Fairfax County reelected him, and he gained a reputation for being honest and friendly. At this time, he exhibited no second thoughts about slavery (later, he criticized it and hoped for its end, although he opposed accomplishing this through the use of force), an institution important to his plantation, and engaged in oftentimes risky but lucrative land speculation.

Had tensions with Britain not increased, Washington would likely have lived his remaining life in quietude, content with farming and minor political duties. He considered himself an Englishman, but clearly disliked the imperial system that indebted him and other planters to British merchants. By the early 1760s, he took the view that at some time—preferably much further down the line—the colonies would have to break with the mother country.

Washington did not take the lead in protesting Parliament's actions in the 1760s, and he disdained extreme responses. Nevertheless, he criticized the 1765 Stamp Act, which placed a tax on printed items used within the colonies, as unconstitutional taxation without representation. He also complained about the British prohibition against the colonists printing their own paper money. While he supported the nonimportation movements that arose at various times to boycott British goods, he criticized the radicals like SAMUEL ADAMS who were involved in the Boston Tea Party.

When Parliament passed the Coercive Acts in 1774, however, that punished Massachusetts for the Tea Party, he called them oppressive and backed the New Englanders. Subsequently, on 17 July, he and George Mason composed the Fairfax Resolves that called for the nonimportation of British goods and provided a mechanism to enforce the ban. The following day, the citizens of Faifax County gathered in a special meeting and approved the document. At a revolutionary convention in Williamsburg, held in August, the representatives made him a delegate to the First Continental Congress, which met in Philadelphia and brought him into contact with leaders from the other colonies, several of whom were immediately impressed with him. Shortly after the Congress met, he was chosen to command the militia companies of Frederick, Fairfax, Prince William, Richmond, and Spotsylvania Counties in Virginia.

Washington attended the Second Continental Congress in 1775 and served on a committee that planned for the defense of New York City. Then came an assignment which he accepted only reluctantly: The Congress, under the urging of Samuel Adams and JOHN ADAMS, selected Washington to command the emerging Continental army. This decision brought a southerner into the revolution's most important position and thus complemented the northern leaders, particularly those from Massachusetts, who had been the most radical, while bridging sectional differences. Washington arrived in Cambridge, Massachusetts, on 3 July 1775 to take over the army. He found a disorganized collection of New England militia, poorly supplied and poorly disciplined. At first, he still hoped for compromise with Britain, but after reading *Common Sense*, the influential pamphlet written by THOMAS PAINE, and noticing its impact, he changed his mind and concluded he must attack Boston and cripple the British military.

Early in 1776, Washington gathered a substantial number of men and fortified Dorchester Heights. This made the British army vulnerable, and on 17 March it evacuated Boston. The Virginian, however, had no opportunity to savor victory. His forces neared collapse, and he had to follow congressional orders and defend New York City—an almost impossible task against the large enemy army and its imposing navy. Until December, Washington suffered numerous setbacks, including the evacuation of New York City and relinquishment of Fort Lee in New Jersey. On Christmas night, however, he launched an attack against Hessian troops at Trenton, and after positioning his men at Morristown he forced the British to fall back.

In 1777, Washington's army began to take shape as Congress extended enlistment periods and the general instilled his troops with discipline. Many historians marvel at his ability to mold the army into a tight unit. In September, British General Howe defeated Washington at Brandywine Creek and soon captured Philadelphia. The following month, Washington lost another battle at Germantown and retreated across New Jersey, events that contributed to the Conway Cabal, an effort by Major General Thomas Conway to have the Virginian dismissed. The plot, however, quickly unravelled, and Washington continued his commitment to winning the war.

In March 1778 France decided to back the United States, a move that proved crucial in bringing victory. French officers, soldiers, supplies, and naval support gave Washington a much-needed boost. In May 1781, he and the French General Rochembeau agreed on a plan to attack New York City. As their armies approached the British-held settlement, the French fleet under Admiral De Grasse arrived in the Chesapeake, and the decision was made to bypass New York and head south to Virginia. This move entrapped Lord Cornwallis and his large British army. The ensuing siege of Yorktown lasted three weeks, and at its conclusion on 19 October 1781, Cornwallis surrendered to the aptly named tune "The World Turned Upside Down." Britain now neared total defeat in North America.

Little happened militarily after Yorktown, but Washington still faced the challenge of keeping his army together amid bickering in Congress and economic discontent. The soldiers did not receive their promised paychecks, while some Americans did business with the British and made substantial profits. At one point, in 1782, a group of his men proposed he become king, an idea Washington quashed immediately. On 19 April 1783, he entered New York City triumphantly. As the year reached its end, he retired to Mount Vernon.

Localized domestic disturbances and the inability of the national government to acquire adequate funding and develop a cohesive foreign policy under the Articles of Confederation led Washington to support the drive for a stronger political system. In 1787, he served as a delegate to the Constitutional Convention in Philadelphia and, in the role of chairman, set the spirit for compromise. His calm demeanor, selflessness, and support of union influenced the delegates when they created the presidency: They shaped the office with him in mind. Although Washington expressed his disdain for monarchy and his support for republicanism, he also believed in tempering popular power, and the Constitution that emerged provided protection for the nation's wealthy elite.

After his unanimous selection by the electoral college, Washington began his first presidential term on 30 April 1789, and with the help of his distinguished cabinet proceeded to develop the financial programs considered essential to establishing governmental stability. An ardent nationalist, he aimed to redirect loyalties away from the states and erode provincialism. His secretary of the treasury, ALEXANDER HAMILTON, advanced this strategy by developing proposals for a national debt and national bank, both approved by Congress.

Hamilton's effort, however, produced a rift with THOMAS JEFFERSON, the secretary of state, who opposed the proposals as concentrating money and power in the hands of an elite while diminishing the state governments. The dispute between Hamilton and Jefferson went well beyond politics and became personal, as each vied for Washington's preference. Washington respected both men but increasingly sided with Hamilton, and as the Federalist Party emerged to support the secretary's programs, the president, who had long been wary of parties as divisive, gravitated toward the new organization. He particularly agreed with Hamilton's criticism of the French Revolution and on more than one occasion chastised Jefferson for supporting the upheaval. To Washington, the French Revolution represented popular power gone wild and threatened stability in America, where the masses might copy the disorderly assaults on leaders and institutions.

Washington ran unopposed and won reelection in 1792. During his second term, alacrity faded and attacks against him increased, encouraged by the expanding contest between Hamilton's Federalists and Jefferson's Republican Party (no relation to the modern Republican Party), which positioned themselves on opposite sides of the French Revolution and struggled to dominate the national government. In 1794, Washington faced a challenge when the Whiskey Rebellion erupted in Pennsylvania. There, farmers refused to pay the excise tax on the spirituous beverage they often used as a form of money. The president called out the militia, which he and Hamilton led into the backwoods, and effectively ended the rebellion. Republicans charged Washington with overreacting, since the rebels had largely rejected violence, but the Virginian had exerted the primacy of the federal government and earned respect for it.

The president faced another controversy in 1795 when he signed Jay's Treaty, an agreement with Britain to relieve the tension emanating from the British raids on American ships engaged in trade with France. Washington had proclaimed America a neutral nation in the war then under way between Britain and France, and the president insisted that the raids violated this neutrality. Many Americans criticized the treaty for gaining no substantial concessions from Britain; they considered it a sellout to avoid war. Angry crowds demonstrated against Washington, and in Virginia some men gathered in taverns and toasted to him a speedy death. Yet Washington had avoided taking a young, weak nation into war and, at about the same time, he signed Pinckney's Treaty, which established the southern boundary of the United States and secured from Spain the right of American ships to navigate the Mississippi River.

As president, Washington set the national government on a firm foundation and established a foreign policy intended to avoid unnecessary entanglements abroad. His tendency, however, to see criticism of his policies as assaults on the government intensified political differences. In 1796, he decided not to seek a third term and issued his notable Farewell Address, in which he warned against party spirit that could tear America apart.

In 1798, after Federalists charged that France might invade the United States, Congress and President John Adams turned to Washington and appointed him lieutenant general and commander in chief of a new army then forming. The dispute with France soon eased, and he never personally commanded the troops. Late in 1799, Washington fell ill, and doctors inadvertently weakened him by engaging in bloodlettings. He died at Mount Vernon on 14 December.

Americans consider Washington the "father" of their nation, and he has been so widely praised that it is difficult to separate the man from the legend. An honest and highly moral man who rejected dictatorial powers and self-aggrandizement, he gave his life to his country, and his sacrifice and sincerity stand as the true monument.

References: Alden, John R., *George Washington: A Biography*, 1984; Cunliffe, Marcus, *George Washington: Man and Monument*, 1958; Davis, Burke, *George Washington and the American Revolution*, 1975; Flexner, James Thomas, *Washington: The Indispensable Man*, 1969; Flexner, James Thomas, *George Washington*, 4 volumes, 1965–1972; Freeman, Douglas Southall, *George Washington: A Biography*, 7 volumes, 1948–1957; Morison, Samuel Eliot, *The Young George Washington*, 1932; Schwartz, Barry, *George Washington*, 1987.

Weizmann, Chaim
(1874–1952)
Israel

Chaim Weizmann was an accomplished scientist who worked tirelessly to advance the Zionist movement. His effort brought the momentous Balfour Declaration, crucial in Israel's emergence.

Chaim Weizmann was born on 27 November 1874 to Oizer and Rachel Weizmann in Motol, a village in Russia. His father was a merchant, successful enough to send 9 of the couple's 15 children to college. From his parents, young Chaim learned a strident Jewish nationalism. They belonged to a Zionist group that advocated Jewish settlements in Palestine. Chaim displayed a brilliant grasp of mathematics and science in his schooling. In 1894, he traveled to Germany, where he attended college, and in 1900, he earned a doctorate in chemistry from the University of Freiburg in Switzerland. While in Berlin, he associated with other students from Russia and headed a group of Jewish intellectuals. Weizmann later claimed that his Zionist ideology "crystallized" in Germany.

In 1901, Weizmann was appointed a lecturer in organic chemistry at the University of Geneva. He also attended the Second Zionist Congress and emerged as a conciliator between two opposing Zionist groups—those who wanted political guarantees from various nations before establishing Jewish settlements in Palestine and those who wanted to proceed with the settlements irrespective of such guarantees. Weizmann later opposed a British offer of land in east Africa, at Uganda, as a site for a Jewish homeland. Nevertheless, he clearly saw Britain as a possible champion of Jewish nationalism and developed a cooperationist stance toward the British government. This feeling deepened when, in 1904, he moved to England with his bride, Vera Khatzman, began a scientific career in organic and biochemistry at the University of Manchester, and became a naturalized British citizen in 1910.

Weizmann led the Manchester Zionists, and his scientific work helped his nationalist effort. First, the money he earned from various patents allowed him to devote time to politics; second, his efforts in discovering a synthetic acetone (used in making smokeless gunpowder) for the British government during World War I and his new position as director of the Admiralty Laboratories brought him into contact with important public figures. His greatest accomplishment soon materialized: the Balfour Declaration. In this document, Britain endorsed the establishment of a Jewish homeland in Palestine.

In 1918, the British government appointed Weizmann chairman of the first Zionist Commission, an advisory group on Jewish questions. That year he visited Palestine and met with emir Faysal of Saudi Arabia, but attempts at cooperation failed when the Western nations did not support Arab nationalist movements in Iraq and Syria. While in Palestine, he laid the cornerstone for Hebrew University in Jerusalem, whose establishment he had championed.

Weizmann served as president of the World Zionist Organization from 1920 to 1931 and again from 1935 to 1946. In that capacity he solicited funds, making several trips to the United States. He suffered, however, two major setbacks. Attacks by Arabs on Jews in Palestine shook the British government, which then became more concerned with Arab discontent than with Jewish nationalism, and in 1929, the British issued a White Paper that in effect canceled their commitment under the Balfour Declaration. Weizmann did lobby successfully in getting Britain to temper the White Paper and support existing Jewish settlements. Still, his strategy of close alliance with the British cost him support and led to the delegates at the World Zionist Congress of 1931 refusing to reelect him as president.

In 1934, Weizmann founded the Sieff Research Institute at Rehovot in Palestine, from which developed the Weizmann Institute of Science. During World War II, he helped the United States develop synthetic rubber, and he continued his diplomatic efforts to get increased British support for Zionism. This, however, came to no avail. Other Zionists, including Abba Hillel Silver and DAVID BEN-GURION wanted more militant action, and in 1946 the World Zionist Congress rejected Weizmann's appeal for a nonconfrontational approach with Britain and his effort to once again become the organization's president. The Zionist movement subsequently sponsored violations of the British immigration restrictions imposed on Palestine and, as represented by Menachem Begin, engaged in sabotage and terrorist activities to secure a Jewish state.

In 1947, Weizmann headed a group of delegates that met with the United Nations Committee on Palestine. He supported the British plan to partition Palestine between Jewish and Arab territory, a position approved later that year by the United Nations. Weizmann also got the U.S. government to promise its support for an independent Israel.

Weizmann never had the influence within Palestine that he had outside, and when Israel gained its nationhood in 1948, the powerful premiership went not to him but to Ben-Gurion. Nevertheless, Weizmann accepted the largely ceremonial post as Israel's first president. Ben-Gurion made it clear that he would not share the leadership spotlight with Weizmann and largely ignored the scientist, even keeping his name off the list of those who signed the Israeli Declaration of Independence.

Weizmann's health soon declined and he died on 9 November 1952. Jews mourned his passing as a great figure in Israel's founding. He left his homeland's further development to Ben-Gurion and other nationalist leaders, including GOLDA MEIR and MOSHE DAYAN.

References: Litvinoff, Barnet, *Weizmann: Last of the Patriarchs,* 1976; Reinharz, Jehuda, *Chaim Weizmann: The Making of a Zionist Leader,* 1985; Rose, Norman, *Chaim Weizmann,* 1986; Weizmann, Chaim, *Trial and Error,* 1949.

William I

(1533–1584)

The Netherlands

In the sixteenth century, dynastic power held an oppressive grip on the Netherlands and produced a drive to form an independent republican nation. William of Orange, also called William the Silent, applied his military and statesman qualities as *stadholder,* or governor, to fight for this goal.

William was born 24 April 1533 in a European environment undergoing enormous change as power shifted from medieval lords to kings ruling consolidated states—the beginning of modern nations. He entered a privileged position: As the eldest son of Count William of Nassau and Countess Juliana of Stolberg-Wernigerode, he stood to inherit land, wealth, and prestige.

On a predominantly Catholic continent, William was raised a Protestant, at least until his eleventh birthday. That year, his cousin René de Chalon died, and he gained the enormous estates from the royal house of Nassau-Breda and Chalon-Orange, thus becoming the Prince of Orange. Habsburg Emperor Charles V, William's overlord who had inherited Spain and the Netherlands (along with Germany and most of Italy), ordered that William henceforth be raised a Catholic and receive an education through tutors in Brussels.

Although owning much land, William lacked liquid assets, an increasingly important possession in an economy becoming commercialized and capitalistic. In 1551, he married Countess Anne of Egmond-Buren, herself wealthy, which brought him several baronies but not much in the way of liquidity. (After she died in 1558, he married Anna of Saxony but divorced her in 1571 and married Charlotte of Bourbon-Montpensier in 1575.)

As Prince of Orange, William faithfully served Charles V, who made him commander of the military in a war against France, and he initially maintained this same loyalty under Charles's successor, Philip II, who in a dynastic arrangement became king of Spain and inherited the Netherlands. Philip appointed William to the Order of the Golden Fleece (an order of knights) in 1555, and made him a member of the Council of State. In 1559, William helped negotiate the Treaty of Cateau Cambresis, which ended the French conflict and freed Orange, his own princedom, from French rule. Philip named William *stadholder* of Holland, Zeeland, Utrecht, and French-Comté.

By this time, though, widespread protest arose in the Netherlands against Philip, a man known for his resentment of any criticism. This region, not really a state but a confusing collection of counties and duchies, was enormously important to the monarch; its bustling commerce and bountiful agriculture provided great revenue. Under Charles V, the Netherlands had experienced substantial autonomy, but Philip determined he must tighten his hold on the region and crush any developments that might challenge him there. He moved strongly against Martin Luther's ideas and the rise of Protestantism by bringing the Jesuits into the Netherlands, censoring writings, and ordering punishments for heresy through the Inquisition.

While these actions antagonized his Netherland subjects, even greater discontent stemmed from the belief among Netherlanders that Philip was cruel and an alien, distant from Dutch culture. They concluded that he wanted to impose an absolutist system and this, they determined, must be stopped.

In 1566, 400 nobles gathered at Brussels and petitioned for an end to the heresy edicts and for regular sessions of the representative body, the States-General. William did not attend this gathering but was linked to the protest by way of his known influence with the delegates. He was cautious and tried to temporize the more radical plans for an armed revolt proposed by others, including his brother. He advised others: "Make as little use as you can of force, for terrible may be the consequences if the people are driven to desperation." William's careful maneuvering and secretive activities in the movement against Philip led to his being called "the Silent."

At about the same time, religious riots erupted—vicious attacks against Catholics prompted in part by a serious economic downturn. Philip retaliated by sending troops under the duke of Alba, who brutally suppressed all dissidents and heretics. The duke began arresting and executing nobles he suspected of disloyalty and included on his list William, who fled to his castle at Dillenberg in Germany.

William began organizing troops, and in April 1568 led two invasions of the Netherlands. These both failed, however, and he retreated to France before returning to Germany in 1569. From there, he allied himself with the Protestant Calvinists to gain much-needed support and issued letters of marque to several vessels—the infamous "Sea Beggars"—that plied the waters and raided Spanish shipping. This proved highly successful (although disruptive of the Netherlands economy), and in 1573, after the Sea Beggars captured Brielle in Zuid-Holland, the provinces of Holland and Dordrecht proclaimed equal rights for Catholics and Calvinist Protestants and provided William supplies for the war. By then, William had become the hero of the Netherlands, the subject of poetic tributes, and he returned there, proclaiming he would die before leaving again.

William used his considerable abilities as a statesman to bring the various towns of Holland closer together and to unite the provinces of Holland, Zeeland, and Utrecht, which in 1576 recognized him as their Chief and Supreme Authority. He continued his fight to gain independence for all 17 provinces of the Low Countries (including present-day Belgium and Luxembourg). Later that year, he arranged the Pacification of Ghent, which brought the provinces together in a mutual pledge to end Spanish rule.

In the late 1570s, Philip sent Alexander Farnese, the duke of Parma, to crush William's rebellion, and the duke succeeded in worsening a split between the Netherland Catholics and Calvinists that caused William to lose the southern provinces. The duke organized the League of Aras in 1579, which united these provinces into a Catholic union and shattered William's hope of unity throughout the Low Countries. The rebellious provinces in the north responded by forming the Union of Utrecht, whose articles became the constitution for the later United Provinces.

In 1581, the seven northern provinces officially pronounced their independence from the Spanish monarch and issued a document, since called the Dutch Declaration of the Rights of Man. In it, they claimed that a prince ruled only for the good of the people and that relations between the ruler and his subjects were defined by a country's laws. Meanwhile, Philip called for William's demise and promised wealth and noble rank to anyone who would capture or kill his opponent. Several attempts were made on William's life; then in July 1584 a religious fanatic entered the *stadholder*'s home and shot him dead.

The struggle for independence continued, and under William's youngest son, Prince Maurice, the Netherlanders, with help from England, gradually expelled the Spanish forces. Peace did not come, however, until after Philip died. A truce signed in 1609 was interrupted by the Thirty Years' War. Finally, Spain recognized the United Provinces as independent in 1648. The Netherlands, or the Dutch Republic as it was called, fell to Napoleon in the late 1700s, but in 1813 a nationalist movement spread, led by Gijsbrecht Karl van Hogendorp, and after the Treaty of Vienna in 1815 the Netherlands regained full independence and developed a constitutional monarchy. Today, as part of their heritage, the Dutch recall how in defeating Spain they had overcome a much larger, wealthier, and populous country, a feat guided in its crucial beginnings by William the Silent.

References: Geyle, Peter, *The Revolt of the Netherlands, 1555–1609*, 1980; Swart, Koenraad W., *William the Silent and the Revolt of the Netherlands*, 1978; Wedgwood, Cicely V., *William the Silent, William of Nassau, Prince of Orange, 1553–1584*, 1968.

William II

(1792–1849)
Luxembourg

As King of the Netherlands and Duke of Luxembourg, William II did not bring the grand duchy its independence; but he did allow it greater autonomy, which made nationhood more possible in the 1860s.

William was born on 6 December 1792 at The Hague. Three years later, he was taken to England after a French conquest forced his family into exile. During the Napoleonic Wars, he served in the British army from 1811 to 1812 as the Duke of Wellington's aide-de-camp. In 1815, he commanded the troops from the Netherlands at the Battle of Waterloo, where he earned a reputation as a hero.

> *"I wish for the good of the Grand Duchy, and I wish it by means of the Luxemburgers."*

William's father, William I, sent him to Belgium (then linked to the Netherlands) in 1830 to end a rebellion there, but his attempts at negotiation failed. The following year, William led a Dutch army against the Belgians, who had proclaimed Leopold I their king. He advanced until the French intervened and halted his attack.

William acceded to the throne in 1840 as king of the Netherlands and at the same time held the title Duke of Luxembourg. His father had abdicated amid discontent in the Netherlands over his authoritarian policies and a widespread dislike in Luxembourg for his interventionism and heavy taxes. Many in Luxembourg feared William would act the same, but on a visit to the grand duchy he promised the people more autonomy. He soon kept that promise. He brought to fruition the administrative separation of Luxembourg from the Netherlands. He also dismissed several Dutch officials and appointed a new governor, who presided over a Council of Government.

He then called to The Hague several leading Luxemburgers and on 12 October 1841 approved a constitution for the grand duchy that provided for an assembly, called the Estates. Also that year a Luxembourg army was formed, although it had as its primary duty service to the German Confederation, of which Luxembourg was a part. The country thus had a complex relationship with its neighbors: It was legally an independent state, as evident in its increased autonomy; but it was linked to the Netherlands because it was William's personal possession by inheritance, and it was included in the German Confederation.

In 1842, William ratified a treaty whereby Luxembourg entered the German Customs Union. Although it infringed on Luxembourg's autonomy, the Union provided numerous economic advantages to the grand duchy, and as a result its agriculture and industry expanded considerably.

The constitution allowed by William did not please many Luxemburgers. They wanted a more liberal document, and when revolutions swept Europe in 1848, Luxembourg demanded additional rights. Demonstrations occurred, particularly in Ettlebruck, and William agreed to a constitution that expanded suffrage and protected basic liberties, such as freedom of the press.

William died at Tilburg in the Netherlands on 17 March 1849. His willingness to accept changes contrasted with his father, and although not a bold reformer, he permitted the political alterations essential in readying the country for greater independence. This came in 1866 when the German Confederation ended, although the grand duchy remained a personal possession of Dutch rulers until 1890, and in World War I and World War II it fell to German occupation.

References: Cooper-Prichard, A. H., *History of the Grand Duchy of Luxembourg*, 1950; Newcomer, James, *The Grand Duchy of Luxembourg: The Evolution of Nationhood, 963 A.D. to 1983*, 1984.

William III
(1650–1702)
Great Britain

William III did not initiate the reform called the Glorious Revolution; rather, the impetus came from Parliament. But he did defeat James II, thus securing a change in government and beginning a new era in British politics.

William was born at The Hague on 4 November 1650, the son of William II, Prince of Orange, and Mary, the daughter of England's future king, James II. He obtained an education at Leyden and in 1667 was admitted to the Council of State of the Dutch Provinces. In 1670, he traveled to London—his first visit to England—where he met his cousin Mary, his future wife, then only eight years old. When William returned to Holland he obtained appointment as captain general of the Dutch army and *stadholder*, or governor, of the United Provinces of the Netherlands, a hereditary position. In 1677, he wed Mary at Saint James Palace in England.

In the 1680s, while William became Prince of Orange and continued as *stadholder* in the Netherlands, England experienced a political crisis that threatened to embroil the nation in a bloody conflict. James II, a Stuart, acceded to the throne in 1685 and brought with him a devout, some would say fanatical, Catholicism fueling a determination to impose his will on Parliament. In a primarily Protestant nation, James's Catholic crusade raised enormous opposition. Early in his reign, James dismissed uncooperative judges, replaced Protestant with Catholic officers in the army, appointed a Catholic to head the British navy, and attacked both Oxford and Cambridge for being centers of Protestantism. He even converted the former college into a Catholic seminary. In 1687, James issued a Declaration of Indulgence granting religious freedom to all denominations—on the surface a libertarian document, but actually written to protect Catholicism. The Church of England opposed him, members of Parliament despised his circumventing them, and many merchants feared an absolutism that would produce crushing taxes.

In 1688, a son was born to James, and many Whigs—opponents to the Stuart monarchs—concluded that England could be in for a long era of Catholic rule. At that point, the Whigs, allied with some Tories—generally supporters of the Stuarts—negotiated with William to assume the English crown. William lost no time in agreeing to head an army against James, both to protect his wife's interest in inheriting the crown and to make sure that England did not ally with France (a move James might undertake as a Catholic monarch assisting a fellow Catholic monarch, Louis XIV).

On 1 November 1688, William sailed for England with 11,000 foot- and 4,000 horse soldiers aboard 49 ships. He outmaneuvered the English fleet and on 5 November landed at Torquay. James had an army of 30,000 men ready to meet the challenge, but he hesitated and returned to London. The English officers subsequently deserted James en masse, and by late November the king decided he would flee. William, however, captured James on 11 December and ordered him to remain at his Rochester estate. He stayed there only 12 days, though, before escaping to France.

William, meanwhile, claimed he would guarantee a free Parliament, and on 24 December, 60 peers formally asked him to lead the realm and hold parliamentary elections. Just two days later 300 former members of the House of Commons supported the request. Parliament convened in a special session on 22 January 1689 and over the next year worked out agreements to guide the government.

The legislators decided to grant the English crown jointly to William and his wife Mary, and in return the new monarchs accepted a Declaration of Rights, later expanded to the Bill of Rights, that covered important principles. For one, it made it illegal to suspend the laws, collect taxes, or maintain a standing army without parliamentary approval; second, it prohibited excessive fines; third, it protected freedom of speech and debate in Parliament; and fourth, it prevented any Catholic from ever inheriting the throne. The document clearly aimed at the absolutist abuses under the Stuarts and is the most important in English constitutional history. On 13 February, William and Mary were installed as monarchs (the formal coronation took place on 11 April), although due to Mary's death in 1694 the joint rule lasted less than six years.

Importantly, Parliament arranged a financial settlement with William and Mary whereby the monarchs had such limited access to revenues they would have to call frequent sessions of the legislature to secure needed funds. Hence, while the Bill of Rights stressed personal liberties, the financial settlement protected Parliament (and guaranteed Parliament's ascendency) and reflected the concern over arbitrary taxation and assaults on property— a concern held dear by the expanding merchant class.

This change in rulers became known as the Glorious Revolution. A largely nonviolent rebellion, it did not eliminate the existing political structure, but rather modified it. The monarchy continued, but within boundaries set by Parliament and under a Declaration and Bill of Rights amounting to a contract between king and subjects. In this sense, William presided over a change establishing the modern, liberal political form upon which present-day England rests.

In 1689, William supported the Toleration Act. This measure allowed nonconformists their own places of worship and their own preachers. They remained, however, excluded from public office. William still had to contend with rebellions against him in Scotland and Ireland. Although his troops lost to the Scottish rebels, the uprising collapsed due to poor leadership. In 1690, William personally led his troops in Ireland, where they defeated the rebels led by James II at the Battle of the Boyne.

William also freed English foreign policy from French domination and began a series of wars against France to protect the Netherlands and project English power against Louis XIV. In the late 1600s, the French had acquired the Spanish Netherlands and Strasbourg. In 1689, William, with Parliament's backing, allied England with Austria and Spain in the League of Augsburg, while Louis XIV backed the rebellion in Ireland and prepared to invade England. As noted, William repelled this invasion but lost many battles on the continent. Nevertheless, his persistence resulted in Louis suing for peace in 1697 and officially recognizing William as king of England. Shortly before William died, however, the war resumed.

Despite his moderating influence on English politics, William was not popular with his subjects. His preference for Dutch customs reinforced his "outsider" status and reminded Englishmen he was a foreigner. In February 1702, William was thrown from his horse. Complications from a broken collar bone led to pleuropneumonia, and on 8 March he died.

The Glorious Revolution and the domestic political developments under William's rule extended the evolution of the English political system since the time of HENRY VII and were important forerunners to later liberalization.

Reference: Jones, J. R., *The Revolution of 1688 in England*, 1972.

Williams, Eric
(1911–1981)
Trinidad and Tobago

An accomplished author, historian, and political scientist, Eric Williams brought to his homeland a strident nationalism that rested on his personal leadership.

Eric Williams was born on 25 September 1911 in Trinidad, which was then, along with Tobago, under British control. He attended Tranquility Intermediate School and Queen's Royal College in Port of Spain before obtaining his bachelor's degree in 1932 at Oxford (where he was an accomplished soccer player). He went on to study for his doctorate in history and political science, which he obtained six years later.

In 1939, he journeyed to the United States and taught at Howard University as an assistant professor of social and political science. Williams claimed that history too often exhibited foreign and neocolonial biases, and he criticized British West Indian education for its categorizing non-British culture as inferior. He believed the slogan "Be British" had infected him and, although it led him to gaining a higher education, it ill-prepared him for Trinidadian society. West Indian students, he believed, should be educated to prepare for life in their homeland. He expressed this view forcefully in his work with the Teachers' Educational and Cultural Association (TECA), a progressive group.

Williams entered politics partly as a result of his experience in the United States. While he was at Howard, he worked with the Caribbean Commission, a group established to promote and coordinate economic development in his home region. He advocated several policies that antagonized the Americans, particularly those reflecting his support of labor. Williams favored a democratic socialism that would encourage widespread political participation and lessen economic injustice.

Through his work with TECA and his many historical speeches, Williams developed admirers who saw him as encouraging black pride. Indeed, TECA established the People's Educational Movement as a vehicle for Williams to tour the islands and build his support. In 1955, he returned to his homeland and on 15 January 1956 launched the Peoples' National Movement (PNM), a political party of middle-class, mainly black, professionals. (Many on the islands were of East Indian heritage, their families having emigrated from Asia, and they formed their own party in opposition to Williams.) The PNM was not leftist, but rather nationalist.

Williams developed a close relationship with the masses and promoted change through his strong will. Numerous observers commented on his seemingly innate talent to attract followers and, through his zeal, the ability to get them to work hard for his cause. He ran a highly personalized party in which he made all the major decisions, and loyalty to the organization came through loyalty to him.

In 1956, the PNM won a plurality of legislative seats in a close election, and Williams became chief minister of Trinidad and Tobago. Under his leadership, the two islands joined with several Caribbean states to form the West Indies Federation. Shortly after this, Williams and the PNM lost their majority in the legislature, and in 1962 the Federation collapsed.

Williams then directed the PNM to a more leftist policy, although maintaining a close attachment to the United States and other Western powers. After obtaining numerous changes in election procedures to help the PNM, he led it to a landslide victory (with 58 percent of the vote) in national elections preparatory to independence. He became prime minister, a position he continued to hold when Trinidad and Tobago gained nationhood in August 1962.

Williams applied what he called "empirical socialism." He developed a free education system and expanded social services, while at the same time encouraging foreign investment. Trinidad and Tobago became the most prosperous of the former British Caribbean colonies.

In foreign policy, he followed a balanced approach, recognizing America's preeminent political and economic strength, while in 1972 establishing diplomatic relations with Communist Cuba. Williams won reelection on several occasions and served as prime minister until his death on 29 March 1981 at St. Anne. He represented the Caribbean man-of-letters as political leader, and while guiding Trinidad and Tobago to independence, he continued as a prolific thinker and author. Writing several articles and more than seven books between 1942 and 1970, he was considered the leading authority on Caribbean history.

References: Brereton, Bridget, *A History of Modern Trinidad, 1783–1962*, 1981; De Suze, J. A., *The New Trinidad and Tobago*, 1965; Deosaran, Ramesh, *Eric Williams: The Man, His Ideas, and His Politics*, 1981; Williams, Eric, *British Historians and the West Indies*, 1964; Williams, Eric, *From Columbus to Castro: The History of the Caribbean, 1492–1969*, 1970; Williams, Eric, *The History of the Negro in the Caribbean*, 1942;

Yahya
(1869–1948)
Yemen

As a young man, Yahya idolized Karb Ali Water, the king who first unified Yemen. An Islamic kingdom became Yahya's goal, one called Great Yemen, and as he fought for it he developed an autocratic regime.

Yahya was born in Sanaa City in June 1869. His father, Mohammed, had attained status as a Zaydi imam (a spiritual authority or "commander of the faithful" within the Zaydi Islamic sect), and shortly after 1890, he began a revolt against the Turks, who ruled North Yemen as part of the Ottoman Empire. By this time, Yahya had been educated by his father and various Zaydi scholars in Islamic law, which imbued him with traditional religious beliefs. Consequently, he supported his father in the rebellion for independence. After his father's death in 1904, Yahya continued the struggle, assuming the title of imam and obtaining for his domain the title Yemeni Mutawakkilite Kingdom.

Yahya faced enormous opposition, not only from the Turks but also from the British, who had colonized neighboring South Yemen; from the Saudis, who would soon occupy southern Hejaz; and from opposing tribes within his own domain. Nevertheless, he committed himself to reuniting historical Yemen under his leadership, an entity called Great Yemen. In ancient times, Yemen had for 4,000 years occupied the southern half of the Arabian Peninsula. In fact, long before Islam the Himyarite king Karb Ali Water, the man who became Yahya's hero, had unified Yemen.

Yahya constructed an effective fighting force that captured Sanaa City in 1905, and by 1911 forced the Turks to recognize his rule over central Yemen. In 1919, the Turks relinquished to him all of North Yemen. In the 1920s and 1930s, Yahya fought to subdue the Idrisis, sheikhs descendant from a Moroccan family, who challenged his authority, and to wrest South Yemen from the British, who controlled the city of Aden. Britain subsequently attacked Yahya's domain, and in a blow to building Great Yemen, Yahya signed a treaty in 1934 recognizing British control over South Yemen.

War next broke out with the Saudis, who backed the Idrisis, after Yahya demanded Asir, an area under Saudi control. The Saudis won important victories in Jizan and central Tihamah where they captured Hudaydah, the leading port. The Saudis demanded that, in return for relinquishing Hudaydah, Yahya release the Idrisis, whom he had captured, and give up his claims to several territories he considered essential in forming Great Yemen. Yahya agreed and this ended his foreign adventure.

He then focused on internal affairs, determined to establish a pure Islamic state under his own absolute power. He oftentimes used violent methods, including a hostage system under which he captured from every tribal sheikh a relative whom he imprisoned and whose safety he assured only with concessions. He also held mass executions, particularly against Muslim scholars and intellectuals who advocated reforms. Yahya opposed modern intrusions, such as schools and newspapers, and himself remained isolated, never leaving the highlands.

He maintained rigid control—all citizens needed his written permission even to travel from one city to another. Yet he imported advanced weaponry to fight his wars and accepted military training from other Arab states. In time, this allowed modern influences and, ultimately, dissent to enter his realm.

With his oppressive tactics, opposition mounted, and in the mid-1930s the Society of Struggle appeared in North Yemen's cities, including San'a. In 1944, the Free Yemenis group organized in Aden and was joined by Ibrahim, Yahya's moderate son. The San'a and Aden opponents subsequently plotted to assassinate Yahya. On 17 February 1948, a 15-man group ambushed Yahya's entourage and killed the aged leader in a hail of machine-gun fire.

After infighting involving considerable bloodshed, Yahya's oldest son Ahmad gained command and ruled North Yemen until his own assassination in 1962. ALI ABDULLAH SALEH then became ruler of the newly proclaimed Yemen Arab Republic. In 1990, this nation merged with the People's Democratic Republic of Yemen (South Yemen), which had developed a Marxist government under SALIM RUBAY ALI and ABD AL-FATTAH ISMAIL. The new nation was named the Yemeni Republic.

References: Bidwell, Robin, *The Two Yemens*, 1983; Wenner, Manfred, *Modern Yemen: 1918–1966*, 1967.

Yameogo, Maurice
(b. 1921)
Burkina Faso

As a leader in Burkina Faso's early struggles against French rule, Maurice Yameogo won the support of his countrymen; as founding president, his extravagance and controversial marriage to a beauty queen brought his demise.

Maurice Yameogo was born into the Mossi, a dominant northern tribe, at Koudougou in December 1921. He attended the Catholic mission secondary school at Pabré. From there, he entered the French civil service and became active in the French Confederation of Christian Workers (CFTC), which brought him a substantial following among his country's educated elite.

Prior to 1983 Burkina Faso was known as Upper Volta. In 1919, France formed this colony and at first made numerous internal improvements. But Upper Volta lost its separate territorial status in 1932 and was largely ignored by French authorities. Then in 1948, while Yameogo was becoming more prominent politically, Upper Volta once again became a separate overseas territory.

In December 1946, Yameogo won election from Koudougou as a representative to the new territorial legislature. A change in the French Constitution allowed Upper Volta this legislature, as well as representation in a Grand Council for all of West Africa, to which Yameogo was elected in 1948. At this time, Yameogo helped lead the Union Voltaic, which as a political party consisted of Catholic-educated Voltaics, such as himself, and traditional tribal chiefs who opposed any domination of Upper Volta by the neighboring Côte d'Ivoire (Ivory Coast).

After Yameogo won election to the Third Territorial Assembly in March 1957, Premier Ouëzzin Coulibaly made him minister of agriculture. A few months later, Yameogo joined Coulibaly's Unified Democratic Party (PDU) to keep it from losing its slim majority in the legislature. Yameogo was rewarded with a higher post, minister of the interior. Coulibaly, however, died in September 1958 and Yameogo's political career soon advanced further: He became leader of the PDU, president of the Council of Ministers and then, in December, premier. When internal dissension tore apart the PDU, Yameogo formed the Democratic Voltaic Union (UDV) and on 11 December 1959, as the UDV obtained 64 of the 75 legislative seats, he won election as president of the newly formed Republic of Upper Volta, a state within the French Community.

In August of the following year, Upper Volta gained its complete independence. Yameogo continued as president and in 1965 won reelection with 99.98 percent of the vote. The result, however, belied his increasing unpopularity. Economically, this poor country had made few advances while Yameogo's appointees spent money extravagantly. Politically, Yameogo strove to outlaw all opposition, calling the competing political party "agitators who represented nothing." Then he married a beauty queen half his age in an elaborate and expensive wedding ceremony. He and his wife honeymooned in Paris and Brazil where they incurred expenses of nearly $100,000. When he returned to Upper Volta, he found that the publicity surrounding his activities had exacerbated discontent. His standing worsened further as the Upper Volta deficit expanded, and he announced an austerity program that included reduced salaries for government bureaucrats and higher taxes. In January 1966 a labor strike began, mass demonstrations besieged Yameogo, and when the military turned against him, he resigned. Yameogo was arrested, failed in a suicide attempt, and then, in 1969, was sentenced to five years of hard labor for embezzlement. Nevertheless, he gained his release in 1970, partly in recognition for the role he had played in gaining Upper Volta's independence.

Upper Volta subsequently experienced a series of adminstrations vacillating between military and democratic rule. Most notably, in 1983 Captain Thomas Sankara, a radical commando, became premier and, in a dispute with the president, seized power and established a revolutionary council. He arrested enemies of the state, nationalized all land, and changed the nation's name in 1984 to Burkina Faso. In 1987, however, a bloody coup ended his rule and resulted in his death.

Reference: McFarland, Daniel M., *Historical Dictionary of Upper Volta*, 1978.

Yeltsin, Boris
(b. 1931)
Russia

As a Communist leader, Boris Yeltsin refused to ride in official limousines, taking the train instead; he criticized corruption, and then relinquished his position on the powerful Politburo. With these actions, he won the hearts and minds of the Russian people and spearheaded a revolution that resulted in the end of the Soviet Union and its Communist system.

Boris Yeltsin was born on 1 February 1931 in Sverdlovsk, a city in the Ural Mountains of the Soviet Union. As a boy, he had a rebellious streak and got into trouble when, during World War II, he and two friends stole hand grenades from a weapons warehouse. One of the grenades exploded, costing Boris his thumb and forefinger.

As a young man, Boris attended the Ural Polytechnical Institute, where he trained to be an engineer. In 1955, he began working on construction projects and in the 1960s advanced to become the engineer of a housing construction combine in Sverdlovsk. At about the same time, he joined the Communist Party and in 1968 presented speeches praising the Soviet leader, Leonid Brezhnev. He aimed for a political career and in 1976 became first secretary of the Sverdlovsk District Party Committee.

Yeltsin earned a reputation as a reformer working to correct a party system rife with corruption and gained the attention of MIKHAIL GORBACHEV, who had recently been chosen general-secretary of the Communist Party, the most powerful position in the Soviet Union. Gorbachev embraced reform, or *perestroika*, and promoted it along with openness, or *glasnost*. At the time, the Soviet Union faced economic difficulties that threatened its stability. In June 1985, Gorbachev appointed Yeltsin as secretary of construction on the powerful Central Committee. In December, he was named first secretary of the Moscow Party Committee, which placed him at the head of the city government. He entered the Communist Party's inner circle in February 1986 after he was named to the Politburo as a nonvoting member.

Yeltsin won extensive popular support when he rejected government privileges, such as the limousine, and visited factories and stores, where he met with the workers. His appeal to the masses became a trademark of his politics. Time and time again, he demanded free-market reforms and an end to Communist political domination. A thorn in Gorbachev's side, he kept prodding the Soviet leader to loosen the Kremlin's grip on Russia and the other republics. Critics called Yeltsin manipulative and essentially autocratic, but supporters saw him as advancing openness and concern where previous party leaders had exhibited none. In April 1987, he allowed a full political debate to take place among representatives from 148 groups who met in Moscow's Hall of Columns.

That same year, Yeltsin's political career took a strange turn and nearly ended. In October, the Communist Party Central Committee met to listen to Gorbachev's policy outline. After the general-secretary completed his presentation, Yeltsin stunned everyone by announcing his resignation from the Moscow Committee and the Politburo. Then he criticized Gorbachev for proceeding too slowly with *perestroika* and warned that the general-secretary might develop a "personality cult."

Gorbachev condemned Yeltsin, and in 1988 the renegade was demoted to a minor post. But events worked in his benefit: Gorbachev's commitment to reform, coupled with the worsening economic pressures and nationalist rumblings in Eastern Europe and the Soviet republics, changed the political system. Debate erupted, as did competitive elections. In March 1989 Yeltsin ran for a seat in the Congress of People's Deputies—the body that was to pick the delegates to the main national legislature, or Supreme Soviet. He effectively appealed to a broad cross-section, rallying both intellectuals and blue-collar workers behind him in calling for direct elections at all levels, popular referendums, and substantial economic reforms. He stunned Gorbachev by winning a landslide victory. The Congress then made him a delegate to the Supreme Soviet of the U.S.S.R.

In 1990, Yeltsin won election to the Supreme Soviet of the Russian Republic, the largest republic within the Soviet Union. Later that year, he became the Supreme Soviet's chairman and from that powerful position continued to warn about a Gorbachev dictatorship, while pressing for a market economy. He emerged as Gorbachev's prime political opponent. By this time, the Soviet Union neared collapse, weakened by the loss of its dominate role in Eastern Europe, by its declining economy, by ethnic disagreements, and by bitter disputes between reformers and conservatives.

On 19 August 1991, conservative Communists attempted to overthrow Gorbachev. While he was away in the Crimea they isolated him and took charge in Moscow. Yeltsin rallied the Russian people; he called for a general strike, promoted huge demonstrations, and defied the conservatives and their military backers to capture him, at one point presenting an emotional speech while standing atop a tank. Yeltsin supporters fortified the parliament building, called the White House, to protect it, and world opinion resoundingly criticized the coup leaders. Within two days, the attempted overthrow collapsed. Gorbachev resumed his position as president of the Soviet Union, but, importantly, Yeltsin emerged an enormous hero, praised for his bravery.

The coup brought the final demise of the Soviet Union. Yeltsin and Gorbachev worked together to form the Commonwealth of Independent States, a confederation consisting of Russia and ten other former Soviet republics. In December, it replaced the Soviet Union and Gorbachev's presidency ended. Yeltsin was now the president of a new nation named after its foremost republic, Russia.

Yeltsin pursued a market economy, but his programs brought considerable criticism from a population beset by high prices and unemployment resulting from communism's collapse. At one point, in March 1992, the Congress of People's Deputies, guided by conservatives, nearly impeached him.

Yeltsin's most dramatic challenge occurred in 1993. On 1 October some 600 armed men joined his conservative political opponents in the White House. At the same time, other Yeltsin opponents staged street demonstrations and set up barricades in Moscow. Former vice-president Aleksandr Rutskoi urged the Russian people to flood the streets and topple Yeltsin. On 3 October, fighting erupted between the anti-Yeltsin rebels and government forces. Rutskoi then appeared on a balcony of the White House, haranguing the crowd below, urging it to overthrow Yeltsin. The rebels assaulted the mayor's office and the television studio. They captured the former, but at the studio, troops turned them back in a hail of gunfire, which resulted in 65 deaths.

Yeltsin's government hung in the balance as chaos broke loose. His supporters entered the streets, while government troops surrounded the White House. On 5 October, amid street fighting, tanks fired on the White House, setting it afire. The rebels, including Rutskoi, surrendered. Later that day, Yeltsin issued orders banning conservative newspapers and dismissing officials who had opposed his military assault on the White House. He scheduled elections to a parliament, along with a referendum on a new constitution. In December, Yeltsin scored a victory in getting the constitution approved, but the results in the parliamentary elections were mixed: While those supporting him did well, so, too, did nationalist extremists led by Vladimir Zhirinovsky.

Yeltsin succeeded in getting economic assistance for his embattled nation from the West, including the United States. Yet the aid was minimal and conditioned on Russia proceeding with additional reforms toward a free market. Although Yeltsin made some economic progress, a poor infrastructure, high unemployment, and massive farmland and water pollution engendered by the old Communist system continued to plague the nation.

Yeltsin still has to deal with continued discontent among ethnic groups within Russia, groups that threaten to follow the former Soviet republics and secede from the national government. In 1994, he sent Russian troops into Chechnya after that area unilaterally declared its independence. A storm of criticism greeted the move, as many liberal democrats in Russia considered it military adventurism that could result in Yeltsin becoming a dictator. In any event, Chechens vowed to fight the invasion, while Yeltsin insisted the rebellion had to be crushed to keep ethnic groups from seceding. He also recognized Chechnya's economic importance with its oil fields and pipelines. After enormously bloody fighting, the Russian army gained the advantage in Cechnya.

Yeltsin faces a presidential election in 1996 with his popularity plummeting. As a revolutionary, he has created a new nation, but it is uncertain whether he can provide the long-term prosperity and stability essential to creating a democratic Russia and breaking with the autoctatic past imposed not just by the Communists, but much earlier by IVAN III, PETER I, and CATHERINE II.

Reference: Smith, Hedrick, *The New Russians,* 1990.

Yoshida Shigeru
(1878–1967)
Japan

Yoshida Shigeru's falling out with Japan's leadership as World War II unfolded served him well. Untainted by the wartime government, he was able to emerge as a leader and rebuilder of Japan after the conflict.

Yoshida Shigeru was born on 22 September 1878 in Tokyo. Although the son of a prominent politician, he was adopted by a wealthy businessman who wanted him to carry on his silk enterprise. Yoshida graduated from Tokyo Imperial University and, in 1906, from the Law College. That same year, he married the daughter of a count, who served as the emperor's close advisor. This union helped his career immensely, and he entered the diplomatic service, where from 1908 to 1916 he held consular posts in China, Manchuria (where Japan gained railway and mining rights after the Russo-Japanese War of 1904–1905), Italy, and Britain.

In 1919, after service as second secretary to the Japanese embassy in Washington, D.C., Yoshida represented this new powerful Japan at the Paris Peace Conference ending World War I. From 1919 to 1922 he served as first secretary to the embassy in London, followed by appointments in China and Manchuria. In 1928, he was appointed minister to Sweden, Norway, and Denmark, and Premier Giichi Tanaka named him vice-minister of foreign affairs.

By the 1930s, the army had gained enormous power (often at odds with the civilian leadership), and in 1936 it rejected Yoshida's appointment as foreign minister, partly because of his criticism of militarists. Yoshida then served as ambassador to Britain but retired from this post in 1939 and left politics to concentrate on his business interests. In June 1945, as Japan faced certain defeat in World War II, the government imprisoned him after he pressed for the nation to surrender to the United States. He remained in jail until the Allied Occupation began in September. Later that year, the new Japanese government appointed him foreign minister. In 1946, he headed the Liberal Party after the Occupation forces prohibited the previous leader from assuming the prime ministry because of his role in the war. Yoshida became prime minister on 22 May 1946, supported by a Liberal Party–Progressive Party coalition representing Japan's more conservative interests, and except for two brief interruptions, he held the post until 1954.

Yoshida took a strong anti-Communist stand, which the United States found desirable since Communists were gaining power in the labor unions. As a man who preferred force and elitism, he purged all Communists from government offices and government corporations and developed a strong personal following in the national assembly, or Diet, which allowed him to rule autocratically. He oversaw an economic resurgence boosted by American aid, negotiated the peace treaty with the United States in 1951, and signed a security pact with America that protected Japan from the Soviet Union. The United States ended its occupation of Japan in 1952. After this, Yoshida enacted more restrictive legislation, including a subversive activities prevention act aimed at the Communists and an act to regulate ideas being communicated in the schools. Under American pressure to rearm, he created a defense force, a move he insisted did not entail giving in to the United States.

Yoshida lost his hold on the Liberal Party leadership in 1954 when factions opposed to his autocratic ways gained the ascendancy. This ended his prime ministry. He subsequently retired from politics, although he remained an influential advisor to the government. He died on 20 October 1967 at his seaside estate located in Osio. Autocratic and often grandiose in his views about himself, he nevertheless led Japan through its difficult postwar adjustment into a more democratic era and thus added to the modernization process begun under ITO HIROBUMI and the Emperor MEIJI.

References: Hellmann, Donald C., *Japanese Foreign Policy and Domestic Politics,* 1969; Yoshida Shigeru, *The Yoshida Memoirs,* 1962.

Zaghlul, Saad
(1859–1927)
Egypt

As a young man at Azhar University, Saad Zaghlul thought about the increasing European influences in Egypt and the sorry state of Egyptian institutions. As a student of Islam, he recoiled at Western accusations that his religion resisted progress. Zaghlul believed in Islam's rational and progressive qualities as well as its moral superiority, and he adopted a reformism and nationalism that helped change Egypt's history.

In 1859, Saad Zaghlul was born in Ibyana, a village on the Egyptian Delta, into a family of modest means. His homeland had not known complete independence for many years, and amid this situation he was influenced by the philosophy of Jamal al-Din al-Afghani that called for a Muslim country to arouse itself, unite the Islamic community, and emulate the more "civilized" nations of the West. Years of submission and apathy, al-Afghani believed, had to be discarded. Zaghlul also absorbed the ideas of Mohammed Abdu, who, less revolutionary than al-Afghani, called for a gradual educating of society in gaining independence from Western domination.

Imbued with these thoughts, Zaghlul became assistant editor of the *Official Journal,* one of several newspapers attached to the Islamic reform movement. In 1882, British forces invaded Egypt and ended the infamous Arabi revolt, and they arrested many of Egypt's reformers, including Zaghlul. Seventy years of British control had begun.

Shortly after his release from prison, Zaghlul became a lawyer and developed links with a wide variety of Egyptian nationalists, both Islamic and secular, whose ideology reflected liberal European nationalism. He continued striving for the reform of Egyptian institutions. He also married the daughter of Egypt's prime minister and established contacts with the British rulers. Zaghlul received numerous appointments within the Egyptian government, including minister of education (1906–1908) and minister of justice (1910–1912). In these positions he proved to be a moderate reformer who steered a middle course between Egyptian nationalists and British occupiers and adopted Abdu's strategy of gradually educating the masses for freedom.

Meanwhile, extremists in the Egyptian nationalist movement organized the National Party in 1907 and demanded an immediate end to British rule. They supported boycotts and public demonstrations; a few even advocated assassinations. Zaghlul rejected these approaches. Yet in 1913 he resigned from the cabinet, disgusted with British support of the ruling Khedive, who had become corrupt. With World War I, his nationalism, along with that of many Egyptians, took on a new urgency and new directions. The ideology of American president Woodrow Wilson proved an enormous influence. Wilson's call for national self-determination at the end of the war stirred Egyptian desires for independence.

Late in 1918, Zaghlul led a group of Egyptians in presenting the British high commissioner with demands. He wanted press censorship ended and the British to support eventual independence. He was willing at this time to allow the continued presence of British forces in the Suez Canal Zone and the appointment of a British financial advisor. Yet Britain rejected his demands. When Zaghlul remained adamant, the British exiled him and three of his colleagues to Malta.

This ignited a rebellion in 1919 that spread from Egypt's cities into the countryside, areas already reeling from rampant inflation. Urban agitators apparently coordinated the peasantry, and the violence mounted against an Egyptian government that had been under the thumb of British rulers. Rebels destroyed railroad lines and attacked government officials.

Meanwhile, Zaghlul obtained his release from Malta and presented his demands to the postwar Peace Conference in Paris. A bitter rejection occurred, however, when the United States backed Britain. In Egypt, Zaghlul's prestige and following grew enormously, he become a hero of the masses, and he continued his agitation. The British deported him again in 1921, this time to the Seychelles. Upon his return in 1923, he helped transform the delegation he had led into a political party, the Wafd.

Although Britain declared Egypt independent in 1922, the Wafd and most Egyptians remained dissatisfied. The independence proved nominal. Britain still controlled four important areas: communications, defense, foreign interests, and the Sudan. Furthermore, a monarch headed the government under a constitution formulated in 1923, and this feature antagonized modernists such as Zaghlul.

The Wafd party won 188 seats out of 215 in Parliament, and in January 1924 Zaghlul became prime minister. This put him in the peculiar position of maintaining law and order while working, as head of the Wafd, for the removal of British troops and advisors. His efforts reached the point of inviting violence, although he openly condemned the assassination in 1924 of a high British official.

Zaghlul fought against the autocratic tendencies of the king and championed more authority for the cabinet and Parliament. His continuing fight for full Egyptian independence caused him to resign as prime minister rather than accept additional British demands. After his death in 1927, the Wafd party grew increasingly conservative and unpopular with the Egyptian masses. For many in Egypt, full independence remained an important goal, but linked with social reform that would alleviate the plight of the working class and the peasants. That the Wafd party did not attack the privileged position of leading industrial capitalists or advocate land redistribution angered reformers. The end of British occupation and the change of Egypt's political and economic structure would await the revolution of 1952 led by GAMAL ABDEL NASSER.

References: Ahmed, Jamal M., *The Intellectual Origins of Egyptian Nationalism*, 1960; Hourani, Albert H., *Arabic Thought in the Liberal Age, 1798–1939*, 1962.

Zapata, Emiliano
(1879–1919)
Mexico

According to legend, Emiliano Zapata, a tenant farmer in Morelos State, began his revolutionary crusade after he noticed the discrepancy between the decrepit housing in which he lived and the luxurious stables maintained for his master's horses. Wearing a sombrero, his face adorned by a drooping black mustache, Zapata rallied the peasants and emerged as a charismatic revolutionary hero.

Emiliano Zapata was born on 8 August 1879 in Anenecuilco to poor mestizo parents (persons of Spanish and indigenous Indian blood). In his youth, he worked as a tenant farmer on a sugar plantation and witnessed the injustice of wealthy landowners—those who had large estates, or haciendas—continuously expanding their holdings by confiscating peasant land. Zapata refused to stand for this and organized the peasants in his village to protest, which resulted in his arrest. After his imprisonment, Zapata served briefly in the army and then trained horses for a wealthy landowner. In 1909, he led a group of peasants in another protest: They forcibly occupied land recently claimed by an owner of a hacienda.

By this time, Mexico had reached a crisis. Since the late colonial period, with the revolutionary uprising led by JOSÉ MARIA MORELOS, and continuing through the independence years of AUGUSTÍN DE ITURBIDE and BENITO JUÁREZ, the nation had been in almost constant turmoil. In particular, the economic gulf between a wealthy few and the impoverished masses produced great tension. This situation resulted in the 1910 Revolution, characterized by disjointed rebellions that shook the countryside. That year, one of the rebels, FRANCISCO MADERO, overthrew the dictatorship of Porfirio Díaz. In the fight between Madero and Díaz, Zapata raised an army to support Madero, a moderate democratic reformer.

Madero, however, soon disappointed Zapata.

When the mustachioed rebel demanded that Madero arrange for land to be returned to the peasants, the incoming president refused and insisted that Zapata and his followers lay down their arms. Zapata considered doing this, but decided against it after Madero's army attacked his men.

Thus Zapata continued fighting—attacking haciendas and government officials and building a larger following among the peasants. In 1911, he issued the *Plan of Ayala* that called for Madero's overthrow and promised democracy and a redistribution of land. Two years later, Madero's regime collapsed, partly because of the disorder promoted by Zapata and other rebel leaders, each fighting their own battles—men such as Pancho Villa and Victoriano Huerta.

In February 1913, Huerta captured the presidency and established a dictatorship. A conservative, he had no desire to redistribute land or establish democracy, and the United States intervened by supporting his overthrow. Zapata now fought Huerta and gained control of the area south of Mexico City. In the territory he ruled, he confiscated the haciendas, redistributed land to the poor, and established an organization to provide the farmers with credit; observers who traveled through the area noted that the peasants worshipped Zapata and that order prevailed. Zapata's military tactics confounded his opponents: He used guerrilla warfare, and oftentimes the peaceful-looking peasant farmers became, at an instant's notice, rifle-wielding fighters.

In July 1914, Huerta's government fell, and Venustiano Carranza became Mexico's ruler. He refused to adopt Zapata's agrarian reform and found himself battling both Zapata, in the south, and Pancho Villa, in the north. In November, representatives of Carranza, Villa, and Zapata met in Aguascalientes, trying but failing to reach an agreement. Carranza soon fled Mexico City for Veracruz, and Villa and Zapata alternately occupied the capital. While turmoil prevailed, Zapata's peasant followers did not loot the city but instead solicited food.

As Villa gained the advantage in the fighting, Zapata agreed late in 1914 to cooperate with him. Carranza's generals, however, developed superb battlefield tactics, and the dictator developed reform programs that appealed to the disadvantaged, issuing decrees that gave them unused lands owned by the national government and that protected industrial workers. By the spring of 1915, Carranza had put both Villa and Zapata on the defensive.

In late 1916, Carranza oversaw a constitutional convention—closed to Villa and Zapata. The Constitution of 1917 was a radical document that gave the government the right to restrict private property in order to more equitably distribute the nation's wealth; it also outlawed child labor and stipulated the eight-hour work day. Although Car-

ranza did not personally care about these provisions other than as a means to consolidate his power, the 1917 constitution appealed to many reformers and deflated Zapata's revolutionary movement.

On 10 April 1919, Colonel Jesús Guajardo arranged a meeting with Zapata and then ambushed and killed him. Thus ended Zapata's revolutionary campaign, one that raised social issues to prominent heights and pressured Carranza into radical reforms that reshaped Mexico and would continue under LÁZARO CÁRDENAS. Mexicans remember Zapata as a revolutionary hero—his influence so great that in 1994 a sizable revolutionary movement in Chiapas State called itself "the Zapatistas."

References: Parkinson, Roger, *Zapata*, 1975; Womack, John, *Zapata and the Mexican Revolution*, 1969.

Zayed bin Sultan al-Nuhayyan
(b. 1918?)
United Arab Emirates

As provincial governor, he held Abu Dhabi together; as emir, he created a new nation: the United Arab Emirates (UAE). For over four decades, Zayed bin Sultan al-Nuhayyan has been a powerful political force in the lower Persian Gulf.

Around 1918, Zayed bin Sultan al-Nuhayyan was born in Abu Dhabi, today the wealthiest and biggest of the emirates within the UAE, with 40 percent of the population and 90 percent of the territorial area. Zayed came from the Al Bu Falah, a subtribe within the larger Bani Yas tribe, and was raised in the rural interior, where he obtained a traditional Islamic education, reading and studying the Koran. He looked up to his grandfather as a role model: Zayed the Great had ruled from the mid-nineteenth century to the early twentieth century and made the Bani Yas the most powerful tribe in the lower gulf. Raised in tribal surroundings, young Zayed learned the attributes his society

prized: physical courage, generosity toward fellow Bedouins, and mediation in settling disputes.

In the mid-1940s, Zayed became governor of al-Ain Province, where he undertook substantial changes to counteract the policies of his incompetent predecessor. Al-Ain was important because its oasis provided water and agricultural goods, and its loss to Oman or Saudi Arabia, both of whom desired it, would mean the destruction of Abu Dhabi. Zayed quickly won the loyalty of the local tribes. He repaired the deteriorating irrigation system, constructed new water channels, and provided water pumps to those farmers who were willing to expand production. Furthermore, he worked to make sure no one person dominated the water rights. He also developed the province's education by building an elementary school.

Zayed gained greater prominence when, in 1966, he was elevated to emir of Abu Dhabi. This occurred after his family persuaded his older brother, who had proved too indecisive, to relinquish his rule. At this time, and indeed ever since the late nineteenth century, Abu Dhabi was under British control, and Zayed wanted to protect British oil interests in the area while gaining the benefit of Britain's help against any external threats.

Zayed firmly believed that educational and economic development would keep his people from adopting radical policies, such as those among the Marxists in nearby South Yemen, and prevent challenges to Abu Dhabi's traditional political structure. This belief, plus his desire to help his fellow Bedouin, led him to build schools and develop oil and trading facilities. Zayed saw stewardship as important and undertook a substantial environmental program, protecting wildlife and developing forests, hoping the latter would change his emirate's climate and reduce its aridity. He promoted recreational activities for his people, activities that he believed encouraged Arab culture, including camel and horse racing and falconry (in which he became such an avid participant that he wrote *Falconry as a Sport: Our Arab Heritage*).

When Britain announced in 1968 its intention to withdraw from the lower gulf, Zayed developed a nationalist position in a land that lacked such. He insisted that his region could protect itself only through a federation that would bring Abu Dhabi together with the nearby emirates. For years he had been at odds with RASHID BIN SAID AL-MAKTUM, who came from a competing family and ruled Dubai, adjacent to Abu Dhabi. Zayed, however, took the lead in opening discussions with Rashid, and in late 1971, Abu Dhabi, Dubai, and several other emirates formed the UAE. Even though Abu Dhabi had the advantage in size and wealth, Zayed agreed to grant Dubai an equal status in the federation with his emirate and also committed himself to using Abu Dhabi's oil income to provide most of the funding for the UAE.

Zayed served as president of the UAE and Rashid as vice-president and prime minister. Zayed strongly supported Arab causes and directed money to the West Bank and to Palestinians in the Gaza. He tried to mediate the Iran-Iraq war and in the 1980s served as spokesman for the Gulf Cooperation Council in that effort. Zayed's prestige suffered a blow in 1991 when investigations revealed fraudulent activities by the Bank of Credit and Commerce International, 70 percent of whose stock was owned by him. It soon became known that, since 1989, Zayed had funneled $1 billion into the bank to keep it afloat.

As UAE leader, Zayed favored a stronger federation with more centralized power. His nationalist desires conflicted with Rashid, who protected Dubai's autonomy and favored a weak federation. Even after Rashid's death in 1990, Dubai continued its intransigent position. Thus Zayed has been frustrated in his goal, but his standing as the foremost leader in founding the UAE and his moderate and generally enlightened policies have earned him considerable respect in the Arab world. He remains embroiled in a dispute with Iran over control of three small islands in the Strait of Hormuz amid indications the Iranians intend to militarize them and threaten the nearby oil-shipping lanes.

References: Abdullah, Mohammed Morsy, *The United Arab Emirates: A Modern History*, 1978; Peck, Malcolm C., *The United Arab Emirates: A Venture in Unity*, 1986.

Zhelev, Zhelyu

(b. 1935)

Bulgaria

Zhelyu Zhelev became an early advocate of Bulgarian reform, and when he ascended to the presidency he joined a select group of other scholars-turned-political leaders in Eastern Europe.

Modern Bulgaria has had to reinvent its political system on several occasions. When Zhelyu Zhelev was born on 3 March 1935 in Vesselinovo to a poor farming family, his country was once again in turmoil. It had a progressive constitution under a limited monarchy, but suffered from numerous changes in governments. Then came World War II and more disruption, followed by Soviet occupation in 1945 and the installation of a Communist regime three years later.

Under Russian domination, Bulgaria developed a totalitarian system and allied itself closely with Soviet policies—perhaps more so than any other Eastern European country. As a young man, Zhelev at first followed the expected route and joined the Communist Party, but he soon rebelled against government oppression and experienced several encounters with the authorities. While pursuing a degree in philosophy at Sofia University, he participated in the 1956 student strike. Later that year, the government ended the "thaw" that had been allowed in academic and artistic pursuits and that it believed, had led to this disorder. As a result, Zhelev was prevented from defending his master's thesis because it contained criticism of Leninist thought. The government also dismissed him from the university and expelled him from the Communist Party.

Zhelev eventually obtained his master's degree, but not until 1974. Despite such persecution, he continued his protest. In 1982, his book *Fascism* was published, in which he criticized totalitarianism. The government immediately banned it. Amid this controversy, Zhelev studied for his doctorate, which he obtained in 1987.

By this time, the Soviet Union had begun to collapse, with important implications for Bulgaria and dissidents such as Zhelev. Within the nation discontent mounted, stirred by economic collapse and problems from industrial pollution. The Bulgarian Communist Party realized it could no longer count on Soviet backing and so tried to retain power by ousting its longtime leader and changing its name to the Bulgarian Socialist Party (BSP). This, however, placated few, and in 1988 Zhelev helped found the Club in Support of Openness and Reform.

One year later, Zhelev's group combined with other opposition groups to form the Union of Democratic Forces (UDF), and he became president of its Coordination Council. The BSP then agreed to an election for 1990, the first open one in more than 40 years. The BSP surprised many observers when it finished ahead of the UDF. Still, Zhelev was elected to the National Assembly and became president of the UDF in the legislature.

The government proved unstable as political factions vied for power, and the UDF refused to enter into a coalition. On 1 August, the National Assembly chose Zhelev to be president of the new Bulgarian Republic. Several months later, Dimitur Popov became prime minister in a coalition cabinet that prepared for new elections in 1991. Zhelev proved instrumental in bringing the various factions together to form this arrangement and save the political system.

The National Assembly adopted a constitution on 12 July 1991, and on 13 October Zhelev issued a decree for the legislative elections. The UDF won a majority, and on 19 January 1992, Zhelev won the first direct election for president.

In his new position, Zhelev favored reconciliation between non-Communists and former Communists and between the minority Turks and majority Bulgars. He also supported economic privatization and a free market. He met with Western officials to promote his nation's entrance into the European Community and gained associate status. In 1992, he pushed for more rapid decollectivization of landholdings while calling for privatization to proceed more cautiously. Zhelev had substantial authority over foreign affairs and improved Bulgaria's relations with Greece and Turkey.

Later in 1992, Zhelev survived a no-confidence measure passed by his opponents in the National Assembly. He continues to follow a cautious path between economic privatization and political stability.

References: Curtis, Glenn, *Bulgaria: A Country Study*, 1993; Kaplan, Robert D., *Balkan Ghosts: A Journey through History*, 1993.

Country Profiles

AFGHANISTAN

This nation is noted for its many independent tribes and its often fractured politics. Nevertheless, there have been important periods of unity. In the sixth century B.C., the Achaemenids governed southern Iran and extended their control into Afghanistan's Kabul Valley. Alexander the Great overcame them in 330 B.C. and brought with him Greek culture. After a Buddhist period, Islam swept across the region in the seventh century A.D., and shortly after A.D. 700 came an Arab conquest. Many years later, in 1219, Mongols under Genghis Khan invaded the region and caused massive destruction.

An Afghan state free of foreign control did not arise until 1747, when the various tribes began uniting under the renowned leader Ahmad Khan Sadozai. He created an empire that in the 1760s stretched from central Asia to Delhi and from Kashmir to the Arabian Sea. But soon after his death in 1772, Afghanistan weakened and became part of the "Great Game"—attempts by Britain and Russia to control the area. The First Anglo-Afghan War produced a British-installed ruler in 1839. British troops reentered Afghanistan in 1878 to prevent the country from developing a close relationship with Russia, and their success in this Second Anglo-Afghan War led to Abdur Rhaman Khan obtaining the throne. He accepted British control of foreign policy and other restrictions imposed on him, while at the same time launching reforms to modernize and unify Afghanistan. An independent modern state free of British control emerged under AMANULLAH KHAN.

ALBANIA

Albanian nationalism arose after the Russo-Turkish War of 1877–1878 that greatly weakened the Ottoman Empire in the Balkans. Albanians organized to protect their land from other nations partitioning it. Abdyl Frasheri emerged as the leading nationalist and in 1878 helped establish the Prizen League to levy taxes, raise an army, and win Albanian freedom. Some League members wanted autonomy within the Ottoman Empire; others desired complete independence. Frasheri represented the latter group.

After the European powers began carving up Albania, the Albanians waged war, only to lose when the Turks, pressured by the European nations, crushed the uprising, arrested Frasheri, imprisoned him, and then, in 1885, exiled him. He died in 1892. Albanians

rebelled again in 1912 and declared their country independent. One year later, the European powers agreed to recognize Albania's nationhood under their protection.

The arrangement resulted in considerable outside interference, and it was not until after World War I that Albania gained real independence with a stable government—and this only after the United States intervened at the Paris Peace Conference to prevent the nation from being partitioned. Ahmed Zogu proclaimed himself president in 1925 and three years later declared himself King Zog I. In 1939, Italy annexed Albania and ended his reign. Albania threw off the foreign rulers in 1944, when the Marxists under Enver Hoxha came to power. After Hoxha's death in 1985, the communist government collapsed, and a new Albania emerged under a revolutionary movement led by SALI BERISHA.

ALGERIA

This country has a long history of foreign occupation and domination. Once part of the Roman Empire, Vandals conquered it in A.D. 430. Later, Algeria was integrated into the Eastern Roman Empire and, after that, the Ottoman Empire. The French occupied Algiers in 1830 but did not secure the inland areas until the 1840s. In 1845, the French appointed a governor-general in a move to make Algeria their central base for expansion in North Africa. European immigration soon became substantial and most economic development favored the European community. A nationalist revolt against French rule occurred in the 1950s and soon produced a strong and controversial leader who led Algeria to independence: AHMED BEN BELLA.

ANGOLA

Evidence exists of a hunter-gatherer culture in Angola that dates back to the late Stone Age. A migration of Bantu-speaking peoples from the Cameroon-Nigeria area began about A.D. 500. The Kongo Kingdom emerged on the Angola-Zaire border in the mid-fourteenth century and became the most powerful kingdom in west-central Africa, with its capital located within Angola at Mbanza Kongo. Southeast of the Kongo, the Ndongo people established a monarchy referred to as *ngola a kiluanje,* from which the Portuguese adopted the name Angola. In the late sixteenth century, a third kingdom emerged in the upper Kasai River, the Lunda.

When the Portuguese arrived in 1483, they began an extensive slave trade between Angola and Brazil. In the nineteenth century, they developed coffee plantations and a system of forced labor. Furthermore, laws passed in 1929 restricted persons of mixed European and African blood to low-level positions in the civil service and established discriminatory pay scales that favored whites. After World War II, Portugal remained unresponsive to African liberation movements, but Angolans took note of the uprisings occurring elsewhere on their continent. When nationalism emerged, it did so within a fractured atmosphere of competing liberation groups that included the Popular Movement for the Liberation of Angola led by AGOSTINHO NETO, a poet who adopted a Marxist ideology. Upon independence on 11 November 1976, he became Angola's first president.

ANTIGUA AND BARBUDA

Christopher Columbus made the European discovery of Antigua in 1463, and Britain colonized the island in the early seventeenth century. The British developed a sugar economy with slaves from Africa working large plantations. Barbuda, dominated by one British family, was used as a site for breeding slaves. Britain did not annex Barbuda until 1860, several decades after Parliament had abolished slavery throughout the colonies. In 1967, Antigua gained internal self-government. Independence came on 1 November 1981, supported hesitantly by VERE CORNWALL BIRD, the nation's first prime minister. Many Barbudans objected to their union with Antigua and preferred separation.

ARGENTINA

Europeans first encountered this country of grass pampas and temperate climate in 1516 when Juan Díaz de Solís planted the Spanish flag at the Río de la Plata. Other explorers soon followed, including Ferdinand Magellan in 1521 and Sebastian Cabot in 1527. Pedro de Mendoza established Buenos Aires in 1536, although it was largely abandoned the following year in favor of Asuncíon.

For much of its colonial era, Argentina remained a backwater within the Spanish Empire. Spain's interest in the area increased only after Portuguese Brazil threatened its security. In 1776, the crown created the Viceroyalty of the Río de la Plata with its center at Buenos Aires. In 1810, shortly after Napoleon conquered Spain, revolutionaries in Buenos Aires deposed the viceroy and established a ruling junta. Led by MANUEL BELGRANO, MARIANO MORENO, and BERNARDINO RIVADAVIA, the rebels professed loyalty to the king but in practice established an autonomous government.

Complete independence was not declared until 1816, after JOSÉ DE SAN MARTÍN moved to the forefront of the revolution. Numerous disputes between Buenos Aires and the outlying provinces prevented national unity until the 1880s. Through the succeeding years, Argentine politics displayed a pattern of instability and military intervention. Notorious dictators ruled the nation, including Juan Manuel de Rosas in the mid-nineteenth century and Juan Perón some hundred years later.

ARMENIA

From 95 to 55 B.C., a kingdom emerged in Armenia under Tigran the Great and encompassed the area from the Caspian to the Mediterranean, and from the Caucuses to Palestine. The Roman Empire eventually absorbed the kingdom, and Armenians succumbed to foreign domination for many centuries. In the late sixteenth century A.D., the Ottoman Turks conquered Armenia and divided it with Persia. Much of Armenia fell to Russian control in the early 1800s, and a nationalist movement against the occupiers emerged shortly after 1900. In 1920, the Bolshevik government in Moscow took control, and Armenia became a part of the Soviet Union. Independence came with the demise of the Soviet state in 1991, and LEVON TER-PETROSYAN guided Armenia to its nationhood.

AUSTRALIA

In the seventeenth century, the Dutch, Portuguese, and Spanish all sighted this vast and largely arid land. In 1770, Captain James Cook sailed along the east coast and claimed the area for Britain. The first Britons, an assortment of soldiers, settlers, and, most numerously, convicts, arrived at Port Jackson (present-day Sydney) in 1788. Until 1839, Britain used the colony as a resettlement point for its prisoners. By 1860, the settlers had established six colonies: New South Wales, Tasmania, Western Australia, South Australia, Victoria, and Queensland. In the 1870s and 1880s, three prominent leaders—James Service, Henry Parkes, and Samuel Walker Griffith—promoted a federation. This, however, did not reach fruition until 1901 when the colonies united into the Commonwealth of Australia under the leadership of EDMUND BARTON.

AUSTRIA

In the sixth century, Germanic tribes raided this mountainous land, which was not united until Charlemagne spread his rule two centuries later and brought Bavaria into his Frankish kingdom. His empire, though, disintegrated in the next century, and the raids began anew. In 955, Otto I restored order by defeating the Magyars and is considered by Austrians to be the initial founder of their country. The Habsburgs began their long dynastic rule of Austria in 1273, expanding and losing lands over the years. For decades, Austria functioned not as an integrated nation but as a dynastic preserve; however, in the late 1600s, Leopold I did throw off Turkish and French domination to create a substantial European power. Still, later in his reign he had less concern for the Empire and more for the Habsburg lands. Indeed, the Habsburgs often strove to keep their states apart in order to protect their right to dispose of their properties as they wished.

The greatest early unification, albeit incomplete, occurred in the eighteenth century under MARIA THERESA, who established the Austrian Empire with her absolutist monarchy; her son, JOSEPH II, built a centralized administration. In 1867, the empire of Austria and the kingdom of Hungary were joined together under Francis Joseph I, but World War I resulted in their separation and left Austria in ruins. Austria became a republic in 1918 with KARL RENNER leading its development and forming the first government. He reestablished the republic after World War II.

AZERBAIJAN

Located in the Caucuses and adjacent to the Caspian Sea, Azerbaijan was conquered by Persians in the sixth century B.C. In the seventh century A.D., Muslims brought their religion into the area. Under the influence of various Turkmen clans, Azerbaijan developed a Turkish culture. Russian domination began in the early 1800s with the acquisition of Kazakh and Shamshadil. After the Bolshevik Revolution, the Soviet Union incorporated Azerbaijan in 1922 as a socialist republic. The country did not gain its independence until 1991, when the Soviet Union collapsed. HEYDAR ALIYEV changed quickly from supporting the Soviet Communist system to leading a nationalist movement.

BAHAMAS

This island chain is most famous in Western history as the site of Christopher Columbus's initial landfall in the Americas. Here he applied the name "Indian" to the indigenous people who greeted him. By 1550, the Spaniards destroyed the Arawak Indian society, its population reduced from about 300,000 to less than 500. British settlers arrived in 1647, and in the eighteenth century the islands became a haven for pirates who plied the Caribbean. In the early 1700s, Britain declared the Bahamas an official Crown colony, and a small white elite monopolized political and economic power. The Bahamas gained internal self-government in the 1960s and then moved toward independence and social reform under the leadership of LYNDON OSCAR PINDLING.

BAHRAIN

This small nation, consisting of several islands in the Persian Gulf, has been the scene of commerce for centuries. Trade from the Middle East passed through Bahrain shortly after 3000 B.C., and around 2000 B.C. the area reached its peak as an economic and military power. Bahrain had a reputation as a source for pearls, and the ancient Greeks and Romans, who called this area Tylos, traded for these. The Portuguese arrived in 1521 and occupied the islands until 1602. Bahrain then came under Persian influence until the British began extending their power into the Persian Gulf in 1820. Britain developed a protectorate over Bahrain in the nineteenth century, a status, which in the ensuing decades relegated the rulers, or emirs, to ceremonial roles. The discovery of oil occurred in the 1930s and enriched both Bahrain and Britain. ISA BIN SULMAN AL-KHALIFAH, who became emir in 1961, led Bahrain to independence in 1971.

BANGLADESH

This nation encompasses much of Bengal and is dominated geographically by two great rivers, the Ganges and the Brahmaputra. About A.D. 1200, Muslim invaders overthrew the existing rulers, and Islam soon gained a widespread following.

A Muslim dynasty ruled East Bengal from the sixteenth into the eighteenth centuries. Its decline facilitated the entry of Britain in the mid-1700s. Although the British left most of the daily administration to the landed nobility, they minimized Indian influence in the colonial government and established a racist system whereby Indians were treated as inferior. Furthermore, they encouraged Muslim-Hindu antagonisms toward each other in a divide-and-rule strategy.

In reaction to these conditions, some upper-class Indians, mostly Hindu lawyers, organized the Indian National Congress Party in 1885. Congress, as it was called, sought more autonomy for Indians, particularly through the Indianization of the government bureaucracy, and civil rights, such as freedom of the press and a greater use of juries. In 1906, some Muslims formed the All-India Muslim League that expressed loyalty to the Crown while calling for the advancement of Muslim political rights. In 1905, Britain divided Bengal Province in two, creating West Bengal and East Bengal. When Pakistan gained its independence from Britain in 1947, its eastern portion encompassed most of East Bengal. Bengalis soon realized that the Pakistani government would be dominated by West Pakistanis, or Punjabis. MUJIBUR RAHMAN subsequently emerged as the leader of a Bengali independence movement that resulted in the formation of Bangladesh.

BARBADOS

This most easterly island in the West Indies gained its independence from Britain in 1966. Back in the fourth century A.D., Amerindians inhabited Barbados, probably migrating from the Orinoco River basin in

South America. They engaged in farming and fishing. Other Amerindians arrived later, including those the Spanish referred to as Arawaks. This civilization fell prey to Spanish slave raids in the early 1500s, and when English colonists arrived in 1627 they found no indigenous population. They transformed the island by developing sugar plantations and importing large numbers of slaves from Africa. Slavery was abolished in 1834, but Barbadian society was still dominated by white plantation owners. Challenges to the political status quo emerged most strongly after World War II, and in the 1950s ERROL BARROW created a reform and nationalist political party that led the drive toward nationhood.

BELARUS

Known in English as "White Russia," this land sits astride a major Baltic-Mediterranean trade route. In the ninth century, it was part of the Kievan Rus state, but 500 years later the Lithuanian Empire controlled it. In the late eighteenth century, Belarus was annexed by the Russian Empire. Rule by the Soviet Union began in 1922 and proved harsh: The Communists forcibly collectivized agriculture and crushed Belorussian cultural practices. In the mid-1980s, nationalism, long expressed by dissidents, spread in the republic at the same time as a reform movment arose in the Soviet Union. When the Soviet government began unravelling in 1991, Belarus declared its independence, spearheaded by the Belarussian Popular Front and supported by the nation's first president, STANISLAU SHUSHKEVICH.

BELGIUM

From 57 B.C. until A.D. 431, the Romans ruled Gaul, which included present-day Belgium. Germanic tribes then penetrated and left a lasting effect: They introduced a language that evolved into Dutch and conflicted with the Latin that evolved into French, hence dividing Belgian society between Dutch-speaking Flemings and French-speaking Walloons. An important era of unity occurred in the Burgundian period from 1384 to 1555, when the dukes of Burgundy united the Lowlands (including Belgium and the Netherlands), and a Golden Age blossomed with substantial economic and cultural development. Periods of foreign domination followed under Spanish, Austrian, French, and Dutch rule. Unification and independence as a modern Belgian nation did not occur until 1830, when Catholics and Liberals under CHARLES LATOUR RO-GIER joined to end Dutch domination.

BELIZE

Mayan Indians occupied Belize long before Europeans arrived. Although the Spanish penetrated the area in the 1500s and 1600s, Britain established a foothold in the late 1700s. In 1798, Belize, which Britain designated a settlement, functioned in all but name as a colony. Beginning in the 1820s, Guatemala challenged British authority and claimed the territory to be its own. Despite this, in 1862 Britain made this land a Crown dependency and shortly thereafter an official colony, calling it British Honduras and guaranteeing its protection. After World War II an independence movement emerged; nationhood, however, came gradually under GEORGE CADLE PRICE, whose careful leadership avoided bloodshed. In 1981, Belize was granted status as an independent nation within the British Commonwealth.

BENIN

This small land, a narrow configuration that stretches from the Gulf of Guinea to the Niger River, has long exhibited a sectional cleavage. Benin contains 46 ethnic groups, with the Bariba most prominent in the North and long isolated from the south. In the nineteenth century, they organized into the Nikki Kingdom, a powerful state. In the south, the Dahomey Kingdom prevailed for hundreds of years and in 1727 gained important access to slave trafficking. The Portuguese arrived in the 1500s as traders. France conquered the area in the late 1800s after expanding outward from Porto Novo. In 1902, Dahomey, as France called this land, became a part of French West Africa. Dahomey's strong ties to French culture and its sectional and ethnic differences influenced development in two important ways: Independence proceeded after World War II along a confusing course of shifting political coalitions, and no one person emerged as a dominant founder. Nevertheless, SOUROU-MIGAN APITHY and HUBERT MAGA shaped Dahomey's move toward independence (gained on 4 December 1960) and its early years of nationhood. Political stability came only with the revolution of 1972 that also resulted in a new name for the nation: Benin.

BHUTAN

Unlike other nations in South Asia, Bhutan does not have a substantial Indian population; rather, its immigrant groups come primarily from Tibet. For centuries, this land of towering mountains and magnificent valleys purposefully isolated itself from outside influences. Prior to unification in the seventeenth century, Bhutan consisted of competing kingdoms closely tied to various Buddhist schools. Consolidation into a single state came in the seventeenth century under NGAWANG NAMGYEL. In modern times, two prominent rulers emerged: Jigme Wangchuck, who reigned from 1926 to 1952 and built many schools, and Jigme Dorji Wangchuck, who reigned from 1952 to 1972 and began a legislature that moved Bhutan toward a constitutional monarchy. He also abolished slavery and serfdom.

BOLIVIA

In its pre-Colombian period, this country, where mountains soar above 14,000 feet, was part of a great Andean Empire. For reasons unclear, it collapsed around A.D. 1200, and by the early 1400s the Quechua, who became known as the Incas, emerged as the most powerful group. They, however, failed to conquer the Indians of the lowlands, an area that constitutes Bolivia's eastern two-thirds. In 1532, the Spaniards arrived under Francisco Pizarro and quickly conquered the Incas. Indian rebellions continued for years, but Spain solidified its hold on this area, which they called Upper Peru. The struggle for independence began after Napoleon invaded Spain in 1807 and disrupted the Empire. The liberation of Upper Peru occurred under SIMÓN BOLÍVAR, who led the effort to end Spanish rule throughout South America. Bolívar's military success in Upper Peru was acutally the work of his great general, ANTONIO JOSÉ DE SUCRE who guided the region to its independent status and became its first president.

BOSNIA-HERZEGOVINA

This mountainous region on the Balkan Peninsula was settled in the seventh century by Slavs. In the fifteenth century, the Ottoman Turks gained control, and many Bosnians adopted Islam. In 1908, the Austro-Hungarian Empire annexed Bosnia, but with the Empire's demise after World War I, the Bosnians joined the Kingdom of Serbs, Croats, and Slovenes, the predecessor to Yugoslavia, which under Josip Broz Tito emerged in the 1940s as a Communist state. Bosnia seceded from Yugoslavia in 1991 and its leader, ALIJA IZETBEGOVIĆ, tried to follow a moderate course in the region's ethnic rivalries. Under attack from Serbs, however, Bosnia's survival remains in doubt.

BOTSWANA

In 1801, the first European visitors arrived in Botswana, a land occupied by the Thalping people. The entire region soon suffered dislocation from the rise in the south of Zulu power. In the late nineteenth century, pressure increased from British and Boer (primarily Dutch) settlers. To offset the Boers, Britain established a protectorate over Botswana (then called Bechuanaland). After border adjustments, this area became a Crown colony in 1885 (later annexed to Cape Colony). In 1961, Britain allowed a representative assembly and three years later granted the colony full internal self-government. Independence followed in 1966 under SIR SERETSE KHAMA.

BRAZIL

Although European maps depicted the Brazilian coastline as early as 1436, Pedro Alavares Cabral, the first explorer from Portugal, did not reach this land until 1500. Colonization began in 1532, when convicts released from Portuguese prisons arrived as the first settlers. Brazil became a royal colony in 1549 and sugar emerged as the leading export, its production heavily dependent on African slave labor. Portuguese expansion met resistance from the Indians, but the light indigenous population and its decimation from European diseases meant the area did not experience substantial warfare.

When Napoleon conquered the Iberian Peninsula in the early nineteenth century, Portugal's king fled to Brazil. After he returned in 1820, he left his son in charge of the country as prince regent. The prince, in turn, declared Brazil independent in 1822 and became King PEDRO I. JOSE BONIFÁCIO emerged as an architect of the new state. Soon after Pedro I abdicated in 1831, his son ruled as PEDRO II, a popular monarch who stabilized the new nation by suppressing separatist rebellions. He, however, was unable to maintain the monarchy against liberalizing pressures, and in 1889 his government fell to a rebellion led by MANUEL DEODORO DA FONSECA, who established the First Republic. Brazil's government changed little after then, at times relying on military dictatorships, at other times displaying civilian control under elite direction. In 1946, the long and influential dictatorship of Getúlio Dornelles Vargas gave way to the Second Republic, which in 1964 succumbed to yet another military rebellion.

BRITAIN

See Great Britain.

BRUNEI

The Brunei sultanate traces its royal line back to the late fourteenth century, about the time Islam spread through the area. The kingdom fell to the Spanish in 1578, but they soon withdrew. After a civil war and attacks by pirates threatened to destroy the entire kingdom, the sultan turned to Britain for protection. In 1839, an Englishman, James Brooke, controlled most of Brunei as his own state. To counter Brooke's power, the sultan leased territory to Americans. Finally, in 1888, Brunei became a British protectorate under which a governor, or resident, exerted the most power. Britain provided military protection while handling Brunei's foreign relations. Signficantly, the British financed drilling and refining operations that expanded Brunei's oil wealth. Independence came in 1964, but only after Sultan HAJI HASSANAL BOLKIAH could no longer forestall the nationalist pressures Brunei's rulers had resisted for years.

BULGARIA

From the ninth to the fourteenth centuries, Bulgaria exerted considerable power in Eastern Europe, but after that time it was largely dominated by outside states. Beginning in the mid-1400s, the Ottoman Turks suppressed Bulgaria culturally and politically. An independence movement emerged in the nineteenth century, and in 1877 the Russians drove the Turks from the country. France and Britain, however, then contained Russian power by establishing Turkish oversight in the Balkans.

Bulgarians declared full independence in 1908, led by Prince Ferdinand of Saxe-Coburg-Gotha, but internal political fighting and the nation's defeat in World War I destabilized the government and failed to bring long-term unity. During World War II, Bulgaria allied with Hitler. Communist rule began in 1948 and lasted until 1989. By the latter year, dissident groups had gained a substantial following, and ZHELYU ZHELEV led the Union of Democratic Forces in ending a totalitarian regime and founding a truly independent nation.

BURKINA FASO

Beginning in the eleventh century, the Mossi people established domination over this land along the Volta Rivers. By the time the first Europeans arrived in the form of German explorer Heinrich Barth in 1853, Mossi rule had deteriorated. The French conquered the territory in 1896 by defeating the Mossi at Ouagadougou in 1896 and Bobo Dioulasso in 1897, although they did not consolidate their rule until 1916.

Formerly known as Upper Volta, Burkina Faso is a poor country, largely arid and subject to frequent droughts and encroachment by the surrounding deserts. The French first established the colony of Upper Senegal and Niger and then established a separate Upper Volta in 1919. It was disbanded, however, in 1932, becoming part of Sudan, Niger, and the Côte d'Ivoire (Ivory Coast). Partly because of Mossi pressure, the French reestablished Upper Volta as a separate territory after World War II. Independence came largely through the leadership of Catholic-educated Voltaics who, while striving for autonomy, resisted pressure to merge Upper Volta into a close union with neighboring lands. Prominent among these leaders was MAURICE YAMEOGO who became his nation's first president. A revolution in the 1980s changed Upper Volta's name to Burkina Faso.

BURMA

See Myanmar.

BURUNDI

This small nation, bordered by Lake Tanganyika in east-central Africa, has a history of sharp ethnic violence between Tutsis and Hutus, the origins of which date from before the fourteenth century when Tutsi herdsmen gradually conquered the Hutu farmers and little assimilation occurred between the two groups.

Thus when Burundi emerged as a state in the 1300s under the rule of a Tutsi mwami, or king, tremendous tension already existed. Euorpeans explored Burundi in the late nineteenth century, and Belgian rule began in 1916. The Belgians affected both the Hutus and the Tutsi: The Hutus had taxes extracted from them, and the Tutsi had many Western political practices imposed on them. In the 1950s, a nationalist movement appeared, one that had to resolve Tutsi and Hutu differences but failed to do so. Prince LOUIS RWAGASORE organized a nationalist political party, which in 1961 gained power. In 1966, MICHEL MICOMBERO ushered in a violent, convulsive era.

CAMBODIA

See Kampuchea.

CAMEROON

Long before recorded history, the West African coastal area that includes Cameroon became home for a people whose culture substantially influenced Africa's development. From this area came great migrations of people who spoke a language ancestral to the Bantu languages that now dominate most of sub-Saharan Africa. Migrations into or within Cameroon took place for centuries before Europeans arrived and continued into the nineteenth century. In 1472, Portuguese mariners appeared, providing the area its modern name of Cameroon, the Portuguese reference to prawns, a fish they found in the waterways (actually, a mistaken identification—they weren't prawns, but actually crayfish). Cameroon became a German protectorate in the late nineteenth century, but with World War I France and Britain gained control, with the former obtaining four-fifths of the territory and Britiain obtaining the remaining one-fifth bordering modern Nigeria. Reunification of Cameroon came under AHMADOU AHIDJO, who represented the moderate wing of Cameroonian nationalism and became his homeland's first president.

CANADA

Leif Eriksson was probably the first European to venture upon this vast country, landing at Labrador in the tenth century. Other explorers followed centuries later, some returning to Europe with stories of great splendor, others with tales of disappointment in trying to find a Northwest Passage to Asia. John Cabot, sailing for England, reached Newfoundland in 1497, but in 1534 Jacques Cartier claimed Canada for France. In 1604, France founded Port Royal in Nova Scotia, followed four years later by Québec. Colonization under France did not go well, hampered by limitations on land ownership. Yet more settlers did arrive, and the famed *coureurs de bois* traveled in their canoes far inland to trade with the Indians. The English began the Hudson's Bay Company that developed an interest in the fur trade, and in 1713, after a war, they obtained Newfoundland, Hudson's Bay, and Nova Scotia from France.

After the Seven Years' War, which lasted from 1756 to 1763, Britain controlled all but a few tiny islands. In the mid-nineteenth century, Canada did not exist as a single entity; the area was called British North America and it consisted of Upper Canada, Lower Canada, and the Maritime Provinces. Tension between English- and French-speaking settlers hampered unification, but in the 1860s several leaders from Ontario, Québec, and the Maritimes led the colonists in forming a unified nation called the Dominion of Canada. These "fathers of confederation" included GEORGE BROWN, GEORGE ÉTIENNE CARTIER, JOHN ALEXANDER MACDONALD, SAMUEL TILLEY, and CHARLES TUPPER.

CAPE VERDE

This archipelago, situated near the west coast of Africa, was uninhabited until the Portuguese arrived in 1462. Through the use of slaves imported from the African mainland, the Europeans developed a cotton economy. In the nineteenth century, a decline in the slave trade (outlawed in 1876) and a severe drought decimated the region. Since that time, the islanders have struggled to develop the area's potential. Nationalism against Portuguese rule grew after World War II, linked to developments in Guinea-Bissau. ARISTIDES PEREIRA helped found the leading anticolonial organization and led Cape Verde as his nation's first president.

CENTRAL AFRICAN REPUBLIC

Landlocked and remote, the Central African Republic, formerly Oubangui-Chari, has been an obscure country in the era of modern nation-states. Settled agricultural society probably began in this area 2,500 years ago. The migratory Aka, more popularly known as Pygmies, have inhabited the region for centuries. Muslim slave traders penetrated the northern reaches while expanding trans-Saharan commerce in the late 1700s. At the same time, Atlantic slavers influenced Oubangui-Chari as tribes preyed upon tribes in rounding up Africans for shipment to the Americas. The Bobangi tribe became prominent raiders, exchanging captives for European goods. Concurrently, Oubangui-Chari's remote regions served as hiding places for Africans from nearby lands fleeing the slave raiders closer to the coast.

France entered Oubangui-Chari in 1887 after having developed an interest in the area because of its proximity to the Upper Nile. In 1910, Oubangui-Chari was affixed to Gabon, Moyen-Congo, and Chad to form French Equatorial Africa. After French armies subdued much of Oubangui-Chari, the government allowed large concessionary companies enormous power; they virtually ruled the land. Although native protests erupted against French practices, nationalism developed slowly. BARTHELEMY BOGANDA strove for African rights while accepting continued allegiance to the French Community. Independence came in 1960 during the presidency of DAVID DACKO, who had not expected such a rapid grant of autonomy.

CHAD

In the eleventh century A.D., Chad was the scene of an important empire, Kanem, situated north of Lake Chad. In 1220, Kanem began expanding across much of present-day Chad, but within a hundred years it deteriorated and fell to outside invaders. In the sixteenth century, Muslims reconquered Kanem and united it with Bornu, located west of Lake Chad. This kingdom served as a major conduit in the transporting of slaves from the Nile Basin to North Africa. By the late 1800s, Kanem had collapsed into disorder. Not until the early 1800s did Europeans begin to explore Chad, and the French did not gain dominance in the country until 1900.

France showed little interest in Chad and administered it halfheartedly. In 1905, the French joined Chad with Oubangui-Chari, Moyen-Congo, and Gabon to form French Equatorial Africa, a curious entity of deserts and forests, Arabs and black Africans. Even then Chad received meager development funds, and French civil servants dreaded any assignment there. In 1920, Chad became a separate colony within French Equatorial Africa. France allowed a territorial legislature and political parties in the late 1940s and membership in a new French Community in 1958. Shortly thereafter, FRANÇOIS TOMBALBAYE became prime minister and presided over the gaining of full independence on 11 August 1960, at which time his controversial rule as president began.

CHILE

When the Spanish began their conquest of this region in the mid-1500s, they initiated 300 years of warfare that resulted in the enslavement and death of most Indians. Chile gained its independence from Spain in 1818, largely due to the efforts of JOSÉ DE SAN MARTÍN, an Argentinean, and BERNARDO O'HIGGINS. As a nation, Chile generally experienced democratic civilian governments dominated by a small economic and social elite that rejected radical changes. A major exception to this moderation occurred in 1970 when the Marxist Salvador Allende Gossens won election as president. Just three years later, however, the military killed him and dismantled most of his reforms. Civilian rule returned in 1990.

CHINA

This country has a vast and complex history. Some three thousand years ago, the Chinese occupied only portions of the Yellow River area, but they expanded outward and mingled with other cultures. The earliest dynasty was the Shang, which emerged in the second millennium B.C. Many others followed, often lasting centuries on end. European traders arrived in 1516, but until the nineteenth century the Chinese prohibited them from traveling inland; thus European culture initially had only minimal impact on China. By the late 1800s, however, European economic and technological penetration had overtaken a weakening Ch'ing Dynasty (which had emerged to rule China in 1644 under the Manchu invaders). Western domination became a reality, coupled with intrusions from Japan.

A drive to regain China's independence, dignity, and power accelerated in the twentieth century and splintered into competing groups, most prominently the leftist Communists and rightist Nationalists, who battled to determine the shape of a new China. Foremost among the leaders in the Nationalist movement was SUN YAT-SEN, considered the father of modern China; MAO TSE-TUNG built the Communist state and developed a Maoist ideology. Other prominent founders included CHIANG CH'ING, CHIANG KAI-SHEK, CHOU EN-LAI, LIN PIAO, and WANG CHING-WEI.

COLOMBIA

Long before the Europeans arrived, Indians from Central America migrated to Colombia. There, around 1200 B.C., they introduced agriculture and were followed by a second wave of settlers in 500 B.C. Near A.D. 1000, warlike Caribs emigrated from the Caribbean onto the coastal islands. By the 1500s, the Chibchas, or Muisca, developed an advanced culture along the plateaus and founded two large confederations. The Tairona, meanwhile, settled the Caribbean lowlands and the highlands of the Nevada de Santa Marta, where they organized towns connected by a sophisticated network of roads. The first Spanish explorers arrived in 1499 and 1500, and in 1510 the Europeans established a settlement on the Golfo de Urabá.

Colonial society emerged highly stratified with *peninsulares* at the top—persons of Spanish descent born in Spain—followed by Creoles, those of Spanish descent born in Colombia. (At the time, the area was called New Grenada, and it did not acquire the name Colombia until 1861.) Black African slaves and *zambos*—persons of mixed African and Indian heritage—stood at the bottom. Pressures between the *peninsulares* and Creoles stimulated nationalism and revolution in the early nineteenth century under the leadership of SIMÓN BOLÍVAR and FRANCISCO DE PAULA SANTANDER. Throughout most of Colombia's history a political elite has ruled, advancing only minor changes while effectively containing both the military and the masses.

COMOROS

This nation of four small islands located in the Indian Ocean came under Arab influence around A.D. 1000. In the fifteenth century, a second large influx of Arab settlers occurred, about the same time Europeans came to the area. The Arabs established a slave system based on African labor. (Other Comorians come from Madagascar and Indonesia.) Between the fifteenth and early twentieth centuries, violence and warfare dominated the islands as various sultans vied for power. In the 1700s and 1800s, raiders from Madagascar often captured Comorians and took them to Africa as slaves, thus reducing the population. France extended a protectorate over two of the islands in the 1880s, but did not gain control over the remaining territory until 1912, after which it administered the Comoros jointly with Madagascar. In 1947, the French assumed exclusive control and in 1962 permitted substantial self-government. Independence came in 1975 under AHMED ABDALLAH.

CONGO

In the sixteenth century, the Kongo Empire reached its peak, stretching from this nation's current boundaries into Angola. In 1483, the Portuguese arrived and established generally amicable ties until, in the 1530s, European demands for slaves caused friction. As the slave trade expanded between 1600 and 1800, various local leaders challenged the larger state rulers, such as the Kongo, and more power flowed to individual chiefs.

The French gained jurisdiction over the Congo River area in 1880 and established the colony of the French Congo in 1891 (frequently referred to as Moyen-Congo). Forced labor and other harsh conditions existed under French rule, but the colony did not develop a strong nationalist movement or produce a single prominent founder. Nevertheless, ALPHONSE MASSAMBA-DEBAT provided leadership that restructured the government and moved the Congo in a more radical direction.

COSTA RICA

In 1502, Christopher Columbus arrived in this land, and a full-scale Spanish conquest began in 1563 that eliminated the indigenous Indian culture. Costa Rica obtained independence in 1821, but lost it two years later when Mexico conquered the region. Shortly after this, it joined the Central American Federation, but seceded from it in 1838. Although JOSÉ CECILIO DEL VALLE helped form the Federation, and FRANCISCO MORAZÁN is considered the liberator of Costa Rica (as well as the founder of Honduras, El Salvador, Guatemala, and Nicaragua), the country did not declare its independence until 1838 and did not become a republic fully committed to exisiting as a separate nation until 1848. In that year JOSE MARIA CASTRO MADRIZ declared that Costa Rica would remain separate from the other Central American countries. Domination by wealthy elite coffee barons followed for many years, but for the most part Costa Ricans avoided oppressive dictatorships. The electoral system was threatened, however, in 1948 and saved through the efforts of JOSE FIGUERES FERRER , who supported democracy and social reform.

CÔTE D'IVOIRE (IVORY COAST)

A difficult coastline and rough seas delayed European penetration of Côte d'Ivoire, but in 1637 French missionaries arrived. They found a land of diverse tribes in the south whose members lived in clusters of villages amid dense forests. Meanwhile, the Muslim kingdom of Kong occupied the north-central region. In the east, the Abron Kingdom was developed by tribesmen who had fled the Asante in Ghana. Around 1750, Akan tribal groups formed the Baoule Kingdom that initially had a centralized governing structure but quickly broke into a loose grouping of chiefdoms. The Baoule developed elaborate bronze works and wood carvings. They also fiercely opposed European intrusion.

In the 1840s, the French established trading posts along the coast and acquired ivory from the indigenous people. In 1893, Côte d'Ivoire became a French colony, but not until the early 1900s did France subdue the interior. Independence came under the leadership of FÉLIX HOUPHOUËT-BOIGNY, who supported many French institutions. In 1958, he served as prime minister of Côte d'Ivoire while it was a republic within the French Community. He became president shortly after complete independence was gained on 4 August 1960.

CROATIA

B eginning in the seventh century, Croats—a Slavic people—settled this area on the Balkan Peninsula. After years of Austrian control, Croatia joined the Kingdom of Serbs, Croats, and Slovenes in 1918. During World War II, Josip Broz Tito led the Balkan fight against the Nazis and after the war established Communist Yugoslavia consisting of six member states, including Croatia. Soon after Tito's death in 1980, Yugoslavia crumbled, and in 1991 Croatia declared its independence, led by FRANJO TUDJMAN, a Communist-turned-nationalist, .

CUBA

I n 1492, Christopher Columbus landed in Cuba and made contact with the Taínos Indians, a sedentary people who raised maize, beans, and tobacco. In 1511, the Spaniards conquered and settled the island. They waged total war against the Taínos and placed them in a forced labor system. As the Indians died from disease and cruelty, the Europeans developed sugar and tobacco plantations by importing black slaves from Africa.

By and large, Cuba remained a backwater within the Spanish Empire; nevertheless, after an independence movement swept Latin America in the early 1800s, Spain determined to hold on to the island. In the 1860s, a revolutionary movement spread to include leaders such as Antonio Maceo and Máximo Gómez, the former a mulatto, the latter a black Dominican exile, whose participation raised the question of ending Cuba's ongoing slavery. The rebellion produced a long, bloody war that did not end until 1878, when Spain defeated the revolutionaries. Another uprising occurred almost immediately, led by Calixto Garcia. He organized the Cuban Revolutionary Committee in New York, and in 1879 several prominent revolutionaries joined him in taking up arms. By September 1880, however, the Spanish crushed this effort, too. Then in 1895 JOSÉ MARTÍ launched a revolution that ended Spain's control. The island, however, found its autonomy greatly restricted by the United States, which supported a series of oppressive dictators. This stimulated another nationalist rebellion led by FIDEL CASTRO, who revolutionized Cuban society.

CYPRUS

T his recently troubled Meditteranean island was first settled around 5800 B.C. By the end of the second millennium B.C., a Hellenic culture emerged, one that today remains the source of tradition and pride for Greek Cypriots. Over the centuries, Cyprus fell under the domination of other civilizations, including the Roman and Byzantine Empires. In the modern era, Britain obtained Cyprus from Turkey in 1878. Meanwhile, a strong movement, called *enosis,* developed among Greek Cypriots to unite their land with Greece. This effort failed in the 1950s and antagonized the minority Turkish community. Unable to achieve *enosis,* MAKARIOS III agreed to independence for Cyprus, which took effect in 1960.

CZECH REPUBLIC

I n this land south of the Carpathian Mountains, Czechs and Slovaks, two Slavic peoples, lived united in the great Moravian Empire of the 900s, but the kingdom collapsed in the following century. In the 1200s, a Czech empire centered in Bohemia became a leading European power under King Charles I, who was hailed as the "father of the country." Beginning in the early seventeenth century, the Czechs were conquered by the Habsburg rulers. In the nineteenth century, a nationalist revival occurred, led by Josef Dobrovsky,

Josef Jungmann, and Frantisek Palacky, and during World War I Czechs and Slovaks agitated for an independent state that would unify their two ethnic groups. Milan Stefánik, Eduard Beneš, and Tomáš Masaryk led this effort, and Czechoslovakia was formed in 1918. Democratic politics and widespread economic growth characterized this First Republic, but internal troubles mounted between Czechs and Slovaks.

Led by Andrej Hlinka, some Slovaks advocated a separate state. This dispute contributed to the partition of Czechoslovakia in 1938 by Germany, Hungary, and Poland; then Hitler's invasion in 1939 ended a short-lived Second Republic. After World War II, Czechs and Slovaks united again in a Third Republic, but in 1948 the Communists gained power and Czechoslovakia lost its autonomy to the Soviet Union. In 1988, a revolution led by VÁCLAV HAVEL ended the Russian occupation. Just four years later, Czechs and Slovaks parted ways and Czechoslovakia split into two nations: the Czech Republic and Slovakia, with the latter led by VLADIMIR MECIAR.

DENMARK

Under the Valdemars in the twelfth century, a Danish kingdom extended around the Baltic Sea and effectively ended German claims to overlordship. This kingdom experienced a tumultuous existence, during which territory was gained and lost. In the fourteenth century, dynastic ties united Denmark with Norway and Sweden in the Kalmar Union. Intermittent wars occurred, however, when Denmark attempted to gain supremacy over Sweden. In 1523, the Kalmar Union dissolved after these two countries chose separate kings. Norway, however, remained linked to Denmark. In 1534, civil war enveloped Denmark, involving a dispute over who should be the new king. The war resulted in the monarchy strengthening itself by confiscating church property.

Until 1616, when Denmark suffered defeat in the Thirty Years' War, Christian IV expanded his country's power; he diversified the economy, founded new towns, acquired overseas colonies, and regained Danish control over the Baltic. Under Frederick II, who reigned from 1648 to 1670, royal absolutism emerged, a system that remained intact for nearly 200 years. During the Napoleonic Wars of the early 1800s, Denmark sided with France and subsequently lost Norway. Modern, liberalized Denmark began with FREDERICK VII, who in 1848 renounced absolute rule and adopted a representative government.

DJIBOUTI

Desert sands cover 90 percent of Djibouti's territory, and the country has few natural resources other than an excellent harbor. Located where the Red Sea and Gulf of Aden meet, Djibouti was acquired by France in the mid-nineteenth century through a series of treaties with Somali clans. France named the area French Somaliland. Substantial nationalist sentiment did not develop until the 1960s, and even then ethnic rivalry dominated the scene as Afars and Issas competed for supremacy. HASSAN GOULED led Djibouti to independence and as president inherited a seemingly hopeless political and economic situation.

DOMINICA

This small, mountainous Caribbean island was sighted by Christopher Columbus in 1493. Settlement by Europeans lagged behind the nearby islands because of its terrain, which made plantation agriculture difficult. Although the French were the first European settlers, Britain seized the island in 1761 and held it almost continuously for over 200 years. The British destroyed the indigenous Indian population and developed Dominica with African slave labor. After World War II, Britain made constitutional changes that provided more autonomy and encouraged political party development. Complete independence occurred in 1978 under PATRICK JOHN with the general support of EUGENIA CHARLES, who also shaped the early government.

DOMINICAN REPUBLIC

In 1492, Christopher Columbus landed and named this area La Española. The Spaniards immediately plundered it for gold and in the process destroyed the indigenous Indian population. They imported slaves from Africa to develop plantations. By the mid-1500s, the area's resources had been largely drained, and it stood as a backwater within the Spanish Empire. In 1795, Spain ceded the colony to France, and in 1801 and again in 1822, neighboring Haiti invaded and established brutal regimes. In 1844, the Dominican Republic won its independence when JUAN PABLO DUARTE and his followers overthrew the Haitians.

ECUADOR

In the high Andes, Indians established the Kingdom of Quito around A.D. 1000. Later, the Inca Empire engulfed it. Europeans conquered the area in 1532, led by the Spaniard, Francisco Pizarro. The extensive use of Indian labor to work the mines made Ecuador a thriving Spanish colony. Under SIMÓN BOLÍVAR and ANTONIO JOSÉ DE SUCRE, Ecuador gained its independence in the early nineteenth century. Initially, it was part of a larger political entity called Gran Colombia. Ecuador gained its status as a separate nation in 1830 under JUAN JOSÉ FLORES.

EGYPT

With its pyramids and Great Sphinx, Egypt displays a timeless appearance. This land of once-great pharaohs fell to foreign rule by the seventh century B.C. In 1798, Napoleon occupied Egypt briefly. With his departure, Mohammed Ali, a Turkish military general, governed until his death in 1849 and established a strong state within the Turkish Empire. After 1863, Mohammed Ali's grandson became ruler and spent huge sums of money on modernization programs that brought enormous debt and intervention by Western nations. In 1882, expeditionary forces from Britain invaded Egypt beginning 70 years of British rule and producing a nationalistic reaction. First, working largely within the existing political structure, SAAD ZAGHLUL emerged as a strong leader of reform and independence. Then, shortly after World War II, GAMAL ABDEL NASSER fulfilled Egypt's long-held desire for nationhood.

EL SALVADOR

The Spanish first entered El Salvador in the early 1500s and encountered the Pipil Indians, who strongly resisted the intrusion. As they conquered the Indians, they searched for gold, but El Salvador offered little reward in this regard. Land and its development then became the main factor in the economy. In the 1820s, when independence movements swept Latin America, a San Salvadoran, José Matías Delgado, led a rebellion, but the Spanish crushed it. In the 1820s, El Salvador became part of the independent Central American Federation, which was crafted by JOSÉ CECILIO DEL VALLE and FRANCISCO MORAZÁN. The country's nationhood was gained in the 1840s under FRANCISCO MALESPIN.

For decades an oligarchy ruled while conservatives and liberals, who had few substantial differences, vied for control. In the 1970s, leftist guerrillas challenged the traditional power structure and gained a substantial following. ALFREDO CRISTIANI reached an agreement in 1991 with the left that recognized some reform and ushered in an era of stability and political change, the degree of which remains uncertain.

EQUATORIAL GUINEA

This tiny nation covers less than 0.1 percent of Africa's total land area and is composed of two islands, Fernando Póo (Bioko) and Annobón, and a mainland province, Río Muni. Various Bantu migrations from the thirteenth to the nineteenth centuries brought in the Ndowe people—who displaced the Pygmies. Later, the Fang settled in Río Muni, and the Bubi occupied the islands. The Portuguese discovered this area for Europeans between 1471 and 1475, establishing trading posts and soon thereafter engaging in the slave trade. With the 1778 Pardo Treaty, Portugal transferred the Guinean Gulf Coast region to Spain.

Under Spanish rule, oftentimes weak, this area was called Spanish Guinea, and its economic and political development favored the Bubi, with Río Muni

largely neglected. As in much of Africa, nationalism stirred after World War II, but here it took a tragic course when FRANCISCO MACÍAS NGUEMA, who did not achieve political prominence until the mid-1960s and then advocated an immediate and violent break with Spain, developed a brutal dictatorship.

ERITREA

Until 1993, this hot, semiarid land was the northernmost province of Ethiopia, a country with whom its history is closely linked. After an invasion of peoples across the Red Sea from Yemen in the first millenium B.C., the Aksum Empire, Ethiopia's first kingdom, expanded along the coast and controlled Eritrea until the eighth century A.D. This linked Eritrea with trade in the Middle East, as well as the eastern Mediterranean and even India. After nomads overran Eritrea, Ethiopia did not again establish authority over the area until the thirteenth century. In 1885, Italy occupied Massawa, Eritrea's leading port, and in 1890 declared Eritrea an Italian colony and Ethiopia a protectorate. Even after Ethiopian forces defeated the Italians at Adwa in 1896, Italy held on to Eritrea. The area received little economic assistance from the Italians until Benito Mussolini conquered all of Ethiopia in 1936. Anxious to boost the Italian economy and develop an overseas showcase for his fascist regime, Mussolini developed ports, roads, and schools. During World War II, Eritrea came under British rule, and in 1952 was federated with Ethiopia.

Eritreans long considered themselves separate from Ethiopians and poorly treated by them. In the 1950s, several prominent Eritreans fled their homeland and organized nationalist groups abroad. These included Woldeab Woldemariam, who helped form the Eritrean Liberation Movement. By the 1960s, other organizations were fighting for Eritrean nationhood. Amid the turmoil, the Ethiopian Peoples Liberation Front became dominant, its efforts embodied in the leadership of ISSAYAS AFEWERKE, noted for his political pragmatism.

ESTONIA

This small nation, tucked between the Gulfs of Finland and Riga, experienced centuries of domination by outside powers, particularly the Germans, Poles, and Russians. The latter seized Estonia in the early 1700s, and in the following century they began an intense Russification campaign to eliminate the indigenous culture. Estonians reacted with their own nationalist drive for autonomy in the early 1900s. After World War I, Estonia declared its independence in 1918 and survived as a nation until 1940, when it was forcibly annexed by the Soviet Union. Germany occupied Estonia during the Second World War, but after it ended the Soviets returned. Despite this, nationalist sentiment continued and in the 1980s it intensified, leading to independence under LENNART MERI.

ETHIOPIA

Ethiopia is a land of ancient kingdoms that for centuries Europeans viewed in mythical proportions. The Kingdom of Aksum emerged in the sixth century B.C. Tradition asserts that it was founded by the Queen of Sheba. By the fourth century A.D., Aksum extended from Nubia to Lake Tana in Gojam, and had been converted to Christianity. With the expansion of Islam into the surrounding area by the seventh century, Ethiopia lost much of its influence and became isolated. Yet European help for a fellow Christian land came in 1453 when Portugal assisted in turning back an Islamic invasion.

During the eighteenth and nineteenth centuries, rival princes competed for control of Ethiopia and chaos prevailed. This changed in 1855 when Emperor Tewodros IV defeated several dissident chiefs and began establishing a centralized government. After Emperor MENELIK II defeated Italian invaders at Aduwa in 1885, Europeans recognized Ethiopia as a modern nation. Emperor HAILE SELASSIE expanded Menelik's modernization efforts and developed a number of programs that left a substantial mark on Ethiopia.

FIJI

Around 2000 B.C., Melanesians arrived on the Fiji Islands and a hierarchical society emerged with chieftains as leaders. Europeans explored Fiji in the seventeenth century, but their political involvement did not become substantial until the nineteenth century. Fearing that France or the United States might annex Fiji, Britain acquired the islands in the 1870s. After World War II, the British encouraged Fiji to develop home rule, and in 1970 independence was granted under RATU KAMISESE MARA. Fiji remained in the British Commonwealth until the prominent Fijian nationalist SITIVENI RABUKA staged a coup in 1985, annulled the exisiting constitution, and proclaimed a republic.

FINLAND

When Swedes arrived in the ninth century A.D., they found in Finland a unique Finno-Ugric linguistic group and a culture that had emerged some 10,000 years before. Finland and Sweden grew closer together, drawn by trade and cultural ties across the Gulf of Bothnia and the Baltic Sea. In the mid-twelfth century, the kingdom of Sweden-Finland emerged, and Swedish language and customs became an integral part of Finland. During the Napoleonic Wars, Sweden lost Finland to Russia. A susbstantial nationalist movement tied to the Finnish language and literature stimulated the drive for independence led by PEHR EVIND SVINHUFVUD.

FRANCE

After Julius Caesar conquered France, or what was then called Gaul, around 51 B.C., Roman rule continued for 500 years. Frankish leadership began when Charlemagne, who reigned from A.D. 768 to 814 , established a kingdom. In 843, the Treaty of Verdun divided the land among Charlemagne's grandsons, with the new borders corresponding roughly to modern France, Germany, and Italy. In 987, the French kingdom passed to Hugh Capet, a prince who controlled the territory surrounding Paris. This began the 350-year Capetian line of rulers, who gradually added to their domain.

In 1328, Philip VI, the first in the Valois line, gained the throne, but England and the House of Burgundy controlled much of France, a situation changed by Charles VII, who began pushing the English out. More substantial gains were made and the foundation of a national state built in the mid-fifteenth century under his son, LOUIS XI. France underwent many changes after Louis's reign, most notably the machinations of CARDINAL DE RICHELIEU, a great statesman whose policies in the 1620s and 1630s advanced French absolutism under the belief that all activities should be dedicated to the good of the state; the French Revolution in 1789 that founded the First Republic; and Napoleon's empire, established in 1804. A revolution in 1848 began the Second Republic, but it collapsed in 1852 when Napoleon III declared himself emperor. His abdication after the Franco-Prussian War in 1871 led to the Third Republic, ended by Germany's invasion in 1940. After World War II, the Fourth Republic emerged in 1946, but it proved incapable of handling the postwar crises within France and in the nation's overseas colonies, thus leading to the Fifth Republic formed in 1958 under the leadership of World War II hero CHARLES DE GAULLE.

GABON

In 1472, the Portuguese arrived in Gabon, where they found the southern part of this land linked to Loango, part of the huge Kongo Kingdom. The Portuguese developed sugar plantations on São Tomé and Príncipe and began trading along the Gabon coast. Beginning in the late 1500s, French, Spanish, Dutch, and English traders entered the area. Slave trafficking became important in the late 1700s, lasting until the 1840s. The slave trade benefited several coastal tribes that obtained slaves from the interior, including the Orungu, who established a kingdom based on this enterprise, and the Mpongwe, who integrated slavery into their already profitable commerce. Only the Fang refused to engage in the trade.

France gained dominance in Gabon during the late 1800s, signing numerous treaties with tribal chiefs who recognized French sovereignty. The Mpongwe proved most recalcitrant and submitted only after the French used force. Gabon became a part of French Equatorial Africa in 1910. Independence, obtained on 17 August 1960, resulted from the actions of disparate, educated anticolonialists who often formed alliances for personal rather than ideological reasons. This group included LÉON M'BA, son of a Fang village chief and Gabon's first prime minister and president.

THE GAMBIA

Closely linked to Senegal's development, The Gambia consists of ethnic groups common to both lands. Most prominent are the Mandingo, who live primarily in the central area, and the Wolof, who live in Banjul and along the coast. Europeans arrived in 1455 when the Portuguese sailed up the Gambia River. They did not have much commercial success, however, nor did the English who arrived in the 1500s. Nevertheless, the British and French, who also had expansionist designs, soon fought for supremacy in the area, with the British obtaining in 1763 all of Senegambia (the territory between the Senegal and Gambia Rivers). Twenty years later, the Treaty of Versailles recognized French authority in the northern region.

After 1848, Britain administered Bathurst and Banjul Island (which they renamed St. Mary's) as the colony of The Gambia. Then, in 1894, Britain declared a protectorate over the inland area along the Gambia River. Gambians did not build a strong nationalist movement after World War II, and independence came only with prodding from Britain. Many Gambians contemplated uniting their area with Senegal. This moderate, halting approach toward nationhood was evident in the efforts of The Gambia's most prominent political leader, DAUDA JAWARA.

GEORGIA

Empires and nations have long contended for control of this land situated between the Black and Caspian Seas. From the tenth to the thirteenth centuries, a united, independent Georgia existed and developed commercial ties with both Europe and the Orient. Mongol invaders, however, destroyed the kingdom, and a series of foreign rulers ensued, with Persia and the Ottoman Turks especially fighting for domination. In 1801, Russia annexed east Georgia and in the 1870s acquired the western portion. Anti-Russian revolts occurred periodically, but Russian control continued almost uninterrupted through the 1980s. In 1991, Georgia, then a republic within the Soviet Union, declared its independence under Zviad Gamsakhurdia. He quickly lost power, and Georgians turned to EDUARD SHEVARDNADZE to protect their independence and eliminate internal revolts that threatened national unity.

GERMANY

The great Charlemagne, ruler of the Franks, consolidated Saxon, Bavarian, Rhenish, and Frankish lands, along with several others, and became Holy Roman Emperor in A.D. 800. After his death, the eastern part of his realm was ceded to the German Prince Louis in 843, with other lands added in 870. The Thirty Years' War of 1618 to 1648 resulted in the splintering of Germany into small principalities and kingdoms. Prussia, however, emerged as a strong state in the mid-eighteenth century under Frederick the Great, and in the early nineteenth century, after Napoleon's defeat in 1815, it contended with Austria for dominance over the German states. Under kings William I and William II, OTTO VON BISMARCK, a great statesman, guided Prussia into forming the new German Empire and establishing German unification. World War I destroyed the empire and caused Germany to lose territory, and World War II shattered German unity by dividing the nation into East and West. Reunification occurred in 1990 under the guidance of HELMUT KOHL.

GHANA

At one time an ancient African empire prospered near, although not within, the current borders of Ghana. It is from this empire, which lasted until the thirteenth century, that modern Ghana gets its name. The people of Ghana likely emigrated into this area some 600 years ago. Several states north of Ghana's forestland, in the dry Sahelian zone, emerged as powerful, but by the end of the seventeenth century the Ashanti Kingdom of the central forest gained dominance.

Earlier, the first Europeans arrived when Portuguese mariners reached the coast in 1471. Initially, Europe's main interest was in gold, hence giving the area its appellation "the Gold Coast." When Britain gained dominance over the littoral in the nineteenth century, tensions grew between them and the Ashanti, who were pressing toward the coast. The British turned back an Ashanti attack in 1874 and declared the Gold Coast a colony. After World War II, nationalism emerged, at first moderate, then increasingly radical under the leadership of KWAME NKRUMAH. He became a strident advocate of Marxism and Pan-Africanism. Britain granted the Gold Coast its independence on 6 March 1957 as the nation of Ghana. Nkrumah became his homeland's leader and quickly established an authoritarian state noted for its personality cult, socialist programs, and appeal to black African pride.

GREAT BRITAIN

This nation, known formally as the United Kingdom of Great Britain and Northern Ireland, encompasses the latter territory and England, Wales, and Scotland. England became a part of the Roman Empire in A.D. 43, but the Romans withdrew in 410 and Germanic tribes—the Jutes, Angles, and Saxons—invaded, establishing several tribal kingdoms. Danes, a related people, also settled the area. Widespread unification did not occur until 1066 when the Normans, led by William the Conqueror, invaded and expanded control. They built castles, and the ensuing feudal era marked by these structures and the adventures of knights has been much popularized in literature and folklore. The institutions peculiar to England began emerging under the Normans, but a nation as such did not evolve until the first Tudor king, HENRY VII, began his reign in the fifteenth century. Further consolidation and a nationalist break with the Roman Catholic Church occurred in the early 1500s, under the infamous Henry VIII.

An important step toward a modern representative state occurred in the late seventeenth century with the Glorious Revolution and the rule of WILLIAM III. England's government liberalized further in the ensuing decades, most notably in the nineteenth century when the House of Commons superseded the House of Lords in power and became more democratic. Various reform acts, such as the one in 1832 passed amid populist demonstrations and riots, broadened the franchise and ended the corrupt borough system.

GREECE

When most people think of Greece, they often remember the ancient civilization at Athens with its democratic politics and its great philosophers, such as Socrates, Plato, and Aristotle. Modern Greece is overlooked, but it too has had a long history, one politically tortuous. In the early 1800s, an independence movement emerged aimed against the Ottoman Turks, who ruled Greece. Alexander Ypislantis earned renown when he led a rebellion in 1821 that ignited a widespread revolution. The rebels put together a constitution in 1822, and won their independence with the help of Russia, Britain, and France. The European powers agreed to a Kingdom of Greece, established in 1831, but limited to the Peloponnesian Peninsula and placed under the rule of a Bavarian who became the nation's king, Otto I. He served from 1833 until 1862, when the Greeks deposed him. In 1864, the Greek legislature developed a new constitution, the most liberal in Europe at the time. In 1909, an army coup toppled King George and later that year the military turned to ELEUTHERIOS VENIZELOS to lead the nation.

In 1923, the monarchy was officially ended and a full republic proclaimed, but in 1935, the king was restored. A military dictatorship ruled shortly before World War II, and both during and after that conflict a civil war raged, not ending until 1949. A tenuous democracy gave way to yet another military dictatorship that continued until CONSTANTINE KARAMANLIS restored democracy in 1974. A more radical change

occurred in the 1980s under the socialist ANDREAS PAPANDREOU.

GRENADA

Although Christopher Columbus sighted this small Caribbean island in 1498, the first European settlers were the French, who arrived in 1650. France and Britain competed for possession of it, and in 1794 the British established their control. Grenada obtained its independence on 7 February 1974 under the leadership of the controversial prime minister ERIC GAIRY.

GUATEMALA

At least as far back as 600 B.C., the Mayans built cities in Guatemala. The Spanish arrived in A.D. 1523 and under Pedro de Alvarado conquered the region. In 1821, a rebellion won indpendence from Spain, but the following year Mexico invaded and took charge. In 1823, Mexican rule collapsed, and Guatemala joined with several other states to form the United Provinces of Central America, led primarily by JOSÉ CECILIO DEL VALLE and FRANCISCO MORAZÁN. An end to this arrangement and complete independence occurred in 1839 under the fanatical RAFAEL CARRERA.

GUINEA

This country, whose name likely derives from the Berber phrase meaning "Land of the Blacks," has a long precolonial history. Hunting and gathering peoples inhabited the region some 30,000 years ago. The dominant Susu and Maninka tribes entered Guinea around A.D. 900, and the Fulbé arrived in the seventeenth century. Much of the area's development became tied to the three great savanna states of Ghana, Mali, and Songhai.

A European presence began in the fifteenth century and linked Guinea to the Atlantic slave network. The French established trading posts in the nineteenth century and expanded inland. They encountered much resistance, however, and did not establish complete control until 1899 when they defeated and captured Almany Samory Touré, considered by many Guineans a great national hero. After World War II, a strong nationalist movement emerged, and AHMED SÉKOU TOURÉ developed a trade union movement into a powerful instrument for radical political and social change.

GUINEA-BISSAU

Long before the Christian era, human beings occupied the northeastern territory of Guinea-Bissau. In the ninth century A.D., the Empire of Ghana expanded trade into the area and Muslims introduced Islam. In the fifteenth century, Portuguese traders arrived, a presence which restricted the expansion of Fulani people into the region. The Portuguese never settled

Guinea-Bissau in large numbers; instead, they focused on establishing trading posts and forts and developing nearby Cape Verde, a country whose history became intimately linked with that of Guinea-Bissau. Initially, Portuguese economic pursuits emphasized the slave trade, but they later shifted to agricultural products and a commercial system using forced labor. After World War II, nationalism grew in Guinea-Bissau and Cape Verde, led by Africans who had obtained a European education. AMILCAR CABRAL became not only the leader of this movement but also an important revolutionary theoretician and writer for all Africa, and, as such, a beacon for African nationalist sentiments. Independence in Guinea-Bissau came only after a long and bloody struggle.

GUYANA

During his third voyage, Christopher Columbus sighted Guyana, a tropical land located along South America's northern coast. The Dutch arrived in 1616, established a trading post, and warred with the Carib and Arawak Indians, whom they destroyed. Dutch settlers gradually drained the swampy coastal areas and developed sugar plantations worked by slaves imported from Africa. After the Napoleonic Wars in 1814, the British obtained Guyana, named it British Guiana, and held it until its independence in 1966. Britain ended slavery and imported large numbers of workers from India. Nationhood came through the efforts of two leaders, CHEDDI JAGAN, a Guyanese of Indian descent who advocated radical programs, and FORBES BURNHAM, a black who established an authoritarian regime.

HAITI

This nation occupies the island of Hispaniola with the Dominican Republic, and like the latter was a landfall for Christopher Columbus in 1492. Columbus found a lush, mountainous land inhabited by various Arawak Indian tribes, but over the years European settlers destroyed the Indians and imported slaves from Africa to develop plantations. Haiti, then called Saint Dominque, became a French possession in 1697 and remained such until uprisings by blacks and mulattos resulted in the country becoming the first independent nation in Latin America. TOUSSAINT L'OUVERTURE led a rebellion in the 1790s that enabled Haiti to end French rule in 1804 under JEAN-JACQUES DESSALINES. In subsequent years, military-supported dictatorships prevailed in Haiti, including the infamous rule by Francois "Papa Doc" Duvalier and his son, "Baby Doc," which lasted from the 1950s into the 1980s.

HONDURAS

When Christopher Columbus arrived here in 1502, he claimed the area for Spain. In 1821, Honduras joined with four other neighboring provinces to declare independence as part of a Central American federation. At the time, this province was poorly developed and sparsely populated. Even so, it produced two great leaders in the Central American independence movement, JOSÉ CECILIO DEL VALLE and FRANCISCO MORAZÁN. After the federation collapsed, FRANCISCO FERRERA led Honduras into nationhood and established a dictatorship.

HUNGARY

Around A.D. 895, the Magyars, pushed westward by the Bulgars, crossed over the Carpathian Mountains and settled in what is today Hungary. They conquered and assimilated the Slavs and developed a loosely organized kingdom under the Árpád Dynasty. In 975, the chieftain Géza accepted Christianity. His son, Stephen I, strengthened Hungary's ties to the West, consolidated his power, and in the year 1000 received recognition from the pope as Hungary's king. Several successor feudal rulers expanded Hungary's size, but a Mongol invasion in 1241 destroyed the kingdom. After the Árpád Dynasty ended in 1301, the nobles chose the kings. By this time, the Turks and the Habsburg rulers threatened Hungary.

Under Matthias I in the fifteenth century, a large consolidated empire emerged that developed some national characteristics. Yet the empire collapsed shortly after his death in 1490, at which time the Turks and Habsburgs partitioned it. After the Turkish Empire weakened, the Habsburgs gained control. In 1848, a nationalist revolt erupted, led by Louis Kossuth, who battled the Austrians and founded a short-lived revolutionary government. It was crushed the following year, and in 1867 a dual monarchy began, establishing Austria-Hungary. After World War I, a republic emerged in Hungary, but it quickly collapsed, followed by Romanian occupation and Hungary's loss of two-thirds of its land. Another brief republic arose after World War II; however, in 1948 the Soviet Union began its domination. Although rebellions occurred against Communist rule, most notably in 1956, Hungarians did not win independence from foreign control until 1990 under JÓZSEF ANTALL JR. and ÁRPÁD GÖNCZ.

ICELAND

An island nation near the Arctic Circle, Icleand is most widely known for its volcanic terrain and fish products. The nation has a history dating back to A.D. 900, when Norsemen arrived. The settlers wrote a constitution in 930 that provided for a general assembly, or Althing. Iceland maintained its status as an independent republic until 1262, when Norway acquired it. In 1381, the Danes gained control (ruling it jointly with Norway for several decades), and in the nineteenth century Icelanders developed a strong nationalism and a desire for autonomy. JÓN SIGURDSSON stirred national consciousness and obtained concessions that paved the way for Iceland's complete independence in 1944.

INDIA

This land had a rich ancient history long before Europeans arrived. Between 1700 and 1200 B.C., Aryans pushed south and southeastward from the Iranian plateau. The Asoka Kingdom ruled most of India in the third century B.C. and established Buddhism, although this religion soon gave way to Hinduism, which eventually dominated. India experienced a golden age of social and cultural development in the fourth to sixth centuries A.D. under the Gupta Kingdom. Arab invaders brought Islam with them in the eighth century, and by 1200 Turkish Muslims gained control over the north. Moguls invaded and ruled from 1526 to 1857.

In 1757, the British East India Company began its presence in the Indian subcontinent and over a period of 100 years expanded its control, often through alliances with local princes. As Britain industrialized, India was relegated to providing raw materials and serving as a market for industrial goods. In 1857, uprisings in the Ganges Valley led to severe British military reaction and the replacement of company rule with direct British rule. The Indian princes had little real authority and few Indians of any persuasion had substantial roles within the colonial government. The British-run Indian Civil Service established a paternalistic authority over India, and its recruits came overwhelmingly from Britain. When Indian nationalism intensified after World War I, three figures dominated the movement: MOHANDAS KARAMCHAND GANDHI with his *satyagraha* approach and moral emphasis, JAWAHARLAL NEHRU with his political and economic orientation, and INDIRA GANDHI with her leadership in a male-dominated political world.

INDONESIA

Srivijaya emerged as the first important state in Indonesia, controlling the straits of Malacca and Srivijaya from the mid-seventh until the thirteenth century. Majapahit, a Javanese state, dominated from about 1300 to 1500, led in the mid-fourteenth century by Gajah Mada, a prime minister and great Indonesian hero. Europeans arrived as the last major Indonesian empire, Mataram, developed in the sixteenth century. Some hundred years later, the Dutch East India Company extended its control over portions of Indonesia, and in 1800 the Netherlands assumed direct control over the company's territory. The European interference with the power of Javanese aristocrats and existing land practices led to a massive revolt in 1825 that the Dutch repressed after a loss of some 200,000 lives.

Until the late 1800s, the Netherlands effectively controlled only Java, but as the twentieth century began, the Dutch expanded their control over all of present-day Indonesia, excepting East Timor. The Dutch trained an Indonesian intellectual elite to help administer the colony, but in the process these intellectuals grew alienated from foreign control. In 1912, the Islamic Union was formed as Indonesia's first truly nationalist organization. By 1920, however, it had lost much vitality, and the Indonesian Communist Party emerged as a power. In 1925, SUKARNO organized a new party to lead the nationalist movement.

IRAN

In 549 B.C., Cyrus the Great united the Medes and Persians and ten years later conquered Babylonia. Soon his Persian Empire extended from the Indus River in the east to the Mediterranean in the west, and from the Caucuses in the north to the Indian Ocean in the south (and later into Egypt). Students of ancient history are familiar with the wars between Greece and Persia. Alexander the Great of Macedonia conquered Persia in 333 B.C., but under the Parthians the Persians regained their independence in the next century. Islam penetrated Persia in the seventh century A.D., replacing the Zoroastrian religion.

In more recent times, Persia experienced numerous invasions, including the Mongols in the thirteenth century and the Afghans and Russians in the eighteenth century. In the early 1900s, an intense rivalry developed between Britain and Russia for influence in Persia, but REZA SHAH PAHLAVI ended foreign control. In 1935, this land was officially renamed Iran, and after World War II an increasingly oppressive regime, supported with American assistance, stimulated a powerful nationalism and with it a desire to reduce Western influences. In the early 1950s, Mohammed Mosaddeq tried to overthrow the pro-American government but failed. A radical revolution occurred in 1979, led by AYATOLLAH RUHOLLA KHOMEINI.

IRAQ

Most students of Western civilization first learn of Iraq by its name in ancient times: Mesopotamia. During the fourth millennium B.C., Sumerians developed an advanced culture along the Tigris and Euphrates Rivers, part of the Fertile Crescent. Later, other formidable empires appeared in this area, particularly the Babylonian, Assyrian, Persian, and Roman civilizations. After the Islamic conquest, Iraq became the center, around A.D. 750, of a powerful Muslim state. The Ottoman Empire spread across Iraq in the sixteenth century and maintained its dominance until World War I.

At that time, British control began, and Iraqi independence efforts focused on ending this influence. Iraq's nationalist struggle went through several phases and by the 1950s and 1960s encompassed revolutionary change. The most prominent leaders in this movement were King FAISAL I, SADDAM HUSSEIN, and ABDUL KARIM QASSEM.

IRELAND

In the tenth century, Danish and Norwegian conquerors penetrated the craggy shoreline and steep mountain ranges of Ireland. King Brian Boru, the Catholic monarch, drove them out, but the Normans invaded in 1170, and for over 700 years the English ruled. They prohibited the Irish language and the intermarriage of English and Irish, confiscated much land from the Catholics, denied them suffrage and public office, and ruthlessly crushed rebellions. While Protestant English landowners grew wealthy, the Catholics lived on potatoes. Agitation by the Irish for independence intensified in the 1790s under Theobald Wolfe Tone. Then the struggle entered a new stage in the early nineteenth century that culminated in nationhood. DANIEL O'CONNELL focused on Catholic political rights, CHARLES STUART PARNELL took up the cause for the peasantry and Irish independence, PATRICK PEARSE embraced mystical nationalism, MICHAEL COLLINS led a wave of terrorist attacks as part of Irish Republican Army strategy, and EAMON DE VALERA became the prominent political leader of Sinn Fein and first president of the independent Irish Republic.

ISRAEL

This land, which borders the southeast Mediterranean, has been the home of many ancient civilizations. The Hebrews arrived early in the second millennium B.C., and from about 1000 to 597 B.C., a Judaic civilization developed, most prominently under King David. Several invasions followed thereafter, including those by Babylonians, Persians, and Greeks. An independent Jewish kingdom reemerged in 168 B.C., but in the next century Rome took control, and from A.D. 70 to 135 the Romans suppressed revolts and dispersed the Jewish population. In 636, Arab invaders arrived and Islam grew dominant, although a Jewish minority continued.

More recently, Palestine, as it was called, fell under the Ottoman Empire, beginning in the sixteenth century and lasting until 1917. The defeat of the Ottomans after World War I opened the way for the Zionist movement to fulfill its goal of establishing a Jewish state in Palestine. Jews battled Arabs and the British, who held a League of Nations mandate to rule Palestine, and in 1948 Israel emerged as an independent nation. Many persons played prominent roles in the Zionist movement and in the establishment of Israel. These included DAVID BEN-GURION, MOSHE DAYAN, GOLDA MEIR, and CHAIM WEIZMANN.

ITALY

When most people think about Italy's history, they recall the grandeur of ancient Rome. Modern nationhood did not come until the nineteenth century. Shortly after 1800, the country was unified under the French ruler Napoleon, who crowned himself King of Italy. But in 1815, the Congress of Vienna restored Austria to the dominant position it had held over Italy since the early 1700s. Soon thereafter, changes swept across Europe as nationalists and republicans challenged the existing national boundaries and monarchical rule.

This movement was especially strong in Italy, which did not exist as a single state but as several separate political units, including the Kingdom of the Two Sicilies, the Kingdom of Sardinia-Piedmont, Tuscany, the Papal States, and Lombardy and Venetia. Many conservatives, especially the various European monarchs, opposed the nationalists and liberals; they wanted to maintain the existing order, and toward this end Austria, Prussia, and Russia formed the Holy Alliance to prevent the spread of popular power. Italian nationalism, however, continued to grow and included four men who led the drive to unify Italy and establish a republican government: CAMILLO BENSO DI CAVOUR, King VICTOR EMMANUEL II, GIUSEPPE GARIBALDI, and GIUSEPPE MAZZINI.

JAMAICA

Arawak Indians inhabited Jamaica when Christopher Columbus landed there in 1494. The Spanish searched for gold and destroyed the indigenous culture. In 1655, the British obtained this island and pirates used it as a base for attacking shipping in the Caribbean. As Britain developed a sugar economy, African slavery grew. In 1807, the British ended the slave trade, and in 1833 the slaves were freed. Jamaica gained internal self-government in the 1950s, and the normally heated political scene intensified as conservatives and socialists vied for power, the former led by WILLIAM BUSTAMANTE and the latter by MICHAEL MANLEY.

JAPAN

Japanese schoolchildren were once taught that the islands on which they lived were created by the gods and that the emperors who ruled Japan descended directly from the sun goddess. Before the American Commodore William C. Perry forced open this mountainous island country to outsiders in 1854, a medieval society prevailed with power wielded under the emperors by shoguns.

A new modernized and Westernized Japan emerged under the emperor MEIJI as leaders such as ITO HIROBUMI advanced reform. The world depression of the 1930s, however, disrupted this society and led to nationalist militancy and fascism. Under the extreme militarists, Japan expanded, attacking China in 1937 and then the United States at Pearl Harbor on 7 December 1941, bringing America into World War II. After the American victory in 1945, Japan faced an enormous rebuilding, not just economic but also political, led by Prime Minister YOSHIDA SHIGERU.

JORDAN

There is evidence that Paleolithic man inhabited the Jordanian deserts, using flint tools for hunting. Biblical accounts mention kingdoms existing before 1300 B.C., such as Gilead in the north and Moab in the south. The Roman Empire spread into Jordan around 64 B.C., and by A.D. 313 Christianity emerged as an important religion. In the sixth and seventh centuries, war between Byzantium and Persia destroyed large areas of Jordan, after which Islamic armies introduced Muslim rule. In the sixteenth century, this area, considered a backwater, succumbed to the Ottoman Turks.

World War I led to a widespread Arab revolt against the Turks in 1916. Turkish domination was replaced by British domination, and in 1920 Abdullah ibn Hussein was backed by Britain in leading the new government of Transjordan. Neither Abdullah nor his grandson, HUSSEIN IBN TALAL (King Hussein I), proved to be strong nationalists, although under the latter, modern Jordan has grown and exhibits a greater independence, particularly toward its former British rulers, and a willingness to ease tensions with Israel, as evident in the 1994 agreement to end the state of belligerency with that nation and pursue a wide-ranging peace treaty.

KAMPUCHEA (CAMBODIA)

The Khmer first settled this area along the Mekong River, and in the first century A.D., Funan, a maritime state, developed into an empire whose trade extended from the Gulf of Thailand to the Mediterranean in the west and the Chinese coast in the east. After Funan declined in the sixth century, the next great empire was Angkor, which became enormously wealthy. In the fifteenth century, it declined rapidly amid attacks from Thai armies. After the Cambodian Empire, smaller and weaker than Angkor, experienced invasions by Thais and Vietnamese in the sixteenth and seventeenth centuries, Cambodia faced extinction.

In 1863, the Cambodian king requested French help in countering these invasions. France agreed and in the process made Cambodia a protectorate. Under this arrangement, the French handled Cambodia's foreign affairs but left to the Cambodians most internal operations. Although Cambodia did not experience the more direct and often onerous colonial rule known in many French colonies, the foreigners intervened extensively in the protectorate. Around 1900, France formed an Indochinese Union encompassing Cambo-

dia, Laos, and Vietnam. Nationalism emerged only gradually in Kampuchea, stirred by World War II and evident in the leadership of Prince SAMDECH NORODOM SIHANOUK.

KAZAKHSTAN

In the fifteenth and sixteenth centuries, the Kazakhs developed a nomadic empire across this vast and largely treeless land. By the early 1700s, Russians penetrated the region and undermined the Kazakh system, and in the following century they crushed the Kazakh hordes and tried to force them into sedentary farming. This produced an uprising, but it failed. Russia then acted to eliminate Kazakh culture and in the late 1800s encouraged ethnic Russians to settle the area and dilute the indigenous practices. In 1916, Russia crushed another uprising with brutal force, resulting in many deaths and some 500,000 Kazakhs fleeing to China.

In 1920, the Soviet Union defeated Kazakh nationalists under Ali Bukneikhanov and annexed Kazakhstan, which in the 1930s became a republic within the Communist nation. The forced collectivization of agriculture resulted in many more deaths, this time from starvation. In the 1980s, nationalism surged, helped by reformist developments within the Soviet Union and, late in 1991, the collapse of that nation. Although reluctant to seek independence, NURSULTAN NAZARBAYEV presided over nationhood and initiated important economic changes in his homeland.

KENYA

This land of white coastal beaches, inland savannas, and forests is perhaps the birthplace of man, the site of *Homo habilis,* predecessor to *Homo sapiens.* In the first millennium A.D., migrations produced three distinct peoples who are still a part of Kenya: Hamitic pastoralists who came from Africa's Horn, Nilotic pastoralists from the Nile, and Bantu agriculturalists from the west and south. Ancient Egyptians, Phoenicians, and Persians conducted trade with coastal Kenya. Arab colonists built cities along the coast before A.D. 700, followed by Chinese and Indian traders. After Vasco da Gama sailed around the Cape of Good Hope in 1498, the Portuguese established trading posts and challenged Arab dominance. But the Arabs maintained their position and in the eighteenth century expanded their trade in slaves and ivory, even journeying far into the interior. Another European presence began when Christian missionaries arrived in the 1840s.

Then, in 1895 Britain included Kenya as part of its East African Protectorate, and the ensuing European monopolization of land and politics provoked Kenyan nationalism. After returning from Europe in 1946, JOMO KENYATTA emerged as his homeland's dominant nationalist figure, organizing new political groups and surviving years of imprisonment after the Mau-Mau uprising of the 1950s to become independent Kenya's first prime minister and president.

KIRIBATI

This nation of 33 low-lying islands located between Polynesia and Micronesia was originally populated by settlers from the latter area. They developed several small kingdoms, one of which appeared in Robert Louis Stevenson's *In the South Seas.* Europeans encountered the islands in the seventeenth century, and the British established a protectorate in 1892. They divided the region into the Gilbert and Ellice Islands and gave them colonial status in 1915 and 1916 respectively. During World War II, the Japanese occupied the Gilbert Islands. In 1975, the Ellice Islands became independent Tuvalu. Kiribati, led in its independence drive by NABOUA RATIETA, became a nation on 12 July 1979.

KOREA (NORTH KOREA AND SOUTH KOREA)

Ancient Korea is known for its three great kingdoms: Silla, established in 57 B.C.; Koguryo, established in 37 B.C.; and Paekche, established in 18 B.C. Silla especially became powerful, spreading across Korea, but it was overthrown by rebels who, in A.D. 918, established the Koryo Dynasty. In 1258, the Mongols penetrated Korea and the Koryos came under their control. In 1392, the Koryo monarchy fell to the Yi Dynasty, which built a capital at Seoul and endorsed Confucianism as the official religion. But the kingdom collapsed due to internal disorder and outside interference, and in the late 1500s and early 1600s both the Japanese and Chinese invaded Korea. Turmoil characterized much of the remaining period up to the domination by Japan beginning in the late 1800s. Japan officially annexed Korea in 1910 and held it until the end of World War II.

In the cold-war competition between the United States and the Soviet Union, Korea was divided at the thirty-eighth parallel between Soviet-dominated North Korea and American-dominated South Korea. In 1950, the North Korean Communist army invaded the South, beginning the Korean War. At the same time, Korean nationalism reflected a longstanding split between capitalists and Communists. In South Korea, SYNGMAN RHEE led the nationalists against foreign domination and promoted a capitalist economy. In 1961, CHUNG HEE PARK began a new third republic under his dictatorship. In North Korea, meanwhile, KIM IL-SÖNG led the Communist nationalists in developing a totalitarian socialist state.

KUWAIT

Prior to the twentieth century, this small arid land tucked between Iraq and Saudi Arabia had been most known for its pearl divers, who searched for the precious jewel in the Persian Gulf. This changed, however, with the discovery of oil. Beginning in the 1940s, unparalleled wealth flooded the land, and Kuwaitis had to come to grips with the social changes brought by their prosperity. Although Kuwait had been ruled since 1799 by the al-Sabah Dynasty, Britain's presence and its establishment of a protectorate in 1914 limited Kuwaiti authority while providing protection from Saudi Arabian claims. ABDALLAH AL-SALIM AL-SABAH led Kuwait's transition into prosperity and, in 1961, independence.

KYRGYZSTAN

Dotted with snow-covered mountains and temperate valleys, Kyrgyzstan became home to the nomadic Kyrgyz herders well before the sixteenth century. The Kyrgyz traded with Turkic peoples in the region. In the early nineteenth century, an Islamic khan controlled the Kyrgyz and completed their conversion to the Muslim faith, a process begun centuries earlier. The Russians penetrated the region in 1862 and conquered the khanate in 1876. Russia then encouraged Ukrainians and Russians to settle the area in order to dilute the Kyrgyz culture.

Shortly after the Bolshevik Revolution in 1918, Soviet Communist rule began, and in 1936 Kyrgyzstan became a full republic within the Soviet Union. As Moscow lost its grip on its republics in the late 1980s, a strong nationalist movement grew. In 1991, Kyrgyzstan gained independence and began substantial economic and political reforms under ASKAR AKAYEV.

LAOS

Jungle-covered hills and valleys dominate Laos, a country whose main highway is the Mekong River. Of all the states in French Indochina, Laos has been the least developed, still reliant on subsistence rice farming. Laotian tribes moved south into this area, probably in the 1200s, when they established city-states not united until the Lan Xang Kingdom arose in the mid-1300s. This kingdom lasted over 300 years, but underwent many attacks and experienced several changes in its borders. In the eighteenth and nineteenth centuries, Thais and Vietnamese threatened to engulf Laos, until the French established a protectorate in the late 1800s.

Around 1900, France made Laos part of an Indochinese Union including Cambodia (Kampuchea) and Vietnam. The French established indirect rule and thus left many daily decisions to the Laotians, but the French resident-general held substantial powers and handled all foreign affairs. When nationalism arose after World War II, it reflected conflicting political personalities and ideologies. By 1975, the leftists prevailed, symbolized by the Marxist and nationalist leadership of SOUPHANOUVONG.

LATVIA

For two centuries, Latvians confronted Russian domination. In the late 1700s, Russia annexed Latvia and enforced a program of Russification. This stirred Latvian nationalism. By the late 1800s, Latvia developed an industrialized society with an excellent educational system. When the Russian Revolution erupted in 1905, a Latvian uprising mixed socialist demands with those for nationhood. Russia crushed this uprising, but in 1918—after the devastation and confusion wrought by World War I—the Latvian National Council declared the country's independence. In 1920, Soviet Russia renounced its claims to Latvia, and the country joined the League of Nations.

Independence, however, proved short-lived: In 1939, the Soviets invaded Latvia, installed a pro-Communist government, and in 1940 formally annexed the country. The Soviet occupation brought severe repression and the unexplained disappearance of several thousand Latvians. The Soviets encouraged Russians to settle Latvia and thus reduce the influence of Latvians within their own country. The desire for autonomy remained strong, however, and in the 1980s a nationalist movement reappeared. Led by ANATOLIJS GORBUNOVS, Latvia declared its independence from the Soviet Union in 1991.

LEBANON

Even before the Christian era, Lebanon was the scene of numerous conquests, such as those by the Egyptians, Assyrians, Persians, Greeks, and Romans. The mountainous interior provided sanctuary for various groups, including the Druze and the Maronites, religious sects that have played important roles in Lebanon's modern history, known for its strife and civil wars. After World War I, France obtained a mandate and replaced the defunct Ottoman Empire as ruler of Lebanon. Although French investments brought prosperity, oppression existed and stirred Lebanese nationalists into challenging French rule. With World War II, Britain supported this effort, and in 1943 France finally agreed to Lebanon's independence. In this maneuvering, CAMILLE CHAMOUN provided perceptive, forceful leadership and later served as his country's president.

LESOTHO

Mshweshwe, a Basuto chief, resisted Zulu invaders in the 1840s by obtaining British protection. In 1868, Britain made Lesotho (then called Basutoland) a territory, thus establishing an integrated state under Mshweshwe's leadership. Three years later, Britain annexed Lesotho to its Cape Colony and attempted to eradicate many Basuto customs.

In 1884, the British again made Lesotho a separate entity, this time as a Crown colony. Britain altered its earlier policy and allowed the tribal chiefs substantial autonomy. Still, the Basuto worried that their homeland might be annexed by South Africa, and indeed, that government attempted to acquire the colony. In 1965, however, South Africa accepted Lesotho's continued existence after LEABUA JONATHAN, a conservative Basuto chief, became his people's leader. The South Africans believed Chief Jonathan would be compliant to their wishes, but he often followed policies that opposed them.

LIBERIA

Liberia has an unusual heritage as a haven for free blacks from the antebellum American South. But the country's history predates this influence. Between the thirteenth and fifteenth centuries, peoples from Songhay, Ghana, and Mali moved into the region, and at least 20 tribes emerged and organized into chiefdoms. They were highly fragmented, although by the early 1800s the Kondo Confederacy had emerged, led by the Mandingo. When in the United States the American Colonization Society sought a home for free blacks in the early nineteenth century, it investigated this Grain Coast area of West Africa and found it highly suitable. In 1820, the first freedmen arrived; shortly thereafter they founded the town of Monrovia. The presence of American blacks caused numerous conflicts with the indigenous tribes. In the late 1830s, JOSEPH JENKINS ROBERTS, an American emigré, helped subdue the Africans and in 1847 led his fellow colonists in establishing the independent Liberian Republic.

LIBYA

Berbers first settled Libya, and the area was once part of the Roman Empire. In the early sixteenth century, the Ottoman Empire prevailed, under which Libya was allowed much autonomy and a dynasty was established, the Karamanli, that ruled from 1711 to 1835. After that time, the Ottomans established more direct rule. Then, in 1911, the Italians, who had developed banking and commercial interests in Libya, invaded. The following year, the Ottomans agreed to relinquish the area, but Italy found it much more difficult to subdue the Libyans, and internal resistance continued into the 1930s. While independence came in 1952, the nation remained under European domination. This disturbed Libyan nationalists, particularly MUAMMAR AL-QADDAFI, who developed a Pan-Arabic view. Qaddafi overthrew the Libyan monarchy in 1969 and thus established his nation's true independence.

LITHUANIA

In the sixteenth century, Lithuania merged with Poland to create a powerful kingdom. Some 200 years later, however, the Russians controlled the area. In 1918, after the Russian Empire collapsed, Lithuania became an independent nation, but this status was disrupted by Poland's occupation of Vilnius. In 1940, the Soviet Union annexed the country. Independence was regained in 1990 under VYTAUTAS LANDSBERGIS.

LUXEMBOURG

At its widest, Luxembourg is 37 miles across, and it has a maximum length of 62 miles. This small nation's history has been closely bound to the other Low Countries, Belgium and the Netherlands. After the Roman era, Luxembourg was at various times included in the Frankish kingdom of Austrasia, in the Holy Roman Empire, and in the Kingdom of Lotharingia. It became independent in A.D. 963 under Siegfried, Count de Ardennes. Subsequent rulers enlarged the country, but in 1443 the Duke of Burgundy acquired it. As a duchy, it passed to the Habsburgs in 1477 and later to other foreign rulers, including the French and Spanish. In 1815, the Congress of Vienna proclaimed Luxembourg a grand duchy under William I, king of the Netherlands. The country gained much autonomy under WILLIAM II, although independence did not come until the 1860s.

MACEDONIA

This Balkan nation has a long history of enduring invasions. In the fourth century B.C., Alexander the Great gained control, and in the sixth century A.D., Slavic tribes overran the area. Eight hundred years later, the Ottoman Turks prevailed. Their rule did not end until 1913, when the country was divided among Greece, Serbia, and Bulgaria. After World War II, Josip Broz Tito joined Macedonia to several other states and formed Yugoslavia, a Communist nation. When Yugoslavia collapsed in 1991, Macedonia declared its independence under the leadership of KIRO GLIGOROV.

MADAGASCAR

By the eighteenth century the Isle of Madagascar, located in the Indian Ocean near Africa's southeast coast, had come under the rule of the Merina tribe. In the early 1800s, King Radama I, enamored of Western modernization, surrounded himself with European advisors. Then, in 1862 King Radama II signed a treaty of friendship with France. This support helped buttress the monarchy against rival tribes.

In the 1880s, however, France extended its influence further and gained control over foreign affairs and rights to the port of Diego Suarez. The Merina rebelled against this, but France, engaged in colonial competition with Britain, overpowered them, and in 1896 annexed the island. The establishment of the First Malagasy Republic within the French Community came in 1958 under President PHILIBERT TSIRANANA and was followed by full independence two years later. A more radical revolution led by Lieutenant Commander DIDIER RATSIRAKA resulted in the new Democratic Republic of Madagascar in 1975.

MALAWI

Enormous Lake Malawi, Africa's third largest, dominates this inland nation. Bantu-speaking peoples arrived here between the first and fourth centuries A.D. and established a number of political states. The Maravi Confederacy emerged in 1480, while to the north the Ngonde established a kingdom around 1600. Slave trading flourished in the eighteenth and nineteenth centuries as the Yao established a sphere of influence, and Arab traders and slavers regained the prominence they had lost to Portuguese merchants, who had arrived in the seventeenth century. With the Arab presence, Islam became the primary religion.

The first substantial European occupation occurred in the 1890s as British missionaries and traders, succeeding David Livingstone's exploration some 30 years earlier, expanded into the area. They ended the slave trade, subdued the tribes that had relied on it, and in 1891 declared a protectorate called Nyasaland.

As British domination increased, so too did tension between Europeans and Africans, and an uprising erupted, led by John Chilembwe. As a young man, Chilembwe adopted apocalyptic visions and egalitarian ideas. He helped found missions in southern Nyasaland and then attended a Negro Baptist seminary in the United States, where he read black intellectual works. After his return to Nyasaland, he condemned the treatment of Africans on European-owned plantations. When the government refused to hear his protests, he and his followers gathered arms and in 1915 attacked white settlements. The whites retaliated, forming a militia and capturing and killing Chilembwe on 3 February 1915. His effort was more of a humanistic protest than a nationalistic one, but many Africans consider Chilembwe an important early leader in their struggle for self-determination. After World War II, HASTINGS KAMUZU BANDA, a doctor by profession, challenged British rule, and Malawi became an independent nation on 6 July 1964.

MALAYSIA

This monsoon-swept tropical land obtained prominence during the fifteenth century, when Malacca emerged as the center of Eastern commerce and controlled the spice trade. Merchants met there and exchanged an array of goods, encouraged by sultans who maintained favorable trading policies. With commerce also came religious influence as the Muslim faith spread, building upon the influence of the powerful Islamic Srivijaya Empire that had prevailed for 500 years, beginning back in the eighth century.

The Portuguese arrived and established military and trading outposts in the early sixteenth century. They were soon followed by the Dutch. In 1786, the British East India Company occupied Pinang Island on the west coast of the Malaysian Peninsula. In 1867, Britain organized Pinang Island, Singapore, and Melaka under direct Crown rule. British influence extended gradually into neighboring states, so that by World War II a complex administrative structure emerged in the region, involving varying degrees of power to the local sultans and the Crown. Two Malaysians led their homeland's nationalist movement after World War II, DATO ONN and TENGKU ABDUL RAHMAN.

MALDIVES

This nation consists of about 1,200 small islands, 200 of which are inhabited. Poor and isolated, the Maldives emerged from an obscure background. People from India and Ceylon (today, Sri Lanka) probably settled the islands in the fifth century B.C. In A.D. 1153, Islam replaced Buddhism as the islanders' religion. Europeans first arrived in 1507 when Portuguese explorers landed. In the mid-seventeenth century, the Dutch dominated the area, but their power declined by 1800, and in 1887 the British, based in Ceylon, established a protectorate over the Maldives. Various sultans ruled in this British system. On 26 July 1965, the Maldives gained their independence, but a substantial change in government did not occur until three years later, when IBRAHIM NASIR established a republic.

MALI

This nation gets its name from the powerful empire that dominated the area in the fourteenth century. Under Emperor Mansa Musa, who ruled from 1307 until 1332, Mali conquered territory along the Niger and the important trade and cultural center of Timbuktu. Mali weakened shortly thereafter and was superseded by the Gao Empire. In the late sixteenth century, this empire collapsed, and by the time France began expanding into the area, some 200 years later, four separate states held sway. French expansion took several decades; in 1894, the Europeans conquered Timbuktu, and near the turn of the century Mali became a colony within French West Africa. MODIBO KEITA led his country to a semi-independent status in 1958 as a member of the French Community, and then gained complete independence in 1960 as the Republic of Mali.

MALTA

Nestled in the Mediterranean between Sicily and northern Africa, Malta was inhabited by a Neolithic society that built huge temples some 5,000 years ago. Over succeeding centuries many different peoples colonized Malta, including Phoenicians, Romans, Arabs, Normans, and Castilians. More recently, in the sixteenth century the Knights of St. John, who had in the eleventh century, and later, waged war in the Holy Land, migrated to Malta and declared it their homeland. They expanded trade, and built roads and hospitals. In 1565, the Knights successfully defended Malta and southern Europe from a Muslim invasion. They then initiated a golden era of development.

In 1798, France seized Malta from the Knights, but two years later Britain helped the Maltese end this rule. British control lasted for 160 years until 1964, when Malta gained its independence under Prime Minister Giorgio Borg Olivier. The drive to nationhood was supported by DOM MINTOFF, who in the 1970s radicalized Maltese politics.

MARSHALL ISLANDS

This archipelago amid the Pacific Ocean encompasses 34 major islands located in eastern Micronesia. The first Europeans to arrive were Spaniards in 1529. Westerners did not explore these islands again until 1767, when the Briton Samuel Wallis landed on Rongerik. In 1788, John Marshall and Thomas Gilbert explored several islands, and Marshall's name was applied to the entire area. In the 1880s, the Marshall Islands became part of a German protectorate, but during World War I Japan acquired them. After World War II, the United States governed the islands and used two of them for testing atomic weapons. An independence movement in the 1980s established a government based on democracy and traditional practices with AMATA KABUA as the nation's first president.

MAURITANIA

Like other Sahelian countries, Mauritania has long exhibited a division between a largely black African and animist population in the south, and a largely Arab and Islamic population in the north. In the third and fourth centuries A.D., and again in the seventh and eighth centuries, Berbers entered Mauritania as herders crossing the broad expanses of desert. In the eleventh century, Mauritania became part of an Islamic empire, the Almoravid. By the 1100s, Sudanic kingdoms dominated by black Africans expanded through southern Mauritania and into Berber areas. Then Yemeni Arabs moved into the north and intermingled with the Berbers, forming the Moor culture. Blacks who had been slaves of the Arabs and assimilated their practices also became Moors. Black Africans, meanwhile, settled in the south, near and along the Senegal River. This cultural division later played a prominent role in Mauritania's emergence as a modern nation.

The French proclaimed jurisdiction over Mauritania in 1840 but did not gain power over the Moors until the early 1900s. In 1920, France made Mauritania a part of French West Africa. Nationalism developed slowly, and under MOKTAR OULD DADDAH, a member of West Africa's modernizing elite congenial to French interests, Mauritania moved haltingly toward independence, declared on 28 November 1960.

MAURITIUS

This island nation, part of the Mascarene group, is situated some 700 miles from the southeast African coast and has a volcanic terrain surrounded by coral reefs. Mauritius has one of the highest population densities in the world—a significant change from just two centuries earlier when it was uninhabited. The Dutch acquired Mauritius in 1598 but abandoned it in 1710, leaving it vacant. The French obtained it in 1721, developed a sugar economy, and imported black slaves from Africa. Britain gained official possession in 1814 and brought in Indian laborers as indentured servants.

Today, Mauritius consists mainly of Creole and Indian peoples. This land's move toward independence proceeded largely nonviolently, led by a Creole-Indian alliance and politicians who stressed negotiation with Britain. SEEWOOSAGUR RAMGOOLAM followed this tactic and became a dominant figure in Mauritian politics, serving as prime minister from the early 1950s into the 1980s.

MEXICO

Well before Europeans arrived, great civilizations existed in Mexico. The Mayas and Toltecs established empires, followed by the Aztecs, who were conquered in 1519 by the Spaniard Hernando Cortés. Spain ruled Mexico for over 300 years, extracting wealth in the form of silver and gold, and decimating the Indian population through warfare, disease, and the infamous *encomienda*, which allowed Spaniards to use Indian laborers in mines and on plantations in a system that approximated slavery. Spain also imported African slaves into the colony and introduced Roman Catholicism.

Mexicans consider 1810 the beginning of their independence, although their homeland remained under Spanish rule for another decade. In 1820, a nationalist revolution erupted under Father Miguel Hidalgo and his fellow priest, JOSÉ MORELOS. The final expulsion of Spain occurred in 1821 under the controversial AUGUSTÍN DE ITURBIDE. Thereafter, turmoil characterized Mexican politics into the early twentieth century. In the mid-1800s, after Mexico's leader General Antonio López de Santa Anna lost over half the nation's territory in a war with the United States, BENITO JUÁREZ initiated reforms that redirected development. Social and economic problems produced a revolution in 1910 that spanned ideologies from the moderate FRANCISCO MADERO to the radical EMILIANO ZAPATA. In the 1930s, LÁZARO CÁRDENAS brought fundamental change to Mexico, including widespread land redistribution and the nationalization of important industries.

MICRONESIA (FEDERATED STATES OF)

In the sixteenth century, this Pacific island area came under Spanish control. In 1899, Germany purchased the islands, but in 1914 Japan captured them. American forces occupied Micronesia during World War II, and in 1947 it became part of the United States Trust Territory of the Pacific under United Nations auspices. BAILEY OLTER played a prominent role in Micronesia's movement toward nationhood.

MOLDOVA

Moldovans consider Stephen the Great, who ruled in the fifteenth century, to be the father of their nation. But the country he led was conquered by the Ottoman Turks. In the early 1800s, amid the Napoleonic Wars, Russia annexed Moldova (then called Bessarabia). While later in the century Russia lost much of this land to Romania, in 1924 the Soviet Union established the Moldovian Republic in western Ukraine.

In 1944 the Soviet army captured Bessarabia from Romania and formed the Moldavian Socialist Republic, a Communist state within the U.S.S.R. The Communist leadership in Moscow worked to end the Moldovan affinity for Romania, a country to which the Moldovans had once been connected, and forcibly collectivized the republic's agriculture. Nationalism remained strong in the region and surged in the 1980s. In 1991, Moldovans officially declared their independence from a disintegrating Soviet Union and turned to MIRCEA SNEGUR to preserve their nation's unity.

MONGOLIA

This arid country, whose plains stretch endlessly under a cold blue sky, is perhaps best known for the reign of Genghis Khan, leader of the nomadic Borjigin Mongols. In the early 1200s, he conquered opposing Mongol and Tatar tribes, unified the Mongol people, and through the use of a mounted army and siege warfare built a vast empire extending from Manchuria in the east to the Black Sea in the west.

In more recent times, the Manchus entered Mongolia from China in the late 1600s with a large army and, taking advantage of the weak contacts among various Mongol tribes, they subjugated much of the region. At about the same time, Russian expansion intruded on Mongolia. These developments ended Mongolian independence in 1732. The southern provinces, or what was known as Inner Mongolia, were absorbed into China (where they remain to this day), while the Manchu Dynasty largely ignored the more remote northern provinces, or Outer Mongolia.

Beginning in the mid-1800s, China resumed an intense interest in Outer Mongolia (after the Russians indicated they wanted to expand there) and exerted its dominance. The Chinese made some economic improvements and commerce expanded, but the Mongols became heavily indebted to the Chinese traders, and this economic oppression coupled with political domination stirred Mongolian nationalism, which was dominated in the early twentieth century by Marxist revolutionaries, most notably HORLOYN CHOIBALSANG and DAMDINY SUKHEBATOR.

MOROCCO

Since ancient times, Morocco has been the site of numerous civilizations. Phoenician traders established coastal posts before the twelfth century B.C., and by the fifth century Carthage had extended domination over the area. In the interior, Berber kingdoms emerged by the second century B.C., generally forming alliances with Carthage and, later, Rome. In A.D. 40, Rome annexed Morocco as part of Mauretania, although Roman influence did not go beyond the towns and surrounding countryside. In 680, an Arab invasion began and with it the conversion of many Berbers to Islam. An Arabic kingdom ruled until the tenth century. After the year 1000, a series of struggles ensued between city and desert areas.

The great Sharifan Dynasties emerged after 1500, named after sharifs, meaning descendants of Mohammed the Prophet. Later, after lengthy internal wars, Mohammed III, who ruled from 1757 to 1790, opened Morocco to trade with France. European penetration now began, and as internal strife renewed itself in the 1800s, Morocco fell to foreign control, with France gaining a major domain in 1904 and Spain obtaining a smaller zone of influence. After World War I, a strong nationalist movement emerged, advanced by two disparate leaders, ALLAL AL-FASI, a scholar and theologian, and MOHAMMED V, Morocco's sultan and Westernized ruler.

MOZAMBIQUE

When Vasco da Gama landed on Mozambique Island in 1498, he began a Portuguese pressence in an area that had been settled and developed for centuries. Early inhabitants were probably related to the hunting and gathering peoples called Bushmen, followed by Bantu-speaking groups who arrived between the first and fourth centuries A.D. and established permanent sedentary settlements. Before the seventeenth century, substantial areas of central Mozambique came under control of two political systems. The Muenenutapa Kingdom stretched from the southern bank of the Zambesi River to the Save River and developed gold mines and extensive trade with Swahili merchants. The Malawi Confederation, northeast of the Muenenutapa Kingdom, gained domination over a vast area and engaged in a lucrative ivory trade.

In the sixteenth century, Portugal competed along the Mozambique coast with Arab traders and, by the late nineteenth century, began developing large agricultural plantations and an oppressive forced-labor system. In the early 1960s, the Mozambique Liberation Front, or FRELIMO, became the main organization for Mozambicans fighting Portuguese rule. EDUARDO MONDLANE began FRELIMO and, until his assassination in 1969, led it to numerous victories. FRELIMO's fight for liberation was continued by SAMORA MACHEL, who in 1975 became Mozambique's first president.

MYANMAR (BURMA)

This country, formerly called Burma, was ruled from A.D. 1044 to 1077 by King Anawrahta, who established an empire that spanned most of today's Myanmar and included the two major ethnic groups, Burmans and Thais. These people populated the lowlands, developed rice cultivation using irrigation, and embraced Buddhism, while in the hills lived tribes who remained animists, believing that all things in nature have a soul. Two other great rulers arose to unite this land: Bayinnaung, from 1551 to 1581, and Alaungpaya, from 1752 to 1760. At other times, warfare among smaller states often prevailed. In 1885, the British completed their conquest of Myanmar and, except for the Japanese invasion during World War II, held on to the country until 1948. Nationalism stirred in the early twentieth century but did not reach great intensity until the 1930s when AUNG SAN and U NU led the drive against Britain.

NAMIBIA

For 75 years, South Africa ruled this arid, impoverished land, but much earlier, even before written history, Khoisan peoples inhabited the area. Europeans arrived in 1484, when the Portuguese navigator Diogo Cão landed on the coast. German missionaries came in the 1840s, thus beginning that nation's interest in the area. In the 1870s, Britain annexed Walvis Bay, but not the interior, and in 1884 Germany developed a greater presence, soon establishing German Southwest Africa. With World War I, South Africa acquired Namibia and began a contract labor system and apartheid. This stirred an independence movement most prominently led by SAM NUJOMA.

NAURU

This tiny Pacific island, only 8 square miles in size, contains an important resource: phosphate that is used as fertilizer. Continuous European contact with Nauru began in the mid-1800s, and phosphate mining began in 1907. After World War I, Britain, Australia, and New Zealand gained the dominant interests in Nauru. In the 1950s, Nauruans increasingly questioned the foreign role in their phosphate mining and a nationalist movement arose, led by HAMMER DERO-BURT. Many outside observers laughed at this settlement of only some 7,000 people becoming a nation, but in 1968 the Nauruans gained their independence and faced the challenge of prosperity amid dwindling phosphate deposits.

NEPAL

This land of towering snow-capped mountains, including the majestic and formidable Mt. Everest, has for years housed a unique civilization, one that combines Buddhism and Hinduism with local cultural influences. For 1,500 years the Kathmandu Valley has been Nepal's center, and throughout its existence Nepal has maintained its independence, albeit under limited British intervention beginning in 1816 and lasting until 1923, and various forms of British influence after that. Until the late eighteenth century, Nepal consisted of many small states or kingdoms.

Although the Lichavi kings in the fourth to eighth centuries and the Malla kings from the twelfth to eighteenth centuries exerted considerable influence, Nepal's unification did not occur until 1769 when Gorkha, a hill kingdom established by Rajputs from India, completed its expansion, largely through military conquest under the leadership of its great king, PRITHVINARAYAN SHAH. Modern political parties did not emerge, however, until after World War I. They challenged the existing dictatorship that was backed by Britain and reflected the nationalist activities then under way in neighboring India. The most prominent party, the Nepali National Congress, patterned itself after the Indian National Congress and even adopted the latter's emphasis on nonviolent protest. In this effort, Bishweshwar Prasad Koirala emerged as the leader and advocated economic self-sufficiency and small-scale production. In 1951, Koirala and his followers toppled the existing ruler, but political maneuvering under a restored monarchy kept him from forming a government until 1959. Political reforms occurred, and for these Koirala should receive much credit; yet his liberal socialist and democratic programs had a short life. In 1991, the Communists did well in free elections and they continue to expand their power.

THE NETHERLANDS

In ancient times, Germanic tribes inhabited the Netherlands and for years effectively resisted Roman rule. Although Julius Caesar conquered them in 55 B.C., the Roman penetration was limited. In the eighth and ninth centuries A.D., the Netherlands became part of Charlemagne's empire. After its demise, the area fell to the Burgundian dukes and later the Spanish Habsburgs. The latter allowed the Netherlands (part of the Low Countries) considerable autonomy, but in the sixteenth century, after Philip II moved to tighten his grip, rebellion ensued, led by the man who is today considered the Father of the Netherlands, WILLIAM I.

NEW ZEALAND

In the seventeenth century, the Maoris, a Polynesian people, resisted the European intrusion on their homeland and turned back a Dutch navigator. The British Captain James Cook explored New Zealand's coasts in 1769. Britain annexed the area in 1840, and the colonists gradually developed a progressive government. New Zealand gained dominion status in 1907 but continued its strong attachments to Britain. The conservative WILLIAM MASSEY first exerted New Zealand's status as a sovereign nation in 1919, but his action did not reflect a strong nationalist movement and, indeed, no such movement ever emerged. Complete independence was gained in 1947.

NICARAGUA

Long before the Spaniards arrived, diverse Indian tribes inhabited Nicaragua. In 1522, Spanish explorers entered, led by Gil González, as part of their expansion into Panama. Within just a few decades, the intruders destroyed the Native American civilization, reducing its population from a million to a few thousand. Nicaragua remained under Spanish control until the nineteenth century. Spain crushed an uprising in 1811, but in 1822 Nicaragua separated from its mother country as part of a rebellion in Mexico. In 1823, the country joined in a federation with other Central American states, led by JOSÉ CECILIO DEL VALLE and FRANCISCO MORAZÁN, that lasted until 1838, when the union collapsed and Nicaragua gained complete independence under the presidency of José Núñez. No strong founding figure emerged, however, and a long period ensued with a series of nearly indistinguishable dictatorships.

In the early twentieth century, the United States occupied Nicaragua, partly to protect its interest in an isthmian canal. Augusto César Sandino led an uprising against the U.S.-backed conservative dictatorship. Although he failed, and the Somoza family began a long, brutal rule, Sandino's nationalism affected many Nicaraguans and stirred a later anti-Somoza movement led by the revolutionary Sandinista National Liberation Front and DANIEL ORTEGA. The Sandinistas succeeded in overthrowing the Somozas but not in retaining power. After ten years, they lost to VIOLETA

CHAMORRO in an election that signaled a conservative reaction and questions as to whether the nation had entered a new era or would revert to its earlier elite domination.

NIGER

Prior to European rule, Niger came under the domination of several different empires. First Mali in the fourteenth century, and then Songhay in the fifteenth and sixteenth centuries, expanded across western Niger. Then Moroccans invading from the north destroyed the Songhay state in 1591. Cattle herders entered Niger and in the eighteenth and nineteenth centuries formed several Muslim states allied with the Sokoto caliphate in Nigeria. When the French arrived in the late 1800s, they ran into especially strong resistance from the Tuareg people and subsequently were unable to establish a civilian colony until 1922.

Niger then became a part of French West Africa, thus joining in a federation with several neighboring territories, including Senegal and Côte d'Ivoire. Consequently, nationalism in Niger was tied to nationalism in these areas. Under French rule, Niger experienced little economic development. No paved roads or railroads were built, nor were any cash crops developed, except for peanuts. France established a forced-labor system, and this, along with economic impoverishment, encouraged an exodus of Nigeriens to Ghana or Côte d'Ivoire. After World War II, nationalism in Niger grew in tandem with movements in the other French West African colonies, all more economically and politically developed than Niger. HAMANI DIORI pursued a moderate path toward Nigerien independence.

NIGERIA

Nigeria has within it several hundred ethnic groups with different cultures and political organizations, a product of a long and complex history; its first high culture emerged in the fourth century B.C. Well before A.D. 1500, Nigeria consisted of competing states, most notably Yoruba west of the Niger River; Benin in the southeast, with its vast trade and centralized government; and the Hausa cities in the north. In the sixteenth century, the Songhai Empire reached its height, stretching from the Senegal and Gambia Rivers into parts of Hausaland in the east. The Sayfawa Dynasty of Borno also extended into Hausaland, and Borno domination continued into the late 1700s, after which there followed a period of instability leading to an uprising of Muslims in the Hausa states and formation of the Sokoto Caliphate in 1809.

During the nineteenth century, Yoruba wars occurred in the south, and Britain, involved in the area's slave trade since the 1700s, increased its presence through additional commerce. The British conquered Benin in 1897 and Sokoto in 1903, and by 1906 they established a protectorate over all of Nigeria. Yet Nigeria's past divisions portended future ones. Amid a weak nationalist movement three prominent individuals guided Nigeria toward independence in 1960: OBAFEMI AWOLOWO, NNAMDI AZIKIWE, and ABUBAKAR TAFAWA BALEWA. These men helped organize Nigerians across ethnic and sectional boundaries but could not overcome their homeland's internal clashes; oftentimes, they spent as much time fighting each other as they spent fighting British rule.

NORWAY

When many people think of ancient Norway, Viking images come to mind. The Vikings ranged across northwestern Europe from the eighth to the eleventh centuries A.D. Beginning in the fourteenth century, Norway was linked to Denmark, a union that lasted until 1814. The Danes allowed the Norwegians to keep most of their own customs and, fearing a Swedish invasion, tended to placate Norway with numerous concessions. After the Napoleonic Wars, the Treaty of Kiel in 1814 ceded Norway to Sweden. Norwegians reacted by writing their own constitution, but in a brief military action, Sweden crushed the independence effort. The constitution, however, remained in effect within the subsequent union of the two countries, which was formalized in November 1814. Under the union, the Swedish king appointed his own ministers, handled foreign policy, and could veto legislation, but the Norwegian legislature initiated legislation and determined taxes.

In the nineteenth century, Norwegians tried to win more autonomy for themselves, and they generally succeeded in gaining concessions. For example, in 1848 a radical labor movement emerged under Marcus Thrane, and he stirred a strong sense of nationalism in promoting the use of the vernacular Norwegian language over the Danish-influenced language. Thrane also organized a political coalition, called the Left. Complete independence for Norway came in 1905 under Prime Minister CHRISTIAN MICHELSEN.

OMAN

Oman has a strong tribal system traceable to the immigration of Arab tribes in the second century A.D. It also strongly supports Islam, a religion introduced in the seventh century. Omani history differs in an important way from other states in the region: This country never became a colony or protectorate during the European imperialism of the nineteenth and twentieth centuries. The Portuguese did occupy the coast beginning in the early 1500s, but the Omanis led by Ahmad ibn Saʿīd ejected them in 1650. Thus began an extended period of rule under the Āl Bū Saʿīd Dynasty. Since this dynasty continues to rule today, Ahmad ibn Saʿīd can be considered the founder of Oman. But in the nineteenth century, the dynasty functioned under substantial British influence and exhibited few modern state characteristics until change occurred in the 1970s under QĀBŪS IBN SA'ĪD.

PAKISTAN

The Indus River courses through this nation on the Indian subcontinent and for centuries has been the conduit for different ethnic and religious groups. Archaeologists have uncovered remains of a civilization dating back to the third millennium B.C., including two cities located in modern Pakistan: Mohenjo-Daro and Harappa. Hindu civilization entered its Golden Age from the fourth to seventh centuries A.D. under the Guptas. This was not a highly centralized empire, however, and after the seventh century northern India went into decline. Islam made its appearance in the eighth century and more forcefully under Turkish and Afghan conquests beginning in the tenth and eleventh centuries. In 1206, a Muslim sultanate arose around Delhi, and Islamic rulers expanded their power over much of the Indian subcontinent. The Muslims protected the region from the Mongols and stimulated a cultural renaissance. In the sixteenth century, the Mughal Empire developed and included the building of the Taj Mahal. As the Mughals arose, the Portuguese arrived in 1498 and conquered Goa in 1510.

The British established their rule in the mid-eighteenth century through the British East India Company and, beginning in 1857, directly through the Crown. Britain established a racist, albeit paternalistic, system that treated Indians as inferior. In reaction to these oppressive conditions, some upper-class Indians, mostly lawyers, organized the Indian National Congress in 1885, which sought civil rights, such as freedom of the press and a greater use of juries, and more autonomy for Indians, particularly the Indianization of the government bureaucracy. Congress included both Hindus and Muslims, who constituted about 25 percent of the Indian population. MOHAMMED ALI JINNAH led the Muslim nationalists and became the most important leader in establishing an independent Pakistan in 1947.

PALAU

This republic occupies the westernmost part of the Caroline archipelago east of the Philippines and shares its history with Micronesia, which after World War II became a Trust Territory supervised by the United States. HARUO REMELIIK authored a controversial constitution that declared Palau a nuclear-free zone. After his violent death, complete independence occurred on 1 October 1994 under KUNIWO NAKAMURA.

PANAMA

In 1502, Christopher Columbus arrived at this site situated strategically at the narrow Central American isthmus, and in 1513 Vasco Núñez de Balboa explored it and found the Pacific Ocean. Spain established control and used Panama as a conduit for supplies shipped between Central and South America. In 1821, the Panamanians joined with Colombia after that nation had gained its independence from Spain. But discontent with the arrangement encouraged several attempts to break away, including one in 1840 by Tomás Herrera that produced a semiautonomous government. Then the United States, seeking to build a canal, interceded and in 1903 backed a revolt led by MANUEL AMADOR GUERRERO that brought Panama its independence. For decades after, an oligarchy ruled the nation. This pattern was not interrupted until the 1970s and 1980s, when OMAR TORRIJOS HERRERA reshaped the government.

PAPUA NEW GUINEA

Humid rain forests and towering mountains cover this nation's main island that was first inhabited by man some 40,000 years ago. Extensive coastal trade emerged 5,000 years ago, as did a social system known for its elaborate ceremonies. The written word, however, did not develop, thus leaving few details about this civilization. Europeans first arrived in the early 1500s, when a Portuguese explorer landed on the main island by accident. In the late nineteenth century, Britain acquired the southern part of New Guinea, but only to frustrate German expansion. Germany controlled the northern part. (The Dutch controlled the western portion of the island of New Guinea, which today is part of Indonesia).

In 1906, Britain transferred its colony to Australia, which obtained the German area during World War I and after the war administered two territories, Papua in the south and New Guinea in the north. Australians, Americans, Papuans, and New Guineans fought together to defeat a Japanese invasion in World War II. The war brought devastation but also introduced the indigenous people to modern technology and, after the conflict, caused Australia to merge the two territories and increase its spending on schools, roads, and other improvements. Westerners, meanwhile, explored the highlands, finding not a largely uninhabitable area as they had imagined, but a population of about 1 million (some of whom lived in a Stone Age culture). When Australia committed itself to independence for the territory in the 1970s, it complemented the efforts of MICHAEL SOMARE, who pushed for nationhood and obtained it in 1975.

PARAGUAY

Europeans penetrated this remote area in the early 1500s, when the Portuguese adventurer Aleixo Garcia crossed the Río Paraná and allied with Indian warriors at what would later become Asuncíon. As the colony developed, the Jesuits assumed a leading role, dominating it from 1608 until their expulsion in 1767. Asuncíon emerged as Paraguay's major city, but it was secondary in the region to Buenos Aires. The colony's status as a backwater, along with oppressive taxes and trade regulations, encouraged nationalist sentiment. Independence and a social revolution came in 1811 under JOSÉ GASPAR RODRÍGUEZ DE FRANCIA. Subsequent governments have followed Francia's pattern of dictatorial rule.

PERU

By the middle of the fifteenth century, Peru emerged as the center of a great Inca civilization. Under the emperor Pachacuti Inca Yupanqui (1438–1471), the Incan conquest expanded rapidly, and a third of South America, encompassing some 9 to 16 million people, came under Incan rule. In 1524, the Spanish conquistador Francisco Pizarro invaded the Incan Empire from his base in Panama. In 1532, he arrived in northern Peru with 180 men and 30 horses. Pizarro wanted gold and soon took advantage of his superior military technology, the European diseases that devastated the indigenous population, and a civil war among the Indians to plunder the empire. By 1533, he captured the imperial city, and Spain subsequently consolidated its control. The Spanish exploited Indian labor and the natural resources, particularly silver, and they monopolized the land, taking much of it as the Indian population declined.

Although colonial Peru experienced some internal upheaval when discontented peasants and Creoles (persons of Spanish blood born in America) rebelled against the Spanish authorities in the late 1700s, the area remained a citadel of royalist support amid the South American liberation movements of the early 1800s. Independence, in fact, came from without, after the armies of SIMÓN BOLÍVAR and JOSÉ DE SAN MARTÍN invaded the country. Since gaining nationhood, Peru has experienced little political and social change, with a small Creole elite holding most of the wealth and power.

PHILIPPINES

This archipelago was originally inhabited by Negritos and Malays who emigrated across land bridges from Southeast Asia. Sometime after A.D. 1000, Arab, Chinese, and Indian traders started to arrive. Although Islam entered the islands, it did not prevail everywhere. Europeans arrived before a centralized government developed; they appeared in 1521 when Ferdinand Magellan debarked under the Spanish flag. Soon, there began conversions to Catholicism and a long period of Spanish rule that lasted until the American takeover in 1898.

Spain provided few social programs, and the Filipinos had little say in the colonial government. Not until the 1860s did the Spaniards act to provide their subjects with compulsory education, and even this effort was incomplete. Philippine nationalism went through several stages, initially directed against Spain and later the United States. The great nationalist writer JOSÉ RIZAL stimulated patriotic activities in the late 1800s, including the organizational efforts of ANDRES BONIFACIO and the revolutionary military commander EMILIO AGUINALDO. An important leader against American rule and the architect of the Philippine constitution was MANUEL ROXAS.

POLAND

Under Wladislaus II in the fifteenth century, the Poles defeated the Prussian Teutonic Knights and regained their Baltic coastline. Poland continued to expand in the fifteenth and sixteenth centuries, winning important victories over the Russians and the Turks. But the Polish monarchy weakened thereafter, and in the 1700s the country lost its autonomy through two partitions after Prussia, Russia, and Austria invaded—Russia originally at the behest of a few Polish nobles who opposed recent internal political reforms—and grabbed Polish land.

The partitions left Poland a feeble and emaciated country. Poles rebelled against this development, but the combined Russian and Prussian forces proved too powerful. This led to a third partition in 1795 when Prussia, Russia, and Austria eliminated Poland from existence. By these agreements and the Congress of Vienna held in 1814, Russia controlled a huge part of former Poland, including Warsaw. In the late 1800s, a strong independence movement emerged, led by JÓZEF PILSUDSKI. Poland gained its nationhood after World War I, but again lost its autonomy, this time after World War II, when the Soviet Union occupied the country. Soviet domination continued until the successful nationalist rebellion under LECH WALESA in the 1980s.

PORTUGAL

This country, tucked along the Atlantic side of the Iberian Peninsula, is the oldest nation in Europe, having emerged as a unified state even before neighboring Spain and France. Its founding occurred in the 1100s under King AFONSO I. Around 1200, Portugal reached the size it is today. The monarchy continued to grow stronger, and under King John II in the early fifteenth century, an absolutist government emerged. His son, Prince Henry the Navigator, promoted Portugal's overseas explorations, and by the mid-1500s this small nation established an empire encompassing areas in West and East Africa, Brazil, Persia, and the Far East.

The monarchy fell in 1910, replaced first by a republican government and then by a dictatorship, which lasted until 1974. A revolution occurred that year; it stemmed from problems within the colonial system and the nation's impoverished economy, and the public criticism offered by ANTONIO DE SPINOLA ultimately led to dramatic changes to the nation's political system.

QATAR

In the 1860s, Britain acquired an influence in Qatar when it negotiated an end to Bahrain's rule over this land. But for the next several decades, it was not the British but rather the Ottoman Turks who occupied Qatar. With the collapse of the Ottoman Empire in World War I, Britain increased its influence in Qatar as part of its expanding power in the Persian Gulf. As the British gained control over Qatar's foreign affairs, they provided the small emirate with military protection. When, in the late 1960s, financial exigencies forced Britain to relinquish its gulf role, KHALIFAH IBN HAMAD AL THANI directed his emirate's independence and the formation of a liberalized government.

ROMANIA

After the Romans abandoned Romania in the third century A.D., Goths, Slavs, and Bulgars invaded the region. By the sixteenth century, Moldavia and Walachia, the two major Romanian provinces, had come under control of the Ottoman Turks. Then, following the Russo-Turkish War of 1828, they fell to Russian domination. Independence came under the leadership of King Carol I and ION BRĂTIANU, who led a nationalist campaign in the mid-nineteenth century. After World War II, the Soviet Union dominated Romania, although the local Communist regime was often able to implement policies opposed by the Soviets. When the Soviet Empire crumbled in the late 1980s, so too did the Romanian dictatorship, and ION ILIESCU developed a more autonomous nation.

RUSSIA

In the ninth century, Scandinavians settled Russia. After Mongols conquered the country 400 years later, Muscovy gradually became the center of Russian authority. Mongol rule did not make Russian society Asian, but it did isolate Russia from many European influences. In the 1320s, Ivan I Kalita collected tribute to give his Asian overlords, and this caused local power to be concentrated in him as the leader of the Grand Dukes of Moscow. Hence emerged the Muscovite state with its absolutism and autocracy that IVAN III expanded in the late fifteenth century. He ended Mongol suzerainty, and under him Russia emerged as a nation ruled by an autocratic tsar.

Beginning in the late 1600s, PETER I consolidated Russia, promoted Western practices, and more firmly established absolutism. CATHERINE II continued his efforts in the eighteenth century and intensified nationalism. In the early 1800s, Tsar Alexander I expanded Russian territory by acquiring Finland and Bessarabia after long and bloody wars. He successfully defeated Napoleon's invasion that began in 1812 and by 1814 was the most powerful ruler in Europe. Despite Russia's prestige, the nation experienced many internal difficulties, in part worsened by tsarist policies. For example, the economy suffered as the peasants, reduced to serfdom, lived in extreme poverty.

The imbalances in society led to the Communist Revolution of 1917 that created the Soviet Union. The Communists, at first under Lenin and then under Joseph Stalin, expected to create a powerful Soviet state based on Marxist principles. Their greatest success, however, came in developing military weaponry and a large army that defeated Germany in World War II and established Soviet domination over Eastern Europe. Economic problems continued, made worse by corruption within the Communist Party and accompanied by ethnic and nationalist pressures. By the 1980s, the Soviet Union faced a crisis of survival, and the Communists turned to MIKHAIL GORBACHEV for leadership. A limited reformer, he inadvertently helped produce the end of the Soviet Union. BORIS YELTSIN was even more instrumental in demanding reforms and leading a revolution that in 1991 created a new Russia.

RWANDA

According to legend, Rwanda—a small landlocked country of plateaus, rolling hills, and mountains tucked among Uganda, Tanzania, Zaire, and Burundi—developed a civilization when the Tutsi tribe arrived and its founding hero, Gihanga, worked miracles. In actuality, Tutsi rule occurred after a migration of many decades through the fourteenth and fifteenth centuries. When the Tutsi, who were nomadic pasturalists, arrived in Rwanda, they found the Hutu, who were agriculturalists, already occupying the area. Through military superiority and possession of cattle, the Tutsi dominated the numerically superior Hutu. Under a feudal system called *ubuhake,* all land was in Tutsi hands under the monarch, or the *mwami.* In 1916, after Rwanda had been under German rule for over a decade, Belgian forces invaded, and in 1923 the kingdom became a Belgian mandated Trust Territory under the League of Nations.

Much like the Germans, the Belgians ruled through Rwanda's *mwami.* When, after World War II, GRÉGOIRE KAYIBANDA became a prominent advocate of Rwanda reform, he and his followers attacked Tutsi domination and Belgian colonialism. Both, they deemed, had to be ended and a new Rwanda created. In 1994, longstanding animosity between the Hutus and Tutsis led to widespread carnage as the former group attacked the latter in a vicious extermination campaign.

ST. KITTS AND NEVIS

Christopher Columbus explored these islands in 1493 and encountered the Carib Indians. British settlers arrived in 1623, although Britain did not gain undisputed possession until the Treaty of Versailles was signed with France in 1783. Along with nearby Anguilla, St. Kitts and Nevis obtained autonomy over their internal affairs in 1967. Within a few months, Anguilla withdrew from the union and decided to remain a British colony. St. Kitts and Nevis obtained their independence as a nation within the British Commonwealth in 1983 under KENNEDY SIMMONDS.

ST. LUCIA

Christopher Columbus may have visited this small Caribbean island in 1502. If he did, he likely faced a hostile reception from the Carib Indians who lived there. They resisted European intrusion for years. Throughout the seventeenth century, Britain and France both claimed the island and control of it shifted between them. After the Napoleonic Wars in 1814, France ceded St. Lucia to Britain for the last time, and the British governed it until 1979. The moderate lawyer JOHN COMPTON led St. Lucia's independence movement.

ST. VINCENT AND THE GRENADINES

Christopher Columbus landed on St. Vincent in 1498 and encountered the Arawak Indians. During the seventeenth and eighteenth centuries, Britain and France competed for control of this Caribbean island. In 1763, St. Vincent became a British colony and remained so until full independence was gained on 27 October 1979, under ROBERT MILTON CATO.

SAN MARINO

Three-tenths the size of Washington, D.C., with its main city clinging to a mountainside, San Marino claims to be the oldest republic in Europe. According to legend, Saint Marino, a Christian stonecutter who fled the persecution of a Roman emperor in the fourth century, founded the nation as a religious community.

By the year 1000, San Marino emerged as a republic, but in succeeding centuries faced numerous challenges to its independence. As the medieval period ended, it had features more akin to an Italian city-state than a modern nation, and its existence in the sixteenth century was precarious. One of the important turning points for San Marino occurred in 1631 when Pope Urban VIII recognized its independence. In its modern era, ANTONIO ONOFRI emerged as a leading figure—the man who prevented a takeover by Napoleon and annexation by the Papal States.

SÃO TOMÉ AND PRÍNCIPE

These two islands, located in Africa's Gulf of Guinea, played an enormously important role in the transatlantic slave trade. The Portuguese arrived in the 1480s and established a plantation system heavily reliant on black slaves imported from the African continent. The sugar-and-slave plantation system became the model for fifteenth-century development of the Americas by Europeans. Portuguese rule continued into the 1970s, when a nationalist movement led by MANUEL PINTO DA COSTA brought independence.

SAUDI ARABIA

In the early seventh century, the Prophet Mohammed withdrew to live in Arabian caves and there received his first revelations. By 630, he entered Mecca, which surrendered itself to Islam and became a sacred city. Ruling from Medina, Mohammed gained control over most of Arabia. After 650, Arabia became the scene of intervention by outside powers and tribal maneuvering, producing a series of states. The Saudi family group emerged as significant around 1450 in east central Arabia. It gained substantial power when, shortly before 1720, Saud ibn Mohammed ibn Miqrin defeated several other families in gaining control of Dariya.

The first unified Saudi state expanded from Nejd in the late 1700s and spread across northern Arabia and into the Islamic holy places located in the Hejaz of western Arabia. This state collapsed in 1818, however, under an Egyptian invasion, and the Saud Dynasty's fortunes underwent a temporary decline. The current Saudi Arabia Kingdom emerged under ABD AL-AZIZ IBN SAUD, who used tribal alliances, military conquests, and agreements with Western powers to build his state.

SENEGAL

Although the Tekrur, Ghana, and Mali Kingdoms extended into Senegal during the eleventh century and later, in its early history this land never served as the base of a major political unit. Instead, there appeared numerous minor states and, near the coast, a variety of small ethnic groups. In the eighteenth and nineteenth centuries, Senegal became an object of rivalry between France and Britain. By virtue of the Treaty of Paris (1814), France gained domination of the area, and French traders penetrated the interior. Along the coast, France established the cities called the Four Communes (Dakar, Goree, Rufisque, and Saint Louis). In each, the French allowed a limited number of black Africans—those with the status of citizens as opposed to subjects—to elect delegates to the city councils and other representative bodies. This provided Senegalese blacks with a Western-style political experience and an organized outlet for protests against various French policies.

The Four Communes were the only locations in French Africa where blacks could vote, and vibrant politics emerged there. Blaise Diagne, a black customs official, organized one of the first modern political parties in Africa: the Republican-Socialists. He declared "Senegal for the Senegalese" and quickly gained the enmity of French officials. Yet Diagne's party won control of the city councils, and in 1914 he became the first black elected to the French Parliament. France, worried about African power, narrowed the duties of the councils, engaged in press censorship, and formed a secret police unit. In time, Diagne became more accommodating to French interests.

Still, the political system had activated blacks in the Four Communes and in those rural areas influenced by urban political activities. This helped foster the rise of political action in the twentieth century by LAMINE GUÈYE, who organized Senegal's first modern political party and pushed for a greater degree of black rights. Later, LÉOPOLD SÉDAR SENGHOR advanced the important concepts of "negritude" and Senegalese political autonomy.

SEYCHELLES

No permanent human settlement occurred on these small islands until 1771, when several whites, their black slaves, and five South Indians arrived from Mauritius and Réunion. At the same time, pirates roamed the islands extensively, including Americans who raided British and French ships. In the nineteenth century, American whalers used the Seychelles for rendering their catches. Although the French first claimed the area in 1756, they turned the islands over to the British in 1814 under the Treaty of Paris. Britain at first merged the Seychelles with Mauritius, but in 1809 the islands obtained their own governor, and formal separation of the two areas occurred in 1903. Britain allowed the Seychelles their first elected legislature in 1948. Universal adult suffrage in 1967 reflected the Seycehellois demand for greater autonomy that culminated ten years later in independence under James Mancham and FRANCE ALBERT RENÉ.

SIERRA LEONE

This small nation has been inhabited for thousands of years. Most residents are descendants of tribes that migrated into the region between the twelfth and fifteenth centuries, particularly the Mende, who organized into small political units, or chiefdoms. Portuguese explorers arrived in the late 1400s and applied the name Serra Lyoa (Lion Mountains), later pronounced as Sierra Leone. British involvement intensified in 1787 when former slaves arrived from England. Nationalism grew slowly in Sierra Leone and generally nonviolently. A largely conservative movement to gain nationhood was led by two brothers, SIR ALBERT

MARGAI and SIR MILTON MARGAI. Their efforts helped produce Sierra Leone's independence on 27 April 1961.

SINGAPORE

In 1284, colonists from Sumatra established a fishing village on this island, called Singa Pura. Later, pirates used the thick mangrove forests as hiding places. Modern Singapore was essentially a British creation. In 1819, Thomas Standford Raffles, an Englishman, acquired the island from a sultan and determined to develop it into a major Asian port. By 1869, this occurred under British Crown rule, and Singapore's population reached 100,000—mainly Chinese merchants and laborers, but also Indians and Malays. During World War II, the Japanese occupied the island and killed thousands of Chinese.

When the British returned in 1945, they began revising the constitution to expand political participation by Singaporeans, but the process was slow, and before 1955 the franchise was limited. At the same time, a strong nationalist movement arose that challenged British rule. LEE KUAN YEW organized the People's Action Party and led the political fight for independence.

SLOVAKIA

Until the collapse of the Great Moravian Empire in the tenth century, Slovaks had lived united with their fellow Slavics, the Czechs. After the empire's demise, they came under the control of the Magyars. Slovak nationalism remained largely dormant until the 1700s when Anton Bernolák tried to develop a Slovak language, an effort continued more successfully in the following century by L'udovit Stúr. This development magnified differences between the Slovaks and the Czechs and encouraged cultural separation. Slovak nationalism, however, remained weak and did not equal the intense desire among the Czechs for an independent nation.

Despite their intensifying differences, numerous Czechs and Slovaks worked together for a state that would unify the two peoples. Tomáš Masaryk led this movement, and in 1918 Czechoslovakia was born. Slovaks soon complained about a secondary status within the nation, and internal disputes between the two ethnic groups facilitated the partitioning of Czechoslovakia by Poland, Hungary, and Germany in 1938. The following year, Hitler conquered what remained of the country and encouraged a separate Slovak nation, established under complete Nazi control. After World War II, Czechs and Slovaks united again to reestablish Czechosolvakia, but in 1948 the Communists gained control, and with them came domination by the Soviet Union. Czechoslovakia did not regain its autonomy until 1989 in a revolution led by VÁCLAV HAVEL. Many Slovaks believed that the outspoken dissident Alexander Dubcek would emerge as their leader in the

Czechoslovakian union, but he died in 1992. Shortly thereafter, the Slovaks declared their independence under VLADIMIR MECIAR, who led the effort to dissolve Czechoslovakia.

SLOVENIA

From the sixth to the eighth centuries, Slavs settled Slovenia. In the 800s, they came under German rule, and from the mid-fourteenth century until the end of World War I they were controlled by the Austrian Habsburg Empire, whose rulers attempted to eliminate Slovene culture. In 1918, the Slovenes joined with the Croats and Serbs to form the Kingdom of Slovenes, Croats, and Serbs.

After World War II, Slovenia united with five other states into a new nation, Yugoslavia. From 1945 to 1980, this nation of disparate ethnic groups and religions was held together by the authoritarian communist ruler Josip Broz Tito. Upon his death the member states formed a collective presidency, but the nation fell victim to intense ethnic strife. Slovenia offically declared its independence on 25 June 1991 under the leadership of MILAN KUCAN.

SOLOMON ISLANDS

When Spaniards first encountered these volcanic islands near Papua New Guinea and Australia in the 1560s, they found an agricultural society. Europeans did not permanently settle the area until the late nineteenth century. In 1893, Britain claimed a protectorate over the islands and developed a plantation economy. Effective control was difficult to accomplish as tribal feuds and head-hunting raids caused disorder, and the last of the major islands was not brought under control until the eve of World War II.

After the war, many on the islands did not want British rule reinstated. In the eastern Solomons, Malaitans organized the Marching Rule, a movement that unified the people in rebuilding homes and the economy, and resisted the British authorities—at first peacefully, then violently. Britain reacted in 1950 by forcefully crushing the Marching Rule. As anticolonial movements developed in the Third World during the 1950s and 1960s, however, the British decided to move the Solomon Islands toward nationhood. This, they believed, could only be done gradually, since the colony had a weak economy. Independence came in 1978 under PETER KENILOREA.

SOMALIA

Well before A.D. 1200, Bantu-speaking peoples migrated northward into Somalia. When persecuted Muslims fled Arabia across the Red Sea, a mass religious conversion of Somalis occurred in the eleventh through thirteenth centuries. Islamization produced a string of city-states along the coast, including Mogadishu, which for several centuries was a prominent urban center. By the 1500s, a series of kingdoms spread from Somalia's interior. Numerous conflicts erupted from the thirteenth to the sixteenth centuries between Ethiopian Christians and Somali Muslims.

Nevertheless, prior to the arrival of Europeans, Somali society was one of the more homogeneous in Africa. Somalis identified with clans, and these entered into shifting alliances. There developed within the clans three major characteristics of Somali society: democracy, equality, and anarchy. Democracy was evident in the widespread male participation in clan councils. Egalitarianism entailed a strong belief in community ahead of personal gain. Anarchy existed in the paucity of institutionalized authority roles.

In the 1880s, this culture was divided into separate territories under British, French, Italian, and Ethiopian rule. In 1899, Mohammed Abdullah Bin Hassan began fighting a guerrilla war against the British in northern Somalia, but in 1920 his rebellion collapsed. In the 1940s, a strong nationalist movement appeared, and in 1960 British and Italian Somaliland merged to form the independent Somali Republic. Somalia's modern nationalism was fuelled in part by the early efforts of MOHAMMED SAYIID 'ABDILLE HASSAN. After independence, national unity in a clan-based society proved difficult. MOHAMMED SAYIID BARRE developed an authoritarian structure to hold Somalia together, which he was able to do for only 22 years.

SOUTH AFRICA

The First European settlers to arrive here were the Dutch, who landed at the Cape of Good Hope in 1652. As they moved inland, they came into contact with Bantu groups, including the Zulu, Xhosa, Swazi, and Sotho. These tribes had occupied much of the area since before the seventeenth century. In 1806, the British seized the cape and eight years later gained official possession. Many of the Dutch settlers, called Afrikaners or Boers, moved inland and established three separate states—Natal, Transvaal, and the Orange Free State. Natal, however, fell to British control in 1843.

Continued friction between the English and Afrikaners led to the Boer War, which resulted in Britain obtaining Transvaal and the Orange Free State. The British soon allowed these areas self-government, and after LOUIS BOTHA and JAN SMUTS led an independence movement, they agreed to the creation of the Union of South Africa, which became a nation in 1910. Over the next few decades a strict color line maintained white supremacy over the majority black population. In the 1990s, a new South Africa emerged, founded on democratic principles, after FREDERIK WILLEM DE KLERK acceded to the demands of the African nationalist leader NELSON MANDELA.

SPAIN

Iberians, Basques, and Celts settled Spain, today the dominant nation on the Iberian Peninsula. Rome conquered this area around 200 B.C., followed in the fifth century A.D. by the Visigoths, a Germanic tribe. They adopted Christianity, but in the eighth century Moslems overran nearly the entire peninsula, and there followed a protracted struggle by Christians to expel them. The kingdoms to the north led in this fight, which by the twelfth century included Castile. In the late fifteenth century, the Castilian Queen ISABELLA I wed the heir to the throne of Aragon, who became King FERDINAND V, to create Spain.

From the mid- to late sixteenth century, Philip II reigned and brought the Spanish Empire to its height of power and wealth. He threatened France and England and the entire European balance of power, but in 1566 failed to crush a rebellion in the Netherlands and in 1588 saw the Spanish Armada go down to defeat in his ill-fated invasion of England. Philip's empire declined after his death in 1598, and the nation experienced numerous political changes over the succeeding years, including the rise of a fascist dictatorship under Francisco Franco in the 1930s that did not end until JUAN CARLOS developed a democracy.

SRI LANKA

Between the third century B.C. and the twelfth century A.D., the Sinhalese developed an impressive culture known for its engineering. Buddhism arrived from India in the third century B.C., and it is here that the Buddha's oral teachings were first put into writing. Between A.D. 1200 and 1500, the Sinhalese Kingdom declined. At the same time, Europeans arrived and developed their hegemony over the island. First, in the 1520s the Portuguese established their rule. Then the Dutch took over in the 1640s and 1650s and monopolized trade.

The most influential European period began with the British, who in the 1790s established a regime that modernized and reformed Sri Lanka. British liberalism brought a representative government and decentralized the executive authority. Economically, the plantation system affected Sri Lanka when Indian Tamil immigrants were brought in as laborers (differing from the Sri Lankan Tamils who had occupied the island for centuries) and conflicted with the dominant Sahels. Nationalism emerged after World War I, and in 1919 the Sinhalese and Tamil political organizations united to form the Ceylon National Congress, which sought numerous governmental reforms. In 1947, Sri Lanka gained its independence and then a further, sharp break with British influence occurred under SOLOMON WEST RIDGEWAY DIAS BANDARANAIKE.

SUDAN

In size, the Sudan is the largest country in Africa. The diverse Sudanese population includes Muslims, Christians, and animists (persons who believe that everything in nature possesses a soul)—a diversity that has made unified rule difficult. The Sudan's recent history begins with Egyptian domination in 1820. This period, called the Turkiyah, produced disastrous results for Sudan. The rulers levied exorbitant taxes on the populace, and Egyptian soldiers ravaged the land while assaulting ancient pyramids in an avaricious search for gold. The Egyptians enslaved and forced into their army some 30,000 Sudanese, most of whom died from the ordeal.

In the 1870s, Britain established domination over Egypt and subsequently developed an increased interest in Sudan. At this point, Muhammad Ahmad, a holy man, emerged to lead the Mahdist movement that stressed religious fundamentalism and a holy war against Britons and infidels, and a Mahdist state was formed in 1884 that presaged later, more nationalistic Sudanese efforts against foreign domination. In 1896, British and Egyptian forces marched into the Sudan; two years later, they defeated the Mahdist army.

The subsequent Anglo-Egyptian Condominium restored Egyptian rule to the Sudan, but the British dominated the administration. Independence from foreign rule did not come until educated groups organized politically. ISMAIL AL-AZHARI founded the Sudan's first political party and in the early 1950s ended foreign control.

SURINAME

In the seventeenth century, the British and the Dutch competed to control this country. Settlers from both nations met fierce resistance from the indigenous population, and this hampered the European expansion. In 1667, the Dutch acquired Suriname through a treaty signed with the British, under which the latter obtained the colony of New York. The Dutch lost Suriname to Britain in the early 1800s, but then regained it in 1815.

Initially, a plantation economy developed that was dependent on African slaves, but after they were freed in the mid-1800s, the Dutch imported contract laborers from China, Indonesia, and India. Following World War II, nationalist sentiment arose, and the drive toward independence worsened racial tensions. HENCK ARRON overcame these differences, compromised with his opponents, and obtained nationhood for Suriname.

SWAZILAND

In the early nineteenth century, King Sobhuza I founded the original Swazi state after Zulu kings forced him and his people, the Ngwane and Dhlamini, to move north toward the Indian Ocean coast. Europeans invaded after gold was discovered in 1879, and in 1894 Swaziland lost its autonomy to the Transvaal, a republic founded by largely Dutch, or Boer, settlers. After Britain gained Transvaal as a result of the Boer War, Swaziland came under its control. Independence was not regained until 1968 under King SOBHUZA II.

SWEDEN

One of the steps toward Sweden's development as a nation occurred under Gustav I (or Gustavus Vasa). His nationalism grew ardent when, during a conflict in 1518, the Danes took him hostage (he escaped the following year) and two years later killed many Swedes, including his father, in the infamous Stockholm Bloodbath. In 1521, Gustav I led a revolt that within months defeated the Danes. This inaugurated an independent Sweden and paved the way for political modernization, but Gustav I ruled in an absolute and oppressive manner, equating Sweden's interests with his own. The establishment of a modern nation, where national interests substantially superseded dynastic ones and a professional administration began, occurred under GUSTAV II, who ruled from 1611 to 1632.

SWITZERLAND

Swiss schoolchildren regularly wind their way down a steep trail to the Rütli, a forest meadow, and pay homage to the place where in 1291 a pact was signed among three small states, or cantons, founding the Swiss Confederation. They also hear about William Tell, a legendary figure who rebelled against foreign oppression. As the story goes, at one point, after being captured, Tell was forced to take an arrow and shoot it through an apple resting on his son's head. In the fourteenth and fifteenth centuries, additional cantons joined the Swiss Confederation, the last to do so until 300 years later. After the Reformation, religious disputes between Protestants and Catholics tore at Switzerland.

The country gained its complete independence from the Holy Roman Empire in 1648, but in the early 1800s Napoleon dissolved the Swiss Confederation. After Napoleon's collapse, the Swiss succumbed to a brief civil war in 1847 that led to a new federal constitution developed by JONAS FURRER and several other statesmen. This document marked the emergence of modern Switzerland.

SYRIA

Syria has been populated since ancient times and Damascus may be the oldest continuously inhabited city in the world. Yet this land in the crossroads of the Middle East has often been dominated by outside powers. When a Muslim army defeated Syria's Byzantine rulers in A.D. 636, an important new stage began with the arrival of Islam.

In more modern times, beginning in the mid-fifteenth century, the Ottoman Empire controlled Syria and held it until World War I. However, after 1700 Ottoman authority was weak and local governors exerted considerable power. With the war, British forces dislodged the Ottomans, and in 1920 Syria became a French-held territory. By this time, nationalism emerged as a strong and vibrant force, and among the movement's heroes SHUKRI AL-KUWATLI gained prominence as a firm advocate of Syrian independence.

TAIWAN (REPUBLIC OF CHINA)

See CHINA.

TAJIKISTAN

Tajik farmers occupied this mountainous land in Central Asia some 3,000 years ago. In the seventh and eighth centuries A.D., Arabs conquered the area, followed two centuries later by Mongols. In the mid-1800s, Russians established Russian Turkestan. After the Bolshevik Revolution swept Russia in 1918 and created the Soviet Union, the Communist army controlled the Tajiks.

In 1924, the Soviets attached Tajikistan to Uzbekistan, and five years later it was made a separate republic. The Communists collectivized agriculture and emphasized cotton production but invested little money in Tajikistan, leaving most of the country underdeveloped. As the Soviet Union collapsed in the early 1990s, Tajikistan moved toward independence, but a chaotic situation emerged, with political, ethnic, and religious differences deteriorating into a civil war. No strong nationalist leader appeared, although RAKHMAN NABIYEV guided the country in its initial break with the Soviet Union.

TANZANIA

The two independent nations of Tanganyika and Zanzibar merged in 1964 to form Tanzania. A huge plateau dominates Tanganyika's topography, with a coastal strip 10 to 40 miles wide to the east. In the eighth century A.D., Arabs, attracted by trade, began settling this area and along with Persian settlers intermixed with the indigenous population, producing a Swahili culture.

Tanganyika's neighbor, Zanzibar, gets its name from a Persian word meaning "Land of the Blacks." Although situated near the African coast, Zanzibar was closely linked to the Middle East. As early as the seventh century B.C., an Arabian state dominated Zanzibar. Trade between this island and Arabia led to Arabs settling and mixing with Africans who had migrated from the mainland. In the ninth and tenth centuries A.D., Zanzibar converted to Islam, and Persian influence also extended over the island.

European penetration of eastern Africa began with the Portuguese in the 1490s. In the 1890s, Germany established a protectorate over Tanganyika while Britain established one over Zanzibar. After World War I, Britain replaced Germany as colonial ruler of Tanganyika. JULIUS KAMBARAGE NYERERE not only became leader of Tanganyika's drive toward independence but also became an important ideological force in Africa and oversaw the merger of Tanganyika and Zanzibar into one nation.

THAILAND

No one is sure about where the Thai people originally came from, but many scholars believe they emigrated from south China in the eleventh and twelfth centuries A.D. and then settled in areas long populated by the Khmers and Mons. Others believe that the Thais actually settled the area first, ahead of the Khmers and Mons, perhaps as far back as 3000 B.C. In any event, in 1238 a Thai chieftain established an independent kingdom in what is today central Thailand. This was succeeded by the Kingdom of Ayutthaya in the fourteenth century, which Burma invaded in 1569. The Thai prince Naresuen restored Ayutthaya's independence in 1590. Burma invaded again in 1765, but in the late eighteenth and early nineteenth centuries, two Thai national heroes, Taksin and Chakkri, reunified and rebuilt the country.

During the nineteenth century, the greatest threat to Thai independence came from Europeans, who expanded their colonial conquests into Southeast Asia. Under MONGKUT, Thailand (at that time Siam) Westernized, escaped European control, and entered the world of modern nations. His son, CHULALONGKORN, expanded the Westernization process.

TOGO

A coastal village, Togo, provided the name for this country; it means "water coast." Togo is a small nation squeezed between Ghana and Benin, with only a 32-mile coastline along the Gulf of Guinea. Before Europeans arrived, dozens of ethnic groups lived in almost total isolation from each other with the Kabré of the north and the Ewe of the South the largest, the latter migrating into the area between the twelfth and fourteenth centuries. A decentralized village environment meant the area lacked a strong state system.

Two Portuguese navigators became the first Europeans to sight the Togolese coast in 1471–1473. In the late nineteenth century, Germany gained prominence, pushing slowly inland and then having its control ratified by the other European powers in 1897. With World War I, however, the Germans lost their possession to the French and English. The territory was subsequently divided, becoming British Togoland and French Togoland. Togo's nationalist movement included an attempt to unite all Ewe peoples into one entity. SYLVANUS EPIPHANIO OLYMPIO led this effort, and with complete independence in 1960, he became his country's first president.

TONGA

This nation, situated in the Pacific Ocean, consists of 170 islands divided into three main regions: Tongatapu, the Ha'apai Group, and the Vava'u Group. The first settlers likely arrived some 3,000 years ago from either Samoa or Fiji. The Tongan monarchy began in the tenth century A.D. and continued in the twentieth century as the oldest and last surviving one in Polynesia. In 1901, Britain established a protectorate over Tonga. Independence as a modern nation occurred in 1970 under King TAUFA'AHAU TUPOU IV.

TRINIDAD AND TOBAGO

These two islands changed hands numerous times after the Europeans arrived. In 1498, Christopher Columbus landed in Trinidad and claimed it for Spain. The Spaniards developed plantations, imported slaves from Africa, and decimated the Indian tribes. Spain held on to Trinidad until 1797, when the British took over. (The British had arrived earlier, only to be driven out by the Carib Indians.) The Dutch and later the French acquired Tobago, but the British took control again in 1814 and united Trinidad and Tobago politically in 1888. Through a charismatic appeal, ERIC WILLIAMS led his countrymen to independence in 1962.

TUNISIA

This nation has been buffeted by two cultural currents: European from the north and Arabic-Islamic from the east. Most Tunisians are Arabs, a group that appeared here in the seventh century A.D. The Arabs conquered the Berbers, some of whom had converted to Judaism and later Christianity under Roman occupation, and brought with them Islam. For centuries after, Arab and Berber rulers vied for power. Then, in 1574, Tunisia fell to the Ottoman Empire, although it still maintained much autonomy.

Gradually, European interests penetrated Tunisia, including a financial commission that was imposed in 1869. With British acquiescence, Tunisia became a French protectorate in 1881, a move that angered Italy, which had a strong interest in the area. Although Tunisians retained their Islamic religion and some internal power, ultimate authority rested with the French. Additionally, France encouraged European immigration and much of the fertile land in northern Tunisia fell into European hands. In the 1890s, some Western-educated Tunisians organized "Young Tunisians" and pushed for schools and a greater Tunisian influence in the government. They, however, did not seek independence.

After World War I, discontent with European rule organized under the Dustur, or Constitutional Party. But a nationalist spirit was most evident beginning in the 1930s when HABIB BEN ALI BOURGUIBA organized the Neo-Dustur Party and led his countrymen to independence on 20 March 1956.

TURKEY

Turkey was once the center of the Ottoman Empire, which had its genesis in the early fourteenth century when Osman I, a sultan, centralized his rule in Sögüt and then expanded outward. His successors continued the expansion, including an important defeat of the Serbs in 1389 and a conquest of Bulgaria in 1393. In the sixteenth century, Palestine, Egypt, and the south Mediterranean littoral all came under Ottoman rule. By the late seventeenth century, the empire encompassed the Balkans and stretched southward into Palestine and westward to include Algeria, Tripoli, and Egypt. Frequent wars in the eighteenth century brought substantial losses of territory, while internal corruption weakened the monarchy.

The European nations would likely have conquered huge areas of the declining empire if not for their own mutual suspicion and distrust. In the mid-nineteenth century, the Ottoman government attempted reforms and tried to incorporate some Western political approaches, but with little success. When foreign armies occupied Constantinople after World War I, ATTATÜRK determined to remove them and build a modern Turkey.

TURKMENISTAN

In the eleventh century, Turkmen tribes founded the Seljuk Empire in this Central Asian land. In the thirteenth century, however, Mongols overran it, and the Turkmen survived through their tribal units. When the Russians arrived in the nineteenth century, they encountered this decentralized system, which proved resilient in resisting their control. The Russians did not conquer the Turkmen until 1881, after winning an important battle and massacring their enemy at Geok-Tepe.

In 1920, following the Bolshevik Revolution, the Communist army defeated a revived Turkmen military at Khiva. Four years later, the Soviets made Turkmenistan a republic within the Soviet Union, although they did not crush the last Turkmen resistance until the 1930s. When the Soviet Union collapsed in 1991, Turkmenistan gained its independence under SAPARMURAD NIYAZOV, who established a stable but authoritarian regime.

TUVALU

In 1892, the British established colonial control over this area, then called the Ellice Islands, linking them with the neighboring Gilbert Islands. After the Gilbertese moved toward independence in the mid-

1960s, the Ellice people decided to separate from the Gilbert Islands and form their own nation. Under the leadership of TOARIPI LAUTI they gained their independence in 1978 as Tuvalu.

UGANDA

Uganda, in the heart of East Africa, has long experienced conflict among tribes and political entities. In the 1700s, the kingdoms of Bunyoro and Buganda engaged in a major power struggle. By the 1800s, Buganda, expanding its boundaries while plundering nearby lands for ivory, most successfully adjusted to the capitalist economy penetrating this region and eclipsed Bunyoro. European interest in Buganda intensified in the late nineteenth century when Britain sought to protect the Upper Nile and promote trade between India and East Africa; subsequently, the British established the Uganda Protectorate in the 1890s, at first encompassing only Buganda and then expanding into other nearby kingdoms, including Bunyoro.

A confusing mix of antagonism subsequently developed: The Kingdom of Buganda conflicted with the colonial administration; the wealthier economy of southern and central Uganda differed from the poor economy of the north; tension arose between areas where the British allowed private African landowner-ship, as in Buganda, and areas where the farmers were tenants on Crown land; and friction increased between urban and rural areas. The division of Uganda into kingdoms and the predominance of Buganda worked against the development of unified political parties and nationalist movements. After World War II, MILTON OBOTE advocated Ugandan unity and independence.

UKRAINE

In the ninth century, Kyyivan Rus emerged as a strong state in this agricultural region. Trade routes also crossed Ukraine and enriched the state, which reached the height of its power under Iaroslav the Wise, who ruled from 1019 to 1054. In the thirteenth century, Kyyivan Rus declined, and Poland and Russia dominated the area. Although Ukranian Cossacks fought against foreign control, by the late eighteenth century the country experienced yet more divisions of its territory. Russia and Austria-Hungary possessed Ukraine at the start of the twentieth century, but after World War I Ukranians declared their independence and established a nation.

This lasted only three years, however, when the Soviet Union forcibly annexed Ukraine in 1921 and declared it a republic within the Communist nation. The Soviets worked to eliminate Ukranian culture and collectivize farming, moves that produced enormous famines and killed some 6 million peasants. In the 1980s, nationalism grew, led by VYACHESLAV CHORNOVIL and adopted by a former Communist, LEONID KRAVCHUK.

UNITED ARAB EMIRATES

This nation, located along the lower Persian Gulf, consists of seven emirates, most prominently Abu Dhabi and Dubai. In ancient times, lush forests dotted the now arid land, and evidence exists that as far back as 2800 B.C. a commercial civilization along the coast traded with Africa and India. Tribes predominated in the interior, and by the early decades of the Christian era they produced a strong Arab influence. By the seventh century A.D., Islam had swept through the area. In the early sixteenth century, the Portuguese captured a port and the island of Hormuz, but they did not establish lasting settlements or greatly influence the Arab culture.

In the nineteenth century, Britain obtained agreements from several sheikhs that recognized its commercial supremacy. Between 1887 and 1892, the British signed treaties resulting in their control of the Trucial States, as they then called the emirates. The United Arab Emirates (UAE) emerged as an independent nation in late 1971 after ZAYED BIN SULTAN AL-NUHAYYAN, the ruler of Abu Dhabi, initiated talks with RASHID BIN SAID AL-MAKTUM, the ruler of Dubai, to form a federation.

UNITED KINGDOM

See Great Britain.

UNITED STATES

Long before Europeans settled this nation, diverse Indian societies inhabited its territory, ranging from the woodland tribes of the Northeast to the cliff dwellers of the Southwest. Spaniards penetrated America in the sixteenth century and settled New Mexico and Florida. The English did not found a permanent settlement until 1607, when they established Jamestown. Around the same time, the French settled near the Great Lakes and along the Mississippi River. In 1763, the British victory in the French and Indian War evicted France from nearly all of North America.

Ironically, this war also weakend Britian's grip, for the tax policies stimulated by the need to support additional administrators and troops and pay the public debt provoked a revolutionary reaction by the colonists. In Massachusetts, SAMUEL ADAMS emerged as an early leader against the infamous Stamp Act of 1765. His more moderate cousin, JOHN ADAMS, soon supported separation from the British Empire. In Virginia, THOMAS JEFFERSON and JAMES MADISON inveighed against British tyranny. In 1775, GEORGE WASHINGTON was appointed to command the emerging Continental Army, and the following year, THOMAS PAINE intensified the revolutionary fervor with his pamphlet *Common Sense*. ALEXANDER HAMILTON served as Washington's aide-de-camp, and BENJAMIN FRANKLIN obtained crucial assistance from France. Most of these men helped craft the Constitution or develop the new national government in the 1790s. In the process, they encouraged a postrevolutionary nationalism that contributed to the nation's westward expansion.

URUGUAY

Sometimes called the "Switzerland of South America" for its relatively peaceful and democratic politics, Uruguay was first encountered by Europeans in 1516 when the Spaniard Juan Díaz de Solís arrived. The Portuguese founded the first European settlement in 1680, however, and the area became a point of contention between Spain and Portugal. In the early nineteenth century, nationalism stirred under JOSÉ GERVASIO ARTIGAS, but the independence he obtained was short-lived. Portuguese Brazil conquered Uruguay in 1821 and nationhood as a republic was not gained until 1828. After a brief civil war in the late 1800s, JOSÉ BATLLE Y ORDÓÑEZ built Uruguay into a democratic and socially progressive nation.

UZBEKISTAN

Turkish-speaking tribes populated this Central Asian region as early as the twelfth century. The Uzbeks consisted of three groups: Kypchak, Turki, and Sart, of which the latter emerged as the largest. Uzbeks consider their period of greatness to have been under the fourteenth-century Mongol leader Tamarlane, and they have erected monuments to him. Ulug Beg was another famous leader who built a large state in the fifteenth century. Russian expansion affected the Uzbek region in the nineteenth century, and in 1865 Tashkent, an important city, fell to the Czarist army. After the Russian Revolution of 1917, the Communist Soviet Union emerged, and in 1925 Moscow created the Uzbek Soviet Socialist Republic as a part of the new nation. As reform movements spread through the Soviet Union in the late 1980s, nationalism surged in Uzbekistan. Under ISLAM KARIMOV the Uzbeks declared their independence in 1991.

VANUATU

This nation of some 80 islands, situated between the Solomons to the north and New Caledonia to the south, has a human history dating back to about 1300 B.C. The first Europeans arrived in 1606 but had little impact until they began to settle on the islands in the 1870s and establish coffee, cacao, banana, and coconut plantations. French citizens and British subjects from Australia both settled what was then called New Hebrides. From the start, tensions with the indigenous Melanesians mounted. In 1906, Britain and France formed an Anglo-French Condominium that provided a joint administration. After World War II, nationalism grew substantial on the islands, and under the leadership of WALTER LINI New Hebrides gained its independence in 1980 as Vanuatu.

VENEZUELA

In 1498, Christopher Columbus sailed along the lush coast of this South American country. Later explorers, impressed by Lake Maracaibo and the Indian huts that dotted it, called the area Little Venice, or Venezuela. The Spaniards founded Caracas in 1567. During the Napoleonic upheaval in Europe, Venezuelans acted to gain their independence. They revolted in 1810 and tried to establish a viable government under FRANCISCO DE MIRANDA, but they did not win their independence until eleven years later. SIMÓN BOLÍVAR, who was born in Caracas, liberated not only Venezuela but also much of Spanish South America. He was ably assisted by his leading general, ANTONIO JOSÉ DE SUCRE. Having gained independence, Venezuela became part of the larger political entity established by Bolívar, called Gran Colombia.

In 1830, Venezuela went its own way as a separate republic, gaining its nationhood under JOSÉ ANTONIO PÁEZ. For decades thereafter, military dictatorships—oftentimes corrupt—dominated the nation. In 1958, a civilian government gained power and subsequent elections relegated the military to the background, although it clearly retained the strength to reassert itself.

VIETNAM

In ancient times, China dominated Vietnam, capturing it in 111 B.C. and controlling it into the tenth century A.D.. Chinese culture had an enormous impact on this country. The great Vietnamese hero Ngo Quyen drove the Chinese out in 939 and established Vietnamese independence that continued almost uninterrupted for over 900 years. During this period, General Tran Hung Dao defeated the Mongols, who invaded in 1284. France conquered Vietnam in 1858 and established Cochin China as a colony in 1867. Several treaties soon extended French control over the area encompassing Annam and Tonkin. Although the French built highways and developed schools, most observers agree that they pauperized the countryside. Tax revolts erupted in 1908, and guerrillas hiding in the mountains attacked French troops.

After World War I, a substantial nationalist movement arose. To regain Vietnam's independence, VO NGUYEN GIAP and HO CHI MINH battled first the French and then the United States. After World War II, America backed France's effort to reconquer Vietnam, seeing it as essential to prevent a Communist takeover. Although Ho had always considered his nationalism primary to his Marxism, the Americans considered the situation just the reverse. In 1954, the United States vi-olated the Geneva Accords by sending military weapons to the government in South Vietnam and later sabotaged the 1956 elections, intended to determine a government for all of Vietnam. This provoked Vietnamese in the South to organize the Viet Cong, a group committed to overthrowing the southern government and its American supporters. The Viet Cong sought and received assistance from Ho and Giap.

WESTERN SAMOA

The rocky, volcanic Samoan islands have a long human history, dating back to at least A.D. 1250. In the eighteenth century, Dutch and French traders visited the islands, and near 1900, Britain, Germany, and the United States competed for influence. Subsequently, the three nations signed a treaty whereby the United States gained control of the eastern islands (today, American Samoa) and Germany gained Western Samoa. After World War I, New Zealand obtained a League of Nations mandate to govern Western Samoa. With World War II, the area became a United Nations Trust Territory, still under New Zealand's control. The arrangement angered many Samoans and stimulated a nationalist movement. Under the leadership of FIAME FAUMUNIA MULINU'U MATA'AFA II, Western Samoa became independent in 1962.

YEMEN

Formally called the Yemeni Republic, Yemen evolved from the union in 1990 of the People's Democratic Republic of Yemen (South Yemen or Aden) and the Yemen Arab Republic (North Yemen). Back in 1839, the British seized South Yemen from the Ottoman Empire and gradually gained control over 20 sultanates, emirates, and sheikhdoms that were consolidated into the Federation of South Arabia in 1959. Centuries earlier, North Yemen had been the center of an important Yemeni civilization, but this area also succumbed to the Ottoman Empire. Here, YAHYA led the fight to end Turkish rule and re-create from North Yemen a great Yemeni kingdom. Upon his death, ALI ABDULLAH SALEH continued the battle. In South Yemen, a radical independence movement led by SALIM RUBAY ALI and ABD AL-FATTAH ISMAIL ended British rule and developed a Marxist state.

YUGOSLAVIA

In 1918, several Slavic states and territories merged to form the Kingdom of Serbs, Croats, and Slovenes. From the beginning, the kingdom experienced ethnic tensions that threatened to tear it apart. To avert this, King Alexander created a dictatorship in 1929. He also changed the country's name to the Kingdom of Yugoslavia. Five years later, he was assassinated by a Macedonian connected to Croatian dissidents. During World War II, the monarchy backed Hitler, but this government was overthrown in March 1941. Germany, Hungary, Italy, and Bulgaria then dismembered Yugoslavia, and a reign of terror prevailed as the German occupiers used violence in trying to crush the Slavic culture. The war unleashed conflict among the Slavs, too: In Croatia, the pro-Nazi Croatian majority viciously attacked Serbs and Jews. Resistance groups emerged to fight the Germans, with Josip Broz Tito leading the Communist Partisans. After the war, Yugoslavia emerged as a Communist country under Tito, who skillfully held the nation together while steering a socialist course independent of the Soviet Union.

Soon after his death in 1980, the ethnic pressures surged again and Yugoslavia disintegrated. In 1991 and 1992, Croatia, Bosnia-Herzegovina, Slovenia, and Macedonia all broke away and became independent nations. This development was accelerated by the efforts of SLOBODAN MILOSEVIC to enforce Serbian domination over Yugoslavia. On 17 April 1992, Serbia and Montenegro, under Milosevic's guidance, declared a new Federal Republic of Yugoslavia, quite different in boundaries, governmental structure, and character from Tito's former nation.

ZAIRE

What is today Zaire has been the site of several African states. The Kingdom of the Kongo emerged in the thirteenth century and thrived for 400 years until European intervention destroyed it. The Songhay developed a highly urbanized civilization along the Lomami River, and in the 1400s established the Luba Empire that reached its height in the late eighteenth century. In the late 1500s, the Lunda Empire emerged, eventually spreading across modern Shaba Province and into Angola and Zambia.

Europeans arrived in 1483 when a Portuguese explorer found the estuary of the Zaire River. In the early nineteenth century, the Zaire Basin became a prominent source for laborers in the Atlantic slave trade. Between 1878 and 1884, Henry Morton Stanley established trading posts and extended Belgian authority in the area, leading to the establishment of the Congo Free State, later called the Belgian Congo. This entity was divided into chiefdoms along lines at variance with local ethnic divisions. Such arbitrary decisions, based in part on cultural ignorance, caused many Africans to condemn Belgian rule as tyrannous. Leadership of Congolese nationalism was dispersed among several prominent figures, including JOSEPH KASAVUBU, PATRICE LUMUMBA, MOBUTU SESE SEKO (JOSEPH MOBUTU), and MOISE TSHOMBE. When independence came in 1960, a tumultuous period of national disorder began, with Mobutu emerging as the dominant founder of a united national state. In 1971, the Congo was renamed Zaire.

ZAMBIA

Archaeological digs over the last three decades have produced evidence of an advanced civilization in Zambia some 1,000 years ago. Europeans arrived in the early sixteenth century when Portuguese traders traveled inland from Africa's southeastern coast and supplanted Arab traders who had dominated the area. By the 1700s, however, Portugal's fortunes had declined and the Arabs returned. David Livingstone, the famous Scottish missionary, traveled through Zambia in the 1850s and made his discovery of Victoria Falls. By the time he died in 1873, he had explored the Zambezi River basin and established several missions while stimulating British interest in colonization. Then, in 1889 Cecil Rhodes obtained a charter for the British South Africa Company that granted it rule over the area, a status it maintained until 1924. Britain combined Barotseland and the northwest and northeast territories in 1911 to form Zambia's predecessor, Northern Rhodesia.

Initially, Northern Rhodesia was a poor stepchild to Southern Rhodesia, Britain's wealthier colony. In fact, when the Crown ended British South African Company rule in 1924 and made Northern Rhodesia a protectorate, the weak economy encouraged direct administrative control. In 1925, huge copper deposits were discovered in Northern Rhodesia, and Europeans flocked northward from Southern Rhodesia. As they did, they sought to minimize Crown interference in their economic pursuits and prevent African political participation. In 1953, Britain combined Northern Rhodesia with Southern Rhodesia and Nyasaland in a federation that enhanced white segregationist power. KENNETH DAVID KAUNDA protested this move and led a surging nationalist movement.

ZIMBABWE

During the 1300s and 1400s, Imbahuru, or the Great House at Great Zimbabwe, arose, constructed by the Karanga, a Bantu people. But around 1500 they abandoned this site, perhaps due to overpopulation. Some Karanga subsequently formed Mutapa, a great kingdom whose influence extended as far east as Mozambique. The Portuguese established themselves along the coast in the early 1500s but were expelled from the plateau region by the Rozvi people in the early 1600s. The Rozvi, however, fell to the Ndebele, who in the 1800s prevailed in the southwest. It was this group that Cecil Rhodes, the great British imperialist, confronted and fought in the 1890s. By 1900, the British South Africa Company dominated the area and ushered in several decades of racial animosity between Africans and Europeans that resulted in a violent fight for independence led by ROBERT MUGABE and JOSHUA NKOMO.

Chronology

This chronology reflects the dates when nations were formed, gained independence, or underwent substantial political change.

Twelfth Century

1130s–1200	Portugal unified

Fifteenth Century

1460s–1480s	France unified
1460s–1490s	Spain unified
1470s–1500	Russia unified and Mongol domination ended
1480s	Britain unified

Seventeenth Century

1610–1630s	Sweden's modern government established
1620s–1650	Bhutan unified
1620s–1630s	France—absolutism is strengthened
1648	The Netherlands gain independence from Spain
1680s	Britain's Parliament ascendant
1690s–1720s	Russia—Western practices and absolutism expanded

Eighteenth Century

1700s	Austria unified
1760s	Nepal unified
1760s–1790s	Russia—Western practices and nationalism expanded
1776	United States gains independence from Britain

Nineteenth Century

1804	Haiti gains independence from France
1810	Mexico revolts against Spanish rule
1810–1816	Argentina gains independence from Spain
1811	Paraguay gains independence from Spain
	Uruguay revolts against Spain
1815	San Marino—independence recognized
	Switzerland—independence recognized
1817	Brazil conquers Uruguay
1818	Chile gains independence from Spain
1819	Ecuador ends Spanish colonial rule
1820s	Central American Federation created
1821	Mexico gains independence from Spain

	Peru gains independence from Spain
	Gran Colombia gains independence from Spain
1822	Brazil gains independence from Portugal
1824	Colombia gains independence from Spain
1825	Bolivia gains independence from Spain
1828	Uruguay gains independence from Brazil
1830	Belgium gains independence from the Netherlands
	Ecuador secedes from Gran Colombia
	Venezuela secedes from Gran Colombia
1838–1841	Central Amercian Federation collapses—Costa Rica, Honduras, Nicaragua, and El Salvador gain independence
1844	Dominican Republic gains independence from Haiti
1847	Liberia unified and independent republic founded
1848	Costa Rica—republican government established
	Denmark establishes representative government
	Switzerland unified
1850s–1860s	Italy unified
	Thailand establishes a westernized government
1855	Mexico—reform government established
1860s–1880s	Germany unified
1860s–1910	Thailand's modernized government expanded
1866	Luxembourg gains independence from Germany
1867	Canada unified and Dominion of Canada founded
1868	Japan's modern government expanded
1881	Romania gains independence from Russia
1885	Ethiopia recognized as modern nation
1890s	Philippines revolt against Spain
1899	Cuba gains independence from Spain
	Brazil—First Republic established

Twentieth Century

1900–1930s	Saudi Arabia unified
1901	Australia unified
1903	Panama secedes from Colombia
1905	Norway gains independence from Sweden

1910	Mexican Revolution begins		Chad gains independence from France
	South Africa gains independence from Britain		Congo gains independence from France
			Côte D'Ivoire gains independence from
1910s	Greece unified	France	
1911	Uruguay establishes reform government		Cyprus gains independence from Britain
1917	Finland gains independence from Russia		Gabon gains independence from France
	In Russia, the Bolshevik Revolution leads to formation of the Soviet Union		Mali gains independence from France
			Mauritania gains independence from France
1918	Poland gains independence from Russia		
	Austrian Republic established		Niger gains independence from France
1920s	Afghanistan unified		Nigeria gains independence from Britain
1920s–1940s	Foreign domination by Britain and Russia ended in Iran		Senegal gains independence from France
			Somalia gains independence from Britain and Italy
1921	Mongolia gains independence from China		
1922	Ireland gains independence from Britain and the Irish Free State is founded		Togo gains independence from France
			Zaire gains independence from Belgium
1923	Turkey establishes a republic	1961	Kuwait gains independence from Britain
1930s	Mexico establishes a reform government		South Korea establishes the Third Republic
1943	Lebanon gains independence from France		
1944	Iceland gains independence from Denmark		Sierra Leone gains independence from Britain
1945	Indonesia gains independence from the Netherlands		Tanganyika gains independence from Britain
	Korea divided at Thirty-eighth parallel	1962	Algeria gains independence from France
1946	Japan establishes post–World War II government		Burundi gains independence from Belgium
	Jordan gains independence from Britain		Jamaica gains independence from Britain
	Philippines gain independence from the United States		Rwanda gains independence from Belgium
	Syria gains independence from France		Trinidad and Tobago gains independence from Britain
1947	India gains independence from Britain		
	New Zealand gains independence from Britian		Western Somoa gains independence from New Zealand
	Pakistan gains independence from Britain		Uganda gains independence from Britain
	Sri Lanka gains independence from Britain	1963	Kenya gains independence from Britain
1948	Israel gains independence from Britain		Malaysia unified
	North Korea establishes a Marxist government		Zanzibar gains independence from Britain
	Myanmar gains independence from Britain	1964	Brueni gains independence from Britain
			Malawi gains independence from Britain
1949	China establishes a Marxist government		Malta gains independence from Britain
1952	Egypt gains independence from Britain		Tanzania formed after Tanganyika and Zanzibar merge
	Libya gains independence from Italy		
1955	Kampuchea gains independence from France		Zambia gains independence from Britain
1956	Morocco gains independence from France	1965	The Gambia gains independence from Britain
	Sri Lanka establishes a radical government		Maldives gains independence from Britain
	Sudan gains independence from Britain and Egypt		Singapore secedes from Malaysia
	Tunisia gains independence from France	1966	Barabados gains independence from Britain
1957	Ghana gains independence from Britain		Botswana gains independence from Britain
	Malaya gains independence from Britain		
1958	Guinea gains independence from France		Guyana gains independence from Britain
	Madagascar gains independence from France		Lesotho gains independence from Britain
	France establishes the Fifth Republic	1968	Equatorial Guinea gains independence from Spain
1959	Cuba establishes a Marxist government		Maldives establishes a republic
1960	Benin gains independence from France		Mauritius gains independence from Britain
	Burkina Faso gains independence from France		Nauru gains independence from Britain, Australia, and New Zealand
	Cameroon gains independence from France		Swaziland gains independence from Britain
	Central African Republic gains independence from France	1969	Libya establishes a revolutionary government

1970	Fiji gains independence from Britain
	Oman establishes a modern government
	Tonga gains independence from Britain
1971	Bahrain gains independence from Britain
	Bangladesh secedes from Pakistan
	Qatar gains independence from Britain
	United Arab Emirates unify and gain independence from Britain
1973	Bahamas gains independence from Britain
	Suriname gains independence from The Netherlands
1974	Greece establishes a democratic government
	Grenada gains independence from Britain
	Portugal establishes a democratic government
1974	Guinea-Bissau gains independence from Portugal
1975	Comoros gains independence from France
	Cape Verde gains independence from Portugal
	Laos establishes a Marxist government
	Madagascar establishes a revolutionary government
	Mozambique gains independence from Portugal
	Papua New Guinea gains independence from Australia
	São Tome and Príncipe gain independence from Portugal
	Spain establishes a democratic government
	Vietnam unifies and gains independence from the United States
1976	Angola gains independence from Portugal
1977	Djibouti gains independence from France
	Seychelles gains independence from Britain
1978	Dominica gains independence from France
	Solomon Islands gains independence from Britain
	Tuvalu gains independence from Britain
1979	Iran establishes an Islamic government
	Iraq establishes a revolutionary government
	Kiribati gains independence from Britain
	St. Lucia gains independence from Britain
	St. Vincent and the Grenadines gains independence from Britain
1980	Zimbabwe ends its white supremacist government and gains independence from Britain

	Vanuatu gains independence from Britain and France
1981	Greece establishes socialist government
	Antigua and Barbuda gains independence from Britain
	Belize gains independence from Britain
1983	St. Kitts and Nevis gains independence from Britain
1985	Albania's Marxist regime ends
1986	Marshall Islands gains independence from the United States
1987	Fiji establishes a republican government
1989	Bulgaria gains independence from the Soviet Union
	Romania regains independence from the Soviet Union
1990	Germany reunified
	Hungary gains independence from the Soviet Union
	Lithuania gains independence from the Soviet Union
	Namibia gains independence from South Africa
	Poland regains independence from the Soviet Union
	Yemen unified
1991	Soviet Union collapses and the following states declare their independence: Armenia; Azerbaijan; Belarus; Estonia; Georgia; Kazakhstan; Kyrgyzstan; Latvia; Moldova; Tajikstan; Turkmenistan; Ukraine; Uzbekistan; and the Russian Federation (Russia) formed
	Yugoslavia collapses and the following states declare their independence: Bosnia-Herezegovina; Croatia; Macedonia; and Slovenia.
	New Yugoslavia declared—Serbia and Montenegro united
	Micronesia gains independence from the United States
1992	Czech Republic is established
1993	Eritrea gains independence from Ethiopa
	Slovakia secedes from Czechoslovakia
1994	Palau gains independence from the United States
	South Africa's white supremacist government toppled

Africa

Asia

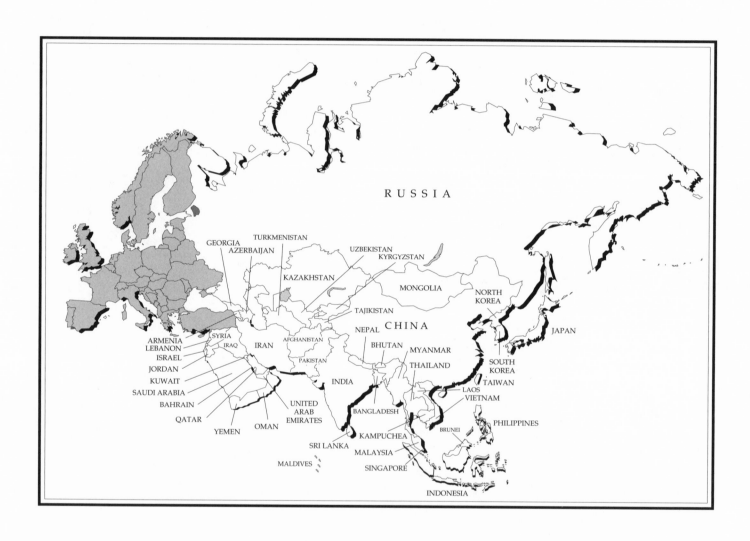

RUSSIA

GEORGIA
TURKMENISTAN
AZERBAIJAN
UZBEKISTAN
KYRGYZSTAN

KAZAKHSTAN

MONGOLIA

NORTH
KOREA

TAJIKISTAN

NEPAL   CHINA

JAPAN

ARMENIA
LEBANON
ISRAEL
JORDAN
KUWAIT
SAUDI ARABIA
BAHRAIN
QATAR
YEMEN

SYRIA
IRAQ

IRAN

AFGHANISTAN

PAKISTAN

BHUTAN

MYANMAR

THAILAND

SOUTH
KOREA

TAIWAN

LAOS
VIETNAM

INDIA

UNITED
ARAB
EMIRATES

OMAN

BANGLADESH

PHILIPPINES

BRUNEI

KAMPUCHEA

SRI LANKA

MALAYSIA

MALDIVES

SINGAPORE

INDONESIA

Europe

ICELAND

SWEDEN

FINLAND

NORWAY

RUSSIA

ESTONIA

LATVIA

LITHUANIA

DENMARK

IRELAND

NETHERLANDS

GREAT
BRITAIN

BELGIUM

LUXEMBOURG

GERMANY

POLAND

BYELARUS

UKRAINE

CZECH
REP.

SLOVAKIA

MOLDOVA

FRANCE

SWITZERLAND

AUSTRIA

HUNGARY

ROMANIA

SLOVENIA

CROATIA

BOSNIA-
HERZ.

SERBIA

BULGARIA

ANDORRA

SAN MARINO

ITALY

YUGOSLAVIA

MACEDONIA

PORTUGAL

SPAIN

ALBANIA

GREECE

TURKEY

CYPRUS

MALTA

North America

GREENLAND

ICELAND

CANADA

UNITED STATES

MEXICO

BAHAMAS

HAITI

DOMINICAN
REPUBLIC

CUBA

ST. KITTS
& NEVIS

JAMAICA

DOMINICA

ANTIGUA &
BARBUDA

ST. LUCIA

BARBADOS

Oceania

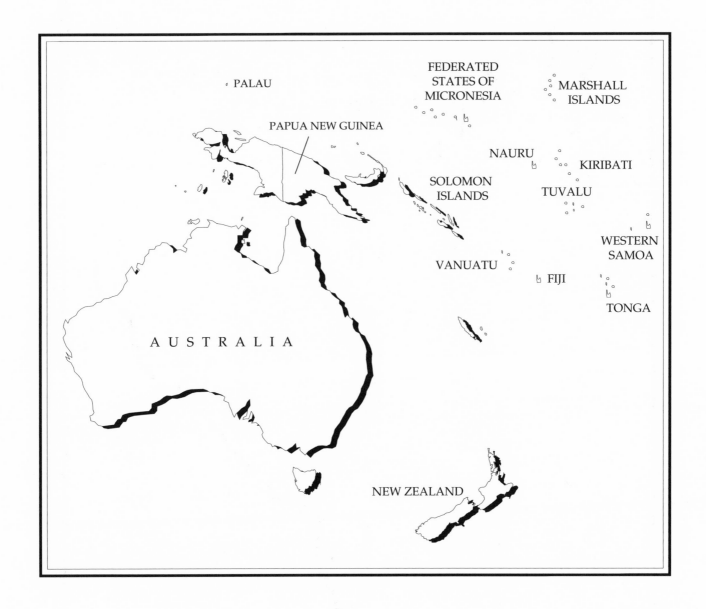

South America

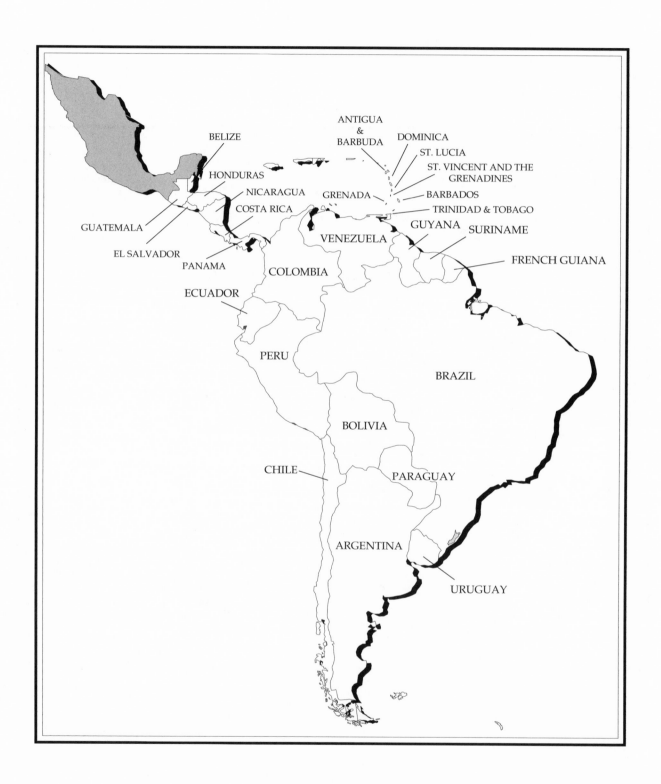

ANTIGUA
&
BARBUDA

DOMINICA

ST. LUCIA

ST. VINCENT AND THE
GRENADINES

BARBADOS

TRINIDAD & TOBAGO

GRENADA

BELIZE

HONDURAS

NICARAGUA

COSTA RICA

GUATEMALA

EL SALVADOR

PANAMA

VENEZUELA

GUYANA

SURINAME

FRENCH GUIANA

COLOMBIA

ECUADOR

PERU

BRAZIL

BOLIVIA

CHILE

PARAGUAY

ARGENTINA

URUGUAY

Bibliography

Abdullah, Mohammed Morsy, *The United Arab Emirates: A Modern History*, 1978.

Abels, Jules, *The Parnell Tragedy*, 1968.

Abu-Hakima, Ahmad Mustafa, *The Modern History of Kuwait*, 1983.

Adamolekun, Ladipo, *Sékou Touré's Guinea: An Experiment in Nation Building*, 1976.

Agoncillo, Teodoro, *The Revolt of the Masses: The Story of Bonifacio and the Katipunan*, 1956.

Agoncillo, Teodoro, *The Writings and Trial of Andres Bonifacio*, 1963.

Aguinaldo, Emilio, *A Second Look at America*, 1957.

Ahmed, Jamal M., *The Intellectual Origins of Egyptian Nationalism*, 1960.

Ahnlund, Nils, *Gustav Adolf the Great*, 1940.

Ajayi, J. F. A., and Michael Crowder, eds., *History of West Africa*, 2d ed., 2 volumes, 1976–1987.

Akbar, M. J., *Nehru: The Making of India*, 1989.

Akita, George, *Foundations of Constitutional Government in Modern Japan, 1868–1900*, 1967.

Albury, Paul, *The Story of the Bahamas*, 1975.

Alden, John R., *George Washington: A Biography*, 1984.

Aldridge, A. Owen, *Tom Paine's American Ideology*, 1984.

Aldridge, Bob, and Ched Myers, *Resisting the Serpent: Palau's Struggle for Self-Determination*, 1990.

Allen, Chris, and Michael Raduin, *Benin and the Congo: Politics, Economics, and Society*, 1987.

Allen, Richard C., *Korea's Syngman Rhee: An Unauthorized Portrait*, 1960.

Alexander, John T., *Catherine the Great: Life and Legend*, 1989.

Almana, Mohammad, *Arabia Unified: A Portrait of Ibn Saud*, 1980.

Alstadt, Audrey L., *The Azerbaijani Turks: Power and Identity Under Russian Rule*, 1992.

Ameringer, Charles D., *Don Pepe: A Political Biography of José Figueres of Costa Rica*, 1978.

Amir, Arjomand Said, *The Turban for the Crown: The Islamic Revolution in Iran*, 1988.

Andrade, Elisa, *The Cape Verde Islands: From Slavery to Modern Times*, 1974.

Angell, Hildegarde, *Simón Bolívar: South American Liberator*, 1930.

Ascherson, Neal, *The Polish August: The Self-Limiting Revolution*, 1981.

Ash, Timothy Garton, *The Magic Lantern: The Revolution of '89 Witnessed in Warsaw, Budapest, Berlin, and Prague*, 1990.

Ash, Timothy Garton, *The Polish Revolution: Solidarity*, 1985.

Ashford, Douglas E., *Political Change in Morocco*, 1961.

Austin, Dennis, *Malta and the End of Empire*, 1971.

Austin, Dennis, *Politics in Ghana: 1946–1960*, 1964.

Awolowo, Obafemi, *Path to Nigerian Freedom*, 1947.

Ayer, A. J., *Thomas Paine*, 1989.

Azikiwe, Nnamdi, *Our Struggle for Freedom*, 1955.

Bachman, Ronald D., ed., *Romania: A Country Study*, 1991.

Bagú, Sergio, *Mariano Moreno*, 1939.

Bakhash, Shaul, *The Reign of the Ayatollahs: Iran and the Islamic Revolution*, 1984.

Barber, James, *Rhodesia: The Road to Rebellion*, 1967.

Barbour, Nevill, *Morocco*, 1965.

Barr, Stringfellow, *Mazzini: Portrait of an Exile*, 1971.

Bar-Zohar, Michel, *Ben-Gurion: The Armed Prophet*, 1967.

Beckles, Hilary, *A History of Barbados: From Amerindian Settlement to Nation-State*, 1990.

Beckmann, George M., *The Making of the Meiji Constitution: The Oligarchs and the Constitutional Development of Japan, 1868–1891*, 1957.

Bell, John Patrick, *Crisis in Costa Rica: The 1948 Revolution*, 1971.

Bellgarde-Smith, Patrick, *Haiti: The Breached Citadel*, 1990.

Bennett, Judith A., *Wealth of the Solomons: A History of a Pacific Archipelago, 1800–1978*, 1987.

Benson, Mary, *Nelson Mandela: The Man and the Movement*, 1986.

Bent, J. Theodore, *A Freak of Freedom, or The Republic of San Marino*, 1879.

Bergin, Joseph, *Cardinal Richelieu: Power and the Pursuit of Wealth*, 1985.

Bhattacharjee, G. P., *Renaissance and Freedom Movement in Bangladesh*, 1973.

Biberaj, Elez, *Albania: A Socialist Maverick*, 1990.

Bidwell, Robin Leonard, *The Two Yemens*, 1983.

Blanksten, George I., *Ecuador: Constitutions and Caudillos*, 1964.

Bligh, Alexander, *From Prince to King*, 1984.

Blundy, David, and Andrew Lycett, *Qadaffi and the Libyan Revolution*, 1987.

Bolitho, Hector, *Jinnah: Creator of Pakistan*, 1954.

Bolland, O. Nigel, *Belize: A New Nation in Central America*, 1986.

Bonjour, Edgar, et al., *A Short History of Switzerland*, 1955.

Booth, A. R., *Swaziland*, 1984.

Boyd, John, *Sir George-Étienne Cartier: His Life and Times*, 1914.

Brant, Irving, *The Fourth President: A Life of James Madison*, 1970.

Brecher, Michael, *Nehru: A Political Biography*, 1959.

Brereton, Bridget, *A History of Modern Trinidad, 1783–1962*, 1981.

Bright, J. F., *Maria Theresa*, 1897.

Brodie, Fawn M., *Thomas Jefferson: An Intimate History*, 1974.

Brown, Archie, ed., *The Soviet Union: A Biographical Dictionary*, 1990.

Buddingh, Hans, *Suriname: Politics, Economics, and Society*, 1987.

Buell, Raymond L., *The Native Problem in Africa*, 2 volumes, 1928, reprint 1965.

Bumgartner, Louis E., *José Cecilio del Valle of Central America*, 1963.

Bunge, Frederica M., ed., *Indian Ocean: Five Island Countries*, 2d. ed., 1983.

Bunge, Frederica, and Melinda W. Cooke, eds., *Oceania: A Regional Study*, 2d. ed., 1984.

Burant, Stephen, ed., *Hungary: A Country Study*, 1990.

Burckhardt, Carl J., *Richelieu and His Age*, 3 volumes, 1972.

Burdette, Marcia, *Zambia*, 1986.

Burrowes, Reynold A., *The Wild Coast: An Account of Politics in Guyana*, 1984.

Burrowes, Robert, *The Yemen Arab Republic*, 1987.

Butler, F., *Indira Gandhi*, 1986.

Butson, Thomas G., *Gorbachev: A Biography*, 1985.

Butwell, Richard, *U Nu of Burma*, 1969.

Cabral, Amilcar, *Our People are Our Mountains: Amilcar Cabral on the Guinean Revolution*, 1971.

Calver, Peter A., *Guatemala*, 1985.

Carr, Raymond, and Juan P. Fusi, *Spain: Dictatorship to Democracy*, 1981.

Cartwright, John R., *Politics in Sierra Leone, 1947–1967*, 1970.

Caruso, J. A., *The Liberators of Mexico*, 1954.

Chabal, Patrick, *Amilcar Cabral: Revolutionary Leadership and Peoples' War*, 1983.

Chamberlain, Robert S., *Francisco Morazán: Champion of Central American Federation*, 1950.

Chandler, David, *A History of Cambodia*, 1983.

Chomchai, Prachoom, *Chulalongkorn the Great*, 1990.

Chrimes, Stanley Bertram, *Henry VII*, 1972.

Church, William F., *Richelieu and Reason of State*, 1972.

Cleugh, James, *Chart Royal*, 1970.

Clissold, Stephen, *Bernardo O'Higgins and the Independence of Chile*, 1969.

Clogg, Richard, *A Short History of Modern Greece*, 1979.

Clogg, Richard, ed., *Greece in the 1980s*, 1983.

Coates, Austin, *Rizal*, 1969.

Cohen, Robin, ed., *African Islands and Enclaves*, 1983.

Collected Works of Patrick H. Pearse: Political Writings and Speeches, 3 volumes, 1917–1922.

Collins, Joseph, *Nicaragua: What Difference Could a Revolution Make?*, 1986.

Cooke, Jacob, *Alexander Hamilton*, 1982.

Cooper-Prichard, A. H., *History of the Grand Duchy of Luxembourg*, 1950.

Correa da Costa, Sergio, *Every Inch a King: A Biography of Dom Pedro I*, 1964.

Cox, Richard, *Kenyatta's Country*, 1966.

Crane, Verner W., *Benjamin Franklin and a Rising People*, 1962.

Craton, Michael, *A History of the Bahamas*, 1986.

Creedman, Theodore S., *Historical Dictionary of Costa Rica*, 1991.

Creighton, Donald, *John A. MacDonald: The Old Chieftain*, 1956.

Creighton, Donald, *John A. Macdonald: The Young Politician*, 1952.

Creighton, Donald, *The Road to Confederation: The Emergence of Canada, 1863–1867*, 1965.

Critchlow, James, *Nationalism in Uzbekistan: A Soviet Republic's Road to Sovereignty*, 1991.

Cronje, Suzanne, *Equatorial Guinea—The Forgotten Dictatorship: Forced Labor and Political Murder in Central Africa*, 1976.

Crozier, Brian, *De Gaulle*, 1973.

Crozier, Brian, *The Man Who Lost China: The Full Biography of Chiang Kai-shek*, 1976.

Crystal, Jill, *Kuwait*, 1992.

Cunliffe, Marcus, *George Washington: Man and Monument*, 1958.

Cunningham, Noble E., *In Pursuit of Reason: The Life of Thomas Jefferson*, 1987.

Curtis, Glenn, *Bulgaria: A Country Study*, 1993.

Curtis, Glenn E., *Yugoslavia: A Country Study*, 1992.

Cvicc, Christopher, *Remaking the Balkans*, 1991.

Dae-Sook Suh, *The Korean Communist Movement, 1918–1948*, 1967.

Dangerfield, George, *The Damnable Question*, 1976.

Dann, Uriel, *Iraq under Qassem: A Political History, 1958–1963*, 1969.

Davies, Robert H., et al., *The Kingdom of Swaziland*, 1986.

Davis, Burke, *George Washington and the American Revolution*, 1975.

Dayan, Moshe, *Story of My Life*, 1976.

Dayan, Yael, *My Father, His Daughter*, 1985.

De Gaulle, Charles, *The Complete War Memoirs*, 1964.

De Gaulle, Charles, *Memoirs of Hope*, 1971.

de Silva, Chandra Richard, *Sri Lanka: A History*, 1987.

De Suze, J. A., *The New Trinidad and Tobago*, 1965.

Deakin, Alfred, *The Federal Story: The Inner History of the Federal Cause, 1880–1900*, 1943.

Decalo, Samuel, *Historical Dictionary of Benin*, 1987.

Decalo, Samuel, *Historical Dictionary of Niger*, 1979.

Del Rio, Daniel, *Simón Bolívar*, 1965.

Demirchian, K. S., *Soviet Armenia*, 1984.

Deosaran, Ramesh, *Eric Williams: The Man, His Ideas, and His Politics*, 1981.

Detwiler, Donald, *Germany: A Short History*, 1989.

Devlin, John F., *Syria: Modern State in an Ancient Land*, 1983.

Dew, Edward, *The Difficult Flowering of Suriname: Ethnicity and Politics in a Plural Society*, 1978.

Dobie, Edith, *Malta's Road to Independence*, 1967.

Dominguez, Jorge I., *Cuba: Order and Revolution*, 1978.

Dupree, Lewis, *Afghanistan*, 1973.

Dutt, Vishnu, *Gandhi, Nehru, and the Challenge*, 1979.

Dyde, Brian, *St. Kitts: Cradle of the Caribbean*, 1993.

Earl of Longford and Thomas P. O'Neill, *Eamon De Valera*, 1976.

Ebon, Martin, *Lin Piao: The Life and Writings of China's New Ruler*, 1970.

Elton, G. R., *England under the Tudors*, 1974.

Engelenburg, Frans V., *General Botha*, 1929.

Entelis, John P., *Algeria: The Revolution Institutionalized*, 1986.

Erikson, Erik H., *Gandhi's Truth: On the Origins of Militant Nonviolence*, 1969.

Evans, Lancelot, ed., *Emerging African Nations and Their Leaders*, 2 volumes, 1964.

Faaniu, Simati et al., *Tuvalu: A History*, 1983.

al-Fasi, Allal, *The Independence Movements in Arab North Africa*, 1954.

Fenn, Charles, *Ho Chi Minh*, 1973.

Fennell, J. L. I., *Ivan the Great of Moscow*, 1961.

Fierman, William, ed., *Soviet Central Asia: The Failed Transformation*, 1991.

First, Ruth, *Libya: The Elusive Revolution*, 1974.

Fischer, Louis, *Gandhi: His Life and Message for the World*, 1954.

Fischer, Louis, *The Life of Mahatma Gandhi*, 1983.

Flexner, James, *The Young Hamilton*, 1978.

Flexner, James Thomas, *George Washington*, 4 volumes, 1965–1972.

Flexner, James Thomas, *Washington: The Indispensable Man*, 1969.

Foner, Eric, *Tom Paine and Revolutionary America*, 1976.

Forero, José Maria, *Santander*, 1937.

Forester, Cecil S., *Victor Emmanuel II and the Union of Italy*, 1927.

Franda, Marcus, *The Seychelles: Unquiet Islands*, 1982.

Franklin, Benjamin, *Autobiography of Benjamin Franklin* (ed. by L. W. Labaree et al.), 1964.

Freeman, Douglas Southall, *George Washington: A Biography*, 7 volumes, 1948–1957.

Friedman, Bernard, *Smuts: A Reappraisal*, 1976.

Fuglestad, Finn, *A History of Niger, 1850–1960*, 1983.

Gaabatshwane, S. M., *Seretse Khama and Botswana*, 1966.

Gailey, Harry A., *A History of The Gambia*, 1963.

Gandhi, Mohandas, *The Story of My Experiments with Truth*, 1983.

Gauze, René, *The Politics of Congo-Brazzaville*, 1973.

Gerson, Noel B., *Grand Incendiary: A Biography of Samuel Adams*, 1973.

Gerteiny, Alfred G., *Mauritania*, 1967.

Geyle, Peter, *The Revolt of the Netherlands, 1555–1609*, 1980.

Gilmore, Robert L., *Caudilloism and Militarism in Venezuela, 1810–1910*, 1964.

Gilmour, David, *Lebanon: The Fractured Country*, 1983.

Giap, Vo Nguyen, *Dien Bien Phu*, 1962.

Giap, Vo Nguyen, *People's War, People's Army* , 1961.

Gjerset, Knut, *History of Iceland*, 1924.

Gopal, Sarvepalli, *Jawaharlal Nehru: An Anthology*, 1980.

Gordon, J., *Nevis: Queen of the Caribees*, 1993.

Gordon, David C., *The Republic of Lebanon: Nation in Jeopardy*.

Graz, Liesl, *The Omanis: Sentinels of the Gulf*, 1982.

Green, Martin B., *Tolstoy and Gandhi: Men of Peace*, 1983.

Greenfield, Richard, *Ethiopia: A New Political History*, 1965.

Gregorian, Vartan, *The Emergence of Modern Afghanistan, 1880–1946*, 1969.

Grey, Ian, *Catherine the Great: Autocrat and Empress of All Russia*, 1961.

Grey, Ian, *Peter the Great, Emperor of All Russia*, 1960.

Griffith, Gwilym O., *Mazzini: Prophet of Modern Europe*, 1970.

Griffiths, John, *The Caribbean in the Twentieth Century*, 1984.

Gunn, Geoffrey C., *Rebellion in Laos: Peasant and Politics in a Colonial Backwater*, 1990.

Haarhoff, Theodore, *Smuts, The Humanist*, 1970.

Haggerty, Richard A., ed., *El Salvador: A Country Study*, 1990.

Halberstam, David, *Ho*, 1987.

Hall, Richard, *The High Price of Principles: Kaunda and the White South*, 1969.

Hall, Richard, *Zambia*, 1965.

Halpern, Joel M., *Laos Profiles*, 1990.

Halstead, John P., *Rebirth of a Nation: The Origins and Rise of Moroccan Nationalism, 1912–1944* , 1968.

Hamada Kengi, *Prince Ito*, 1936.

Hanna, Willard A., *Eight Nation Makers: Southeast Asia's Charismatic Statesmen*, 1964.

Hardy, William George, *From Sea unto Sea: Canada, 1850 to 1910—The Road to Nationhood*, 1960.

Hargreaves, John D., *West Africa: The Former French States*, 1967.

Harlow, Ralph V., *Samuel Adams: Promoter of the American Revolution*, 1972.

Hawke, David F., *Franklin*, 1976.

Hedin, Sven Anders, *Chiang Kai-shek, Marshall of China*, 1975.

Hellmann, Donald C., *Japanese Foreign Policy and Domestic Politics*, 1969.

Helms, C. M., *Iraq: Eastern Flank of the Arab World*, 1984.

Helpern, Jack, *South Africa's Hostages*, 1965.

Henderson, K. D. D., *The Making of the Modern Sudan*, 1952.

Henderson, Lawrence W., *Angola: Five Centuries of Conflict*, 1979.

Higbie, Janet, *Eugenia: The Caribbean's Iron Lady*, 1993.

Hiro, Dilip, *Desert Shield to Desert Storm: The Second Gulf War*, 1992.

Hiro, Dilip, *Inside India Today*, 1979.

Hodges, Tony, and Malyn Newitt, *Sao Tome and Principe*, 1988.

Hoensch, Jorg, *A History of Modern Hungary, 1867–1986*, 1988.

Holden David, and Richard Johns, *The House of Saud*, 1981.

Holt, P. M., *A Modern History of the Sudan*, 1979.

Honychurch, Lennox, *The Dominica Story: A History of the Island*, 1984.

Hoskyns, Catherine, *The Congo Since Independence, January, 1960–December, 1961*, 1965.

Hourani, Albert H., *Arabic Thought in the Liberal Age, 1798–1939*, 1962.

Howe, John R., and Edward H. Tebbenhoff, *John Adams*, 2 volumes, 1987.

Hughes, John, *Indonesian Upheaval*, 1967.

Hussein ibn Talal, *Uneasy Lies the Head: The Autobiography of His Majesty King Hussein I of the Hashemite Kingdom of Jordan*, 1962.

Hymans, Jacques L., *Léopold Sédar Senghor: An Intellectual Biography*, 1971.

Ingham, Kenneth, *Jan Christiaan Smuts*, 1986.

Isaacman, Allen, and Barbara Isaacman, *Mozambique: From Colonialism to Revolution, 1900–1982*, 1983.

Iskandar, Amir, *Saddam Hussein: The Fighter, the Thinker, and the Man*, 1980. Marr, Phebe, *The Modern History of Iraq*, 1985.

Jackson, Robert H., and Carl Rosberg, *Personal Rule in Black Africa*, 1982.

Jagan, Cheddi, *The West on Trial: My Fight for Guyana's Freedom*, 1966.

Jalal, Ayesha, *The Sole Spokesman: Jinnah, the Muslim League, and the Demand for Pakistan*, 1985.

James, C. L. R., *The Black Jacobins: Toussaint L'Overture and the San Domingo Revolution*, 1963.

Jedrzejewicz, Waclaw, *Pilsudski: A Life for Poland*, 1982.

Jeffries, Charles, *Ceylon: The Path to Independence*, 1963.

Johnson, John J., *Simón Bolívar and Spanish American Independence, 1783–1830*, 1968.

Jones, J. R., *The Revolution of 1688 in England*, 1972.

Jorgensen, Jan Jelmert, *Uganda: A Modern History*, 1981.

Josey, Alex, *Lee Kuan Yew and the Commonwealth*, 1969.

Kahin, George McTurna, *Intervention: How America Became Involved in Vietnam*, 1987.

Kai-yu Hsu, *Chou En-lai: China's Gray Eminence*, 1968.

Kalck, Pierre, *Central African Republic: A Failure in De-Colonisation*, 1971.

Kaplan, Irving, ed., *Zaire: A Country Study*, 1979.

Kaplan, Robert D., *Balkan Ghosts: A Journey through History*, 1993.

Karnow, Stanley, *In Our Image: America's Empire in the Philippines*, 1989.

Karnow, Stanley, *Mao and China: Inside China's Cultural Revolution*, 1972.

Karnow, Stanley, *Vietnam: A History*, 1983.

Karugire, Samwiri Rubaraza, *A Political History of Uganda*, 1980.

Kau, Michael Y. M., *The Lin Piao Affair: Power Politics and Military Coup*, 1975.

Kaufman, Michael, *Jamaica under Manley: Dilemmas of Socialism and Democracy*, 1985.

Kaunda, Kenneth David, *The Riddle of Violence*, 1981.

Keane, John, *Tom Paine: A Political Life*, 1995.

Kelley, Michael P., *A State in Disarray: Conditions of Chad's Survival*, 1986.

Kendall, Paul M., *Louis XI: The Universal Spider*, 1986.

Kent, Raymond K., *From Madagascar to the Malagasy Republic*, 1976.

Kerofilas, C., *Eleutherios Venizelos: His Life and Work*, 1915.

Ketcham, R. L., *Benjamin Franklin*, 1965.

Ketcham, Ralph, *James Madison: A Biography*, 1990.

Kilson, M., *Political Change in a West African State*, 1966.

Kinross, Patrick, *Atatürk: The Rebirth of a Nation*, 1981.

Kipel, Vitaut, ed., *Byelorussian Statehood: Reader and Bibliography*, 1988.

Kirk, John M., *José Martí, Mentor of the Cuban Nation*, 1983.

Kjersgaard, Erik, *A History of Denmark*, 1974.

Koch, Adrienne, *Jefferson and Madison: The Great Collaboration*, 1950.

Kohn, Hans, *Nationalism and Liberty: The Swiss Example*, 1956.

Korngold, Ralph, *Citizen Toussaint*, 1979.

Kossmann, E. H., *The Low Countries, 1780–1940*, 1978.

Kostiner, Joseph, *The Struggle for South Yemen*, 1984.

Kottak, Conrad, ed., *Madagascar: Society and History*, 1986.

Kousoulas, D. George, *Modern Greece: Profile of a Nation*, 1974.

Kurzman, Dan, *Ben-Gurion: Prophet of Fire*, 1983.

Lackner, Helen, *P.D.R. Yemen: Outpost of Socialist Development in Arabia*, 1985.

Lacouture, Jean, *De Gaulle: The Rebel, 1890–1944*, 1990.

Laitin, David D., and Said S. Samatar, *Somalia: Nation in Search of a State*, 1987.

Landau, Rom, *Mohammed V, King of Morocco*, 1957.

Lattimore, Owen, *Nationalism and Revolution in Mongolia*, 1955.

Lattimore, Owen, *Nomads and Commissars: Mongolia Revisted*, 1962.

Lawson, Fred H., *Bahrain: The Modernization of Autocracy*, 1989.

Le Roux, Lois, *Patrick H. Pearse*, translated by Desmond Ryan, 1932.

Le Vine, Victor T., *The Cameroons: From Mandate to Independence*, 1977.

Leff, Carol Skalnik, *National Conflict in Czechoslovakia: The Making and Remaking of the State, 1918–1987*, 1988.

Lenczowski, George, ed., *Iran under the Pahlavis*, 1978.

Levene, Ricardo, *A History of Argentina*, 1937.

Levi, Darrell E., *Michael Manley: The Making of a Leader*, 1989.

Levy, Leonard, *Jefferson and Civil Liberties: The Darker Side*, 1972.

Lewis, Bernard, *The Emergence of Modern Turkey*, 1968.

Lewis, Gordon K., *Grenada: The Jewel Despoiled*, 1987.

Lewis, I. M., *The Modern History of Somalia*, 1980.

Li Tien-min, *Chou En-lai*, 1970.

Lijphart, Arend, ed., *Conflict and Coexistence in Belgium: The Dynamics of a Culturally Divided Society*, 1981.

Lindgren, Raymond E., *Norway-Sweden: Union, Disunion, and Scandinavian Integration*, 1959.

Lini, Walter, *Beyond Pandemonium: From the New Hebrides to Vanuatu*, 1980.

Litvinoff, Barnet, *Weizmann: Last of the Patriarchs*, 1976.

Livermore, H. V., *A New History of Portugal*, 1969.

Lodge, Tom, *Black Politics in South Africa since 1945*, 1983.

Loeber, Dietrich Andre et al., *Regional Identity under Soviet Rule: The Case of the Baltic States*, 1990.

Longley, James W., *Sir Charles Tupper*, 1917.

Lopez, Claude-Anne, and E. W. Herbert, *The Private Franklin*, 1975.

Lord Chalfont, *By God's Will: A Portrait of the Sultan of Brunei*, 1989.

Lusignan, Guy de, *French-Speaking Africa since Independence*, 1969.

Lyons, Francis Stewart, *The Fall of Parnell*, 1960.

Macaulay, Neill, *Dom Pedro*, 1986.

McCaffey, Lawrence, *Irish Federalism in the 1870s: A Study in Conservative Nationalism*, 1962.

McCartney, C. A., *The Habsburg Empire, 1790–1918*, 1968.

McCoy, D. R., *The Last of the Fathers*, 1989.

McDermott, Anthony, *Egypt from Nasser to Mubarak: A Flawed Revolution*, 1988.

MacDonald, Alexander, *Tanzania: Young Nation in a Hurry*, 1966.

MacDonald, Barrie, *Cinderellas of the Empire: Towards a History of Kiribati and Tuvalu*, 1982.

McDonald, Forrest, *Alexander Hamilton: A Biography*, 1979.

McFarland, Daniel M., *Historical Dictionary of Upper Volta*, 1978.

McKenzie, Frederick A., *The Tragedy of Korea*, 1969.

Mackey, Sandra, *Lebanon: The Death of a Nation*, 1989.

McLaren, Walter W., *A Political History during the Meiji Era, 1867–1912*, 1965.

Magas, Branka, *The Destruction of Yugoslavia: Tracking the Break-up of 1980–1992*, 1993.

Magner, James A., *Men of Mexico*, 1942.

Maier, Pauline, *The Old Revolutionaries: Political Lives in the Age of Samule Adams*, 1982.

Malone, Dumas, *Jefferson and His Time*, 6 volumes, 1948–1981.

Mandela, Nelson, *The Struggle Is My Life*, 1986.

Maniruzzaman, Talukder, *The Bangladesh Revolution and Its Aftermath*, 1980.

Manley, Michael, *Jamaica: Struggle in the Periphery*, 1982.

Manley, Michael, *The Politics of Change: A Jamaican Testament*, 1974.

Marcus, Harold G., *The Life and Times of Menelik II: Ethiopia, 1844–1913*, 1975.

Marinelli, Lawrence, *The New Liberia: A Historical and Political Survey*, 1964.

Marr, Phebe, *The Modern History of Iraq*, 1985.

Martí, José, *On Education*, 1979 (translated and edited by Philip Foner).

Martí, José, *Our America: Writings on Latin America and the Cuban Struggle for Independence*, 1978 (translated and edited by Philip Foner).

Masani, Zaheer, *Indira Gandhi*, 1976.

Massie, Robert K., *Peter the Great: His Life and World*, 1980.

Masur, Gerhard, *Simón Bolívar*, 1969.

Matteini, Nevio, *The Republic of San Marino: Historical and Artistic Guide*, 1981.

Mayes, Stanley, *Makarios: A Biography*, 1981.

Meir, Golda, *My Life*, 1975.

Melady, Thomas Patrick, *Burundi: The Tragic Years*, 1974.

Meleisea, Malama, *The Making of Western Somoa: Traditional Authority and Colonial Administration in the History of Western Somoa*, 1987.

Merle, Robert, *Ben Bella*, 1965.

Merriam, Allen Hayes, *Gandhi vs. Jinnah: The Debate over the Partition of India*, 1980.

Merrill, Tim, ed., *Guyana and Belize: Country Studies*, 1993.

Metford, John C. J., *San Martín: The Liberator*, 1950.

Miller, John C., *Sam Adams: Pioneer in Propaganda*, 1936.

Miller, John C., *The Wolf by the Ears: Thomas Jefferson and Slavery*, 1980.

Miller, Norman N., *Kenya: The Quest for Prosperity*, 1988.

Miller, Townsend, *The Castles and The Crown: Spain, 1451–1555*, 1963.

Mitre, Bartolomé, *The Emancipation of South America*, 1969.

Mlambo, Eshmael E. M., *Rhodesia: The Struggle for a Birthright*, 1972.

Moffat, Abbot L., *Mongkut, The King of Siam*, 1961.

Mondlane, Eduardo, *The Struggle for Mozambique*, 1969.

Morison, Samuel Eliot, *The Young George Washington*, 1932.

Morton, William L., *The Critical Years: The Union of British North America, 1857–1873*, 1964.

Munslow, Barry, *Mozambique: The Revolution and Its Origin*, 1983.

Nakhleh, Emile A., *Bahrain: Political Development in a Modernizing Society*, 1976.

Nanda, Bal R., *Majhatma Gandhi: A Biography*, 1968.

Nazarbayev, Nursultan, *Without Left or Right*, 1991.

Nedelcvic, Vasile, *The Republic of Moldova*, 1992.

Nelson, Harold D., *Costa Rica: A Country Study*, 1983.

Nelson, Harold D., ed., *Liberia: A Country Study*, 1985.

Nelson, Harold D., ed., *Zimbabwe: A Country Study*, 1983.

Nettleford, Rex, *Caribbean Cultural Identity: The Case of Jamaica*, 1980.

Neumann-Hoditz, Reinhold, *Portrait of Ho Chi Minh: An Illustrated Biography*, 1972.

Newcomer, James, *The Grand Duchy of Luxembourg: The Evolution of Nationhood, 963 A.D. to 1983*, 1984.

Newton, Clarke, *The Men Who Made Mexico*, 1973.

Nicholls, David, *From Dessalines to Duvalier: Race, Colour, and National Independence in Haiti*, 1979.

Nicolson, I. F., *The Administration of Nigeria, 1900–1960: Men, Methods, and Myths*, 1969.

Niemier, Jean Gilbreath, *The Panama Story*, 1968.

Nkomo, Joshua, *Nkomo, The Story of My Life*, 1984.

Nkrumah, Kwame, *Ghana*, 1957.

Nowell, Charles, *Portugal*, 1973.

Nyerere, Julius K., *Uhuru na Maendeleo (Freedom and Development)*, 1973.

Nyerere, Julius K., *Uhuru na Umoja (Freedom and Unity)*, 1967.

Nyrop, Richard F., Brenneman, Lyle E., et al., eds., *Rwanda: A Country Study*, 1982.

O'Brien, Richard Barry, *The Life of Charles Stewart Parnell*, 2 volumes, 1968.

O'Brien, Steve, *Alexander Hamilton*, 1989.

O'Connor, Frank, *The Big Fellow: Michael Collins and the Irish Revolution*, 1937.

O'Faolain, Sean, *King of the Beggars: A Life of Daniel O'Connell, The Irish Liberator*, 1938.

O'Neill, Robert J., *General Giap*, 1969.

O'Toole, Thomas, *The Central African Republic: The Continent's Hidden Heart*, 1986.

Oakley, Stewart, *A Short History of Denmark*, 1972.

Oh, John Kie-chiang, *Korea: Democracy on Trial*, 1968.

Olcott, Martha Brill, *The Kazakhs*, 1987.

Oliver, W. H., ed., *The Oxford History of New Zealand*, 1981.

Omari, T. Peter, *Kwame Nkrumah: The Anatomy of an African Dictatorship*, 1971.

Osias, Camillio, *José Rizal: His Life and Times*, 1949.

Padover, Saul K., *The Revolutionary Emperor: Joseph the Second, 1741–1790*, 1934.

Page, Stephen, *The Soviet Union and the Yemens: Influence in Asymmetrical Relationships*, 1985.

Painter, James, *Guatemala*, 1989.

Parkinson, Roger, *Zapata*, 1975.

Parkinson, Wenda, *This Gilded African: Toussaint L'Overture*, 1978.

Parris, John, *The Lion of Caprera*, 1962.

Pateman, Roy, *Eritrea: Even the Stones are Burning*, 1990.

Payne, Robert, *The Life and Death of Mahatma Gandhi*, 1969.

Peck, Malcolm C., *The United Arab Emirates: A Venture in Unity*, 1986.

Pendle, George, *Paraguay: A Riverside Nation*, 1967.

Perkins, Kenneth J., *Tunisia: Crossroads of the Islamic and European Worlds*, 1986.

Peterson, Merrill, *Adams and Jefferson: A Revolutionary Dialogue*, 1976.

Peterson, Merrill, *The Jefferson Image in the American Mind*, 1960.

Peterson, Merrill, *Thomas Jefferson and the New Nation*, 1986.

Pick, Robert, *Empress Maria Theresa*, 1966.

Pike, John G., *Malawi: A Political and Economic History*, 1968.

Porch, Douglas, *The Portuguese Armed Forces and the Revolution*, 1977.

Pro Mundi Vita, *Rwanda: The Strength and Weakness of the Christian Center of Africa*, 1963.

Qaddafi, Mummar, *The Green Book*, 2 volumes, 1976 and 1980.

Räikkönen, Erik, *Svinhufvud, The Builder of Finland: An Adventure in Statecraft*, 1938.

Ramazani, R. K., *Revolutionary Iran: Challenge and Response in the Middle East*, 1986.

Randall, Willard Sterne, *Thomas Jefferson: A Life*, 1993.

Raun, Toivo U., *Estonia and the Estonians*, 1987.

Recto, Claro M., *Three Years of Enemy Occupation: The Issue of Political Collaboration in the Philippines*, 1946.

Reddaway, W. F., *Marshal Lisudski*, 1939.

Reinharz, Jehuda, *Chaim Weizmann: The Making of a Zionist Leader*, 1985.

Remeikis, Thomas, *Opposition to Soviet Rule in Lithuania, 1945–1980*, 1980.

Reynolds, John, *Edmund Barton*, 1948.

Rickett, Richard A., *A Brief Survey of Austrian History*, 1977.

Ridley, Jaspar, *Garibaldi*, 1974.

Riker, T.W., *The Making of Roumania*, 1971.

Riviére, Claude, *The Mobilization of a People*, translated by Richard Adloff and Virginia Thompson, 1977.

Roberts, Michael, *Gustavus Adolphus and the Rise of Sweden*, 1973.

Robertson, William S., *The Life of Miranda*, 1929.

Robertson, William Spence, *Iturbide of Mexico*, 1952.

Robie, David, *Blood on Their Banner: Nationalist Struggles in the Pacific*, 1989.

Robinson, Richard Alan Hodgson, *Contemporary Portugal: A History*, 1979.

Robinson, Thomas W., *A Politico-Military Biography of Lin Piao, Part I, 1907–1949*, 1971.

Rodman, Selden, *Quisqueya: A History of the Dominican Republic*, 1964.

Roeder, Ralph, *Juárez and His Mexico*, 2 volumes, 1947.

Roider, Karl Jr., ed., *Maria Theresa*, 1973.

Rojas, Ricardo, *San Martín: Knight of the Andes*, 1945.

Roots, John M., *An Informal Biography of China's Legendary Chou En-lai*, 1978.

Ropp, Steve C., *Panamanian Politics: From Guarded Nation to National Guard*, 1982.

Rose, Norman, *Chaim Weizmann*, 1986.

Rosenthal, Mario, *Guatemala*, 1962.

Ross, S. R., *Francisco I. Madero: Apostle of Mexican Democracy*, 1955.

Rossiter, Clinton, *Alexander Hamilton and the Constitution*, 1964.

Rotberg, R. I., *The Rise of Nationalism in Central Africa*, 1966.

Rubin, Neville, *Cameroun: An African Federation*, 1971.

Rudolph, James D., ed., *Honduras: A Country Study*, 1984.

Rupen, Robert, *How Mongolia Is Really Ruled: A Political History of the Mongolian People's Republic, 1900–1978*, 1979.

Rush, Alan, *Al-Sabah: History and Genealogy of Kuwait's Ruling Family, 1752–1987*, 1987.

Rutherford, Noel, *Friendly Islands: A History of Tonga*, 1977.

Rutland, Robert A., *James Madison*, 1987.

Rutland, Robert A., *The Presidency of James Madison*, 1990.

Sadik, Mohammed T., and William P. Snavely, *Bahrain, Qatar, and the United Arab Emirates: Colonial Past, Present Problems, and Future Prospects*, 1972.

Safran, Nadav, *Israel the Embattled Ally*, 1981.

St. John, Robert, *The Boss*, 1961.

Salvadori, M., *Cavour and the Unification of Italy*, 1961.

Salvemini, Gaetano, *Mazzini*, 1957.

Savada, Andrea Matles, ed., *Nepal and Bhutan: Country Studies*, 1993.

Scarr, Deryck, *Fiji: A Short History*, 1984.

Schiffrin, Harold Z., *Sun Yat-sen and the Origins of the Chinese Revolution*, 1968.

Schoeman, Stanley, and Elna Schoeman, *Namibia*, 1985.

Schram, Stuart R., ed., *Chairman Mao Talks to the People*, 1975.

Schwartz, Barry, *George Washington*, 1987.

Shao Chuan Leng, and Norman D. Palmer, *Sun Yat-sen and Communism*, 1960.

Sharman, Lyon, *Sun Yat-sen: His Life and Its Meaning*, 1934.

Shaw, Peter, *The Character of John Adams*, 1976.

Sheehan, Neil, *A Bright Shining Lie: John Paul Vann and America in Vietnam*, 1988.

Sherman, Richard, *Eritrea: The Unfinished Revolution*, 1980.

Sherwell, Guillermo Antonio, *Antonio José de Sucre: Hero and Martyr of American Independence*, 1924.

Shinn, Rinn S., *Greece: A Country Study*, 1986.

Sicker, Martin, *The Making of a Pariah State: The Adventure Politics of Muammar Qaddafi*, 1987.

Simmons, Adele Smith, *Modern Mauritius: The Politics of Decolonization*, 1982.

Simons, Charles Willis, *Marshal Deodoro and the Fall of Dom Pedro II*, 1966.

Singh, Akhileshwar, *Political Leadership: Jawaharlal Nehru*, 1986.

Smart, Charles A., *Viva Juarez*, 1963.

Smelser, Marshall, *The Democratic Republic, 1801–1815*, 1968.

Smith, David, and Colin Simpson, *Mugabe*, 1981.

Smith, D. Mack, *Garbaldi: A Great Life in Brief*, 1956.

Smith, Dennis Mack, *Victor Emanuel, Cavour, and the Risorgimento*, 1971.

Smith, Hedrick, *The New Russians*, 1990.

Smith, Page, *John Adams*, 2 volumes, 1962.

Snow, Edgar, *Red Star over China*, 1974.

Snow, Peter, *Hussein: A Biography*, 1972.

Soggot, David, *Namibia: The Violent Heritage*, 1986.

Solchanyk, Roman, ed., *Ukraine, From Chernoybl to Sovereignty: A Collection of Interviews*, 1992.

Solsten, Eric, ed., *Finland: A Country Study*, 1990.

Somare, Michael, *Sana*, 1975.

Somerville, Keith, *Angola: Politics, Economics, and Society*, 1986.

Spencer, John H., *Ethiopia at Bay: A Personal Account of the Haile Selassie Years*, 1984.

Spender, Harold, *General Botha: The Career and The Man*, 1916.

Stadler, Karl R., *Austria*, 1971.

Starr, John Bryan, *Continuing the Revolution: The Political Thought of Mao*, 1979.

Stefansson, Vilhjalmur, *Iceland: The First American Republic*, 1943.

Steinberg, David Joel, *Philippine Collaboration in World War II*, 1967.

Stevens, Richard P., *Lesotho, Botswana, and Swaziland*, 1967.

Stevens, Rita, *Madagascar*, 1988.

Stiller, Ludwig, *The Rise of the House of Gorkha*, 1973.

Stookey, Robert W., *South Yemen: A Marxist Republic in Arabia*, 1982.

Storey, R. L., *The Reign of Henry VII*.

Stourzh, Gerald, *Alexander Hamilton and the Idea of Republican Government*, 1970.

Street, John, *Artigas and the Emancipation of Uruguay*, 1959.

Sullivan, Keith A., *A History of New Zealand*, 1986.

Suny, Ronald, *The Making of the Georgian Nation*, 1989.

Suny, Ronald G., *Looking Toward Ararat: Armenia in Modern History*, 1993.

Swart, Koenraad W., *William the Silent and the Revolt of the Netherlands*, 1978.

Szulc, Tad, *Fidel: A Critical Portrait*, 1986.

Tai Sung An, *North Korea in Transition: From Dictatorship to Dynasty*, 1983.

Talbott, Strobe et al., *Mikhail S. Gorbachev: An Intimate Biography*, 1988.

Talu, Alaima et al., *Kiribati*, 1979.

T'ang Leang-li, *Wang Ching-wei: A Poltical Biography*, 1931.

Terrill, Ross, *Mao*, 1981.

Tholomier, Robert, *Djibouti: Pawn of the Horn of Africa*, 1981.

Thompson, Virginia, and Richard Adloff, *The Malagasy Republic*, 1965.

Thompson, Virginia M., and Richard Adloff, *Conflict in Chad*, 1981.

Thorning, Joseph F., *Miranda: World Citizen*, 1952.

Tibawi, A. L., *A Modern History of Syria Including Lebanon and Palestine*, 1969.

Timmons, Wilbert H., *Morelos: Priest, Soldier, Statesman of Mexico*, 1970.

Townsend, William Cameron, *Lázaro Cárdenas: Mexican Democrat*, 1979.

Trager, Frank N., *Burma, From Kingdom to Republic: A Historical and Political Analysis*, 1966.

Trend, J. B., *Bolívar and the Independence of Spanish America*, 1946.

Tubangui, Helen R., ed., *The Filipino Nation: A Concise History of the Philippines*, 1982.

Tudjman, Franjo, *Wastelands—Historical Truth*, 1988.

Tupper, Charles, *Recollections of Sixty Years in Canada*, 1914.

Turnbull, C. M., *A History of Singapore, 1819–1975*, 1984.

Turnbull, C. Mary, *A History of Malaysia, Singapore, and Brunei*, 1989.

U Maung Maung, ed., *Aung San of Burma*, 1962.

Upton, Joseph M., *The History of Modern Iran: An Interpretation*, 1960.

Vaillant, Janet G., *Black, French, and African: A Life of Léopold Sédar Senghor*, 1990.

Van Lierde, Jean, *Lumumba Speaks: The Speeches and Writings of Patrice Lumumba, 1958–1961*, 1972.

Vanger, Milton I., *José Batlle y Ordóñez of Uruguay: The Creator of His Times, 1902–1907*, 1963.

Volkan, Vamik, and Norman Itzkowitz, *The Immortal Attatürk*, 1984.

Wade, Mason, *The French Canadians, 1760–1945*, 1968.

Walker, Thomas, *Nicaragua: The First Five Years*, 1985.

Walker, Thomas, *Nicaragua: The Land of Sandino*, 1991.

Webster, John, *The Political Development of Rwanda and Burundi*, 1966.

Wedgwood, Cicely V., *William the Silent, William of Nassau, Prince of Orange, 1553–1584*, 1968.

Weinstein, Warren, and Robert Schrire, *Political Conflict and Ethnic Strategies: A Case Study of Burundi*, 1976.

Weizmann, Chaim, *Trial and Error*, 1949.

Wenner, Manfred, *Modern Yemen: 1918–1966*, 1967.

Wheelock, Keith, *Nasser's New Egypt*, 1960.

Whyte A. J., *The Early Life and Letters of Cavour, 1810–1848*, 1976.

Whyte A. J., *The Political Life and Letters of Cavour, 1848–1861*, 1975.

Wiarda, Howard J., and Michael J. Kryzanek, *The Dominican Republic: A Caribbean Crucible*, 1992.

Williams, Eric, *British Historians and the West Indies*, 1964.

Williams, Eric, *From Columbus to Castro: The History of the Caribbean, 1492–1969*, 1970.

Williams, Eric, *The History of the Negro in the Caribbean*, 1942.

Williams, John Hoyt, *The Rise and Fall of the Paraguayan Republic, 1800–1870*, 1979.

Williams, Mary W., *Dom Pedro the Magnanimous*, 1966.

Wilson, A. Jeyaratnam, *Politics in Sri Lanka, 1947–1979*, 1979.

Wilson, Mary C., *King Abdullah, Britain, and the Making of Jordan*, 1987.

Wolff, Leon, *Little Brown Brother: How the United States Purchased and Pacified the Philippine Islands at the Century's Turn*, 1961.

Wollper, Stanley, *Jinnah of Pakistan*.

Womack, John, *Zapata and the Mexican Revolution*, 1969.

Woolford, Don, *Papua New Guinea: Initiation and Independence*, 1976.

Worcester, Donald, *Brazil: From Colony to World Power*, 1973.

Wright, E., *Benjamin Franklin: His Life As He Wrote It*, 1990.

Wright, E., *Franklin of Philadelphia*, 1986.

Wylie, Raymond, *The Emergence of Maoism*, 1980.

Yeager, Rodger, *Tanzania: An African Experiment*, 1989.

Yoshida Shigeru, *The Yoshida Memoirs*, 1962.

Young, Crawford, *Politics in the Congo: Decolonization and Independence*, 1965.

Young, Crawford, and Thomas E. Turner, *The Rise and Decline of the Zairian State*, 1985.

Zaide, Gregorio, *José Rizal*, 1970.

Zickel, Raymond, and Walter R. Iwaskiw, eds., *Albania: A Country Study*, 1994.

Zwerling, Philip, and Connie Martin, *Nicaragua: A New Kind of Revolution*, 1985.

Illustration Credits

Illustration Credits

Index